AMERICA'S CHILDREN

AMERICA'S CHILDREN

Resources from Family, Government, and the Economy

Donald J. Hernandez

With

David E. Myers

MATHEMATICA POLICY RESEARCH INC.

for the
National Committee for Research
on the 1980 Census

RUSSELL SAGE FOUNDATION / NEW YORK

Library of Congress Cataloging-in-Publication Data

Hernandez, Donald J.
America's children : resources from family, government, and the economy / Donald J. Hernandez.
  p.   cm.—(The Population of the United States in the 1980s)
Includes bibliographical references and index.
ISBN 0-87154-381-8
  1. Children—United States. 2. Family—United States. 3. Child welfare—United States. 4. Children—Government policy—United States. I. Title. II. Series.
HQ792.U5H47 1993
305.23'0973—dc20

92-9368
CIP

The paper used in this publication meets the minimum requirements of American National Standard for Information Sciences—Permanence of Paper for Printed Library Materials, ANSI Z39.48-1984.

RUSSELL SAGE FOUNDATION
112 East 64th Street, New York, New York 10021

10 9 8 7 6 5 4 3 2 1

The National Committee for Research on the 1980 Census

The committee is sponsored by the Social Science Research Council, the Russell Sage Foundation, and the Alfred P. Sloan Foundation, in collaboration with the U.S. Bureau of the Census. The opinions, findings, and conclusions or recommendations expressed in the monographs supported by the committee are those of the author(s) and do not necessarily reflect the views of the committee or its sponsors.

Foreword

America's Children is one of an ambitious series of volumes aimed at converting the vast statistical yield of the 1980 census into authoritative analyses of major changes and trends in American life. This series, "The Population of the United States in the 1980s," represents an important episode in social science research and revives a long tradition of independent census analysis. First in 1930, and then again in 1950 and 1960, teams of social scientists worked with the U.S. Bureau of the Census to investigate significant social, economic, and demographic developments revealed by the decennial censuses. These census projects produced three landmark series of studies, providing a firm foundation and setting a high standard for our present undertaking.

There is, in fact, more than a theoretical continuity between those earlier census projects and the present one. Like those previous efforts, this new census project has benefited from close cooperation between the Census Bureau and a distinguished, interdisciplinary group of scholars. Like the 1950 and 1960s research projects, research on the 1980 census was initiated by the Social Science Research Council and the Russell Sage Foundation. In deciding once again to promote a coordinated program of census analysis, Russell Sage and the Council were mindful not only of the severe budgetary restrictions imposed on the Census Bureau's own publishing and dissemination activities in the 1980s, but also of the extraordinary changes that have occurred in so many dimensions of American life over the past two decades.

The studies constituting "The Population of the United States in the 1980s" were planned, commissioned, and monitored by the National Committee for Research on the 1980 Census, a special committee appointed by the Social Science Research Council and sponsored by the Council, the Russell Sage Foundation, and the Alfred P. Sloan Foundation, with the collaboration of the U.S. Bureau of the Census. This committee includes leading social scientists from a broad range of fields—

demography, economics, education, geography, history, political science, sociology, and statistics. It has been the committee's task to select the main topics for research, obtain highly qualified specialists to carry out that research, and provide the structure necessary to facilitate coordination among researchers and with the Census Bureau.

The topics treated in this series span virtually all the major features of American society—ethnic groups (blacks, Hispanics, foreign-born); spatial dimensions (migration, neighborhoods, housing, regional and metropolitan growth and decline); and status groups (income levels, families and households, women). Authors were encouraged to draw not only on the 1980 census but also on previous censuses and on subsequent national data. Each individual research project was assigned a special advisory panel made up of one committee member, one member nominated by the Census Bureau, one nominated by the National Science Foundation, and one or two other experts. These advisory panels were responsible for project liaison and review and for recommendations to the National Committee regarding the readiness of each manuscript for publication. With the final approval of the chairman of the National Committee, each report was released to the Russell Sage Foundation for publication and distribution.

The debts of gratitude incurred by a project of such scope and organizational complexity are necessarily large and numerous. The committee must thank, first, its sponsors—the Social Science Research Council, the Russell Sage Foundation, and the Alfred P. Sloan Foundation. The long-range vision and day-to-day persistence of these organizations and individuals sustained this research program over many years. The active and willing cooperation of the Bureau of the Census was clearly invaluable at all stages of this project, and the extra commitment of time and effort made by Bureau economist James R. Wetzel must be singled out for special recognition. A special tribute is also due to David L. Sills of the Social Science Research Council, staff member of the committee, whose organizational, administrative, and diplomatic skills kept this complicated project running smoothly.

The committee also wishes to thank those organizations that contributed additional funding to the 1980 census report—the Ford Foundation and its deputy vice president, Louis Winnick, the National Science Foundation, the National Institute on Aging, and the National Institute of Child Health and Human Development. Their support of the research program in general and of several particular studies is gratefully acknowledged.

The ultimate goal of the National Committee and its sponsors has been to produce a definitive, accurate, and comprehensive picture of the

U.S. population in the 1980s, a picture that would be primarily descriptive but also enriched by a historical perspective and a sense of the challenges for the future inherent in the trends of today. We hope our readers will agree that the present volume takes a significant step toward achieving that goal.

CHARLES F. WESTOFF

Chairman and Executive Director
National Committee for Research
on the 1980 Census

*I dedicate this book to Lyla, Erik,
and Tresne, my wife and our children*

Acknowledgments

I devoted many years to writing this book, and numerous people have contributed in various ways.

Foremost were my wife and children. Lyla was a constant intellectual companion, an astute critic and editor, a sensitive source of personal and emotional sustenance, and generous with her time. Erik and Tresne were a continual inspiration and joy.

Arthur J. Norton's institutional leadership, scholarly counsel, and personal enthusiasm and encouragement created an indispensable and nurturing home in the Census Bureau for writing the book. Art conceived the book as one of my central Bureau responsibilities, allowing the time needed to bring it to fruition; he was always available with insightful reactions to questions or problems; and his enthusiasm for the project, reflected, for example, in his thorough reading and invaluable comments on the draft manuscript, were greatly appreciated.

Charles F. Westoff, Chairman and Executive Director of the National Committee for Research on the 1980 Census, and the advisory panel for this volume, Judith Blake, Paul C. Glick, Glen H. Elder, Jr., and Martin O'Connell, provided extremely valuable, thoughtful and thought-provoking commentary on the draft manuscript, as did Harold W. Watts.

The empirical research for this book was an enormous and complex effort involving the creation of massive extract files and the comprehensive recoding and multi-level reformatting of five distinct decennial census PUMS and three separate Current Population Survey public use files. David E. Myers had to leave the project before the analysis was well underway, because of responsibilities in a new job, but before leaving he oversaw the development of a series of computer programs required to put the data into a form capable of analysis. David's efforts were indispensable.

Additional technical assistance with computers and computer programming were provided by many persons. Most important was Catherine Schmitt for her assistance in transforming SPSS programs that created decennial census extract files into SAS programs that created CPS extract files.

Financial support was provided by the Russell Sage Foundation and the National Institute for Child Health and Human Development, through the National Committee for Research on the 1980 Census. The National Science Foundation provided major funding under grant SES-8411350. Murray Aborn's foresight was indispensable to this project. He played a central role in National Science Foundation support for use of 1940 and 1950 census date in this research, and for the essential prior step—the creation of the PUMS files for these censuses through a special joint project of the University of Wisconsin at Madison and the U.S. Bureau of the Census.

My colleagues within the Marriage and Family Statistics Branch also provided valuable assistance, and a professionally productive and cheerful work environment. Robert O. Grymes, Arlene F. Saluter, and Steve W. Rawlings guided me through official conceptual schemes and provided baseline and analytical data. Edith L. Reeves, Gerda K. Mudd, and Catherine O'Brien provided statistical and graphical assistance. Peggy A. Armstrong and Debra N. Middleton provided secretarial support.

Warren Gaskill's editorial insights regarding the draft manuscript served as a beacon for developing the final shape of the book.

The research and the book benefited enormously from the contributions acknowledged here, but responsibility for the final content and interpretation remains solely with the author.

DONALD J. HERNANDEZ

Contents

List of Tables

List of Figures

RESOURCES FOR CHILDREN: AN INTRODUCTION AND OVERVIEW

The Needs of Children

A WELL-WORN cliché, it is nevertheless true that the children of today are the adults—the parents, workers, and citizens—of tomorrow. Childhood is a time for learning and developing abilities that will be essential during adulthood. Yet children depend almost entirely upon adults to meet their needs and to make decisions on their behalf. Parents and families bear direct responsibility for the care and nurturing of children. But the larger public also has a stake in their development, because the kind and quality of resources available to children influence the kind of parents, workers, and citizens they will become and therefore the kind of society in which everyone will live. In addition, many public policies—including employment, income, and tax policies—alter parents' choices in ways that influence, for better or worse, the resources that are available to their children.[1]

Because there have been revolutionary changes in the American family, society, and economy during the past century, an understanding

[1]For a more extensive theoretical analysis of resources for childrearing, see Harold W. Watts and Fredricka Pickford Santos, *The Allocation of Human and Material Resources to Childbearing in the United States: A Theoretical Framework and Analysis of Major Data Sources*, prepared for the Foundation for Child Development (New York: Center for Social Sciences, Columbia University, 1978).

of how the current circumstances of children came about, and of what the future may hold, is not possible without examining earlier historical changes. But national studies that focused on children were virtually nonexistent before 1960. (The most noteworthy exception, the 1950 census monograph by Eleanor H. Bernert entitled *America's Children*, dealt almost exclusively with school and work among children because the published tabulations on children so necessary to the study were largely limited to these two topics.)[2] Only during the past 15 years have sociologists, demographers, and economists begun to conduct national studies that focus on children and the wide range of relationships linking them to their families and to society as a whole.[3]

The purpose of this book is to help fill the void that exists in our historical knowledge of the changing resources available to children. This will be done by analyzing data from each Census of the Population conducted between 1940 and 1980, as well as data from Current Population Surveys (CPS) conducted during the 1980s, supplemented by additional research for this and earlier periods wherever necessary. We begin with the 1940 census because it was the first effort to collect national family data on number of times married and children ever born to women; national educational attainment data for all persons school age or older; and national economic data on wage and salary income, employment, unemployment, number of hours worked, and number of weeks worked.[4]

These censuses and surveys allow children born between the 1920s and the 1980s to be studied, beginning during the Great Depression, with a series of comparatively rich, historical data.[5] Since families pro-

[2]Eleanor H. Bernert (Sheldon), *America's Children*, prepared for the Social Science Research Council in cooperation with the U.S. Department of Commerce Bureau of the Census (New York: Wiley, 1958). A total of 88 text pages explored various aspects of education and work among children and youth, while 13 pages focused on the number and geographical distribution of children and youth. Another 13 pages compared U.S. states according to the ratio of children to adults in the state, the median family income of the state, the median educational level of adults in the state, current expenditures per pupil, and childhood school enrollment and educational success. Only 7 pages focused on living arrangements in families with children, and only 3 pages presented results on the income of families by number of children and working mothers.

[3]For a review of recent social and demographic literature, and citations to reviews of related sociological studies, see Donald J. Hernandez, "Childhood in Sociodemographic Perspective," *Annual Review of Sociology*, vol. 12, Ralph H. Turner and James F. Short, Jr., eds. (Palo Alto, CA: Annual Reviews, 1986), pp. 159–180.

[4]Frederick G. Bohme, U.S. Bureau of the Census, *200 Years of U.S. Census Taking: Population and Housing Questions, 1790–1990* (Washington, DC: U.S. Government Printing Office, 1989).

[5]Public Use Microdata Samples (PUMS) for the 1940 and 1950 Censuses of the Population were not available until 1983, when the collaborative effort between the U.S. Bureau of the Census and the Center for Demography and Ecology of the University of Wisconsin at Madison to produce them was completed. Hence only recently did it become possible to study the family and the social and economic circumstances of individual children with 1940 and 1950 census data. Processing procedures, including data coding

vide the day-to-day care and most intimate and long-lasting personal relationships for the majority of children, the resources available to children depend largely on the number, characteristics, and activities of family members—within, of course, constraints set by society, the economy, and public policy. For this reason, the book attempts to answer the following questions about children and their families during the course of the past 50–150 years.

What changes have occurred for children in the number of siblings and other dependent family members who may act both as companions and competitors for family resources, and in the number of parents and grandparents available to provide care or economic support? What changes have occurred for children in the ways in which parents provide economic support, and in who provides child care? What changes have occurred for children in their parents' educational attainments, in their parents' work, in their family's income, in their chances of living in poverty or luxury, and in their chances of living in a working-poor or welfare-dependent family? To what extent have changes in the income of fathers, mothers, other relatives, and welfare programs accounted for changes in childhood poverty? Finally, what are the important causes and consequences of these changes in the lives of children and their families?

The answers to these questions portray, with a broad brush, a series of revolutionary changes in childhood that have occurred within the past century, sometimes within the past few decades—changes that can be attributed to the fundamental social, demographic, and economic processes experienced in all developed countries. Yet when viewed from an international perspective, direct public support for children in economic need is substantially more limited in the United States than in most, if not all, other industrialized countries. Before proceeding, we will briefly discuss major conceptual approaches and distinctions used throughout this study, the plan of the book, and an overview.

---

and editing for these censuses, were designed to be as similar as possible to subsequent censuses, while also taking advantage of the unique detail available in these censuses. The PUMS for the 1980 census also became available in 1983. The PUMS for the 1970 census were released in 1972, and directly comparable PUMS for the 1960 census were released in 1975. The actual comparability of particular kinds of data across censuses, and additional procedures designed specifically for this book to maximize the comparability of data across each census from 1940 to 1980, are discussed in the context of specific analyses in subsequent chapters and an appendix.

The Life Course of Children

Despite the paucity of national data on children, historical studies of families and their members have developed conceptual approaches that are valuable for the present research. Paul C. Glick initiated a series of classic studies dating from 1947 that characterized the beginning, middle, and end of the "family life cycle" according to the ages of husbands and wives when they form a family through marriage, bear their first and last child, see their first and last child marry, and experience marital dissolution through death.

The family life-cycle perspective emphasizes that children are a central defining feature of family life, making it clear that the development of children and the circumstances of parents have profound consequences for each other.[6] Glick focuses especially on the "typical" family, but he also highlights important ways in which many families differ from the typical family, both in the age at which family-defining events occur and in the extent to which family members experience events—such as separations, divorces, and remarriages—that lead to serial family living.[7]

[6] For a review of national studies of the consequences of parents' behavior for children, and of the consequences children themselves have for parents' family and economic behavior, see Donald J. Hernandez, "Childhood in Sociodemographic Perspective," pp. 159–180 in Ralph H. Turner and James F. Short, Jr., eds., *Annual Review of Sociology*, vol. 12 (1986). In a review of the early days of family studies in the United States in honor of the fiftieth anniversary of the National Council of Family Relations, Carlfred B. Broderick emphasizes that "[t]he man most responsible for grafting the (family life cycle) concept back into the main body of family theory and research is unquestionably Paul Glick of the U.S. Bureau of the Census" (p. 572); "To Arrive Where We Started: The Field of Family Studies in the 1930s," *Journal of Marriage and the Family* 50, 3 (August 1988): 569–584. Spanning 40 years, Glick portrayed the history and evolution of the family life cycle in the United States in four classic articles: Paul C. Glick, "The Family Cycle," *American Sociological Review* 12 (1947): 164–174; Paul C. Glick, "The Life Cycle of the Family," *Marriage and Family Living* 17 (1955): 3–9; Paul C. Glick and Robert Parke, Jr., "New Approaches in Studying the Life Cycle of the Family," *Demography* 2 (1965): 187–202; Paul C. Glick, "Updating the Life Cycle of the Family," *Journal of Marriage and the Family* 39 (1977): 5–13. More recent extensions of this approach with results are presented by Graham B. Spanier and Paul C. Glick, "The Life Cycle of American Families: An Expanded Analysis," *Journal of Family History* 5 (Spring 1980): 97–111; Arthur J. Norton, "Family Life Cycle: 1980," *Journal of Marriage and the Family* 45, 2 (May 1983): 267–275; Arthur J. Norton and Louisa F. Miller, "The Family Life Cycle: 1985," in *Work and Family Patterns of American Women*, U.S. Bureau of the Census, Current Population Reports, Series P-23, No. 165 (Washington, DC: U.S. Government Printing Office, 1990), pp. 1–10; and Arthur J. Norton and Louisa F. Miller, "*Marriage, Divorce, and Remarriage in the 1990's*" (Washington, DC: U.S. Government Printing Office, 1992), pp. 23–180.

[7] For example, Glick devoted considerable attention to variations in first marriage and to separation, divorce, and nonmarriage in his 1950 census monograph and a subsequent monograph, as well as many articles. Paul C. Glick, *American Families* (New York: Wiley, 1957); Hugh Carter and Paul C. Glick, *Marriage and Divorce: A Social and Economic Study* (Cambridge, MA: Harvard University Press, 1970).

In addition to family studies, a wide range of social science disciplines have developed and contributed ideas on the family life cycle. This is reflected in David L. Featherman's state-of-the-art review of "life-span perspectives."[8] Especially noteworthy for present purposes are the ideas of the "cohort" and the "life course" as valuable approaches in the study of individual and social change.

Offering a demographic approach to the study of social change, Norman B. Ryder persuasively recommends a focus on successive cohorts, or groups of children born during successive years or sets of years.[9] Because successive cohorts are born at various points in history, they experience specific historical, social, and economic events at different ages, with potentially unique implications for their development. These differences in childhood experiences and development can in turn influence the subsequent nature and direction of historical, social, and economic change.

The family life cycle and cohort perspectives have evolved and merged with other lines of theoretical work and research spanning the twentieth century to become an approach known, especially among sociologists and demographers, as the life course perspective. Glen H. Elder, Jr., who initiated a series of classic studies using this approach (beginning most notably with research published in 1974 on child development during the Great Depression), describes the following key aspects of the life course perspective.[10]

According to Elder, the similarities and differences in the life course experiences, or trajectories, of various people are based on certain factors: whether they experience a specific kind of event—such as marriage, the birth of a child, job loss, or a spell of poverty; the timing and sequencing of such events—that is, their age and the order in which these events occur; and the duration of time between these events. Differences in life course trajectories can therefore lead to important differences in individual development. The fact that some trajectories are more conventional, or conform more closely to normative expectations, than others is only one of the reasons for differences in individual development. Other differences emerge because individuals differ in the specific configurations of life course trajectories found among the family mem-

[8]David L. Featherman, "Life-Span Perspectives in Social Science Research," in Paul B. Baltes and Orville G. Brim, Jr., eds., *Life-Span Development*, vol. 5 (New York: Academic, 1983), pp. 1–51.

[9]Norman B. Ryder, "The Cohort as a Concept in the Study of Social Change," *American Sociological Review* 30, 6 (1965): 843–861.

[10]Glen H. Elder, Jr., *Children of the Great Depression* (Chicago: University of Chicago Press, 1974). Elder's overview of the life course perspective is presented in Glen H. Elder, Jr., "Perspectives on the Life Course." In Glen H. Elder, Jr., ed., *Life Course Dynamics* (Ithaca, NY: Cornell University Press, 1985), pp. 23–49.

bers with whom they are intimately associated. And further individual differences in development can be expected to result from the ways in which historical, social, or economic events impinge upon families with similar or different configurations of life course trajectories. To reflect the complexities of child development suggested by these perspectives, we have adopted several specific strategies in analyzing and interpreting the data presented in this book.

First, in addition to discussing the circumstances and resources available to children at specific points in time, we also present results for young children beginning life as well as for older children who are at the end of the childhood life course. For example, since the needs of preschool children (aged 0–5) are very different from those of adolescents (aged 12–17), we often focus on these groups in each census year. Since children aged 2–5 in one census are aged 12–15 in the next census, the children in this four-year age group constitute about two-thirds of the six-year age range 0–5 in one census and about two-thirds of the six-year age range 12–17 in the next census. Taking advantage of this substantial overlap in membership, we often treat children aged 0–5 in one census and aged 12–17 in the next census as "quasi" cohorts and compare changes across successive quasi cohorts.

For example, our quasi cohorts born during the 1930s consists of children aged 0–5 in 1940 who were born mainly between 1934 and 1939, and children aged 12–17 in 1960 who were born mainly between 1932 and 1937.[11] Results for quasi cohorts correspond fairly closely to results that would be derived from "genuine" cohorts.[12] For present purposes, the advantage of using quasi cohorts instead of actual cohorts is that life course changes can be studied across successive cohorts from the very beginning of childhood to the end of childhood as conventionally defined.[13] To simplify discussion in subsequent chapters, we refer

[11]Since the census date is April 1 in specified years, most of the children who were under age 1 in that year were born during the preceding calendar year.

[12]Insofar as the circumstances of successive cohorts at specific ages change little across the 20-year periods between censuses, the estimates for these "quasi" cohorts will be quite similar to estimates that would be derived if "genuine" cohort data were used. In addition, insofar as the circumstances of successive cohorts at specific ages change greatly across the 10-year periods between censuses, the estimates of change across quasi cohorts will be generally similar to estimates of change that would be derived if genuine cohort data were used, as reflected by the following. Since children aged 0–5 in one census are aged 10–15 in the next census, the age group 12–17 in the second census is, on average, 2 years older. But if change across successive cohorts is fairly uniform through time, then the 2-year difference between the quasi and genuine cohorts will be only one-fifth as large as the 10-year difference between censuses. Finally, comparisons across successive cohorts at either the preschool ages or the adolescent ages do reflect genuine 10-year changes across cohorts, albeit slightly different preschool and adolescent cohorts.

[13]For purposes of family study, for example, the U.S. Bureau of the Census generally defines persons aged 0–17 as children. Since the population censuses are conducted only

to quasi cohorts simply as cohorts born in specific decades, especially between the 1920s and the 1980s. In addition, we sometimes focus on children by single year of age. For example, the analysis of potential child care providers distinguishes preschool children by single year of age—including newborns under age 1—since children's needs for personal care change very rapidly during these early ages. At the other extreme, since the analysis of experience with one-parent family living focuses in part on cumulative experience spanning the entire childhood life course, it is necessary to focus on children at age 17—that is, at the end of childhood—in order to fully portray the cohort experience.

These distinctions by age and cohort are implemented through analyses that, insofar as possible, link the life course trajectories of children with those of other family members. For example, marital and fertility history data, and work experience data for children's parents from each census, are used to develop measures reflecting the number, timing, and sequencing of parental marriages, divorces, and births, and changing childhood exposure to the interrelated family and economic experiences of parents. These results are then supplemented by the research of other social scientists using data (though this pertains only to comparatively recent cohorts) that provide the basis for a more detailed study of the life course trajectories of children and their parents.

Because black and Hispanic children (of any race) are large minority populations whose historical experiences have differed in important ways from those of non-Hispanic white children, we also refine our analyses of children to study these subgroups separately. Black children are studied as of each census date, while Hispanic children (of any race) are studied only as of the 1980s. But to provide historical perspective, we characterize Hispanic children in the 1980 census as "old-family" or "first-generation" Americans, depending upon whether the mother was born a U.S. citizen.[14]

Based on estimates by Jeffrey S. Passel and Barry Edmonston regarding the foreign or native parentage of Hispanic persons in the U.S. in

---

every 10 years, genuine cohorts might be identified at ages 0–5 and 10–15 in successive censuses, or at ages 2–7 and 12–17. Because of the large developmental differences between the beginning and the end of childhood, and because estimates of change across quasi cohorts should be fairly similar to estimates for actual cohorts, quasi cohorts are used here as the best compromise available for studying the full life course of children. The changing nature of the transition to adulthood is a major topic in itself and cannot be explored within the context of this book. But for a recent social history on this topic, see John Modell, *Into One's Own: From Youth to Adulthood in the United States 1920–1972* (Berkeley: University of California Press, 1989).

[14]The measurement of Hispanic origin in the 1980 census is substantially different from that of earlier censuses.

1980, we have estimated that among Hispanic children (of any race) in 1980 whose mothers were born U.S. citizens, approximately 63–68 percent also had grandparents who were born in the U.S.[15] As of 1980, therefore, it is possible to compare the experience of three groups: (1) first-generation Hispanic children (of any race)—that is, those who represent the first generation within their families to be born U.S. citizens; (2) old-family Hispanic children (of any race), about two-thirds of whom are third-, fourth-, or later-generation Americans; and (3) non-Hispanic children.

Of course, Hispanics (of any race) differ substantially in their social and economic characteristics and circumstances depending upon their country or region of origin.[16] But because of the small sample sizes for

[15]These results are derived as follows from 1980 estimates in Table 1, Jeffrey S. Passel and Barry Edmonston, "Immigration and Race: Recent Trends in Immigration to the United States," paper presented at conference on "Immigration and Ethnicity: The Integration of America's Newest Immigrants," The Urban Institute, Washington, DC (June 1991). The 1980 estimates are used. Hispanic children (of any race) aged 0–17 in 1980 were mainly born to women aged 15–51 in 1980. Among native U.S. Hispanic persons (of any race) in 1980, the proportions who themselves were born of native parents (both parents native) was 63 percent for persons 15–49 years old, 66 percent for persons aged 20–44 years old, and 68 percent for persons 25–39 years old. Hence, somewhere between 63–68 percent of the children of these women had maternal grandparents who both were U.S. natives.

In addition, since, for example, women aged 20–44 in 1980 were born mainly to women aged 35–78 in 1980, we can calculate the approximate proportion of maternal great-grandparents who themselves were U.S. natives. The proportion of Hispanics with two U.S. native parents was 60 percent for persons aged 35–75+, 57 percent for persons aged 40–74, and 53 percent for persons aged 45–69. These last proportions were calculated as the means of the proportions for five-year age groups (and the 75+ age group), in order to treat each age group equally, since mortality has substantially reduced the actual size of these populations.

Multiplying these proportions (53–60 percent) for the maternal great-grandparental generation by the earlier proportions (63–68 percent) for the maternal grandparental generation suggests that approximately 33–41 percent of these great-grandparents were U.S. natives, that is, U.S. born.

Taken together, these results suggest that for Hispanic children (of any race) in 1980 with native, U.S.-born mothers, 63–68 percent of their maternal grandparents were U.S. natives and 33–41 percent of their maternal great-grandparents were U.S. natives. Hence, about two-thirds of these children can be viewed, at least on their maternal side, as third- or later generation Americans, and approximately one-third to two-fifths can be viewed, again on the maternal side, as fourth- or later generation Americans. In other words, for Hispanic children (of any race) in 1980 with native, U.S.-born mothers, 63–68 percent had at least two (out of a total of four) grandparents who were U.S. natives, although the total proportion of such children who had at least four (out of a total of eight) great-grandparents cannot be directly estimated from available data, since the precise level depends on the extent to which marriages between foreign-born and U.S.-native Hispanics (of any race) occurred among earlier generations.

[16]For detailed and recent studies of Hispanic subgroups (of any race), see Frank D. Bean and Marta Tienda, The Hispanic Population of the United States (New York: Russell Sage Foundation, 1987); and Jesus M. Garcia and Patricia A. Montgomery, The Hispanic Population in the United States: March 1990. U.S. Bureau of the Census, Current Population Reports. Series P-20, No. 449 (Washington, DC: U.S. Government Printing Office, 1991).

Hispanic children (of any race) in the data sets used here, and because there are limits in the number of topics that can be covered in this book, results are not presented separately for subgroups of Hispanic children (of any race). In preparing this book, we were guided by past studies showing, or suggesting, which specific features of children's life course and family origins have important consequences for children's well-being and development throughout childhood and into adulthood. Each chapter summarizes the results of past research to highlight why we should care about the topic under study. Of course, the topics included in the book and the ways in which we approach them are shaped by the nature of the data available from the census and the CPS. Fortunately, these databases were specifically designed to provide information about fundamental social and economic phenomena in American society.

Because parents, citizens, public policymakers, and scholars also have a considerable interest in the causes of historical change in the resources available to children, the present research has been designed, and past studies of long-term social and economic change have been drawn upon, to provide at least partial explanations for why important changes in the childhood life course have occurred.

In short, the object of this book is to rectify the scant historical knowledge that exists on the changing resources available to children. This will be done by presenting a broad yet detailed assessment of major changes that have taken place in the life course of American children, drawing upon both new analyses of recently available historical data and past research. Still, any such effort must be selective, given limits on available data, the author's time, and publication space. An important decision was to restrict this research to national-level analyses. To provide up-to-date geographical detail, however, we are planning a U.S. Bureau of the Census Special Report based on the 1990 census to replicate as much as possible many of the major analyses in this book with state-level data. The specific topics chosen for study here and an overview of conclusions are presented in the following section.

Plan and Overview of the Book

The life course trajectories of most children, and the resources available to them, are most directly influenced by the number, characteristics, and past and present activities of the family members with whom they live. For this reason, we begin in Chapters 2 and 3 by focusing on changes in the number and nature of family experiences that link siblings, parents, and grandparents in the homes of children.

Chapter 2 discusses the revolutionary decline in the number of siblings in families that has occurred during the past 150 years, highlighting the postwar baby boom, and expected future changes. Since siblings are the family members who are most similar in age and needs, a corresponding revolution occurred in potential sibling companionship and sibling competition for family resources.

Chapter 3 shows that of the children born from at least the late nineteenth to the mid-twentieth centuries, about one-third were exposed to the potential disadvantages associated with not having two parents in the home; and this figure increased to about one-half for children born in 1980. During the past 50 years at least, fewer than one-half of children in one-parent families had a grandparent in the home who could help fill the resource gap left by the absent parent.

Following the portrayals of change in sibling, parental, and grandparental living arrangements, Chapters 4 and 5 discuss where and how children and parents actually spend their time. These two chapters also examine the two revolutions that have occurred in these aspects of family living during the past century or more.

Chapter 4 focuses on the double revolution that took place in the parents' workplace. First, when the breadwinner-homemaker family displaced the farm family, family members no longer worked together to support themselves. Instead, fathers devoted much of the week to work away from the home, while mothers remained at home to care for the children. Even before this revolutionary transformation was complete, however, the dual-earner or /parent family system had begun to rise to the fore. This was because mothers, too, were leaving home for paid work in great numbers. By 1980, in fact, about 60 percent of all children lived in dual-earner or one-parent families.

The first revolution in parents' work was accompanied by an idealized perception, in mid-twentieth century America, that breadwinner-homemaker families involved a father who worked full-time year-round, a mother who was a full-time homemaker, and a (nonfarm) family situation in which all the children were born after the parents' only marriage. But the second revolution in parents' work followed closely upon the first, and, combined with instability in family living arrangements and in the father's work, led to a situation throughout the last half century in which, even among newborn children, only a minority could claim to have been born into supposedly typical "Ozzie and Harriet" families.

Chapter 5 analyzes the corresponding double revolution in child care arrangements—that is, where and how children spend their time. First, as fathers increasingly became nonfarm breadwinners, children aged 5–17 began to leave home to attend school for part of the day. The resulting decline in the need for mothers to provide child care contributed to the rise in mothers' paid work after 1940. Second, between 1940 and 1987, the proportion of preschoolers who did not have a parent at home full-time nearly quadrupled from about 13 to 50 percent, and by 1987 about 40 percent of preschoolers were regularly being cared for by someone other than their parents.

The ongoing revolution in child care for preschoolers is not pervasively harmful, but the quality of care received appears to have important consequences, and children from low-income families are especially at risk. In general, the time that mothers devoted to child care as a primary activity increased between the 1920s and the early 1960s, but since then it has declined.

Chapter 6 shows how the first child-care revolution led to a revolution in parents' education, since the children of one era are the parents of the next. Because children with highly educated parents are themselves more likely to achieve high levels of education when they reach adulthood, and to obtain jobs with relatively high social prestige and income, successive cohorts of children have benefited from the ongoing revolution in parents' education. Chapter 6 also discusses how successive cohorts have benefited educationally from other changes in family origins—namely the near extinction of the farm, the associated rise in the father's occupational prestige, and the decline in number of siblings. But these effects were partially offset by the rise in one-parent families.

In addition, educational opportunities became substantially more equal, especially for children born after 1936, but this improvement was noted only for educational attainments through high school. Opportunities to go beyond high school and complete at least one year of college have become less equal, as family origins have become more influential in determining post-high school educational attainments.

While Chapters 2–6 focus on changes in the number, characteristics, and activities of children and their family members, especially their parents, Chapters 7–9 focus on changes in the family income available to children that in turn resulted from changes in the family and the broader economy and society. Family income is important, of course, because whether children live in material deprivation or in comfort or luxury largely depends upon the income level of their families. Furthermore, the children's chances of having a low or high income when they reach adulthood is greatly influenced by their childhood family income. Particularly noteworthy is the extent to which children live in low-income families, because these children may experience marked deprivation in such basic areas as nutrition, clothing, housing, and healthcare.

Chapter 7 shows that the absolute income levels of American families increased greatly during the 1940s, 1950s, and 1960s, but that income growth nearly ceased during the 1970s and the 1980s. The data on absolute income levels tell little about the extent to which children lived in relative deprivation or luxury compared with the standards of the time in which they were growing up, however. The reason for this is that a family's status on the economic scale—i.e., whether that family is judged to be living in deprivation or luxury—is based on its income and whether this income is especially low or high compared with the income of typical families in the same historical period.

Measuring relative poverty in comparison to median family income in various years, our results indicate that the proportion of children living in relative poverty declined sharply during the 1940s and more slowly during the 1950s and the 1960s. This figure then increased after 1969, especially during the 1980s, to reach a level in 1988 that equaled the figure recorded almost 40 years earlier in 1949. Despite these important changes, the relative poverty rate for children has remained substantially higher than for adults throughout the era since the Great Depression. Taking into account the proportion of children at both extremes of the income distribution in various years, children experienced a large decline in income inequality between 1939 and 1959 and a substantial increase in income inequality after 1969, primarily during the 1980s.

Chapter 8 shows that most relatively poor children since 1939 have lived in fully self-supporting, working-poor families. Welfare dependence (measured as the receipt of public assistance or Social Security) increased especially during the 1970s. But by 1988, 52 percent of relatively poor children were living in fully self-supporting families, compared with 18 percent in fully welfare-dependent families. Although the poverty rate for children in mother-only families is much higher than for those in two-parent families, most relatively poor children in 1988 (more than 85 percent) would have been poor even if the remarkable post-1959 increase in mother-only families had not occurred.

In addition, the increasing value of welfare benefits after 1959 apparently encouraged some women not to marry the fathers of their children, leading to an increase of about 1–2 percentage points in the proportion of children living in mother-only families. Still, most relatively poor children in 1988 (more than 90 percent) would have been poor even if this welfare-incentive effect had not occurred.

Turning to specific sources of family income, Chapter 9 indicates that changes in available fathers' income can account for much of the post-Depression decline and subsequent increase in the relative poverty rate of children. Meanwhile, increasing mothers' income acted to speed the earlier decline and then to slow the subsequent increase. By 1988, 13.9 percent of children depended on their mothers' income to lift them out of relative poverty, and another 15 percent lived in relative poverty despite the mothers' work. Income from family members other than parents acted to reduce childhood relative poverty by 8–9 percentage points in 1939, but neither the post-Depression decline nor the subsequent increase in childhood relative poverty is accounted for by such relatives.

Beyond income from family members, major cash welfare programs acted to lift a nearly constant 1–2 percent of children out of relative poverty between 1939 and 1988. Welfare benefits lift few relatively poor children out of poverty. Finally, although larger families need more income than do smaller families to lift themselves out of poverty, decade-by-decade changes in dependent sibsizes since the Great Depression can account for changes of only 1–2 percentage points in relative childhood poverty. The exception to this is the 1970s, when a declining number of dependent siblings accounted for a 4–5 percentage point reduction in childhood relative poverty.

Taken together, Chapters 2–9 discuss profound changes in the lives of children associated with major trends in family size and composition; parents' education, work, and income; and child care arrangements and childhood poverty. Chapter 10 portrays the ways in which these and other trends are related to one another by exploring some fundamental causes of changes in fathers' income, the rise of mothers' labor-force participation, and the rise of mother-only families.

Chapter 10 also shows that the relative poverty rate for children declined greatly during the post–World War II economic boom, because it brought declines in fathers' unemployment, increases in fathers' absolute income levels, and increases in equality in the distribution of fathers' income. But relative poverty then increased for children after 1969, and official poverty increased after 1979, reflecting the increasing proportions of children who lived with comparatively low-income fathers and in mother-only families. Contributing to the rising proportion of children who lived with comparatively low-income fathers was the increasing competition for jobs, which resulted from rapid labor-force growth as the large baby-boom cohorts reached working and parenting ages. To a lesser extent, an increase in immigration also contributed to this trend.

Contributing to increasing mothers' labor-force participation was a continuing desire of couples to maintain or improve their relative economic standing, combined with the limited availability of historic avenues to achieving this desire—namely, to have husbands shift from farming to comparatively well-paid nonfarm jobs, to have families with comparatively few children, and to obtain comparatively high educational attainments that provide access to well-paid jobs. By 1940, most couples already had husbands with nonfarm jobs and families with few children, and beyond age 25 it is often difficult or impractical to return to school. As a result, paid work for wives and mothers became a major avenue to improving family income after 1940, as the traditional non-farm female labor force (unmarried women) ceased growing or declined in size, while demand for female workers increased.

Also, compared with earlier generations, mothers in 1940 were relatively well qualified and potentially available for work outside the home because of their comparatively higher educational attainments, and because their homemaker-mother role had become constricted by small family sizes and compulsory universal school attendance of children over age 6. Finally, as mothers' labor-force participation increased, this in itself fostered further increases, because in our competitive consumer-oriented society, families in which the mother was not in the labor force, even ones with well-paid husbands, increasingly found themselves at a comparative disadvantage; this in turn made mothers' work increasingly attractive.

The historic shift away from farming also contributed to the rise in separation, divorce, and mother-only families by removing fathers from face-to-face interaction with their families during much of the day and by providing them with increasing opportunities for extramarital relationships—especially since behavior could no longer be inhibited or controlled by rural and small-town censorship. The more recent rise in mothers' labor-force participation contributed further to the rise in divorce and mother-only families by providing mothers with similar opportunities and with income that made it feasible for them to live away from their husbands.

Simultaneously, the rise in divorce contributed to mothers' labor-force participation as women found a hedge against the increasingly possible economic disaster of losing most or all of their husband's income through divorce. Finally, in the context of these socioeconomic changes, economic insecurity and need have also contributed to increasing separation and divorce. Instability in husbands' work, drops in family income, and a low ratio of family-income-to-needs have been found to lead to increased hostility between husbands and wives, and, correspondingly, to increased risk of divorce. Not surprisingly, then, each economic recession since at least the early 1970s has brought a substantially larger increase in mother-only families for children than was the case during each preceding nonrecessionary period.

An oft-noted difference between black children and white children is the prevalence of mother-only families in the black community. The analysis in Chapter 10 suggests that the main reason for this difference may be that blacks began the postwar era with extraordinarily high levels of economic insecurity, and that this, combined with the high level of residential segregation and changes in the economy that affected them more severely than whites, is what led to larger increases in mother-only families among blacks. Much more limited results for old-family Hispanic children (of any race) are consistent, at least, with the view that they have faced changes and constraints similar to, but in some ways less severe than, those experienced by black children.

In concluding this monograph, Chapter 11 provides a detailed summary of changes in the resources available to children and in their life course circumstances, with special emphasis on important differences by race and Hispanic origin. Basic results for children in other developed countries are also presented in order to highlight international similarities and differences in resources, circumstances, and public policies pertaining to children.

As has been indicated above, the research for this book is necessarily limited in both breadth and depth. Because the primary objective is to study major long-term changes, we have attempted to devise and use measures of resources for children and their life course circumstances that are maximally refined and relevant. In addition, these measures are based upon the longest available set of historically consistent and comparatively rich social, economic, and family data for the United States—namely, data from the Census of the Population and the Current Population Survey.

We have therefore focused primarily on decade-to-decade changes in historically consistent measures and devoted comparatively little attention to short-term fluctuations, precise turning points, or more refined measures available for some topics in recent years. More work needs to be done, but we hope that this book will help to fill the present void in our knowledge of the changing resources available to America's children and, in doing so, help to point the way toward future research and public policies that will ameliorate the condition of these children.

THE FAMILY-SIZE REVOLUTION:
FROM MANY TO FEW SIBLINGS

Introduction and Highlights

WE ARE approaching the end of a historic, revolutionary shift toward small families. At the beginning of this century, most children grew up in families with 5 or more children, but today the overwhelming majority live in families with only 1, 2, or 3 children. In this chapter we will explore the nature, causes, and consequences this family-size revolution has for children by addressing the following questions.

How are the welfare of children and their future life chances during adulthood influenced by growing up in a large or a small family? What family-size changes for children occurred during the long-term fertility decline that had begun by 1800 and continued through the Great Depression? What effect did the postwar baby boom and the subsequent baby bust have on family size? What caused the historic fertility decline and the subsequent postwar swings in fertility and family size? How will family size change in the future? In brief, this chapter offers the following answers to these questions.

First, children who have many siblings also have greater opportunities for caring sibling companionship. But large families usually reduce both the amount of time and the resources parents can devote to each child.[1] Second, although the size of a child's family appears to have little effect on his or her psychological well-being later during adulthood, children who grow up in large families (i.e., families with 5 or more children) tend to complete fewer years of school than do children from smaller families. Consequently, children from large families are less likely to enter high-status occupations with high incomes when they reach adulthood.

Third, as the historic, nineteenth century decline in fertility in the United States continued into the twentieth century, median family size declined from 6.6 for children born in 1890 to 2.9 for those born in the 1940s. Meanwhile, the proportion of children living in families with 5 or more siblings declined from 77 percent in 1890 to 32 percent in the 1940s.

Fourth, despite the jump in fertility rates during the baby boom (1946–1964), the size of the average (median) family increased only from about 2.9 to 3.4 siblings, and the proportion of children in families with 5 or more siblings increased by only about 6 percentage points. Fifth, the subsequent baby bust brought a much larger drop in family size, primarily because of the substantial reduction in families with 5 or more children. Hence, the small increase in family size that took place during the baby boom had little effect on the future life chances of children born during that period, but the substantial shift away from large families during the baby bust tended to foster higher educational attainments and occupational achievements among these children than was the case among children born during earlier decades.

Still, among children born in 1973, about 1 out of every 7 adolescents (15 percent) lived in families with 5 or more siblings, and the proportion was about one-half again as large for black adolescents. Within 25–35 years, however, white, black, and Hispanic children (of any race) are all expected to have nearly identical and comparatively small family sizes, with an average of fewer than 2 children per family and more than 80 percent living in families with only 1, 2, or 3 siblings.

Fifth, the historic fertility decline in this country resulted from social, economic, and political changes that increased the costs of having a large family while reducing its benefits. As social, political, and economic circumstances changed during the past two centuries, adults sought either to improve their relative social and economic standing or to keep

---

[1]Many studies on the effect of number of children on marital and parental satisfaction also suggest that parents who have a small number of children (or no children at all in the case of marital satisfaction) are more satisfied than those who have a large number of children. For a review of these studies, see Donald J. Hernandez, "Childhood in Sociodemographic Perspective," in Ralph H. Turner and James F. Short, Jr., eds., *Annual Review of Sociology* 12 (1986): 159–180.

from losing ground compared with others who were taking advantage of emerging economic opportunities. To achieve these goals, couples pursued a variety of strategies—including limiting the size of their families in order to maximize the time and resources that would be available to advance their own work and careers as well as the work and careers of their children.

Following the hard times of the Great Depression, the postwar economic boom appears to have provided such large and immediate opportunities for social and economic advance that many couples decided they could both satisfy their economic aspirations and have an additional child or two, often at an early age and with close spacing. But when the postwar economic boom drew to a close, fertility again began to decline, as many families found it necessary to limit themselves to fewer children in order to improve their relative social and economic standing or at least keep from losing ground compared with others. These highlights are drawn from the following discussion of past studies and new results.

Advantages and Disadvantages of Large and Small Families

For most children, having brothers and sisters is a mixed blessing. Growing up in a large family can be beneficial, because brothers and sisters share the companionship of childhood—a time of play that may be far removed from the work and responsibilities of their parents. The love and friendship shared by siblings may last a lifetime. On the other hand, siblings are also competitors for the limited time and financial resources of their parents. As a result, the larger the number of siblings, the less time parents can devote exclusively to each child and the fewer are their financial resources.

Dependent brothers and sisters under age 18 are especially likely to compete for parental time and income. Most of these siblings live with their parents, spend much of their nonschool time with family members, and seldom have jobs that provide a substantial independent income. Older brothers and sisters, however, are less likely to compete for their parents' time and attention. They may live in a separate household and have many interests outside the home. In fact, instead of competing for parental attention, young adult siblings may actually supplement it by providing child care for younger siblings. Financially, older siblings can be either a greater burden than younger siblings or no burden at all, depending upon whether they earn a substantial income of their own or are incurring high costs that must be paid by the parents, such as those associated with owning a car or attending college.

Clearly, then, the number of siblings in a child's family influences his or her current interpersonal and economic situation. In addition, although the number of siblings children have appears to have little effect on their psychological well-being later during adulthood,[2] sociologists have found that family size does have important consequences for a child's subsequent social and economic situation during adulthood.[3] In a classic study done more than two decades ago, Peter M. Blau and Otis Dudley Duncan found that children with few siblings are more likely to finish high school and college than are children with many siblings. Consequently, since children who finish more years of schooling are more likely to enter higher-status occupations with higher incomes, children with few siblings are more likely to earn relatively high incomes as adults.[4]

More recently, David L. Featherman and Robert M. Hauser found that educational opportunities have increased during the twentieth century for children whose fathers had comparatively few years of schooling; and Judith Blake has found that much of this increase in educational opportunities occurred among children in families with 1–4 children.[5] In families with 5 or more children, opportunities for upward educational mobility have not increased by the same percentage as they have for children in smaller families. The reason appears, at least in part, to be that child-parent interaction is diluted in large families, while children in small families have more interaction with parents, develop better verbal ability, and therefore experience greater success in school.

In general, then, the number of siblings children have has important consequences for their current interpersonal and economic situation, their ultimate educational attainments, and their occupation and income when they reach adulthood.[6] Thus, the results presented in this chapter concerning long-term changes in family size are important not only because

---

[2]For a review of studies concerning the effects of sibling size on the psychological well-being of adults, see Hernandez, pp. 159–180.

[3]For a review of relevant sociodemographic studies, see Hernandez, pp. 159–180.

[4]Peter M. Blau and Otis Dudley Duncan, *The American Occupational Structure* (New York: Wiley, 1969).

[5]David L. Featherman and Robert M. Hauser, *Opportunity and Change* (New York: Academic, 1978); and Judith Blake, "Family Size and the Quality of Children," *Demography* 18 (1981): 321–342; "Number of Siblings and Educational Mobility," *American Sociological Review* 50 (1985): 84–94. Judith Blake, "Differential Parental Investment: Its Effects on Child Quality and Status Attainment," in Jane B. Lancaster et al., *Parenting Across the Life Span: Biosocial Dimensions* (New York: Aldine de Gruyter, 1987), pp. 351–375; Judith Blake, *Family Size and Achievement* (Berkeley: University of California Press, 1989).

[6]For a review of additional studies concerning the effect of sibling size on later adult educational attainments, see Hernandez, pp. 159–180.

they contribute to our understanding of changes in the current situation of children, but also because they add to our understanding of changes in the economic attainments of these children when they reach adulthood.

Fertility Change Among Women Since 1800

One fertility measure used by demographers, the General Fertility Rate (GFR), is calculated as the annual number of births per 1,000 women aged 15–44. Using this measure, fertility declined during each of the 14 decades spanning 1800 to 1940, and by the time of the Great Depression and World War II, the GFR was less than one-third as large as it was in 1800 (Figure 2.1 and Table 2.1). With the post–World War II baby boom, the GFR increased, for example, by about 50 percent between 1940 and 1957, returning to the level experienced in 1916.

A second fertility measure used by demographers, the Total Fertility Rate (TFR), indicates the mean number of births that would occur to a hypothetical cohort of 1,000 women over the course of their childbearing years if they were to experience the age-specific fertility rates for a given year. Divided by 1,000, the TFR indicates the average number of children that would be born to one woman in that hypothetical cohort. By this oft-cited measure, fertility increased by about 60 percent during the baby boom—from an average of 2.3 births per woman in 1930–1945 to a peak of 3.7 in 1957.

After the postwar baby boom the historic fertility decline resumed, and by the early 1970s, both the GFR and the TFR had fallen below the level recorded during the Great Depression, with the TFR fluctuating narrowly between 1.7 and 1.9 births per woman (Figure 2.1 and Table 2.1).

Family-Size Change Among Women Since 1865

A more direct measure of actual family size is the average (mean) number of children ever born to specific 5-year cohorts of women by the end of their childbearing years. Since the average childbearing age is about 27, estimates are graphed in Figure 2.1 and Table 2.2 at the point about 27 years later than the average year of birth for each cohort of

FIGURE 2.1

*General and Total Fertility Rates, Number of Children Ever Born,
and Lifetime Expected Births: 1800–1994*

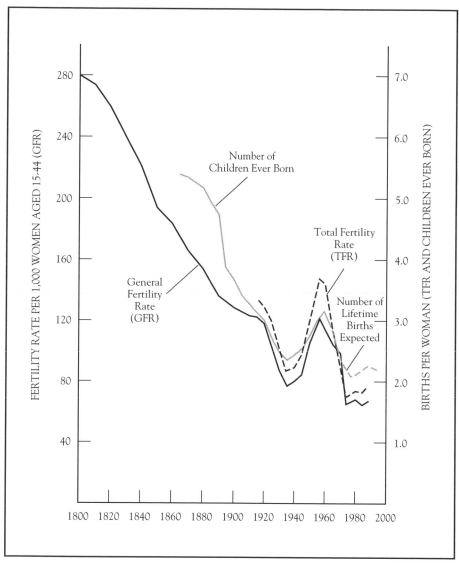

SOURCES: See Tables 2.1 and 2.2.

TABLE 2.1
General and Total Fertility Rates: 1800–1988

Year	General Fertility Rate	Total Fertility Rate	Year	General Fertility Rate	Total Fertility Rate
1988	67.2	1,932.0	1950	106.2	3,028.0
1987	65.7	1,871.0	1949	107.1	3,036.2
1986	65.4	1,836.0	1948	107.3	3,026.2
			1947	113.3	3,181.2
1985	66.2	1,842.5	1946	101.9	2,857.9
1984	65.4	1,805.5			
1983	65.8	1,802.5	1945	85.9	2,421.8
1982	67.3	1,828.5	1944	88.8	2,494.5
1981	67.4	1,815.0	1943	94.3	2,640.2
			1942	91.5	2,554.8
1980	68.4	1,839.5	1941	83.4	2,331.5
1979	67.2	1,808.0			
1978	65.5	1,760.0	1940	79.9	2,229.0
1977	66.8	1,789.5	1939	77.6	2,171.7
1976	65.0	1,738.0	1938	79.1	2,221.7
			1937	77.1	2,173.3
1975	66.0	1,774.0	1936	75.8	2,145.6
1974	67.8	1,835.0			
1973	68.8	1,879.0	1935	77.2	2,188.7
1972	73.1	2,010.0	1934	78.5	2,232.0
1971	81.6	2,266.5	1933	76.3	2,172.0
			1932	81.7	2,318.6
1970	87.9	2,480.0	1931	84.6	2,401.7
1969	86.1	2,455.5			
1968	85.2	2,464.2	1930	89.2	2,532.5
1967	87.2	2,557.7	1929	89.3	2,532.0
1966	90.8	2,721.4	1928	93.8	2,659.8
			1927	99.8	2,824.3
1965	96.3	2,912.6	1926	102.6	2,900.7
1964	104.7	3,190.5			
1963	108.3	3,318.8	1925	106.6	3,011.6
1962	112.0	3,461.3	1924	110.9	3,120.7
1961	117.1	3,620.3	1923	110.5	3,101.2
			1922	111.2	3,109.4
1960	118.0	3,653.6	1921	119.8	3,326.2
1959	118.8	3,638.2			
1958	120.0	3,628.9	1920	117.9	3,263.3
1957	122.7	3,682.4	1919	111.2	3,067.7
1956	121.0	3,604.7	1918	119.8	3,312.2
			1917	121.0	3,333.3
1955	118.3	3,498.3	1916	123.4	
1954	117.9	3,461.2			
1953	115.0	3,349.4	1915	125.0	
1952	113.8	3,286.5	1914	126.6	
1951	111.4	3,199.1	1913	124.7	

TABLE 2.1 (*continued*)

Year	General Fertility Rate	Total Fertility Rate	Year	General Fertility Rate	Total Fertility Rate
1912	125.8		1890	137	
1911	126.3		1880	155	
1910	126.8		1870	167	
1909	126.8		1860	184	
			1850	194	
			1840	222	
			1830	240	
			1820	260	
1910	123.8		1810	274	
1900	130		1800	278	

SOURCES: General Fertility Rates for 1909–1988, Table 1.1, and Total Fertility Rates for 1960–1988, Table 1.6, National Center for Health Statistics: *Vital Statistics of the United States, 1988*, Vol. I, Natality, DHHS Pub. No. (PHS) 90-1100. Public Health Service, Washington, D.C.: U.S. Government Printing Office, 1990. General Fertility Rates for 1800–1910, Series B 4, U.S. Bureau of the Census, *Historical Statistics of the United States, Colonial Times to 1970*, Bicentennial Edition, Part 1, Washington, D.C.: U.S. Government Printing Office, 1975. Total Fertility Rates for 1917–1959, Table 1, Robert L. Heuser, National Center for Health Statistics, *Fertility Tables for Birth Cohorts by Color: United States, 1917–73*, Washington, D.C.: U.S. Government Printing Office, April 1976.

NOTES: General Fertility Rate is fertility rate per 1,000 women aged 15–44 in specified years. General Fertility Rates for 1800 through 1910 are for white women. General Fertility Rates for 1909 through 1988 are for all women.

women.[7] For women who have not yet completed their childbearing, expected family size can be calculated from data on the total number of births these women expect to have during their lifetime. Martin O'Connell has shown that such birth expectation data, collected by the Census Bureau since 1976, may predict actual childbearing behavior with a high degree of accuracy.[8]

The general pattern of family-size change indicated by this measure is similar to the pattern of change shown in the GFR and the TFR. The

[7]The mean age of childbearing varied between 26.4 and 28.0 for women born between 1910 and 1930. See Gregory Spencer, *Projections of the Population of the United States, by Age, Sex, and Race: 1988 to 2080* (Washington, DC: U.S. Government Printing Office, 1989). See Appendix A, "Fertility," U.S. Bureau of the Census, *Current Population Reports*, Series P-25, No. 1018.

[8]Martin O'Connell, "Late Expectations: Childbearing Patterns of American Women for the 1990's," in *Studies in American Fertility*, U.S. Bureau of the Census, *Current Population Reports*, Series P-23, No. 176 (Washington, DC: U.S. Government Printing Office, 1991).

TABLE 2.2

*Number of Children Ever Born and Lifetime Births Expected
for Women Born 1835–1969*

Year of Birth of Women	Children per 1,000 Women
1963–69	2,045
1958–62	2,116
1953–57	2,057
1948–52	2,088
1943–47	2,297
1935–39	2,918
1930–34	3,106
1925–29	2,978
1920–24	2,738
1915–19	2,496
1910–14	2,402
1905–09	2,355
1900–04	2,492
1895–99	2,706
1890–94	2,998
1885–89	3,146
1880–84	3,301
1875–79	3,462
1870–74	3,700
1865–69	3,901
1860–64	4,744
1855–59	4,972
1850–54	5,218
1845–49	5,266
1840–44	5,364
1835–39	5,395

SOURCES: Women born 1943–52, Table 5, women born 1953–69, Table 7, Amara Bachu, U.S. Bureau of the Census, Current Population Reports, Series P-20, No. 436, *Fertility of American Women: June 1988* U.S. Government Printing Office, Washington, D.C.: 1989. Women born 1915–39, Table 270, U.S. Bureau of the Census, *1980 Census of Population, Volume 1, Characteristics of the Population, Chapter D, Detailed Population Characteristics, Part 1, Suited Statues Summary,* PC80-1-D1-A, U.S. Government Printing Office, Washington, D.C., March 1984. Women born 1835–1914, Series B 48, U.S. Bureau of the Census, *Historical Statistics of the United States, Colonial Times to 1970,* Bicentennial Edition, Part 1, Washington, D.C. 1975, U.S. Government Printing Office.

NOTES: Data for ever-married women born 1835–1914 and for all women born 1915–1969. Women born 1943–69 were aged 18–24, 25–29, 30–34 in 1988, aged 30–34 in 1983 and 1978. Women born 1915–29 were aged 40–44, 45–49, 50–54, 55–59, and 60–64 in 1980.

mean number of children ever born declined from more than 5.0 children in 1865 to only 2.4 children in the mid-1930s (Figure 2.1). During the baby boom it then increased to 3.1 children per woman in the late 1950s and declined during the baby bust to about 2.1 children per woman since 1975.[9]

By this measure, then, the actual family size of women increased by about 30 percent during the baby boom—that is, by about only one-half as much as the TFR—and the baby-bust decline also was about one-half as large as the decline measured by the TFR. Why were the postwar swings in family size so much smaller than the corresponding swings in fertility?

Norman B. Ryder has provided the answer to this question, calculating that one-half of the baby-boom increase in the TFR was due to: (1) childbearing among older women who had postponed having children during the economic hard times of the Great Depression; (2) a shift toward earlier childbearing among young women after World War II; and (3) the tendency of these young women to space their children's births more closely.[10]

Similarly, more than one-half of the baby-bust decline in the TFR between 1957 and 1976 occurred because: (1) young women who during the baby boom started their childbearing at an early age also finished at an early age, and hence had relatively fewer births later in life; and (2) a shift toward later childbearing and longer spacing of births occurred among women who were beginning to bear children during the late 1960s.

We now turn to a discussion of the effect these changes in women's fertility and family size had on the family size of children.

Family Size Among Children Aged 0–17

Since large families include many children but only one mother, the average family size as calculated for children is larger than the average as calculated for mothers. Nevertheless, trends in children's family size have been broadly similar to trends in the family size of mothers. To

---

[9]Estimates of the number of children ever born may be about 10 percent too high for 1865–1890 because stillbirths may have been reported as live births; and estimates pertaining to more recent years may be too low by as much as 5 percent because of the inappropriate exclusion of out-of-wedlock births. See U.S. Bureau of the Census, *Historical Statistics of the United States, Colonial Times to 1970, Bicentennial Edition, Part 2*, Series B 42-48 (Washington, DC: U.S. Government Printing Office, 1975), p. 46.

[10]Norman B. Ryder, "Components of Temporal Variations in American Fertility," in R. W. Hiorns, ed., *Demographic Patterns in Developed Societies* (London: Taylor & Francis, 1980).

FIGURE 2.2

Dependent and Total Siblings for Children Aged 0–17: 1940–1980

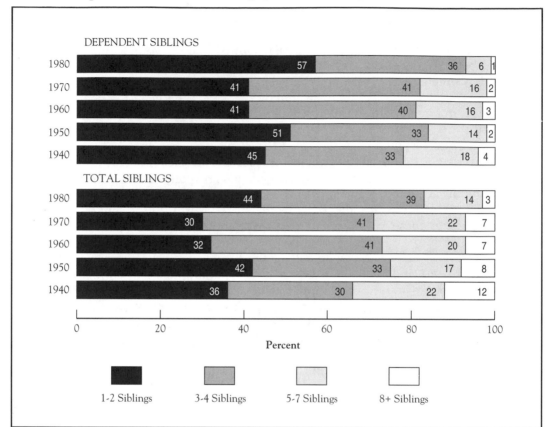

SOURCE: Table 2.3.

NOTES: Dependent siblings calculated for children aged 0–17 living with at least one parent as number of siblings aged 0–17 (including the child) living in the household. Total siblings calculated for children aged 0–17 and living with a mother who has borne at least one child as number of children ever born to the mother.

study family-size change for children since the Great Depression, we begin by focusing broadly on all children under age 18 at three census dates (1950, 1970, and 1980) because these children were born mainly before the baby boom (1932–1949), during the baby boom (1952–1969), and after the baby boom (1962–1979).

For children, the median number of siblings in the family increased by only 20 percent between 1950 and 1970, from 2.4 to 2.9 (Table 2.3).[11] Changes in the distribution of children by family size were also small (Figure 2.2). Between 1950 and 1970, the proportion of children who were in families with 1–2 children declined by 12 percentage points. Since most of this decline is accounted for by the 8 percentage point increase in the proportion living in families with 3–4 siblings, the baby boom brought an increase of only 4 percentage points in the proportion of children living in families with 5 or more siblings.

The baby bust through 1980 brought a drop in children's family size that was larger than the baby-boom increase. Between 1970 and 1980, the median number of siblings dropped by 0.63 siblings, compared with the baby-boom increase of .49 siblings (Table 2.3). Perhaps more important than the size of the sibsize decline, however, is the way in which it occurred. The proportion of children in families with 1–2 children increased by 14 percentage points, mainly because there was an 11–12 percentage point drop in the proportion living in families with 5 or more siblings (Figure 2.2 and Table 2.3).

Still, by 1980, 17 percent of children lived in families with a total of 5 or more siblings. Hence, in 1980 about one-sixth of all children aged 0–17 were growing up in families whose opportunities for upward educational mobility tended to be especially limited by competition among siblings for parental time and attention.

Family Size Among Preschoolers and Adolescents

Competition for the time parents can devote to child care is most keenly experienced by preschool-age children, because preschoolers can be left on their own for only comparatively brief periods. As children grow older, they require less parental attention, but since, as Thomas J. Espenshade has shown, the financial cost of childrearing is greatest during the teenage years, competition among siblings for financial resources is experienced most keenly by adolescents.[12]

Preschoolers Born Between the 1930s and the 1970s

Beginning with preschoolers aged 0–5 who were born between the 1930s and the 1980s, four features of family size have been particularly

---

[11]The "median" is used to measure average family size here because it best represents the situation of the typical child, since one-half of children fall above and one-half fall below the median. Dependent siblings are siblings under age 18 who are living in the home. Total siblings is the number of children ever born to the child's mother, where the child has a mother in the home and the mother has given birth to at least one child.

[12]See Thomas J. Espenshade, *Investing in Children: New Estimates of Parental Expenditures* (Washington, DC: Urban Institute, 1984), pp. 30–31.

TABLE 2.3
Sibsizes of Children Born 1865–1994

Children Aged 0–17 — Percent with Dependent Sibsize

Census Year	Total	Percent	1	2	3	4	5	6	7	8	9+	Median Number of Siblings
1940	37,344	100.0	19.5	25.7	19.7	13.5	8.9	5.9	3.3	2.0	1.6	2.24
1950	43,520	100.0	20.4	30.4	21.0	11.7	7.0	4.6	2.5	1.3	1.1	1.97
1960	62,264	100.0	14.2	27.0	23.9	15.9	8.2	5.0	2.8	1.7	1.3	2.37
1970	67,298	100.0	14.5	26.7	24.0	16.6	9.3	4.5	2.1	1.2	1.2	2.37
1980	61,294	100.0	20.7	36.7	24.6	11.3	4.3	1.4	0.5	0.3	0.3	1.80

Children Aged 0–17 — Percent with Total Sibsize

Census Year	Total	Percent	1	2	3	4	5	6	7	8	9+	Median Number of Siblings
1940	35,783	100.0	15.1	21.2	17.0	13.3	9.4	7.1	5.1	4.1	7.7	2.81
1950	42,126	100.0	14.7	27.2	20.4	12.2	8.1	5.4	4.0	2.7	5.3	2.40
1960	60,605	100.0	8.8	23.2	23.9	16.8	10.0	6.2	3.8	2.7	4.6	2.75
1970	65,007	100.0	8.5	21.4	22.6	18.4	11.0	6.9	4.0	2.6	4.5	2.89
1980	59,072	100.0	12.7	30.8	25.1	14.1	7.5	4.1	2.3	1.3	2.2	2.26

Preschool Children Aged 0–5 — Percent with Total Sibsize

Year of Child's Birth	Total	Percent	1	2	3	4	5	6	7	8	9+	Median Number of Siblings
1930s	11,392	100.0	24.2	26.0	17.1	10.8	6.6	4.8	3.4	2.5	4.6	1.99
1940s	17,208	100.0	17.7	29.3	20.0	11.3	7.2	4.7	3.3	2.2	4.3	2.15
1950s	23,507	100.0	12.6	26.0	24.6	15.4	8.5	5.2	2.8	2.1	2.8	2.46
1960s	19,618	100.0	18.6	30.2	20.9	13.5	7.1	4.0	2.1	1.3	2.3	2.06
1970s	18,195	100.0	24.9	39.2	20.5	8.6	3.4	1.4	0.7	0.4	0.7	1.64

TABLE 2.3 (continued)

Year of Child's Birth	Total	Percent	Adolescent Children Aged 12–17 Percent with Total Sibsize									Median Number of Siblings
			1	2	3	4	5	6	7	8	9+	
1865	—	100.0	1.4	3.5	5.5	7.3	8.9	9.9	10.2	11.0	42.2	7.29
1890	—	100.0	2.2	5.1	7.2	9.0	9.7	10.3	10.2	10.1	36.3	6.64
1920s	12,486	100.0	9.6	17.3	16.0	14.7	11.2	8.7	6.5	5.6	10.4	3.48
1930s	11,407	100.0	12.6	24.7	19.7	12.6	8.9	6.1	4.7	3.4	7.2	2.64
1940s	16,625	100.0	7.6	22.8	22.1	16.0	10.5	6.3	4.6	3.4	6.9	2.89
1950s	21,889	100.0	4.0	16.4	21.9	20.4	13.1	8.7	5.4	3.6	6.5	3.38
1960s	21,286	100.0	5.1	21.4	26.4	18.8	11.4	6.9	3.8	2.4	3.8	2.89
1973 *	—	100.0	6.9	32.7	28.8	16.3	7.8	4.7	1.1	0.7	1.1	2.36
1983 *	—	100.0	7.8	42.1	29.8	13.0	2.9	1.8	1.0	0.6	1.0	2.00
1994 *	—	100.0	5.7	51.2	26.5	11.0	2.3	1.4	0.8	0.5	0.8	1.86

SOURCES: Tables 1 and 2, U.S. Bureau of the Census, *Population. Differential Fertility 1940 and 1910, Fertility for States and Large Cities* (Washington, D.C.: U.S. Government Printing Office, 1943); Series B-48, U.S. Bureau of the Census, *Historical Statistics of the United States, Colonial Times to 1970, Bicentennial Edition, Part 1* (Washington, D.C.: U.S. Government Printing Office, 1975); Amara Bachu, U.S. Bureau of the Census, Current Population Reports, Series P-20, No. 436, *Fertility of American Women: June 1988* (Washington, D.C.: U.S. Government Printing Office, 1989); and unpublished U.S. Census Bureau data provided by Martin O'Connell.

NOTES: Estimates for 1865 and 1890 cohorts based on children ever born data for women aged 45–49 and 70–74 in 1910. These estimates are approximate because they exclude children born to women who did not live to the specified ages. Estimate for census years and for children born between the 1920s and the 1970s derived from 1940–1980 PUMS, based on mothers' children ever born for children living with a mother with at least one child ever born. Estimates for 1973–1994 derived from birth expectation data for women aged 18–24, 30–34, and 40–44 in 1988 Current Population Survey. Estimates for women aged 18–24 and 30–34 are made assuming mean number of births to women with 5+ births are 5.5, and for women aged 40–44 assuming mean number of births to women with 7+ births is 7.5. For the younger age groups, changing the assumption sharply from a mean of 5.5 to 7.5 would increase the proportion of children in such large families, for blacks for example, aged 18–24, by only about 2.5 percentage points. After obtaining estimates of the children in the highest parity categories, these children are distributed through the 9+ category by assuming the distribution corresponds to the most recent distribution based on PUMS data.

* Expected.

— Not available.

prominent (Figure 2.3 and Table 2.3). First, for preschoolers born between the 1930s and the 1970s, the proportion living in families with 8 or more siblings declined from a small 7 percent to only 1 percent. Second, the proportion in families with 5–7 siblings fluctuated between only 13 and 17 percent for cohorts born between the 1930s and the 1960s, then dropped to only 6 percent for the 1970s cohort. Hence, among preschoolers born since at least the 1930s, no more than 22 percent lived in families with 5 or more children, and at least 78 percent lived in families with only 1–4 children.

Third, the proportion of preschoolers living in small families as only-children or with 1 sibling declined from 50 to 39 percent during the baby boom, but this 11 percentage point decline is accounted for by the corresponding increase in the proportion in moderate-size families of 3–4 children. Fourth, among members of the 1970s cohort born during the baby bust, 64 percent lived in small families with 1–2 children, and 93 percent lived in families with 1–4 children.

As each cohort of preschoolers became older and reached adolescence, its average family size increased, because younger siblings were added to many families. If the number of such additional younger siblings had differed substantially across various cohorts of children, then family-size trends across these cohorts as of adolescence would have differed from family-size trends as of the preschool ages. In fact, this was not the case; for each cohort born since the 1930s, the median number of siblings increased by 0.65–0.92 siblings between the preschool and the adolescent ages.

As a result, between the preschool and the adolescent years, the typical child in each cohort born between the 1930s and the 1960s experienced the additional benefits as well as the competition for parental time and financial resources that result from having somewhat less than an additional sibling in the home.[13] We now turn to a longer-term view of family-size trends across successive cohorts of children as of adolescence.

Adolescents Born Between the 1860s and the 1990s

Family size, as of adolescence, can be calculated for children at 10-year intervals between the 1920s and the 1960s using census data for

---

[13]Increases in the number of siblings over the course of childhood have been shown to have a negative effect on the educational attainments of children later in life. See Duane F. Alwin and Arland Thornton, "Family Origins and the Schooling Process: Early Versus Late Influence of Parental Characteristics," *American Sociological Review* 49 (1984): 784–802; and Donald J. Hernandez, "Childhood in Sociodemographic Perspective," in Ralph H. Turner and James F. Short, Jr., eds., *Annual Review of Sociology*, vol. 12 (1986), pp. 159–180.

1940 to 1980.[14] These estimates can be extended back in time for children born as early as 1865 using published 1910 census data, and they can be extended forward in time for children who will be born as late as 1994, using birth expectation data for women now in their childbearing ages.[15]

The median number of siblings in the families of adolescents born in 1994 is expected to be about 1.9—that is, 75 percent smaller than the median of 7.3 siblings recorded for adolescents born in 1865.[16] By the end of the Great Depression—that is, by the 1940s—about four-fifths of this total decline had already occurred, and more than three-fifths of the decline occurred during the 55 years between 1890 and 1945. This re-markable drop in median family size was brought about by a revolutionary shift from large to small families (Figures 2.3 and 2.4 and Table 2.3).

For example, the proportion of adolescents in families with 8 or more siblings declined from 53 percent for the 1865 cohort to only 10 percent for the 1940s cohort, and only 2 percent of the 1973 cohort is expected to live in such families. Hence, about four-fifths of the decline to nearly 0 percent had occurred by the end of the Great Depression, and two-thirds occurred between 1890 and the 1940s.

Meanwhile, the proportion of adolescents in families with 5–7 siblings also declined markedly—from 29–30 percent for adolescents born between 1865 and 1890 to 21 percent for the 1940s cohort, 13 percent

[14]For example, since most adolescents aged 12–17 in 1940 were born in 1922–1927—but some were also born in the first quarter of 1928, and none was born in the first quarter of 1922—the year of birth nearest the midpoint for these adolescents is 1925. For adolescents, the total family size (total number of siblings) is estimated for children living with their mothers as their mothers' past fertility (that is, the number of children ever born to their mothers by the census date). We calculated these estimates from the Public Use Microdata Samples (PUMS).

[15]Using historical data on the number of children ever born to women by the end of their childbearing years, we have calculated family-size estimates for children born, on average, in about 1865. Data on the number of children ever born are available from the 1910 census for women as old as ages 70–74 (that is, for women born as early as 1835–1839). Since the average age of childbearing was about 27 years, the children of these women were born, on average, in about 1865. Similar data are used to estimate the family sizes of children born in 1890 and 1935. Since these estimates for children born in 1935 (adjusted for early childhood mortality) are quite similar to our earlier estimates for children born in 1935 based on PUMS for children aged 12–17 in the 1940 census, the two approaches appear to portray a consistent historical time series. The estimate for the 1973 cohort of children is based on Current Population Survey (CPS) estimates of children ever born to women aged 40–44 in 1988, and the estimate for the 1983 and 1994 cohorts are based on CPS estimates of total births expected by women aged 30–34 and 18–24 in 1988. Martin O'Connell kindly provided estimates of lifetime birth expected for women in 1988 aged 40–44 for births 1, 2, 3, 4, 5–6, and 7+, and for women age 30–34 and 18–24, for births 1, 2, 3, 4, and 5+.

[16]The median is used to measure average family size in this chapter because it represents the situation of the typical adolescent, since one-half of adolescents fall above the median and one-half fall below it.

FIGURE 2.3

Total Sibsizes for Preschoolers and Adolescents Born 1865–1994

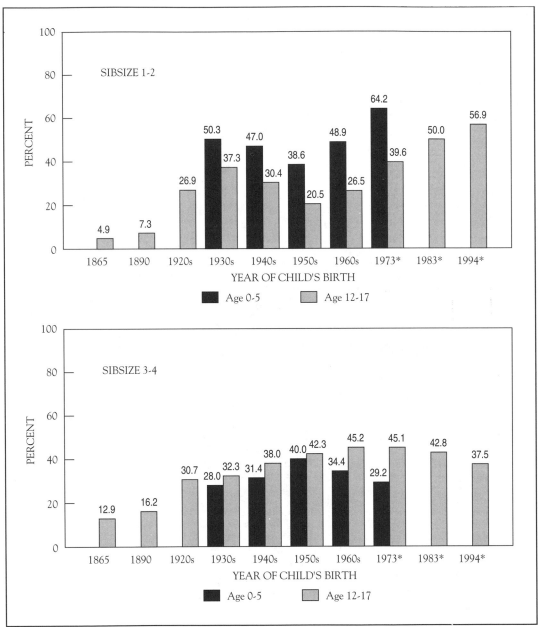

SOURCE: Table 2.3.

FIGURE 2.3 (*continued*)

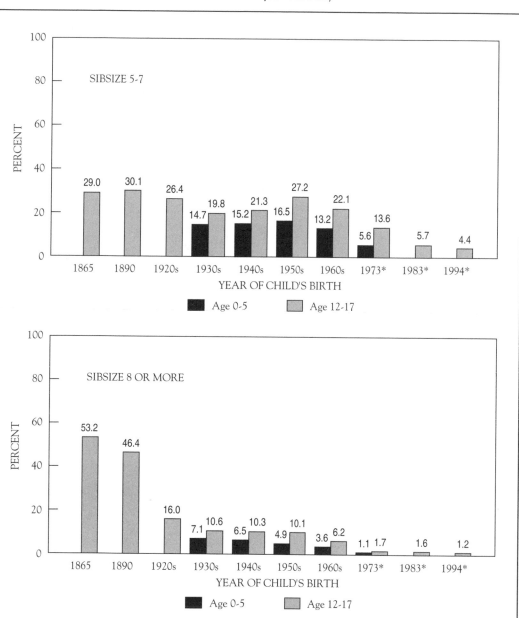

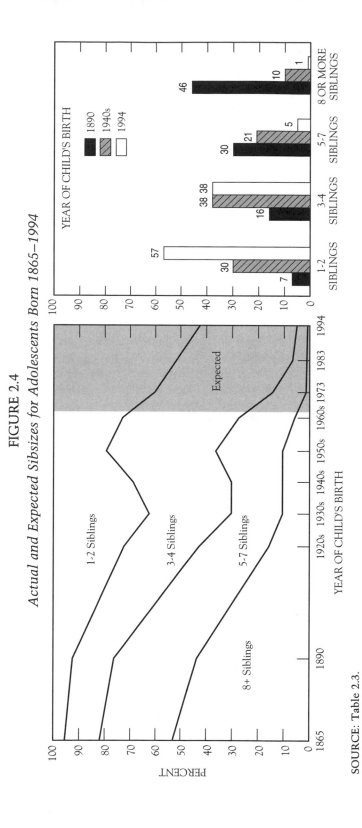

FIGURE 2.4

Actual and Expected Sibsizes for Adolescents Born 1865–1994

SOURCE: Table 2.3.

for the 1973 cohort, and only an expected 5 percent for the 1994 cohort. Although little change occurred between 1865 and 1890, one-third of the expected total decline occurred between 1890 and the 1940s.

Taken together, as of adolescence, 82 percent of the 1865 cohort lived in large families with 5 or more siblings, compared with only 15 percent for the 1973 cohort, and only 6 percent of the 1994 cohort is expected to live in such families. In other words, only 18 percent of adolescents in the 1865 cohort lived in small and moderate-size families with 1–4 children, but this figure increased to 85 percent for the 1973 cohort and is expected to rise to 94 percent for the 1994 cohort. Of the expected 76 percentage point shift from families with 5 or more siblings to families with 1–4 siblings, two-thirds had occurred by the Great Depression, and about three-fifths of the total change occurred during the 55 years between 1890 and the 1940s.

Since only-children as a proportion of all adolescents increased by only 4 percentage points between 1865 and 1994, more than 90 percent of the shift away from large families between 1890 and 1994 is accounted for by the increase in families with 2–4 siblings.

In short, the revolutionary shift toward small families has transformed the family-size experience of adolescents born since 1890, and more than one-half of the change had occurred by the time of the Great Depression. These family-size estimates tend, however, to exaggerate somewhat the decline in sibling companionship and competition experienced by successive cohorts of adolescents, because a century ago many children died at an early age. For example, between 1900 and 1902 and 1939 and 1941, the proportion of children who died before age 1 declined from 14 to 5 percent, and the proportion who died before age 5 declined from 20 to 6 percent.[17]

Alternative family-size estimates that crudely take this mortality decline into account suggest that about (slightly less than) one-half of the shift from large to small families after 1890 had occurred by the Great Depression (Table 2.5).[18] Siblings who die early are a lesser source of companionship and competition than are siblings who survive to adulthood, but since preschoolers make such great demands on their

---

[17]U.S. National Center for Health Statistics, *Vital Statistics of the United States, 1973, Volume II—Section 5, Life Tables* (Rockville, MD: 1975). Calculated from Table 5.4, assuming nonwhites account for 14 percent of the population at each age. Additional deaths by age 20 amounted to only about 3 percent in 1900 and 1 percent in 1940.

[18]These estimates of family size assume that the mortality rates of siblings in the same family are independent—that is, equal. If, however, children in large families actually had higher mortality rates than did children in small families, then the decline in family size was somewhat smaller than indicated here, and the proportion living in families with a large number of siblings who lived to adulthood would be smaller than was indicated by these crude estimates—especially in 1900.

parents' time, and since pregnancy itself may be a considerable drain on the energy of most mothers, siblings who die before adulthood do represent an important source of competition, if not companionship, despite their early death. Taking the decline in childhood mortality into account, then, it is probably best to conclude that about one-half of the expected decline in sibling competition between 1890 and 1994 had occurred by the Great Depression.

As we look toward the future, it appears that one-third of the total expected shift from large families to families with 1–4 siblings has yet to occur, since two-thirds of that shift had occurred as of the 1960s cohort, and this cohort was beyond college age at the time this book was written. If, as expected, the proportion of adolescents in families with 5 or more siblings becomes approximately constant after 1983, then the remaining one-third of the potential improvement in educational opportunities associated with the family-size revolution will have occurred by about 2010—only 18 years from now—when the 1983 cohort has passed through the prime ages of college enrollment.

What Caused the Historic Decline and Recent Swing in Family Size?

The historic decline in U.S. fertility and family size was not unique; all currently developed countries have experienced similar declines. What caused these fertility declines? Kingsley Davis and Judith Blake provide a general explanation.[19] Fundamental social, economic, and political changes since the beginning of the Industrial Revolution had two sets of

[19]Kingsley Davis, "The Theory of Response and Change in Modern Demographic History," *Population Index* 29 (1963):345–366; Judith Blake, "Fertility Control and the Problem of Voluntarism," in Scientists and World Affairs (proceedings of the Twenty-second Pugwash Conference on Science and World Affairs, September 7–12, 1973, London (pp. 279–283)); and Judith Blake, "Demographic Science and the Redirection of Population Policy," Mindel C. Sheps and Jeanne Clare Ridley, eds., *Public Health and Population Change* (Pittsburgh: University of Pittsburgh Press, 1965). For research on more recent fertility declines in Third World countries, see Donald J. Hernandez, *Success or Failure? Family Planning Programs in the Third World* (Westport, CT: Greenwood, 1984), pp. 11–12. The central sociological focus of this explanation of the desire to improve one's relative social and economic status, or to keep from losing ground compared with others, in light of changing social, economic, and political circumstances, remains at the core of much subsequent research concerned with fertility change. Subsequent research, however, tends to concentrate more on the nature of the social, economic, and political processes to which individuals ultimately respond with changes in fertility behavior. For a discussion of more recent studies, see Susan Greehalgh, "Toward a Political Economy of Fertility: Anthropological Contributions," *Population and Development Review* 16, 1 (March 1990): 85–106.

interrelated effects. First, these changes increased opportunities for upward social and economic mobility, and they increased the costs of having children while at the same time reducing parental benefits. In response to these changes, adults sought to improve their relative social and economic standing, or at least to keep from losing ground compared with others who were taking advantage of emerging economic opportunities, in part by limiting their fertility.

In terms of employment, a shift from farming to urban occupations was typically required in order to achieve an improved relative economic status, or to keep from losing ground compared with others.[20] But this shift meant that housing in dense urban areas, food, clothing, and other necessities had to be purchased with cash, making the increasing cost of supporting each additional child increasingly apparent. Yet the potential economic contribution children made to their parents and families was sharply reduced by the passage of laws restricting child labor and mandating compulsory education.

At the same time, as economic growth led to increases in the quality and quantity of available consumer products and services, expected consumption standards rose, and individuals were required to spend more money simply to maintain the new "normal" standard of living. Hence, the costs of supporting each additional child at a "normal" level increased as time passed.

In addition, the newly available goods and services competed with children for parental time and money. Since each additional child in a family requires additional financial support and makes greater demands on parental time and attention, the birth of each child reduces the time and money parents can devote to their own work or careers as well as to recreation and to older children.

Between the beginning of the Industrial Revolution and the Great Depression, then, parents sought to improve their relative economic standing, or to keep from losing ground compared with others who were taking advantage of gradually emerging opportunities, at least in part by

---

[20]The decline in fertility and family size within rural America during the early and mid-1800s also appears to have resulted from the desire of couples to maintain or improve their relative economic status as well as that of their children. In response to the declining availability and increasing cost of farmland, the major source of economic opportunity for most Americans during that time, many individuals may have postponed or forgone marriage and, when married, limited their family size in order to avoid fragmentation of the family farm or to increase their chances of accumulating the financial resources required to establish an independent farm for themselves or their children. For a summary, critique, and citations to this research, see Tamara K. Hareven and Maris A. Vinovskis, eds., *Family and Population in Nineteenth-Century America* (Princeton, NJ: Princeton University Press, 1978), pp. 4–10. Kingsley Davis provides a similar explanation regarding the European agricultural peasantry in "The Theory of Response and Change in Modern Demographic History," *Population Index* 29 (1963): 345–366.

limiting their fertility. This resulted in a substantial, long-term fertility decline.[21] But why was there a reversal in this fertility decline between the end of the Great Depression and the early 1960s, and why did the decline subsequently resume?

In answer to this question, Richard A. Easterlin has made the following suggestions.[22] The postwar baby boom resulted from postwar improvements in the relative incomes of young men compared with the past incomes of their parents during the Great Depression; and the subsequent post-1960 baby bust resulted from a deterioration in the relative incomes of young men compared with the past incomes of their fathers during the postwar economic boom.

Valerie Kincade Oppenheimer extends and refines this explanation, suggesting that young couples judge themselves to be relatively affluent or deprived not only by comparing their own current incomes with their parents' past incomes, but also (1) by comparing both their current and expected incomes with those of older couples who currently are rearing children in fully furnished households, and (2) by comparing their current incomes with the cost of setting up a household furnished to allow for a "normal" adult life, especially one that is suitable for raising a family.[23]

This explanation of the postwar baby boom and subsequent baby bust is generally consistent with available evidence concerning the relative incomes of various groups. The postwar economic boom appears to have provided such immediate opportunities for economic advance that many couples decided they could both satisfy their economic aspirations *and* have an additional child or two, often at an early age and with close spacing. Faced with the sudden postwar explosion of opportunities for young men to advance their education at government expense through the GI Bill, obtain comparatively high-paying jobs with little difficulty, and buy homes with great ease, many couples also decided that they could afford to have an additional child or two, while achieving a comparatively affluent economic status.[24]

Of course, the baby boom was short-lived, lasting little more than

[21]Other responses by individuals and couples to fundamental social, economic, and political changes since the beginning of the Industrial Revolution are discussed in greater detail in Chapter 10.

[22]For a recent summary of this research and references to the early work, see Richard A. Easterlin, *Birth and Fortune: The Impact of Numbers on Personal Welfare* (New York: Basic Books, 1980), especially pp. 41–44.

[23]Valerie Kincade Oppenheimer, *Work and the Family* (New York: Academic, 1982). Especially see pp. 26–27, 123–164.

[24]For a fascinating discussion of how federal policies made homeownership much easier after the Great Depression and World War II, see especially Chapter 11 in Kenneth T. Jackson, *Crabgrass Frontier: The Suburbanization of the United States* (New York: Oxford University Press, 1985).

a decade and a half beyond the end of World War II. The subsequent post-1960 baby bust appears to have resulted from a turnaround in factors that were responsible for the baby boom. After 1960 the relative incomes of young men deteriorated substantially, and after the late 1960s sharp increases occurred in the costs of such normal consumer durables as homes, home furnishings including home appliances, new and used automobiles, and medical care.[25] Many couples responded by postponing marriage and childbearing, then limiting themselves to no more than 3 children.

For example, between 1960 and 1988, the proportion of women aged 20–24 who had never married jumped from 28 to 61 percent, and the proportion who were childless jumped from 47 to 69 percent. Meanwhile, women born between 1930 and 1934—that is, women who were in the primary childbearing ages during the baby boom—had an average of 3.1 births by the end of their childbearing years, the highest average number of births of any women during the twentieth century. But by age 40–44, women born between 1943 and 1947 had an average of only 2.1 births per women, and 85 percent had given birth to no more 3 children.[26]

Although improved birth-control methods, especially the oral contraceptive pill, are sometimes cited as causing the post-1960 baby bust, Judith Blake and Prithwis Das Gupta have calculated that no more than one-fourth of the decline in national fertility between 1960 and 1970 was due to improved birth-control effectiveness; at least 75 percent of the decline was due to the drop in the number of births that women wanted to have in view of their current and expected social and economic circumstances.[27]

[25]Richard A. Easterlin, *Birth and Fortune: The Impact of Numbers on Personal Welfare* (New York: Basic Books, 1980), pp. 44–48; Valerie Kincade Oppenheimer, *Work and Family* (New York: Academic, 1982), pp. 65–164.

[26]Arlene F. Saluter, U.S. Bureau of the Census, *Current Population Reports, Marital Status and Living Arrangements: March 1985.* Series P-20, No. 410. (Washington, DC: U.S. Government Printing Office, 1986), p. 68; Arlene F. Saluter, "Singleness in America," U.S. Bureau of the Census, Current Population Reports, Series P-23, No. 162, (*Studies in Marriage and the Family.* (Washington, DC: U.S. Government Printing Office, 1989), p. 2; Amara Bachu, U.S. Bureau of the Census, Current Population Reports Series P-20, No. 436, *Fertility of American Women: June 1988* (Washington, DC: U.S. Government Printing Office, 1986), pp. 15, 30; Robert L. Heuser, *Fertility Tables for Birth Cohorts by Color: United States, 1917–73*, National Center for Health Statistics, Public Health Service, DHEW No. (HRA) 76-1152 (Washington, DC: U.S. Government Printing Office, 1976), p. 224; U.S. Bureau of the Census, 1980 Census of the Population, Chapter D, Table 270.

[27]See p. 240 in Judith Blake and Prithwis Das Gupta, "Reproductive Motivation Versus Contraceptive Technology: Is Recent American Experience an Exception?" *Population and Development Review* 1: 229–249. For a discussion of the role of modern contraception in fertility declines of newly developed and currently developing countries, see Donald J. Hernandez, *Success or Failure? Family Planning Programs in the Third World* (Westport, CT: Greenwood, 1984); Donald J. Hernandez, "Organizing for Effective Family Planning

The broad explanations offered for both the historic fertility decline and the recent fertility swings, then, involve essentially the same factors—namely, the desire of individuals and couples to improve their relative social and economic standing, or to keep from falling behind, in competition with other couples and in light of changing economic opportunities, assisted during recent decades by technical refinements in birth-control methods.

The Changing Racial Gap in Family Size

Children Aged 0–17 Between 1940 and 1980

Black and white children aged 0–17 experienced quite different changes in median family size between 1940 and 1980 (Table 2.4 and Figure 2.5). For blacks the median number of total siblings increased during the 1940s and the 1950s, but this figure declined during the 1960s and 1970s. For whites, sibling size decreased during the 1940s, but increased during the 1960s and the 1970s, only to fall during the 1980s. The result was that the racial gap in median number of siblings *expanded* sharply by eight-tenths of a sibling during the 1940s, contracted *slightly* by two-tenths of a sibling during the 1950s, and contracted *sharply* by five-tenths of a sibling during the 1960s. Finally, during the 1970s both black and white children experienced declines in sibling size, but the decline was much larger for blacks, and the racial gap continued to contract sharply, by six-tenths of a sibling. Overall, then, the racial gap in median number of siblings nearly doubled, from 1.1 siblings in 1940 to 1.9 in 1950. But it then shrank by more than two-thirds, reaching only 0.6 of a sibling in 1980.

Adolescents Born Between 1865 and 1994

Despite a sizable racial gap, trends in family size by race were broadly similar for adolescents born between 1865 and the 1920s (Figure 2.6 and Table 2.4). The proportion of adolescents in families with 8 or more

---

Programs," a review of a National Research Council report in *Population and Development Review* 14, 1 (1988):198–201; and Donald J. Hernandez, "A Comment on Barbara Entwisle's 'Measuring Components of Family Planning Program Effort,'" *Demography* 26, 1 (1989): 77–80. For a comprehensive summary of population policies, see Donald J. Hernandez, "Population Policy," in Adam Kuper and Jessica Kuper, eds., *The Social Science Encyclopedia* (London: Routledge, 1985), p. 628.

TABLE 2.4
Sibsizes of White and Black Children Born 1865–1994

White

Children Aged 0–17
Percent with Dependent Sibsize

Census Year	Total	Percent	1	2	3	4	5	6	7	8	9+	Median Number of Siblings
1940	33,620	100.0	20.2	26.6	19.9	13.4	8.5	5.4	2.9	1.7	1.4	2.16
1950	39,036	100.0	21.3	31.9	21.5	11.5	6.1	4.0	2.0	1.0	0.8	1.90
1960	55,114	100.0	14.7	28.5	24.9	15.8	7.6	4.2	2.1	1.3	0.9	2.27
1970	58,545	100.0	14.9	27.9	24.9	16.6	8.3	3.9	1.7	0.8	1.0	2.29
1980	52,676	100.0	21.0	38.0	24.8	10.7	3.5	1.1	0.4	0.2	0.2	1.76

Children Aged 0–17
Percent with Total Sibsize

Census Year	Total	Percent	1	2	3	4	5	6	7	8	9+	Median Number of Siblings
1940	32,363	100.0	15.6	22.0	17.2	13.4	9.3	6.8	4.9	3.9	7.0	2.72
1950	37,968	100.0	15.3	28.7	21.2	12.2	7.6	5.0	3.4	2.3	4.4	2.28
1960	53,844	100.0	9.1	24.8	25.1	17.2	9.7	5.4	3.0	2.2	3.4	2.64
1970	56,661	100.0	8.6	22.7	23.8	19.0	10.7	6.4	3.6	2.1	3.2	2.79
1980	50,832	100.0	12.8	32.2	25.9	14.1	6.9	3.8	1.9	1.1	1.4	2.20

Preschool Children Aged 0–5
Percent with Total Sibsize

Year of Child's Birth	Total	Percent	1	2	3	4	5	6	7	8	9+	Median Number of Siblings
1930s	10,211	100.0	25.4	27.0	17.1	10.5	6.3	4.4	3.0	2.4	3.9	1.91
1940s	15,560	100.0	18.5	30.8	20.6	11.4	6.5	4.2	2.8	1.8	3.5	2.04
1950s	20,748	100.0	13.2	27.4	25.8	15.5	8.0	4.3	2.1	1.6	2.1	2.36
1960s	19,988	100.0	19.0	31.7	21.6	13.4	6.5	3.5	1.8	1.0	1.6	1.98
1970s	15,696	100.0	25.4	40.4	20.8	8.1	2.9	1.2	0.6	0.4	0.4	1.61

41

TABLE 2.4 (continued)

White

Year of Child's Birth	Total	Percent	Adolescent Children Aged 12–17 Percent with Total Sibsize									Median Number of Siblings
			1	2	3	4	5	6	7	8	9+	
1865	—	100.0	1.5	3.6	5.7	7.6	9.4	10.3	10.4	11.3	40.2	7.14
1890	—	100.0	2.3	5.5	7.7	9.6	10.3	10.8	10.6	10.3	33.1	6.37
1920s	11,384	100.0	9.6	17.7	16.4	15.1	11.4	8.6	6.4	5.3	9.6	3.42
1930s	10,235	100.0	13.1	26.1	20.9	12.6	8.6	5.7	4.1	2.9	6.1	2.52
1940s	14,987	100.0	7.8	24.3	23.1	16.4	10.3	5.8	4.0	2.9	5.3	2.77
1950s	19,251	100.0	4.0	17.7	23.2	21.2	13.1	8.2	4.9	2.9	4.7	3.24
1960s	18,302	100.0	5.1	22.7	27.8	19.4	10.8	6.4	3.3	2.0	2.5	2.80
1973*	—	100.0	7.0	33.3	29.8	15.7	7.1	4.2	1.2	0.7	0.9	2.33
1983*	—	100.0	7.6	43.9	30.1	12.5	2.6	1.5	0.8	0.5	0.6	1.97
1994*	—	100.0	4.9	51.8	26.7	11.2	2.4	1.4	0.7	0.4	0.5	1.87

Black

Census Year	Total	Percent	Children Aged 0–17 Percent with Dependent Sibsize									Median Number of Siblings
			1	2	3	4	5	6	7	8	9+	
1940	3,725	100.0	13.3	17.7	17.5	14.4	12.4	10.7	6.3	4.4	3.3	3.11
1950	4,483	100.0	13.0	17.2	16.3	13.4	15.0	10.2	7.0	4.3	3.7	3.21
1960	7,150	100.0	10.0	15.5	16.3	16.5	12.6	11.3	7.8	5.1	4.8	3.50
1970	8,753	100.0	11.6	18.7	18.0	16.7	15.6	8.3	4.7	3.5	2.9	3.10
1980	8,618	100.0	18.9	29.0	23.4	14.5	8.8	3.2	1.0	0.4	0.8	2.09

Census Year	Total	Percent	Children Aged 0–17 Percent with Total Sibsize									Median Number of Siblings
			1	2	3	4	5	6	7	8	9+	
1940	3,420	100.0	10.8	14.2	14.7	12.4	10.4	9.4	7.4	6.6	14.3	3.84
1950	4,157	100.0	8.9	13.8	12.8	12.0	12.7	9.7	9.1	7.1	13.8	4.19
1960	6,761	100.0	6.0	11.8	14.2	13.8	12.3	12.0	9.8	6.6	13.6	4.34
1970	8,346	100.0	7.9	13.2	14.6	14.9	13.2	10.3	6.9	6.3	12.9	3.97
1980	8,240	100.0	12.0	22.8	19.7	14.0	11.4	6.4	4.3	2.8	6.8	2.76

FIGURE 2.5

Total and Dependent Sibsizes for White and Black Children Aged 0–17:
1940–1980

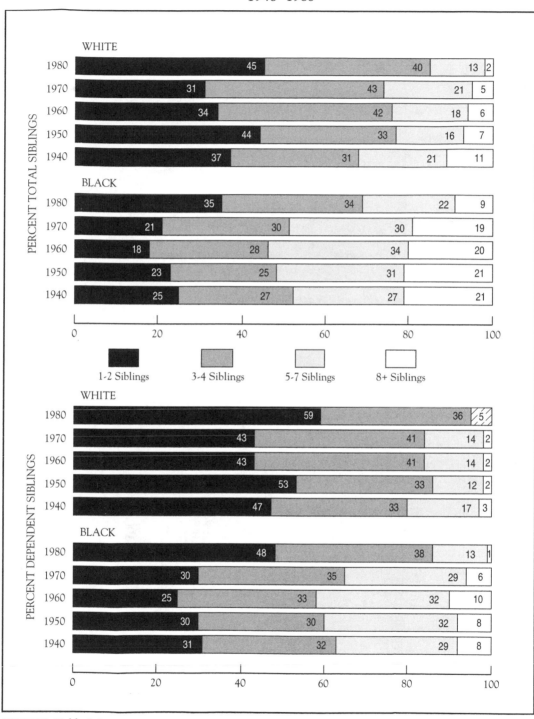

SOURCE: Table 2.4.

TABLE 2.4 (continued)

Year of Child's Birth	Total	Percent	Preschool Children Aged 0-5 Percent with Total Sibsize									Median Number of Siblings
			1	2	3	4	5	6	7	8	9+	
1930s	1,181	100.0	13.6	17.6	17.7	13.4	9.7	8.2	6.3	3.6	10.0	3.09
1940s	1,648	100.0	10.1	15.7	14.9	10.8	12.9	9.5	8.5	6.1	11.5	3.86
1950s	2,759	100.0	7.8	15.6	15.5	14.6	12.4	12.0	8.1	5.6	8.6	3.76
1960s	2,630	100.0	15.9	20.5	16.4	14.3	11.3	7.2	4.2	3.6	6.6	2.83
1970s	2,499	100.0	22.0	32.1	19.2	11.6	7.0	3.2	1.8	0.9	2.2	1.87

Year of Child's Birth	Total	Percent	Adolescent Children Aged 12-17 Percent with Total Sibsize									Median Number of Siblings
			1	2	3	4	5	6	7	8	9+	
1865	—	100.0	1.2	2.0	3.6	4.1	4.8	6.2	7.8	7.5	62.9	9.11
1890	—	100.0	1.6	2.7	3.7	5.2	5.7	6.7	7.3	8.9	58.3	9.00
1920s	1,102	100.0	9.2	13.2	12.5	10.6	9.8	9.3	7.6	9.0	18.9	4.47
1930s	1,173	100.0	8.4	12.7	9.6	12.5	11.8	10.2	10.1	8.1	16.7	4.58
1940s	1,638	100.0	5.7	8.4	12.2	11.8	11.8	10.7	10.1	8.0	21.3	5.02
1950s	2,638	100.0	3.8	7.6	12.2	14.2	13.3	12.0	8.8	8.5	19.5	4.92
1960s	2,984	100.0	5.0	13.3	17.8	15.1	15.1	10.0	6.7	4.9	12.2	3.92
1973*	—	100.0	7.1	26.9	22.1	20.0	13.3	8.8	0.5	0.4	1.0	2.73
1983*	—	100.0	10.0	32.7	26.0	16.9	4.5	2.9	2.0	1.4	3.6	2.28
1994*	—	100.0	12.3	44.7	25.9	10.0	2.2	1.5	1.0	0.7	1.8	1.84

SOURCES: See Table 2.3.

NOTES: See Table 2.3.

* Expected.

— Not available.

FIGURE 2.6

Actual and Expected Sibsizes for White and Black Adolescents Born 1865–1994

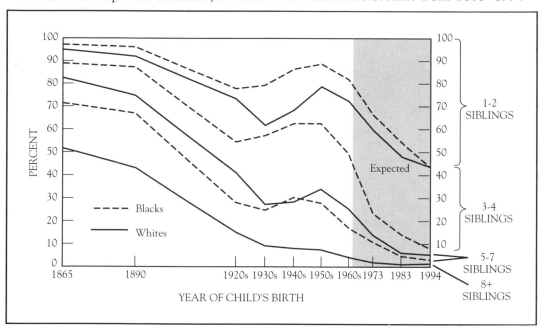

SOURCE: Table 2.4.

siblings declined greatly—from 70 and 52 percent for blacks and whites, respectively, to only 28 and 15 percent. Meanwhile, the proportion of adolescents in families with 1–4 siblings increased greatly—from 11 to 46 percent for blacks and from 18 to 59 percent for whites. Most of these shifts from large to small and moderate-size families occurred for cohorts born between 1890 and the 1920s.

Then racial trends in family size diverged sharply for adolescents born between the 1920s and the 1940s, because the proportion in families with 1–4 children continued to increase for whites, but declined for blacks by 13 and 8 percentage points, respectively. As a result, the racial gap in the proportion of adolescents living in families with 1–4 children more than doubled, jumping from 8–14 percentage points for the 1865–1920s cohorts to 34 percentage points for the 1940s cohort.

For adolescents born after 1945, however, racial trends in family size converged sharply, first because family-size increases were smaller for blacks than for whites during the baby boom and then because family-size declines were larger for blacks than for whites during the baby bust. During the baby boom, for adolescents born between the 1940s

45

and the 1950s the proportion living in families with 1–2 children declined for blacks and whites by 3 versus 10 percentage points, respectively. Increases for blacks and for whites occurred mainly in the proportions with 4–6 siblings.

Then during the baby bust, for black adolescents born between the 1950s and 1973, the proportion living in families with 8 or more siblings plummeted from 28 to 1 percent, and the racial gap of 20 percentage points vanished. Similarly, the proportion of black adolescents living in families with 1–4 children jumped from 38 to 76 percent, and the racial gap narrowed from 28 to 10 percentage points.

If the birth expectations of women currently in their childbearing ages are realized, the racial gap will essentially vanish for adolescents born in 1994, with only 5 percent in families with 5–7 siblings, 57 percent in families with 1–2 children, and 83 percent in families with 1–3 children. In short, the family-size revolution for both black and white adolescents, involving a shift from at least 80 percent in families with 5 or more siblings to at least 90 percent in families with 1–4 children, will have occurred in little more than a century. Of the total increase expected to occur in the proportion of adolescents living in families with 1–4 children, about 40 percent occurred for both blacks and whites born between 1890 and the 1920s, and an additional 20 percent had occurred for whites born by the 1940s.

Despite the subsequent small reversal, for baby-bust children born in 1973, who were age 18 as of this writing in 1991, about 80 percent of the expected increase for blacks and 90 percent of the expected increase for whites living in families with 1–4 children has occurred, and the remaining expected increase will occur for both blacks and whites born as of 1994. Hence, the family-size revolution is nearly complete, and only 30 years from now children born in the new family-size era will already have passed through the main ages of college attendance.

The Drop in Childhood Mortality

Around 1890, the proportion of children who died before age 1 was about 23 percent for blacks and 12 percent for whites, and the proportion of those who died before age 15 was about 40 percent for blacks and 20 percent for whites. Only 40 years later, the proportion of children who died before age 15 had plummeted to 10 and 6 percent for blacks and whites, respectively; and by 1973 the proportion who died by age 15 had experienced a further drop to 4 percent for blacks and 2 percent for whites.[28]

[28]National Center for Health Statistics, *Vital Statistics of the United States, 1973. Volume II, Section 5. Life Tables* (Rockville, MD: 1975), Table 5–4.

Particularly for blacks, high childhood mortality rates, combined with very large proportions in large families in 1890, imply that many children lived in families that experienced the death of one or more siblings (see derivation of results in Table 2.5). For example, among blacks living in families with 8 siblings, 68 percent lost 3 or more siblings through death by age 15, and 40 percent lost 4 or more siblings.

Hence, although 67 percent of black children born in 1890 had a total of 8 or more siblings, only 18 percent lived in families in which 8 or more siblings survived to age 15. Similarly, although 43 percent of white children lived in families with 8 or more siblings, only 26 percent lived in families in which 8 or more siblings survived to age 15.

By the 1930s, however, because childhood mortality had dropped greatly, the distribution of children age 15 by number of living siblings was fairly similar to the distribution of children age 15 by the total number of siblings that had ever been born into their families. Hence, the declines in total family size between about 1890 and 1925–35 tend to exaggerate, as we discussed earlier, the magnitude of the decline in sibling companionship and competition that occurred. This is especially true for blacks. Although we have seen that the proportion of blacks with a total of 8 siblings declined by about 40 percentage points for black children born between 1890 and the 1930s (Table 2.4), crude estimates indicate that the proportion in families with 8 or more siblings surviving to age 15 actually increased by approximately 13 percentage points (Table 2.5).

Children who die at an early age may provide only limited companionship, but they still represent a substantial demand on the time of parents (or older siblings). Among adolescents born between 1890 and the 1930s, we saw that blacks experienced a greater decline than did whites in the proportion in families with a total of 8 or more siblings (Table 2.4). But blacks appear to have experienced an increase in the proportion in families with 8 or more siblings surviving to age 15, while whites experienced an equally large decline, of about 13 percentage points (Table 2.5). Hence, it appears likely, overall, that the racial gap in sibling competition increased somewhat for adolescents born between 1890 and the 1930s.

Causes of Change in the Family-Size Racial Gap

The increasing family-size racial gap between the 1920s and the 1950s, and the subsequent narrowing of the racial gap, cannot be explained without exploring the causes of the earlier family-size changes among blacks and whites. Since family-size declines for black and white

TABLE 2.5
Adolescents Born Circa 1890 and 1935, by Total Siblings Surviving Past Age 15, by Race

Year of Child's Birth	Percent	Total Mortality-Adjusted Sibsize										Median Number of Siblings
		1	2	3	4	5	6	7	8	9	10+	
Circa 1890	100.0	4.8	8.7	11.3	12.8	13.1	12.7	11.6	10.1	7.5	7.4	4.95
Circa 1935	100.0	10.5	20.4	18.1	13.8	9.9	7.3	5.3	3.7	1.9	9.2	3.08

Year of Child's Birth	Percent	White Mortality-Adjusted Sibsize										Median Number of Siblings
		1	2	3	4	5	6	7	8	9	10+	
Circa 1890	100.0	4.7	8.7	11.4	12.8	13.0	12.3	11.2	9.9	8.4	7.8	4.96
Circa 1935	100.0	10.7	21.4	18.9	14.1	9.9	7.1	5.0	3.6	1.8	7.4	2.94

Year of Child's Birth	Percent	Black Mortality-Adjusted Sibsize										Median Number of Siblings
		1	2	3	4	5	6	7	8	9	10+	
Circa 1890	100.0	5.5	8.5	11.0	12.9	14.3	15.2	14.9	12.3	0.9	4.5	4.84
Circa 1935	100.0	8.7	11.7	11.5	11.0	10.0	8.8	7.2	4.6	3.2	23.2	4.72

SOURCES: See Table 2.3, and Footnotes 17 and 18.

NOTES: Premortality-adjusted sibsizes were derived as indicated in Table 2.3 from results on children ever born for women aged 45–49 in 1910 and aged 50–54 in 1960. The children of these women were born, on average, in about 1890 and 1935. Over the course of childhood, these cohorts of children experienced, at least approximately, the mortality rates of 1900 and 1940. These results are necessarily crude, but in view of the large mortality changes in the first part of the 1900s, they provide some indication of the magnitude of changes in surviving sibsizes that actually occurred, for children who themselves survived to age 15. These estimates are only approximate, as reflected in the differences between mortality adjusted estimates here and corresponding estimates for the 1920 cohort derived from PUMS in Tables 2.3 and 2.4. Still, mortality-adjusted estimates for the white 1930 cohort appear to lie about midway between the PUMS-based estimates for the 1920s and 1930s cohorts, and the mortality-adjusted results for the black 1930 cohort are fairly similar to the 1920s and 1930s cohort derived from the PUMS.

children born between 1865 and the 1920s are generally similar, we can only conclude that the declines resulted largely from the same factors.

In fact, after the Civil War and emancipation, blacks as well as whites moved away from farming communities and into cities and other urban areas. On the eve of the Civil War in 1860, 89 percent of blacks lived in slavery, most, no doubt, on farms.[29] The proportion of blacks living in urban areas increased after the Civil War—from 13 percent in 1880 to 20–23 percent in 1900 and 34 percent in 1920. For whites, the corresponding increases were from 28 percent to 40–43 percent to 53 percent.[30]

Perhaps equally important, as early as 1900, only 53 percent of employed blacks worked as agricultural laborers or farmers; nearly one-half worked in nonagricultural occupations.[31] Hence, although it is clear that blacks lagged behind whites in their movement off the farm through 1920, it is equally clear that after the Civil War, blacks as well as whites moved from farms to cities, no doubt with the hope that obtaining nonagricultural occupations would allow them to improve, or at least maintain, their relative economic standing. In doing so many blacks, like many whites, were exposed to the increasing costs and declining benefits of children.

In addition, however, in reviewing existing research Reynolds Farley and Walter R. Allen suggest that the sharp increase in tuberculosis (TB) reported during the decades following the Civil War may have contributed to the family-size decline among blacks.[32] Tuberculosis often leads to sterility, and

The diet of blacks, which may have been adequate during slavery, probably deteriorated as they became sharecroppers and entered the cash economy to buy food. . . . By the 1890s tenant farmers' diets included few proteins or vitamins, a diet that would encourage TB. Those blacks who moved to the cities probably increased their risk because of their poverty, the absence of health programs, and their greater exposure to the infected white population.

Since about 1905 tuberculosis has declined in the United States, with the rate of decrease among nonwhites being much greater after

[29]Reynolds Farley and Walter R. Allen, *The Color Line and the Quality of Life in America* (New York: Russell Sage Foundation, 1987), p. 13.

[30]U.S. Bureau of the Census, *Historical Statistics of the United States, Colonial Times to 1970, Bicentennial Edition, Part 1* (Washington, DC: U.S. Government Printing Office, 1975) Series A, 76–79, p. 12.

[31]U.S. Bureau of the Census, *Negro Population 1790–1915* (Washington, DC: U.S. Government Printing Office, 1918), p. 88; U.S. Bureau of the Census, *Negroes in the United States*, Bulletin 8 (Washington, DC: U.S. Government Printing Office, 1940), p. 57.

[32]Farley and Allen, pp. 20–21.

1935 than before. Trends in fertility among blacks—especially child-lessness—match the trends in TB.[33]

Trends in childlessness among whites have been similar to those reported for blacks, although the increase from 7 to 29 percent for black women born between 1850 and 1909 was 10 percentage points greater than the increase from 8 to 20 percent recorded for white women.[34]

After reviewing additional existing research, Farley and Allen go on to suggest that the comparatively high rates of gonorrhea and syphilis found among blacks may also have contributed to the low family size of blacks during the 1920s and 1930s by producing increases in sterility, stillbirths, and spontaneous abortions.[35]

For children born in a specific year, most siblings are born no more than 10 years earlier or 10 years later, with, on average about one-half of the siblings being born earlier and about one-half being born later. For example, for adolescents born in 1925, most siblings were born before 1935; for adolescents born in 1935, about one-half of siblings were born after 1935; and for adolescents born in 1945, nearly all siblings were born after 1935. Since the rate of decrease in TB among blacks was much greater after 1935 than before, and since public health programs during the late 1930s and the discovery of penicillin in 1943 led to a sharp drop in venereal disease during the 1940s, these health improvements may be responsible for much of the increasing racial gap in family size among adolescents born between the 1920s and the 1950s.[36]

In addition, for adolescents born between the 1940s and the 1950s, it seems likely that unprecedented prosperity following World War II allowed significant proportions of both whites and blacks to achieve their economic desires and still have an additional child or two. The much smaller proportion of black children in families with only one or two siblings in the 1940s may, however, at least partly account for the smaller shift away from small families recorded for blacks than for whites among adolescents born between 1945 and 1955 (see Chapter 7).

Finally, the family-size declines and the narrowing of the racial gap in family size for adolescents born between the 1940s and 1973 are expected to continue until the racial gap essentially vanishes for adolescents born in 1994. In general, it appears that about two-thirds of the expected racial convergence between the 1940s and 1994 had occurred for children born by 1973 who are now approaching college age. For example, for children born between the 1940s and 1973, the racial gap is

[33]Farley and Allen, pp. 20–21.
[34]For source, see Table 2.1.
[35]Farley and Allen, pp. 21–23.
[36]Farley and Allen, pp. 21–23.

expected to decline from 34 to 10 percentage points for the proportion in families with 5 or more siblings, and from 18 to 6 percentage points for the proportion in families with 1–2 siblings (Table 2.4).

Family Size Among Hispanics and Non-Hispanics

Hispanic children (of any race) in 1980 were nearly identical to non-Hispanic black children in family size (Figure 2.7 and Table 2.6). For example, among Hispanic children (of any race) the proportions living in families with a total of 5–7 and 8 or more siblings were 20 and 7 percent, respectively, compared with 22 and 10 percent for non-Hispanic blacks. The small 5 percentage point difference is accounted for by the slightly larger proportion of Hispanic children (of any race) living in families with 2–4 children.

In addition, first-generation Hispanics (of any race) have family sizes only slightly larger than old-family Hispanics (of any race). In 1980 the proportion of children living in families with a total of 5 or more siblings was 30 percent for first-generation Hispanics (of any race) and 26 percent for old-family Hispanics (of any race), a difference accounted for by the 6 percentage point gap in the proportion living in small families with 1–3 children.

Looking toward the future, birth expectations for current U.S. residents suggest that Hispanic adolescents (of any race) born in 1994 will be only 6 percentage points less likely than non-Hispanic blacks and non-Hispanic whites to live in families with 1–2 siblings (51 versus 57 percent), and only 4 percentage points more likely to live in families with 4 or more siblings. Hence, median family sizes are expected to be almost identical: 1.97 for Hispanics, 1.84 for non-Hispanic blacks, and 1.87 for non-Hispanic whites.

Conclusions

Children experienced a revolutionary shift from large to small families during the past 100 years. Comparing adolescents born in 1890 with today's adolescents (born in 1973), the proportions living in families with 5–7 and 8+ siblings plummeted from 30 and 46 percent, respectively, to only 14 and 2 percent, while the proportions living in families with 1–2 and 3–4 siblings jumped from 7 and 16 percent, respectively, to 40 and 45 percent. As the family-size revolution continues, among adoles-

FIGURE 2.7

Sibsizes for Hispanic and Non-Hispanic Children Aged 0–17: 1980

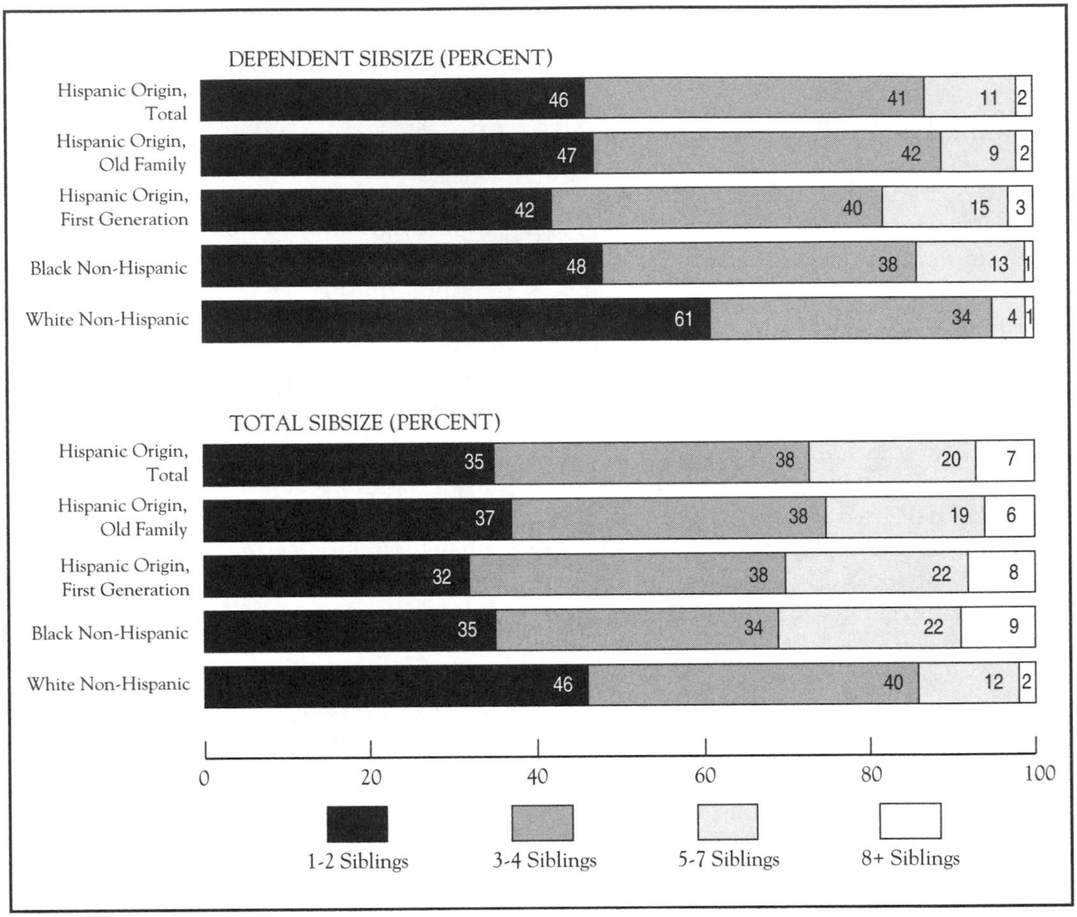

DEPENDENT SIBSIZE (PERCENT)

Hispanic Origin, Total	46	41	11 2
Hispanic Origin, Old Family	47	42	9 2
Hispanic Origin, First Generation	42	40	15 3
Black Non-Hispanic	48	38	13 1
White Non-Hispanic	61	34	4 1

TOTAL SIBSIZE (PERCENT)

Hispanic Origin, Total	35	38	20 7
Hispanic Origin, Old Family	37	38	19 6
Hispanic Origin, First Generation	32	38	22 8
Black Non-Hispanic	35	34	22 9
White Non-Hispanic	46	40	12 2

0   20   40   60   80   100

■ 1-2 Siblings   ▨ 3-4 Siblings   ▢ 5-7 Siblings   □ 8+ Siblings

SOURCE: Table 2.6

cents born during the mid-1990s, the proportion living in families with 5+ siblings is expected to fall to only 6 percent, and the proportion living in families with 1–2 and 3–4 siblings is expected to rise to 57 and 38 percent, respectively.

One consequence of this family-size revolution was a decline in the number of siblings who would be available as potential companions during childhood and through adulthood. However, because children also compete with siblings for parental attention and financial resources during childhood, and because children from smaller families experience

TABLE 2.6

Sibsizes of Hispanic and Non-Hispanic Children Born 1960s–1994

Hispanic Origin and Race	Total	Percent	Children Aged 0–17 in 1980 Percent with Dependent Sibsize									Median Number of Siblings
			1	2	3	4	5	6	7	8	9+	
Hispanic (Living with Mother)	5,294	100.0	16.3	29.9	24.9	16.4	6.7	2.8	1.1	0.6	1.3	2.15
Old family	3,409	100.0	16.3	31.2	26.4	15.8	6.2	1.9	0.6	0.7	0.9	2.09
First generation	1,795	100.0	15.5	26.8	22.3	18.0	8.2	4.7	2.0	0.5	2.1	2.36
Non-Hispanic White	47,495	100.0	21.5	38.9	24.8	10.1	3.2	0.9	0.3	0.2	0.1	1.73
Non-Hispanic Black	8,505	100.0	18.9	28.9	23.5	14.6	8.8	3.3	1.0	0.4	0.7	2.09

	Total	Percent	Children Aged 0–17 in 1980 Percent with Total Sibsize									Median Number of Siblings
			1	2	3	4	5	6	7	8	9+	
Hispanic (Living with Mother)	5,139	100.0	11.2	24.0	21.5	16.3	9.3	5.9	4.8	2.2	4.8	2.65
Old family	3,362	100.0	11.6	25.1	22.1	15.8	9.5	5.2	4.3	2.0	4.5	2.60
First generation	1,777	100.0	10.5	22.0	20.3	17.4	8.8	7.4	5.6	2.7	5.4	2.87
Non-Hispanic White	45,802	100.0	13.0	33.0	26.4	13.8	6.6	3.5	1.6	1.0	1.1	2.15
Non-Hispanic Black	8,131	100.0	11.8	22.8	19.8	14.1	11.4	6.4	4.3	2.8	6.7	2.78

Year of Child's Birth 1970s	Total	Percent	Preschool Children Aged 0–5 Percent with Total Sibsize									Median Number of Siblings
			1	2	3	4	5	6	7	8	9+	
Hispanic (Living with Mother)	1,835	100.0	21.7	34.7	18.9	12.9	5.1	2.5	1.9	0.8	1.7	1.82
Old family	1,180	100.0	22.9	35.9	19.2	11.3	5.2	2.0	1.7	0.5	1.4	1.75
First generation	655	100.0	19.5	32.4	18.5	15.7	4.9	3.4	2.3	1.2	2.1	1.94
Non-Hispanic White	13,906	100.0	25.9	41.1	21.0	7.5	2.6	1.0	0.4	0.3	0.3	1.59
Non-Hispanic Black	2,454	100.0	21.8	32.1	19.2	11.8	7.0	3.3	1.8	0.9	2.2	1.88

TABLE 2.6 (continued)

Year of Child's Birth 1960s	Total	Percent	Adolescent Children Aged 12–17 Percent with Total Sibsize									Median Number of Siblings
			1	2	3	4	5	6	7	8	9+	
Hispanic (Living with Mother)	1,570	100.0	3.8	13.9	20.1	18.5	13.4	9.9	8.2	3.8	8.3	3.66
Old-family	1,067	100.0	3.8	14.3	20.6	19.2	14.2	9.0	7.7	3.7	7.6	3.59
First generation	503	100.0	4.0	12.9	19.1	16.9	11.9	11.7	9.3	4.2	9.9	3.83
Non-Hispanic White	16,770	100.0	5.2	23.6	28.5	19.4	10.6	6.1	2.9	1.8	2.0	2.74
Non-Hispanic Black	2,946	100.0	4.8	13.3	17.9	15.0	15.2	10.1	6.7	4.9	12.1	3.93

Year of Child's Birth Hispanic Origin	Total	Percent	Adolescent Children Aged 12–17 Expected Percentage with Sibsize						Median Number of Siblings
			1	2	3	4	5–6	7+	
1973	—	100.0	4.4	20.6	21.9	13.3	28.8	11.1	3.23
		Percent	1	2	3	4	5+		
1983	—	100.0	6.6	35.4	30.4	17.4	10.3		2.26
1994	—	100.0	4.2	47.1	28.0	14.2	6.5		1.97

SOURCES: See Table 2.3.

NOTES: See Table 2.3.

—Not available.

greater opportunities for educational advancement, as well as for obtaining occupations with a relatively high social status and income during adulthood, the family-size revolution has also had beneficial consequences for childhood experience and for achieving success during adulthood.

Since we were approximately midway through the family-size revolution by the end of the Great Depression, about half of ultimate consequences had occurred among children born by then, and since the postwar baby boom had a small, short-term effect on family size, the baby boom is best viewed as a brief lull in the revolution rather than as a sharp reversal.

The historic cause of the family-size revolution appears to have been social, economic, and political changes that have taken place since the beginning of the Industrial Revolution—including gradually emerging social and economic opportunities—that acted to increase the costs, while at the same time reducing the benefits, of having children. These changes required couples to limit their family size in order to improve their relative social and economic status, or to keep from falling behind others who were taking advantage of emerging opportunities.

The brief postwar shift toward slightly larger families appears to have resulted from a sharp change in conditions—namely, the postwar economic boom and the resulting rapid increase in relative incomes that allowed some couples to both achieve their economic goals and have an additional child or two. Following the postwar economic boom, the historic family-size decline resumed.

Finally, despite historically significant racial differences in family size, racial trends in family size were generally similar for adolescents born between the Civil War and the 1920s. Then, after a brief 20-year hiatus of family-size divergence, apparently resulting from comparatively rapid reductions among blacks in TB and venereal diseases, which can lead to sterility, spontaneous abortions, and still births, the family size of black and white children converged. Among children born during the next few years, family-size differences between black and white children, and between Hispanic children (of any race) and non-Hispanic children, are expected to virtually vanish.

Of course, companionship and resources available to children in their homes depend not only on the number of siblings in the family but also upon the number of parents and other adults who live with children. In the next chapter we will focus on historic changes in the life course experience of children that resulted from changes in the living arrangements of their parents and grandparents.

3

THE CHANGING MIX OF PARENTS
AND GRANDPARENTS
IN CHILDHOOD HOMES

Introduction and Highlights

B IOLOGICALLY, every child has two parents, and it is a social fact that most newborns live with both of their biological parents. Yet historically a large minority of children have spent part of their childhood living with only one (or neither) biological parent, and this will increase to a majority for children born since 1980. Since most children depend primarily upon the parents in their homes for financial support and day-to-day care, children living with one (or neither) parent may experience financial difficulties, and they may also receive less parental attention than do children living with both parents. Of course, other adult family members, such as grandparents or stepparents, may fill the gap left by an absent parent. In this chapter we will discuss the transformation in family life that is associated with the changing mix of parents and grandparents in the homes of children born during the past century.

More specifically, we will address the following questions. How do the current welfare and future life chances of children who do not spend their entire childhood in a two-parent family differ from those who do? With the current rise in separation, divorce, remarriage, and out-of-wedlock childbearing among adults, how typical has it become for children not to spend their entire childhood in an intact two-parent family? For children in one-parent families, to what extent have grandparents in the home acted to fill the gap left by the absent parent? This chapter provides some answers to these questions.

First, in the short run, for many children the separation or divorce of their parents brings a sharp drop in family income as well as substantial psychological trauma, but when the lone parent in a one-parent family (re)marries to form a stepfamily, the children often experience a sharp increase in family income. Still, children in stepfamilies are more likely to have a low family income than are children in intact two-parent families. In addition, since one parent is absent from the home in one-parent families, children in these families may receive substantially less day-to-day care and attention from parents than do children in two-parent families. Similarly, compared with children in intact two-parent families, children in one-parent families are more likely, on average, to be exposed to parental stress, exhibit behavioral problems, receive or need professional psychological help, perform poorly in school, and experience health problems. Stepchildren are virtually indistinguishable, on average, from children in one-parent families in their chances of having behavioral, psychological, academic, and health problems.

Second, in the long run, children who do not spend most of their childhood in an intact two-parent family tend, as they reach adulthood, to complete fewer years of schooling, enter lower-status occupations, and earn lower incomes than do adults who did spend most of their childhood in an intact two-parent family. Some children from one-parent families may finish fewer years of school because fathers who can afford to do so may not provide financial support when the child reaches college age. In fact, the comparatively low incomes available to children in one-parent households and stepfamilies may account for an important part of many of the other differences between these children and those who are raised in intact two-parent families.

Third, focusing on all children at specific points in time, the proportion not living in an intact two-parent family—that is, those not living in a family in which both parents were married only once and all of the children were born after the marriage—increased from 30–35 percent in 1940–1960 to about 50 percent in 1988. For white children, the increase was from 25–30 percent in 1940–1960 to nearly 40 percent in 1980. For black children, the increase was from 55–60 percent in 1940–1960 to nearly 75 percent in 1980. The single, most significant cause of these increases is the rise in mother-only families. Among both white and black children living in mother-only families at any single point in time, the proportion with a grandparent in the home declined from 20–27 percent in 1940–1960 to about 11–14 percent in 1970–1980.

Fourth, focusing on cohorts of children, the proportion who spend part of their childhood with only one parent (or no parent) in the home is expected to increase from a large minority of 30–40 percent for children born between 1920–1960 to a projected majority of 50–60 percent for children born in 1980. Among white children, the proportion will increase from about 30 percent for the 1920–1960 cohorts to nearly 50 percent for the 1980 cohort; and among black children it will increase from 55–60 percent for the 1920–1950 cohorts to about 80 percent for the 1980 cohort. However, since the proportion of children in one-parent families who also have a grandparent in the home has declined, the proportion of all children ever living in a one-parent family with a grandparent in the home remained roughly constant—at 5–10 percent for white children and somewhere between 20 and 35 percent for black children.

Finally, in 1980 Hispanic children (of any race) were more similar to non-Hispanic whites than to non-Hispanic blacks in their parental and grandparental family living arrangements. These highlights are drawn from the more detailed discussion of past studies and new results that follow.

Advantages and Disadvantages of One- and Two-Parent Families

According to the Current Population Survey, the median annual family income in 1989 for children living with two parents ($39,076) was more than three times as large as that for children living with their mother only ($12,005). Similarly, 75 percent of children living with two parents had annual family incomes of $25,000 or more, compared with 22 percent for children living with their mother only.[1]

Using data from the National Panel Study of Income Dynamics (PSID), Greg J. Duncan, Saul D. Hoffman, Robert S. Weiss, and their colleagues have shown that this difference results in part from the sharp drop in family income that many children experience when their parents become separated or divorced.[2] This sharp drop in family income is further accentuated by the fact that the children living with one parent

---

[1]Arlene F. Saluter, *Marital Status and Living Arrangements: March 1990*, U.S. Bureau of the Census, Current Population Reports, Series P-20, No. 450 (Washington, DC: Printing Office, 1990), Table 6.

[2]Greg J. Duncan, *Years of Poverty, Years of Plenty* (Michigan: Survey Research Center, Institute for Social Research, University of Michigan, Ann Arbor, 1980), p. 21; Robert S. Weiss, "The Impact of Marital Dissolution on Income and Consumption in Single-Parent Households," *Journal of Marriage and the Family* 46 (1984): 115–127. Saul D. Hoffman and Greg J. Duncan, "What *Are* the Economic Consequences of Divorce?" *Demography* 25, 4 (November 1988): 641–645.

usually live with their mother, and not only do mothers generally earn less than their husbands, but many of them lack access to most, if not all, of the father's income.

For example, in 1985, 8.8 million women had children under age 21 with no father in the home, but 52 percent of these women either had not been awarded any child support by the courts or had not received child support payments during the past year. Even among the women who did receive child support, the average annual payment was only $2,220, which amounted to only 15 percent of their total money income.[3] As we will see in Chapters 9 and 10, however, many absent fathers, especially among blacks, earn so little that not even access to their entire income would raise the family out of poverty. Nevertheless, for an important proportion of children, it is a fact that absent fathers can afford (larger) child support payments that would substantially enhance their children's economic well-being.

As time passes, if and when a mother (re)marries, the income of the new stepfamily often substantially exceeds the income of the former mother-only family.[4] Despite this income jump, however, we have documented (using the Marital and Fertility Histories of the Current Population Survey) that families with a stepfather are substantially more likely to have low income levels than are intact two-parent families, and there are a larger average number of siblings in the home competing for that income. Since families with a stepfather are more likely to have both parents working in the labor force than are intact two-parent families, the difference in income may be due primarily to the comparatively low educational levels of parents in families with stepfathers compared with the educational achievements of adults in intact two-parent families.[5]

Psychologically, in two separate in-depth studies following members of divorced families for long periods of time, Judith S. Wallerstein, E. Mavis Hetherington, and their colleagues have documented the immediate and sometimes enduring feelings of distress, depression, fear, sadness, yearning, worry, rejection, loneliness, and anger that children often experience when their parents become separated or divorced.[6]

In addition, children in one-parent families may also receive substantially less direct, day-to-day care and attention from their parents

[3]Ruth A. Sanders Hanlon, U.S. Bureau of the Census, Current Population Reports, *Child Support and Alimony: 1985 (Supplemental Report).* Series P-23, No. 154 (Washington, DC: U.S. Government Printing Office, 1989), pp. 2–4.

[4]Duncan, *Years of Poverty.*

[5]Jeanne E. Moorman and Donald J. Hernandez, "Married-Couple Children with Step, Adopted, and Biological Children," *Demography* 26 (1989): 267–277; Louisa F. Miller and Jeanne E. Moorman, "Married-Couple Families with Children," U.S. Bureau of the Census, Current Population Reports, *Studies in Marriage and the Family.* Series P-23, No. 162 (Washington, DC: U.S. Government Printing Office, 1989).

[6]See Judith S. Wallerstein and Joan Berlin Kelly, *Second Chances* (New York: Ticknor & Fields, 1989); Judith S. Wallerstein and Joan Berlin Kelly, *Surviving the Breakup*

than do children in two-parent families. For example, Joseph H. Pleck reports the following from the 1975–1976 National Study of Time Use. Of total parent time devoted to *child care as a primary activity*, in families where the youngest child is aged 6–17, husbands account for 33 or 20 percent of the total depending, respectively, upon whether the mother is or is not employed outside the home; and in families where the youngest child is aged 0–5, husbands account for 26 or 17 percent of the total depending upon whether the mother is or is not employed in the labor force.[7]

From an earlier 1965–1966 National Study of Time Use, John P. Robinson also reports that men account for a larger proportion of the *total contact time that parents spend with their children*. Compared with employed wives, men account for about 50 percent of the total contact time spent with children; and compared with wives not in the labor force, men account for nearly 30 percent of the total contact time spent with children.[8]

Focusing on the amount of contact that children living with a divorced mother have with their father, Frank F. Furstenberg and his colleagues (using the National Survey of Children) found that 36 percent of these children aged 11–16 in 1981 had had no contact with their father during the past five years and did not even know where he was living. Furstenberg also found that an additional 33 percent of these children had seen their father an average of less than once per month during the preceding year. Only 33 percent saw their father an average of once per month, and only 16 percent saw him an average of once per week.[9]

(New York: Basic Books, 1980); Judith S. Wallerstein, Shauna B. Corbin, and Julia M. Lewis, "Children of Divorce: A 10-Year Study," in E. Mavis Hetherington and Josephine D. Arasteh, eds., *Impact of Divorce, Single Parenting, and Stepparenting on Children* (Hillsdale, NJ: Lawrence Erlbaum, 1988); E. Mavis Hetherington, M. Cox, and R. Cox, "The Aftermath of Divorce," in J.H. Stevens, Jr., and M. Matthews, *Mother-Child, Father-Child Relations*, National Association for the Education of Young Children, Washington, DC, 1978; E. Mavis Hetherington, M. Cox, and R. Cox, "Long-term Effects of Divorce and Remarriage on the Adjustment of Children," *Journal of the American Academy of Child Psychiatry* 24: 518–30. Also see other chapters in the volume cited above and edited by E. Mavis Hetherington and Josephine Arasteh; Cynthia Longfellow, "Divorce in Context: Its Impact on Children," in George Levinger and Oliver C. Moles, eds., *Divorce and Separation* (New York: Basic Books, 1979), pp. 287–306; and Donald J. Hernandez, "Childhood in Sociodemographic Perspective," in Ralph H. Turner and James J. Short, Jr., eds., *Annual Review of Sociology* 12 (1988): 159–180.

[7]Calculated from Tables 2.5 and 2.6, Joseph H. Pleck, *Working Wives/Working Husbands* (Beverly Hills: Sage Publications), 1985.

[8]Calculated from Table 3.8 assuming men have the same total time contact with children regardless of whether their wives are employed. In John P. Robinson, *How Americans Use Time* (New York: Praeger, 1977). This assumption is consistent with Pleck's finding for child care as a primary activity. See preceding footnote.

[9]Table 6, Frank F. Furstenberg, Jr., Christine Winquist Nord, James L. Peterson, and

If, as seems plausible, children living with a never-married mother are less likely to see their father than are children who live with a divorced mother, and if, as also seems plausible, many mothers in one-parent families do not increase contact with their children enough to make up for time lost with the absent father, then many children in one-parent families have less day-to-day contact with their parents than do children in two-parent families.

Mothers in mother-only families are also more likely to experience stress. Using the PSID, Sara S. McLanahan found that mothers in one-parent families are more likely than fathers in married-couple families to experience chronic stress in the form of low income and low levels of social support (from relatives and neighbors), and that they are also more likely to experience acute stress in the form of major life transitions (such as unemployment, job changes, persons moving in and out of the home, and residential moves). These differences in stress result primarily from the process of marital disruption.[10] As a result, children in mother-only families are exposed to more parental stress than are children who live with two parents.

Focusing specifically on the behavior, schooling, and health of children, Nicholas Zill and James L. Peterson have drawn upon the Child Health Supplement to the National Health Interview Survey and the National Survey of Children to document specific disadvantages experienced by children living in one-parent families and in blended families that include a stepparent.[11] For example, compared with children living in intact two-parent families, Zill reports that both children in one-parent families and stepchildren experience an average of one-fourth to one-half more behavioral problems (an average of 7.3–8.6 vs. 5.8); they are three to five times as likely to have needed or received psychological help within the past year (9–15 vs. 3 percent); and they are one-third more likely to have repeated a grade in school (17–18 vs. 13 percent).[12]

Nicholas Zill, "The Life Course of Children of Divorce: Marital Disruption and Parental Contact," *American Sociological Review* 48 (1983): 656–668.

[10]Sara S. McLanahan, "Family Structure and Stress: A Longitudinal Comparison of Two-Parent and Female-Headed Families," *Journal of Marriage and the Family* 45 (1983): 347–357.

[11]Nicholas Zill, "Behavior, Achievement, and Health Problems Among Children in Stepfamilies: Findings from a National Survey of Child Health," in E. Mavis Hetherington and Josephine D. Arasteh, *Impact of Divorce, Single Parenting, and Stepparenting on Children* (Hillsdale, NJ: Lawrence Erlbaum Associates, 1988), pp. 325–368; James L. Peterson and Nicholas Zill, "Marital Disruption and Behavioral Problems in Children," *Journal of Marriage and the Family* 48 (1986): 295–307.

[12]Results presented in the text are effects that remain after controlling for age, sex, education, income, ethnicity, family size and identify of parent respondent. See Nicholas Zill, "Behavior, Achievement, and Health Problems Among Children in Stepfamilies:

In addition, compared with children in intact two-parent families, children in mother-only families and children with a stepfather in the home—that is, most children not living in an intact two-parent family—have an average of one-fifth to one-fourth more absences from school during the past year (5.1–5.5 vs. 4.3), and their average standing in class rating is lower.

In deriving these estimates, Zill controls for a number of factors—including the child's ethnicity, the level of parental education, family income, and family size. Hence, these differences in children's families do not account for the behavioral, academic, and health differences among children in one-parent families, stepchildren, and children in intact two-parent families. It is also important to note that children in one-parent families experience substantially more behavioral problems than do children in intact two-parent families, regardless of whether the one-parent family was formed through divorce, out-of-wedlock childbearing, or the death of the father.

Finally, Zill found that children in one-parent families and children with a stepfather were somewhat less likely to be reported as being in excellent health than were children in intact two-parent families, but these differences disappeared when income and other variables were controlled. This suggests that the health deficit of children not living in intact two-parent families may result at least in part from the comparatively low family incomes available to these children.

In the long run, too, children who spend part of their childhood in a one-parent or blended two-parent family tend, on average, to be disadvantaged in their future life chances. More than two decades ago, Peter M. Blau and Otis Dudley Duncan found that children who do not spend most of their childhood in an intact two-parent family tend, as they reach adulthood, to complete fewer years of schooling, enter lower-status occupations, and earn lower incomes than is the case among adults who did spend most of their childhood in an intact two-parent family.[13]

More recently, David L. Featherman and Robert M. Hauser found that the negative effect that not living in an intact two-parent family has on a son's chances of completing at least one year of college was twice as great, on average, for sons born in 1927–1931 as for sons born in 1907–1911. They also found that the larger negative effect of not

---

Findings from a National Survey of Child Health," in E. Mavis Hetherington and Josephine D. Arasteh, *Impact of Divorce, Single Parenting, and Stepparenting on Children,* (Hillsdale, NJ: Lawrence Erlbaum Associates, 1988) pp. 325–368.

[13]Peter M. Blau and Otis Dudley Duncan, *The American Occupational Structure* (New York: Wiley, 1967).

living in an intact two-parent family has continued for sons born more recently.[14]

Unfortunately, since these studies do not control for family income during childhood, we do not know to what extent low family income for children not living in intact two-parent families may account for their lower educational and occupational achievements. For example, in her recent study of the social and economic consequences of divorce, Lenore J. Weitzman has identified part of the reason for the negative effect that living in a one-parent family has on completing at least one year of college. Many children with divorced parents may not receive the financial support from fathers needed to attend college, and fathers of such children may not be required to provide such financial support because children over age 18 are not considered to be minors.[15]

In the final analysis, then, children living in one-parent and blended two-parent families tend, on average, to be at a disadvantage compared with children in intact two-parent families with regard to their economic circumstances, psychological functioning, behavioral problems, education, and health; and some of these disadvantages last a lifetime. Despite these differences, however, it is not possible to conclude that the experience of entering or living in a one-parent or blended two-parent family is the only or even the primary cause of any specific disadvantage.

For example, as we will discuss in Chapters 9 and 10, children who experience a parental separation and divorce tend to have lower family incomes before the marital disruption than do children living in intact two-parent families who do not experience such a disruption. Similarly, it appears that children born to unmarried mothers tend to have fathers with very low incomes, and that these low incomes may contribute to the mother's decision not to marry the father. Hence, many of the economic disadvantages experienced by children in mother-only families would have existed even if the children had remained in or been born into an intact two-parent family.

More broadly, it seems likely that many children who experience a parental marital disruption are also exposed to more parental conflict and that, on average, they experience greater psychological, behavioral, and educational difficulties prior to the marital disruption than do children who remain in intact two-parent families. Insofar as this is true, then, the childhood disadvantages associated with not living in an intact

[14]David L. Featherman and Robert M. Hauser, *Opportunity and Change* (New York: Academic, 1978), pp. 242–243.

[15]Lenore J. Weitzman, *The Divorce Revolution* (New York: Free Press, 1985), pp. 278–281.

two-parent family are not the result of living in one-parent or blended two-parent families but are more likely to have resulted from the same factors that contributed to the original creation of the one-parent or blended two-parent families.

Parents in the Homes of Children Aged 0–17

At any specific time since the Great Depression, a large majority of children have lived with two parents, although the proportion has declined from 85 to 87 percent in 1940–1960 to 77 percent in 1980 and an estimated 71 percent in 1988 (Table 3.1).[16] Notably smaller, however, has been the proportion of children living in intact two-parent families—that is, primary two-parent families in which both parents were in their first (primary) marriage and all the children were born after the marriage. In fact, a substantial minority of 30 percent did not live in intact two-parent families in specific years between 1940 and 1960, and this figure increased to 43 percent in 1980 and to about 50 percent in 1988.[17]

Most of the decline in two-parent families is accounted for by the rise in mother-only families from 6–8 percent in 1940–1960 to 21 per-

[16]The estimate for 1988 is obtained from the Current Population Survey (CPS) as follows. The CPS indicated that 61,271,000 children under 18 lived with at least one parent in 1988. Assuming that the proportion living with no parent was 5 percent, as in the 1980 census estimate, total persons under 18 in the United States was estimated to be 64,496,000. Of these, the CPS indicates that 45,942,000 lived with two parents, for a proportion of 71 percent. Arlene F. Saluter, U.S. Bureau of the Census, Current Population Reports, *Marital Status and Living Arrangements: March 1988.* Series P-20, No. 433 (Washington, DC: U.S. Government Printing Office, 1989), Table 9. The estimates for 1940 and 1950 of the proportion living with at least one parent and with two parents are slightly too low, because we excluded from them children who lived in unrelated subfamilies (that is, children living with parents but in households maintained by someone who was not related to the children and parents).

[17]The values of 51 and 6 percent in Table 3.1 for two-parent families in 1988 are derived as follows. Using the Marital and Fertility History from the 1980 CPS, Moorman and Hernandez estimated that 83.7 percent of children in two-parent families lived with their biological mother and father. Applied to the total of 76.7 percent living in two-parent families in Table 3.1, this suggests that 64.2 percent of all children lived with their biological parents. This is only about 1.2 percentage points larger than the estimate in Table 3.1 that 63.0 percent of children lived in families with only biological children, of which 56.8 percent lived with parents who were both married only once. Miller and Moorman used the 1985 CPS to estimate that the proportion of children living in two-parent families with biological parents was 82.1 percent in 1985. Applied to the estimated 71.2 percent of children in two-parent families in Table 3.1, the results indicate that 58.5 percent lived in families with biological parents. Subtracting the 1.2 percentage point difference in 1980, and the 6.2 percent living in families with two biological parents where one was remarried in 1980, the result is that about 51 percent lived in two-parent families in which all of the co-resident siblings were born after the parents' only marriage.

TABLE 3.1

Living Arrangements of Children Aged 0–17: 1940–1988

	1940	1950	1960	1970	1980	1988
Total Number (in thousands)	40,035	46,306	64,782	70,129	64,586	64,496
Percent	100.0	100.0	100.0	100.0	100.0	100.0
Two-Parent Family	84.6	86.1	87.2	82.5	76.6	71.2
Children born after marriage (one or both parents married only once)	75.2	74.5	77.7	72.0	63.0	57.0
Parents married once (intact two-parent family)	69.6	69.8	70.6	65.5	56.8	51.0
Father remarried, mother married once	NA	NA	4.8	4.5	4.6	6.0
Mother remarried, father married once	5.6	4.7	2.3	2.0	1.6	NA
At least one stepchild in family	9.4	11.5	6.0	6.5	8.2	NA
Mother married once	8.2	6.2	2.6	3.0	3.8	NA
Mother remarried	1.2	5.4	3.4	3.5	4.4	NA
Both parents remarried	NA	NA	3.6	4.0	5.5	NA
One-Parent Family	8.8	7.8	8.7	13.6	18.3	23.8
Mother-only family	6.7	6.4	7.7	11.8	16.2	21.0
Mother never married	0.1	0.1	0.3	1.1	3.0	6.7
Mother separated or married spouse absent	2.1	2.7	3.6	4.7	4.4	5.2
Mother divorced	0.9	1.4	1.9	3.5	7.2	7.8
Mother widowed	3.6	2.2	1.9	2.5	1.6	1.3
Father-only family	2.1	1.4	1.0	1.8	2.1	2.8
Father never married	0.1	0.0	0.0	0.1	0.3	0.6
Father separated or married spouse absent	0.6	0.6	0.6	1.0	0.5	0.7
Father divorced	0.1	0.2	0.1	0.3	1.0	1.3
Father widowed	1.3	0.6	0.3	0.4	0.3	0.2
No Parent in Home	6.7	6.0	3.9	4.1	5.1	5.0
Grandparent family	2.0	1.9	1.4	1.5	1.5	NA
Child is married householder or householder's spouse	0.2	0.3	0.3	0.3	0.2	NA
Child is unmarried householder	0.0	0.0	0.0	0.1	0.1	NA
Child is other relative of householder	2.1	1.7	1.0	1.0	1.7	NA
Child not related to householder	1.2	0.8	0.5	0.6	1.1	NA
Child in group quarters	1.2	1.3	0.7	0.6	0.4	NA

SOURCES: Calculated from 1940–1980 PUMS and 1988 March CPS.

NOTES: Estimates for two-parent families in 1940 and 1950 are derived using marital history information for mothers but not fathers. When both parents remarried, it is not possible to ascertain whether children were born before or after current marriage, that is, whether any children in home are stepchildren.

NA indicates cannot be estimated from available data.

cent in 1988. By 1988, 7 percent of children lived in mother-only families with a never-married mother, 13 percent lived in mother-only families with a separated or divorced mother, 24 percent lived in one-parent families, and 20 percent lived in blended two-parent families with at least one remarried parent or stepchild.

Parents in the Homes of Newborns and 17-Year-Olds

Even among newborns under age 1, a significant minority since 1940 did not begin life in a two-parent family (Tables 3.2 and 3.4). Although only 4–5 percent of children were born to unmarried mothers between 1940 and 1960, at any specific time twice as many newborns under age 1 (9–10 percent) did not live with two parents, and this figure had increased to 19 percent for newborns by 1980. The proportion of newborns not living in an intact two-parent family has been almost twice as large, increasing from 19–25 percent for newborns in 1940–1960 to 38 percent for newborns in 1980.

As each cohort grew older, many experienced a parental separation, divorce, or death. By age 17, then, the proportion of children not living with two parents will increase from 25–30 percent for children born between 1920 and 1960 to a projected 43 percent for children born in 1980, while the proportion not living in an intact two-parent family is expected to increase from 40–46 percent to 62 percent.[18]

Children Ever Living with Fewer Than Two Parents

The proportion of children who have ever lived with fewer than two parents before age 18 is greater than the proportion not currently living with two parents at age 17. The reason for this is that at age 17 some

[18]The proportion projected as not living in a two-parent family by ages 8–9 is 30 percent, based on the simple assumption that the proportion will continue to rise slightly above the estimated value of 29 percent in 1988 for children aged 6–11. The estimate of 29 percent is drawn from CPS data with the further assumption that the proportion of children not living with any parents was 5 percent. The proportions projected as not living in a two-parent family by age 17 for children born in 1970 and 1980 were obtained by adding to the corresponding proportion for children born in 1960 the differences between the 1960, 1970, and 1980 cohorts at ages 8–9. The proportions projected as not living in intact two-parent families at age 17 for children born in 1970, and at ages 8–9 and 17 for children born in 1980, were derived by adding, for each cohort and age, to the corresponding proportion of children born a decade earlier the difference between the current cohort and the preceding cohort at the next earlier age in Table 3.4.

TABLE 3.2

Living Arrangements of Newborns Under 1 Year: 1940–1980

	1940	1950	1960	1970	1980
Total Number (in thousands)	1,757	3,092	4,270	3,440	3,637
Percent	100.0	100.0	100.0	100.0	100.0
Two-Parent Family	91.4	91.2	89.8	85.1	80.9
Children born after marriage (one or both parents married only once)	84.7	83.9	82.5	77.4	70.3
Parents married once (intact two-parent family)	80.6	77.7	75.1	70.6	62.5
Father remarried, mother married once	NA	NA	4.9	4.9	5.5
Mother remarried, father married once	4.1	6.2	2.5	1.9	2.3
At least one stepchild in family	6.7	7.3	4.9	5.3	6.8
Mother married once	5.9	3.8	2.7	2.5	3.5
Mother remarried	0.8	3.5	2.2	2.8	3.3
Both parents remarried	NA	NA	2.4	2.4	3.8
One-Parent Family	3.3	3.9	7.0	11.7	13.1
Mother-only family	2.8	3.6	6.3	10.4	11.3
Mother never married	0.1	0.2	0.5	3.2	5.9
Mother separated or married spouse absent	1.9	2.6	4.4	5.0	2.6
Mother divorced	0.2	0.4	0.7	1.2	2.3
Mother widowed	0.6	0.4	0.7	1.0	0.5
Father-only family	0.5	0.3	0.7	1.3	1.8
Father never married	0.1	0.0	0.0	0.2	1.0
Father separated or married spouse absent	0.4	0.3	0.7	1.0	0.3
Father divorced	0.0	0.0	0.0	0.0	0.4
Father widowed	0.0	0.0	0.0	0.1	0.1
No Parent in Home	5.4	4.7	3.2	3.1	5.4
Grandparent family	1.4	1.2	1.6	1.8	2.2
Child is married householder or householder's spouse	0.0	0.0	0.0	0.0	0.0
Child is unmarried householder	0.0	0.0	0.0	0.0	0.0
Child is other relative of householder	1.8	1.5	0.8	0.5	1.9
Child not related to householder	1.0	1.0	0.5	0.5	1.2
Child in group quarters	1.2	1.0	0.3	0.3	0.1

SOURCES: Calculated from 1940–1980 PUMS.

NOTES: Estimates for two-parent families in 1940 and 1950 are derived using marital history information for mothers but not fathers. When both parents remarried, it is not possible to ascertain whether children were born before or after current marriage, that is, whether any children in home are stepchildren.

NA indicates cannot be estimated from available data.

children in two-parent families were born out of wedlock, or they experienced a parental separation, divorce, or death; but they also experienced a subsequent parental reconciliation or (re)marriage between birth and age 17. On the other hand, the proportion of children who have ever

TABLE 3.3

Living Arrangements of Children Aged 17 Years: 1940–1980

	1940	1950	1960	1970	1980
Total Number (in thousands)	2,468	2,095	2,789	3,816	4,198
Percent	100.0	100.0	100.0	100.0	100.0
Two-Parent Family	72.9	71.6	75.2	75.4	70.4
Children born after marriage (one or both parents married only once)	65.3	60.4	64.7	66.3	58.9
Parents married once (intact two-parent family)	59.4	56.7	60.1	60.1	53.6
Father remarried, mother married once	NA	NA	3.1	3.9	3.5
Mother remarried, father married once	5.9	3.7	1.5	2.3	1.8
At least one stepchild in family	7.6	11.2	6.2	4.6	5.8
Mother married once	6.2	5.6	2.1	2.0	2.3
Mother remarried	1.4	5.6	4.1	2.6	3.5
Both parents remarried	NA	NA	4.3	4.5	5.7
One-Parent Family	10.8	13.0	11.3	14.9	18.2
Mother-only family	7.0	10.2	9.3	12.7	15.7
Mother never married	0.0	0.2	0.3	0.4	0.9
Mother separated or married spouse absent	0.0	2.3	3.2	4.0	3.5
Mother divorced	0.0	1.7	2.1	3.5	7.7
Mother widowed	7.0	6.0	3.7	4.8	3.6
Father-only family	3.8	2.8	2.0	2.2	2.5
Father never married	0.1	0.0	0.0	0.0	0.1
Father separated or married spouse absent	1.0	0.8	0.9	0.9	0.7
Father divorced	0.3	0.4	0.2	0.4	1.2
Father widowed	2.4	1.6	0.9	0.9	0.5
No Parent in Home	12.5	15.5	13.7	9.8	11.2
Grandparent family	1.5	1.4	1.3	1.2	1.2
Child is married householder or householder's spouse	2.7	4.2	4.2	3.0	2.0
Child is unmarried householder	0.1	0.1	0.3	0.3	0.5
Child is other relative of householder	4.1	3.6	3.4	2.0	3.0
Child not related to householder	2.4	2.0	1.0	1.2	2.1
Child in group quarters	1.7	4.2	3.5	2.1	2.4

SOURCES: Calculated from 1940–1980 PUMS.

NOTES: Estimates for two-parent families in 1940 and 1950 are derived using marital history information for mothers but not fathers. When both parents remarried, it is not possible to ascertain whether children were born before or after current marriage, that is, whether any children in home are stepchildren.

NA indicates cannot be estimated from available data.

lived with fewer than two parents before age 18 is smaller than the proportion not currently living in a primary two-parent family, because some of these families were formed before the child was born (Table 3.3).

Based on these considerations, we estimate that approximately 33 percent of most cohorts of children born between 1920 and 1950 spent part of childhood in either a one-parent family or a no-parent situation, although the proportion may have been slightly higher for children born at the beginning of the Great Depression (Table 3.4). For an earlier period, estimates by Peter Uhlenberg suggest that if a cohort of children had experienced the parental mortality rates of 1900 as they passed through ages 0–17, then approximately 28 percent would have experienced a parental death during childhood.[19]

If, as seems likely, at least an additional few percent of children around the turn of the century experienced an extended period of parental separation or divorce, then approximately one-third of most cohorts of children born between the late 1800s and 1950 spent part of their childhood living with fewer than two parents.[20] From the perspective of children, then, it appears that declines in parents' death rates were approximately counterbalanced by increases in parents' separation and divorce from at least the late 1800s to the mid-1900s.[21]

For children born after 1950, the proportion who did not have two parents in the home throughout childhood increased—primarily because of increasing separation, divorce, and out-of-wedlock childbearing—to

[19]Uhlenberg estimates that 24 percent would have experienced at least one parental death by age 15. Since children aged 17 in a census are on average about 17.5 years old, we calculated the proportion who would experience a parental death by age 17 to be census-consistent as follows: 17.5 (years) divided by 15 (years) times 24 percent equals 28 percent. Since mortality rates declined sharply after 1900 (see Chapter 2), this approach to estimating parental mortality experience probably corresponds most closely with an actual cohort of children born sometime between 1880 and 1890. See Peter Uhlenberg, "Death and the Family," *Journal of Family History* (Fall 1980): 313–320.

[20]These estimates are generally consistent with new results from the National Survey of Families and Households (NSFH), which indicate that for persons aged 19 and over in 1987–1988, about 31 percent did not live with both biological parents from the time they were born until age 19 or until they left home to be on their own (*Codebook and Documentation: Introduction* (October 1988), p. M-44). Most of these persons were born before 1968. The NSFH estimate counts children through age 18 but excludes those who left home to be on their own, while our estimate counts children as of age 17 and includes children who have left home to be on their own.

[21]Another estimate by Peter Uhlenberg suggests that about 11.7 percent of a cohort exposed to 1940 mortality rates would have experienced at least one parental death by age 17. The cohort that came closest to actually experiencing these mortality rates was probably born around 1930. Our census-derived estimates for children born mainly in 1932 indicate that about 9.2 percent were living with a widowed parent at age 17. Assuming some remarriage of widowed parents, our estimates and those by Uhlenberg are generally consistent with each other. The overall stability in the rate of marital dissolutions between 1860 and 1960 due to the counterbalancing of declining mortality and rising divorce has been demonstrated and highlighted by Paul H. Jacobson, *American Marriage and Divorce* (New York: Rinehart, 1959), pp. 141–144; and Kingsley Davis, "The American Family in Relation to Demographic Change," in U.S. Commission on Population Growth and the American Future, pp. 237–265. Charles F. Westoff and Robert Parke, Jr., eds., *Demographic and Social Aspects of Population Growth*, vol. 1 of Commission Research Reports (Washington, DC: U.S. Government Printing Office, 1972).

TABLE 3.4

Children Ever Living with Fewer than Two Parents: 1920s–1980s Cohorts

Percent	1920	1930	1940	1950	1960	1970	1980	1990
Percent Born Out of Wedlock			3.8	3.7	5.2	10.0	17.1	25.7
Not Living with Two Parents								
Newborn under 1 year			8.6	8.7	10.3	14.9	19.1	
Age 8–9		13.5	13.5	11.6	16.1	22.9*	29.0*	
Age 17	27.1	28.4	24.8	24.6	29.6	36.0*	43.0*	
Not Living in Intact Two-Parent Family								
Newborn under 1 year			19.4	22.3	24.9	29.4	37.5	
Age 8–9		30.1	31.1	29.4	34.3	47.7	52.0*	
Age 17	40.6	43.3	39.9	39.9	46.4	55.0*	62.0*	
Ever Living with 0–1 Parent by Age 17	34.0	36.0	32.0	32.0	38.0	46.0*	53.0*	
Living with Mother Only, Widowed								
Newborn under 1 year			0.6	0.4	0.7	1.0	0.5	
Age 8–9		2.9	2.0	1.7	2.2	1.3		
Age 17	7.0	6.0	3.7	4.8	3.6			
Living with Father Only, Widowed								
Newborn under 1 year			0.0	0.0	0.0	0.1	0.1	
Age 8–9		1.1	0.5	0.3	0.4	0.2		
Age 17	2.4	1.6	0.9	0.9	0.5			
Living with One Parent, Widowed								
Newborn under 1 year			0.6	0.4	0.7	1.1		
Age 8–9		4.0	2.5	2.0	2.6	1.5		
Age 17	9.4	7.6	4.4	5.7	4.1			

SOURCE: Percent born out of wedlock obtained from National Center for Health Statistics: Vital and Health Statistics of the United States, 1988, Vol. 1, Natality, DHHS Pub. No. (PHS)90-1100. Public Health Service (Washington, DC: U.S. Government Printing Office, 1990), p. 57, and 1940–1980 PUMS. Except for 1940, out-of-wedlock data are for year prior to the census year indicated, since, for example, children age 0 in the 1950 census were born mainly in 1949.

NOTES: Ever living with 0–1 parents by age 17 estimated as the mean of percentage not living with two parents at age 17 and percentage not living in intact two-parent family at age 17.

* Numbers are projections derived by combining race-specific projections in Table 3.9.

about 38 percent for children born in 1960 and to projected values of 46 and 53 percent for children born in 1970 and 1980, respectively.[22] Our projection for the 1980 cohort lies near the middle of the range of projections developed by other scholars. Larry Bumpass projects that 49 percent of children born in 1977–1979 will spend time in a one-parent family by age 16; Arthur J. Norton and Paul C. Glick project that 59 percent of children born in 1983 will live in a one-parent family before reaching age 18; and Sandra L. Hofferth projects that 74 percent of children will live in a one-parent family before they reach age 18.

As discussed by Bumpass and recorded in Footnote 31 of this chapter, the values projected by Hofferth are probably too high.[23] In addition, since the value projected by Bumpass is to age 16, an extension to age 18 would increase the projected value somewhat, and both the Bumpass projections and the new projections presented here fail to take into account the parental separations that end in reconciliation. Hence, it appears that 55–60 percent of children born in 1980 will have lived in either a one-parent family or a no-parent situation before age 18. Approximately one-half of the post-1950 rise in the proportion of children who have ever lived with one parent or no parents is accounted for by the increase in out-of-wedlock childbearing and the proportion who did not live with two parents even as newborns, while the remainder is accounted for by the rise in parental separation and divorce.

For many children, the experience of living in a one- or no-parent situation is not short-lived. For children born around 1980, Larry Bumpass projects that the majority of those experiencing a marital disruption will live in a family maintained by a mother for five years before she remarries, and that about one-half of children living with remarried mothers will experience a second parental divorce. Applied to the projections presented here, Bumpass's results suggest that about 20 percent of children born into a two-parent family in 1980 will experience at least five years of living in a mother-only family after experiencing their parents' divorce.

---

[22]These projections are based on separate projections for white and black children as described in Footnote 31.

[23]Larry L. Bumpass, "Children and Marital Disruption: A Replication and Update," *Demography* 21 (1984):71–83; and "Bigger Isn't Necessarily Better: A Comment on Hofferth's "Updating Children's Life Course," *Journal of Marriage and the Family* 47 (1985): 797–798; Sandra L. Hofferth, "Children's Life Course: Family Structure and Living Arrangements in Cohort Perspective, in Glen H. Elder, ed., *Life Course Dynamics: Trajectories and Transitions, 1968–1980* (Ithaca, NY: Cornell University Press, 1985), pp. 75–112; and "Updating Children's Life Course," *Journal of Marriage and the Family* 47(195): 93–115; Arthur J. Norton and Paul C. Glick, "One-Parent Families: A Social and Economic Profile," *Journal of Family Relations* 35 (1986): 9–17. Also for further discussion, see Donald J. Hernandez, "Childhood in Sociodemographic Perspective," in Ralph H. Turner and James J. Short, Jr., eds., *Annual Review of Sociology,* 12 (1986): 159–180.

Overall, then, for children born between the late 1800s and 1950, a substantial minority of about 33 percent experienced life in either a one-parent family or a no-parent situation; and for children born since about 1970, a majority will spend part of their childhood either living with only one parent or with no parents.

Grandparents in the Homes of Children

With the recent significant decline in two-parent living for children, have grandparents moved into children's homes to fill the gap? The answer is no. Between 1940 and 1980, the proportion of children aged 0–17 living with a grandparent, but no parent, in the home remained nearly stable (1.4–2.0 percent), and the proportions were essentially the same for newborns and 17-year-olds (Tables 3.1, 3.2, and 3.3).[24] Even more striking among children in one-parent families, however, is the fact that the proportion with a grandparent in the home dropped by about one-half between 1960 and 1980 (Figure 3.1).

Between 1940–1960 and 1980, the proportion of children living in mother-only families more than doubled—from 6–8 percent to 16 percent—and the proportion with two or more living grandparents increased; yet the proportion of children in mother-only families who had a grandparent in the home dropped by one-half (from 20–27 percent to only 12 percent).[25] Although children living with a never-married mother were roughly twice as likely to have a grandparent in the home as were children in other mother-only families, by 1980 nearly 80 percent of children living with never-married mothers *did not* have a grandparent in the home. Among children living in father-only families, the changes have been nearly identical to those in mother-only families.

Among newborn children in mother-only families, the decline in the presence of grandparents in the home has been even more striking (Table 3.5). For newborn children living with an ever-married (separated, divorced, or widowed) mother, the proportion who had a grandparent in the home declined from 52 percent in 1950 to only 25 percent in 1980. Even among newborns living with a never-married mother, although a

[24]Estimates of grandparents in the home were obtained based on a collapsing of family relationship categories in certain censuses so that identical categories could be used across all censuses.

[25]For example, based on mortality rates Peter Uhlenberg calculates that the proportion of 15-year-olds who have two or more living grandparents increased from 71 to 88 percent between 1940 and 1976. In "Death and the Family," *Journal of Family History* (Fall, 1980): 313–320.

Grandparents in the Homes of Children Aged 0–17: 1940–1980

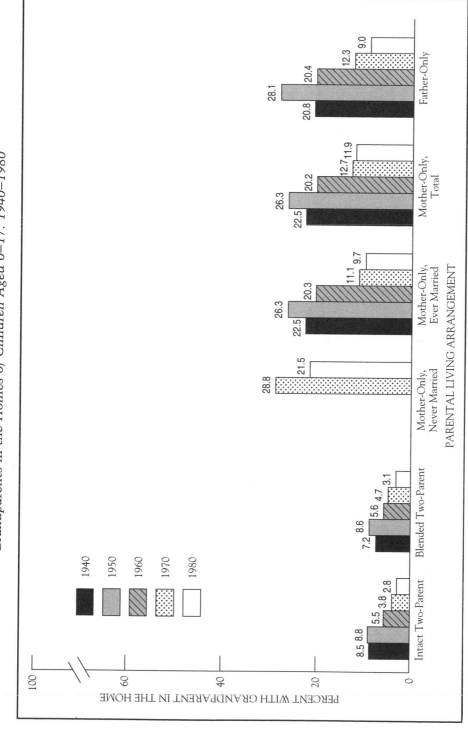

SOURCES: Calculated from 1940–1980 PUMS.

TABLE 3.5

Percentage of Newborns Aged 0 in Mother-Only Families Who Have Grandparents in the Home: 1950–1980

Year	Total		White		Black	
	Parent Never Married	Parent Ever Married	Parent Never Married	Parent Ever Married	Parent Never Married	Parent Ever Married
1950	NA	51.9	NA	58.7	NA	NA
1960	NA	36.2	NA	39.2	NA	NA
1970	52.3	32.0	NA	38.5	NA	NA
1980	41.8	25.3	47.0	29.6	38.5	NA

Year	Non-Hispanic White		Non-Hispanic Black		Hispanic	
	Parent Never Married	Parent Ever Married	Parent Never Married	Parent Ever Married	Parent Never Married	Parent Ever Married
1980	NA	31.0	38.4	NA	NA	NA

SOURCE: Calculated from 1950–1980 PUMS.

NOTE: NA indicates sample base of 75 or less.

majority of 52 percent had a grandparent in the home in 1970, this fell to 42 percent in 1980.

Based on separate estimates for black and white children described below, it appears that the proportion of children who ever lived in a one-parent or no-parent situation with a grandparent before age 18 has for the most part been constant, lying somewhere between 5 and 15 percent. Hence, for some children who lacked two parents in the home, grandparents have helped to fill the gap by either providing a home or joining the one-parent family of these children; yet for a majority of children born since at least the 1920s who did not spend their entire childhood in a two-parent family, no grandparent was available.

Among children living with two parents, the proportion with a grandparent in the home has also fallen since 1950. All together, we estimate that the proportion of these children who have ever lived with a grandparent has, at somewhere between 10 and 30 percent, generally been constant. Hence, most children born since at least the 1920s did not spend any of their childhood living in extended family homes that included a grandparent.

Summarizing existing historical findings, Tamara K. Hareven and

FIGURE 3.2

Percentage of White and Black Newborn Children
Not Living with Two Parents: 1940–1980

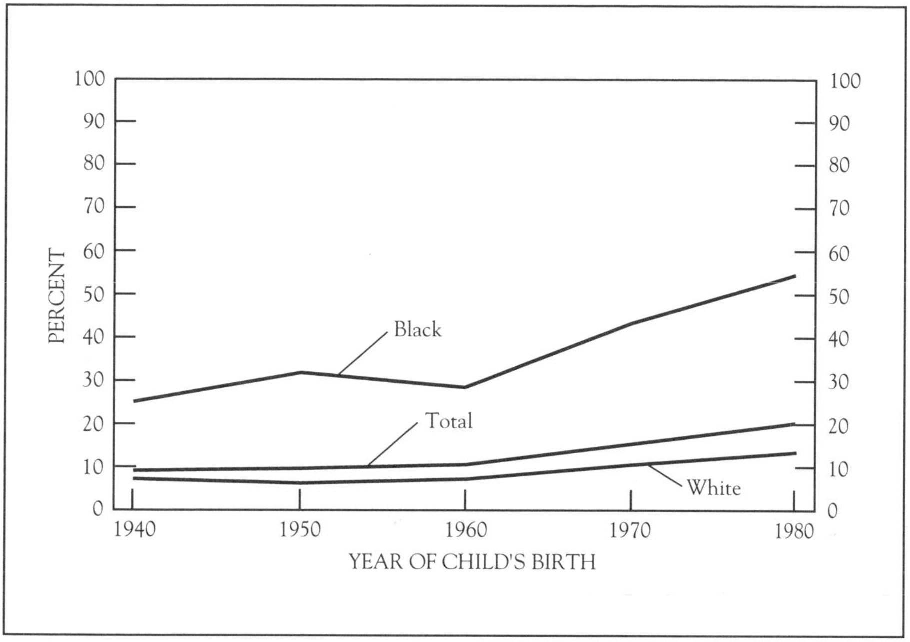

SOURCES: Tables 3.4 and 3.9.

Maris A. Vinovskis report that U.S. communities during the second half of the nineteenth century and, in fact, all European societies during the past 300 years had *few* households that consisted of three-generation extended families.[26] It appears, then, that the limited experience of American children with extended family living during the twentieth century is actually a continuation of the experience of children in Western society during preceding centuries.

Parents in the Homes of Black and White Children Aged 0–17

Between the Great Depression and 1988, the proportion of black children who had two parents in the home dropped from 67 percent to

[26]Tamara K. Hareven and Maris A. Vinovskis, eds., *Family and Population in Nineteenth-Century America* (Princeton, NJ: Princeton University Press, 1978), pp. 14–15.

38 percent, but at no time during this period did as many as 50 percent of black children live in intact (primary) two-parent families (Table 3.6). Between 1940–1960 and 1980, the proportion of children living in intact two-parent families fell, resulting in a drop from 43–46 percent to only 27 percent for black children and from 73–75 to 62 percent for white children. Hence, the racial gap in intact family living expanded from 27 to 35 percentage points between 1940 and 1980.

At the opposite extreme, the proportion of children who lived with neither parent also declined with the coming of the postwar era, dropping by as much as 4–6 and 2–3 percentage points for blacks and whites, respectively, between 1940 and 1960.[27] For both races, the proportion of children living with grandparents in the home probably declined by less than the figure that was recorded for the total proportion living with neither parent.

For black children, the declines in the proportion of those living in either intact two-parent families or with no parents in the home at all are explained by the rise in mother-only families from only 12 percent in 1940 to 39 percent in 1980 and 50 percent in 1988. For white children, the corresponding declines are largely explained by the increase in mother-only families from 6 to 16 percent between 1940 and 1988. But the proportion of white children living in blended two-parent families also increased by about 6 percentage points between 1940 and 1980; that is, a 6 percentage point increase occurred in the proportion in families where at least one parent was married more than once or at least one of the children was born before the parents' (current) marriage.

For black children, the source of the increase in mother-only families shifted after 1960. Between 1940 and 1960, the proportion of black children living with a never-married mother increased by only 1 percentage point, compared with the 9 percentage point increase reported for the proportion living with a separated or divorced mother. Between 1960 and 1988, however, the proportion of black children living with a never-married mother increased by 26 percentage points (mainly after 1970), while the proportion living with a separated or divorced mother increased by only 6 percentage points (all during the 1960s).[28]

[27]Estimates of the proportion of children living as nonrelatives of the household and in group quarters include children who were living in "unrelated subfamilies" (that is, with at least one parent present but in the home of a nonrelative). In 1940 and 1950, as many as 2.5 percent of black children and 1 percent of white children may have lived in unrelated subfamilies.

[28]The estimates of change in the proportion living in mother-only families between 1960 and 1988 are somewhat crude. New procedures implemented in the Current Population Survey in 1982 and 1983 acted to improve the identification of related subfamilies, and most of the improvement was among mother-child subfamilies. Hence, some of the increase in mother-only families for 1980–1988 actually occurred during the preceding years, mainly since 1960, but especially since 1970, when the largest measured increases

By contrast, among white children each passing decade between 1940 and 1980 brought a somewhat larger increase in the proportion who lived with a separated or divorced mother. Not until after 1970 did a noteworthy increase occur in the proportion of white children living with a never-married mother, and even then the increase in the proportion who lived with a separated or divorced mother was larger than that for those living with a never-married mother (5.6 vs. 2.5 percentage points between 1970 and 1988).

What caused these increases in mother-only families, and, especially among black children, the shift toward mother-only families with never-married mothers? When we address these questions in Chapter 10, we will see that the causes appear to lie in fundamental social and economic changes that have occurred since the Great Depression. For this reason, our discussion of the causes in the rise in mother-only families will be deferred until we have explored in detail other changes in the lives of children during the past half century.

Parents in the Homes of Black and White Newborns and 17-Year-Olds

Among newborn children (under age 1) in 1940–1960, 25–32 percent of blacks and 5–7 percent of whites did not live with two parents (Figure 3.2 and Tables 3.7 and 3.8).[29] But by 1980, these proportions had jumped to 55 percent for blacks and 13 percent for whites due to corresponding increases in the proportion of children who were born out of wedlock. As a result, the racial gap in the proportion of newborns not living with two parents more than doubled, going from 18 to 42 percentage points between 1940 and 1980.

As each cohort of children grew older, an increasing proportion did not live with two parents. For children aged 17 in census years between 1940 and 1970, that is, for children born between about 1920 and 1950,

---

in mother-only families occurred among both black and white children. Arlene F. Saluter, U.S. Bureau of the Census, Current Population Reports, *Marital Status and Living Arrangements: March 1984.* Series P-20, No. 399 (Washington, DC: U.S. Government Printing Office, 1985), p. 8.

[29]Since newborns in unrelated subfamilies in 1940 and 1950 are classified here as having no parent in the home and either as not being related to the householder or as living in group quarters, if no change occurred between 1940 and 1960, then the total proportion of newborns not living with two parents may have been as much as 1.3 and 0.6 percentage points smaller for whites in 1940 and 1950 and as much as 0.9 and 5.6 percentage points smaller for blacks during these years than is suggested by estimates in Tables 3.7 and 3.8.

TABLE 3.6

Living Arrangements of White and Black Children Aged 0–17: 1940–1988

White	1940	1950	1960	1970	1980	1988
Total Number (in thousands)	35,487	40,808	56,648	60,422	54,788	
Percent	100.0	100.0	100.0	100.0	100.0	100.0
Two-Parent Family	86.7	88.8	90.1	86.5	81.9	77.7
Children born after marriage (one or both						
parents married only once)	78.0	78.2	81.4	76.6	68.6	NA
Parents married once (intact two-parent family)	72.6	73.5	74.5	70.2	62.1	NA
Father remarried, mother married once	NA	NA	4.6	4.4	4.8	NA
Mother remarried, father married once	5.4	4.7	2.3	2.0	1.7	NA
At least one stepchild in family	8.7	10.6	5.2	5.7	7.4	NA
Mother married once	7.6	5.6	1.8	2.2	2.8	NA
Mother remarried	1.1	5.0	3.4	3.5	4.6	NA
Both parents remarried	NA	NA	3.5	4.2	5.9	NA
One-Parent Family	8.0	6.9	6.9	10.4	14.0	18.5
Mother-only family	6.0	5.7	6.2	8.8	12.1	15.7
Mother never married	0.0	0.1	0.1	0.4	1.0	2.9
Mother separated or married spouse absent	1.9	2.1	2.6	3.0	3.1	4.0
Mother divorced	0.9	1.4	1.9	3.2	6.7	7.8
Mother widowed	3.2	2.1	1.6	2.2	1.3	1.0
Father-only family	2.0	1.2	0.7	1.6	1.9	2.8
Father never married	0.1	0.0	0.0	0.1	0.2	0.5
Father separated or married spouse absent	0.5	0.5	0.4	0.8	0.4	0.6
Father divorced	0.2	0.2	0.0	0.3	1.0	1.5
Father widowed	1.2	0.5	0.3	0.4	0.3	0.2
No Parent in Home	5.2	4.4	2.7	3.0	4.1	4.0
Grandparent family	1.3	1.1	0.7	0.9	1.0	NA
Child is married householder or householder's spouse	0.2	0.3	0.3	0.3	0.2	NA
Child is unmarried householder	0.0	0.0	0.0	0.0	0.1	NA
Child is other relative of householder	1.6	1.2	0.7	0.8	1.3	NA
Child not related to householder	1.0	0.7	0.4	0.5	1.1	NA
Child in group quarters	1.1	1.1	0.6	0.5	0.4	NA

TABLE 3.6 *(continued)*

Black	1940	1950	1960	1970	1980	1988
Total Number (in thousands)	4,548	5,497	8,134	9,707	9,707	
Percent	100.0	100.0	100.0	100.0	100.0	100.0
Two-Parent Family	67.2	65.3	66.5	57.3	46.7	37.5
Children born after marriage (one or both parents married only once)	52.8	47.4	51.1	42.1	30.7	NA
Parents married once (intact two-parent family)	46.0	42.8	43.3	35.9	26.5	NA
Father remarried, mother married once	NA	NA	6.1	4.6	3.4	NA
Mother remarried, father married once	6.8	4.6	1.7	1.6	0.8	NA
At least one stepchild in family	14.4	17.9	11.1	12.2	13.1	NA
Mother married once	12.1	10.5	7.7	8.5	9.5	NA
Mother remarried	2.3	7.4	3.4	3.7	3.6	NA
Both parents remarried	NA	NA	4.3	3.0	2.9	NA
One-Parent Family	14.5	16.2	21.4	33.0	42.0	52.5
Mother-only family	11.5	13.7	19.1	30.1	39.2	49.6
Mother never married	0.6	0.7	1.4	5.4	14.0	27.4
Mother separated or married spouse absent	3.7	7.8	11.1	14.8	11.7	11.7
Mother divorced	0.7	1.9	2.4	5.2	10.0	8.1
Mother widowed	6.5	3.3	4.2	4.7	3.5	2.4
Father-only family	3.0	2.5	2.3	2.9	2.8	2.9
Father never married	0.0	0.0	0.1	0.6	0.9	1.1
Father separated or married spouse absent	1.2	1.1	1.3	1.6	1.0	0.8
Father divorced	0.1	0.2	0.4	0.2	0.6	0.9
Father widowed	1.7	1.2	0.5	0.5	0.3	0.1
No Parent in Home	18.1	18.3	12.0	9.9	11.1	11.0
Grandparent family	7.6	7.6	6.2	4.9	4.8	NA
Child is married householder or householder's spouse	0.4	0.3	0.2	0.3	0.1	NA
Child is unmarried householder	0.1	0.0	0.0	0.1	0.0	NA
Child is other relative of householder	5.8	5.8	3.4	2.5	4.2	NA
Child not related to householder	2.4	1.9	1.0	1.0	1.5	NA
Child in group quarters	1.8	2.7	1.2	1.1	0.5	NA

SOURCES: Calculated from 1940–1980 PUMS.

NOTES: Estimates for two-parent families in 1940 and 1950 are derived using marital history information for mothers but not fathers. When both parents remarried, it is not possible to ascertain whether children were born before or after current marriage; that is, whether any children in home are stepchildren.   NA indicates cannot be estimated from available data.

TABLE 3.7

Living Arrangements of White Children Aged 0 and 17: 1940–1980

White Newborns Under Age 1	1940	1950	1960	1970	1980
Total Number (in thousands)	1,562	2,733	3,696	2,955	3,091
Percent	100.0	100.0	100.0	100.0	100.0
Two-Parent Family	93.4	94.5	92.7	89.8	87.0
Children born after marriage (one or both parents married only once)	87.0	87.7	86.2	82.6	76.6
Parents married once (intact two-parent family)	82.9	81.4	78.8	75.6	68.0
Father remarried, mother married once	NA	NA	4.7	5.1	6.1
Mother remarried, father married once	4.1	6.3	2.7	1.9	2.5
At least one stepchild in family	6.4	6.8	4.3	4.5	6.2
Mother married once	5.6	3.5	2.1	1.7	2.7
Mother remarried	0.8	3.3	2.2	2.8	3.5
Both parents remarried	NA	NA	2.2	2.7	4.2
One-Parent Family	2.5	2.8	6.3	8.3	9.1
Mother-only family	2.1	2.6	4.9	7.2	7.6
Mother never married	0.0	0.0	0.2	1.3	2.7
Mother separated or married spouse absent	1.5	2.0	3.5	4.1	2.9
Mother divorced	0.2	0.4	0.7	1.2	1.7
Mother widowed	0.4	0.2	0.5	0.6	0.3
Father-only family	0.4	0.2	1.4	1.1	1.5
Father never married	0.0	0.0	0.0	0.1	0.8
Father separated or married spouse absent	0.4	0.2	0.7	0.9	0.3
Father divorced	0.0	0.0	0.0	0.0	0.4
Father widowed	0.0	0.0	0.7	0.1	0.0
No Parent in Home	4.0	2.6	1.7	1.9	3.9
Grandparent family	0.7	0.5	0.7	0.9	1.1
Child is married householder or householder's spouse	—	—	—	—	—
Child is unmarried householder	—	—	—	—	—
Child is other relative of householder	1.3	0.9	0.4	0.3	1.6
Child not related to householder	0.9	0.7	0.4	0.4	1.1
Child in group quarters	1.1	0.5	0.2	0.3	0.1

the proportion not living with two parents at age 17 was 45–50 percent for blacks and 21–26 percent for whites.[30] But for children born around

[30]Since 17-year-olds in unrelated subfamilies in 1940 and 1950 (born in 1920 and 1930) are classified here as having no parent in the home and as being either unrelated to the householder or as living in group quarters, if there was actually no change between 1940 and 1960, then the total proportion of 17-year-olds not living with two parents may have been as much as 1.2 and 1.1 percentage points smaller for whites in 1940 and 1950 and as much as 2.5 and 4.7 percentage points smaller for blacks during these years than is suggested by estimates in Tables 3.7 and 3.8.

TABLE 3.7 (*continued*)

White Children Age 17	1940	1950	1960	1970	1980
Total Number (in thousands)	2,223	1,841	2,481	3,479	3,579
Percent	100.0	100.0	100.0	100.0	100.0
Two-Parent Family	75.1	74.2	77.7	78.9	74.9
Children born after marriage (one or both parents married only once)	67.8	63.7	67.7	70.5	64.1
Parents married once (intact two-parent family)	62.1	60.0	63.2	64.2	58.6
Father remarried, mother married once	NA	NA	3.0	4.0	3.5
Mother remarried, father married once	5.7	3.7	1.5	2.3	2.0
At least one stepchild in family	7.3	10.5	5.7	3.8	5.0
Mother married once	6.0	5.3	1.7	1.5	1.6
Mother remarried	1.3	5.2	4.0	2.3	3.4
Both parents remarried	NA	NA	4.3	4.6	5.8
One-Parent Family	13.7	11.7	9.8	12.2	14.5
Mother-only family	10.1	9.1	7.9	10.2	12.1
Mother never married	0.0	0.1	0.1	0.1	0.2
Mother separated or married spouse absent	2.0	1.6	2.7	2.3	2.3
Mother divorced	1.3	1.7	2.1	3.4	6.9
Mother widowed	6.8	5.7	3.0	4.4	2.7
Father-only family	3.6	2.6	1.9	2.0	2.4
Father never married	0.1	0.0	0.0	0.0	0.0
Father separated or married spouse absent	0.9	0.7	0.8	0.7	0.5
Father divorced	0.3	0.4	0.2	0.4	1.3
Father widowed	2.3	1.5	0.9	0.9	0.6
No Parent in Home	11.1	13.9	13.1	9.0	10.5
Grandparent family	1.3	1.1	1.0	0.8	0.9
Child is married householder or householder's spouse	2.5	4.2	4.4	3.1	2.2
Child is unmarried householder	0.0	0.1	0.4	0.3	0.6
Child is other relative of householder	3.4	2.8	2.7	1.9	2.4
Child not related to householder	2.3	1.8	1.1	1.1	2.2
Child in group quarters	1.6	3.9	3.5	1.8	2.2

SOURCES: Calculated from 1940–1980 PUMS.

NOTES: Estimates for two-parent families in 1940 and 1950 are derived using marital history information for mothers but not fathers. When both parents remarried, it is not possible to ascertain whether children were born before or after current marriage, that is, whether any children in the home are stepchildren.

NA indicates cannot be estimated from available data.

TABLE 3.8

Living Arrangements of Black Children Aged 0 and 17: 1940–1980

Black Newborns Under Age 1	1940	1950	1960	1970	1980
Total Number (in thousands)	195	381	574	485	546
Percent	100.0	100.0	100.0	100.0	100.0
Two-Parent Family	75.3	68.1	71.3	56.7	45.5
Children born after marriage (one or both parents married only once)	65.9	55.3	59.1	45.8	34.5
Parents married once (intact two-parent family)	61.9	49.8	51.4	40.2	31.0
Father remarried, mother married once	NA	NA	6.1	3.7	2.4
Mother remarried, father married once	4.0	5.5	1.6	1.9	1.1
At least one stepchild in family	9.4	12.8	8.9	9.9	9.7
Mother married once	8.3	6.6	6.8	7.4	7.9
Mother remarried	1.1	6.2	2.1	2.5	1.8
Both parents remarried	NA	NA	3.3	1.0	1.3
One-Parent Family	4.4	11.6	16.1	33.2	41.6
Mother-only family	3.6	10.2	15.1	31.4	37.6
Mother never married	0.7	1.5	2.1	14.8	23.8
Mother separated or married spouse absent	0.0	6.6	10.8	11.1	6.8
Mother divorced	0.0	0.4	0.5	1.8	5.5
Mother widowed	2.9	1.7	1.7	3.7	1.5
Father-only family	0.8	1.4	1.0	1.8	4.0
Father never married	0.4	0.0	0.0	0.6	2.4
Father separated or married spouse absent	0.4	1.0	0.6	1.2	0.6
Father divorced	0.0	0.2	0.2	0.0	0.6
Father widowed	0.0	0.2	0.2	0.0	0.4
No Parent in Home	15.4	20.4	12.7	9.8	13.5
Grandparent family	6.8	6.6	7.0	7.0	8.2
Child is married householder or householder's spouse	—	—	—	—	—
Child is unmarried householder	—	—	—	—	—
Child is other relative of householder	5.8	6.3	3.8	1.6	3.5
Child not related to householder	1.4	3.3	0.9	1.0	1.6
Child in group quarters	1.4	4.2	1.0	0.2	0.2

1980, we project that the proportion not living with two parents at age 17 will jump to 72 percent for blacks and 34 percent for whites (Table 3.9). As a result the racial gap in the proportion of 17-year-olds not living with two parents is projected to increase from 23 to 38 percentage points for children born between about 1920 and 1980.

Since some two-parent families include either children who were born before the parents' marriage or parents who have been married more

TABLE 3.8 (continued)

Black Children Age 17	1940	1950	1960	1970	1980
Total Number (in thousands)	246	253	308	475	619
Percent	100.0	100.0	100.0	100.0	100.0
Two-Parent Family	52.2	52.1	54.7	50.1	43.9
Children born after marriage (one or both parents married only once)	41.9	36.5	40.2	36.6	28.1
Parents married once (intact two-parent family)	34.5	32.6	34.4	30.9	24.6
Father remarried, mother married once	NA	NA	4.2	3.6	2.9
Mother remarried, father married once	7.4	3.9	1.6	2.1	0.6
At least one stepchild in family	10.3	15.6	10.0	9.7	10.8
Mother married once	7.4	7.8	5.5	5.5	6.6
Mother remarried	2.9	7.8	4.5	4.2	4.2
Both parents remarried	NA	NA	4.5	3.8	5.0
One-Parent Family	21.4	21.2	25.5	34.7	40.4
Mother-only family	15.7	17.0	22.6	31.6	37.2
Mother never married	0.3	0.5	1.6	2.7	5.2
Mother separated or married spouse absent	5.7	7.3	9.1	16.6	11.0
Mother divorced	0.9	1.6	2.5	4.7	12.3
Mother widowed	8.8	7.6	9.4	7.6	8.7
Father-only family	5.7	4.2	2.9	3.1	3.2
Father never married	0.0	0.0	0.0	0.2	0.5
Father separated or married spouse absent	2.0	1.6	2.3	1.7	1.6
Father divorced	0.3	0.3	0.0	0.4	0.8
Father widowed	3.4	2.3	0.6	0.8	0.3
No Parent in Home	26.3	26.9	19.4	13.2	15.7
Grandparent family	3.1	3.9	3.9	3.4	3.2
Child is married householder or householder's spouse	4.8	3.9	2.6	2.1	1.1
Child is unmarried householder	1.1	0.5	0.0	0.6	0.2
Child is other relative of householder	10.5	9.4	9.4	3.0	6.5
Child not related to householder	3.7	2.9	0.3	1.1	1.1
Child in group quarters	3.1	6.3	3.2	3.0	3.6

SOURCES: Calculated from 1940–1980 PUMS.

NOTES: Estimates for two-parent families in 1940 and 1950 are derived using marital history information for mothers but not fathers. When both parents remarried, it is not possible to ascertain whether children were born before or after current marriage, that is, whether any children in home are stepchildren.

NA indicates cannot be estimated from available data.

than once, the proportion of children who do not live in an intact two-parent family is larger than the proportion of those who do not live with two parents. For black newborns, the proportion not living in an intact two-parent family increased from 38 percent in 1940 to 69 percent in 1980, while among whites the proportion, at 18 percent in 1940, remained nearly one-half as large as for blacks but rose to 32 percent in 1980. Hence, the racial gap nearly doubled from 20 to 37 percentage points.

Among children born between 1920 and 1950, by the time they were 17, the proportion of those not living in intact two-parent families was 66–69 percent for blacks and 36–40 percent for whites. For children born in 1980, we project that the proportion not living in intact two-parent families at age 17 will jump to 88 percent for blacks and 58 percent for whites. The racial gap will have remained within the range of 27–34 percentage points throughout that period, however.

Overall, then, although the racial gap in the proportion of newborns not living with two parents expanded by 24 percentage points between 1940 and 1980, the increase is expected to be one-half as large for 17-year-olds born between 1920 and 1980. Similarly, although the racial gap in the proportion of newborns not living in an intact two-parent family increased by 16 percentage points between 1940 and 1980, the increase for 17-year-olds born between 1920 and 1980 will be only 2 percentage points. The racial gap expanded more among newborns than among 17-year-olds, because blacks experienced a larger increase in births out of wedlock while whites experienced a larger increase in parental separation and divorce.

Black and White Children Ever Living With Fewer Than Two Parents

About 57–60 percent of all black children born between 1920 and 1950 spent at least part of their childhood living in either a one-parent family or with no parents at all, and we project that this figure will increase to 80 percent for blacks born in 1980 (Figure 3.3 and Table 3.9). Among white children the proportions have been substantially smaller, yet 28–34 percent of whites born between 1920 and 1960 spent at least part of their childhood living with only one parent or with no parents; we project that this figure will jump to about 46 percent for children born in 1980.[31]

[31]These projections for children born in 1970 and 1980 are derived as follows. For whites, the percentage point increase across each age span for a cohort is assumed to be

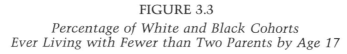

FIGURE 3.3

Percentage of White and Black Cohorts
Ever Living with Fewer than Two Parents by Age 17

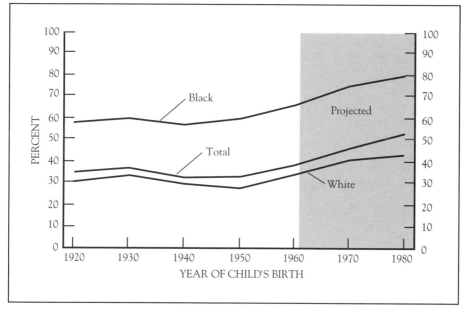

SOURCES: Tables 3.4 and 3.9.

NOTE: Actual years of birth were mainly two years later than indicated.

In earlier times, based on mortality rates in 1900, the proportion of 17-year-olds who would have experienced the death of at least one parent was about 40 percent for blacks and 23 percent for whites, while the corresponding proportions based on the mortality rates in 1940 were about

the same as the percentage point increase across the same age span for the cohort of children born 10 years earlier. This approach takes as given the proportion of newborns not living with two parents or in an intact two-parent family for children born in 1970 and 1980, and it takes as given the proportion of children aged 8–9 and living in such families as given for children born in 1970. Hence, the procedure assumes that the combined percentage point effect of separation, divorce, and widowhood among white children overall was the same as for the next earlier cohort. But this assumption also implies that the effect of separation, divorce, and widowhood on children in intact two-parent families after the specified age was somewhat larger for a specific cohort than for the earlier cohort, proportionately. The procedure does not fully take into account the long-term separations and reconciliations, since the separations are identified only at ages 0, 8–9, and 17. The projected proportion who ever lived with fewer than two parents is then calculated as the average of the proportion at age 17 who lived in an intact two-parent family and lived

TABLE 3.9

White and Black Children Ever Living with Fewer than Two Parents:
1920s–1980s Cohorts

Percent	1920	1930	1940	1950	1960	1970	1980	1990
Black								
Percent born out of wedlock			16.8	16.8	21.8	32.5	48.8	63.5
Not living with two parents								
Newborn under 1 year			24.7	31.9	28.7	43.6	54.5	
Age 8–9		31.3	33.5	32.9	39.5	52.7	61.8 *	
Age 17	47.5	50.2	48.6	50.2	56.1	65.7 *	72.2 *	
Not living in intact two-parent family								
Newborn under 1 year			38.6	50.2	48.6	59.8	69.0	
Age 8–9		53.4	59.2	58.2	64.8	77.4	82.4 *	
Age 17	65.5	67.4	65.6	69.1	75.4	84.4 *	87.9 *	
Ever living with 0–1 parent by age 17	57	59	57	60	66	75 *	80 *	
White								
Percent born out of wedlock			2.0	1.7	2.2	5.5	10.2	17.7
Not living with two parents								
Newborn under 1 year			6.6	5.5	7.3	10.7	13.0	
Age 8–9		11.0	10.7	8.7	12.6	18.0	20.3 *	
Age 17	24.9	25.8	22.3	21.1	26.7	32.1 *	34.4 *	
Not living in intact two-parent family								
Newborn under 1 year			17.1	18.6	21.2	24.4	32.0	
Age 8–9		26.9	27.2	25.2	29.7	38.7	46.3 *	
Age 17	37.9	40.0	36.8	35.8	41.4	50.4 *	58.0 *	
Ever living with 0–1 parent by age 17	31	33	30	28	34	41 *	46 *	

SOURCES: Percent born out of wedlock obtained from National Center for Health Statistics: Vital and Health Statistics of the United States, 1988, Vol. 1, Natality, DHHS Pub. No. (PHS)90-1100. Public Health Service (Washington, DC: U.S. Government Printing Office, 1990), p. 57, and calculated from 1940–1980 PUMS. Except for 1940, out-of-wedlock data are for year prior to the census year indicated, since, for example, children age 0 in the 1950 census were born mainly in 1949.

NOTES: Ever living with 0–1 parent by age 17 estimated as mean of percentage not living with two parents at age 17 and percentage not living in intact two-parent family at age 17.

* Numbers are projections as indicated in Footnote 31.

29 percent for blacks and 12 percent for whites.[32] Since children born around 1890 and around 1930, respectively, experienced approximately these mortality rates, they would also have experienced approximately these chances of facing a parental death during childhood. Although

with two parents.
    For blacks, we used a somewhat different procedure in order to take into account the large shift from separation and divorce toward out-of-wedlock childbearing as the major source of increase in mother-only families. The percentage point increase for each age span

mortality rates in 1987 imply that children born around 1980 are much less likely to experience a parental death than were children born during the 1930s, the estimated proportion of 12 percent for blacks born around 1980 is nearly the same as that for whites born during the 1930s and is more than twice as large as the estimate of 5 percent for whites born around 1980.[33]

Since the overall rate of marital dissolutions between the mid-1800s and the mid-1900s remained relatively constant as the rise in divorce counterbalanced the decline in mortality, and since the proportions of black and white women aged 30–54 who were currently divorced in-

---

for the next younger cohort in the same age span was divided by the following: 100 percent minus the proportion already not in an intact two-parent family at the next earlier age for the preceding cohort. This estimates the proportionate increase across the age span for the preceding cohort, and this proportion is multiplied by the following: 100 percent minus the proportion already not in a (primary) two-parent family at the earlier age for the current cohort whose value is being projected. The projected value for the proportion ever not living with two parents is then estimated (as for whites) as the mean at age 17 living in an intact two-parent family and living with two parents.

Using this procedure, the results for blacks are substantially smaller than they would be if the procedure used for whites were applied to blacks. For example, the projected proportion ever living in a fragmented family among black children born in 1980 is 80 percent, but the alternative procedure would produce a projection of 91 percent. The difference is that the alternative procedure effectively assumes that no major shift from separation and divorce to out-of-wedlock childbearing has occurred.

As we saw earlier in this chapter, the projections developed here imply that about 53 percent of all children born in 1980 will spend time in a non-two-parent family—a result generally consistent with the range of 49 percent by age 16 projected by Larry Bumpass and 59 percent by age 18 projected by Arthur J. Norton and Paul C. Glick. The probable reason the projection by Bumpass is slightly smaller than the one developed here is that it refers to an end point two years younger. The probable reason the projection by Norton and Glick is larger than the ones developed here and by Bumpass is that it includes more parental separations that end in reconciliation. But all of these projections are much smaller than the 74 percent projected by Sandra L. Hofferth. In fact, Hofferth projects that for children born in 1980 an enormous 70 percent of whites and an astounding 94 percent of blacks will spend time in a fragmented family. At least part of the difference, especially for blacks, may be that the projections developed here, and by Bumpass, Norton, and Glick, effectively take into account the shift among blacks from separation and divorce to out-of-wedlock childbearing, while the projections by Hofferth do not.

[32]These calculations follow the same "census-consistent" procedures used in Footnote 19, but separately for blacks and whites, using data from the citations in that footnote. Fifteen-year mortality for whites is calculated as the mean for females beginning at ages 25 and 30, and for males beginning at age 30. Fifteen-year mortality for blacks is calculated beginning at age 25 for females and for males as the mean beginning at ages 25 and 30. The estimates correspond with the approximate median ages of childbearing of 25 for black women and 27.5 for white women. Husbands are assumed to be about 2.5 years older than wives. Median age of childbearing calculated from Tables 6B and 6C, Robert L. Heuser, *Fertility Tables for Birth Cohorts by Color: United States, 1917–73* (Washington, DC: National Center for Health Statistics, 1976).

[33]Estimates for children born around 1980 are based on mortality rates in 1987. See Table 6–4, National Center for Health Statistics, *Vital Statistics of the United States, 1987*, vol. 2, Mortality, Part A (Washington, DC: Public Health Service, 1990).

creased by approximately equal amounts, it seems likely that changes in mortality and divorce approximately counterbalanced each other for both blacks and whites.[34] If so, then, between the late 1800s and about 1950, the proportions of children who ever lived with either one or no parents remained roughly constant at 55–60 percent for black children and about 28–33 percent for white children.

Therefore, the racial gap in the proportion of children who ever lived with fewer than two parents remained at 26–32 percentage points, roughly constant between the late 1800s and 1950. Since the proportions of black and white children who ever lived with fewer than two parents are projected to increase equally for children born through 1980, the racial gap, too, is projected to increase only slightly to 34 percentage points.

Grandparents in the Homes of Black and White Children

Throughout the period since the Great Depression, black children have been five to nine times more likely to have lived with a grandparent but no parent in the home (Table 3.10) than have whites. Despite the increases in one-parent families, the proportion of children living in grandparent-only families declined slightly for blacks from 8 to 5 percent between 1940 and 1980 but remained constant for whites at 1 percent.

Among the sharply increasing proportion of children living in one-parent families since 1960, as of 1980, the chances of having a grandparent in the home declined by about one-half for both black and white children. Between 1940–1960 and 1980, among children living with a separated, divorced, or widowed mother, the proportion who had a grandparent in the home dropped from 20–25 percent to 11 percent for blacks and from 21–27 percent to 9 percent for whites. Nearly identical declines occurred in the proportion of children in father-only families who also had a grandparent in the home. Even among children living in mother-only families with a never-married mother, only 20 percent of blacks and 26 percent of whites also lived with a grandparent in 1980. The proportions were higher for newborns, but the declining proportions with grandparents in the home were equally striking (Table 3.5).

[34]See citations in Footnote 21, and Table 25, U.S. Bureau of the Census, *Abstract of the Twelfth Census of the United States* (Washington, DC: U.S. Government Printing Office, 1902); and Table 177, U.S. Bureau of the Census, *U.S. Census of the Population: 1960. Vol. I, Characteristics of the Population*. Part 1, United States Summary (Washington, DC: U.S. Government Printing Office, 1964).

TABLE 3.10

White and Black Children with Grandparents in Home: 1940–1980

	1940 White	1940 Black	1950 White	1950 Black	1960 White	1960 Black	1970 White	1970 Black	1980 White	1980 Black
Percentage of all Children with Grandparents in Home, and 0, 1, or 2 Parents in Home										
No parent in home	1.3	7.6	1.1	7.6	0.7	6.2	0.9	4.9	1.0	4.8
One parent in home	1.8	3.1	1.8	4.0	1.4	4.4	1.2	4.6	1.5	5.7
Two parents in home	7.2	5.3	7.7	6.9	4.7	5.2	3.3	3.5	2.3	1.7
Total with grandparent	10.3	16.0	10.6	18.5	6.8	15.8	5.4	13.0	4.8	12.2
Within Parental Living Arrangement, Percentage with Grandparents in Home										
Intact two-parent	8.6	8.3	8.7	10.7	5.2	8.3	3.6	5.6	2.7	3.4
Blended two-parent	7.2	7.1	8.2	10.5	5.3	6.8	4.3	6.8	2.9	4.0
Mother-only	22.7	21.5	26.9	24.2	20.4	19.6	11.9	14.1	10.7	14.0
Mother-only, never married	—	—	—	—	—	—	28.8	28.8	26.2	19.6
Mother-only, ever married	22.8	21.5	26.8	24.7	20.5	19.6	11.2	10.9	9.3	10.9
Father-only	21.0	19.8	28.4	27.2	17.8	28.2	12.1	13.2	8.9	9.1

SOURCES: Calculated from 1940–1980 PUMS.

Overall, the increases in one-parent families and the declines in grandparents in the homes of children in one-parent families balanced each other almost perfectly (Table 3.10). Among children aged 0–17, the proportion living in either one-parent families with a grandparent in the home or in grandparent-only families remained unchanged between 1940 and 1980 at 10–12 percent for blacks and 2–3 percent for whites. If it is reasonable to assume that the proportion of children who ever lived in such families during their childhood was two to three times as large as the proportion who lived in such families at a specific point in time, then for children born during the middle of this century, the proportion who were ever either taken in by their grandparents or lived in one-parent families with grandparents was nearly stable (somewhere between 20–35 percent for blacks and 5–10 percent for whites).

Clearly, grandparents have played an important role for many children, especially blacks, in easing the difficulties associated with living in one-parent families. Yet for both black and white children, there is evidence to suggest that fewer than one-half who ever lived with fewer than two parents also had grandparents in the home to fill the gap created by the absent parent. In addition, during this time the proportion of children living in two-parent families with at least one grandparent declined between 1940–1960 and 1980 from 5–7 percent to 2 percent for both blacks and whites. Although many of these grandparents may have provided child care or some other form of assistance, it should be noted that many were probably also living as physical or economic dependents of their own adult children. In any event, it is possible that at mid-century an additional 5–15 percent of children lived in two-parent families that also had a grandparent sometime during their childhood, but this figure dropped to only about 5 percent for children born later in the century.

All told, then, at mid-century, the proportion of children who either lived with a grandparent or had one in the home sometime during childhood was probably somewhere between 25–50 percent for blacks and 10–25 percent for whites. With the decline in grandparents living in two-parent families, however, these proportions had dropped by as much as 10 percentage points by the latter part of the century.[35] From the perspective of children, then, the extended family has remained a vital institution, especially for black children and children whose parents do

[35]These ranges are generally consistent with the estimates from the National Survey of Families and Households (NSFH) for persons aged 19 and over in 1986 that 11 percent ever lived in the home of a grandparent for up to four months while growing up, and that 18 percent ever had a grandparent living in their home (pp. M-52 and M-55, *Codebook and Documentation: Introduction*, University of Wisconsin, Madison). Taken together, NSFH results indicate that for all adults in 1986, 18–29 percent ever lived with a grandparent during childhood.

not live together, but it is also true that a majority of children in one-parent families have never had a grandparent live in their home.

Parents and Grandparents in the Homes
of Hispanic and Non-Hispanic Children

In 1980, Hispanic children (of any race) were 12 percentage points less likely than non-Hispanic whites to be living with two parents, but they were 24 percentage points more likely than non-Hispanic blacks to be living with two parents (Table 3.11). Similarly, Hispanic children (of any race) were 13 percentage points less likely than non-Hispanic whites and 26 percentage points more likely than non-Hispanic blacks to be living in an intact two-parent family. Among children aged 17, but not among newborns, however, Hispanics (of any race) are about midway between non-Hispanic whites and non-Hispanic blacks in their chances of living with two parents or in an intact two-parent family (Table 3.12).

Hispanic children (of any race) are also more comparable to non-Hispanic whites than to non-Hispanic blacks in their chances of living in a mother-only family. Hispanic children (of any race) are about 9 percentage points more likely than non-Hispanic whites to live with a mother only, but about 19 percentage points less likely than non-Hispanic blacks to live in such families. Among newborns and 17-year-olds, the differences are quite similar. Much of this difference is due to variations in the proportion of these children who live with never-married mothers. For example, and most important, newborn Hispanic children (of any race) were 6 percentage points more likely than non-Hispanic whites to be living with a never-married mother only, but they were 16 percentage points less likely than non-Hispanic blacks to be living in such a family.

Combined with our earlier projections of the proportion of children who will ever live with only one or no parent, these results suggest that among Hispanic children (of any race) born in 1980, between 55 and 65 percent may spend part of their childhood living with either one or no parent in the home.

In their chances of living in a grandparent-only family, Hispanic children (of any race) were, again, more similar to non-Hispanic whites (2 vs. 1 percent) than to non-Hispanic blacks (5 percent) (Table 3.13). However, the proportion of Hispanic children (of any race) in mother-only families with a grandparent in the home was 2 percentage points smaller than for non-Hispanic whites and 5 percentage points smaller than for non-Hispanic blacks.

All together, Hispanic children (of any race) aged 0–17 were slightly

TABLE 3.11

Living Arrangements of Hispanic and Non-Hispanic Children Aged 0–17: 1980

	Non-Hispanic			Hispanic Living with Mother	
	White	Black	Total Hispanic	Old Family	First Generation
Total Number (in thousands)	49,294	9,568	5,724	3,409	1,795
Percent	100.0	100.0	100.0	100.0	100.0
Two-Parent Family	83.0	46.7	71.1	73.4	87.3
Children born after marriage (one or both parents married only once)	69.9	30.8	57.1	57.6	72.7
Parents married once (intact two-parent family)	63.2	26.6	52.2	52.2	67.2
Father remarried, mother married once	4.9	3.4	3.7	3.8	4.6
Mother remarried, father married once	1.8	0.8	1.2	1.6	0.9
At least one stepchild in family	6.9	13.1	10.9	11.9	12.0
Mother married once	2.3	9.5	6.6	6.5	8.6
Mother remarried	4.6	3.6	4.3	5.4	3.4
Both parents remarried	6.3	3.0	3.1	3.9	2.6
One-Parent Family	13.3	42.0	21.5	26.6	12.7
Mother-only family	11.4	39.1	19.9	26.6	12.7
Mother never married	0.7	14.0	3.9	5.4	2.0
Mother separated or married spouse absent	2.7	11.6	6.9	8.5	5.8
Mother divorced	6.7	10.0	7.7	10.7	4.2
Mother widowed	1.3	3.5	1.4	2.0	0.7
Father-only family	1.9	2.9	1.6	NA	NA
Father never married	0.1	0.9	0.5	NA	NA
Father separated or married spouse absent	0.4	1.0	0.6	NA	NA
Father divorced	1.1	0.7	0.3	NA	NA
Father widowed	0.3	0.3	0.2	NA	NA
No Parent in Home	3.7	11.1	7.6	NA	NA
Grandparent family	0.9	4.9	1.8	NA	NA
Child is married householder or householder's spouse	0.2	0.1	0.4	NA	NA
Child is unmarried householder	0.1	0.0	0.1	NA	NA
Child is other relative of householder	1.1	4.1	3.4	NA	NA
Child not related to householder	1.0	1.5	1.5	NA	NA
Child in group quarters	0.4	0.5	0.4	NA	NA

SOURCES: Calculated from 1980 Census PUMS.

NA indicates cannot be estimated from available data.

more likely than non-Hispanic whites to live in a family that included a grandparent in the home (7 vs. 5 percent), but they were substantially less likely than non-Hispanic blacks (at 12 percent) to live in such a family.

Focusing only on children aged 0–17 who live with their mother (including 86–91 percent of all Hispanic children [of any race] and non-Hispanic white and black children), first-generation Hispanics (of any race) are nearly identical to non-Hispanic whites in their chances of living with two parents or in mother-only families (86–87 and 12–13 percent). Furthermore, these first-generation Hispanics (of any race) living with a mother are as likely as non-Hispanic whites living with a mother to live in an intact two-parent family (67 percent).

Since first-generation Hispanic children (of any race) are generally more similar than Hispanic children, taken as a whole, to non-Hispanic whites in the parental living arrangements, old-family Hispanic children (of any race) are less similar than Hispanic children (of any race), taken as a whole, to non-Hispanic whites. Nevertheless, old-family Hispanic children (of any race) are more similar to non-Hispanic whites than to non-Hispanic blacks in their parental living arrangements. Among children living with their mother, the gap between old-family Hispanics (of any race) and non-Hispanic whites in the proportion living with two parents is 13 percentage points, compared with a gap of 33 percentage points separating old-family Hispanics (of any race) from non-Hispanic blacks.

Conclusions

Children in one-parent families tend, on average, to experience disadvantages compared with children in intact two-parent families for several reasons: (1) their families tend to have lower incomes; (2) they may receive less care and attention from parents; (3) they tend to be exposed to greater personal and parental stress; (4) they tend to experience more school-related, health, and behavioral problems; and (5) they tend to complete fewer years of education, enter lower-status occupations, and earn lower incomes during adulthood. Children in stepfamilies also experience some of these disadvantages. For many children, however, these disadvantages may result not only from the family's living arrangements but from other factors, such as low parental income, that also contribute to the creation of non-intact family living arrangements (see Chapters 9 and 10).

TABLE 3.12

Living Arrangements of Hispanic and Non-Hispanic Children Aged 0 and 17: 1980

Newborns Under Age 1	Non-Hispanic		Total Hispanic	Hispanic Living with Mother	
	White	Black		Old Family	First Generation
Total Number (in thousands)	2,733	527	376	235	111
Percent	100.0	100.0	100.0	100.0	100.0
Two-Parent Family	88.5	45.7	74.1	75.4	91.0
Children born after marriage (one or both parents married only once)	78.3	34.3	61.8	63.1	75.7
Parents married once (intact two-parent family)	69.5	30.9	55.1	56.2	67.6
Father remarried, mother married once	6.1	2.3	6.1	6.0	8.1
Mother remarried, father married once	2.7	1.1	0.5	0.9	0.0
At least one stepchild in family	5.8	10.1	9.4	8.9	12.6
Mother married once	2.2	8.2	6.7	5.5	10.8
Mother remarried	3.6	1.9	2.7	3.4	1.8
Both parents remarried	4.4	1.3	2.9	3.4	2.7
One-Parent Family	8.4	40.7	19.9	24.6	9.0
Mother-only family	6.5	37.0	18.1	24.6	9.0
Mother never married	2.2	23.7	7.7	9.8	5.4
Mother separated or married spouse absent	2.4	6.5	7.2	10.6	1.8
Mother divorced	1.6	5.3	2.9	3.8	1.8
Mother widowed	0.3	1.5	0.3	0.4	0.0
Father-only family	1.9	3.7	1.6	NA	NA
Father never married	0.8	2.5	0.8	NA	NA
Father separated or married spouse absent	0.3	0.4	0.5	NA	NA
Father divorced	0.4	0.4	0.3	NA	NA
Father widowed	0.0	0.4	0.0	NA	NA
No Parent in Home	3.6	13.6	6.2	NA	NA
Grandparent family	1.2	8.5	0.8	NA	NA
Child is married householder or householder's spouse	0.0	0.0	0.0	NA	NA
Child is unmarried householder	0.0	0.0	0.0	NA	NA
Child is other relative of householder	1.4	3.4	3.2	NA	NA
Child not related to householder	0.9	1.5	2.4	NA	NA
Child in group quarters	0.1	0.2	0.0	NA	NA

TABLE 3.12 (*continued*)

Children Aged 17	Non-Hispanic White	Black	Total Hispanic	Hispanic Living with Mother Old Family
Total Number (in thousands)	3,287	600	310	175
Percent	100.0	100.0	100.0	100.0
Two-Parent Family	76.6	44.1	57.4	74.4
Children born after marriage (one or both parents married only once)	65.5	28.4	48.3	61.2
Parents married once (intact two-parent family)	59.9	24.7	43.2	54.3
Father remarried, mother married once	3.6	3.0	3.2	4.0
Mother remarried, father married once	2.0	0.7	1.9	2.9
At least one stepchild in family	4.9	10.7	7.2	10.3
Mother married once	1.5	6.5	3.6	5.7
Mother remarried	3.4	4.2	3.6	4.6
Both parents remarried	6.2	5.0	1.9	2.9
One-Parent Family	14.1	40.6	20.0	25.7
Mother-only family	11.6	37.7	18.0	25.7
Mother never married	0.1	5.0	1.9	3.4
Mother separated or married spouse absent	1.9	11.2	6.1	6.9
Mother divorced	6.8	12.7	7.7	11.4
Mother widowed	2.8	8.8	2.3	4.0
Father-only family	2.5	2.9	2.0	NA
Father never married	0.0	0.5	0.0	NA
Father separated or married spouse absent	0.5	1.3	1.0	NA
Father divorced	1.4	0.8	0.0	NA
Father widowed	0.6	0.3	1.0	NA
No Parent in Home	9.4	15.3	22.6	NA
Grandparent family	0.8	3.3	1.9	NA
Child is married householder or householder's spouse	2.1	1.0	3.6	NA
Child is unmarried householder	0.5	0.0	1.9	NA
Child is other relative of householder	1.9	6.5	8.1	NA
Child is not related to householder	2.0	1.2	4.2	NA
Child in group quarters	2.1	3.3	2.9	NA

SOURCES: Calculated from 1980 Census PUMS.

NA indicates cannot be estimated from available data.

Although most newborn children live with both biological parents, among children born between the late 1800s and 1950, a large and nearly stable minority (about 33 percent) spent part of their childhood with fewer than two parents in the home. In addition, by the time they had reached age 17, about 40 percent of these children were no longer living

TABLE 3.13

Hispanic and Non-Hispanic Children with Grandparents in the Home: 1980

	Non-Hispanic			Hispanic Living with Mother	
	White	Black	Total Hispanic	Old Family	First Generation
Percentage of all Children with Grandparents in Home, and 0, 1, or 2 Parents in Home					
No parent in home	0.9	4.9	1.8	NA	NA
One parent in home	1.4.	5.7	2.1	2.7	0.8
Two parents in home	2.2	1.7	2.8	2.0	5.0
Total with grandparent	4.5	12.3	6.6	4.8	5.8
Within Parental Living Arrangement, Percentage with Grandparents in Home					
Two-parent family	2.7	3.7	3.9	2.8	5.8
Mother-only family	11.0	14.0	9.4	10.3	5.7
Mother-only, never married	33.1	19.6	14.5	14.1	—
Mother-only, ever married	9.5	10.9	8.2	9.3	4.1
Father-only	8.6	9.2	12.2	NA	NA

SOURCES: Calculated from 1980 Census PUMS.

in an intact two-parent family in which both parents were married only once and all the siblings were born after the marriage. Little change occurred for more than a half century, however, because the effects of declining parental mortality were counterbalanced by increases in the incidence of parental separation and divorce.

Since then, however, as was recently highlighted by Andrew J. Cherlin, the link between marriage and the b ing and rearing of children has weakened further.[36] The proportion o. newborns who are not living with two parents doubled between 1940 and 1960, rising from 9 to 19 percent, because of the increase in out-of-wedlock childbearing. In addition, combined with the continuing rise in the rates of separation and divorce, the proportion of children who will ever live with fewer than two parents is projected to increase to 55–60 percent for children born in 1980.

Among black children, a high rate of exposure to living arrangements with fewer than two parents has long been common. For ex-

[36]Andrew J. Cherlin, "The Weakening Link Between Marriage and the Care of Children," *Family Planning Perspectives* 20 (December 1988): 302–306.

ample, in 1940 the proportion of newborns not living with two parents was about 25 percent for blacks compared with only 7 percent for whites; and for children born between the late 1800s and 1940 it appears that a majority of blacks (55–60 percent) and a large minority of whites (28–33 percent) spent part of their childhood in families with fewer than two parents. Subsequently, the racial gap in out-of-wedlock childbearing more than doubled, and in 1980 about 55 percent of black newborns did not live with two parents, compared with 13 percent for whites. However, since separation and divorce have increased less for blacks than for whites, we project that for children born in 1980, the proportion who have ever lived with fewer than two parents will increase between ages 0 and 17 by 25 percentage points for blacks to 80 percent at age 17, compared with a 33 percentage point increase for whites to 46 percent at age 17.

Although grandparents have played an important role for many children, especially blacks, in easing the difficulties associated with living in one-parent families, among both black and white children during the past 50 years, it is probably true that for children who have ever lived with fewer than two parents, less than one-half also had grandparents in the home to fill the gap left by the absent parent. Recently at least, Hispanic children (of any race) have been found to be more similar to non-Hispanic whites than to non-Hispanic blacks in their parental and grandparental living arrangements.

In Chapter 2 as well as in this chapter, we saw that the family life of the typical child was transformed during the past century by the revolutionary decline in family size and by the changing mix of parents and grandparents in the home. Beyond these living arrangements, the nature of family life for children also depends upon the kind of productive activities in which parents are engaged. In the next chapter, we will discuss the two transformations in parental work that have accompanied historic changes in the family living arrangements of children.

4

PARENTS' WORK AND
THE FAMILY ECONOMY
TWICE TRANSFORMED

Introduction and Highlights

NOT ONLY did the past century and a half bring a revolutionary decline in children's family size and a large increase in their experience with one-parent family living, it also brought two distinct transformations in parents' work and hence in the economic foundation of family life.

When the United States was primarily an agricultural country, parenting, child care, and economic production were combined. Children and their parents lived and worked together on the family farm to support themselves. This changed during the Industrial Revolution. Fathers became breadwinners who worked at jobs away from the family home in order to earn the income that was necessary to support the family, while mothers became homemakers who stayed home to personally care for their children, as well as to clean, cook, and perform other domestic functions for the family. Since the Great Depression, parents' work and the family economy have again been transformed. The result is that most children today live either in dual-earner families, where both parents maintain jobs away from home, or in one-parent families. In this chapter we will discuss the nature of these changes by addressing the following questions.

Which periods of history were dominated by each of the three major forms of family organization—that is, by the farm family, the breadwin-ner-homemaker family, and the dual-earner/one-parent family systems? When and how rapidly did the transformation from one family system to the next occur? To what extent did the various family systems over-lap in time? To what extent did children actually experience the appar-ent mid-twentieth century ideal of an intact two-parent family in which the father was the full-time breadwinner and the mother was the full-time housewife and mother? What associated changes occurred in the work of older children during the era? Briefly, this chapter offers the following answers to these questions.

A majority of children probably lived in two-parent farm families until around 1870, and not until after 1900 did the number of children living in nonfarm breadwinner-homemaker families substantially ex-ceed the number in two-parent farm families. The transformation began earlier as the proportion of children living in nonfarm breadwinner-homemaker families rose fairly steadily from about 15–20 percent in 1840 to about 50 percent in 1920. Less than 50 years later, the propor-tion of children in nonfarm breadwinner-homemaker families again fell below 50 percent, and the dominance of this family form ended.

Much of the era of dominance for breadwinner-homemaker families was simultaneously marked by the continuing shift away from the farm family system and the new shift toward the dual-earner/one-parent fam-ily system. After the rise of breadwinner-homemaker families to a ma-jority around 1920, the proportion of children living in two-parent farm families continued to decline until it reached a very low level. In addi-tion, only two decades later, after 1940, the proportion of children living in dual-earner families began to rise sharply, and after 1960 the propor-tion living in one-parent families began to rise sharply.

Since the mid-1970s, therefore, a new system of family organization has been dominant, and by the year 2000 the proportion of children liv-ing in dual-earner or one-parent families may exceed 80 percent. But even in specific years between 1920 and 1970, when a majority of chil-dren did live in breadwinner-homemaker families, only a minority lived in the mid-twentieth century ideal form of the breadwinner-homemaker family—namely, in a nonfarm two-parent family in which the father worked full-time year-round, the mother was not in the labor force, and all the children were born after the parents' only marriage. In fact, throughout the industrial era a majority of American children were born into families that did not conform to this ideal, and by the end of their childhood an overwhelming majority of children were no longer living in such an idealized family situation.

For white children, the chances of living in the idealized form of the breadwinner-homemaker family were only slightly larger than they were for children as a whole. Among newborn black children at least since 1940, however, no more than 25 percent have lived in such idealized families, and this figure fell to 8 percent for black children born in 1980. Among blacks born in 1920, by the end of childhood only 15 percent still lived in such families at age 17, and among blacks born in 1960, only 3 percent lived in such families at age 17.

Finally, in 1980, among Hispanic children (of any race), only a minority lived in such idealized families—21 percent of newborns and 10 percent of 17-year-olds. Hispanic children (of any race) were slightly closer to non-Hispanic whites than to non-Hispanic blacks in their chances of living in such families.

Overall, then, a majority of children born throughout the industrial era have lived in families that experienced at least one of the following: a parental separation, divorce, or death; a sibling born out of wedlock; a spell of unemployment, job search, or part-time employment of the father; or paid employment of the mother. Exposure to these experiences is important for many reasons. For example, as we saw in Chapter 3, a parental separation and divorce may have negative consequences for children, even if they removed the children from a conflict-ridden family situation. As Glen Elder and his colleagues have suggested, if the drop in income resulting from a father's unemployment or part-time employment is severe enough to require major hardship adaptations, then family members may experience psychological difficulties, as well, of course, as the opportunity to rise above life's disadvantages.[1] And as we will see in Chapters 9 and 10, many mothers apparently work out of economic necessity, while many others do so in order to improve their relative social and economic status, or to receive other benefits. But

[1]See Glen H. Elder, Jr., *Children of the Great Depression: Social Change in Life Experience* (Chicago: University of Chicago Press, 1974); Glen H. Elder, Jr., "Scarcity and Prosperity in Postwar Childbearing: Explorations from a Life Course Perspective," *Journal of Family History* 5:410–433; Glen H. Elder, Jr., "Household, Kinship, and the Life Course: Perspectives on Black Families and Children, in M. Spencer, G. Brookins, and W. Allen, eds., *Beginnings: The Social and Affective Development of Black Children*, pp. 39–43; Glen H. Elder, Jr., Avshalom Caspi, and Tri van Nguyen, "Resourceful and Vulnerable Children: Family Influences in Stressful Times," in R. K. Silbereisen and K. Eyferth, eds., *Development as Action in Context: Integrative Perspectives on Youth Development* (CITY: Springer, 1986), pp. 167–187; Glen H. Elder, Avshalom Caspi, and Geraldine Downey, "Problem Behavior and Family Relationships, in Aage Sorenson, Franz Weinert, and Lonnie Sherrod, *Human Development: Multi-Disciplinary Perspectives* (Hillsdale, NJ: Erlbaum, [in press]), pp. 293–340; R. D. Conger, et. al., "Linking Economic Hardship to Marital Quality and Instability," *Journal of Marriage and the Family* 52 (1990): 643–656; Glen H. Elder, Jr. and Tamara K. Hareven, "Rising Above Life's Disadvantage: From Great Depression to World War," in Glen H. Elder, Jr., John Modell, and Ross Parke, eds., selections from *Children in Time and Place* (Cambridge: Cambridge University Press, 1992); and Glen H. Elder, Jr., Rand D. Conger, E. Michael Foster, and Monika Ardelt, "Families Under Economic Pressure," *Journal of Family Issues* (in Press).

whatever their reasons for working, mothers' work brings into the home income that would not otherwise be available to the family.

Finally, the work of adolescents has also undergone a transformation since the mid-1800s. On the family farm, adolescent labor contributed to the survival of the family and provided adolescents with the opportunity to learn the work they would do as adults. During the early part of the industrial era, adolescents also often worked in the nonagricultural economy to help support their families. But labor force participation by adolescents declined greatly after 1900 with the general rise in affluence, the efforts of labor unions to ensure jobs for adults by limiting child labor, the success of child labor laws, and the passage of laws mandating compulsory education. Since the 1950s, however, adolescent students have greatly increased their labor force participation, largely in jobs that will not be pursued into adulthood and mainly to pay for items of personal consumption rather than to provide basic family support.

Let's take a more a detailed look at the historic transformations in parents' and adolescents' work, and hence in the family economy, that have occurred during the past century and a half.

Historical Transformation of Parents' Work

For hundreds, if not thousands of years, agriculture and the two-parent farm family were primary forms of economic production and family organization in western countries. The tradition to and through the nonfarm father-as-bread-winner family system in the U.S. was extremely lopsided by comparison. The subsequent transition to a dual-earner/one-parent system of family organization occurred three times as quickly, and is nearly complete. For children, the heyday of nonfarm families in which fathers were the sole breadwinners lasted for little more than 50 years; in only five censuses did at least a majority of children live in such families.[2]

Between the first U.S. census in 1790 and the one taken in 1840, at least two-thirds of all children lived on farms, and fewer than one-fifth lived in nonfarm families in which the father worked outside the home and the mother did not (Figure 4.1).[3] With increasing urbanization and industrialization during the next 50 years, however, the proportion of

[2]For a discussion of the transformation from the farm family to the father-as-bread-winner family to the dual-earner family, see Kingsley Davis, "Wives and Work: The Sex Role Revolution and Its Consequences," *Population and Development Review* 10: 397–417.

[3]For the derivation of these estimates, see Appendix 4.1.

children living in two-parent farm families declined by about 25 percentage points, while the proportion living in nonfarm breadwinner-homemaker families increased by about 25 percentage points.

By 1890, then, approximately equal proportions of children (41–43 percent) lived in two-parent farm families and nonfarm breadwinner-homemaker families. Not until 30 years later, however, in about 1920, did a bare majority of children live in this new form of family organization. During the next 50 years, nonfarm breadwinner-homemaker families remained dominant, but the proportion of children living in such families never reached 60 percent.

Then, after only a half century of dominance, the nonfarm breadwinner-homemaker family went into rapid decline. During the 20 years from 1960 to 1980, the proportion of children living in such families dropped precipitously by 21 percentage points—from 56 to 35 percent. The corresponding increase from 33 to 55 percent had required a period three times as long, specifically, the 60 years between 1870 and 1930. By 1989, preliminary estimates indicated that only 25 percent of children still lived in nonfarm breadwinner-homemaker families.[4] Hence, during the short 29 years following 1960, the increase that was about 90 years in the making was completely wiped out. This sharp decline in nonfarm breadwinner-homemaker families is accounted for by increases in dual-earner and one-parent families.

Between 1920 and 1960, when a majority of children lived in nonfarm breadwinner-homemaker families, the proportion living on farms continued its historic decline, dropping from 32 to 9 percent, while the proportion living in dual-earner or one-parent families jumped from 13 to 30 percent. Virtually all of this increase is accounted for by the rise in dual-earner families.

As of the Great Depression, then, children were in the middle of a rapid transition that simultaneously encompassed all three major forms of family organization (Figure 4.2). In 1940, 25 percent of children lived in two-parent farm families, a bare majority of 52 percent lived in nonfarm families in which fathers were the sole breadwinners, and 23 percent lived in either dual-earner, one-parent, or no-parent situations. In 1960, as the heyday of the nonfarm breadwinner-homemaker family reached its zenith, did somewhat more than one-half of children live in such families, while the proportion living in two-parent farm families had dropped to 10 percent and the proportion living with either two working parents, one parent, or no parent had increased to 30 percent.

In 1980, after another 20 years, virtually no children lived in two-

---

[4]Estimates for 1989 were obtained from the Current Population Survey.

FIGURE 4.1

Children Aged 0–17 in Farm Families, Father-as-Breadwinner Families, and Dual-Earner Families: 1790–1989

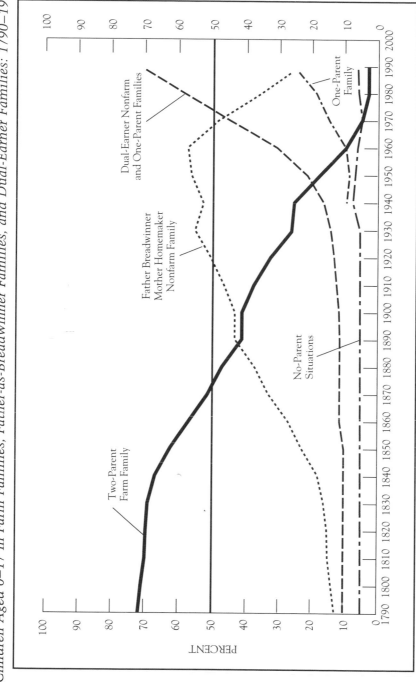

SOURCES: Census PUMS for 1940–1980, CPS for 1980 and 1989, and Appendix 4.1.

NOTES: Estimates for 10-year intervals to 1980, and for 1989.

FIGURE 4.2

Children Aged 0–17, by Three Major Family Forms: 1940, 1960, 1980, and 1989

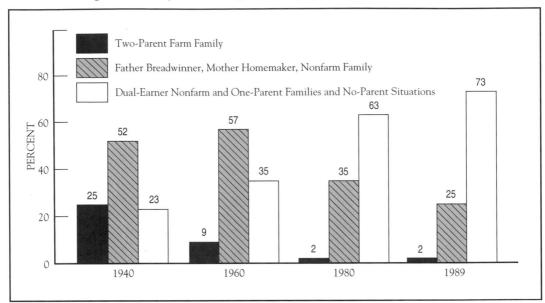

SOURCES: Census PUMS for 1940, 1960, 1980, and CPS for 1989.

parent farm families, the proportion living in nonfarm breadwinner-homemaker families had dropped by 22 percentage points, and the proportion living with two employed parents or with one parent had jumped by a startling 28 percentage points. By 1980, therefore, the proportion of children living in dual-earner and one-parent families had grown to 58 percent—a figure that was larger than the proportion who had lived in nonfarm breadwinner-homemaker families in any census year.

This rise in dual-earner and one-parent families from about one-fifth to nearly three-fifths of children occurred between 1950 and 1980, a period spanning only three decades. The corresponding rise in nonfarm breadwinner-homemaker families had required the nine decades from 1840 to 1930—a period about three times as long. Since 1980, the rise in dual-earner and one-parent families has continued. By 1989, about 68 percent of children lived in such families, while the proportion living in nonfarm breadwinner-homemaker families had fallen to 25 percent, essentially the same as the 24 percent living in one-parent families!

Although much attention has quite properly been focused on the recent rise in one-parent families, the rapid increase in dual-earner and one-parent families has been due primarily to the large increase in dual-earner families, and only secondarily to the increase in one-parent families. In Chapter 10 we will discuss the reasons for this rise in dual-earner and one-parent families.

Based on recent trends it appears that by the year 2000, a scant 8 years from now, the proportion of children living in dual-earner or one-parent families may exceed 80 percent, and the proportion living in either farm families or nonfarm breadwinner-homemaker families will have fallen to about 15 percent. The decline of nonfarm breadwinner-homemaker families from a position of dominance to one of minor importance will have occurred in the brief span of 40 years.

Idealized Breadwinner-Homemaker Families Among Children Aged 0–17

During the 1950s the urban family was idealized in such television programs as "Ozzie and Harriet" and "Father Knows Best." These programs portrayed as ideal a nonfarm two-parent family in which the father was the full-time year-round breadwinner, the mother was a full-time homemaker, and the children were all born after the parents' only marriage. Although more than one-half of children in specific years between 1920 and 1970 lived in nonfarm breadwinner-homemaker families, at no time during this period did a majority live in the idealized vision of American family life. During the century from 1850 to 1950, it may have seemed that reality was approaching this ideal, however, since most of the decline in farm families was accounted for by a corresponding increase in nonfarm breadwinner-homemaker families. As late as 1950, of the total children living in nonfarm two-parent families, about 81 percent lived in breadwinner-homemaker families.

Similarly, the role of fathers as employed breadwinners has been obvious. For example, between 1940 and 1980, only 3–4 percent of children lived with fathers who were not in the labor force, and except during the Great Depression, only 2–3 percent lived with fathers who were unemployed. Even during the Great Depression year of 1940, 73 percent of children lived with fathers who were employed in the regular economy, and another 6 percent lived with fathers who were employed in government emergency work programs that had been funded to help families work through the Great Depression (Figure 4.3 and Table 4.1). Hence, between 1940 and 1970, 79–83 percent of children lived with employed fathers, and the subsequent decline to 72 percent in 1980 is mostly accounted for by the decline in the proportion of children with a father in the home.

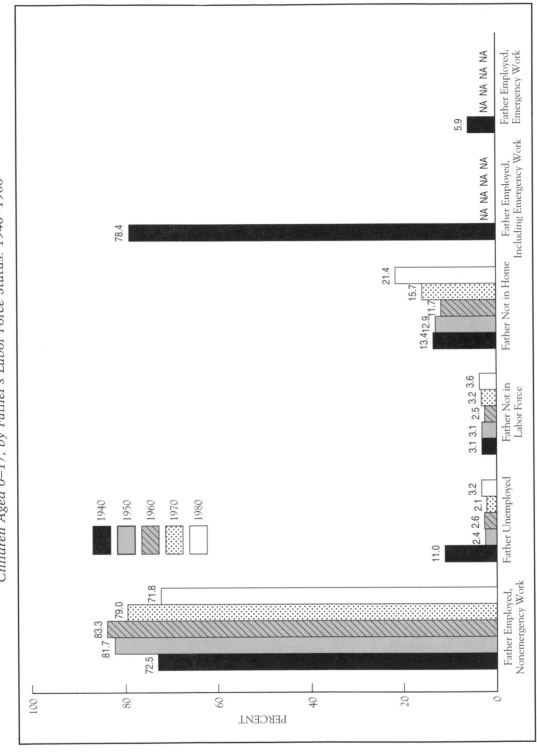

FIGURE 4.3

Children Aged 0–17, by Father's Labor Force Status: 1940–1980

SOURCE: Table 4.1.

NOTE: See Table 4.1.

While 72–83 percent of children lived with employed fathers between 1940 and 1980, many children lived with fathers who were not employed full-time year-round (Figure 4.4 and Table 4.1).[5] In 1940, counting fathers employed in government emergency work as less than full-time, 40 percent of all children lived with fathers who did not work full-time, year-round.[6] In 1950, 32 percent of all children lived with fathers who did not work full-time year-round, and this figure slowly declined to 24 percent in 1980. The 8 percentage point decline between 1950 and 1980 is equal to the increase in the proportion of children who did not have a father in the home. Hence, at any specific time, no more than 60 percent of children, including those on farms, lived with fathers who were employed full-time on a year-round basis.

Since between 1940 and 1980 at least 24 percent of children lived with fathers who were *not* full-time year-round breadwinners, and since, historically, mothers on farms had contributed greatly to the economic support of the family, it is not surprising that the proportion of children with employed mothers has increased sharply since the Great Depression. In 1940 only 6 percent of all children lived in two-parent families in which the mother was employed (in nonemergency work), but this figure doubled to 12 percent in 1950, and each of the next three decades brought an additional increase of 8 percentage points (Figure 4.5 and Table 4.1). Hence, the proportion of children living in dual-earner families grew to 36 percent in 1980, then to 43 percent in 1989, seven times greater than it had been in 1940. Of those children who lived with two parents, the proportion whose mothers were employed had expanded to 47 percent by 1980 and to about 60 percent by 1989.

Taking labor force participation of mothers into account, at no time since the Great Depression have a majority of children lived in two-parent families in which the father worked full-time year-round *and* the mother was *not* in the labor force (Figure 4.6 and Table 4.1). Between 1940 and 1960, 43–47 percent of children lived in two-parent families in which the father was employed full-time year-round and the mother was not employed; this figure had fallen to 26 percent by 1980 and to only 19 percent by 1989.

It should also be noted that when parental divorce and out-of-wedlock childbearing are taken into account, the proportion of children who

[5]Full-time is calculated as at least 35 hours during the week preceding the census, and year-round is calculated as at least 48 weeks during the previous year. Since some fathers who worked at least 48 weeks during the preceding year did not work at least 35 hours during each of those weeks, the proportion who worked full work weeks during the entire year has probably been overestimated somewhat by the measure calculated and reported here.

[6]In the 1940 census, hours worked during the previous week were not obtained for persons employed in emergency government work.

TABLE 4.1

Children Aged 0–17, by Father's and Mother's Work Status: 1940–1980

	1940	1950	1960	1970	1980
Father's Presence in Household and Labor Force Status					
Total (thousands)	40,035	45,190	64,782	70,129	64,586
Percent	100.0	100.0	100.0	100.0	100.0
Father employed, nonemergency work	72.5	81.7	83.3	79.0	71.8
Father unemployed	11.0	2.4	2.6	2.1	3.2
Father not in labor force	3.1	3.1	2.5	3.2	3.6
Father not in home	13.4	12.9	11.7	15.7	21.4
Father employed, including emergency work	78.4	NA	NA	NA	NA
Father employed, emergency work	5.9	NA	NA	NA	NA
Father's Presence in Household, Father's Weeks Worked Last Year, Father's Hours Worked Last Week, Intact Family Status, and Farm Residence					
Total	100.0	100.0	100.0	100.0	100.0
Father worked full-time last week and year, intact family	38.9	44.1	49.3	47.4	41.3
Father worked full-time last week and year, not intact family	8.3	11.3	10.5	11.6	13.8
Father did not work full-time last week and year	39.5	31.7	28.5	25.3	23.5
Father worked less than full-time, intact farm family	5.0	3.5	1.7	0.5	0.3
Father worked less than full-time, not intact farm family	1.3	1.3	0.5	0.1	0.0
Father not in household	13.4	12.9	11.7	15.7	21.4

lived in the mid-twentieth century idealized version of the breadwinner-homemaker family declined even more. Throughout the era since the Great Depression, fewer than 40 percent of children lived in the idealized "Ozzie and Harriet" family. Between 1940 and 1960, 36–38 percent of children lived in two-parent families in which the father worked full-time year-round, the mother was not in the labor force, and all of the children were born after the parents' only marriage. By 1980 only 21 percent of children lived in such families, and between 11 and 16 percent or fewer lived in such families by 1989. Since at least the Great Depression, then, the mid-twentieth century ideal of family living has been just that—an ideal; for in any single year the reality has been that more than 60 percent of children lived in families that did not conform to this model.

TABLE 4.1 *(continued)*

	1940	1950	1960	1970	1980
Father's Presence, Weeks Worked Last Year, Hours Worked Last Week, Intact Family Status, and Mother's Labor Force Status					
Total	100.0	100.0	100.0	100.0	100.0
Father worked full-time last week and year, intact family, mother not in labor force	36.3	38.1	37.8	30.9	20.6
Father worked full-time last week and year, not intact family, mother present but not in labor force	6.8	9.0	6.9	6.3	5.7
Father present, other work arrangements	43.6	40.0	43.6	47.1	52.3
Father not in household	13.4	12.9	11.7	15.7	21.4
Mother's Labor Force Participation and Number of Parents in the Home					
Total	100.0	100.0	100.0	100.0	100.0
Mother employed, nonemergency work	8.6	14.9	24.0	33.9	45.0
Two-parent family	6.3	12.0	20.3	27.8	36.0
Mother unemployed	1.0	0.7	1.7	2.2	3.7
Two-parent family	0.5	0.5	1.3	1.7	2.4
Mother not in labor force	81.5	76.8	69.2	58.0	44.2
Two-parent family	77.7	73.3	65.6	52.9	38.2
Father but not mother in household	2.1	1.3	1.1	1.8	2.0
Neither parent in household	6.7	6.2	3.9	4.0	5.1

NOTES: Estimates from 1940–1980 Census PUMS. Full-time work last week is 35 hours or more during the week. Full-time work last year is 48 weeks or more during the year. Intact family is one in which all the children were born after the parent's only marriage. In 1940, father employed in emergency work is included in category for father unemployed. In all years, father worked less than full-time includes only those who worked at least some time. In all years, father did not work full-time includes those who worked less than full-time and those who did not work at all.

NA Not applicable.

Idealized Breadwinner-Homemaker Families from Birth Through Age 17

Even among newborn children under age 1, a majority since 1940 have not begun life in breadwinner-homemaker families in which the father worked full-time year-round, the mother was a full-time home-maker, and all of the children were born after the parents' only marriage. A large majority of newborns between 1940 and 1980 (75–86 percent) did live with employed fathers, but only a minority (42–49 percent) were born into families in which the father worked full-time year-round

FIGURE 4.4

Children Aged 0–17, by Father's Amount of Work: 1940–1980

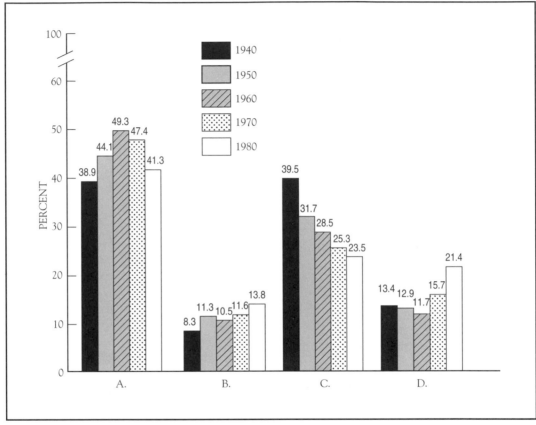

SOURCE: Table 4.1.

NOTES: See Table 4.1.
A. Father worked full-time last week and year, intact family
B. Father worked full-time last week and year, not intact family
C. Father did not work full-time last week and year
D. Father not in household

and all the children were born after the parents' only marriage (Figure 4.7 and Table 4.3).

Counting newborns with a mother in the labor force, between 1940 and 1960 a smaller minority (41–45 percent) were born into two-parent families in which the father was a full-time year-round breadwinner, the mother was a full-time homemaker, and all the children were born after the parents' only marriage. With the subsequent rise in mothers' labor-

110

FIGURE 4.5

Children Aged 0–17, by Mother's Labor Force Status: 1940–1980

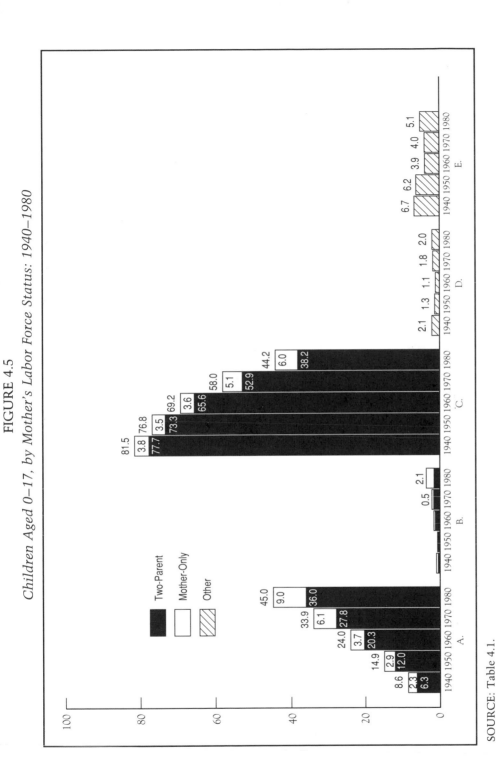

SOURCE: Table 4.1.

NOTES: See Table 4.1.
A. Mother employed, nonemergency work
B. Mother unemployed
C. Mother not in labor force
D. Father but not mother in household
E. Neither parent in household

FIGURE 4.6

Children Aged 0–17, by Father's and Mother's Amount of Work: 1940–1980

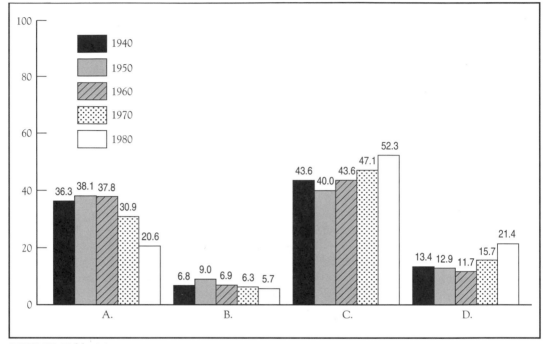

SOURCE: Table 4.1.

NOTES: See Table 4.1.
A. Father worked full-time last week and year, intact family, mother not in labor force
B. Father worked full-time last week and year, not intact family, mother present but not in labor force
C. Father present, other work arrangements
D. Father not in household

force participation, the proportion of newborns living in this idealized situation fell to 27 percent in 1980 and to only 17–22 percent in 1988 (Figure 4.7 and Table 4.3).

Focusing on mothers' employment, the proportion of newborns living in dual-earner families with an employed mother increased from 3 to 10 percent between 1940 and 1960, then jumped to 26 percent in 1980 and to about 37 percent in 1989 (Table 4.3). Meanwhile, the proportion of all newborns living with an employed mother increased from 4 to 29 percent between 1940 and 1980, then to about 50 percent in 1989.[7]

Children aged 17 have been found to be more likely than children

[7]The estimate is 50.9 percent in 1988 based on Table C, Amara Bachu, U.S. Bureau of the Census, Current Population Reports, Series P-20, No. 436, *Fertility of American Women: June 1988* (Washington, DC: U.S. Government Printing Office, 1989).

FIGURE 4.7

Children in Ozzie and Harriet Families at Ages 0 and 17 for 1920–1980 Birth Cohorts

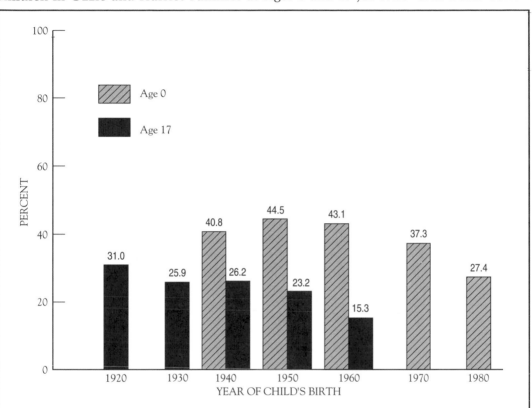

SOURCE: Tables 4.2 and 4.3.

NOTES: See Tables 4.3 and 4.5. Ozzie and Harriet families are two-parent families with all the children born after the parents' only marriage, the father works full-time year-round, and the mother is not in the labor force. Since these results are based on census data, children aged 0 were mainly born 1 year before the indicated year ending in zero, and children aged 17 were mainly born 2 years after the indicated year ending in zero.

as a whole to have no father in the home or a father who is unemployed or does not work full-time year-round. Hence, they are also more likely to live in families that do not conform to the mid-twentieth century ideal.

Between 1940 and 1980, only 64–72 percent of 17-year-olds lived in families in which the father was employed, and only 33–44 percent lived in a two-parent family in which the father worked full-time year-round and all the children were born after the parents' only marriage (Table 4.4). The proportion living in families in which the father worked full-time year-round, the mother was a full-time homemaker, and the chil-

TABLE 4.2

White and Black Children Aged 0–17, by Father's and Mother's Work Status: 1940–1980

	White					Black				
	1940	1950	1960	1970	1980	1940	1950	1960	1970	1980
Father's Presence in Household and Labor Force Status										
Total (thousands)	35,487	39,786	56,648	60,422	54,879	4,548	5,403	8,134	9,707	9,707
Percent	100.0	100.0	100.0	100.0	100.0	100.0	100.0	100.0	100.0	100.0
Father employed, nonemergency work	74.3	84.5	86.5	83.3	77.2	58.3	60.5	61.2	51.9	41.2
Father unemployed	11.2	2.2	2.5	2.0	3.2	9.2	3.5	3.4	2.5	3.5
Father not in labor force	3.1	3.0	2.2	2.8	3.4	2.8	3.3	4.1	5.7	4.9
Father not in home	11.3	10.2	8.9	11.9	16.2	29.7	32.8	31.3	39.9	50.4
Father employed, including emergency work	80.3	NA	NA	NA	NA	63.6	NA	NA	NA	NA
Father employed, emergency work	6.0	NA	NA	NA	NA	5.3	NA	NA	NA	NA
Father's Presence in Household, Father's Weeks Worked Last Year, Father's Hours Worked Last Week, Intact Family Status, and Farm Residence										
Total	100.0	100.0	100.0	100.0	100.0	100.0	100.0	100.0	100.0	100.0
Father worked full-time last week and year, intact family	41.0	47.1	53.2	51.8	46.0	22.4	21.5	21.9	20.1	15.1
Father worked full-time last week and year, not intact family	7.9	11.0	10.4	11.6	14.1	11.9	13.4	11.3	11.7	12.3
Father did not work full-time last week and year	39.8	31.7	27.6	24.7	23.7	36.0	32.3	35.5	28.3	22.2
Father worked less than full-time, intact farm family	4.7	3.4	1.6	0.5	0.3	7.1	4.9	2.7	0.3	0.0
Father worked less than full-time, not intact farm family	1.0	1.0	0.4	0.1	0.0	3.0	3.2	1.5	0.4	0.0
Father not in household	11.3	10.2	8.9	11.9	16.2	29.7	32.8	31.3	39.9	50.4

Father's Presence, Weeks Worked Last Year, Hours Worked Last Week, Intact Family Status, and Mother's Labor Force Status	White					Black				
	1940	1950	1960	1970	1980	1940	1950	1960	1970	1980
Total	100.0	100.0	100.0	100.0	100.0	100.0	100.0	100.0	100.0	100.0
Father worked full-time last week and year, intact family, mother not in labor force	38.6	41.0	41.2	34.3	23.4	18.5	16.8	14.3	9.8	4.9
Father worked full-time last week and year, not intact family, mother present but not in labor force	6.5	8.9	7.1	6.5	6.2	9.1	9.6	5.9	4.9	3.0
Father present, other work arrangements	43.7	39.9	42.9	47.4	54.2	42.7	40.8	48.6	45.4	41.6
Father not in household	11.3	10.2	8.9	11.9	16.2	29.7	32.8	31.3	39.9	50.4
Mother's Labor Force Participation and Number of Parents in the Home										
Total	100.0	100.0	100.0	100.0	100.0	100.0	100.0	100.0	100.0	100.0
Mother employed, nonemergency work	7.5	14.5	23.2	33.1	44.8	17.5	18.2	30.3	38.9	45.5
Two-parent family	5.6	12.0	20.2	28.2	37.4	11.3	12.3	21.5	25.7	27.7
Mother unemployed	1.0	0.6	1.4	1.8	3.1	1.9	1.2	3.2	4.4	6.7
Two-parent family	0.5	0.4	1.2	1.6	2.4	0.6	0.8	2.2	2.6	2.7
Mother not in labor force	84.3	79.2	71.7	60.2	46.1	59.5	59.2	52.2	43.9	33.7
Two-parent family	80.7	76.2	68.8	56.7	42.1	55.2	51.6	42.8	28.8	16.4
Father but not mother in household	1.9	1.2	0.9	1.6	1.9	3.0	2.5	2.2	2.9	2.8
Neither parent in household	5.3	4.5	2.7	3.1	4.0	18.1	18.8	12.1	9.8	11.2

NOTES: Estimates from 1940–1980 Census PUMS. Full-time work last week is 35 hours or more during the week. Full-time work last year is 48 weeks or more during the year. Intact family is one in which all the children were born after the parent's only marriage. In 1940, father employed in emergency work is included in category for father unemployed. In all years, father worked less than full-time includes only those who worked at least some time. In all years, father did not work full-time includes those who worked less than full-time and those who did not work at all.

NA Not applicable.

TABLE 4.3

Children Under Age 1, by Father's and Mother's Work Status: 1940–1980

	1940	1950	1960	1970	1980
Father's Presence in Household and Labor Force Status					
Total (thousands)	1,757	2,930	4,270	3,440	3,636
Percent	100.0	100.0	100.0	100.0	100.0
Father employed, nonemergency work	77.8	85.2	85.8	81.1	74.8
Father unemployed	11.7	2.9	3.1	2.4	4.7
Father not in labor force	2.3	3.3	1.7	3.0	3.2
Father not in home	8.2	8.6	9.4	13.5	17.4
Father employed, including emergency work	84.0	NA	NA	NA	NA
Father employed, emergency work	6.2	NA	NA	NA	NA
Father's Presence in Household, Father's Weeks Worked Last Year, Father's Hours Worked Last Week, Intact Family Status, and Farm Residence					
Total	100.0	100.0	100.0	100.0	100.0
Father worked full-time last week and year, intact family	42.5	47.5	49.2	46.2	42.0
Father worked full-time last week and year, not intact family	5.2	8.9	8.6	9.3	11.7
Father did not work full-time last week and year	44.1	35.0	32.8	31.1	29.0
Father worked less than full-time, intact farm family	6.1	3.1	1.4	0.2	0.2
Father worked less than full-time, not intact farm family	1.2	0.9	0.4	0.3	0.0
Father not in household	8.2	8.6	9.4	13.5	17.4

dren were all born after the parents' only marriage was still smaller; only 31 percent of 17-year-olds lived in such families in 1940, and this declined further to 15 percent in 1980 and to between 8 and 11 percent in 1989 (Figure 4.7 and Table 4.4).

Hence, fewer than one-third of children born since 1920 were living in an idealized breadwinner-homemaker family situation by the end of their childhood. Since it was not until 1920 that nonfarm homemaker-breadwinner families became the dominant form of family organization for children as a whole, these results suggest that for no cohort of children born in any years since the Industrial Revolution have a majority lived in the idealized nonfarm family situation by the end of their childhood.

Meanwhile, the proportion of 17-year-olds living with an employed mother in a two-parent family jumped from 7 percent in 1940 to 40

TABLE 4.3 (*continued*)

	1940	1950	1960	1970	1980
Father's Presence, Weeks Worked Last Week, Hours Worked Last Year, Intact Family Status, and Mother's Labor Force Status					
Total	100.0	100.0	100.0	100.0	100.0
Father worked full-time last week and year, intact family, mother not in labor force	40.8	44.5	43.1	37.3	27.4
Father worked full-time last week and year, not intact family, mother present but not in labor force	4.9	8.1	7.0	6.3	6.8
Father present, other work arrangements	46.1	38.7	40.5	43.0	48.4
Father not in household	8.2	8.6	9.4	13.5	17.4
Mother's Labor Force Participation and Number of Parents in the Home					
Total	100.0	100.0	100.0	100.0	100.0
Mother employed, nonemergency work	4.1	6.4	11.8	18.8	29.2
Two-parent family	3.2	5.7	10.3	15.4	26.0
Mother unemployed	0.6	0.7	1.7	2.7	4.2
Two-parent family	0.4	0.6	1.3	2.3	2.9
Mother not in labor force	89.6	87.4	82.4	74.1	59.4
Two-parent family	87.8	84.5	78.2	67.6	51.9
Father but not mother in household	0.4	0.4	0.8	1.3	1.8
Neither parent in household	5.3	4.9	3.2	3.1	5.3

NOTES: Estimates from 1940–1980 Census PUMS. Full-time work last week is 35 hours or more during the week. Full-time work last year is 48 weeks or more during the year. Intact family is one in which all the children were born after the parent's only marriage. In 1940, father employed in emergency work is included in category for father unemployed. In all years, father worked less than full-time includes only those who worked at least some time. In all years, father did not work full-time includes those who worked less than full-time and those who did not work at all.

NA Not applicable.

percent in 1980 and about 46 percent in 1989. In addition, the total proportion living with an employed mother increased from 10 to 50 percent between 1940 and 1980, then to about 60 percent in 1989 (Figure 4.7 and Table 4.3).

Over the course of childhood, as each cohort of children born between 1940 and 1960 grew older, a steady increase occurred in the proportion who did not live in an idealized breadwinner-homemaker family in which the father worked full-time year-round, the mother was a full-time homemaker, and all of the children were born after the parents' only marriage. Consequently, the average proportion of childhood that each cohort spent in a family that did not conform to this ideal is ap-

TABLE 4.4

White and Black Children Under Age 1, by Father's and Mother's Work Status: 1940–1980

	White					Black				
	1940	1950	1960	1970	1980	1940	1950	1960	1970	1980
Father's Presence in Household and Labor Force Status										
Total (thousands)	1,562	2,549	3,696	2,955	3,094	195	381	574	485	542
Percent	100.0	100.0	100.0	100.0	100.0	100.0	100.0	100.0	100.0	100.0
Father employed, nonemergency work	79.5	88.7	89.0	86.0	80.7	64.0	61.8	64.8	51.1	41.0
Father unemployed	11.9	2.4	3.0	2.3	4.7	10.5	5.7	4.2	3.1	4.8
Father not in labor force	2.4	3.2	1.5	2.8	3.2	1.4	3.8	3.1	4.3	3.1
Father not in home	6.2	5.6	6.5	8.9	11.5	24.1	28.7	27.9	41.4	51.1
Father employed, including emergency work	85.7	NA	NA	NA	NA	70.5	NA	NA	NA	NA
Father employed, emergency work	6.2	NA	NA	NA	NA	6.5	NA	NA	NA	NA
Father's Presence in Household, Father's Weeks Worked Last Year, Father's Hours Worked Last Week, Intact Family Status, and Farm Residence										
Total	100.0	100.0	100.0	100.0	100.0	100.0	100.0	100.0	100.0	100.0
Father worked full-time last week and year, intact family	44.4	50.9	53.1	50.4	46.4	27.7	24.6	24.0	20.6	16.4
Father worked full-time last week and year, not intact family	4.9	9.0	8.5	9.5	12.4	7.2	8.3	9.2	8.2	7.2
Father did not work full-time last week	44.5	34.5	31.9	31.2	29.6	41.0	38.4	38.8	29.7	25.3
Father worked less than full-time, intact farm family	5.6	3.0	1.3	0.2	0.2	10.4	4.2	2.4	0.0	0.0
Father worked less than full-time, not intact farm family	1.1	0.6	0.3	0.3	0.0	2.2	2.9	0.7	0.2	0.0
Father not in household	6.2	5.6	6.5	8.9	11.5	24.1	28.7	27.9	41.4	51.1

TABLE 4.4 (continued)

	White					Black				
Father's Presence, Weeks Worked Last Year, Hours Worked Last Week, Intact Family Status, and Mother's Labor Force Status	1940	1950	1960	1970	1980	1940	1950	1960	1970	1980
Total	100.0	100.0	100.0	100.0	100.0	100.0	100.0	100.0	100.0	100.0
Father worked full-time last week and year, intact family, mother not in labor force	42.8	48.1	47.0	41.4	30.9	24.8	20.6	18.3	12.2	7.6
Father worked full-time last week and year, not intact family, mother present but not in labor force	4.6	8.2	7.1	6.7	7.6	7.2	7.4	6.8	3.3	2.6
Father present, other work arrangements	46.4	38.0	39.4	42.9	50.1	43.9	43.3	47.0	43.1	38.7
Father not in household	6.2	5.6	6.5	8.9	11.5	24.1	28.7	27.9	41.4	51.1
Mother's Labor Force Participation and Number of Parents in the Home										
Total	100.0	100.0	100.0	100.0	100.0	100.0	100.0	100.0	100.0	100.0
Mother employed, nonemergency work	3.3	6.0	10.9	17.1	29.2	10.4	9.4	18.1	29.1	30.1
Two-parent family	2.8	5.5	9.7	14.5	26.9	6.5	7.1	13.6	20.4	21.2
Mother unemployed	0.4	0.6	1.4	2.5	3.5	2.2	1.7	3.5	4.1	8.1
Two-parent family	0.3	0.5	1.2	2.3	3.0	1.1	1.0	2.3	2.5	2.6
Mother not in labor force	91.8	90.3	85.2	77.2	62.0	71.3	67.8	64.5	55.0	44.6
Two-parent family	90.3	87.9	81.8	73.1	57.1	67.7	61.4	55.1	33.8	21.6
Father but not mother in household	0.4	0.3	0.8	1.2	1.5	0.7	1.2	0.9	1.9	3.5
Neither parent in household	4.0	2.8	1.7	2.0	3.9	15.5	19.2	12.7	9.9	13.7

NOTES: Estimates from 1940–1980 Census PUMS. Full-time work last week is 35 hours or more during the week. Full-time work last year is 48 weeks or more during the year. Intact family is one in which all the children were born after the parent's only marriage. In 1940, father employed in emergency work is included in category for father unemployed. In all years, father worked less than full-time includes only those who worked at least some time. In all years, father did not work full-time includes those who worked less than full-time and those who did not work at all.

NA Not applicable.

proximately the average of the proportions not living in such families as newborns and as 17-year-olds.

For children born between 1940 and 1960, then, an average of about 65–70 percent of their childhood years were not spent in families that conformed to the mid-twentieth century ideal, and there were several reasons for this: the father did not work full-time year-round, the mother was employed, at least one parent had been married more than once, at least one child was born before the parents' marriage, or at least one parent was not living in the home. For children born after 1960, this average is expected to rise further—by at least 10–15 percentage points among children born in 1980, since newborns in 1980 were 16 percentage points more likely not to be living in such families than were newborns in 1960. Hence, children born in 1980 may spend an average of at least 80 percent of their childhood in families that do not conform to the mid-twentieth century breadwinner-homemaker ideal. Furthermore, with continuing changes during the 1980s, it appears that children born during the 1990s may spend an average of at least 85 percent of their childhood in families that do not conform to this ideal. For children born in 1920 and 1930, the proportion living in such families by age 17 was no more than 5 percentage points larger than it had been for children born in 1940. Hence, for children born as early as 1920, the average proportion of childhood not spent in idealized breadwinner-homemaker families was probably 60–65 percent.

In addition, since 1920 marks the approximate beginning of the dominance of nonfarm families in which fathers were the sole breadwinners, it appears that the proportion of childhood spent in idealized nonfarm breadwinner-homemaker families by children born before 1920 was probably smaller than for children born after 1920. As we go back in time before 1920, we find that increasing proportions of childhood were spent in farm families in which parental living and work arrangements were quite different from those of the nonfarm breadwinner-homemaker family—a difference that can be explained by the fact that both parents typically lived and worked on the family farm.

It is likely, then, that the average proportion of childhood spent in the idealized urban breadwinner-homemaker family was the highest for children born around 1920 or later. But as we have seen, even among children born in 1920, the average proportion of childhood spent in this idealized family situation was less than 40 percent. In fact, more than 60 percent of childhood was spent in families that did not conform to this ideal. During the transition from the farm family system to the dual-earner/one-parent family system, then, for no cohort of children, on average, was a majority of childhood spent in idealized nonfarm families in which the father worked full-time year-round, the mother was a full-time homemaker, and the children were all born after the parents' only marriage.

These results suggest that a majority of children born throughout the industrial era have lived in families that experienced at least one of the following: a parental separation, divorce, or death; a sibling born out of wedlock; a spell of unemployment, job search, or part-time employment of the father; or paid employment of the mother. Of course, not all of these experiences involve personal difficulty or economic insecurity for children and their parents, but most of the associated transitions are, to some degree, stressful for the persons involved.

For example, as we saw in Chapter 3, a parental separation and divorce may have negative consequences for children even if they removed the children from a conflict-ridden family situation. As Glen Elder and his colleagues have suggested, if the drop in income resulting from a father's unemployment or part-time employment is severe enough to require major hardship adaptations, then family members may experience psychological difficulties, as well, of course, as the opportunity to rise above life's disadvantages.[8] And as we will see in Chapter 10, many mothers apparently work out of economic necessity, while many others do so in order to improve their relative social and economic status, or for other related benefits. But whatever the reason for mothers' work, it brings income into the home that would not otherwise be available to the family.

[8]See Glen H. Elder, Jr., *Children of the Great Depression: Social Change in Life Experience* (Chicago: University of Chicago Press, 1974); Glen H. Elder, Jr., "Scarcity and Prosperity in Postwar Childbearing: Explorations from a Life Course Perspective," *Journal of Family History* 5:410–433; Glen H. Elder, Jr., "Household, Kinship, and the Life Course: Perspectives on Black Families and Children, in M. Spencer, G. Brookins, and W. Allen, eds., *Beginnings: The Social and Affective Development of Black Children*, pp. 39–43; Glen H. Elder, Jr., Avshalom Caspi, and Tri van Nguyen, "Resourceful and Vulnerable Children: Family Influences in Stressful Times," in R. K. Silbereisen and K. Eyferth, eds., *Development as Action in Context: Integrative Perspectives on Youth Development* (CITY: Springer, 1986), pp. 167–187); Glen H. Elder, Avshalom Caspi, and Geraldine Downey, "Problem Behavior and Family Relationships, pp. 293–340 in Aage Sorenson, Franz Weinert, and Lonnie Sherrod, *Human Development: Multi-Disciplinary Perspectives* (Hillsdale, NJ: Erlbaum, in press), pp. 293–340; R. D. Conger, et al. "Linking Economic Hardship to Marital Quality and Instability," *Journal of Marriage and the Family* 52 (1990): 643–656; Glen H. Elder, Jr. and Tamara K. Hareven, "Rising Above Life's Disadvantages: From Great Depression to World War," in Glen H. Elder, Jr., John Modell, and Ross Parke, eds., selections from *Children in Time and Place* (Cambridge: Cambridge University Press, 1992); and Glen H. Elder, Jr., Rand D. Conger, E. Michael Foster, and Monika Ardelt, "Families Under Economic Pressure," *Journal of Family Issues*, (in Press).

Idealized Breadwinner-Homemaker Families Among Black and White Children

Since at least the Great Depression, black and white children have differed substantially in their parents' work pattern and family economy. Between 1940 and 1960, for example, only 62–71 percent of black newborns lived with fathers who worked, and this figure dropped to only 41 percent in 1980. For white newborns the proportion living with a working father has been much higher throughout the era—81–89 percent (Table 4.5).

At no time since the Great Depression have a majority of black newborns lived with a father who worked full-time year-round; the proportion dropped from only 35 percent in 1940 to 24 percent in 1980. Hence, throughout the era since the Great Depression, a substantial majority of black children (65 percent or more) were born into families without a father who worked full-time year-round. For white newborns the proportion living with a father who worked full-time year-round increased from 49 percent in 1940 to a nearly stable 59–62 percent between 1950 and 1980. Despite the substantial racial gap, then, even among white newborns, between 1950 and 1980 a substantial minority of about 40 percent did not live with a father who worked full-time year-round.

More striking still is the fact that the proportion of black newborns who began life in the idealized form of a breadwinner-homemaker family, in which the father worked full-time year-round, the mother was a full-time homemaker, and all the children were born after the parents' only marriage, was only 25 percent in 1940, and this dropped to 8 percent by 1980 and was 6 percent or less by 1989 (Figure 4.8). Although the proportions were larger for white newborns—at 41–48 percent between 1940 and 1970—at no time since the Great Depression did a majority of white newborns live in the idealized form of a breadwinner-homemaker family. By 1980 only 31 percent lived in such families, and by 1989 this figure had fallen to about 20–25 percent. For neither black nor white children born since the Great Depression, then, did a majority begin life in a family situation that was for so many years portrayed as the ideal American experience.

As early as the Great Depression, only about one-half of black children had an employed father in the home at age 17 (Table 4.6), and the proportion declined from 46–52 percent in 1940–1970 to 38 percent in 1980. Among white 17-year-olds, a large majority of 69–76 percent have had such a father in the home. The proportion of 17-year-olds living in families in which the father worked full-time year-round was smaller,

FIGURE 4.8

White and Black Children in Ozzie and Harriet Families at Ages 0 and 17 for 1920–1980 Birth Cohorts

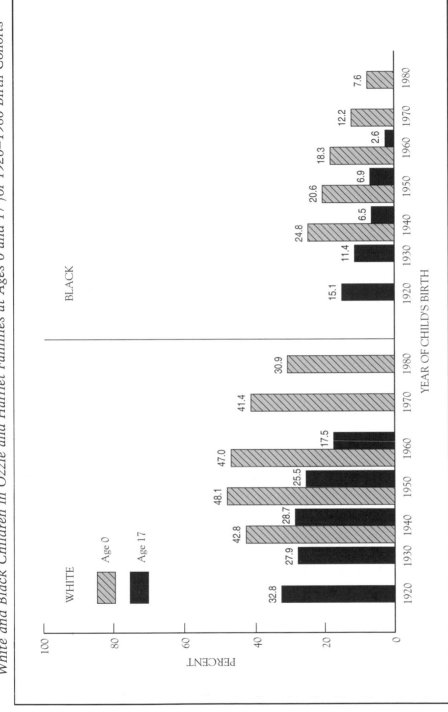

SOURCE: Tables 4.3 and 4.5.

NOTES: See Tables 4.3 and 4.5. Ozzie and Harriet families are two-parent families with all the children born after the parents' only marriage, the father works full-time year-round, and the mother is not in the labor force. Since these results are based on census data, children aged 0 were mainly born 1 year before the indicated year ending in zero, and children aged 17 were mainly born 2 years after the indicated year ending in zero.

123

TABLE 4.5

Children Aged 17, by Father's and Mother's Work Status: 1940–1980

	1940	1950	1960	1970	1980
Father's Presence in Household and Labor Force Status					
Total (thousands)	2,468	1,985	2,789	3,816	4,197
Percent	100.0	100.0	100.0	100.0	100.0
Father employed, nonemergency work	63.6	66.4	71.5	72.1	65.6
Father unemployed	8.9	1.9	2.4	1.7	2.4
Father not in labor force	4.2	4.6	3.2	3.8	5.0
Father not in home	23.4	27.1	22.9	22.5	27.0
Father employed, including emergency work	68.2	NA	NA	NA	NA
Father employed, emergency work	4.6	NA	NA	NA	NA
Father's Presence in Household, Father's Weeks Worked Last Year, Father's Hours Worked Last Week, Intact Family Status, and Farm Residence					
Total	100.0	100.0	100.0	100.0	100.0
Father worked full-time last week and year, intact family	34.0	33.2	42.0	43.8	39.3
Father worked full-time last week and year, not intact family	8.5	12.3	9.9	11.1	12.5
Father did not work full-time last week and year	34.1	27.4	25.3	22.6	21.2
Father worked less than full-time, intact farm family	3.8	3.3	2.3	0.8	0.4
Father worked less than full-time, not intact farm family	0.8	1.2	0.6	0.1	0.0
Father not in household	23.4	27.1	22.9	22.5	27.0

falling slightly for blacks from 31–32 percent in 1940–1950 to 25–27 percent in 1960–1980 and rising slightly for whites from 44–48 percent in 1940–1950 to 55–59 percent in 1960–1980. Hence, among 17-year-olds in 1980 only one-fourth of blacks and a small majority of whites lived in families in which the father worked full-time year-round.

At no time since the Great Depression among either blacks or whites have a majority of 17-year-olds lived in the idealized form of the breadwinner-homemaker family (Figure 4.8). For black 17-year-olds, the proportion living in such families was only 15 percent in 1940, and it fell to 3 percent in 1980, while the proportion of white 17-year-olds living in such families fell from 33 percent in 1940 to 18 percent in 1980 and to about 9–13 percent in 1989.

These results demonstrate that for children born since at least 1920,

TABLE 4.5 (*continued*)

	1940	1950	1960	1970	1980
Father's Presence, Weeks Worked Last Year, Hours Worked Last Week, Intact Family Status, and Mother's Labor Force Status					
Total	100.0	100.0	100.0	100.0	100.0
Father worked full-time last week and year, intact family, mother not in labor force	31.0	25.9	26.2	23.2	15.3
Father worked full-time last week and year, not intact family, mother present but not in labor force	6.1	7.9	4.8	5.4	3.9
Father present, other work arrangements	39.6	39.2	46.1	49.0	53.7
Father not in household	23.4	27.1	22.9	22.5	27.0
Mother's Labor Force Participation and Number of Parents in the Home					
Total	100.0	100.0	100.0	100.0	100.0
Mother employed, nonemergency work	10.2	20.9	33.3	41.6	49.7
Two-parent family	6.7	15.2	27.2	33.7	39.9
Mother unemployed	1.4	0.8	1.8	1.9	2.7
Two-parent family	0.4	0.4	1.5	1.4	1.8
Mother not in labor force	72.1	59.0	49.3	44.5	33.9
Two-parent family	65.7	54.4	46.4	40.3	28.7
Father but not mother in household	3.8	2.9	2.0	2.2	2.5
Neither parent in household	12.7	16.3	13.7	9.7	11.2

NOTES: Estimates from 1940–1980 Census PUMS. Full-time work last week is 35 hours or more during the week. Full-time work last year is 48 weeks or more during the year. Intact family is one in which all the children were born after the parent's only marriage. In 1940, father employed in emergency work is included in category for father unemployed. In all years, father worked less than full-time includes only those who worked at least some time. In all years, father did not work full-time includes those who worked less than full-time and those who did not work at all.

NA Not applicable.

a large majority among both blacks and whites have experienced families that did not conform to the ideal portrayed in the "Ozzie and Harriet" and "Father Knows Best" television programs of the 1950s. Many children have lived in families that experienced a parental separation, divorce, or death; a spell of unemployment, job search or part-time employment of the father; employment of the mother outside the home; or the absence of at least one parent from the home.

The preceding results for newborns and 17-year-olds imply that the average proportion of childhood *not* spent in families in which the father worked full-time year-round, the mother was a full-time homemaker, and the children were all born after the parents' only marriage

TABLE 4.6

White and Black Children Aged 17, by Father's and Mother's Work Status: 1940–1980

	White					Black				
	1940	1950	1960	1970	1980	1940	1950	1960	1970	1980
Father's Presence in Household and Labor Force Status										
Total (thousands)	2,223	1,741	2,481	3,341	3,584	246	244	308	475	613
Percent	100.0	100.0	100.0	100.0	100.0	100.0	100.0	100.0	100.0	100.0
Father employed, nonemergency work	65.3	68.9	74.4	75.9	70.3	48.4	48.6	47.7	45.5	37.7
Father unemployed	9.1	1.9	2.2	1.7	2.2	6.3	2.2	3.9	1.5	3.4
Father not in labor force	4.3	4.7	2.9	3.4	4.9	3.1	3.8	6.2	6.3	5.7
Father not in home	21.3	24.5	20.5	19.0	22.5	42.2	45.4	42.2	46.7	53.2
Father employed, including emergency work	70.0	NA	NA	NA	NA	52.1	NA	NA	NA	NA
Father employed, emergency work	4.7	NA	NA	NA	NA	3.7	NA	NA	NA	NA
Father's Presence in Household, Father's Weeks Worked Last Year, Father's Hours Worked Last Week, Intact Family Status, and Farm Residence										
Total	100.0	100.0	100.0	100.0	100.0	100.0	100.0	100.0	100.0	100.0
Father worked full-time last week and year, intact family	35.6	35.6	45.3	47.8	43.6	19.4	16.8	15.6	16.2	14.4
Father worked full-time last week and year, not intact family	8.0	12.0	10.0	11.2	12.6	12.8	14.3	9.4	10.1	11.4
Father did not work full-time last week and year	35.1	27.9	24.2	22.1	21.3	25.6	23.5	32.7	26.9	21.0
Father worked less than full-time, intact farm family	3.6	3.3	2.0	0.9	0.5	5.7	3.5	4.2	0.2	0.0
Father worked less than full-time, not intact farm family	0.6	0.9	0.4	0.1	0.0	2.3	3.0	1.9	0.6	0.0
Father not in household	21.3	24.5	20.5	19.0	22.5	42.2	45.4	42.2	46.7	53.2

TABLE 4.6 (continued)

	White					Black				
Father's Presence, Weeks Worked Last Year, Hours Worked Last Week, Intact Family Status, and Mother's Labor Force Status	1940	1950	1960	1970	1980	1940	1950	1960	1970	1980
Total	100.0	100.0	100.0	100.0	100.0	100.0	100.0	100.0	100.0	100.0
Father worked full-time last week and year, intact family, mother not in labor force	32.8	27.9	28.7	25.5	17.5	15.1	11.4	6.5	6.9	2.6
Father worked full-time last week and year, not intact family, mother present but not in labor force	5.9	8.0	4.9	5.5	4.1	8.0	7.3	3.9	4.6	2.8
Father present, other work arrangements	40.1	39.6	46.0	50.0	55.8	34.8	35.9	47.4	41.7	41.4
Father not in household	21.3	24.5	20.5	19.0	22.5	42.2	45.4	42.2	46.7	53.2
Mother's Labor Force Participation and Number of Parents in the Home										
Total	100.0	100.0	100.0	100.0	100.0	100.0	100.0	100.0	100.0	100.0
Mother employed, nonemergency work	9.1	20.4	32.7	41.6	50.1	19.9	24.6	37.6	41.9	47.3
Two-parent family	6.1	15.4	27.6	35.0	41.9	12.9	14.0	24.0	25.0	28.2
Mother unemployed	1.4	0.8	1.7	1.7	2.4	1.4	0.8	2.6	3.4	4.2
Two-parent family	0.4	0.5	1.5	1.4	1.9	0.0	0.3	1.0	1.5	1.3
Mother not in labor force	75.0	61.4	50.8	45.7	34.6	46.4	42.4	37.3	36.4	29.5
Two-parent family	68.7	56.9	48.5	42.6	31.2	39.4	35.9	29.9	23.6	14.2
Father but not mother in household	3.6	2.7	1.9	2.0	2.4	5.7	4.3	2.9	3.2	3.1
Neither parent in household	11.1	14.7	12.9	8.9	10.4	26.5	27.8	19.5	15.2	15.8

NOTES: Estimates from 1940–1980 Census PUMS. Full-time work last week is 35 hours or more during the week. Full-time work last year is 48 weeks or more during the year. Intact family is one in which all the children were born after the parent's only marriage. In 1940, father employed in emergency work is included in category for father unemployed. In all years, father worked less than full-time includes only those who worked at least some time. In all years, father did not work full-time includes those who worked less than full-time and those who did not work at all.

will have increased from 70–80 percent for black children born in 1920 to at least 95 percent for black children born in 1980. Among white children, the average proportion who did *not* spend their childhood in such an idealized family situation will have increased from 55–65 percent for children born in 1920 to 70–80 percent for children born in 1980 and to 80–90 percent for children born in 1989.

In short, the childhood years of a vast majority of black children and a majority of white children born throughout the industrial era have been marked by exposure to one or more of the following: a parental separation, divorce, or death; a spell of unemployment, job search, or part-time employment of the father; work outside the home by the mother; or the absence of at least one parent from the home.

Idealized Breadwinner-Homemaker Families by Hispanic Origin

In 1980 Hispanic children (of any race) were generally about midway between non-Hispanic blacks and non-Hispanic whites in their chances of living in families in which the father was employed or worked full-time year-round and the family structure conformed to the mid-twentieth century ideal (Table 4.7).

For example, among newborns in 1980, the proportion living with a father who worked full-time year-round, a mother who was a full-time homemaker, and children who were all born after the parents' only marriage was 21 percent for Hispanics (of any race)—14 percentage points more than for non-Hispanic blacks and 11 percentage points less than for non-Hispanic whites. Similarly, the proportion of 17-year-olds living in such families was 10 percent for Hispanics (of any race)—8 percentage points more than for non-Hispanic blacks and 8 percentage points less than for non-Hispanic whites. Consequently, it seems likely that, on average, for Hispanic children born in 1980, more than 85 percent of their childhood years will be spent in families that do not conform to the mid-twentieth century ideal.

The Transformation of Adolescents' Work

As the nature and physical location of parents' work was transformed during the past century and a half, so, too, was work among older children. When the United States was primarily an agricultural country, both children and their parents lived and worked together on the family farm to support themselves. Ellen Greenberger and Laurence Steinberg describe adolescent work during that era as follows: In agricultural societies "[t]he worlds of work and education are merged. Working side by side with adults, young people learn the tasks that they will be expected to perform on their own—and to pass on to a new generation of youngsters—when they themselves attain adult status."[9] Similarly, off the farm ". . . at least up until the end of the nineteenth century—many young people were socialized into adult work roles through apprenticeships, both formal and informal, in which they were paired with adult workers in order to learn a specific (skilled) craft or trade. . . . The adolescent apprenticeship provided for a continuous transition into adult work roles—the work performed during adolescence was essentially the same as the work performed during adulthood."[10]

Before the Industrial Revolution, both on and off the farm, then, adolescents worked directly under the supervision of adults who had a strong personal and economic stake in their training and socialization for adult roles. Equally important, the labor of young people was essential for the survival of the family and the community.[11] With the Industrial Revolution, however, the amount, social context, nature, and purpose of adolescent work changed greatly.

As Eleanor Bernert Sheldon highlighted in her 1950 census monograph on children, by the beginning of the twentieth century, when children were about equally likely to live in two-parent farm families and nonfarm breadwinner-homemaker families, only 50–60 percent of males aged 14–19 worked in the labor force while school was in session, and this declined further to about 35–36 percent in 1940–1950. Meanwhile, the proportion of females aged 14–19 who were in the labor force appears to have declined slightly from 25–28 percent to about 19–23 percent.[12]

The decline in adolescent labor-force participation between the inception of the Industrial Revolution and the mid-twentieth century appears to have had several interrelated causes: the shift from farming,

[9]Ellen Greenberger and Laurence Steinberg, *When Teenagers Work: The Psychological and Social Costs of Adolescent Employment* (New York: Basic Books, 1986), p. 52.

[10]Greenberger and Steinberg, pp. 53–54.

[11]Greenberger and Steinberg, pp. 52–89.

[12]Eleanor H. Bernert (Sheldon), *America's Children* for the Social Science Research Council in cooperation with the U.S. Department of Commerce Bureau of the Census (New York: Wiley, 1958), p. 36. Also see John D. Durand, *The Labor Force in the United States 1890–1960* (New York: Social Science Research Council, 1948), pp. 208–209. The proportions aged 10–13 in the labor force also declined from 10–20 percent to less than 5 percent for males and from about 5 percent to negligible for females.

TABLE 4.7

Hispanic and Non-Hispanic Children, by Father's and Mother's Work Status: 1980

	Total			Under Age 1			Age 17		
	Non-Hispanic Origin		Total Hispanic Origin	Non-Hispanic Origin		Total Hispanic Origin	Non-Hispanic Origin		Total Hispanic Origin
	White	Black		White	Black		White	Black	
Father's Presence in Household and Labor Force Status									
Total (thousands)	49,294	9,568	5,734	2,733	527	376	3,287	600	310
Percent	100.0	100.0	100.0	100.0	100.0	100.0	100.0	100.0	100.0
Father employed, nonemergency work	78.5	41.3	64.5	82.3	41.4	67.0	72.0	37.7	51.0
Father unemployed	3.2	3.5	3.5	4.8	4.7	3.5	2.2	3.5	2.3
Father not in labor force	3.2	4.9	4.7	2.9	3.2	5.1	4.8	5.8	6.1
Father not in home	15.1	50.3	27.3	10.0	50.7	24.5	21.0	53.0	40.6
Father's Presence in Household, Father's Weeks Worked Last Year, Father's Hours Worked Last Week, Intact Family Status, and Farm Residence									
Total	100.0	100.0	100.0	100.0	100.0	100.0	100.0	100.0	100.0
Father worked full-time last week and year, intact family	47.6	15.2	30.7	48.1	16.7	32.7	45.2	14.5	24.8
Father worked full-time last week and year, not intact family	14.3	12.3	12.3	12.5	7.4	11.7	12.8	11.3	10.6
Father did not work full-time last week and year	23.0	22.2	29.7	29.2	25.2	31.1	20.9	21.2	23.9
Father worked less than full-time, intact farm family	0.4	0.0	0.0	0.2	0.0	0.0	0.5	0.0	0.0
Father worked less than full-time, not intact farm family	0.0	0.0	0.0	0.0	0.0	0.0	0.0	0.0	0.0
Father not in household	15.1	50.3	27.3	10.0	50.7	24.5	21.0	53.0	40.6

Father's Presence, Weeks Worked Last Year, Hours Worked Last Week, Intact Family Status, and Mother's Labor Force Status	Total			Under Age 1			Age 17		
	Non-Hispanic Origin		Total Hispanic Origin	Non-Hispanic Origin		Total Hispanic Origin	Non-Hispanic Origin		Total Hispanic Origin
	White	Black		White	Black		White	Black	
Total	100.0	100.0	100.0	100.0	100.0	100.0	100.0	100.0	100.0
Father worked full-time last week and year, intact family, mother not in labor force	24.1	4.9	16.6	32.1	7.6	21.3	18.1	2.7	10.3
Father worked full-time last week and year, not intact family, mother present but not in labor force	6.2	3.1	6.0	7.6	2.7	6.6	4.3	2.7	2.9
Father present, other work arrangements	54.6	41.8	50.2	50.3	39.1	47.6	56.6	41.7	46.1
Father not in household	15.1	50.3	27.3	10.0	50.7	24.5	21.0	53.0	40.6
Mother's Labor Force Participation and Number of Parents in the Home									
Total	100.0	100.0	100.0	100.0	100.0	100.0	100.0	100.0	100.0
Mother employed, nonemergency work	45.9	45.6	35.6	29.2	30.3	28.2	51.6	47.9	33.6
Two-parent family	38.4	27.9	28.1	27.2	21.8	24.0	43.2	28.6	26.7
Mother unemployed	3.0	6.7	4.2	3.4	8.2	3.7	2.3	4.3	3.2
Two-parent family	2.3	2.7	2.9	3.0	2.7	2.9	1.9	1.3	2.6
Mother not in labor force	45.5	33.7	51.0	62.2	44.3	60.1	34.2	29.5	38.7
Two-parent family	42.3	16.3	40.1	58.3	21.3	47.1	31.5	14.0	28.1
Father but not mother in household	1.9	2.8	1.6	1.5	3.6	1.6	2.5	3.0	1.9
Neither parent in household	3.6	11.1	7.5	3.6	13.7	6.4	9.4	15.3	22.6

NOTES: Estimates from 1940–1980 Census PUMS. Full-time work last week is 35 hours or more during the week. Full-time work last year is 48 weeks or more during the year. Intact family is one in which all the children were born after the parent's only marriage. In all years, father worked less than full-time includes only those who worked at least some time. In all years, father did not work full-time includes those who worked less than full-time and those who did not work at all.

where young people could provide valuable labor, to an evolving industrial economy that increasingly required workers who were stronger, more experienced, and capable of operating the machinery of the time; the success of trade unions in fighting the employment of young workers, thereby increasing employment opportunities for adults; the success of the child welfare movement in obtaining the passage of child labor laws intended to protect young people from workplace exploitation and dangerous working conditions; the rise of compulsory education laws; and the rising level of affluence that allowed families to survive without the labor of adolescent children.[13]

Since the mid-1900s, labor force participation rates for adolescents during the school year (as of March) have continued to decline somewhat for males but have increased somewhat for females. In 1950, among adolescents aged 16–17, for example, the employment rate was 45 percent for males and 26 percent for females, respectively, but by 1988 the proportion was 37–38 for both males and females. Similarly, among adolescents aged 18–19 in 1950, 67 percent of males and 46 percent of females were employed, but by 1988 the proportions were 58 and 55 percent, respectively.[14]

Meanwhile, the social context, nature, and purpose of adolescent work also underwent substantial transformation. Apart from the change in family composition, the most important transformation in the social context has been the rise in school enrollment associated with compulsory education laws and with increasing levels of formal education needed to obtain employment in the nonfarm economy. As early as 1910, for example, school enrollment rates (in April) among adolescents aged 16–17 were 42 percent for males and 45 percent for females, and by 1950 these figures had climbed to 75 percent.[15]

The increase has since continued. Among adolescents aged 16–17 in October 1955, approximately 80 percent of males and 73 percent of females were enrolled in school, and these figures climbed to 91–92 percent in October 1988. Corresponding increases in school enrollment among adolescents aged 18–19 were from 43 percent for males and 23 percent for females in 1955 to 55–56 percent in 1988.[16] As school en-

[13]See Bernert (Sheldon), pp. 111–112; Greenberger and Steinberg, pp. 68–79.

[14]U.S. Department of Labor, Bureau of Labor Statistics, *Handbook of Labor Statistics*, Bulletin 2340 (August 1989) (Washington, DC: U.S. Government Printing Office), pp. 71–72.

[15]Bernert (Sheldon), p. 44.

[16]Rosalind R. Bruno U.S. Bureau of the Census, Current Population Reports, Series P-20, No. 443 *School Enrollment—Social and Economic Characteristics of Students: October 1988 and 1987* (Washington, DC: U.S. Government Printing Office, (1990), p. 168. Estimates for adolescents aged 16–17 in 1955 were derived for each sex, assuming that 97 percent of adolescents aged 14–15 were enrolled and that one-half of the adolescents aged 14–17 were aged 16–17. Our estimates for ages 16–17 may be slightly too low.

rollment rates have increased since the 1950s, so, too, have the labor-force participation rates of students. In 1953, among students aged 16–17 and 18–19, labor-force participation rates were 29–32 percent for males and 18 percent for females, but by 1989 they had increased to 44–47 percent for males and 42–51 percent for females.[17]

As formal schooling has become increasingly important in providing the knowledge and skills needed to obtain adult employment, the nature of adolescent work has been transformed. Greenberger and Steinberg point out that as late as 1940, about 60 percent of employed adolescents aged 16–17 worked in "old" workplace settings, such as farms or factories, where the work might well continue into adulthood. By 1980, however, only 14 percent of adolescents worked in such settings. Meanwhile, the proportion employed in "new" settings involving service or sales work increased from about 12 percent in 1940 to 56 percent in 1980.[18]

Greenberger and Steinberg argue that compared with the old work settings, the new ones tend not to require skills (reading, writing, arithmetic) that will be useful in jobs adolescents secure as adults; tend to involve adult supervisors with little stake in the personal socialization or development of adolescents; and tend to promote a peer culture that fosters some forms of delinquent behavior (alcohol and marijuana use, for example) and cynicism about the value of productive labor. On the other hand, Jeylan T. Mortimer and colleagues, reporting preliminary results from a more recent longitudinal study of the life course of children, suggest that work, in and of itself, may have no specific psychological or behavioral consequences, but that the depending on the nature of the work, adolescents may experience either harmful or helpful consequences.[19]

Hence, the most appropriate conclusion that can be drawn at this time is that the nature of adolescent work has been transformed during the past century and a half from one that provides on-the-job training for adult work, usually as a farmer, to one that provides work experience that is often less directly relevant to subsequent adult employment than

[17]U.S. Department of Labor, Bureau of Labor Statistics, Bulletin 2217, *Handbook of Labor Statistics* (Washington, DC: U.S. Government Printing Office, June 1985), p. 139; and unpublished data from the October 1989 Current Population Survey, U.S. Department of Labor Bureau of Labor Statistics.

[18]Greenberger and Steinberg, *When Teenagers Work: The Psychological and Social Costs of Adolescent Employment*, pp. 58–65.

[19]Jeylan T. Mortimer, Michael D. Finch, Michael Shanahan, and Seongryeol Ryu, "Work Experience, Mental Health and Behavioral Adjustment in Adolescence," 1990 Biennial Meeting of the Society for Research in Adolescence, Atlanta, and 1990 Meeting of the World Congress of Sociology, Madrid; and Jaeylan T. Mortimer, Michael D. Finch, Seongryeol Ryu, and Michael Shanahan, "Evidence from a Prospective Longitudinal Study of Work Experience and Adolescent Development" (forthcoming).

was previously the case. Additional, possibly helpful or harmful effects associated with the changing nature of work among adolescent students have yet to be demonstrated but are currently being investigated in important studies.

Finally, the purpose of adolescent work has been transformed since the mid-twentieth century. Before that time, the labor of adolescents and the income they earned contributed directly to the support and survival of their families. By 1980, however, it was found that comparatively few high school students worked as a result of financial need. Lloyd Johnston, Jerald Bachman, and Patrick O'Malley report from the Monitoring the Future Survey of high school seniors that only a small minority of adolescents contribute most or all of their earnings to basic family living expenses or to saving for their future education, and more than half spend none of their income for basic family living expenses.[20]

Hence, adolescents today spend much of their income on items related to personal consumption, such as clothing, stereos, records or compact discs, and recreation. Although Greenberger and Steinberg characterize this transformation in the purpose of adolescent work as "the rise of luxury youth employment," adolescents themselves may view such expenditures as necessary for "normal" adolescent living.[21]

Conclusions

During the past 150 years, parents' work and the family economy have undergone two transformations. Until around 1840, at least two-thirds of children lived in two-parent farm families in which both parents and children lived and worked together to support the family. As the Industrial Revolution proceeded, however, an increasing proportion of fathers became breadwinners who worked at jobs located away from home in order to earn the income necessary to support their families. At the same time, mothers became homemakers who remained in the home to care personally for their children and to perform other domestic functions.

Around the turn of the century, approximately equal proportions of children lived in breadwinner-homemaker and two-parent farm families, and by about 1920 a majority of children lived in breadwinner-homemaker families—compared with only 15–20 percent in 1840—and only one-third lived in two-parent farm families. Although it appears that the proportion of children living in breadwinner-homemaker families never

[20]Greenberger and Steinberg, pp. 74–75.
[21]Greenberger and Steinberg, pp. 68–79.

reached 60 percent, a majority of children did live in such families during the half century between 1920 and 1970.

Even as the breadwinner-homemaker family was in its heyday, however, a second transformation in parents' work had begun to occur. While the proportion of children living in two-parent farm families continued to fall between 1920 and 1970, it became apparent that an increasing proportion were living with breadwinner mothers who worked at jobs located away from home; and after 1960, an increasing proportion of children lived in families in which their mother but no father was present in the home. The rise in the dual-earner/one-parent family system was extremely rapid, requiring only one-third as long (30 years) as the breadwinner-homemaker system required (90 years) to rise from only minor importance (15–20 percent) to it current position of dominance as the family living arrangement for a majority of children.

By 1980 nearly 60 percent of children lived in dual-earner or one-parent families, by 1989 70 percent lived in such families, and by the year 2000 the proportion of children living in such families could exceed 80 percent. Equally striking is the fact that even between 1920 and 1970, only a minority of children lived in the mid-twentieth century idealized form of the nonfarm breadwinner-homemaker family in which the father worked full-time year-round, the mother was a full-time homemaker, and all the children were born after the parents' only marriage. In fact, a majority of newborn children under age 1 did not live in such families between 1920 and 1970, and the overwhelming majority of children born since 1920 no longer lived in such families by age 17.

Historically, children living on farms were likely to experience one or both of the following: a parental death or other parental loss, or the economic insecurity associated with drought, crop disease, collapse of commodity prices, and the like. As we have seen in this chapter, a majority of children born since at least the 1920s have been exposed to at least one of the following: a parental separation, divorce, or death; a sibling born out-of-wedlock; a spell of unemployment, job search, or part-time employment of the father; or paid employment of the mother. Hence, it is apparent that neither historically nor during the industrial era have a majority of children experienced the family stability, economic stability, or homemaking-mother image that was idealized as the typical family system in mid-twentieth century America.

The work of adolescents has also been transformed since the mid-1800s. On the family farm, the labor of adolescents contributed to the family's survival and provided the opportunity for them to learn the work they would perform as adults. During the early part of the industrial era, adolescents also often worked in the nonagricultural economy to help support their family. But the proportion of adolescents engaged in such work declined greatly with the general rise in affluence, the efforts of labor unions to ensure jobs for adults by limiting child labor, the success of the child welfare movement in obtaining the passage of laws restricting child exploitation in the workplace, and the passage of compulsory education laws. Between the mid-1800s and the mid-1900s, then, adolescents through at least age 17 shifted from focusing primarily on farm work to focusing on schoolwork.

Since the mid-1900s, even as school enrollment among adolescents aged 16–19 has increased, the labor-force participation rates of students have also climbed. The new labor force participation of adolescents, like that of parents, is often located away from the family home. However, compared with the old adolescent work before 1950, this new work is much less likely to involve direct training for adult employment and much more likely to provide earnings that the adolescent spends only for personal consumption.

Overall, then, the family economy before the Industrial Revolution engaged parents and able-bodied children in work together on the family farm to provide for family support. With the Industrial Revolution, however, the family economy was transformed. Fathers became breadwinners who had to take jobs away from home in order to support their families, while mothers remained at home to care for children, and adolescent work supporting the family was replaced by schoolwork that provided abstract knowledge and training needed for nonfarm jobs in adulthood. But this family economy represented only a brief transition to one in which both parents worked outside the home as family breadwinners or the father was absent from the home, and in which many adolescents not only attended school but also worked to supplement family earnings that would support a "normal" lifestyle during the transition to adulthood.

In short, most children in preindustrial America lived in families in which both parents and children worked together on the farm to support themselves. But by the end of the twentieth century, most children are expected to live in families in which both parents work away from home to support the family, or in which the father is simply absent from the home on a full-time basis. With the shift away from farming, older children increasingly devoted their work time to obtaining the education required for employment during adulthood; but with the rise in dual-earner and one-parent families, older children have increasingly entered the labor force to supplement the family income that will support a "normal" adolescent lifestyle.

The family economy of children today is increasingly similar to that of children in preindustrial America in that there are parents as well as older children who work to support the family by contributing to production for the broader market economy. But today's family economy is quite different from that of the preindustrial family farm in that family members today typically work at very different jobs and at locations scattered far from home, and in that today's work provides for a much more affluent standard of living. As first fathers and then mothers left the home to work at jobs in the growing nonfarm sectors of the economy, child care, once an at-home activity of parents, underwent two revolutionary transformations. These child care revolutions will be discussed in the next chapter.

Appendix 4.1. Derivation of Results for Figure 4.1

Results for 1940–1980 were derived directly from PUMS tapes. Results for earlier years were estimated as follows: First, the proportion of children living with no parents was assumed to be constant at 5 percent for 1790 through 1930. The proportion remained within the narrow range of 4–7 percent between 1940 and 1980, and 5 percent is the average value for 1940–1980. Since the proportion of children living on farms is greater as we go further back in time, if the proportion of children who are not living with a parent is lower on farms than nonfarm settings, then the assumed value of 5 percent may be slightly too large, particularly for the earlier years. On the other hand, parental mortality was higher in earlier years, and some historical data indicate that in earlier years the proportion of older children living with no parents was larger, because apprenticeships, etc., were more common. Overall, it seems likely that our assumption of no change is correct within 0–5 percentage points, particularly in view of the fact that children may obtain new parents though the remarriage of a parent or through adoption. The magnitude of any error is probably less, the more recent the year to which the estimate pertains.

Second, the proportion of children living in a nonfarm dual-earner family or in a one-parent family was estimated as follows. For census years from 1890 through 1940, the proportion of married women who were in the labor force was obtained from two data series measuring (1) the number of married women, and (2) the number of married women in the labor force (Historical Statistics of the United States, Colonial Times to 1970). The value for 1910 was obtained by linear interpolation since the value for this year appears to be an overestimate compared to surrounding years due to a change in Census Bureau procedures for the 1910 census (see Valerie Oppenheimer, *The Female Labor Force in the United States*, Population Monograph Series, No. 5, Institute of International Studies, University of California, Berkeley, p. 3). The estimates of the proportion of married women in the labor force for 1890–1940 were 4.6, 5.6, 7.3, 9.0, 11.7, and 15.5 percent.

The proportion of children living in dual-earner or one-parent families as derived from the 1940 PUMS was 15.0 percent. The components of this value are 8.7 percent living in one-parent families and 6.3 percent living in nonfarm dual-earner families. Dividing 6.3 (the proportion of children in dual-earner families) by 15.5 (the proportion of married women in the labor force) produced an adjustment factor from estimates for 1940 of 0.41. This adjustment factor was multiplied by the proportion of married women in the labor force for 1890–1930 to estimate the proportion of children in dual-earner families for these years. The estimates are 1.9, 2.3, 3.0, 3.7, and 4.8 percent for 1890–1930. Then proportionate changes in the percentage of all persons gainfully employed in agriculture were applied to the estimate of 1.9 percent for 1890 to derive estimates for earlier dates back to 1850, that is, estimates of the proportion of children living in dual-earner families in 1850–1880. The estimates for each year of the proportion living in dual-earner families was then added to the value of 8.7 percent of children living in one-parent families to obtain combined estimates of the proportion of children living in nonfarm dual-earner families and in one-parent families for 1850–1930. Finally, the total proportion of 10 percent for 1850 in dual-earner nonfarm and one-parent families was assumed to have been constant since 1790.

The most important assumption underlying these estimating procedures is that the proportion of children living in one-parent families remained constant between 1790 and 1940 at 8.7 percent. For 1860–1930, this assumption is probably correct within 0–2 percentage points (as decade-long averages), because parental death or divorce probably account for most children living with one-parent during this era (in 1940 only 0.1 percent of children were living with an unmarried mother, 8.6 percent were living with an ever-married mother or with a father), and because the proportion of all marriages ending in death or divorce was approximately stable between 1860 and 1940 (see Kingsley Davis, "The American Family in Relation to Demographic Change," pp. 235–265 in Charles F. Westoff and Robert Parke, Jr., eds., Commission on Population Growth and the American Future, *Research Reports, Volume I, Demographic and Social Aspects of Population Growth*, Washington, DC: U.S. Government Printing Office). Prior to 1860, it is possible that the value tended to be a little higher, because parental mortality was probably a little higher. In any event, in terms of decade-long averages, our assumption that the proportion living with one parent remained stable at 8.7 percent between 1790 and 1850 is probably correct within 2–4 percentage points, particularly since children can obtain a new (step)parent through a co-resident parent's remarriage.

The second most important assumption underlying our procedures for estimating the proportion of children in dual-earner/one-parent families is that the proportion of children in nonfarm dual-earner families changed in concert between 1890 and 1930 with changes in the proportion of married women who were in the labor force. In 1940, of the 7.3 percent of all children who lived in nonfarm dual-earner families, about one-third lived in families with neither parent in the labor force and about two-thirds lived in families in which both parents worked. (Families with neither parent in the labor force are included in this category as a residual, rather than in the "traditional" farm family as father-as-breadwinner categories.) Since mothers have become a larger proportion of the female and married-female labor force through time, it seems likely that the proportion of children living in two-parent families with a working mother may have declined more rapidly, as we move back through time, than did the proportion of married women who worked. In this case the proportion of children living in nonfarm dual-earner families will be overestimated by our procedures the further back in time we go. Also, since the U.S. was historically a country with a labor shortage, it is possible that the proportion of children living in families with neither parent working was less, the further back in time we go, but such a change is in effect built into our procedures.

On the other hand, female labor force participation, especially for married women and mothers, may be underestimated in censuses prior to 1940. In this case, our procedures would tend to underestimate the proportion of children living in two-parent families with a working mother. Overall, these possible problems probably tend to counterbalance each other, and it seems likely that our estimates of the proportion in dual-earner nonfarm families are probably correct within 0–3 percentage points for 1790–1930.

Taken together, our results for the proportion of children living with no parent and in nonfarm dual-earner or in one-parent families probably are correct within 0–5 percentage points for the years beginning with 1860–1930, and they probably are correct within 0–10 percentage points for 1790–1850. Any such errors should have no effect on our broad conclusions regarding the relative dominance of two-parent farm families and breadwinner/homemaker nonfarm families, because the errors almost surely occur in a fashion that is approximately proportionate to the distribution of children across these two latter types of families at any give point in time.

For example, if the proportion of children in no-parent, dual-earner, and one-parent families were underestimated in 1790 by 10 percentage points, then it is likely that the proportion in two-parent farm families would be overestimated by approximately 8 percentage points and the proportion living in breadwinner/homemaker nonfarm families would be overestimated by approximately 2 percentage points. If this were the case then the proportion in two-parent farm families and breadwinner/homemaker nonfarm families would be 64 and 11 percent, respectively, instead of 72 and 13 percent. But these results would leave our broad conclusions unchanged, namely, that a large majority of children lived in two-parent farm families, and a small minority lived in breadwinner/homemaker nonfarm families. Similarly, if the total proportion of children in no-parent, dual-earner, and one-parent families were underestimated by 5 percentage points in 1890, it is seems likely that this error is about equally distributed between two-parent farm families and breadwinner/homemaker nonfarm families. Again the estimated and the "correct" results would lead to the same broad conclusion; children were about equally likely to live in two-parent farm families and breadwinner/homemaker nonfarm families in 1890.

After deriving estimates for children living with no parent or in dual-earner/one-parent families, we focused on the proportion of children living living in two-parent farm families. The proportions of children aged 0–19 who were living on farms in 1920, 1930, and 1940 were obtained from published census data. The published proportion of children aged 0–19 living on farms in 1940 was 3.6 percentage points more than the proportion of children aged 0–17 living in two-parent farm families. Consequently, the estimates of the proportion of children aged 0–17 who lived in two-parent farm families in 1920 and 1930 were obtained by subtracting 3.6 percentage points from the proportion aged 0–19 for those years. (The adjustment factor would have been 4.1 percentage points if we had based it on the proportion of children aged 0–14 living on farms, but our final estimates rounded to the nearest percentage point would have been unchanged).

Then the proportion of the total population living on farms was obtained from published census data for 1880–1920. The estimated values for 1880–1920 were 43.8, 39.4, 39.3, 34.7, and 30.0 percent. Our previously estimated value for the proportion of children living in two-parent farm families in 1920 was 2.0 percentage points greater, at 32.0 percent. Consequently, this 2.0 percentage point difference was added to the series of proportions of all persons living on farms to obtain estimates of the proportion of children living in two-parent farm families. Since farmers consistently had higher fertility rates than non-farmers during this era, it is reasonable to assume that children were more likely than adults to live on farms.

Then the proportion of gainful workers who were farmers was obtained from published census data for 1820–1880. Since our previous estimate for 1880 that 47.4 percent of children living in two-parent farm families was 2.0 percentage points less than the published estimate that 49.4 percent of gainfully employed workers who were farmers, we subtracted 2.0 percentage points from the estimates of the gainfully employed who were farmers to estimate the percentage of children living in two-parent farm families for 1820–1880. Then the proportion of the population living in rural areas was obtained from published census data for 1790–1820, and decade-to-decade changes in the proportion were assumed to apply to the proportion of children living in two-parent farm families to obtain estimates of the proportion of children living in two-parent farm families for 1790–1810.

The estimates for the most recent years of 1920–1930 are based on a small adjustment (3.6 percentage points) to a variable (children aged 0–19 on farms), which is closely related to the estimated variable (children aged 0–17 in two-parent farm families). Since the adjustment is small and the time period short, the resulting estimates probably are accurate within 0–2 percentage points. The direction of error, if any, probably leads to a slight underestimate in the proportion of children in two-parent farm families in 1920, since the adjustment factor is derived as of 1940, a time when the Great Depression may have led to a slightly larger amount of temporary family disruption than had been the case in 1920.

The estimates of the proportion of children living in two-parent farm families for the next most recent years of 1880–1910 are based on an even smaller adjustment (2.0 percentage points). However, since the adjustment variable (proportion of the total population on farms) is somewhat less closely related to the estimated variable (children aged 0–17 in two-parent farm families), and since the estimation period is further removed from directly derived results and is longer (40 years instead of 20 years), the possible error may be somewhat larger, but probably no larger than 0–5 percent.

As we move further back to estimates for 1820–1870, the adjustment factor remains small at only 2 percentage points, but the adjustment variable (percentage of gainful workers employed on farms) is still less closely related to the estimated variable, and the estimation period is still further removed from the directly derived results and still longer (60 years). Hence, the possible error may be still larger, at perhaps 0–10 percent. Finally, possible errors for the earliest years of 1790–1810 may be prone to still more error since the adjustment variable (proportion of the total population living in rural areas) is still less closely related to the estimated variable. Possible errors for these years may be in the range of 0–15 percent. The direction of any errors in the estimates for 1790–1810 probably tends to underestimate change since they are based on shifts between the rural-nonrural population, but more rapid changes may have been occurring in the shift from farm to other nonrural.

Despite the possibility of errors in our estimates of the proportion of children living in two-parent farm families, our broad conclusions about the relative dominance of the two-parent family farm versus breadwinner/homemaker nonfarm families should not be affected, because the possible magnitude of the errors is probably less than the differences between our estimates of these two variables, except in the years of 1890 and 1900 when children were about equally likely to be living in each type of family situation. But for these years, our conclusion is that, from the perspective of children, these two types of families were about equally prevalent.

Finally, we estimated the proportion of children living in breadwinner/homemaker nonfarm families by subtracting from 100 percent for each decade between 1790 and 1930 our previous estimates of the proportion of children living in two-parent farm families, the proportion of children living in nonfarm dual-earner families and one-parent families, and the proportion in no-parent situations.

Overall, in view of available data, the estimates for 1790–1930 appear reasonable. Nevertheless, in view of the nature and magnitude of possible errors, conclusions drawn in the text are based on broad levels and trends especially for years before 1880, so that possible errors should not materially affect conclusions drawn.

5

TWO CHILD-CARE REVOLUTIONS

Introduction and Highlights

CHILDREN experienced two revolutionary increases in nonparental care during the past 120 years. The total time that children aged 5–17 spend in school, and hence away from the family, nearly quadrupled, as more and more fathers took jobs away from home, as school attendance became compulsory, and as affluence increased and advanced formal education became increasingly necessary for many jobs. Within the past 50 years, the proportion of younger children aged 0–5 who have had no specific parent at home on a full-time basis has also nearly quadrupled as more and more mothers work away from home. As a result, many preschool children today receive substantial child care from someone other than their parents. In this chapter we will discuss the nature of these child care revolutions, especially the second one for preschool children, by addressing the following questions.

For school-age children, when and how rapidly did time spent in school increase; what increases have occurred in the proportion of children who do not have a parent at home full-time; and what proportion are not cared for by parents after school? For preschool-age children, what changes have occurred in the amount of parental time that is potentially available to children, and in the availability of other relatives in the home who might act as surrogate parents by providing child care when parents are not available? Also for preschoolers, to what extent is child care the primary focus of parental activity; who actually provides care when parents are not available, and in what ways is nonparental child care beneficial or detrimental to the child? Briefly, this chapter offers the following answers to these questions.

With the transition from farming to an industrial economy in which fathers worked away from the home, and with the rise of compulsory education and child labor laws, the average number of days during which children aged 5–17 attended school, as a proportion of the days in the year, nearly quadrupled between 1870 and 1988, climbing from about 12 to 43 percent. By comparison, an adult five-day work week includes about 65 percent of the days in a year.[1] Most of the increase for children aged 7–14 occurred between 1870 and 1930 and for those aged 16–17, between 1920 and 1970.

By 1930, then, a large reduction had occurred in the time that mothers with school-age children might need to devote to the care and supervision of their children, making these mothers potentially available for paid work outside the home for more than 60 percent of the days in a work year. After 1940 mothers did in fact—and in large numbers—follow fathers into the paid labor force. The proportion of school-age children who had no specific parent at home on a full-time basis tripled, climbing from about 20 percent in 1940 to 59 percent in 1980 and 66 percent in 1989. By 1984, then, about 24 percent of children aged 5–13, and a similar proportion of children aged 5–8, not only attended school but were also cared for after school by someone other than their parents.

The post-1940 rise in mothers' labor-force participation was not limited to school-age children, however, and among preschool-age children the proportion who have no specific parent at home on a full-time basis quadrupled between 1940 and 1989, climbing from 13 to 53 percent. Consequently, the amount of parental time that is potentially available to preschoolers has declined substantially and the need for nonparental care has increased substantially. Despite the increasing need for nonparental care, however, the proportion of preschoolers who have a relative in the home who might act as a surrogate parent declined between 1940 and 1980 (from 19–20 percent to 4–5 percent among preschoolers living in dual-earner families and from 51–57 percent to 20–25 percent for preschoolers living in one-parent families with an employed parent).

Among mothers of preschoolers in the mid-1970s, mothers who were not in the labor force devoted about twice as much time to child care as

[1]Assuming 5 days per week, 2–4 weeks vacation, 10 holidays, and no sick days, an adult would work 63–66 percent of the days in a year.

a primary activity as did employed mothers (2.2 vs. 1.2 hours per day). Among fathers of preschoolers, the time devoted to child care as a primary activity was the same regardless of whether the mother was employed, and it amounted to one-fifth (20 percent) as much time as nonemployed mothers and about two-fifths (36 percent) as much time as employed mothers devoted to such child care.

Earlier, between 1926–1935 and 1943, the time that mothers who were not in the labor force devoted to child care as a primary activity increased by 50–100 percent, and during the subsequent 20 years it may have increased a bit more. Between the early 1960s and early 1980s, however, the average amount of time that all mothers of preschoolers devoted to child care as a primary activity declined, because employment among the mothers of preschoolers increased and these mothers were then able to devote only about one-half as much time to child care as a primary activity as did nonemployed mothers of preschoolers.

By 1989, 48 percent of preschoolers had a specific nonemployed parent at home full-time, and 12 percent had employed parents who personally provided their preschoolers' care, often by working different hours or days. In addition, 15 percent of preschoolers were cared for by relatives who often did not live in the preschoolers' home; and 25 percent were cared for by nonrelatives—about half in such organized care facilities as nursery schools.

One beneficial consequence of having two parents in the labor force is that two can earn more income than one, as we will discuss in detail in Chapters 9 and 10. Additional potentially beneficial and detrimental effects of mothers' employment and nonparental care for children, especially for preschoolers, have been studied recently, but most of the results must be viewed as both preliminary and tentative.

Available evidence suggests that nonparental child care is neither necessarily nor pervasively harmful; nor is it a form of maternal deprivation, since children form attachments to multiple caregivers if the number of caregivers is limited, the relationships are long-lasting, and the caregivers are responsive to the child's needs. Available evidence also suggests that the quality of care that children receive is important, and that some children, especially those from low-income families, are in double jeopardy from psychological and economic stress at home as well as from stress imposed by low-quality, nonparental child care environments.

Let's turn to a more detailed discussion of these results.

Nonparental Care for School-Age Children

In 1870 children aged 5–17 attended school an average of about 11 percent of the days during the year, but this figure quadrupled to about 43 percent of the year in 1988.[2] Two changes contributed fairly equally to this increase in the proportion of days per year spent in school by children aged 5–17: School enrollment doubled from about 50 to 98 percent; and the average number of days of attendance per enrolled student doubled from about 78 to 162 days per year.

Most of the increase for children aged 7–14 occurred between 1870 and 1930, as the average proportion of days per year spent in school rose from about 15 to 38 percent. Much of this rise, in turn, is accounted for by a four-fifths increase in the average number of days during which school was attended per student (from 78 to 143 days per year), while a smaller proportion of the rise is accounted for by a school-enrollment rate increase of roughly one-third (from 70–75 percent to 95 percent).[3]

[2]The data for 1850–1870 was obtained from Series H 433, U.S. Bureau of the Census, *Historical Statistics of the United States, Colonial Times to 1970, Bicentennial Edition, Part 1* (Washington, DC: U.S. Government Printing Office, 1975). Estimates of the enrollment rates per 100 children aged 5–19 are slightly too large because enrollment pertains to persons of all ages, while the population of children aged 5–19 is used as the denominator. For the calculation in the text, the published enrollment rate was 48.4 percent for 5–19-year-olds. However, since enrollment rates for persons aged 18–19 were much lower than those for children aged 5–17 historically, the enrollment rate for 5–19-year-olds tends to be too large as an estimate of the enrollment rate for 5–17-year-olds. Since the latter effect is probably larger than the former, for the calculation in the text we assume crudely that the enrollment rate for children aged 5–17 was about 50 percent in 1870. If the actual enrollment rate lies in the range from 40 to 60 percent, which seems likely, then the actual proportion of childhood days per year spent in school is in the range of 9–13 percent for 1870. Enrollment rates for 1955–1988 are drawn from Table A-3, U.S. Bureau of the Census, Current Population Reports, Series P-20, No. 443, *School Enrollment—Social and Economic Characteristics of Students: October 1988 and 1987* (Washington, DC: U.S. Government Printing Office, 1990). Average number of days attended per enrolled pupil per year was obtained from Series H 522, in *Historical Statistics of the United States* cited above. The average for 1970 is assumed to have continued unchanged through 1988.

[3]The estimate that the enrollment rate for children aged 7–13 in 1870 was about 70–75 percent is derived as follows. First, as of 1910 the enrollment rate for children aged 10–14 was 2.1 percentage points larger than that for children aged 7–13, at 88.2 vs. 86.1 percent. See U.S. Bureau of the Census, Thirteenth Census of the United States taken in the year 1910, *Population, Volume I, 1910* (Washington, DC: U.S. Government Printing Office, 1913), Tables 5 and 12. Since the enrollment rate for children aged 10–14 increased by 8.5 percentage points between 1890 and 1910, if the difference remained constant, the enrollment rate for children aged 7–13 would have been about 77.6 percent in 1890. See the 1910 census, U.S. Bureau of the Census, *Report on the Population of the United States at the Eleventh Census: 1890, Part II* (Washington, DC: U.S. Government Printing Office, 1897), p. xxviii. Now the enrollment rate for children aged 5–19 increased by about 5.9 percentage points between 1870 and 1890 (Series H 433, *Historical Statistics of the United States*). If the same change occurred for children aged 7–13, then their enrollment rate in 1870 was about 71.7 percent, or about 70–75 percent. If the actual enrollment rate was

For children aged 16–17, most of the increase in the average proportion of days per year spent in school occurred between 1920 and 1970, as the proportion rose from about 14 to 39 percent of the days per year. Most of this rise is accounted for by the doubling of the school enrollment rate for children aged 16–17 (from 43 to 90 percent), while a smaller proportion of the rise is explained by a one-third increase in the average school days attended per student (from 121 to 162 days per year).

More recently, among young adults aged 18–19, school attendance has increased largely because of increasing college enrollment. Between 1940 and 1970, the enrollment rate for young adults aged 18–19 increased by two-thirds (from 29 to 48 percent); and during 1986–1988, about 55–56 percent were enrolled in school.[4]

As early as 1850–1870, then, nearly half of children aged 5–17 were attending school at any given time, and the prevalence of a minimal formal or informal education—at least for whites—was reflected in the fact that by 1870, only 20 percent of persons 10 years and older were classified as illiterate and only 11.5 percent of whites were so classified.[5] During the next 100 years, both school enrollment rates and the average number of days per year during which students attended school doubled, producing a quadrupling in the proportion of childhood days spent in school between the ages of 5 and 17.

The factors that contributed to these increases in formal schooling were probably the same as those that contributed to the decline in child labor during the era (Chapter 4)—namely, the shift from farming to industrial jobs requiring stronger, more experienced workers; the enactment of child labor and compulsory education laws; and the rising level of affluence that made it possible for families to survive without child labor. Also contributing to the rise in formal education was the fact that many occupations, especially those characterized by high incomes and high prestige, increasingly required advanced knowledge and skills that could be obtained only through formal schooling.

Although after the beginning of the Industrial Revolution mothers were viewed as homemakers who remained at home to personally care

---

between 60 and 80 percent, as seems quite likely, then school days as a proportion of the year were within the range of 13–17 percent—not greatly different from our approximate estimate of 15 percent in the text.

[4]In October 1988, 75 percent of persons aged 18–19 who were enrolled in school were enrolled in college, while 25 percent were enrolled below the college level. U.S. Bureau of the Census, Current Population Reports, Series P-20, No. 443, *School Enrollment—Social and Economic Characteristics of Students: October 1988 and 1987* (Washington, DC: U.S. Government Printing Office, 1990), Table A-1.

[5]U.S. Bureau of the Census, *Historical Statistics of the United States, Colonial Times to 1970, Bicentennial Edition*, Part 2, Series H 664–668 (Washington, DC: U.S. Government Printing Office, 1975).

for their children and perform other domestic functions (Chapter 4), the expanding amount of time spent by children aged 5–17 in the care of schools implied a commensurate constriction in the role of mothers as child care providers. In 1870, about one-half of children aged 5–19 spent no time in school; and for the remaining one-half of children aged 5–19, school days represented an average of only 21 percent of the total days in the year. By 1940, however, school days represented an average of 42 percent of the days in the year for 95 percent of children aged 7–13 and for 79 percent of children aged 14–17.

Since a five-day work week for an adult requires about 65 percent of the days in the year, it is apparent that by 1940 most mothers had a substantial amount of time, formerly required for child care, that had become potentially available for work in the labor force.[6] It appears, then, that the large increases in school enrollment between 1870 and 1940 should be viewed as one of the underlying factors that facilitated the rise in mothers' labor-force participation after 1940, and hence the rise in the proportion of school-age children who did not have a specific parent at home full-time.

In 1940, 8 percent of school-age children did not live with a parent, and 13 percent lived with parents who were in the labor force. Taken together, in 1940 a total of 20 percent of children aged 6–17 had no specific parent in the home full-time, but by 1989 this proportion had more than tripled to 66 percent (Table 5.1). Most of this 46 percentage point rise resulted from the 39 percentage point increase in the proportion living in dual-earner families, which in turn was split roughly equally between the increases in two-parent families in which both parents worked full-time and at least one parent worked part-time.

Since a typical school day for students lasts only 5–6 hours, some mothers may find it difficult to find part-time work with hours that correspond precisely to the school day, while for other mothers full-time employment may be either preferable or financially necessary.[7] Since 63

[6]"The passage of the Fair Labor Standards Act of 1938 (FLSA) established a standard workweek of 40 hours' duration for nonsupervisory employees of firms engaged in Interstate commerce. Over the ensuing years, concern about workers' health led to many Federal and State statutes and union contracts, which stipulated a second standard: the 8-hour day." In Shirley J. Smith, "The Growing Diversity of Work Schedules," *Monthly Labor Review* 109, 11 (November 1986): 7–13. Smith also indicates that the FLSA became effective in 1940 (p. 13). "From 1900 to 1946, the average workweek shrank from about 53 to 44 hours." In Philip L. Rones, "Moving to the Sun: Regional Job Growth, 1968 to 1978," *Monthly Labor Review* 103, 3 (March 1980): 3–11.

[7]Even schoolteachers have a 7–8-hour workday, since they must arrive at school earlier and leave later than the students do. Among employed women who were married, spouse present between 1960 and 1988, 27–35 of those with children aged 6–17 worked part-time, compared with 18–25 percent of those who had no children under 18 years of age in the home, and compared with 30–38 percent for those with children aged 0–5. The small difference in the proportion between mothers with school-age children and mothers

148

percent of school-age children in 1989 lived in dual-earner families or in one-parent families with a working parent, it would not be surprising to find that the increase in mothers' labor-force participation after 1940 also led to an increase in the proportion of children who were cared for by someone other than their parents not only during school but after school as well.

Unfortunately, historical data on after-school care for children are not available, but Census Bureau data collected in 1984 show that 24 percent of children aged 5–13 were cared for after school by someone other than their parents.[8] More specifically, 9 percent were cared for by adult siblings or other relatives, 8 percent were cared for by nonrelatives, and 7 percent were "taking care of themselves." Among the youngest children aged 5–8, 25 percent were cared for by someone other than their parents: 9 percent by relatives, 13 percent by nonrelatives, and 3 percent were taking care of themselves.

Of all the children aged 5–13 who were taking care of themselves after school, about 90 percent had employed mothers, 69 percent of whom were employed full-time. Viewed from another perspective with slightly different data, of the children aged 5–14 who were in school most of the time while their mothers were at work, 20 percent were taking care of themselves before or after school, compared with only 4 percent of other children.[9]

Without historical data we cannot be certain, but these results are consistent with the possibility that increased employment among mothers since 1940 fostered a substantial increase in after-school nonparental care for school-age children. Hence, increasing school enrollment between 1870 and 1940 may have facilitated the rise in mothers' employment after 1940, and the rise in mothers' employment may in turn have fostered further increases in nonparental care for school-age children.

---

of preschoolers who were employed part-time suggests that school attendance has only a slight effect, overall, on whether a mother works part-time or full-time. The somewhat larger difference in the proportion between mothers with children in the home and married women without children in the home who were employed part-time suggests that having a child in the home does to some degree foster part-time, as opposed to full-time, work. U.S. Department of Labor, Bureau of Labor Statistics, *Handbook of Labor Statistics*, Bulletin 2340 (Washington, DC: U.S. Government Printing Office, August 1989), Table 57, pp. 242–244.

[8]Rosalind R. Bruno, U.S. Bureau of the Census, Current Population Reports, Series P-23, No. 149, *After-School Care of School-Age Children: December 1984* (Washington, DC: U.S. Government Printing Office, 1987), Table 1.

[9]Martin O'Connell and Amara Bachu, U.S. Bureau of the Census, Current Population Reports,Series P-70, No. 9, *Who's Minding the Kids? Child Care Arrangements: Winter 1984–1985* (Washington, DC: U.S. Government Printing Office, 1987), Table F.

Parental Time Potentially Available to Preschoolers

For preschool children aged 0–5, despite the drop in the proportion living in two-parent families (from 90 to 75 percent between 1940–1960 and 1989), the proportion living in dual-earner families multiplied nearly eightfold (from 5 to 38 percent). Meanwhile, the proportion living in one-parent families in which there was an employed parent also multiplied sixfold (from 2 to 13 percent) (Table 5.2). Overall, then, a sevenfold increase (from 7 to 51 percent) occurred in the proportion of preschoolers who had employed parents. Counting preschoolers who had no parent in the home, the proportion without a specific parent in the home full-time—that is, the proportion without a specific parent potentially available to provide full-time care—jumped from 13 to 52 percent between 1940 and 1989.

More specifically, among preschoolers who lived with two parents, the proportion who had both parents in the labor force increased from 6 to 51 percent between 1940 and 1989, and one-fourth of this increase occurred during the single decade between 1970 and 1980. Among preschoolers living with their mother only, the proportion whose mother was employed increased from 39–42 percent in 1940–1960 to about 49–51 percent in 1970–1989. Hence, the sharp rise in one-parent families for preschoolers after 1960 was accompanied by a rise in mothers' employment among such preschoolers.

Newborn infants and other children through age 2 are more dependent on adults than are older preschoolers aged 3–5 because they require more intensive adult care. Yet since 1940, the proportion of these children who had a specific parent at home full-time—that is, the proportion with a specific parent who is potentially available to provide full-time care—has dropped nearly as much for newborn children under age 1 as for older children. Between 1940 and 1980, the proportion with a specific parent at home full-time declined by 29 percentage points for newborns under age 1, by 33 percentage points for children aged 5, and by 38 percentage points for children aged 6–17 (Tables 5.1 and 5.3).

More specifically, between 1940 and 1980, the proportion of children who had a parent at home full-time declined from 90 to 60 percent for newborns under age 1, from 84 to 52 percent for children aged 5, and from 80 to 42 percent for children aged 6–17. The largest declines are recent. One-half of the 50-year decline for newborns occurred between 1970 and 1980, and 70 and 60 percent of the declines for children aged 5 and 6–17, respectively, occurred between 1960 and 1980. In addition, for each age, the rise in dual-earner families accounts for more than 80 percent of the decline in the proportion for whom a specific parent was

TABLE 5.1

Children Aged 6–17, by Parental Presence and Employment Status: 1940–1989

	1940	1950	1960	1970	1980	1989
Total Number (in thousands)	27,651	27,505	39,974	49,234	44,867	41,598
Percent	100.0	100.0	100.0	100.0	100.0	100.0
Breadwinner-homemaker total	71.9	59.9	58.3	46.7	32.1	21.5
Breadwinner-homemaker intact	58.6	48.0	47.5	37.7	24.2	NA
Breadwinner-homemaker blended	13.3	11.9	10.8	9.0	7.8	NA
Two-parent, father not breadwinner	3.3	5.7	2.6	3.3	3.7	4.7
One-parent family, not a breadwinner	4.6	3.9	3.7	5.1	5.8	7.5
Dual-earner family, employed full time	3.3	3.9	12.5	15.3	20.8	23.1
One-parent family employed full time	3.6	2.6	4.3	6.3	9.5	11.8
Dual-earner family, employed part time	3.5	14.0	12.3	16.1	19.1	22.7
One-parent family, employed part time	2.4	3.1	1.8	2.7	3.9	5.5
No parent in home	7.5	6.9	4.5	4.5	5.2	3.3

NOTES: Estimates derived from 1940–1980 Census PUMS and 1989 CPS. Estimates for 1940 and 1950 based on mother's marital history only (see Chapter 4).

Breadwinner-Homemaker: Two-parent family with father in labor force and mother not in labor force.

Intact: Two-parent family with all children born after parents' only marriage.

Blended: Two-parent family other than intact.

Two-Parent, Father not breadwinner: Father not in labor force, mother may or may not be in labor force.

One-Parent Family, Not a Breadwinner: Mother-only or father-only family with parent not in labor force.

Dual-Earner Family, Employed Full-time: Two-parent family, both parents employed 35 or more hours last week.

One-Parent Family, Employed full-time: Mother-only or father-only family with parent employed 35 or more hours last week.

Dual-Earner Family, Employed Part-time: Two-parent family, both parents in labor force, at least one employed less than 35 hours last week.

One-Parent Employed Part-time: Mother-only or father-only family with parent in labor force employed less than 35 hours last week.

No Parent in Home: Child does not reside with biological, step, or adoptive parent.

NA Not Available

potentially available to provide full-time care. The rise in one-parent families accounts for less than 20 percent of the decline in the full-time availability of a specific parent.

More recently (between 1980 and 1989), the decline in the proportion of newborns who had a parent at home full-time was about two-thirds as large as that recorded during the 1970s, and by 1989 only 51 percent of newborns had a specific parent at home full-time. Hence, 60 percent of the five-decade change occurred during the two decades between 1970 and 1989.

In each year between 1940 and 1989, the differences between preschoolers and school-age children in the proportion who had a specific

TABLE 5.2

Children by Parental Presence and Employment Status for Cohorts Born Between 1920s and 1980s

	1920s	1930s		1940s		1950s		1960s		1970s		1980s
	Age 12–17	Age 0–5	Age 12–17	Age 0–5	Age 12–17	Age 0–5	Age 12–17	Age 0–5	Age 12–17	Age 0–5	Age 12–17	Age 0–5
Total Number (in thousands)	14,534	12,384	12,718	18,801	18,322	24,808	24,132	20,895	23,753	19,719	20,168	22,303
Percent	100.0	100.0	100.0	100.0	100.0	100.0	100.0	100.0	100.0	100.0	100.0	100.0
Breadwinner-homemaker total	67.6	82.9	60.0	78.3	51.3	72.9	42.0	60.7	29.0	45.5	18.7	31.6
Breadwinner-homemaker intact	55.0	70.7	47.6	65.6	41.6	61.0	33.7	50.4	22.1	35.2	NA	NA
Breadwinner-homemaker blended	12.6	12.2	12.4	12.7	9.7	11.9	8.3	10.3	6.9	10.3	NA	NA
Two-parent, father not breadwinner	3.7	2.1	3.5	3.0	3.2	1.8	3.7	2.5	4.3	2.6	4.9	4.9
One-parent family, not a breadwinner	5.5	2.3	4.7	2.9	3.7	3.9	4.9	5.6	5.5	7.2	6.6	11.0
Dual-earner family, employed full-time	3.4	2.5	9.4	4.5	15.1	6.6	17.2	10.1	22.3	13.8	25.1	17.5
One-parent family, employed full-time	4.3	1.4	5.2	1.7	5.2	2.4	6.9	4.4	9.8	5.6	13.2	7.0
Dual-earner family, employed part-time	3.6	2.9	6.9	4.3	13.0	8.4	16.5	11.7	19.1	17.0	22.1	20.8
One-parent family, employed part-time	2.8	0.9	1.6	0.7	2.2	1.2	2.9	2.1	3.9	3.4	5.2	5.5
No parent in home	9.0	5.0	8.7	4.7	6.2	2.9	5.8	3.0	6.2	4.9	4.3	1.7

SOURCES: Estimates derived from 1940–1980 Census PUMS, and 1989 CPS.

NOTES: See Table 4.1 for explanation, and Table 5.1 Notes.

parent at home full-time suggest that the extreme dependency associated with the earliest years of life has encouraged some parents to maintain two-parent families, with the mother potentially available to provide full-time care (Tables 5.1 and 5.2). Yet through time, the proportion of children with a specific parent at home full-time has declined greatly for all ages—for example, from 87 to 48 percent for preschoolers and from 80 to 34 percent for school-age children. Hence, despite the deterring effect that early childhood dependency appears to exercise on mothers' employment outside the home, the overall effect of this dependency on mothers' employment outside the home has diminished greatly since the Great Depression, but especially since 1960 or 1970.

If, as seems likely, this revolutionary transformation in family life continues, then within 20 to 30 years only a small minority of preschool children will be living in families in which there is a specific parent who is potentially available to provide full-time care.

Surrogate Parents Potentially Available to Preschoolers

As the amount of parental time potentially available to care for preschoolers has declined, what changes have occurred in the potential availability of other relatives in the home who might act as surrogate parents by providing child care when parents are not available? In the absence of parents, other adult relatives who live in a preschooler's home may be viewed by parents as particularly appropriate care providers, since they tend to share the same values as the parents. Furthermore, since they share the same home, these relatives are fully integrated into the daily life and share in the responsibilities of the family. In fact, adult relatives living in the homes of preschoolers often may act as substitute or surrogate parents.

To measure the extent to which relatives in the homes of preschoolers have been potentially available to act as surrogate parents and thereby fill the increasing need for nonparental care when parents are at work, we define a potential surrogate parent as any relative (other than the parents) who (1) lives in the home with preschoolers and their parents, (2) is at least 18 years of age, (3) is not enrolled in school, and (4) either is not in the labor force or works less than full-time.

Our findings indicate that for preschoolers in two-parent and those in one-parent families, the chances of having a potential surrogate parent in the home are quite different. But within each family situation, preschoolers whose parents were employed were only slightly more likely than other preschoolers to have a potential surrogate parent in the home;

TABLE 5.3

Children Aged 0–5, by Parental Presence and Employment Status: 1940–1989

Age	1940	1950	1960	1970	1980	1989
Breadwinner-Homemaker, Total						
0	85.6	82.6	76.8	65.2	49.9	33.8
1	85.1	79.9	74.5	63.8	47.2	33.0
2	84.5	78.2	74.5	60.1	45.4	31.5
3	81.4	78.2	70.8	59.4	44.5	30.6
4	81.7	74.8	71.8	59.4	43.2	30.1
5	79.4	74.5	68.9	56.9	42.0	30.2
Breadwinner-Homemaker, Intact						
0	75.8	70.6	64.8	54.8	39.2	NA
1	74.4	67.6	63.3	52.8	35.9	NA
2	72.0	65.6	61.9	50.1	35.5	NA
3	68.6	65.3	58.5	49.6	34.3	NA
4	68.2	61.9	60.1	48.8	33.7	NA
5	66.1	61.1	57.0	46.7	32.0	NA
Breadwinner-Homemaker, Blended						
0	9.8	12.0	12.0	10.4	10.7	NA
1	10.7	12.3	11.2	11.0	11.3	NA
2	12.5	12.6	12.6	10.0	9.9	NA
3	12.8	12.9	12.3	9.8	10.2	NA
4	13.5	12.9	11.7	10.6	9.5	NA
5	13.3	13.4	11.9	10.2	10.0	NA
Two-Parent, Father Not Breadwinner						
0	2.3	3.5	1.7	2.9	2.9	4.2
1	1.6	2.9	1.9	2.2	2.7	5.0
2	1.9	3.3	1.8	2.6	2.6	5.4
3	2.4	2.9	1.7	2.2	2.4	5.7
4	2.3	2.9	1.7	2.0	2.6	4.1
5	2.3	2.6	1.9	2.8	2.5	4.9
One-Parent Family, Not a Breadwinner						
0	1.8	2.8	4.2	6.6	7.6	13.1
1	2.2	2.8	4.1	5.2	7.4	11.6
2	1.6	2.6	3.9	5.9	7.6	11.0
3	2.7	2.7	3.9	5.5	6.7	9.8
4	2.6	3.2	3.5	5.4	7.1	10.2
5	2.7	3.2	4.0	5.3	7.0	10.3
Dual-Earner Family, Employed Full Time						
0	1.7	2.3	4.9	7.4	10.9	13.9
1	2.3	4.3	6.4	9.3	13.1	18.0
2	2.3	4.3	6.1	10.4	14.6	18.0
3	2.6	5.0	7.4	10.3	14.7	18.9
4	3.0	5.7	7.1	10.7	14.6	17.8
5	3.0	6.0	8.1	12.1	15.1	18.5

TABLE 5.3 (*continued*)

Age	1940	1950	1960	1970	1980	1989
One-Parent Family, Employed Full Time						
0	0.9	0.6	1.8	3.4	2.9	4.8
1	1.2	1.4	1.9	3.8	4.8	6.5
2	1.3	2.1	2.3	4.5	5.9	7.2
3	1.6	1.7	2.8	4.8	6.3	7.5
4	1.7	2.3	2.4	5.1	6.6	7.7
5	1.6	2.5	3.0	4.6	7.2	8.7
Dual-Earner Family, Employed Part Time						
0	1.9	3.0	6.4	9.8	17.0	23.1
1	2.7	3.9	7.6	10.4	16.1	20.0
2	2.9	4.1	7.7	11.7	16.3	19.3
3	3.3	4.5	9.3	12.5	16.5	20.4
4	2.5	4.9	9.4	12.4	18.0	22.2
5	3.6	5.4	9.9	13.3	18.2	19.4
One-Parent Family, Employed Part Time						
0	0.6	0.5	1.0	1.7	3.4	5.5
1	0.9	0.6	0.9	2.2	3.2	4.7
2	1.0	0.6	1.0	2.0	3.2	5.5
3	1.0	0.6	1.3	2.2	3.9	5.0
4	1.0	1.0	1.4	2.2	3.5	6.3
5	1.1	0.6	1.2	2.2	3.4	6.1
No Parent in Home						
0	5.3	4.7	3.2	3.1	5.3	1.7
1	4.0	4.3	2.7	3.0	5.6	1.3
2	4.5	4.7	2.6	2.9	4.5	1.9
3	5.0	4.4	2.9	3.0	5.0	2.0
4	5.2	4.9	2.7	2.8	4.3	1.7
5	6.2	5.2	3.1	2.9	4.7	1.9
Total (in thousands)						
0	1,757	3,092	4,270	3,440	3,636	3,892
1	2,045	3,303	4,233	3,321	3,333	3,751
2	2,181	3,520	4,197	3,292	3,269	3,666
3	2,092	3,553	4,061	3,884	3,188	3,681
4	2,160	2,641	4,016	3,530	3,114	3,633
5	2,148	2,690	4,031	3,928	3,179	3,680

SOURCES: Estimates derived from 1940–1980 Census PUMS, and 1989 CPS.

NOTES: See Table 4.1 for explanation and Table 5.1 NOTES.

TABLE 5.4

Children Aged 0–5 Separately,
by Presence of Surrogate Parent and School Enrollment: 1940–1980

	1940	1950	1960	1970	1980
Total Number (in thousands)	12384	18801	24808	20895	19719
Percent with Surrogate Parent in Home					
Breadwinner-homemaker total	15.1	11.8	6.3	4.7	3.6
Breadwinner-homemaker intact	14.9	11.4	5.7	4.4	3.2
Breadwinner-homemaker blended	16.1	13.9	9.4	6.4	4.9
Two-parent, father not breadwinner	25.6	15.7	18.3	10.0	6.4
One-parent family, not a breadwinner	51.6	44.3	31.2	24.5	21.6
Dual-earner family, employed full time	18.8	22.9	11.1	7.4	4.9
One-parent family, employed full time	57.1	50.0	43.3	32.3	20.1
Dual-earner family, employed part time	20.4	15.8	8.7	6.3	4.0
One-parent family, employed part time	51.2	54.8	34.6	21.4	25.1
Total	16.5	14.0	9.0	7.8	6.7
Percent with No Surrogate Parent in Home, but Enrolled in Kindergarten or Elementary School					
Breadwinner-homemaker total	2.6		6.5	9.6	9.1
Breadwinner-homemaker intact	2.6		6.6	9.7	8.9
Breadwinner-homemaker blended	2.7		6.0	9.3	9.6
Two-parent, father not breadwinner	4.3		6.3	12.1	10.2
One-parent family, not a breadwinner	3.2		6.6	9.9	9.1
Dual-earner family, employed full time	4.7		7.6	13.0	12.6
One-parent family, employed full time	0.8		6.8	11.5	12.3
Dual-earner family, employed part time	4.0		8.3	13.1	11.0
One-parent family, employed part time	3.0		5.9	13.2	9.7
Total	2.7		6.7	10.7	10.2
Percent with No Surrogate Parent in Home, but Enrolled in Nursery School					
Breadwinner-homemaker total				5.2	12.1
Breadwinner-homemaker intact				5.2	12.7
Breadwinner-homemaker blended				5.2	10.3
Two-parent, father not breadwinner				4.1	10.6
One-parent family, not a breadwinner				5.0	10.8
Dual-earner family, employed full time				7.4	20.7
One-parent family, employed full time				5.8	21.2
Dual-earner family, employed part time				6.8	17.4
One-parent family, employed part time				7.7	16.9
Total				5.7	14.8

SOURCES: Estimates derived from 1940–1980 Census PUMS.

NOTES: See Table 4.1 for explanation and Table 5.1 NOTES. Enrollment in kindergarten or elementary school not calculated for 1950 because data were collected for sample line persons only. Nursery school data available only for 1970 and 1980.

and the proportion living with such a person has dropped greatly since 1940 for preschoolers in both two-parent and one-parent families (Table 5.4).

Among preschoolers living in two-parent families in 1940, 15–16 percent in breadwinner-homemaker families had a potential surrogate parent in the home, compared with 19–20 percent in dual-earner families. Subsequently, the small gap narrowed, and by 1980, regardless of parents' employment status, only 3–6 percent of preschoolers living in two-parent families had a potential surrogate parent in the home. In 1940, among preschoolers living in one-parent families with a parent who was employed full-time, part-time, or not at all, the proportions with a potential surrogate parent in the home were 57, 51, and 52 percent, respectively. By 1980, these proportions had fallen by at least one-half to 20, 25, and 22 percent, respectively.

In comparing preschoolers under age 1 with 5-year-olds, it was found that if they lived in two-parent families and had parents whose work patterns were the same, then in any given year these children were equally likely to have a potential surrogate parent in the home (Tables 5.5 and 5.6). Comparing preschoolers under age 1 with 5-year-olds living in one-parent families in which the parent was not employed, however, newborns were found to be about 10 percentage points more likely than 5-year-olds to have a potential surrogate parent in the home in any given year.

Among preschoolers living in one-parent families with an employed parent, in 1940–1950 newborns and 5-year-olds were roughly equal in their chances of having a potential surrogate parent in the home. After 1950, however, the proportion declined less for newborns than for 5-year-olds, and by 1980 newborns were roughly 20 percentage points more likely to have a surrogate parent in the home than were 5-year-olds. Still, by 1980 newborns living in one-parent families with an employed parent were only 4–6 percentage points more likely to have a potential surrogate parent in the home than were newborns living in one-parent families with a parent who was not employed.

The small differences in the availability of potential surrogate parents within families that have the same number of parents but across parental employment situations suggest, from the perspective of children, that, at least since 1940, the need for nonparental child care associated with mothers' employment had little effect on the availability of potential surrogate parents for preschoolers. Of course, some potential surrogate parents (such as grandparents) live with the family either because they themselves have special care needs or because they provide other valuable resources, such as income.[10] Insofar as this is more often

[10]The contribution of relatives other than parents to family income is discussed in Chapter 9.

TABLE 5.5

*Children Aged 0 and 5, by Parental Presence and Employment Status
for Cohorts Born Circa 1940 to 1980*

Family Situation and Age	Year of Child's Birth				
	1940	1950	1960	1970	1980
Dual-Earner Family					
0	3.6	5.3	11.3	17.2	27.9
5	9.0	14.7	21.7	29.4	
One-Parent Family, Parent Employed					
0	1.5	1.1	2.8	5.1	6.3
5	2.9	3.7	5.5	8.7	
Total with Parent(s) Employed					
0	5.1	6.4	12.5	22.3	34.2
5	11.9	18.4	27.2	38.1	
Increase in Parent Employment Between Ages 0 and 5					
Dual earner	5.4	9.4	10.4	12.2	
One parent	1.4	2.6	2.7	3.6	
Total	6.8	12.0	13.1	15.8	

SOURCES: Estimates derived from 1940–1980 Census PUMS.

NOTES: Since data pertain to census years, children aged 0 were born mainly one year before the one indicated. Results for age 5 calculated as mean at aged 5 across two census years. For example, results for aged 5 in 1940 calculated as mean of estimates for aged 5 in 1940 and 1950. See Table 4.1 for explanation and Table 5.1 NOTES.

true in preschooler's families in which a parent is not employed than in families in which the parent(s) are employed, the need for nonparental child care associated with parents' employment may have had a greater effect on the availability of potential surrogate parents than is suggested by the results presented here.

Earlier in this chapter we saw that a large increase occurred between 1940 and 1989 in the potential need for nonparental care among preschoolers, due to the rise in dual-earner families and one-parent families in which the parent is employed. But we have also just seen that given a specific potential need for nonparental care, reflected in a specific pattern of parental presence and employment, a large drop occurred between 1940 and 1980 in the chances of preschoolers having a potential surrogate parent in the home. What was the overall effect of these two trends on the chances that a preschooler was both potentially in need of nonparental care and had a potential surrogate parent in the

TABLE 5.6

Children, by Single Year of Age 0–5 with Surrogate Parent or Enrolled in School: 1940–1980

	Percent with Surrogate Parent in Home				
Age	1940	1950	1960	1970	1980
Breadwinner-Homemaker, Intact					
0	15.1	12.4	6.0	5.1	3.3
1	14.2	11.4	5.0	4.2	4.0
2	14.4	10.6	5.5	3.1	2.7
3	14.1	11.4	5.0	4.2	3.2
4	15.2	10.7	6.4	4.1	2.7
5	16.4	12.0	6.2	5.2	3.4
Breadwinner-Homemaker, Blended					
0	13.5	14.1	8.6	5.0	4.1
1	14.6	13.7	9.9	5.5	4.5
2	18.5	13.8	10.6	5.5	6.5
3	17.3	12.4	10.2	7.2	3.4
4	15.1	14.7	8.5	7.0	4.7
5	16.7	15.5	8.2	8.0	6.6
Two-Parent Family, Father Not Breadwinner					
0	24.6 *	15.4	27.8 *	11.1 *	9.4
1	27.1 †	13.7	19.8 *	10.8 *	4.4 *
2	22.4 *	14.1	21.3 *	11.9 *	7.0 *
3	25.4 *	13.5	13.0 *	5.5 *	7.7 *
4	25.7 *	20.5	17.4 *	11.1 *	4.9 *
5	28.2 *	19.4	10.5 *	9.1	3.8 *
One-Parent Family, Not a Breadwinner					
0	69.6 †	50.0	34.8	38.3	29.5
1	53.1 *	47.9	35.8	36.4	26.0
2	49.0 *	47.8	33.7	23.2	18.5
3	63.0 *	42.8	31.0	21.4	15.4
4	44.3 *	38.5	23.0	14.8	19.4
5	37.8 *	38.5	26.9	12.5	18.9
Dual-Earner Family, Employed Full Time					
0	25.6 †	20.9	14.3	7.9	3.8
1	13.6 *	25.8	12.3	6.5	4.6
2	21.9 *	21.7	9.7	5.9	4.6
3	20.3 *	26.5	9.3	6.3	5.5
4	14.9 *	22.6	11.3	10.3	5.9
5	19.8 *	18.9	10.8	7.2	4.6

TABLE 5.6 (continued)

Age	Percent with Surrogate Parent in Home				
	1940	1950	1960	1970	1980
One-Parent Family, Employed Full Time					
0	68.2†	43.3†	46.1*	41.4	33.6
1	54.3†	55.9*	46.3*	37.0	25.6
2	62.5†	49.1	43.9*	32.9	21.4
3	53.2†	46.7*	44.2	32.3	20.9
4	45.3*	52.7*	38.8*	28.3	14.0
5	66.0*	49.5	42.0	26.7	13.6
Dual-Earner Family, Employed Part Time					
0	12.5†	14.2	8.8	7.1	4.5
1	31.3*	16.0	8.4	6.1	4.9
2	18.9*	17.0	9.9	4.2	3.4
3	21.0	15.3	7.9	5.9	3.0
4	16.9*	19.7	7.4	7.7	4.1
5	18.9	12.8	10.0	6.7	4.0
One-Parent Family, Employed Part Time					
0	50.0†	70.8†	48.8†	27.1*	36.1
1	64.0†	48.4†	36.8†	30.1*	38.1
2	43.3†	55.9†	29.5†	19.4*	15.5
3	46.7†	55.9†	37.0*	17.3*	22.8
4	59.4†	52.4†	22.4*	19.5*	20.2
5	45.7†	47.8†	36.7†	17.0*	16.8
Total					
0	16.1	13.9	9.4	9.3	7.6
1	16.1	13.9	8.8	8.3	7.8
2	16.2	13.4	9.1	6.7	6.1
3	16.8	13.7	8.8	7.4	6.2
4	16.4	14.4	8.7	7.7	6.1
5	17.6	14.5	9.3	7.5	6.1

TABLE 5.6 (*continued*)

Percent Enrolled in Kindergarten or Elementary School	Age 4		Age 5	
	1970	1980	1970	1980
Breadwinner-Homemaker, Intact	4.2	4.9	54.4	57.7
Breadwinner-Homemaker, Blended	4.0	6.4	49.3	58.8
Two-Parent Family, Father Not Breadwinner	15.3 *	9.9 *	54.5	60.3 *
One-Parent Family, Not a Breadwinner	9.0	9.5	52.9	60.8
Dual-Earner Family, Employed Full Time	7.1	9.0	56.8	64.6
One-Parent Family, Employed Full Time	8.9	9.2	61.7	60.5
Dual-Earner Family, Employed Part Time	7.5	5.9	57.2	59.7
One-Parent Family, Employed Part Time	10.4 *	6.4 *	64.8	59.9
No Parent in Home	11.2 *	14.2	55.8	63.6
Total	5.9	7.0	55.9	57.3

Percent Enrolled in Nursery School	Age 3		Age 4		Age 5	
	1970	1980	1970	1980	1970	1980
Breadwinner-Homemaker, Intact	8.5	19.1	16.2	40.4	7.9	20.0
Breadwinner-Homemaker, Blended	7.8	15.1	17.2	31.1	8.0	19.2
Two-Parent, Father Not Breadwinner	12.3 *	21.8 *	8.3 *	23.5 *	5.5	11.5 *
One-Parent Family, Not a Breadwinner	9.6	18.7	15.3	34.7	8.2	14.9
Dual-Earner Family, Employed Full Time	14.6	31.8	23.5	51.4	5.5	17.7
One-Parent Family, Employed Full Time	15.5	37.8	24.4	45.4	6.7	20.6
Dual-Earner Family, Employed Part Time	11.8	26.9	20.5	47.4	6.5	21.8
One-Parent Family, Employed Part Time	13.3 *	25.2	27.3 *	52.3	11.4	21.5
No Parent in Home	16.5	17.0	16.3 *	36.6	4.4	20.0
Total	10.3	23.2	18.1	42.1	7.3	19.4

SOURCES: Estimates derived from 1940–1980 Census PUMS.

NOTES: See Table 4.1 for explanation and NOTES, Table 5.1.

* Sample size is at least 50 and less than 100.

† Sample size is less than 50.

TABLE 5.7

Children Aged 0–5 with Either a Surrogate Parent Present or Enrolled in School:
1940–1980

Total, Aged 0–5	1940	1950	1960	1970	1980
Employed Parent(s)					
Total	7.7	11.2	18.5	28.3	39.7
Two Parents	5.4	8.8	15.0	21.8	30.8
One Parent	2.3	2.4	3.5	6.5	8.9
Parent(s) Not Employed					
Total	87.3	84.1	78.6	68.8	55.3
Two Parents	85.0	81.3	74.7	63.1	48.1
One Parent	2.3	2.9	3.9	5.6	7.2
No Parent in Home					
Total	5.0	4.7	2.9	3.0	4.9
Employed Parent(s) and Potential Surrogate Parent in Home					
Total	2.3	2.9	2.9	3.3	3.3
Two parents	1.1	1.7	1.5	1.5	1.3
One parent	1.3	1.2	1.4	1.9	2.0
Employed Parent(s) and Either Potential Surrogate Parent in Home or Enrolled in Kindergarten or Elementary School					
Total	2.6	—	4.3	7.0	7.9
Two parents	1.3	—	2.7	4.3	4.9
One parent	1.3	—	1.7	2.6	3.0
Employed Parent(s) and Either Potential Surrogate Parent in Home or Enrolled in Kindergarten, Elementary School, or Nursery School					
Total	—	—	—	8.9	15.5
Two parents	—	—	—	5.9	10.8
One parent	—	—	—	3.1	4.7

SOURCES: Estimates derived from 1940–1980 Census PUMS.

NOTES: See Table 4.1 for explanation and Table 5.1 NOTES. Enrollment in kindergarten and elementary school not calculated for 1950 because data were collected for sample line persons only. Nursery school data available only for 1970 and 1980.

home? The answer is that between 1940 and 1980, the proportion of preschoolers who had both employed parents and a potential surrogate parent in the home remained remarkably stable at 2–3 percent (Table 5.7).

Since the proportion of preschoolers living in dual-earner or one-parent families with an employed parent increased from 8 to 40 percent during these years, the largest proportion of the need for nonparental care that could have been met by surrogate parents in the home dropped from less than one-third in 1940 to less than one-tenth in 1980. Clearly, potential surrogate parents in the homes of a small 2–3 percent of pre-schoolers may have provided needed child care that allowed parents to work. But it was equally clear that potential surrogate parents have not stepped in to fill the increasing need for nonparental care among pre-schoolers that resulted from the rise in parental employment between 1940 and 1980.

Parental Time Spent Caring for Preschoolers

The amount of time that parents devote to child care as their primary activity is only a portion of the time that is potentially available outside of paid work time, because parents have other responsibilities (such as meal preparation, housecleaning, yard work, laundry, and shopping) and because they engage in other personal-care and free-time activities (such as eating, sleeping, socializing, and other leisure and recreational pastimes). Of course, even when they are engaged in some of these other activities, parents may be providing child care as a secondary activity or their children may be present with them.

Estimates of the amount of time that parents devote to child care defined in various ways are available from four national studies of Americans' use of time conducted between 1965 and 1985. In a diary of daily activities, respondents were asked, What did you do during each hour of the day? Were you doing anything else, and with whom?[11] These results provide estimates of the time spent in child care as a primary activity, as a secondary activity, and as a "total contact time" with children.

Joseph H. Pleck found that among mothers in 1975 whose youngest child was aged 0–5, employed mothers devoted about one-half as much time to child care as a primary activity as did mothers who were not in the labor force (1.2 vs. 2.2 hours per day).[12] Compared with correspond-

[11]"Historical Changes in the Household Division of Labor," *Demography* 25, 4 (November 1988): 537–552; John P. Robinson, *How Americans Use Time* (New York: Praeger, 1977), p. 7; J. Thomas Juster and Frank P. Stafford, "Introduction and Overview," in F. Thomas Juster and Frank P. Stafford, eds., *Times, Goods, and Well-Being* (Ann Arbor: Survey Research Center, Institute for Social Research, University of Michigan, 1985), pp. 1–18; and Richard C. Taeuber and Richard C. Rockwell, "National Social Data Series: A Compendium of Brief Descriptions," *Review of Public Data Use* 10, 1–2 (May 1982): 23–111.

[12]Joseph H. Pleck, *Working Wives/Working Husbands* (Beverly Hills: Sage, 1985), p. 45.

ing mothers of preschoolers, employed and nonemployed mothers whose youngest child was aged 6–17 devoted about one-half as much time to primary-activity child care (about 0.5 and 1.2 hours per day, respectively).

Fathers devoted the same amount of time to primary-activity child care regardless of whether their wives worked (0.4 hours per day for fathers of preschoolers and 0.3 hours per day for fathers of school-age children). Hence, of the total parental time devoted to primary-activity child care, fathers in dual-earner families accounted for 26–33 percent and those in breadwinner-homemaker families accounted for 17–20 percent.

By comparison, of the total parental time devoted to primary-activity housework in 1975, fathers in dual-earner families accounted for 28–33 percent of the total and those in breadwinner-homemaker families accounted for 17–20 percent of the total. Of the total parental time devoted to primary-activity paid work, fathers in dual-earner families accounted for 59–63 percent, and by definition those in breadwinner-homemaker families accounted for 100 percent. Combining parental time devoted to housework, child care, and paid work as primary activities, fathers accounted for 49–57 percent of the total, depending upon the age of the youngest child as well as the mother's employment status. Of course, these estimates do not count secondary-activity child care and housework, which may differ substantially for fathers and mothers.

In their findings, Susan Goff Timmer, Jacquelynne Eccles, and Kerth O'Brien focused more precisely on "quality time" spent with children (of all ages)—that is, time that parents themselves report as having spent doing "quality child-related activities" as a primary activity, including, for example, time spent reading to a child or conversing or playing with the child."[13] They found that working mothers devoted about one-half as much time to quality child-related activities as did homemaker mothers, but that this time was comparatively small for both groups (only 1.9 and 3.7 hours per week, respectively). Fathers, they found, devoted about 1.1 hours per week to "quality child-related primary activity," which represents about 37 percent of the total time spent in dual-earner families and 23 percent of the total spent in breadwinner-homemaker families.

John P. Robinson found (using the 1965 survey) that only one-third of the time parents devoted to primary-activity child care (for children of all ages) was "interactional" (reading, playing, etc.) in nature, while two-thirds was "custodial" (feeding, clothing, chauffeuring, etc.). He also

[13]Susan Goff Timmer, Jacquelynne Eccles, and Kerth O'Brien, "How Families Use Time," *ISR Newsletter* (Ann Arbor: Institute for Social Research, University of Michigan, winter 1985–86), pp. 3–4.

found, however, that the bulk of *secondary*-activity child care consisted of interactional activities, and that the time devoted to secondary-activity child care was 50 percent as great as the time devoted to primary-activity child care.[14] Robinson's results imply, then, that the *total time* parents devoted to interactional child care was about two to three times as great as the time devoted to quality child-related *primary* activities.

Robinson further argues that the total contact time between parents and children—that is, the time they spend with one another—can be considered ". . . the upper limit of time that they would have available for their children."[15] In 1965, the total contact time employed and nonemployed women spend with their children (of all ages) was about 5.3 and 3.8 times, respectively, as great as that spent in primary-activity child care. Hence, employed women had about 39 percent as much total contact time with their children as did nonemployed mothers. Of the total parent-child contact time, the proportions accounted for by mothers and fathers were approximately 63 and 37 percent, respectively.

Historically, Joann Vanek analyzed about two dozen studies, apparently pertaining to "primary activities," showing that the time nonemployed mothers devoted to child care increased by 50–100 percent between 1926–1935 and 1943 and may have increased a bit more during the subsequent 20 years through 1965. The reason for this increase, Vanek suggests, is that "[t]oday's mother is cautioned to care for the child's social and mental development in addition to the traditional concerns of health, discipline and cleanliness."[16]

Pleck cites results for roughly the same period from one of the classic American community studies of a single town, indicating ". . . that both fathers and mothers spent more time with their children in 1978 than in 1924. About 10 percent of working class fathers were reported by their wives as spending no time with their children, compared to 2 percent in 1978—a change from one father in ten, to one in 50. The percentage of fathers spending more than an hour per day with their children increased significantly from 68 to 77 percent in the same group. . . . Figures in the 'business class' families were quite parallel."[17]

Unfortunately, direct estimates of change in the amount of time that mothers and fathers devoted to child care between 1965 and 1985 do not appear to have been published. Fortunately, however, studies concerned with the household division of labor have published relevant

[14]Robinson, *How Americans Use Time*, pp. 70–73.
[15] Robinson, p. 70.
[16]Joann Vanek, "Time Spent in Housework." In Alice H. Amsden, ed., *The Economics of Women and Work* (New York: St. Martin's), pp. 83–90. Reprinted from *Scientific American* 231 (November 1974): 116–120.
[17]Pleck, p. 142.

results concerning the primary-activity child care of all women and all men, whether or not they have children at home, and regarding all family work by men, including not only child care but also housework, yard work, and related tasks.[18]

In one of these studies, Gershuny and Robinson report that the primary-activity child care of all women aged 25–45 declined by about one-third (from about 71 to 47 minutes per day) between 1965 and 1985.[19] Since the proportion of women aged 25–44 who had a child aged 0–17 in the home declined by 10 percentage points during these two decades, the average amount of time that mothers devoted to primary-activity child care apparently declined by about 20–25 percent (from approximately 94 to 72 minutes per day). This was largely attributed to the fact that employment among the mothers of children increased, and employed mothers devoted about one-half as much time to child care as did nonemployed mothers.[20]

For men aged 25–44, primary-activity child care declined slightly between 1965 and 1985. But since the proportion of men with a child aged 0–17 in the home declined by about 19 percentage points between 1965 and 1985, it appears that fathers may have increased their primary-activity child care by about 15–20 percent from 24 to 28 minutes per day. Overall, then, since the time devoted to primary-activity child care declined substantially for mothers and appears to have increased for fathers between 1965 and 1985, the proportion of the total parental time accounted for by fathers appears to have increased across these two decades.

[18]Jonathan Gershuny and John P. Robinson, "Historical Change in the Household Division of Labor," *Demography* 25, 4 (November 1989): 537–552; and Pleck, pp. 145–146, citing F. Thomas Juster (in press), "A Note on Recent Changes in Time Use," in F. Thomas Juster and Frank Stafford, eds., *Studies in the Measurement of Time Allocation* (Ann Arbor: Institute for Social Research, University of Michigan), pp. 397–422.

[19]Gershuny and Robinson, pp. 537–552. These estimates are obtained by visual inspection from Figure 1.

[20]Estimates of the proportion of women and men aged 25–44 who had a child aged 0–17 in the home during various years were kindly provided by Arlene F. Saluter, based on data for married-couple and one-parent families and subfamilies. Ninety percent of one-parent families and subfamilies in 1965 were assumed to be maintained by mothers. Ages 25–44 pertains to the age of the reference person in married-couple families and subfamilies. Among persons aged 25–44, the proportion of females who had a child in the home was 75.6 percent in 1965 and 65.4 percent in 1985; for males, it was 72.8 percent in 1965 and 54.2 percent in 1985. These results were calculated from Arlene F. Saluter, U.S. Bureau of the Census, Current Population Reports, Series P-20, *Marital Status and Living Arrangement* (Washington, DC: U.S. Government Printing Office). Table 1, March 1965 and March 1985. See also Steve W. Rawlings, *Household and Family Characteristics*, Table 7, March 1965 and Tables 3 and 14, March 1985. Report numbers are 140, 144, 410, and 411.

Kindergarten and Nursery School Enrollment

With the rapid postwar expansion of kindergarten, the proportion of 5-year-olds who were enrolled in school on April 1 nearly quadrupled, climbing from only 19–20 percent in 1920–1940 to 76 percent in 1980.[21] More recently, nursery school enrollment also expanded rapidly, more than doubling between 1970 and 1980 (from 7 to 19 percent for 5-year-olds, 18 to 42 percent for 4-year-olds, and 10 to 23 percent for 3-year-olds). Since kindergarten and nursery school last at least several hours per school day, it is clear that organized educational programs have become an important component of the care received by many children beginning by age 3.

One might suppose, then, that the large increase in parental employment during the same decades, and the associated rise in the need for nonparental care, contributed to these increases in kindergarten and nursery school enrollment. In fact, however, parental employment appears to have had little, if any, effect on kindergarten enrollment, since the kindergarten enrollment rates in each census year from 1940 to 1980 differed by no more than a few percentage points for children living with the same number of parents but with different patterns of parental employment (Tables 5.4 and 5.6).

As might be expected, since parents may exercise more discretion over whether their children attend nursery school than over whether they attend kindergarten, parental employment appears to have had a larger, but still small, effect on nursery school enrollment. For example, Paul M. Siegel and Rosalind R. Bruno estimate that the increase in mothers' labor-force participation accounted for no more than 10 percent of the rise in nursery school enrollment among children aged 3–5 during the decade from October 1972 to October 1982.[22]

[21]Enrollment and age data as of April 1 during census years. In 1950–1980, 78–89 percent of 5-year-olds enrolled in school were attending kindergarten or a higher grade. Tables 166–167, U.S. Bureau of the Census, *U.S. Census of Population: 1960. Vol. I, Characteristics of the Population. Part 1. United States Summary* (Washington, DC: U.S. Government Printing Office, 1986); U.S. Bureau of the Census, *Census of the Population: 1970. Vol. I, Characteristics of the Population. Part 1, United States Summary—Section 2* (Washington, DC: U.S. Government Printing Office, 1973), Table 197; U.S. Bureau of the Census, *1980 Census of the Population. Vol. I. Characteristics of the Population. Chapter D. Detailed Characteristics of the Population. Part 1. United States Summary. PC80-1-D1-A. Section A: United States. Tables 253–310.* (Washington, DC: U.S. Government Printing Office, March 1984), Table 260.

[22]Paul M. Siegel and Rosalind R. Bruno, U.S. Bureau of the Census, Current Population Reports, Series P-20, No. 408. *School Enrollment—Social and Economic Characteristics of Students: October 1982* (Washington, DC: U.S. Government Printing Office, 1986), p. 2.

Decennial Census Data for April 1 of 1970 and 1980 indicate that nursery-school enrollment rates approximately doubled for 3- and 4-year-olds within specific categories of parental presence and employment status. For example, among children who had a parent at home full-time in a breadwinner-homemaker family, nursery school enrollment jumped from 8–9 to 15–19 percent for 3-year-olds and from 16–17 to 31–40 percent for 4-year-olds. Similarly, at the opposite extreme among children with parents who worked full-time, nursery school enrollment jumped from 15–16 to 32–38 percent for 3-year-olds and from 24 to 45–51 percent for 4-year-olds.

The large increases for all children, regardless of the number and employment status of parents in the home, indicate that much of the increase in nursery school enrollment resulted from forces other than the rise in parental employment. Still, in both 1970 and 1980 nursery-school enrollment rates for children with parents employed part-time or full-time were substantially higher than for children who had a specific parent at home full-time, and the enrollment rate gap approximately doubled during the 1970s. Taken together, these results suggest that the rise in dual-earner and one-parent families with an employed parent were responsible for a noteworthy, albeit fairly small, proportion of the rise in nursery school enrollment for children aged 3–5.

Although increasing kindergarten and nursery school enrollment apparently did not result mainly from increasing parental employment, enrollment increases have continued to represent a potentially important source of child care for the increasing proportion of preschool children living in dual-earner and one-parent families with employed parents. In fact, as the proportion of the potential need for nonparental care that might be met by potential surrogate parents declined among preschool children with working parents, an approximately offsetting increase occurred in the enrollment rates recorded for organized educational programs.

Between 1940 and 1980, the proportion of preschool children living in dual-earner and one-parent families in which there was an employed parent increased from 8 to 40 percent. Of these children, while the proportion who had a potential surrogate parent declined from 30 to 8 percent between 1940 and 1980, the proportion who had a potential surrogate parent *or* were enrolled in nursery school, kindergarten, or elementary school increased somewhat from about 34 to 39 percent. These estimates indicate that organized educational programs for pre-elementary school children have become important sources of nonparental care, and at least potentially important as sources of nonparental care while parents are at work.

Child Care Arrangements While Parents Work

Who provides the child care for preschoolers whose parents are employed in the labor force? Special child care surveys conducted by the U.S. Bureau of the Census provide the answer for children who live with employed mothers.[23] Among preschoolers whose mothers were employed during the winter of 1984–1985, for example, 8 percent had mothers who managed to work and care for them simultaneously; and about one-half of these preschoolers (4 percent) had mothers who were employed as private household workers or as child care workers. An additional 16 percent of preschoolers whose mothers were employed were cared for by their fathers while their mothers worked. Many of these latter preschoolers probably had parents who worked different hours or days and who, consequently, spent comparatively little time together.[24]

Relatives other than parents provided care for about 24 percent of preschoolers with an employed mother, and about two-thirds of this child care was provided by grandparents. Since about 8 percent of preschoolers in dual-earner and one-parent families with a working parent had a potential surrogate parent in the home in 1980, and since 9 percent of preschoolers with an employed mother were cared for by nonparental relatives in a home other than the preschoolers' home during the winter of 1984–1985, it appears that when potential surrogate parents are available in the home, they often do provide necessary child care when parents are at work. But there is also evidence that at least 60 percent of the care provided by nonparental relatives was supplied by relatives who did not live with the child.

Finally, 50 percent of preschoolers with an employed mother were cared for by nonrelatives—specifically, 6 percent in the preschoolers' own home, 22 percent in another home, and 24 percent in an organized child care facility such as a nursery school or day-care center. Since the proportion of preschoolers who were cared for in an organized facility is only slightly larger than the proportions living in dual-earner or one-parent families who had an employed parent but no potential surrogate parent in the home (17–21 vs. 24 percent), it again appears that if a potential surrogate parent is available in the home, it is that person rather than an organized child care facility who provides care.

[23]Martin O'Connell and Amara Bachu, U.S. Bureau of the Census, Current Population Reports, Series P-70, No. 9, *Who's Minding the Kids? Child Care Arrangements: Winter 1984–1985* (Washington, DC: U.S. Government Printing Office, 1987), Table B.

[24]For an analysis of parental work schedules and child care needs, see Harriet B. Presser, "Can We Make Time for Children? The Economy, Work Schedules, and Child Care," *Demography* 26 (1989): 523–543.

Despite this apparent preference, however, preschoolers with an employed mother who were cared for by nonparental relatives declined by 9 percentage points (from 31 to 22 percent between 1977 and 1987), and the proportion in an organized child care facility increased by 11 percentage points (from 13 to 24 percent).[25]

When these estimates of the proportion of preschoolers living in families with various parental living and employment arrangements are combined with those made for 1989, we can then calculate the proportion of all preschoolers who have various child care arrangements.[26] Among all preschoolers in 1989, about 48 percent had a specific parent in the home full-time who was not in the labor force. An additional 12 percent had parents who personally provided their preschoolers' care (often by working different hours or days, or by the mother combining work and child care), and about 15 percent were cared for by other relatives who often did not live in the preschoolers' home. Hence, a total of 27 percent of preschoolers were cared for by relatives—including parents— other than a specific parent who was available full-time for child care; and about 25 percent were cared for by nonrelatives, approximately half of these in organized care facilities.

Potential Effects of Nonparental Child Care

Since the decline in the proportion of children who had a specific parent at home full-time, as well as the rise in nonparental care, are accounted for by the rise in mothers' labor-force participation in association with continued high labor-force participation rates among fathers in the home and the rise of mother-only families, there has been increasing interest in another question: What are the beneficial and detrimental effects of mothers' employment and nonparental care on children, especially preschoolers? The research addressing this question is recent and few effects have yet been found, but both beneficial and detrimental factors have recently been identified, though in only a preliminary and tentative way.

One obvious and beneficial effect of mothers' employment, at least in two-parent families, is that two working parents can earn more income than one parent alone is likely to earn. In Chapters 9 and 10, we

[25]Martin O'Connell and Amara Bachu, U.S. Bureau of the Census, Current Population Reports, Series P-70, No. 20. *Who's Minding the Kids? Child Care Arrangements: 1986–87* (Washington, DC: U.S. Government Printing Office, 1990), Table C.

[26]The latest estimates of child care arrangements made for preschoolers with employed mothers in 1986 and 1987 are not statistically significantly different from the estimates for the winter of 1984–1985. See O'Connell and Bachu, 1990.

will discuss in detail the important role mothers' work plays in helping to maintain or improve the family incomes of children and in reducing childhood poverty.

Focusing on children themselves, a 1983 National Academy of Sciences report on the children of working parents concluded that existing research had not demonstrated that mothers' employment has either beneficial or detrimental effects on either children's development or their educational future. The report went on to emphasize, however, that because of limitations in existing research, it also was not possible to conclude that mothers' employment is irrelevant to children's development.[27]

More recent research has identified, largely in a preliminary and tentative way, specific potentially beneficial and potentially detrimental effects of mothers' employment and nonparental child care. The most recent National Academy of Sciences report on child care reviews this burgeoning literature in some detail.[28]

One of the best-documented but potentially detrimental effects of day care is Harriet B. Presser's finding that preschool children cared for outside their home have a substantially higher prevalence of medicated respiratory illness than do preschoolers who are cared for solely in their own homes (by parents or others).[29] Within a two-week period, about 27 percent of preschoolers cared for at home experience such an illness, compared with about 38 percent for preschoolers in formal day-care settings. Presser emphasizes that these differences remain after controlling for the age, sex, and race of the child, and for family income, number of siblings, number of persons in the household, and number of caretakers.

Presser also points out, however, the possibility that day care itself may not be the cause of these differences. It is conceivable that parents who rely on day care outside the home are more likely (for some reason other than the factors controlled for and listed above) to medicate their children for respiratory illnesses. Nevertheless, Presser points out that whatever the cause of the differences, respiratory illnesses are discomforting, and medicated illnesses may involve economic costs for medication, physician visits, and work missed by employed parents who may need to stay home in order to care for a sick child.

[27]Cheryl D. Hayes and Sheila B. Kamerman, eds., *Children of Working Parents: Experiences and Outcomes*, a report of the Panel on Work, Family and Community of the Committee on Child Development Research and Public Policy (Washington, DC: National Academy, 1983), pp. 221–222.

[28]Cheryl D. Hayes, John L. Palmer, and Martha J. Zaslow, eds., *Who Cares for America's Children?*, a report of the Panel of Child Care Policy, Committee on Child Development Research and Public Policy (Washington, DC: National Academy, 1990).

[29]Harriet B. Presser, "Place of Child Care and Medicated Respiratory Illness Among Young American Children," *Journal of Marriage and the Family* 50 (1988): 995–1005.

In addition, the recent National Academy of Sciences review of research on physical health and safety in child care cites the possibility (which is in "urgent" need of further study) that the comparatively frequent respiratory illnesses among children under age 3 who participate in child care outside the home may lead to more frequent middle-ear infections and, hence, to lasting harmful effects on hearing and language development.[30]

Turning to the effects of early childhood education programs, such as Head Start, Ron Haskins concludes in his review of research done through 1988 that by the end of a year, the programs produce beneficial effects on intellectual performance, socioemotional development, and social competence.[31] However, the size of these effects declines within a few years of leaving the programs. Haskins also concludes that limited but intriguing evidence suggests that model (experimental) preschool education programs may have beneficial effects on teen pregnancy, delinquency, welfare use, and employment, but that there is little evidence linking Head Start to these beneficial outcomes.

In a more recent longitudinal study of children born in 1981–1982 to women who gave birth between the ages of 16 and 25, Sonalde Desai, P. Lindsay Chase-Lansdale, and Robert T. Michael report that among 4-year-old boys living in families whose income is at least somewhat above the poverty threshold, mothers' employment appears to have an adverse effect on intellectual performance if the mother is employed during the first year of the child's life.[32] Since the children in this study were born to relatively early childbearers, they have mothers whose education and family incomes are somewhat lower than children as a whole. But as a national study providing the first large sample estimates of this type, the conclusions are potentially quite important.

In reviewing research on the effects of mothers' employment in two-parent families, Lois Wladis Hoffman concludes that parents in dual-earner families place greater stress on independence training for children than do other parents. This is a potentially important finding because, as we will see in Chapter 6, independence is a characteristic that becomes advantageous during adulthood when occupations with high social prestige and high incomes are at stake.[33]

Hoffman and, in another review of research on womens' employ-

[30]Hayes, Palmer, and Zaslow, pp. 109, 115.

[31]Ron Haskins, "Beyond Metaphor: The Efficacy of Early Childhood Education," *American Psychologist* 44 (1989): 274–282.

[32] Sonalde Desai, P. Lindsay Chase-Lansdale, and Robert T. Michael, "Mother or Market? Effects of Maternal Employment on Intellectual Ability of 4-Year-Old Children," *Demography* 26 (1989): 545–561.

[33]Lois Wladis Hoffman, "Effects of Maternal Employment in the Two-Parent Family," *American Psychologist* 44 (1989): 283–299.

ment and family relations, Glenna Spitze also conclude that children whose mothers are employed exhibit less sex-role traditionalism and more egalitarian sex-role attitudes than do children whose mothers are not employed. They further conclude that daughters may benefit from mothers' employment in their social adjustment, school performance, and occupational attainments.[34]

In two additional reviews of research on the effects of day care, Jay Belsky and K. Alison Clarke-Stewart conclude that infants in day care whose mothers work full-time are less likely than other infants to positively greet their mothers following a brief separation and more likely to avoid psychological contact with the mother by moving away from her or by avoiding direct eye contact after a brief separation.[35] Clarke-Stewart estimates that the proportion of infants who avoid their mothers after a brief separation is 36 percent for infants whose mothers work full-time, compared with 29 percent for other infants. Researchers disagree on the implications and causes of this difference, however.

Belsky points out that infants who exhibit the mother-avoiding behavior tend later, as toddlers and preschoolers, to be less able to empathize with others, less compliant, and less cooperative, as well as more at risk of developing behavioral problems by the age of 5 or 6. On the other hand, Clarke-Stewart presents reasons to believe that this behavior may have a different meaning for infants in day care than for infants in home care, and that it is not yet known whether the mother-avoiding infants of employed mothers experience these problems later in childhood.

Belsky and Clarke-Stewart also conclude that children who were placed in day care as infants are more likely than other children to disobey their mothers and to be aggressive toward other children. While disobedience and aggression are usually viewed as negative behaviors, Clarke-Stewart suggests that it is possible that these behaviors reflect greater independence rather than negative behavioral responses: "Children who have spent time in day care, then, may be more demanding and independent, more disobedient and aggressive, more bossy and bratty than children who stay at home, because they want their own way and do not have the skills to achieve it smoothly, rather than because they are maladjusted."[36]

Although scholars do not agree on the meaning and implications of

[34]Glenna Spitze, "Women's Employment and Family Relations: A Review," *Journal of Marriage and the Family* 50 (1988): 595–618.

[35]Jay Belsky, "Developmental Risks Associated with Infant Day Care: Attachment Insecurity, Noncompliance, and Aggression?" In S. Chehrazi, ed., *Balancing Working and Parenting: Psychological and Developmental Implications of Day Care* (New York: American Psychiatric, 1990), pp. 37–68; and K. Alison Clarke-Stewart, "Infant Day Care: Maligned or Malignant?" *American Psychologist* 44 (1989): 266–273.

[36]K. Alison Clarke-Stewart, p. 269.

these differences between day-care and home-care children with regard to mother-avoiding, noncompliant, and aggressive behavior, they do agree that the cause of the differences is not clear. While the differences may be due to day care as such, it is also possible that they are partly or completely due to other preexisting differences between families themselves, or that they depend on the quality of the day care provided. With regard to the measurement and possible consequences of high-quality child care, a recent review by Deborah A. Phillips and Carollee Howes highlights the difficulties and complexities in this new but important area of research.[37]

Despite limitations in the existing research, the recent National Academy of Sciences review suggests the following broad conclusions.

> Child care participation is not a form of maternal deprivation. Children can and do form attachment relationships to multiple caregivers, if the number of caregivers is limited, the relationships enduring, and the caregivers are responsive to the individual child.
>
> Child care is not inevitably or pervasively harmful to children's development. Indeed, the evidence points to aspects of development for which child care is beneficial.
>
> The quality of child care . . . is important to children's development, whatever their socioeconomic levels. . . .
>
> Children from families enduring greater psychological and economic stress are more likely to be found in lower quality care settings. Thus, there are children in the United States, especially those from low-income families, in double jeopardy from stress both at home and in their care environments.
>
> There is no strong basis in our review for urging parents toward or away from enrolling children in child care settings.[38]

Because most of the more specific research findings about the potential psychological and behavioral effects of day care for preschoolers remain quite tentative, it is apparent that this area of research is in its infancy and much remains to be done. Since the proportion of preschoolers who have a specific parent at home full-time declined from about 89 to 48 percent between 1960 and 1989, it also appears that we are roughly midway through the preschool child-care revolution and that this revolution may be complete within 30 years. Hence, it is possible that the preschool child-care revolution will be complete before we have

[37]Deborah A. Phillips and Carollee Howes, "Indicators of Quality in Child Care: Review of Research." In Deborah A. Phillips, ed., *Quality in Child Care: What Does Research Tell Us?* (Washington, DC: National Association for the Education of Young Children, 1987), pp. 1–20.

[38]Hayes, Palmer, and Zaslow, p. 77.

a detailed understanding of the effects, or lack of effects, that day care has on children aged 0–5.

The Racial Gap
in Potential Parental Time for Children

Between 1940 and 1989, the racial gap in the proportion of children who had a specific parent at home full-time narrowed from about 24 to 11 percentage points. Specifically, in 1940 the proportion of children who had a specific parent at home full-time was about 61 percent for blacks and 85 percent for whites (Table 5.8).[39] By 1989, the proportions had declined to 37 percent for blacks and 39 percent for whites.

In 1940, racial differences in dual-earner families and one-parent families with an employed parent accounted for approximately equal proportions of the overall racial gap in a child's chances of having a specific parent at home full-time. Between 1940 and 1989, the rise in dual-earner families accounted for about 60 percent of the decline in the proportion of black children who had a parent at home full-time and for 80 percent of the decline for white children.

The racial gap among adolescents who had a parent at home full-time essentially vanished, shrinking from 27 percentage points in 1940 to no difference in 1989 (Table 5.8). As of 1989, only 30 percent of black adolescents and 30 percent of white adolescents had a parent at home full-time, while the proportion in one-parent families with an employed parent was 32 percent for blacks and 16 percent for whites and the proportion in dual-earner families was 28 percent for blacks and 51 percent for whites. Among adolescents living with two parents, however, blacks were substantially more likely than whites to live in a dual-earner family both in 1940 (21 vs. 8 percent) and 1980 (63 vs. 55 percent), but by 1989 the racial gap had vanished (66–67 percent).

Among preschool children, the racial gap in the proportion who had a parent at home full-time remained fairly constant (18–23 percentage points) between 1940 and 1980 but had nearly vanished by 1989 (3 percentage points). In 1940, about 69 percent of black preschoolers and 90 percent of white preschoolers had a parent at home full-time. During the next 40 years, both proportions declined by about 30 percentage points

[39]Because children living in unrelated subfamilies with one or both parents in 1940 and 1950 are classified in Table 5.8 as living in a no-parent situation, the proportion living with parents in 1940 and 1950 is 0–6 percentage points greater for black children than is indicated in Table 5.8, and about 0–2 percentage points greater for white children.

TABLE 5.8

*White and Black Children, by Parental Presence and Employment Status:
1940–1989*

White Aged 0–17	1940	1950	1960	1970	1980	1989
Total Number (in thousands)	35,487	40,808	56,648	60,422	54,879	53,982
Percent	100.0	100.0	100.0	100.0	100.0	100.0
Breadwinner-Homemaker, total	78.1	73.7	67.3	54.9	40.2	28.1
Breadwinner-Homemaker, Intact	65.7	61.3	56.3	45.5	31.0	} NA
Breadwinner-Homemaker, Blended	12.5	12.4	11.0	9.5	9.1	
Two-Parent Family, Father Not Breadwinner	3.0	3.1	2.1	2.7	3.2	4.7
One-Parent Family, Not a Breadwinner	3.8	3.1	2.9	3.6	4.2	6.1
Dual-Earner Family, Employed Full Time	2.9	6.8	10.4	13.7	19.0	22.3
One-Parent Family, Employed Full Time	2.6	2.8	3.1	4.9	7.1	8.7
Dual-Earner Family, Employed Part Time	2.8	5.4	10.4	15.2	19.6	24.3
One-Parent Family, Employed Part Time	1.6	0.8	1.1	1.9	2.8	4.1
No Parent in Home	5.3	4.3	2.7	3.1	4.0	1.8

Black Aged 0–17	1940	1950	1960	1970	1980	1989
Total Number (in thousands)	4,548	5,497	8,134	9,707	9,707	9,920
Percent	100.0	100.0	100.0	100.0	100.0	100.0
Breadwinner-Homemaker, total	53.5	48.5	40.0	25.7	13.7	8.1
Breadwinner-Homemaker, Intact	36.7	32.1	26.9	16.9	8.1	} NA
Breadwinner-Homemaker, Blended	16.8	16.4	13.1	8.8	5.6	
Two-Parent Family, Father Not Breadwinner	2.6	3.0	3.6	5.0	4.4	5.2
One-Parent Family, Not a Breadwinner	4.5	7.7	9.8	15.6	17.8	23.3
Dual-Earner Family, Employed Full Time	3.8	6.2	9.3	14.4	16.9	14.7
One-Parent Family, Employed Full Time	5.4	5.8	6.8	11.0	15.2	18.0
Dual-Earner Family, Employed Part Time	7.4	7.6	13.6	12.1	11.7	9.8
One-Parent Family, Employed Part Time	4.7	2.7	4.7	6.4	9.0	13.2
No Parent in Home	18.1*	18.4	12.1	9.8	11.2	7.7

TABLE 5.8 (*continued*)

White Aged 0–5	1940	1950	1960	1970	1980	1989
Total Number (in thousands)	10,890	16,608	21,503	17,865	16,725	18,895
Percent	100.0	100.0	100.0	100.0	100.0	100.0
Breadwinner-Homemaker, total	85.6	81.4	77.1	65.9	50.7	35.5
Breadwinner-Homemaker, Intact	74.0	69.2	65.6	55.5	39.6	NA
Breadwinner-Homemaker, Blended	11.6	12.2	11.5	10.4	11.0	
Two-Parent Family, Father Not Breadwinner	2.1	3.0	1.7	2.2	2.6	4.9
One-Parent Family, Not a Breadwinner	2.1	2.2	2.9	3.7	4.8	7.6
Dual-Earner Family, Employed Full Time	2.4	4.5	6.4	9.4	13.8	18.5
One-Parent Family, Employed Full Time	1.2	1.5	2.0	3.6	4.4	5.6
Dual-Earner Family, Employed Part Time	2.4	4.0	7.7	11.8	18.0	23.0
One-Parent Family, Employed Part Time	0.6	0.5	0.8	1.5	2.2	3.9
No Parent in Home	3.6	2.9	1.5	1.9	3.6	1.1

Black Aged 0–5	1940	1950	1960	1970	1980	1989
Total Number (in thousands)	1,494	2,193	3,305	3,030	2,994	3,408
Percent	100.0	100.0	100.0	100.0	100.0	100.0
Breadwinner-Homemaker, total	63.0	54.2	45.7	30.0	16.4	9.8
Breadwinner-Homemaker, Intact	46.3	37.8	31.1	20.2	10.4	NA
Breadwinner-Homemaker, Blended	16.7	16.4	14.7	9.8	6.0	
Two-Parent Family, Father Not Breadwinner	2.2	3.5	2.6	4.1	2.7	5.0
One-Parent Family, Not a Breadwinner	3.3	7.7	10.8	16.9	21.1	30.0
Dual-Earner Family, Employed Full Time	3.3	4.9	7.9	13.8	13.7	12.1
One-Parent Family, Employed Full Time	2.9	3.6	5.0	8.9	12.3	15.2
Dual-Earner Family, Employed Part Time	6.5	5.8	12.3	11.5	11.4	8.2
One-Parent Family, Employed Part Time	3.2	2.1	3.6	5.7	9.8	14.4
No Parent in Home	15.7	18.2	12.0	9.1	12.5	5.3

TABLE 5.8 (continued)

White Aged 12–17	1940	1950	1960	1970	1980	1989
Total Number (in thousands)	12,978	11,178	16,280	20,971	20,237	16,997
Percent	100.0	100.0	100.0	100.0	100.0	100.0
Breadwinner-Homemaker, total	70.4	62.5	54.0	45.2	31.9	20.9
Breadwinner-Homemaker, Intact	58.2	50.5	44.3	36.7	24.7	} NA
Breadwinner-Homemaker, Blended	12.2	12.0	9.7	8.5	7.3	
Two-Parent, Father Not Breadwinner	3.8	3.6	3.0	3.3	4.1	4.7
One-Parent Family, Not a Breadwinner	5.5	4.3	3.1	3.5	3.7	4.7
Dual-Earner Family, Employed Full Time	3.2	9.8	15.7	17.6	22.9	26.5
One-Parent Family, Employed Full Time	4.0	4.8	4.6	6.0	8.6	11.8
Dual-Earner Family, Employed Part Time	3.1	6.6	12.7	17.2	20.4	24.2
One-Parent Family, Employed Part Time	2.3	1.3	1.6	2.3	3.0	3.9
No Parent in Home	7.6	7.2	5.3	4.8	5.4	3.3

Black Aged 12–17	1940	1950	1960	1970	1980	1989
Total Number (in thousands)	1,556	1,540	2,042	3,161	3,516	3,172
Percent	100.0	100.0	100.0	100.0	100.0	100.0
Breadwinner-Homemaker, total	44.0	41.6	30.6	21.1	12.1	7.4
Breadwinner-Homemaker, Intact	28.5	26.5	20.4	13.9	7.1	} NA
Breadwinner-Homemaker, Blended	15.5	15.1	10.2	7.2	5.1	
Two-Parent Family, Father Not Breadwinner	3.1	2.8	5.0	6.2	5.6	5.8
One-Parent Family, Not a Breadwinner	5.8	7.7	8.5	14.0	15.9	16.8
Dual-Earner Family, Employed Full Time	4.6	7.0	10.5	14.5	18.3	17.5
One-Parent Family, Employed Full Time	6.9	8.1	10.1	13.1	16.8	20.5
Dual-Earner Family, Employed Part Time	7.8	9.2	15.1	11.8	11.7	10.5
One-Parent Family, Employed Part Time	6.2	3.8	6.4	7.3	8.8	11.8
No Parent in Home	21.5	19.8	13.8	12.1	10.7	9.7

SOURCES: Estimates derived from 1940–1980 Census PUMS.

NOTES: See Table 4.1 for explanation and NOTES, Table 5.1.

NA Not available.

(to 40 percent for blacks and 58 percent for whites), and by 1989 they had declined further (to 45–48 percent for both blacks and whites).

In 1940 the proportion of preschoolers living in dual-earner families was 10 percent for blacks and 5 percent for whites, but these proportions had jumped to 25 and 32 percent, respectively, by 1980; by 1989 they had increased to 42 percent for whites but declined to 20 percent for blacks. However, among preschoolers living with two parents, blacks were substantially more likely than whites to live in a dual-earner family in 1940 (13 vs. 5 percent), 1980 (57 vs. 37 percent), and 1989 (58 vs. 51 percent). The proportion of all black preschoolers living in a one-parent family with an employed parent has also been larger than that for whites. The proportion was 6 percent for blacks and 2 percent for whites in 1940, but by 1980 these figures had increased—for both blacks and whites—to 22 and 7 percent, respectively, and to 30 and 10 percent, respectively, by 1989.

Overall, in 1980 about one-half of the racial gap in the proportion of preschoolers who did not have a parent at home full-time was accounted for by the racial difference in the proportion whose parents were employed (47 vs. 38 percent), and about one-half was accounted for by the racial difference in the proportion who had no parent in the home (13 vs. 4 percent). This was not greatly different in 1940.

The Racial Gap in Nonparental Child Care

Despite the differences between black and white preschoolers in the proportion whose families have specific parental living and employment arrangements, black and white preschoolers in similar family situations have been fairly similar in their chances of having a potential surrogate parent in the home (Table 5.9).

For example, in 1940 across parental employment situations, about 40–60 percent of black and white preschoolers living with one parent had a potential surrogate parent in the home, compared with only 15–25 percent for preschoolers living with two parents. Hence, the differences of 15–45 percentage points between preschoolers in two-parent and those in one-parent families were generally larger than the 10-20 percentage point differences found to exist within two-parent and one-parent families by parental employment status. By 1980 the patterns had changed little, but the proportions who had a potential surrogate parent in the home dropped substantially (to 18–31 percent for preschoolers living with one parent and 3–10 percent for preschoolers living with two parents).

TABLE 5.9

White and Black Children Aged 0–5 with Surrogate Parent Present in Home: 1940–1980

White	1940	1950	1960	1970	1980
Percent with Surrogate Parent in Home					
Breadwinner-Homemaker, total	14.6	11.0	5.6	4.2	3.3
Breadwinner-Homemaker, Intact	14.6	10.8	5.0	4.0	3.0
Breadwinner-Homemaker, Blended	14.6	12.0	8.6	5.1	4.4
Two-Parent Family, Father Not Breadwinner	24.7	12.7	16.9	8.5	4.8
One-Parent Family, Not a Breadwinner	52.3	42.0	31.1	25.6	18.1
Dual-Earner Family, Employed Full Time	18.9	22.4	10.6	7.3	4.6
One-Parent Family, Employed Full Time	57.8	52.5	45.5	30.1	19.4
Dual-Earner Family, Employed Part Time	20.7	15.1	7.2	5.7	3.9
One-Parent Family, Employed Part Time	59.2 *	61.5	31.9	21.7	20.5
Total	16.1	12.9	7.8	6.7	5.3

Black	1940	1950	1960	1970	1980
Percent with Surrogate Parent in Home					
Breadwinner-Homemaker, total	19.9	21.7	14.2	11.1	9.1
Breadwinner-Homemaker, Intact	18.4	20.4	14.7	9.5	8.7
Breadwinner-Homemaker, Blended	23.8	24.6	13.2	14.5	10.0
Two-Parent Family, Father Not Breadwinner	31.9 *	35.0	24.1 *	14.4	14.6 *
One-Parent Family, Not a Breadwinner	48.6 *	49.2	31.5	23.2	26.1
Dual-Earner Family, Employed Full Time	18.6 *	26.5	13.8	7.7	6.6
One-Parent Family, Employed Full Time	54.8 *	42.0	37.8	37.5	21.5
Dual-Earner Family, Employed Part Time	19.4	19.7	15.0	10.3	5.3
One-Parent Family, Employed Part Time	39.7 *	43.7 *	38.3	20.9	31.0
Total	19.5	21.6	16.7	14.6	14.6

SOURCES: Estimates derived from 1940–1980 Census PUMS.

NOTES: See Table 4.1 for explanation, and NOTES, Table 5.1.

* Sample size is at least 50 and less than 100.

Hence, for both black and white preschoolers, as the chances of living in dual-earner and one-parent families with an employed parent rose sharply, there was a corresponding sharp drop in the chance that these children would have a potential surrogate parent in the home. These changes tended to offset each other, however, and the proportion of all preschoolers who had both employed parents and a potential surrogate parent remained fairly constant between 1940–1980—at 5–7 percent for black preschoolers and 2–3 percent for white preschoolers (Table 5.10).

Because the need for nonparental care was increasing rapidly, the proportion of preschoolers in need of nonparental care who had a potential surrogate parent in the home dropped from 30 percent for both blacks and whites in 1940 to 15 percent for blacks and 7 percent for whites in 1980. These proportions for 1980 were about the same as the proportions recorded in the winter of 1984–1985 for preschoolers with an employed mother whose primary child-care arrangement was provided by a nonparental relative in the child's home (19.3 and 7.6 percent for blacks and whites, respectively).

Overall, however, between 1940 and 1980, among preschoolers who did not have a specific parent at home full-time, the proportion who had no potential surrogate parent and were not enrolled in nursery school, kindergarten, or elementary school declined from 68 to 51 percent for blacks and remained constant at 63–65 percent for whites (Table 5.10).

Parental Time and Child Care for Hispanic Children

In 1980, Hispanic children (of any race) were quite similar to non-Hispanic whites in their parental living and work arrangements with two exceptions (Table 5.11). Hispanic children (of any race) were 8 percentage points less likely to live in a dual-earner family in which at least one parent worked part-time and 8 percentage points more likely to live in a one-parent family in which the parent was not employed. Hence, Hispanic children (of any race) were generally similar to non-Hispanic whites in their chances of having a specific parent at home full-time. These same conclusions generally apply to Hispanic preschoolers and school-age children (of any race).

Despite the large differences between the parental living and employment arrangements of Hispanic preschoolers (of any race) and non-Hispanic white preschoolers on one hand, and those of non-Hispanic black preschoolers on the other, all three groups are fairly equal in their chances of having a potential surrogate parent in the home, given a specific parental living and employment arrangement. Similarly, large dif-

TABLE 5.10

White and Black Children Aged 0–5 with Either a Surrogate Parent or Enrolled in School: 1940–1980

White	1940	1950	1960	1970	1980
Employed Parent(s)					
Total	6.6	10.5	16.9	26.3	38.4
Two parents	4.8	8.6	14.2	21.2	31.8
One parent	1.8	2.0	2.7	5.1	6.6
Parent Not Employed					
Total	89.8	86.6	81.6	71.8	58.1
Two parents	87.7	84.4	78.8	68.1	53.3
One parent	2.1	2.2	2.9	3.7	4.8
No Parent in Home					
Total	3.6	2.9	1.5	1.9	3.6
Employed Parent(s) and Potential Surrogate Parent in Home					
Total	2.0	2.7	2.4	2.8	2.6
Two parents	0.9	1.6	1.2	1.4	1.3
One parent	1.1	1.1	1.1	1.4	1.3
Employed Parent(s) and Either Potential Surrogate Parent in Home or Enrolled in Kindergarten or Elementary School					
Total	2.3	—	3.7	6.2	6.9
Two parents	1.2	—	2.4	4.1	4.9
One parent	1.1	—	1.3	2.1	2.1
Employed Parent(s) and Either Potential Surrogate Parent in Home or Enrolled in Kindergarten or Elementary School or Nursery School					
Total	—	—	—	8.1	14.2
Two parents	—	—	—	5.6	10.7
One parent	—	—	—	2.4	3.4

ferences between Hispanic preschoolers (of any race) and non-Hispanic preschoolers do not exist in the proportion enrolled in elementary school, kindergarten, or nursery school.

More recent results for the winter of 1984–1985 concerning the actual primary child-care arrangement for preschoolers with employed

TABLE 5.10 (*continued*)

Black	1940	1950	1960	1970	1980
Employed Parent(s)					
Total	15.9	16.4	28.8	39.8	47.2
Two parents	9.8	10.7	20.2	25.2	25.1
One parent	6.1	5.7	8.6	14.6	22.1
Parent Not Employed					
Total	68.5	65.4	59.2	51.1	40.3
Two parents	65.2	57.7	48.4	34.2	19.2
One parent	3.3	7.7	10.8	16.9	21.1
No Parent in Home					
Total	15.7	18.2	12.0	9.1	12.5
Employed Parent(s) and Potential Surrogate Parent in Home					
Total	4.7	4.9	6.2	6.8	7.2
Two parents	1.9	2.4	2.9	2.2	1.5
One parent	2.9	2.4	3.3	4.5	5.7
Employed Parent(s) and Either Potential Surrogate Parent in Home or Enrolled in Kindergarten or Elementary School					
Total	5.1	—	8.2	11.6	13.4
Two parents	2.1	—	4.4	5.5	5.3
One parent	3.0	—	3.8	6.0	8.1
Employed Parent(s) and Either Potential Surrogate Parent in Home or Enrolled in Kindergarten or Elementary School or Nursery School					
Total	—	—	—	14.1	22.9
Two parents	—	—	—	7.2	10.9
One parent	—	—	—	6.8	12.0

SOURCES: Estimates derived from 1940–1980 PUMS.

NOTES: Surrogate parent: Any relative of the child (other than the parents) who (1) lives in the home of the preschoolers and their parents, (2) is age 18 or over, (3) is not enrolled in school, and (4) either is not in the labor force or works less than 35 hours per week. Enrollment in kindergarten and elementary school not calculated for 1950 because data were collected for sample line person only. Nursery school data available only for 1970 and 1980.

TABLE 5.11

Hispanic and Non-Hispanic Children,
by Parental Presence and Employment Status: 1980

	Aged 0–17			Aged 0–5		
	Non-Hispanic Origin White	Non-Hispanic Origin Black	Hispanic	Non-Hispanic Origin White	Non-Hispanic Origin Black	Hispanic
Total Number (in thousands)	49,294	9,568	5,724	14,742	2,943	2,034
Percent	100.0	100.0	100.0	100.0	100.0	100.0
Breadwinner-Homemaker, total	40.5	13.6	36.8	51.9	16.3	41.5
Breadwinner-Homemaker, Intact	31.3	8.0	27.9	40.6	10.3	32.1
Breadwinner-Homemaker, Blended	9.1	5.5	8.9	11.3	6.0	9.4
Two-Parent Family, Father Not Breadwinner	3.1	4.4	4.5	2.4	2.8	3.8
One-Parent Family, Not a Breadwinner	3.4	17.8	11.1	3.9	20.9	11.6
Dual-Earner Family, Employed Full Time	19.1	17.1	17.5	13.3	13.9	16.8
One-Parent Family, Employed Full Time	7.2	15.3	6.6	4.3	12.2	4.8
Dual-Earner Family, Employed Part Time	20.4	11.8	12.3	18.8	11.0	11.8
One-Parent Family, Employed Part Time	2.7	8.9	3.7	2.2	9.8	2.9
No Parent in Home	3.6	11.1	7.5	3.1	12.6	6.9

	Aged 6–11		
	Non-Hispanic Origin White	Non-Hispanic Origin Black	Hispanic Origin
Total Number (in thousands)	16,074	3,163	1,877
Percent	100.0	100.0	100.0
Breadwinner-homemaker, total	39.7	12.7	38.1
Breadwinner-homemaker, intact	30.3	7.0	29.0
Breadwinner-homemaker, blended	9.5	5.7	9.1
Two-parent family, father not breadwinner	2.6	4.6	3.8
One-parent family, not a breadwinner	3.4	16.9	11.1
Dual-earner family, employed full time	19.4	18.7	17.8
One-parent family employed full time	8.0	16.4	7.6
Dual-earner family, employed part time	21.1	12.0	12.5
One-parent family employed part time	3.0	8.3	4.2
No parent in home	2.7	10.4	4.9

TABLE 5.11 *(continued)*

	Aged 12–17		
	Non-Hispanic Origin White	Non-Hispanic Origin Black	Hispanic Origin
Total Number (in thousands)	18,478	3,462	1,813
Percent	100.0	100.0	100.0
Breadwinner-homemaker, total	32.1	12.0	30.1
Breadwinner-homemaker, intact	24.9	7.0	22.0
Breadwinner-homemaker, blended	7.2	5.0	8.2
Two-parent family, father not breadwinner	4.0	5.6	6.0
One-parent family, not a breadwinner	3.0	16.0	10.6
Dual-earner family, employed full time	23.4	18.4	18.1
One-parent family, employed full time	8.7	16.8	7.5
Dual-earner family, employed part time	21.1	11.8	12.7
One-parent family, employed part time	2.9	8.8	4.0
No parent in home	4.9	10.5	10.9

SOURCES: Estimates derived from 1980 Census PUMS.

NOTES: See Table 4.1 for explanation and NOTES, Table 5.1.

mothers are generally consistent with these results for 1980.[41] The only important difference is that in 1984–1985, Hispanic children (of any race) were substantially more likely than whites to be cared for by a grandparent (29 vs. 15 percent), and substantially less likely to be cared for by a nonrelative (19 vs. 29 percent). Overall, then, the need for nonparental child care and the family life situation of Hispanic children (of any race) lies between that of non-Hispanic whites and non-Hispanic blacks, but the situation of Hispanic children (of any race) is generally more similar to that of non-Hispanic whites than to that of non-Hispanic blacks.

Conclusions

Two revolutions in nonparental child care, first for children over age 6 and then for younger children, have accompanied the double trans-

[41]Martin O'Connell and Amara Bachu, U.S. Bureau of the Census, *Current Population Reports, Who's Minding the Kids? Child Care Arrangements: Winter 1984–85,* Series P-70, No. 9, (Washington, DC: U.S. Government Printing Office, 1987), Table 4.

formation in the family economy that marks the era since the beginning of the Industrial Revolution.

Most important, even as farming was becoming overshadowed by an industrial economy in which fathers secured jobs located away from home, there were corresponding landmark changes that made school attendance compulsory and enacted child labor laws to ensure that children would be protected from unsafe and unfair working conditions, excluded from jobs that adults needed, and received at least a minimal education. Also, as time passed, increasing affluence allowed families to support themselves without child labor, and higher educational attainments became increasingly necessary in order to obtain jobs that offered higher incomes and greater prestige.

Hence, in 1870 only 50 percent of children aged 5–19 were enrolled in school, and their attendance averaged only 21 percent of the days in the year. But 70 years later, in 1940, 95 percent of children aged 7–13 and 79 percent of children aged 14–17 attended school for an average of 42 percent of the days in the year. Even as mothers were increasingly viewed as full-time child care providers and homemakers, the need for them to act as full-time child care providers was diminishing, both because of the revolutionary decline in family size discussed in Chapter 2 and because of the revolutionary increase in nonparental child care provided by teachers in school.

Since a full adult workday amounts to about 8 hours (plus commuting time), and since a full adult work year requires only 65 percent of the days in a year, by 1940 school days of 5–6 hours (plus commuting time) amounted to about two-thirds of a full workday for about two-thirds of a full work year. As of 1940, then, childhood school attendance had effectively released mothers from personal child care responsibilities for a time period equivalent to about two-thirds of a full-time adult work year—the exception being the few years before children entered elementary school.

By reducing the time required for a mother's most important homemaker responsibility—the personal care of her children—the first childcare revolution, and additional social and economic changes discussed in Chapter 10, led to the large increase in mothers' labor-force participation after 1940, not only for school-age children but for preschoolers as well, and the second child-care revolution was under way. Subsequently, between 1940 and 1989, the proportion of children who had no specific parent at home full-time more than tripled for school-age children (from 20 to 66 percent) and quadrupled for preschoolers (from 13 to 53 percent).

Despite the associated decline in the amount of parental time potentially available to care for preschoolers, and the associated increase in the potential need for nonparental care, the proportion of pre-schoolers who had another relative in the home who might act as a surrogate parent also declined between 1940 and 1980 (from 19–20 percent to 4–5 percent for preschoolers in dual-earner families and from 51–57 percent to 20–25 percent for preschoolers in one-parent families with an employed parent).

Time-use studies of nonemployed mothers indicate that actual time devoted to child care as a primary activity probably increased between 1926–1935 and 1943 by about 50–100 percent and may have increased by a bit more during the 20 years that followed. But between the early 1960s and the early 1980s, the average amount of time that all mothers of preschoolers devoted to child care as a primary activity declined, due in large part to both increased employment outside the home and the fact that mothers of preschoolers devote about one-half as much time to child care as a primary activity as do nonemployed mothers (1.2 vs. 2.2 hours per day during the mid-1970s).

Overall, by 1989, about 48 percent of preschoolers had a specific nonemployed parent at home full-time (usually the mother), and 12 percent had employed parents who personally provided their preschoolers' care (often by working different hours or days). An additional 15 percent of preschoolers were cared for by relatives who often did not live in the preschoolers' home; and 25 percent were cared for by nonrelatives, about half in organized care facilities such as nursery schools.

The beneficial effect of mothers' employment on the family income will be discussed in Chapters 9 and 10. Past research suggests, broadly, that mothers' employment and nonparental care are not inherently and pervasively harmful to preschoolers; nor is nonparental care a form of maternal deprivation, since children can and do form attachments to multiple caregivers if the number of caregivers is limited, the child-care-giver relationships are long-lasting, and the caregivers are responsive to the child's needs.

Available evidence also suggests that the quality of care children receive is important and that some children, especially those from low-income families, are in double jeopardy from psychological and economic stress at home as well as from exposure to low-quality nonparental child care. Additional potentially beneficial and detrimental effects of mothers' employment and nonparental care for preschoolers have also been identified, but most of these results must be viewed as both preliminary and tentative. Overall, research on the consequences of nonparental care for preschoolers is in its infancy, and much remains to be done.

Since the proportion of preschoolers who had a specific parent at home on a full-time basis declined from about 79 to 48 percent in the

29 years between 1960 and 1989, it appears that we are roughly halfway through the preschool child-care revolution and that this second child-care revolution may be complete within 30–40 years, quite possibly before we have gained a detailed understanding of the effects, or lack of effects, that nonparental care has for preschoolers.

Taking a long view, then, as the Industrial Revolution removed fathers from the home for much of the day to work, the first child-care revolution also removed children over age 6 from the home for much of the day in order for them to attend school. Subsequently, as the post-1940 rise in mothers' labor-force participation removed many mothers from the home for much of the day, the second child-care revolution led to declines in parental care and increases in nonparental care for children aged 0–5.

We are now in the midst, in fact probably within 30–40 years of the end, of the second child-care revolution, yet potentially important effects for preschoolers remain uncertain. One major consequence of the first child-care revolution is clear, however: Successive cohorts of children attained increasingly higher levels of education. Since the children of today are the parents of tomorrow, the first child-care revolution subsequently brought a revolution in parents' education. In the next chapter, we will focus on the revolution in parents' education, its apparent consequences for children, and its relationship to the family-size revolution and the transformations in the family economy that were discussed in earlier chapters.

6

PARENTS' EDUCATION, OTHER FAMILY ORIGINS, AND THE AMERICAN DREAM

Introduction and Highlights

THE AMERICAN DREAM promises each new generation of children the opportunity to rise above their social and economic origins, no matter how humble, through initiative and hard work. Yet family origins continue to act as important steppingstones for some children and as stumbling blocks for others along the road to success. Opportunities to achieve educational success, and hence occupational and economic success, have tended to become more equal during the twentieth century, because family origins have become less influential in determining children's educational attainments. The overall increase in the equality of educational opportunities was restricted, however, to the opportunity to achieve only as much as a high school education. Beyond the high school level, educational opportunities became less equal.

In this chapter we will focus both on changes that have taken place in the equality of educational opportunities and on major changes in the proportion of children who, because of their family situation, were especially advantaged or disadvantaged in their chances of achieving success during adulthood. Since educational accomplishments are often viewed as the first step toward achieving success in this country, we will begin this chapter by presenting evidence on the extent to which high educational attainments have, in fact, led to occupational and economic success during adulthood. We will then focus on major features of family origins that influence children's chances of achieving high educational levels, including not only parents' education but also parents' occupational status, number of siblings, family intactness, farm residence, and race.

Children whose parents are highly educated are substantially more likely to achieve high educational levels than are children whose parents are less educated, although the degree of advantage or disadvantage associated with parents' education has become smaller over time. This increasing equality of opportunity has been especially noteworthy among children who have very few or only a moderate number of siblings. For children with many siblings, the parents' educational level continues to act as either an important steppingstone or as a stumbling block.

Historically, children's educational attainments have also been influenced by their parents' occupation, by whether they lived in an intact two-parent family for most of their childhood, by whether they lived on a farm, and by their race. The degree of advantage or disadvantage associated with these factors, especially farm origin and race, has also decreased over time, at least through high school. But fathers' education, number of siblings, family intactness, and farm origins have become more influential in determining a child's chances of completing at least one year of college.

Insofar as family origins continue to influence children's educational attainments, it was found that successive cohorts of children born during the twentieth century benefited from the revolutionary increases in parents' education and fathers' occupational prestige, the revolutionary decline in family size, and the near extinction of the family farm, but that these effects were partially offset by the rise in one-parent families. Although black children have also benefited or been hindered by similar changes, and although the educational disadvantage of black children, compared with white children, has decreased, a substantial number of black children are still educationally disadvantaged, and old-family Hispanic children (of any race) have progressed roughly as far as non-Hispanic black children.

In addition to these features of family origins, family income has also acted as a steppingstone or a stumbling block to children in their efforts to achieve educational, social, and economic success during adulthood. Beginning in Chapter 7, therefore, we will examine historic changes in parents' and family incomes.

Education as a Path to Success

It is widely believed that higher educational attainments provide a direct path to social and economic success—that is, that the completion of many years of schooling often provides access to high-prestige occupations that guarantee high incomes. Is this belief correct? The answer clearly is yes.

For example, Robert Kominski recently estimated that as of spring 1987, the *monthly* income of individuals with a doctorate was $4,118— nearly twice the $2,109 earned by individuals with a bachelor's degree and three and one-half times the $1,135 received by those who have only a high school diploma.[1] Looking back in time, in a classic study done on education, occupation, and earnings, William H. Sewell and Robert M. Hauser developed a sophisticated model of the effects of fathers' education, occupation, and income on sons' education, occupation, and earnings.[2] They found, controlling for other factors, that each additional year of education sons received led to an increase of 8.1 points in occupational prestige on a 100-point scale. In 1967, when average annual earnings in their sample were $7,022, they also found that each additional year of education led to an increase of $261 in annual earnings. In other words, controlling for other factors, the difference in annual earnings between men who had completed exactly four years of college and those who had completed exactly four years of high school was $1,044, which, taking inflation into account, was equal in value to $3,699 in 1988.

In general, then, additional years of schooling provide a stepping-stone to occupations that offer higher prestige and guarantee greater incomes. Let us now examine the features of family origins that influence children's chances of attaining comparatively high, or comparatively low, educational levels during adulthood.

Family Influences on Children's Education

It would be surprising if the level of education parents themselves received did not influence their children's ultimate educational attain-

[1]Robert Kominski, U.S. Bureau of the Census, *Current Population Reports, What's It Worth?, Educational Background and Economic Status, Spring 1987,* Series P-70, No. 21 (Washington, DC: U.S. Government Printing Office, 1990), Table 2.

[2]William H. Sewell and Robert M. Hauser, *Education, Occupation, and Earnings* (New York: Academic, 1975), pp. 71–75.

ments. In fact, parents' educational attainments are important, in part because they reflect the knowledge, experience, and aspirations that parents bring to their children. Many sociological and demographic studies have documented the importance of parents' education in determining their socialization values as well as their occupation and income, and in influencing the levels of education and income their children achieve when they in turn become adults. These studies suggest that in both the short term and the long run, parents' relatively high educational attainments represent an important resource from which children benefit—a steppingstone to success. Conversely, children whose parents have completed relatively few years of school were found to be comparatively disadvantaged in their chances of achieving success.

In the short run, parents with higher educational attainments tend to work in occupations that offer high prestige and correspondingly high incomes, and it is parental income that provides the most important basis for the material standard of living that will be enjoyed by children (see Chapters 8 and 9). Furthermore, highly educated parents tend to value self-direction, autonomy, and independence in their children—characteristics that are advantageous in occupations marked by high social prestige and high incomes.[3] At the other extreme, parents who have completed fewer years of schooling tend to value conformity and obedience to externally imposed rules—characteristics that are a disadvantage in obtaining and keeping high-prestige and high-income occupations. Partly for these reasons, in the long run children whose parents are highly educated are themselves more likely to achieve high levels of education as they reach adulthood and subsequently work in relatively prestigious occupations that pay well, while children whose parents are less educated tend to end their formal educational experience earlier and go on to work in less prestigious jobs that offer less income.[4]

Many studies have focused on the effect that fathers' education has on their sons' educational and occupational attainments, but recent research has expanded to include the effects of both fathers' and mothers' education on the attainments of both sons and daughters. This research shows that the occupational attainment process differs in important ways for sons and daughters, but that the factors that influence their attainments are generally the same. The most interesting difference between

---

[3]Melvin L. Kohn, *Class and Conformity* (Homewood, IL: Dorsey, 1969); and Melvin L. Kohn and Carmi Schooler, *Work and Personality* (Norwood, NJ: Ablex, 1983). Duane F. Alwin, "Trends in Parental Socialization Values: Detroit, 1958–1983," *American Journal of Sociology* 90, 2 (September 1984): 359–382.

[4]For example, see Peter M. Blau and Otis Dudley Duncan, *The American Occupational Structure* (New York: Wiley, 1967); David L. Featherman and Robert M. Hauser, *Opportunity and Change* (New York: Academic, 1978); and Sewell and Hauser, *Education, Occupation, and Earnings* (1975).

sons and daughters, in the present context, is that fathers' education has a greater influence on sons' educational attainments than does mothers' education, but mothers' education has a greater influence on daughters' educational attainments than does fathers' education.[5]

These differences in process would produce differences in the educational attainments of sons and daughters if it were the case that sons and daughters differed substantially with regard to either the education of their fathers or the education of their mothers. But it turns out that these differences are quite small. In other words, fathers' educational attainments are similar for sons and daughters, and mothers' educational attainments are likewise similar for sons and daughters. Consequently, in this chapter we will present results for all children rather than for boys and girls separately.

In short, children whose parents have completed many years of schooling are at a distinct advantage in their educational attainments and in their chances of achieving social and economic success during adulthood, while children whose parents are less educated are at a comparative disadvantage. Parents' education is not the only feature of family origins that influences children's educational attainments, however, and in fact the role of parents' education itself depends in part on the number of siblings who are in the family.

In their classic research on the educational attainment process, David L. Featherman and Robert M. Hauser studied not only fathers' education but also five additional features of family origins that have influenced the educational attainments of American men born during the 45 years spanning 1907–1951.[6] Each of these six features of family origins— fathers' education, fathers' occupational status, number of siblings, farm origin, family intactness during childhood, and race—have acted as steppingstones to higher educational attainments for some children but as stumbling blocks for others.

Featherman and Hauser further estimate the extent of the structural effect of each feature of family origins while controlling for the other five. These estimates indicate the extent to which the position of children in the social structure along a specific dimension of family origins acted to influence their educational attainments, independently of the other family circumstances. Although each of these six features of family origins had a substantial independent effect on children's educational attainments for men born early in this century, five effects diminished in importance for later cohorts.

---

[5]William H. Sewell, Robert M. Hauser, and Wendy C. Wolf, "Sex, Schooling, and Occupational Status," *American Journal of Sociology* 83, 3 (1980): 551–583.

[6]Featherman and Hauser, *Opportunity and Change.* See especially Table 5.9 and the associated text.

When Featherman and Hauser compared various sons born in the 1907–1911 cohort, they found that: each additional 10 points on a father's occupational prestige scale led on average to .306 additional years of schooling; each additional year of a father's education led on average to .284 additional years of schooling; each additional sibling led on average to .202 fewer years of schooling; family intactness, or not living with both parents during most of childhood, led on average to .845 fewer years of schooling; farm origin led on average to .966 fewer years of schooling; and being black led to 1.730 fewer years of schooling.

The structural effect of number of siblings remained fairly constant across cohorts born between 1907–1911 and 1947–1951. But the structural effects declined substantially for fathers' occupation, fathers' education, and family intactness by 49, 39, and 34 percent, respectively; and they essentially vanished for farm origin and race, dropping by 98 and 95 percent, respectively. Hence, during the 45 years spanning 1907–1951, later cohorts benefited substantially from the decline in the effects of these five features of family origins. In other words, educational opportunities became more equal, overall, because family origins became less of an advantage or a handicap as time passed. In fact, much of the 45-year change occurred among cohorts born during the short 15-year span encompassing 1937–1951. Compared with children born in earlier years, these cohorts experienced about 50 percent of the declines that occurred in the effects of fathers' occupation and education, about 80 percent of the decline in the effect of family intactness, and about 95 percent of the decline in the effect of farm origin. Only for race did a majority (70–75 percent) of the decline occur among earlier cohorts.

Judith Blake documented additional findings in a more recent and in some ways more refined study. Among white men who grew up in intact, two-parent families, the decline in the structural effect of fathers' education did not occur across the board but mainly for children who had very few or a moderate number of siblings.[7] Among children born early in the twentieth century, the effect of fathers' education on years (0–12) of graded schooling for sons in very large families (i.e., 8 or more siblings) was about twice as large as the effect of fathers' education for sons in small families (i.e., 1–2 children). In other words, the negative effect of one less year of fathers' education or, equivalently, the positive effect of one additional year of fathers' education was twice as great for sons who grew up in very large families as for sons who grew up in small families.

Subsequently, the extent of the effect that fathers' education had on

[7]Judith Blake, "Number of Siblings and Educational Mobility," *American Sociological Review* 50, 1 (1985): 84–94. See especially Table 7.

sons' education declined regardless of family size, but the declines were 2–3 times larger among sons in families with 1–4 children than among sons in families with 8 or more children.[8] Comparing sons born during the 1930s and the 1940s with those born earlier in the century, the effect of fathers' education had declined among sons in families with 1–2, 3–4, 5–7, and 8 or more children by 57–61 percent, 41–48 percent, 26–29 percent, and 9–14 percent, respectively. Hence, much of the 36–45 percent decline in the total structural effect of fathers' education across these cohorts taken as a whole can be accounted for by the larger declines among sons from smaller families. Overall, then, for more recent cohorts born during the twentieth century, but especially those born since 1937, family origins have tended to play a smaller role in determining children's ultimate educational attainments. The comparative advantage or disadvantage experienced by successive cohorts is influenced, however, not only by the size of these *structural effects*, but by the *changing distribution of children* with regard to important features of family origins, as we will see in the following section.

The Parents' Education Revolution and Other Family Origins

Insofar as family origins have continued to influence the educational attainments of children, changes in the distribution of successive cohorts with regard to important features of family origins imply that later cohorts tended to be more (or less) advantaged in their family origins than were earlier cohorts. The revolutionary increase in parents' education is one change in family origins that was highly advantageous to more recent cohorts.

Comparing children born during the mid-1920s with those born during the mid-1980s, it was found that the proportion with fathers who completed only 0–8 years of schooling plummeted from 73 to 15 percent, while the proportion with fathers who completed at least 4 years of high school jumped from 15 to 85 percent (Figure 6.1 and Table 6.1). Although these cohorts were separated by 60 years, about half of the change occurred in only 20 years, and two-thirds of the change occurred

---

[8]Blake, "Number of Siblings." See especially Table 7. Blake presents estimates from two sets of data. For children in families with 5–7 children, one estimate indicates an absolute decline in the size of the effect of fathers' education roughly equal to that of sons in families with 1–4 children, while the second estimate indicates that the absolute decline was about one-half as large as that for children in families with 1–4 children and hence roughly equal to the decline for children in families with 8 or more children.

FIGURE 6.1

Distribution of Children Born between 1920s and 1980s, by Fathers' and Mothers' Educational Attainments

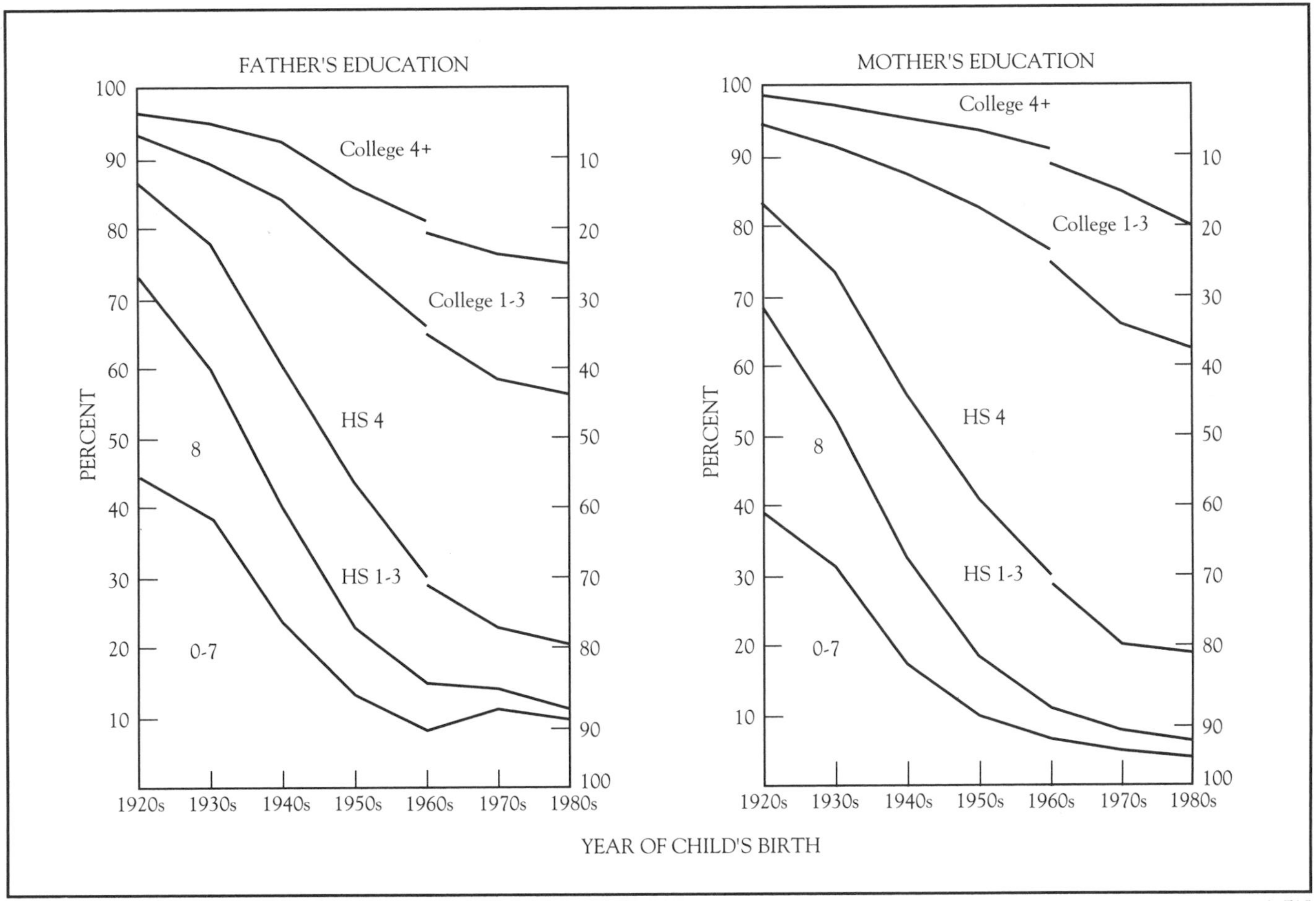

SOURCE: Appendix Table 6.1.
NOTE: See Appendix Table 6.1.

TABLE 6.1

Children Born Between 1920s and 1980s,
by Fathers' and Mothers' Educational Attainments

Years of School Completed	1920s	1930s	1940s	1950s	Census 1960s	CPS 1960s	1970s	1980s
Percent with								
Father								
Elementary 0–7 years	43.5	36.7	22.9	12.9	8.5	8.2	5.7	3.5
Elementary 0–8 years	72.7	60.4	40.4	23.6	14.9	14.7	9.1	5.2
High school 4 years or more	14.7	22.1	39.2	55.7	70.3	71.7	81.6	85.4
College 1 year or more	7.2	9.7	16.7	24.9	34.4	35.5	44.9	47.4
College 4 years or more	3.7	5.0	8.2	14.2	19.4	21.1	25.9	27.5
Mother								
Elementary 0–7 years	39.4	30.6	17.0	9.9	6.6	6.4	5.3	4.1
Elementary 0–8 years	68.1	52.4	32.4	18.2	11.5	11.3	7.8	6.4
High school 4 years or more	16.8	26.6	44.3	58.0	70.4	70.9	79.7	80.9
College 1 year or more	5.8	9.0	13.3	17.0	24.4	25.0	34.1	37.9
College 4 years or more	1.7	2.8	4.7	6.6	9.2	10.9	15.2	18.8

SOURCES: Estimates derived from 1940–1980 Census PUMS and March CPS 1980 and 1989.

NOTES: Estimates based only on children living with father or mother. Results for cohorts of 1920s through 1970s based on children at age 12–17. Estimates for 1980s cohort based on children aged 0–5 in 1989. Since some parents complete additional years of schooling after bearing children, children aged 0–5 will have parents with somewhat higher educational attainments when they reach age 12–17.

in only 30 years (following the mid-1930s). At still higher educational levels, the proportions with fathers who completed at least 1 or 4 years of college jumped, respectively, from 7 and 4 percent for the 1920s cohort to 47 and 28 percent for the 1980s cohort. These changes were also especially large for children born after the mid-1930s, but they were spread more evenly through the 40 years spanning the mid-1930s and the mid-1970s.

It appears, then, that fathers' education has increased greatly for successive cohorts of children born since the mid-1920s, and especially for those born since the mid-1930s; but the pace of this improvement slowed noticeably for the 1970s cohort, and the 1980s cohort experienced comparatively little improvement.

The revolution in mothers' education has generally paralleled the revolution in fathers' education. The main difference is that for cohorts born between the 1930s and the 1960s, the proportions whose mothers completed at least either 1 or 4 years of college increased *less* than did the proportions whose fathers completed the same years of education. For cohorts born since then (Figure 6.1 and Appendix Table 6.1), however, the proportions whose mothers completed this much education increased about the same as did the proportions whose fathers completed the same number of years of education. Rosalind R. Bruno suggests that the widening difference in the proportion of mothers and fathers who completed at least 4 years of college may be at least partly accounted for by the GI Bill, which provided funding for young men to attend college, augmented later by the incentives to attend college associated with the Vietnam-era draft deferment for men in college.[9] These sources of college enrollment were curtailed after the Vietnam era.

Hence, mothers' education, like fathers' education, has increased greatly for successive cohorts of children born since the mid-1920s, especially for those born since the mid-1930s. But the pace of increase slowed noticeably for the 1980s cohort, except perhaps for the rise in the proportion of mothers who completed at least 4 years of college.

Of course, as we saw in the preceding section, the structural effect of the level of fathers' education on that of sons' education became 39 percent smaller for cohorts born between 1907–1911 and 1947–1951, and one-half of this reduction was experienced by the cohorts born between 1937 and 1951. In addition, as we also saw in the preceding section, the amount of advantage (or disadvantage) associated with additional (or fewer) years of parents' education has depended, to an important extent, on the number of siblings in the family.

Among children born early in the century, a comparatively high proportion were concentrated in large families in which there were 5 or more siblings, where the low level of the parents' education proved to be especially disadvantageous. But among children born recently, a comparatively high proportion were concentrated in families with 1–4 children, where the parents' high level of education had comparatively little effect on the children's educational attainments. From estimates presented by Blake, for example, it appears that the structural effect of fathers' education on sons' education was roughly 44–81 percent smaller for cohorts born during the 1930s and the 1940s in families with 1–4 children than it was for cohorts born earlier in the century in families with 5 or more siblings.[10]

[9]Rosalind R. Bruno, U.S. Bureau of the Census, Current Population Reports, Series P-20, No. 415, *Educational Attainment in the United States: March 1982 to 1985* (Washington, DC: U.S. Government Printing Office, 1987), pp. 1–2.

[10]Blake, "Number of Siblings." For children born between 1894 and 1924 in families with 5 or more siblings, roughly one-half lived in families with 5–7 siblings, and roughly one-half lived in families with 8 or more siblings. Hence, to approximate the size of the structural effect of education for each of Blake's two oldest cohorts (one from each OCG), we calculated the mean of the separate estimates for these two sibsizes in Blake's Table 7. Similarly, except during the baby boom, for children born in later years in families with 1–4 siblings, roughly one-half lived in families with 1–2 siblings, and roughly one-half lived in families with 3–4 siblings. Hence, to approximate the size of the structural effect

Although similar results for more recent cohorts are not available, these results strongly suggest that the revolutionary rise in parents' education across cohorts had a smaller salutary effect on the educational attainments of successive cohorts of children than is suggested by results that focus only on the changing distribution of children as measured by parents' education. Still, results on the *joint distribution* of children as measured by parents' education *and* number of siblings indicate that the revolutionary rise in parents' education did have an important effect on the educational attainments of successive cohorts of children.

For example, the proportion of children in families with 5 or more siblings and mothers who completed 0–11 years of schooling dropped from 39 percent for the 1920s cohort to 14 percent for the 1960s cohort and is probably less than 6 percent for the 1980s cohort (Table 6.2).[11] This shift of about 32 percentage points between the 1920s and the 1980s is about one-half the size of the 62–71 percentage point shift in the proportions whose father or mother completed 0–8 years of school or at least 4 years of high school (Table 6.1). Three-fifths of the change in the joint distribution of mothers' education and family size occurred between the 1920s and the pre-baby-boom 1940s cohorts, and two-fifths of it occurred between the 1940s and 1980s cohorts.

Simply controlling for other features of family origins, Featherman and Hauser found that number of siblings had a comparatively stable effect on children's education for cohorts born between 1907 and 1951. Hence, the revolutionary decline in family size discussed in Chapter 2 implies that successive cohorts benefited educationally from ever smaller families, with the single noteworthy exception of baby-boom children. Between the 1920s and 1940s cohorts, the proportion of children in families with 5 or more siblings declined 11 percentage points, then a one-decade 6 percentage point increase during the baby boom was followed by a one-decade 9 percentage point decline (Table 6.2).

Featherman and Hauser also found, among cohorts born between 1907 and 1936, that children of farm origin attained an average of .826 to 1.225 fewer years of schooling than did nonfarm children. But this negative structural effect declined in size to only .162 years of schooling

---

for each of Blake's two youngest cohorts, we calculated the mean of the separate estimates for these two sibsizes in Blake's Table 7.

[11]Mothers' education is used here because number of siblings is measured as the number of children ever born to the mother, and because fathers' education is not available for the increasingly large proportion of children living in mother-only families. Since only 7 percent of the 1980s cohort is expected in families with 5 or more siblings by adolescence (Table 2.3), the proportion who also have a mother who has had 0–11 years of education must be at least slightly smaller.

TABLE 6.2

Children Born Between 1920s and 1960s,
by Mothers' Education, Family Size, and Farm Origin

Number of Siblings and Mothers' Years of School Completed	1920s	1930s	1940s	1950s	1960s
Total Number (in thousands)	12,486	11,119	16,625	21,889	21,286
Percent with					
1–2 Siblings					
College 1 year or more	2.5	4.3	5.5	4.3	8.4
High school 4 years	4.6	7.9	12.1	9.5	13.5
High school less than 4 years	19.7	17.3	12.8	6.6	4.6
3–4 Siblings					
College 1 year or more	2.1	3.3	5.5	8.3	11.3
High school 4 years	4.0	6.5	13.2	18.8	22.5
High school less than 4 years	24.7	23.4	19.4	15.2	11.4
5 or More Siblings					
College 1 year or more	1.1	1.4	2.3	4.2	4.6
High school 4 years	2.5	3.1	5.9	12.7	10.2
High school less than 4 years	38.8	32.6	23.4	20.3	13.6
Percent	100.0	100.0	100.0	100.0	100.0
Number of Siblings					
1–2	26.9	29.6	30.4	20.4	26.5
3–4	30.7	33.3	38.0	42.3	45.2
5 or more	42.4	37.2	31.6	37.3	28.3
Percent	100.0	100.0	100.0	100.0	100.0
Mothers' Years of School Completed					
College 1 year or more	5.7	9.0	13.3	16.8	24.2
High school 4 years	11.0	17.6	31.1	41.0	46.1
High school less than 4 years	83.2	73.4	55.6	42.2	29.7
Percent	100.0	100.0	100.0	100.0	100.0
Percent Living on Farm	28.3	22.5	12.1	5.6	3.1
Percent Living in Intact Two-Parent Family	73.2	71.2	72.1	68.0	60.5
Percent	100.0	100.0	100.0	100.0	100.0

SOURCE: Estimates derived from 1940–1980 Census PUMS.

NOTES: Estimates of number of siblings and mothers' years of school completed based only on children living with mother having at least 1 child ever born. Number of siblings estimated as number of children ever born to mother. Farm origin measured as farm residence. Intact two-parent families include only those with all children living in the home born after the parent's only marriage, and 1940 and 1950 estimates based only on mothers' marital history. Results based on children at age 12–17.

for the 1937–1941 cohort and to .050 years of school, or less, for 1942–1951 cohorts. Hence, the 28 percent of the 1920s cohort and the 23 percent of the 1930s cohort who lived on farms were substantially disadvantaged by this aspect of family origins, but among subsequent cohorts the much smaller proportions living on farms were only minimally affected in their overall educational attainments (Table 6.2).

Regarding fathers' occupational prestige, Featherman and Hauser report that for cohorts born between 1907–1911 and 1947–1951, the increase in fathers' average occupational prestige was similar to the increase in fathers' average education (about 50 percent). It appears that perhaps 40–60 percent of the increase in average fathers' occupational prestige can be accounted for simply by the shift from farming to nonfarm occupations, since the proportion of children whose fathers were farmers declined from 40 to 11 percent across these cohorts, and since the occupational prestige of farmers as of 1960 was extremely low (only 10–14 points on a scale ranging from 0–96 points in which the occupations with the highest prestige had point values of 90–96 points).[12]

Regarding family composition, Featherman and Hauser found that for the 1907–1936 cohorts, not spending *most* of their childhood in a two-parent family led, on average, to .713–.899 fewer years of schooling, but for the 1937–1951 cohorts, this figure fell to .558–.660 fewer years of schooling. The results discussed in Chapter 3 indicate that the chances of not spending *at least part* of childhood in a two-parent family remained fairly stable across cohorts born between the late 1800s and the 1950s (about 30–35 percent), but that this proportion is projected to increase for the 1960s, 1970s, and 1980s cohorts (to about 38, 46, and 53 percent, respectively). Not all of these children spend a major proportion of their childhood in a one-parent family; of children in early cohorts who spent time in a one-parent family between two-fifths and three-fifths report spending most of childhood not living with both parents.[13] Still, these projections suggest that the proportion who do spend a major portion of childhood in a one-parent family may increase substantially, perhaps by as much as 10–20 percentage points between the 1950s and 1980s cohorts.

Finally, although Featherman and Hauser found that black children experienced a large but decreasing educational disadvantage of 1.730 to .535 fewer years of schooling for cohorts born between 1907 and 1936, the disadvantage nearly disappeared thereafter, and black children as a

---

[12]Featherman and Hauser, *Opportunity and Change*, Table 5.4; and Blau and Duncan, *Occupational Structure*, Table 4.1.

[13]According to Featherman and Hauser, 13–18 percent of men born between 1907 and 1951 reported themselves as not "living with both . . . parents most of the time up to age 16." Featherman and Hauser, *Opportunity and Change*, p. 501 and Table 5.4.

proportion of all children have changed little during the twentieth century.[14]

How did these various changes in family origins affect the total proportion of various cohorts who were disadvantaged by at least one feature of family origins? Our results suggest the following necessarily crude answers.

As we saw above, the proportion of children living in families in which there were 5 or more siblings and a mother who had completed 0–11 years of schooling dropped from 39 to 14 percent for cohorts born between the 1920s and the 1960s—a decline of 25 percentage points. In addition, if we count either having a mother who completed less than 4 years of high school and living in a family with a large number of siblings *or* not living in a primary (intact, two-parent) family as a disadvantage, it becomes clear that there was much less of a decline in the proportion of children who had either of these disadvantages (from 56 to 46 percent).

Although some children who did not live in primary families spent little time in a one-parent family, these results suggest that a portion of the declining disadvantage associated with the declining proportion of children living in large-size families in which the parents had a low level of education tended to be partly counterbalanced by the rise in the proportion living in one-parent families. Even with the declining size of the structural effect of not living in a two-parent family, according to the Featherman and Hauser study, the effect of not living in a one-parent family for most of childhood for the cohort born as late as 1947–1951 was equivalent to having an additional 2.8 siblings in the family or a father who received 3.2 fewer years of education.

Remember that 23–28 percent of the 1920s and 1930s cohorts tended to be educationally disadvantaged by farm origin. Among these cohorts, compared with the proportions who were disadvantaged by (1) living in families with 5 or more siblings and mothers who completed only 0–11 years of education *or* (2) not living in an intact family, an additional 8–10 percent were disadvantaged by farm origin. All told, then, the proportion who experienced at least one of these potentially disadvantageous features of family origins fell from about 66 percent for the 1920s cohort to 60 percent for the 1930s cohort and 43–46 percent for the 1940s through 1960s cohorts (Table 6.3).

Hence, it appears that the proportion of children who were educationally disadvantaged by family size and parents' education, by not living in a two-parent family, or by farm residence declined by about 20

[14]Featherman and Hauser report that for men, for example, the proportion who were black varied from 8–10 percent for various cohorts born between 1907 and 1911 and 1947 and 1951.

TABLE 6.3

Children Born Between 1920s and 1960s Disadvantaged by Family Origins

	1920s	1930s	1940s	1950s	1960s
Percent with					
At Least 1 Disadvantage					
5 siblings or more and mother completed less than 4 years of high school	38.8	32.6	23.4	20.3	13.6
5 siblings or more and mother completed less than 4 years of high school *or* not in intact two-parent family	56.1	51.6	43.0	43.8	46.0
5 siblings or more and mother completed less than 4 years of high school *or* farm origin	51.5	43.6			
5 siblings or more and mother completed less than 4 years of high school *or* not in intact two-parent family *or* farm origin	65.7	60.0			
Multiple Disadvantages					
5 siblings or more and mother completed less than 4 years of high school and not in intact two-parent family	9.5	9.8	8.3	8.6	7.1
5 siblings or more and mother completed less than 4 years of high school and farm origin	15.6	11.6			
5 siblings or more and mother completed less than 4 years of high school and not in intact two-parent family and farm origin	3.1	2.8			

SOURCE: Estimates derived from 1940–1980 Census PUMS.

NOTES: Estimates of number of siblings and mothers' years of school completed based only on children living with mother having at least 1 child ever born. Number of siblings estimated as number of children ever born to mother. Farm origin measured as farm residence. Intact two-parent families include those with all children living in the home born after the parent's only marriage, and 1940 and 1950 estimates based only on mothers' marital history. Results based on children at age 12–17.

percentage points between the 1920s and the 1940s, both because of the 15 percentage point drop in children in large families whose mothers had a comparatively low level of education and because the structural effect of farm origin nearly vanished. Between the 1940s and 1960s cohorts, however, the decline in the proportion who lived in large families and had mothers who completed only 0–11 years of schooling was at least partly counterbalanced by the negative educational effects of the 12 percentage point rise in the proportion who did not live in an intact two-parent family (Tables 6.2 and 6.3).

On the other hand, the proportion of children who were multiply disadvantaged by several features of their family origins has remained fairly constant. For example, there was little change in the proportion who were multiply disadvantaged by living in a large family in which the mother had only 0–11 years of schooling *and* by not living in an intact family (7–10 percent for cohorts born between the 1920s and the 1960s). The proportion who were multiply disadvantaged by living in a large family in which the mother who had 0–11 years of schooling *and* by farm origin was 2–6 percentage points larger (12–16 percent for the 1920s and 1930s cohort). Meanwhile, the proportion who were multiply disadvantaged by a large family in which the mother had 0–11 years of schooling *and* by farm origin *and* by not living in an intact family was only 3 percent for the 1920s and 1930s cohorts. Hence, the vanishing educational disadvantage of farm origin had fairly little effect on the proportion of children who experienced multiple disadvantages associated with their family origins.

As we look toward the future, it appears that the proportion of children who are disadvantaged by a large number of siblings cannot shrink much below the small, approximately 6 percent of the early 1990s cohort who are expected to live in families in which there are 5 or more siblings (see chapter 2). A potentially large shift above the 50 percent of the early 1990s cohort expected to live in families with only 1–2 children could occur but is not currently expected. In addition, even if such a shift to 1–2-child families did occur, its effect on educational attainments might be small compared with earlier sibsize changes, since by mid-century the difference in the size of the structural effects between children living in families in which there were 1–2 vs. 3–4 children was much smaller than the historic and current differences between those living in families in which there were 1–4 children and 5 or more siblings.

Regarding the proportion of children living in two-parent families, if divorce and out-of-wedlock childbearing remain comparatively stable after 1990, little change in this source of educational disadvantage is expected. Regarding farm origin, only 2–3 percent of children currently live on farms, a major increase does not seem likely, and a decline of more than 2–3 percentage points is not possible. It may be, then, that fathers' education and occupational status are the only two remaining features of family origins—except for income (as discussed in Chapters 7–9)—that will have a noteworthy potential for influencing the educational distribution of successive cohorts born after 1990.

Equality of Educational Opportunity

The preceding discussion has shown us that various cohorts have differed not only in the structural effects of specific features of family origins and the proportions who were advantaged or disadvantaged by specific features of family origins, but also in the overall extent to which family origins led to unequal educational attainments. Featherman and Hauser found, for example, that six features of family origins together explain about 33.3 percent of the variations noted in the educational attainments for men born in 1907–1911, but this proportion fell by one-fourth (to 25.5 percent) for men born in 1947–1951. In other words, since family origins became one-fourth less important, overall, in determining men's educational attainments, opportunities to achieve educational success became more equal during the twentieth century.

Between one-third and one-half of this 7.8 percentage point improvement occurred among men born in 1937–1941. Family origins explained 30.4 and 31.7 percent of the variation in educational attainments for men born in 1927–1931 and 1932–1936, respectively, compared with 27.6 percent for men born in 1937–1941—a decline of between 2.8 and 4.1 percentage points. An additional one-fourth of the improvement also occurred across two five-year cohorts, as the variation in educational attainments explained by family origins declined from 27.6 percent for men born in 1942–1946 to 25.5 percent for men born in 1947–1951.

All told, then, of the total increase in the equality of educational opportunities that occurred across cohorts born during the 45 years from 1907 to 1951, between 60 and 80 percent of the improvement was experienced by men born during the 15 years from 1937 to 1951. Important contributors to this increase in the equality of educational opportunities between 1937 and 1951 appear to be the corresponding declines in the structural effects for fathers' education and occupational prestige, farm origin, and two-parent family living.

According to estimates by Featherman and Hauser, of the total declines in the structural effects that occurred between cohorts born in

1907–1911 and 1947–1951, the proportion that occurred between co-horts born in 1932–1936 and 1947–1951 was 51–53 percent for fathers' education and occupational prestige, 96 percent for farm origin, and 79 percent for not living in an intact two-parent family. Of course, as Blake found, much of the decline in the structural effect of fathers' education occurred among men in families in which there were 1–4 siblings.

In addition, Featherman and Hauser found that the distribution of men with regard to number of siblings, farm origin, fathers' education, and living in a two-parent family was more equal among men born in 1947–1951 than among those born in 1932–1936. These changes, too, contributed somewhat to the overall reduction in the extent to which family origins led to unequal educational attainments—that is, to the reduction in the amount of variation in men's educational attainments that could be explained by differences in family origins.[15]

As emphasized by Feathermann and Hauser[16] and by Blake[17], how-ever, this increasing equality of educational opportunities has occurred *only* in the opportunities to complete at least 4 years of high school. Featherman and Hauser report, for example, that 30.0 percent of the variation in educational attainments associated with 0–12 years of schooling among men born in 1907–1911 can be explained by the six features of family origins that they studied, but this figure fell (by 17.2 percentage points) to only 12.8 percent for men born in 1947–1951.

Contributing to this 57 percent reduction in educational inequality through 4 years of high school were very large reductions in the struc-tural effects of family origins, with the possible exception of number of siblings. For example, focusing on the first 12 years of schooling for men born between 1907–1911 and 1947–1951, Featherman and Hauser re-port 63 and 95 percent reductions, respectively, in the sizes of structural effects recorded for fathers' education and occupational prestige, 70–71 percent reductions in the sizes of the structural effects associated with farm origin and not living in a two-parent family, and a 96 percent re-duction for the structural effect of race.[18]

Beyond the high school level, however, educational opportunities have become *less equal* for men and women born between the begin-ning and the middle of the twentieth century. For example, most esti-mates by Featherman and Hauser as well as by Blake indicate that the proportion of the variation in postsecondary education that can be ex-plained by family origins was 17–21 percent for men and women born

[15]Featherman and Hauser, *Opportunity and Change*, Table 5.4.

[16]Featherman and Hauser, *Opportunity and Change*, pp. 241–252.

[17]Judith Blake, *Family Size and Achievement* (Berkeley: University of California Press, 1989), pp. 55–61.

[18]Featherman and Hauser, *Opportunity and Change*, Table 5.9.

between the mid-1940s and the early 1950s. But this is 3–13 percentage points larger than the proportion of the variation in postsecondary education that can be explained by family origins among men and women born early in the century.

This increased *in*equality of educational opportunities beyond the high school level appears to have resulted, at least in part, from the increasing size of structural effects for at least four of the six aspects of family origins discussed here. For example, focusing specifically on the determinants of completing at least one year of college, Featherman and Hauser found that for men born between 1907–1911 and 1947–1951,[19] the size of the structural effects approximately doubled for fathers' education, number of siblings, and not living in a two-parent family. Meanwhile, farm origin shifted from having a slightly negative effect to having a substantial positive effect on children's chances of completing at least one year of college, and there was comparatively little change in the effect of fathers' occupational prestige.

For men born in 1947–1951, their chances of going beyond high school to finish at least one year of college were *increased* by 4.3 percentage points for each additional 10 points of fathers' occupational prestige; *increased* by 3.0 percentage points for each additional year of fathers' education; were *reduced* by 3.4 percentage points for each additional sibling in the home; *increased* by 8.4 percentage points if their father was a farmer; and was *reduced* by 10.0 percentage points if they did not spend most of their childhood in a two-parent family.

For men born by mid-century, then, not spending most of their childhood in a two-parent family had a negative structural effect on their chances of completing at least one year of college, one that was roughly equal in size to the effect of having a father who had three fewer years of schooling or to that of having three additional siblings. Similarly, among these men, farm origin had a positive structural effect on their chances of going on to complete at least one year of college, and this was greater in size than the effect of having a father who had two or three additional years of schooling or to that of having two or three fewer siblings.

Between mid-century and the 1980s, in accordance with Featherman and Hauser's suggestion, the secular rise in parents' education and the post-baby-boom decline in fertility and family size acted together to produce successive cohorts of young persons who tended to have configurations of social background that were more favorable to a continuation of schooling into the college years.[20] On the other hand, this is at least partly counterbalanced by the projected shift away from two-par-

[19]Featherman and Hauser, *Opportunity and Change,* Table 5.12.
[20]Featherman and Hauser, *Opportunity and Change,* p. 251.

ent families. For cohorts born after 1990, potential changes in the size of the *structural effects* also might have important effects on the equality of postsecondary educational opportunity, but as discussed above, the effect of future changes in the *distribution* of children with regard to farm origin, family size, and two-parent family living may be relatively small compared with earlier historic changes, and compared with the *potential* for changes in parents' education and occupational prestige.

Featherman and Hauser summarize their findings with regard to changes in the equality of educational opportunities as follows: ". . . [A]s average education has risen in the society to a level that approximates the high school diploma, the historic socioeconomic differentials in schooling have not disappeared. Instead, they have merely shifted up the range of education into the transition into postsecondary, college years. . . . Still, the total impact of social origin on college access and continuation is modest even among the most recent cohorts to complete their college training. Less than one-quarter of the variance in college education . . ."[21] is explained by the social background variables in their study.

Before closing this section, however, we should note that much of the sociological research on this topic does not include the effects of at least one potentially important feature of family origins—namely, family income. The reason is that until recently most of the data sources available questioned adults about childhood years that were already distant and removed, and as such did not include questions about family income during childhood because such questions would tend to yield rather inaccurate results. One early study by William H. Sewell and Robert M. Hauser did study how sons' earnings were affected by fathers' incomes, as well as how fathers' education and occupation affected sons' education and occupation.

For sons with a nonfarm background Sewell and Hauser report that ". . . [a]s soon as father's income is entered as a variable, . . . [the structural effects] of father's education and occupation are reduced to . . . nonsignificance."[22] They further report that 84 percent of the effect of fathers' incomes on sons' earnings is independent of—that is, *not* mediated by—its effect on sons' educational attainments or occupational status.[23] These results suggest that fathers' incomes, and hence family income, are potentially important in providing the resources that will be valuable to children in achieving comparatively high incomes during adulthood.

[21]Featherman and Hauser, *Opportunity and Change*, p. 251.
[22]Sewell and Hauser, *Education, Occupation, and Earnings*, p. 71.
[23]Sewell and Hauser, *Education, Occupation, and Earnings*, pp. 72–73.

Although the Sewell and Hauser models do not include other potentially important variables studied by Featherman and Hauser and by Blake—such as number of siblings and not living in a two-parent family—and although their model explains only 6.6 percent of the variation in sons' earnings, their results suggest that the family income of children is a comparatively important feature of family origins in influencing children's social and economic success during adulthood.

Because of its potential importance, the changing distribution of children with regard to family income is studied from several different vantage points in the following chapters. But before turning to this topic, the remainder of this chapter will focus on differences by race and Hispanic origin in five of the six features of family origin that have been the focus of much sociological research on the educational and occupational attainments of children.

Family Origin Differences by Race

Both black and white children experienced revolutionary increases in parents' education after the 1920s, but blacks continued to lag substantially behind whites. Among children born during the 1920s and living with their fathers at age 12–17, most had fathers who had completed at least 1 year of elementary school (88 percent for blacks and 96 percent for whites) (Appendix Table 6.1). But blacks were only one-third as likely as whites to have fathers who had completed 8 or more years of elementary school (19 vs. 60 percent) (Table 6.4). Subsequently, this racial gap narrowed greatly, mainly for children born between the 1940s and the 1960s; and among children born by the 1970s, the gap had essentially vanished when it was found that 93–95 percent had fathers who had completed 8 or more years of schooling.

With generally rising educational levels, however, the narrowing of the elementary education gap in fathers' education was accompanied by an expansion in the racial gap among the proportion who completed high school, at least for a while. For example, among the 1920s cohort only 5 percent of blacks and 16 percent of whites had fathers who had completed at least 4 years of high school (12 years of schooling). But the racial gap then tripled from 11 percentage points to a peak of 34 percentage points for the 1950s cohort, as the proportion with fathers who had completed at least 4 years of high school rose to 25 percent for blacks and 59 percent for whites. For the 1980s cohort, however, this racial gap narrowed to 4 percentage points, as the proportion with co-

TABLE 6.4

White and Black Children Born Between 1920s and 1980s,
by Fathers' and Mothers' Educational Attainments

Years of School Completed	1920s	1930s	1940s	1950s	Census 1960s	CPS 1960s	CPS 1970s	CPS 1980s
Percent with								
Elementary 0–7 Years								
Father white	40.1	32.5	19.4	10.2	7.4	7.3	5.5	3.6
Father black	81.4	75.9	59.7	38.9	18.9	17.6	7.4	2.3
Mother white	36.0	27.1	14.2	8.3	6.1	5.8	5.5	4.4
Mother black	73.7	60.4	42.1	22.0	9.5	9.8	4.2	2.0
Elementary 0–8 Years								
Father white	71.0	57.7	37.4	20.8	13.7	13.7	8.7	5.2
Father black	91.4	85.8	72.4	51.3	26.3	25.3	12.3	4.6
Mother white	66.3	49.8	29.3	16.2	10.7	10.5	8.0	6.8
Mother black	86.5	74.2	60.3	32.7	16.3	16.5	7.0	4.4
High School 4 Years or More								
Father white	15.7	23.9	41.7	58.8	72.9	73.9	82.8	85.7
Father black	4.8	6.0	11.8	24.6	46.1	47.6	69.4	81.6
Mother white	18.0	28.6	47.2	61.9	73.6	73.9	81.3	82.4
Mother black	5.0	9.2	18.4	29.8	50.6	51.4	71.0	72.3
College 1 Year or More								
Father white	7.6	10.5	17.8	26.7	36.2	37.2	46.3	48.5
Father black	2.8	1.9	5.3	7.5	17.8	16.2	31.0	34.5
Mother white	6.1	9.7	14.1	18.3	25.7	26.6	35.2	40.0
Mother black	1.9	2.8	6.0	7.5	16.3	15.0	27.4	25.4
College 4 Years or More								
Father white	3.9	5.4	8.8	15.3	20.8	22.6	27.0	28.6
Father black	1.5	1.1	1.5	3.2	6.6	4.1	13.6	13.2
Mother white	1.8	3.1	5.0	7.1	10.0	11.9	16.2	20.4
Mother black	1.0	0.8	1.8	2.8	4.2	4.1	9.5	9.1

SOURCES: Estimates derived from 1940–1980 Census PUMs and March CPS 1980 and 1989.

NOTES: Estimates based only on children living with father or mother. Results for cohorts of 1920s through 1970s based on children at age 12–17. Estimates for 1980s cohort based on children aged 0–5 in 1989. Since some parents complete additional years of schooling after bearing children, children aged 0–5 will have parents with somewhat higher educational attainments when they reach age 12–17.

resident fathers who had completed at least 4 years of high school increased to 82 and 86 percent for blacks and whites, respectively.

The racial gap in the proportion of children whose fathers had completed at least 4 years of college (16 years of schooling) continued to expand for an additional decade beyond the 1950s, from only 2 percent-

FIGURE 6.2

Proportion of Children Born Between 1920s and 1980s Whose Parents Have Specified Educational Attainments

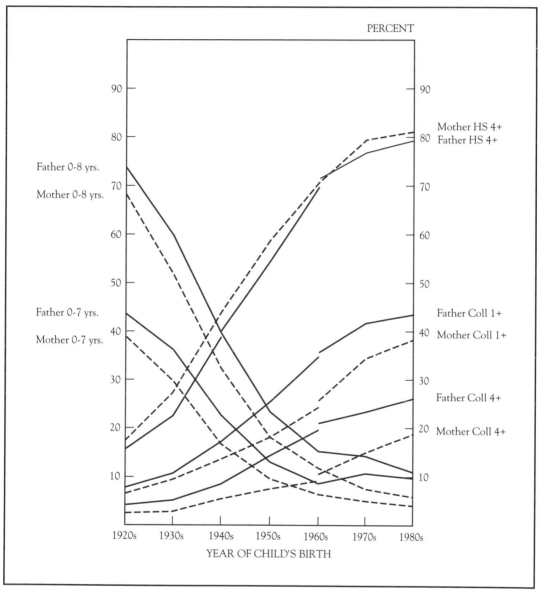

SOURCE: Appendix Table 6.1.

NOTE: See Appendix Table 6.1.

age points, when 2–4 percent for the 1920s cohort had fathers with such high educational attainments, to a gap of 14–19 percentage points, when the proportion of the 1960s cohort whose fathers had attained such a high educational level had increased somewhat (to 4–7 percent) for blacks, but greatly (to 21–23 percentage points) for whites. Among the 1980s cohort, the racial gap was 15 percentage points, as the proportion of blacks with (co-resident) fathers who had completed at least 4 years of college increased to 13 percentage points—still only one-half as large as the 29 percent of whites whose fathers had attained such a high level of education.

Changes in mothers' educational levels and the racial gap in mothers' education across successive cohorts of children have been broadly similar to changes for fathers (Table 6.4). The main differences are the following. First, for earlier cohorts, mothers were somewhat more likely than fathers to have completed at least 8 years of education, and the difference expanded to a peak for the 1930s or 1940s cohorts. But this difference in mothers' and fathers' education fell to 5–6 percentage points for whites born during the 1950s and for blacks born during the 1970s. In addition, the racial gap at this level of education was somewhat smaller for mothers than for fathers, and the racial gap for mothers' educational levels narrowed and vanished earlier.

Second, for earlier cohorts, mothers were also somewhat more likely than fathers to have completed at least 4 years of high school, but the difference reached a peak during the 1940s and then narrowed and reversed. For the 1980s cohort, co-resident mothers were less likely than co-resident fathers to have completed at least 4 years of high school, with differences of 9 and 3 percentage points for blacks and whites, respectively. Insofar as separation, divorce, and out-of-wedlock childbearing are more common among parents with lower educational attainments (Chapters 9 and 10), however, at least part of this reversal may be due to the rise in mother-only families, since fathers with comparatively low levels of education tend to be absent from the home. Also partly for this reason, at this educational level, the racial gap for the 1980s cohort was larger for co-resident mothers than for co-resident fathers (10 vs. 4 percentage points).

Third, for earlier cohorts, mothers were less likely than fathers to have completed at least 4 years of college, and this difference tended to increase through the 1970s, especially for whites. The difference then narrowed between the 1970s and the 1980s for whites. As indicated earlier, Rosalind R. Bruno suggests that the widening difference in the proportion of mothers and fathers who have completed at least 4 years of college may be at least partly accounted for by the GI Bill, which provided funding for young men to attend college, and later augmented by the incentive to attend college associated with the Vietnam-era draft deferment for men in college.[24] These sources of college enrollment were curtailed after the Vietnam era.

Meanwhile, the racial gap in the proportion of parents who had completed at least 4 years of college increased more for fathers than for mothers among cohorts born between the 1920s and the 1960s. But then the racial gap continued to expand for mothers, though not for fathers— a difference that might also be explained by the increasing absence of low-education fathers in mother-only families, especially among blacks.

The changing racial gap in parents' education can be measured in another way: by calculating the number of decades by which black children have lagged behind white children in their chances of having parents who have achieved specific educational levels (Table 6.4). Of course, at the lowest educational levels the time lag has vanished. For example, in the 1920s cohort 60–64 percent of whites had parents who had at least 8 years of education, but the earliest black cohorts to reach these levels weren't born until the 1940s or 1950s—a 2–3-decade time lag. By the 1970s, black and white children were nearly identical in their very high chances of having parents who had at least 8 years of education.

At higher educational levels the time lag has constricted slightly. For example, 16–18 percent of the 1920s cohort of whites had parents who had completed at least 12 years of education—a level first achieved among the black cohorts born during the 1940s or 1950s—again a 2–3-decade time lag. Then the time lag narrowed to little more than 1 decade for the 1970s cohort of black children. For the 1980s cohort, the time lag in the proportion who had at least 12 years of education remained at 1 decade for (co-resident) fathers' education but expanded to a 2-decade lag for (co-resident) mothers' education.

Since, as discussed above (also see Chapters 9 and 10), the rise in mother-only families appears to account for at least part of the racial convergence between the 1970s and the 1980s in the proportion of *co-resident* fathers who had completed at least 4 years of high school, the expansion to a 2-decade time lag reflected in data for mothers may more accurately reflect racial trends in parents' education for black and white children *as a whole*, including those who did not reside with their fathers.

Finally, the time lag in the proportion of black children whose fathers had completed at least 4 years of college (16 years of schooling) was compressed from about 3 decades for the 1950s and 1960s cohorts of blacks to about 2 decades for the 1970s cohort, but then expanded

---

[24]Rosalind R. Bruno, U.S. Bureau of the Census, *Current Population Reports*, Series P-20, No. 415, *Educational Attainment in the United States: March 1982 to 1985* (Washington, DC: U.S. Government Printing Office, 1987), pp. 1–2.

again to about 3 decades for the 1980s cohort. Similarly, the time lag in the proportion of black children with mothers who had completed at least 4 years of college was compressed from about 2 decades for the 1940s, 1950s, and 1960s cohorts of blacks to about 1 decade for the 1970s cohort, but then it expanded again to about 2 decades for the 1980s cohort.

In short, as revolutionary increases occurred in fathers' and mothers' education among successive cohorts of both black and white children, the black disadvantage effectively shifted upward but constricted substantially in size. For example, among the 1920s cohort, the maximum racial gaps were in the proportions whose fathers or mothers had completed at least 7 and 8 years of education, respectively, at 43 and 38 percentage points (Table A-6.1). But among the 1980s cohort, the maximum racial gap was in the proportion whose fathers and mothers had completed 14–15 and 13 years of education, respectively, at 16 and 15 percentage points. Hence, the maximum racial gap in parents' education among the 1980s cohort, while still substantial, was only about two-fifths as large as it had been among the 1920s cohort.

When the black disadvantage in parents' education is measured in terms of the number of decades by which blacks lagged behind whites, the comparative improvement of blacks at the bottom end of the educational distribution is quite impressive. The 1940s and 1950s black cohorts lagged 2–3 decades behind white children in having parents who had completed at least 8 years of education, but the difference had essentially vanished for the 1970s cohort.

On the other hand, the 1940s and 1950s black cohorts lagged behind whites by 2–3 decades in the proportion whose parents had completed at least 12 years of education, and this gap narrowed to about 1 decade for the 1970s cohort, but expanded again to about 2 decades for the 1980s cohort. Similarly, the 1940s and 1950s black cohorts lagged behind whites in the proportion whose fathers and mothers had completed at least 4 years of college by 3 and 2 decades, respectively, and each lag became about 1 decade shorter for the 1970s cohort but expanded by about 1 decade for the 1980s cohort.

Historically, black children have also been disadvantaged in other features of family origins that affect children's chances of attaining high educational achievements, and hence their chances of attaining high prestige and high income occupations during adulthood. As we saw in Chapter 2, the racial gap in the proportion of children living in families in which there are 5 or more siblings increased from 13 percentage points for the 1920s cohort to 34 percentage points for the 1940s cohort, but declined to 24 percentage points for the 1960s cohort and is expected to essentially vanish among children born during the 1990s.

For successive cohorts, then, what changes occurred in the joint distribution of children by parents' education and family size? Table 6.5 shows the proportion who had large families consisting of 5 or more siblings and mothers who had completed only 0–11 years of schooling. The racial gap in this proportion increased by 19 percentage points (from 15 to 34 percent) for children born between the 1920s and the 1940s, then narrowed by 12 percentage points for the 1960s cohort.

Between the 1920s and the 1940s, the racial gap in the proportion of children whose mothers had 0–11 years of school increased 16 percentage points for these cohorts, while the racial gap in the proportion who lived in large families increased by 21 percentage points. Subsequently, for the 1960s cohort the racial gap in the proportion whose mothers had completed 0–10 years of schooling narrowed by 6 percentage points, while the racial gap in the proportion who lived in large families narrowed by 11 percentage points. Hence, both trends contributed both to the 19 percentage point rise and the subsequent 12 percentage point decline in the racial gap of the two combined. Since the changes in the family-size gap have been one-third to two-thirds larger than the changes in the gap in mothers' education, the changing family-size gap appears to have been more important in determining the size of the changes that occurred in the joint distribution.

If, as expected, the family-size gap essentially vanishes for the 1990s cohort, then the racial gap in the joint distribution of family size and parents' education will also become small, and the disadvantage of these features of family origins among blacks will be equally small. All the same, if the disadvantage in parents' education among blacks continues into the 1990s, this feature of family origins will continue to have a depressing effect on the educational attainments of black children.

The increases in the disadvantage experienced by blacks between the 1920s and the 1940s due to the increasing racial *gaps* in parents' education and family size were counterbalanced, at least in part, by the declines in the racial *gap* for the proportions living on farms (from 13 percentage points during the 1920s and 1930s to 3 percentage points during the 1940s). Table 6.5 shows, however, that the racial gap in the proportion who lived on farms *or* had large families and a mother with low education during the 1920s and 1930s, when the structural effect of farm origins was substantial, was essentially the same as the racial gap in the joint distribution of family size and mothers' education in the same decades.

But the proportion of both white and black children who were disadvantaged by at least one of these two sets of factors was much greater than the proportions who were disadvantaged only by their mothers' education and family size. Among the 1920s cohort, 50 percent of whites

TABLE 6.5

White and Black Children Born Between 1920s and 1960s, Disadvantaged by Family Origins

	1920s	1930s	1940s	1950s	1960s
Number of white children (in thousands)	11,384	9,992	14,987	19,251	18,302
Number of black children (in thousands)	1,102	1,127	1,638	2,638	2,984
Percent with					
At Least 1 Disadvantage					
5 siblings or more and mother completed less than 4 years of high school					
White	37.4	29.8	20.1	16.5	10.6
Black	52.5	58.2	53.6	48.4	32.4
5 siblings or more and mother completed less than 4 years of high school, *or not in intact two-parent family*					
White	54.0	48.3	39.1	38.6	40.6
Black	78.0	81.6	78.8	81.9	78.8
5 siblings or more and mother completed less than 4 years of high school, *or farm origin*					
White	50.1	41.0			
Black	66.2	66.8			
5 siblings or more and mother completed less than 4 years of high school, *or not in intact two-parent family, or farm origin*					
White	63.8	57.0			
Black	86.0	86.2			
Percent living on farm					
White	27.1	21.2	11.8	6.0	3.6
Black	40.5	34.2	14.9	3.2	0.3
Multiple Disadvantages					
5 siblings or more and mother completed less than 4 years of high school and not in intact two-parent family					
White	8.5	8.0	6.3	5.9	5.9
Black	20.5	25.6	26.1	28.2	22.6
5 siblings or more and mother completed less than 4 years of high school and farm origin					
White	14.6	10.0			
Black	26.9	25.6			

216

TABLE 6.5 (*continued*)

	1920s	1930s	1940s	1950s	1960s
5 siblings or more and mother completed less than 4 years of high school and not in intact two-parent family and farm origin					
White	2.6	2.0			
Black	9.0	9.4			

SOURCES: Estimates derived from 1940–1980 PUMS.

NOTES: Estimates of number of siblings and mothers' years of schooling based only on children living with mother having at least 1 child ever born. Number of siblings estimated as number of children ever born to mother. Farm origin measured as farm residence. Intact two-parent families include those in which all children living in the home were born after the parents' only marriage, and 1940 and 1950 estimated based on mothers' marital history. Results based on children at age 12–17.

and 66 percent of blacks were disadvantaged by at least 1 of these 2 sets of factors, but by the 1940s, when the structural effect of farm origins was much smaller overall and the racial gap in farm origins was only 3 percentage points, the proportions who were disadvantaged only by mothers' education and family size declined to 20 and 54 percentage points for whites and blacks, respectively (declines of 30 and 12 percentage points). Taking into account, as well, the potential disadvantage of not living in an intact family (for at least part of childhood), the proportion of the 1920s cohort who were disadvantaged by at least one feature of family origins, excluding race itself, was as much as 14 percentage points larger for whites and 20 percentage points larger for blacks. Counting all these features of family origins, the proportions who were disadvantaged by at least one feature of family origins declined from 64 and 86 percent, respectively, for whites and blacks during the 1920s to 39–41 and 79–82 percent for whites and blacks, respectively, during the 1940s, 1950s, and 1960s.

Black children also continue to be substantially disadvantaged, compared with whites, in the proportion who were disadvantaged by at least two features of family origins, although this disadvantage diminished greatly between the 1920s and the 1940s with the reduction in the structural effect of race. The proportion who were potentially disadvantaged by large families and low mothers' education *and* by not living in an intact family (for at least part of childhood) was 6–9 percent for whites and 21–28 percent for blacks born between the 1920s and the 1960s. However, since Featherman and Hauser found that race had a large structural effect during the 1920s but very little effect during the 1940s, the proportion of blacks who were disadvantaged by race *and* by at least one other feature of family origins was as much as 86 percent during the 1920s.

Hence, the proportion of blacks who were disadvantaged by at least two features of family origins, including race, dropped from 86 percent during the 1920s to 23–28 percent during the 1940s, 1950s, and 1960s. This drop produced a correspondingly large decline of perhaps 60 percentage points in the racial gap in the proportion who were disadvantaged by at least two features of family origins. Finally, the proportion who were disadvantaged by at least three features of family origins was quite small for whites (2–3 percent) during the 1920s and the 1930s, but, if we include race, quite substantial (26–27 percent) for blacks born during these decades.

Overall, then, the racial gap in the proportion of blacks and whites disadvantaged by family origins has declined greatly since the 1920s, especially between the 1920s and the 1940s for multiple disadvantages. Since then, however, the smaller but important decline in the proportion who were disadvantaged by large families and low mothers' education has been at least partly counterbalanced by the increasing racial gap in one-parent family living (during at least part of childhood). By the 1960s, the proportion who were disadvantaged by at least one of these features of family origins was as much as 32 percent for white children and as much as 79 percent or more for black children.

Looking forward from the 1960s, changes in the racial gaps for children born through the 1990s may be roughly the following. First, if, as expected, the racial gap in family size vanishes for children born during the 1990s, then its effect will diminish to negligible levels (Chapter 1). Second, based on mothers' education, it appears that the racial gap in the proportion of children whose parents completed at least 4 years of high school diminished substantially between the 1960s and the 1970s, but then this gap remained constant, and the racial gap in the proportion whose parents completed at least 4 years of college increased. Hence, the racial gap in parents' education became less important between the 1960s and the 1970s, but unless there is a turnaround in the current trend, it may become more important between the 1970s and the 1990s.

Third, although the proportion of children ever living with fewer than two parents is projected to increase substantially for both blacks and whites born between 1960 and 1980, the projected increase is slightly larger for whites, and 1980 to 1990 may bring little change (Chapter 3). If this occurs, the slightly narrowing racial gap between 1960 and 1980 may have a salutary effect on the black educational disadvantage—an effect that would be a reversal of the one that occurred between 1940 and 1960.

Taking changes in family size, parents' education, and one-parent family living into account, then, the educational disadvantage of black children, compared with white children, may become smaller between the 1960s and the 1990s, mainly because of the vanishing racial gap in family size. But blacks will continue to be educationally disadvantaged compared with whites, mainly because of continuing race differences in parents' education and two-parent family living. Because family income and poverty also have important consequences for the educational attainments of children and for two-parent family living, however, we must view these conclusions as incomplete until we have discussed income and poverty trends (see Chapters 7–10).

Family Origin Differences by Hispanic Origin

Hispanic children (of any race) born during the 1960s and 1970s were 17–26 percentage points less likely than non-Hispanic black children to have a parent who had completed at least 8 years of schooling, but most of this educational disadvantage is accounted for by Hispanic children (of any race) whose parents were not born U.S. citizens (Appendix Tables 6.2 and 6.3). Such first-generation Hispanic children (of any race) were 32–42 percentage points less likely than non-Hispanic blacks to have a parent who had at least 8 years of schooling, while old-family Hispanic children (of any race) were 2–18 percentage points less likely to have parents who had 8 years of schooling.

Similarly, first-generation Hispanic children (of any race) were 14–35 percentage points less likely than non-Hispanic blacks to have parents who had completed at least 4 years of high school, while old-family Hispanic children (of any race) were 2–11 percentage points less likely than non-Hispanic black children to have parents who had completed less than 4 years of high school. At the top of the education distribution, however, first-generation and old-family Hispanic children (of any race) and non-Hispanic black children were nearly equal in their chances of having parents who had completed at least 4 years of college.

Hence, by 1980 old-family Hispanic children (of any race) appeared to have experienced a revolution in parents' education during the twentieth century that was about as great as that experienced by non-Hispanic black children. By 1980, however, old-family Hispanic children (of any race) were still somewhat disadvantaged in parents' education compared with non-Hispanic black children, and substantially disadvantaged compared with non-Hispanic white children. First-generation Hispanic children (of any race) were greatly disadvantaged compared with both old-family Hispanics (of any race) and non-Hispanics, no doubt because many (or most) of their foreign-born parents spent their childhood in countries that have much lower general levels of educational attainment than is common in the United States.

Based on the Current Population Survey for 1980 and 1989 (Appendix Table 6.3), among Hispanic children born between the 1970s and the 1980s, the increases of 5–7 percentage points in the proportion whose parents had completed at least 4 years of high school were generally similar to the corresponding increases for non-Hispanic blacks (1–13 percentage points) and somewhat larger than for non-Hispanic whites (2–3 percentage points).

These results are somewhat puzzling since, according to the 1990 census, the total population of Hispanic origin (of any race) grew by 53 percent between 1980 and 1990. By 1990, then, about 25 percent of the total Hispanic population (of any race) was foreign-born and had entered the United States during the 1980s.[25] But, for example, if these new Hispanic migrants were similar to earlier migrants in their educational attainments, and if the educational attainments of Hispanics (of any race) in the United States had by 1980 increased in a fashion similar to increases reported for non-Hispanic blacks, then we would expect the educational distribution of all Hispanics (of any race) to have shifted downward. The reasons this did not occur will emerge during the next few years as more detailed results from the 1990 census become available. Of course, one such reason that merits exploration is the fact that new migrants tend to be underrepresented in the 1989 Current Population Survey.

Finally, regarding other features of family origins among children born during the 1970s, old-family Hispanic children (of any race) and non-Hispanic black children were roughly equal (32–34 percent) in their chances of living in large families with a mother who had completed 0–11 years of education. The proportion who were disadvantaged in this respect is four times as great as the 8 percent recorded for non-Hispanic white children born during the 1970s. The disadvantage was still larger (40 percent) for first-generation Hispanic children (of any race). On the other hand, because both old-family and first-generation Hispanic children (of any race) are substantially more likely than non-Hispanic blacks to live in an intact two-parent family, both old-family and first-genera-

[25]Press Release, Monday, March 11, 1991, CB91-100, U.S. Bureau of the Census (Washington, DC: Government Printing Office).

TABLE 6.6

Hispanic and Non-Hispanic Children in 1980, Disadvantaged by Family Origins

| | Non-Hispanic | | | Hispanic Living with Mother | |
	White	Black	Hispanic	First Generation	Old Family
Number of Children (in thousands)	16,770	2,940	1,570	503	1,067
Percent with					
At least 1 Disadvantage					
5 siblings or more and mother completed less than 4 years of high school	8.3	32.4	35.6	40.2	33.5
5 siblings or more and mother completed less than 4 years of high school, *or* not in intact two-parent family	38.5	78.6	65.1	63.2	66.0
Multiple Disadvantages					
5 siblings or more and mother completed less than 4 years of high school and not in intact two-parent family	3.6	22.6	15.7	12.5	17.2

SOURCE: Calculated from 1980 PUMS.

NOTES: Estimates of number of siblings and mothers' years of schooling based only on children living with mother having at least 1 child ever born. Number of siblings estimated as number of children ever born to mother. Farm origin measured as farm residence. Intact two-parent families include those in which all children living in the home were born after the parents' only marriage. Results based on children at age 12–17.

tion Hispanic children (of any race) were less likely than non-Hispanic blacks, but more likely than non-Hispanic whites, to live in a large family with a mother who had completed 0–11 years of schooling *and/or* not to live in an intact family (Table 6.6).

As we look beyond the 1970s to children born during the 1990s, Hispanic children (of any race) born of mothers in the United States by 1988 are expected to have family sizes similar to those of non-Hispanic whites and blacks by the 1990s. If, in addition, their parents' educational attainments remain similar to those of non-Hispanic blacks, and Hispanics (of any race) continue to have a proportion in intact two-parent families that is between that for non-Hispanic blacks and non-Hispanic whites, then Hispanics (of any race) born to mothers in the United States by 1988 will also continue to have a proportion who are disadvantaged by one or two features of family origins that fall between that of non-Hispanic blacks and non-Hispanic whites. Meanwhile, the comparative disadvantages, or advantages, of Hispanics (of any race) whose parents are recent migrants may depend to an important degree on the characteristics of those migrants when they enter the United States.

Conclusion

Since at least early in the twentieth century, the family origins of children have had a substantial influence on their ultimate educational attainments, and hence their chances, as adults, of entering occupations marked by high social prestige as well as high incomes. Features of family origins that were known to be disadvantageous were (1) having parents with low educational attainments or with occupations of low social prestige, (2) having families with many siblings, (3) not spending most of childhood living with two parents, (4) coming from a farm family, or (5) being black.

By mid-century, educational opportunities had become more equal for children, particularly for those born between 1937 and 1951 because of declines in the size of the negative effects associated with having parents of low education and low occupational prestige and with not living in a two-parent family, and because the negative effects of farm origin and being black had nearly vanished. This overall increase in the equality of educational opportunities was restricted to the opportunity to achieve only as much as a high school education, however.

Beyond the high school level, educational opportunities became *more unequal*, as four features of family origins became more influential. The size of the structural effects for children's chances of completing at least one year of college approximately doubled when measured by fathers' education, number of siblings, and family intactness, while farm origins shifted from a small negative to a substantial positive factor. For the mid-century cohort, not living in a two-parent family had a negative effect on their chances of going on to college that was equal to the structural effect of having a father with 3 fewer years of education or a family with 3 additional siblings, and coming from a farm family had a positive effect 84 percent as large as the negative effect of not living in a two-parent family.

Insofar as family origins continued to influence children's educational attainments, changes across successive cohorts in their distribution with regard to specific features of family origins placed more recent cohorts at an advantage compared with earlier cohorts. The revolutionary increase in parents' education and fathers' occupational prestige, the revolutionary decline in family size, and the near extinction of the family farm all contributed to higher educational attainments among later cohorts of children, although the rise in one-parent families was found to have a partially countervailing influence.

For future cohorts born during the 1990s and beyond, the proportion who are disadvantaged by a large family of 5 or more siblings can shrink no more than the approximate 6 percent of the 1990s cohorts who are expected to live in such families. The proportion in small families with 1–2 children could increase, but with only small effect compared with historic changes. Since only 2–3 percent of children live on farms, the potential for a further decline in the farm population is also small.

If the stabilization of divorce rates since the late 1970s continues and is accompanied by a slowing in the growth of the proportion of births to unmarried women as a proportion of all births, then comparatively little change may occur in the proportion of children born after 1990 who are disadvantaged by not spending most of their childhood in two-parent families.[26] A continued rise in the proportion born out of wedlock could, however, lead to an increasing proportion who are disadvantaged by this feature of family origins.

Finally, changes in parents' educational attainments and occupational prestige could be substantial during the 1990s and beyond, but the direction and magnitude of any such changes is difficult to judge. Of course, the importance of the changing distribution of children with regard to these features of family origins depends on the size of the structural effect associated with each, but the future direction of change in such structural effects is also difficult to judge.

Distinguishing children by race, both blacks and whites experienced revolutionary increases in parents' education during the twentieth century, ensuring that most children of either race born since the 1970s have parents who had at least some high school education. Despite a substantial narrowing of the racial gap in parents' education, however, black children continue to be at a disadvantage and to lag substantially

[26]For births per 1,000 married women 15 years of age and over, see Table 2-1, National Center for Health Statistics: *Vital Statistics of the United States, 1985, Vol. III, Marriage and Divorce.* DHHS No. 9PHS 89–1103. Public Health Service (Washington, DC: U.S. Government Printing Office, 1989). Births to unmarried women as a proportion of all births increased more per year between 1980 and 1988 than between 1970 and 1980 for whites (0.835 vs. 0.449 percentage points per year), but it increased by less for blacks (1.03 vs. 1.788 percentage points per years). For birth data, see Table 1-31, National Center for Health Statistics: *Vital Statistics of the United States, 1986, Vol. I, Natality.* DHHS No. PHS 88–1123. Public Health Service (Washington, DC: U.S. Government Printing Office, 1988); and National Center for Health Statistics, Advance Report of Final Natality Statistics 1988, *Monthly Vital Statistics Report* 39, 4 (August 15, 1990): Suppl. Hyattsville, Maryland: Public Health Service.

behind white children in their chances of having parents who have completed at least 4 years of high school or college. For example, among the 1920s cohort, the largest disadvantages in parents' education among blacks were of 38–43 percentage points for fathers and mothers who had completed at least 7–8 years of education, while among the 1980s cohort the maximum gaps were about two-fifths as large (15–16 percentage points for the proportions whose parents had completed at least 13–15 years of education). Still, the 1980s cohort of black children lagged 2–3 decades behind white children in their chances of having parents who had completed at least 4 years of college.

Black children have also been disadvantaged by other features of family origins. Especially noteworthy is the fact that, over and above five other features of family origins, being black itself had a very large negative effect on educational attainments for the 1920s cohort—an effect equal to having 7–8 additional siblings in the family or a father who had 5–6 fewer years of schooling. But this negative effect declined sharply and essentially vanished for children born after about 1940.

On the other hand, the racial gap in large family living increased sharply (by 20 percentage points) between the 1920s and 1940s cohorts, and the racial gap in the proportion of children living in large families with mothers who had completed only 0–11 years of education increased about as much (by 19 percentage points). Meanwhile, however, the racial gap in the proportion of children who belonged to farm families declined substantially (by 10 percentage points). Overall, then, for blacks the disadvantage in family origins probably declined substantially between the 1920s and 1940s cohorts, mainly because the large disadvantage associated with being black vanished during the decades.

Subsequently, the 20 percentage point racial gap in the proportion of children living in families with 5 or more siblings for the 1940s cohort is expected to disappear for the 1990s cohort, and the maximum racial gaps in parents' education declined 16–23 percentage points between the 1940s and 1980s cohorts. On the other hand, the racial gap in one-parent family living is projected to increase by about 5–10 percentage points between the 1940 and 1980 cohorts. Overall, then, the disadvantage in family origins experienced by blacks, compared with whites, will have declined substantially between the 1940s and the 1980s or 1990s, but it appears that a substantial disadvantage will remain in parents' education and one-parent family living.

Compared with non-Hispanic whites born during the 1960s, old-family Hispanic children (of any race) were fairly similar to non-Hispanic blacks in their chances of having parents with low educational attainments and 5 or more siblings in the home, and they were closer to non-Hispanic blacks than to non-Hispanic whites in their chances of living in a one-parent family. First-generation Hispanic children (of any race) born during the 1960s were much more likely than old-family Hispanics (of any race) or non-Hispanics to have parents with low educational levels, were fairly similar to old-family Hispanics (of any race) and non-Hispanic blacks in their chances of living in a large family, and fairly similar to non-Hispanic whites in their chances of living in a one-parent family.

Overall, then, by the time of the 1970s cohort, old-family Hispanic children (of any race) and non-Hispanic blacks were about equal in their chances of being educationally disadvantaged by family origins, and first-generation Hispanic children (of any race) were somewhat more disadvantaged. Since the expected family size of Hispanics (of any race) born in the 1990s to mothers in the United States as of 1988 is similar to that of non-Hispanic blacks and non-Hispanic whites, Hispanic children (of any race) born of parents in the United States by 1988 may continue to be fairly similar to non-Hispanic blacks in their chances of being disadvantaged by family origins.

Beyond the features of family origins discussed in this chapter, however, children's educational attainments have in the past and will in the future be influenced by parents' and family incomes. In the next three chapters, we will turn our attention to an examination of historic changes in parents' and family incomes.

TABLE A-6.1

Total, White, and Black Children with Parents Completing Specified or Fewer Years of Education

All Races

Parents' Education	1920s	1930s	1940s	1950s	Census 1960s	CPS 1960s	CPS 1970s	CPS 1980s
Number of Children (in thousands)	11,860	10,060	15,450	19,679	18,320	17,895	14,075	16,069
Percent with Father Completing Specified or Fewer Years of Schooling								
0	4.9	2.3	1.4	1.0	0.5	0.6	0.5	0.3
1	6.1	3.6	2.1	1.4	0.7	0.8	0.6	0.4
2	8.7	5.7	3.2	2.1	1.4	1.4	1.0	0.7
3	12.5	9.5	5.5	3.0	2.2	2.1	1.6	1.1
4	19.9	14.7	8.6	4.3	3.0	2.9	2.0	1.4
5	26.4	19.8	11.5	6.2	4.4	4.0	2.7	1.9
6	35.4	27.4	15.9	9.1	6.5	5.8	4.3	3.0
7	43.5	36.7	22.8	12.9	8.5	8.2	5.7	3.5
8	72.7	60.4	40.3	23.6	14.9	14.7	9.1	5.2
9	78.0	67.0	46.8	29.7	19.6	18.8	11.8	7.8
10	83.2	74.2	55.3	37.9	25.2	24.2	15.0	11.3
11	85.2	77.9	60.8	44.4	29.7	28.3	18.4	14.6
12	92.8	90.4	83.3	75.1	65.6	64.5	55.1	52.6
13	94.0	92.1	86.6	79.2	70.9	69.8	61.3	59.4
14	95.5	94.3	90.3	84.1	78.0	76.6	71.0	68.9
15	96.3	95.0	91.8	85.8	80.6	78.9	74.1	72.5
16	98.7	97.9	95.9	93.1	89.5	89.4	87.4	87.3

TABLE A-6.1 (continued)

					All Races			
Parents' Education	1920s	1930s	1940s	1950s	Census 1960s	CPS 1960s	CPS 1970s	CPS 1980s
Number of children (in thousands)	12,745	11,332	16,892	22,222	21,719	21,685	18,627	21,387
Percent with Mother Completing Specified or Fewer Years of Schooling								
0	4.1	1.7	1.0	0.7	0.6	0.5	0.5	0.4
1	5.0	2.5	1.2	0.9	0.7	0.5	0.6	0.5
2	6.8	3.9	1.8	1.2	1.0	0.8	1.1	0.7
3	9.6	6.6	3.0	2.0	1.6	1.3	1.6	1.1
4	15.2	10.3	4.8	2.9	2.1	2.0	2.0	1.5
5	21.5	14.6	7.3	4.3	2.9	2.9	2.8	1.7
6	29.5	21.3	10.8	6.5	4.7	4.4	4.4	3.2
7	39.4	30.6	17.0	9.9	6.6	6.4	5.3	4.1
8	68.1	52.4	32.4	18.2	11.5	11.3	7.8	6.4
9	74.0	60.3	39.8	24.6	16.7	16.4	11.4	10.0
10	80.2	68.3	49.1	34.2	24.0	23.7	16.5	14.6
11	83.2	73.4	55.7	42.0	29.6	29.1	20.3	19.1
12	94.3	91.0	86.7	83.0	75.7	75.0	65.9	62.1
13	95.7	93.3	90.4	87.5	82.4	80.6	73.2	69.2
14	97.8	96.0	93.8	91.6	87.9	86.9	82.1	78.3
15	98.3	97.2	95.3	93.4	90.9	89.1	84.8	81.2
16	99.7	99.3	98.8	98.2	96.8	96.6	94.7	93.9

TABLE A-6.1 *(continued)*

Parents' Education	1920s White	1920s Black	1930s White	1930s Black	1940s White	1940s Black	1950s White	1950s Black	Census 1960s White	Census 1960s Black	CPS 1960s White	CPS 1960s Black	CPS 1970s White	CPS 1970s Black	CPS 1980s White	CPS 1980s Black
Number of Children (in thousands)	10,872	988	9,071	989	14,131	1,319	17,884	1,795	16,536	1,784	16,390	1,505	12,861	1,214	14,906	1,164
Percent with Father Completing Specified or Fewer Years of Schooling																
0	4.3	11.9	1.8	7.3	1.1	4.4	0.8	2.8	0.5	0.6	0.6	0.4	0.5	0.5	0.3	0.0
1	5.2	15.9	2.7	11.5	1.6	7.1	1.0	4.7	0.7	1.0	0.8	1.0	0.7	0.5	0.4	0.0
2	7.4	23.0	4.3	18.4	2.2	13.0	1.5	7.9	1.2	2.5	1.3	2.4	1.0	0.9	0.7	0.3
3	10.7	32.4	7.2	29.9	4.1	21.2	2.1	12.5	2.0	4.4	1.9	4.8	1.6	1.4	1.1	0.5
4	17.1	50.7	11.6	42.7	6.5	30.6	3.1	16.0	2.6	7.0	2.5	6.7	2.0	1.7	1.4	0.7
5	22.9	65.0	16.2	52.8	9.1	37.5	4.5	23.2	3.6	11.2	3.5	9.8	2.7	2.4	1.9	1.0
6	31.8	75.1	23.4	64.1	12.9	48.2	6.9	30.5	5.7	14.4	5.1	13.7	4.3	4.0	3.1	1.3
7	40.1	81.4	32.5	75.9	19.4	59.7	10.3	38.9	7.4	18.9	7.3	17.6	5.5	7.4	3.6	2.3
8	71.0	91.4	57.7	85.8	37.4	72.4	20.8	51.3	13.7	26.3	13.7	25.3	5.7	12.3	5.2	4.6
9	76.6	93.2	64.5	89.6	43.9	77.2	26.8	58.0	17.9	34.9	17.6	32.2	11.3	17.3	7.8	7.7
10	82.2	94.7	72.2	92.7	52.5	84.8	34.9	68.2	23.0	45.1	22.5	43.1	14.2	23.3	11.2	12.4
11	84.3	95.2	76.1	94.0	58.3	88.2	41.2	75.4	27.1	53.9	26.1	52.4	17.2	30.6	14.3	18.4
12	92.4	97.2	89.5	98.1	82.2	94.7	73.3	92.5	63.8	82.2	62.8	83.8	53.7	69.0	51.6	65.5
13	93.7	97.4	91.4	98.2	85.8	96.1	77.6	94.3	69.2	86.8	68.0	89.6	60.0	74.6	58.3	74.2
14	95.3	98.0	93.8	98.8	89.6	98.0	82.9	96.3	76.5	91.4	75.0	94.5	69.9	82.4	67.7	84.1
15	96.1	98.5	94.6	98.9	91.2	88.5	84.7	96.8	79.2	93.4	77.4	95.9	73.0	86.4	71.4	86.8
16	98.6	99.3	97.7	99.5	95.0	99.5	92.6	98.1	88.7	97.1	88.6	98.8	86.8	93.0	86.7	95.5
17											91.1	99.3	89.6	94.8	89.8	96.4

TABLE A-6.1 (continued)

Parents' Education	1920s White	1920s Black	1930s White	1930s Black	1940s White	1940s Black	1950s White	1950s Black	Census 1960s White	Census 1960s Black	CPS 1960s White	CPS 1960s Black	CPS 1970s White	CPS 1970s Black	CPS 1980s White	CPS 1980s Black
Number of Children (in thousands)	11,586	1,159	10,157	1,175	15,200	1,692	19,547	2,675	18,686	3,033	18,747	2,937	15,871	2,755	18,238	3,104
Percent with Mother Completing Specified or Fewer Years of Schooling																
0	3.8	6.7	1.7	2.0	1.0	1.0	0.7	0.6	0.6	0.3	0.5	0.2	0.6	0.3	0.5	0.1
1	4.7	8.5	2.3	4.1	1.1	1.5	0.8	1.1	0.7	0.4	0.6	0.2	0.6	0.4	0.5	0.1
2	6.1	13.6	3.3	9.1	1.5	3.7	1.1	2.2	1.1	0.8	0.8	0.5	1.1	0.8	0.8	0.2
3	8.3	22.4	5.5	15.9	2.6	6.1	1.8	3.4	1.6	1.5	1.3	1.2	1.7	0.9	1.3	0.2
4	13.1	25.8	8.5	25.3	3.8	12.8	2.5	5.5	2.1	2.5	2.0	2.0	2.1	1.3	1.7	0.3
5	18.7	49.7	12.2	34.5	5.8	20.2	3.6	9.5	2.8	3.5	2.8	3.2	3.0	1.8	1.9	0.5
6	26.2	62.7	18.2	47.7	8.7	29.3	5.5	14.3	4.4	6.1	4.1	6.3	4.6	3.1	3.5	1.0
7	36.0	73.7	27.1	60.4	14.2	42.1	8.3	22.0	6.1	9.5	5.8	9.8	5.5	4.2	4.4	2.0
8	66.3	86.5	49.8	74.2	29.3	60.3	16.2	32.7	10.7	16.3	10.5	16.5	8.0	7.0	6.8	4.4
9	72.2	91.5	57.8	81.2	36.8	67.0	22.1	42.5	15.2	25.5	15.2	24.5	11.2	12.5	10.1	9.5
10	78.8	93.7	66.1	87.0	46.2	75.1	31.1	56.9	21.6	38.6	21.6	37.3	15.5	22.2	14.0	18.2
11	82.0	95.0	71.4	90.8	52.8	81.6	38.1	70.2	26.4	49.4	26.1	48.6	18.8	29.0	17.6	27.7
12	93.9	98.1	90.3	97.2	85.9	94.0	81.7	92.5	74.3	83.7	73.4	85.0	64.8	72.6	60.0	74.6
13	95.4	98.6	92.8	97.9	89.8	95.6	86.5	94.7	81.1	90.1	79.2	89.6	72.1	79.4	67.2	81.1
14	97.6	98.9	95.7	99.0	93.3	97.7	90.9	96.6	86.8	94.5	85.7	94.5	81.1	87.9	76.5	88.5
15	98.2	99.0	96.9	99.2	95.0	98.2	92.9	97.2	90.0	95.8	88.1	96.0	83.8	90.5	79.6	90.9
16	99.7	99.6	99.2	99.7	98.7	99.5	98.1	98.9	96.5	98.1	96.3	98.9	94.2	97.5	93.3	97.5
17											97.8	99.7	96.2	98.3	95.4	98.2

SOURCES: Estimates derived from 1940–1980 PUMS and March CPS 1980 and 1989.

NOTES: Results for cohorts of 1920s through 1970s based on children at age 12–17. Estimates for 1980s cohort based on children aged 0–5 in 1989. Since some parents complete additional years of schooling after bearing children, children aged 0–5 will have parents with somewhat higher educational attainments when they reach age 12–17.

TABLE A-6.2

Hispanic and Non-Hispanic Children, by Parents' Years of Education: Census-Based

| | 1960s | | | | | 1970s | | | | |
| | Non-Hispanic | | | Hispanic Living with Father | | Non-Hispanic | | | Hispanic Living with Father | |
	White	Black	Hispanic	First Generation	Old Family	White	Black	Hispanic	First Generation	Old Family
Number of Children (in thousands)	15,319	1,762	1,239	450	789	12,960	1,415	1,534	635	899
Percent with Father Completing Specified or Fewer Years of Schooling										
0	0.3	0.6	3.6	6.2	2.2	0.1	0.4	2.5	4.7	0.9
1	0.4	1.0	5.0	7.3	3.7	0.1	0.5	3.1	6.1	1.0
2	0.6	2.4	9.0	12.7	6.8	0.2	0.5	4.8	9.3	1.7
3	1.0	4.2	14.3	20.0	11.0	0.4	0.8	7.3	13.7	2.8
4	1.3	6.8	18.2	24.9	14.3	0.6	1.6	9.1	16.5	3.9
5	2.1	10.8	23.2	32.7	17.9	0.8	3.0	12.5	23.1	5.0
6	3.6	14.0	32.4	48.7	23.2	1.4	4.6	23.5	44.3	8.9
7	5.2	18.5	35.5	50.9	26.7	2.2	6.2	26.3	47.2	11.6
8	11.4	26.0	42.5	57.6	33.8	4.3	9.4	31.2	52.8	15.9
9	15.5	34.7	47.9	59.1	41.4	7.6	13.6	37.6	58.0	23.2
10	20.5	44.9	54.4	63.6	49.2	11.4	21.6	44.3	63.1	31.0
11	24.5	53.8	59.7	67.3	55.4	14.8	30.2	49.0	65.5	37.3
12	62.4	82.2	80.8	84.2	78.8	52.0	71.4	75.8	79.8	73.0
13	68.0	86.8	84.4	86.2	83.4	59.9	78.2	82.7	85.2	80.9
14	75.4	91.4	90.2	90.2	90.2	69.1	85.3	88.0	89.6	86.9
15	78.1	93.4	92.3	91.8	92.6	73.2	88.6	90.8	92.0	90.0
16	88.1	97.0	95.7	96.4	95.3	86.1	94.8	93.8	93.4	94.1

TABLE A-6.2 (continued)

	1960s					1970s				
	Non-Hispanic		Hispanic	Hispanic Living with Mother		Non-Hispanic		Hispanic	Hispanic Living with Mother	
	White	Black	Hispanic	First Generation	Old Family	White	Black	Hispanic	First Generation	Old Family
Number of Children (in thousands)	17,136	2,994	1,589	508	1,081	14,067	2,469	1,863	662	1,201
Percent with Mother Completing Specified or Fewer Years of Schooling										
0	0.3	0.3	4.2	6.5	3.1	0.2	0.2	2.4	4.1	1.4
1	0.3	0.4	4.6	7.3	3.3	0.3	0.2	2.5	4.4	1.4
2	0.4	0.8	8.2	13.6	5.7	0.3	0.2	4.1	8.3	1.8
3	0.6	1.5	12.5	20.5	8.8	0.4	0.3	6.7	13.7	2.7
4	0.7	2.4	16.7	27.6	11.6	0.5	0.4	8.4	16.9	3.7
5	1.2	3.5	20.3	32.5	14.6	0.7	0.6	11.1	22.4	4.9
6	2.1	6.0	29.3	48.2	20.4	1.0	1.5	18.3	39.3	6.7
7	3.5	9.4	35.2	51.4	27.6	1.8	2.8	21.8	41.4	11.1
8	7.5	16.1	45.5	60.2	38.6	4.5	6.4	28.7	48.8	17.6
9	11.8	25.3	52.6	64.6	47.0	8.2	13.6	38.4	54.7	29.5
10	18.1	38.5	59.7	70.1	54.8	12.8	23.5	46.2	61.6	37.6
11	22.9	49.3	64.4	73.6	60.0	17.3	34.7	51.8	64.8	44.6
12	73.1	83.7	87.9	90.9	86.4	63.7	76.6	84.1	84.0	84.1
13	80.1	90.1	91.8	93.9	90.8	72.2	84.6	89.7	88.8	90.2
14	86.0	94.6	95.3	95.3	95.3	80.2	90.6	94.2	93.4	94.7
15	89.4	95.9	96.9	96.9	96.9	83.7	93.3	96.0	95.3	96.3
16	96.3	98.0	98.9	99.2	98.7	93.9	97.9	98.1	97.6	98.4

SOURCE: Estimates derived from 1980 Census PUMS.

NOTES: Estimates based only on children living with father or mother. Results for 1960s cohort based on children at age 12–17. Results for 1970s cohort based on children aged 0–5. Since some parents complete additional years of schooling after bearing children, children aged 0–5 will have parents with somewhat higher educational attainments when they reach age 12–17.

TABLE A-6.3
Hispanic and Non-Hispanic Children, by Parents' Years of Education: CPS-Based

| | 1960s | | | 1970s | | | 1980s | | |
	Non-Hispanic White	Non-Hispanic Black	Hispanic	Non-Hispanic White	Non-Hispanic Black	Hispanic	Non-Hispanic White	Non-Hispanic Black	Hispanic
Number of Children (in thousands)	15,180	1,479	1,236	11,579	1,198	1,298	13,282	1,148	1,639
Percent with Father Completing Specified or Fewer Years of Schooling									
0	0.3	0.4	5.2	0.1	0.5	4.2	0.1	0.0	1.5
1	0.3	1.0	6.8	0.1	0.5	5.2	0.2	0.0	2.7
2	0.6	2.4	9.1	0.3	0.7	7.9	0.2	0.3	4.5
3	0.9	4.9	13.8	0.4	1.2	11.8	0.4	0.5	7.0
4	1.4	6.9	16.9	0.7	1.3	13.7	0.4	0.7	9.9
5	2.2	9.5	19.4	1.0	2.1	18.5	0.5	1.0	13.7
6	3.3	13.4	28.0	1.6	3.7	28.1	0.8	1.3	22.1
7	5.3	17.0	32.5	2.6	7.2	31.4	1.1	2.3	24.1
8	11.3	24.5	44.3	5.5	12.1	37.9	2.2	4.7	29.4
9	15.1	31.6	49.3	7.7	17.1	43.5	4.2	7.8	37.0
10	19.9	42.7	54.3	10.5	23.2	47.5	7.3	12.5	42.8
11	23.6	52.0	58.2	13.3	30.7	51.9	10.2	18.6	47.4
12	61.2	83.8	82.8	51.1	69.0	77.9	48.4	65.8	77.3
13	66.6	89.6	86.4	57.5	74.5	82.4	55.0	74.3	84.8
14	73.8	94.5	90.4	67.8	82.3	89.1	64.9	84.3	90.3
15	76.2	96.0	92.0	70.9	86.3	91.8	68.8	87.1	92.5
16	87.9	98.8	96.5	85.7	93.0	96.7	85.4	95.5	97.2
17	90.6	99.3	97.8	88.7	94.9	97.5	88.8	96.3	97.7

TABLE A-6.3 (continued)

	1960s			1970s			1980s		
	Non-Hispanic White	Non-Hispanic Black	Hispanic	Non-Hispanic White	Non-Hispanic Black	Hispanic	Non-Hispanic White	Non-Hispanic Black	Hispanic
Number of Children (in thousands)	17,265	2,901	1,519	14,033	2,726	1,867	15,858	3,045	2,484
Percent with Mother Completing Specified or Fewer Years of Schooling									
0	0.3	0.2	3.1	0.4	0.2	2.1	0.4	0.1	1.1
1	0.3	0.2	3.9	0.4	0.3	2.6	0.4	0.1	1.6
2	0.4	0.6	5.8	0.5	0.7	6.4	0.4	0.2	3.1
3	0.5	1.1	10.2	0.6	0.8	10.0	0.5	0.2	6.3
4	0.9	1.9	14.8	0.8	1.1	12.3	0.6	0.2	9.1
5	1.4	3.1	19.1	1.1	1.6	17.4	0.7	0.4	10.1
6	2.2	6.0	27.3	1.5	2.9	28.0	0.8	0.8	20.8
7	3.6	9.5	31.8	2.2	4.0	31.0	1.3	1.9	24.1
8	7.8	16.0	42.3	4.0	6.7	38.4	2.9	4.3	31.6
9	12.2	24.2	49.9	6.5	12.1	46.9	5.4	9.3	40.2
10	18.7	36.9	55.5	10.7	22.0	51.9	8.9	18.1	46.6
11	23.2	48.4	59.5	13.7	28.8	57.2	12.2	27.5	52.7
12	72.2	85.0	87.5	62.2	72.6	83.9	56.1	74.6	85.1
13	78.2	89.6	90.5	70.1	79.5	87.0	63.9	81.0	88.4
14	84.9	94.5	94.2	79.5	87.9	93.1	73.9	88.6	93.8
15	87.4	96.0	95.4	82.4	90.5	94.6	77.2	90.9	94.9
16	96.1	98.9	98.7	93.6	97.5	98.9	92.4	97.5	98.6
17	97.7	99.6	99.0	95.7	98.3	99.5	94.8	98.1	99.2

SOURCES: 1980 and 1989 CPS

NOTES: Estimates based only on children living with father or mother. Results for 1960s and 1970s chart based on children at age 12–17 and for 1980s cohort based on children aged 0–5. Since some parents complete additional years of schooling after bearing children, children aged 0–5 will have parents with somewhat higher educational attainments when they reach age 12–17.

233

7

CHILDREN OF POVERTY AND LUXURY

Introduction and Highlights

IN THE United States it is family income that determines whether children live in material deprivation, comfort, or luxury. Children in low-income families may experience marked deprivation in such basic areas as nutrition, clothing, housing, and healthcare, while children in middle-income families generally live in material comfort and those in high-income families have access to the many luxuries that are available in the U.S. marketplace. Differences in family income also influence a child's chances of achieving economic success during adulthood: Children from low-income families are less likely to earn high incomes when they reach adulthood than are children from high-income families.[1]

The Great Depression was a time of economic deprivation for many

[1] For example, see William H. Sewell and Robert M. Hauser, *Education, Occupation, and Earnings* (New York: Academic, 1975). For discussions of additional studies, see Irwin Garfinkel and Sara S. McLanahan, *Single Mothers and Their Children* (Washington, DC: Urban Institute, 1986), pp. 31–37; Martha S. Hill and Greg J. Duncan, "Parental Family Income and the Socioeconomic Attainment of Children," *Social Science Research* 16, 1 (March 1987): 39–73; and Greg J. Duncan and Willard Rodgers, "Lone-Parent Families and Their Economic Problems: Transitory or Persistent?" in *Lone-Parent Families*, Organization for Economic Co-operation and Development, Social Policy Studies No. 8, Organization for Economic Co-operation and Development, pp. 61–62.

Americans, but especially for children. The post-Depression years through the 1960s brought large increases in absolute family income, and large reductions both in relative poverty and economic inequality. Measuring relative poverty in comparison to median family income in various years, it was found that the proportion of children living in relative poverty dropped sharply (from 38 to 24 percent) between 1939 and 1959, while the proportion living in relative luxury also declined (from 23 to 15 percent).[2] The corresponding proportion of children whose parents had comfortable, middle-class incomes increased greatly (from 28 to 42 percent between 1939 and 1959), and the proportion living in near-poor frugality increased somewhat (from 12 to 18 percent).

Only slight improvements occurred during the 1960s, and the next two decades brought a sharp reversal. Between 1969 and 1988, the proportion of children living in relative poverty increased from 23 to 27 percent, and the proportion living in relative luxury increased from 15 to 22 percent, as the proportion with comfortable middle-class incomes declined from 43 to 37 percent and the proportion living in relatively frugal circumstances declined from 19 to 14 percent.

For children, then, the 1940s and the 1950s brought a large decline in economic deprivation and a large reduction in economic inequality; the 1960s brought a slight additional improvement; and the 1970s and the 1980s brought substantial increases in both relative poverty and economic inequality. By 1988 relative poverty and inequality among children had returned to levels not seen since 1949 or earlier; the gains of the 1950s and the 1960s vanished during the 1970s and the 1980s. These trends were largely the result of changes among white children.

Among black children, relative poverty declined during each decade between 1939 and 1979, especially during the 1940s, 1960s, and 1970s. During the 1980s, the economic situation of young black children deteriorated. By 1988 a large proportion (22 percent) of white children and a much larger proportion (53 percent) of black children lived in relative poverty, and the proportion whose family incomes fell below the comfortable middle class was 37 percent for whites and 67 percent for blacks, while the proportion living in luxury was 25 percent for whites and only 8 percent for blacks. By 1980, both old-family and first-generation Hispanic children were similar to black children in their chances of living in relative poverty.

---

[2]As discussed later in this chapter, relative poverty is defined as an income that is less than one-half as large as the median family income in the specified year, adjusted for family composition. Similarly, relative luxury is defined as an income that is at least 50 percent larger than the median family income, adjusted for family composition. Definitions of middle-class comfort and near-poor frugality used here, as well as differences between these measures of relative income, and the official absolute poverty measure of the U.S. government are discussed later in this chapter.

Throughout the era, children have been more likely than adults to live in deprived economic circumstances, but the gap narrowed from 9 percentage points in 1939 to 4–6 percentage points in 1949–1969 only to return to 10 percentage points by 1988. The narrowing of the gap between adults and children during the 1940s occurred because the proportion living in relative poverty declined more for children than for adults, while the expansion in the gap during the 1970s and the 1980s occurred mainly because of increased relative deprivation among children. Adults, as was true for children, experienced a large increase in economic equality between 1939 and 1969, and a substantial increase in economic inequality between 1969 and 1988.

This chapter discusses in detail the changes in family income experienced by children since the Great Depression, and hence the changing proportion of children who have lived in relative poverty, comfort, and luxury. To accomplish this, the advantages and disadvantages of several alternative measures of family income are discussed. In this chapter family income includes all sources of cash income, but it does not include the effects of changes in tax laws and noncash transfers, such as public or employer-provided health-insurance benefits, food stamps, and the like. But our review of other studies and supplementary data pertaining to taxes and noncash benefits indicates the following.

First, relative poverty and economic inequality for children were actually greater than was suggested by the cash-income measures in each year between 1949 and 1988. Second, the reduction in relative poverty and economic inequality for children during the 1940s and the 1950s was actually somewhat less than was indicated by cash-income measures. Third, access to noncash health benefits became more equal during the 1960s and the 1970s, but the tax burden became less equal between the mid-1960s and the mid-1980s. Fourth, the increase in relative poverty and economic inequality for children during the 1980s was actually somewhat greater than was indicated by cash-income measures.[3]

In subsequent chapters, we will focus on how changes in the economic circumstances of children have been influenced by changes in parents' labor-force participation and earnings, family composition, government welfare (income transfer) programs, and by other social changes in the United States.

[3]Joseph A. Pechman, *Who Paid the Taxes, 1966–1985?*, (Washington, DC: Brookings Institution, 1985), pp. 4–6, 68. See later sections in this chapter for a discussion of tax laws and noncash health benefits, as well as relevant data.

The Post-Depression Boom in Absolute Income

Following the Great Depression and World War II, real median family income (controlling for inflation) increased greatly (by 35–45 percent per decade during the 1940s, 1950s, and 1960s). Similar decade-by-decade increases in real median family income per family member also occurred during these years, despite the shifts in family composition associated with the baby boom and the baby bust, and the increases, especially after 1960, in divorce and out-of-wedlock childbearing. Since the high level it reached in about 1969, however, real family income has increased comparatively little.

Despite increasing labor-force participation rates for wives and mothers, real median family income increased by only 5 percent during the 1970s and 1 percent between 1979 and 1988. Similarly, real median family income per family member increased by only 13 percent during the 1970s and 7 percent between 1979 and 1988.

The large increases in family income following the Great Depression were accompanied by a proliferation of consumer goods and by remarkable increases in the quality of many consumer products. As a result, the typical American during the 1970s lived in a world of abundance that Americans 30 years earlier could hardly have imagined, let alone hoped for.[4]

Children benefited from this large, absolute increase in the American standard of living. For example, controlling for inflation (by expressing incomes in 1988 dollars), 64 percent of children in 1939 lived in families whose annual incomes were less than $12,200, compared with only 14–15 percent in 1979 and 1988. At the opposite extreme, a tiny 3

[4]Estimates from the Census of the Population indicate that real median family income (controlling for inflation) increased by 47 percent between 1939 and 1949, by 51 percent between 1949 and 1959, by 35 percent between 1959 and 1969, and by 5 percent between 1969 and 1979. Estimates from the Current Population Survey for the last three sets of decades indicate that the increases were 43, 38 and 5 percent, respectively. Since income was probably underestimated somewhat more in the census than in the Current Population Survey (CPS) in 1949, the census probably somewhat overestimates the 1949–1959 change. Similarly, since the census' underestimate of income was probably somewhat greater in 1939 than in 1949, the estimate of change for 1939–1949 is probably somewhat too large. Additional noncensus data for earlier years also support the latter conclusion. See Edward J. Welniak, Jr., U.S. Bureau of the Census, Current Population Reports, Series P-60, No. 151, *Money Income of Households, Families, and Persons in the United States: 1984* (Washington, DC: U.S. Government Printing Office, 1986), Table 11. Despite the census' underestimates of total income for 1939 and 1949, results pertaining to differences between groups within a given census year are reasonably accurate and the best available. For example, see Herman P. Miller, *Income of the American People* (New York: Wiley, 1955).

percent of children in 1939 had annual family incomes of at least $32,600, compared with 51 percent in 1979 and 1988.

Another indicator of absolute income levels, for persons with low incomes, is the official poverty rate. Applying the official poverty thresholds for 1988 to historical data, but controlling for inflation, we find that the official poverty rate for children dropped sharply from a huge 72 percent in 1939 to 48 percent in 1949, 26 percent in 1959, and 16 percent in 1969 and 1979; it then rose to 20 percent in 1988.[5] Clearly, the three decades following the Great Depression brought large increases in absolute income and large reductions in absolute want.

Measuring Relative Income and Relative Poverty

Despite these economic improvements, statistics about absolute income levels tell us little about the extent to which children were living

[5]Poverty rates are calculated in this book using the official poverty threshold for 1979 (controlling for inflation). But "negative" incomes are ignored, since they are largely a creation of the tax code, and the actual cash income available to a family or person for spending in any particular year does not fall below zero. Census income data for 1939 pertain only to wage and salary income, while census data for later years include all sources of income. To derive estimates for 1939 that are comparable to estimates for later years, two sets of estimates are derived for income measures as of 1949. The first set is based on all sources of income for all persons; the second is based only on wage and salary income for persons or families with some wage and salary income. For income measures presented in this chapter, although the two sets of results for 1949 are fairly similar to each other, the percentage point differences are calculated and then applied as "adjustment factors" to the corresponding results for 1939, which are based only on wage and salary income for persons or families with some wage and salary income, in order to derive "adjusted" estimates for income from all sources for 1939. In Table 7.1, for example, the estimates of relative poverty have been adjusted by the following percentage point values: 0.73 for children, 5.63 for adults, −0.42 for parents, 7.06 for potential parents, 7.35 for post-parental adults aged 45–64, and 16.73 for postparental adults aged 65+. The importance and appropriateness of making these somewhat crude adjustments is reflected in the fact that without the adjustments, the measured relative poverty rate would have increased between 1939 and 1949 for potential parents and postparental adults. Our estimates of the official poverty rates from censuses taken between 1939 and 1979 are similar to those presented on p. 33 of Eugene Smolensky, Sheldon Danziger, and Peter Gottschalk, "The Declining Significance of Age in the United States: Trends in the Well-Being of Children and the Elderly Since 1939." In John L. Palmer, Timothy Smeeding, and Barbara Boyle Torrey, eds., The Vulnerable (Washington, DC: Urban Institute, 1988), pp. 29–54. See also, Christine Ross, Sheldon Danziger, and Eugene Smolensky, "The Level and Trend of Poverty in the United States, 1939–1979," Demography 24, 4 (November 1987): 587–600. Compared with their estimates, our estimates of the official poverty rate are about 6 percentage points smaller for 1939, 1 percentage point larger for 1949, and 1 percentage point smaller for 1979. These differences for the total population may exist because we use the official 1980 poverty thresholds as the starting point, while they appear to use the 1959 thresholds as the starting point, and the latter varied by the age and sex of the household head, and by farm-nonfarm residence, while the 1980 thresholds do not.

in relative deprivation or luxury compared with the standards of the times in which they were growing up. The reason is that *within a specific historical period, what determines whether a family (and its members) is judged to be living in deprivation or luxury is that family's income and whether it is especially low or especially high compared with typical families in the same historical period.*

For example, the few children in 1939 whose annual family incomes were $32,000 or more (in 1988 dollars) were judged, correctly by the standards of the time, to be living in luxury. But with the enormous general increase in income levels that followed, the median family income in 1988 was $32,080. In other words, about half of all families had incomes below $32,000 and about half had incomes above $32,000. By contemporary standards in 1988, then, many children whose family incomes were $32,000 or more were judged, correctly, to have an average American standard of living and not a life of luxury.

Because a family's income relative to the standards of the time in which they live determines whether their income is viewed as inadequate, acceptable, or luxurious, economic reports often classify families (and their members) as having relatively low or relatively high incomes compared with the income of the typical (median) family or compared with that of families in the bottom, middle, or top fifths of the income distribution.[6] These median and quintile-based measures of relative income are limited in their usefulness for describing the standard of living among children, however, because in order to maintain a specified standard of living, families that have a large number of children need a higher income than do families that have a small number of children.

One approach to reducing this problem is to calculate median and quintile income distributions based on "family income per family member"—that is, family income divided by the number of people in the family.[7] But these income measures also are limited in two important

[6]For example, see U.S. Bureau of the Census, *Historical Statistics of the United States, Colonial Times to 1970, Bicentennial Edition, Part 1;* or U.S. Bureau of the Census, *Current Population Reports,* various issues (Washington, DC: U.S. Government Printing Office, 1975). See also Frank Levy, *Dollars and Dreams: The Changing American Income Distribution* (New York: Russell Sage Foundation, 1987), p. 44. Our estimates show that for each census year between 1939 and 1979, about one-half of children had family incomes above and about one-half had family incomes below the median, and that about one-fifth of children had family incomes that fell within each quintile of the family income distribution.

[7]Focusing on family income per family member, a very large 70–73 percent of children were below the median during census years since the Great Depression, and a very large 60–62 percent were in the two lowest quintiles. Only 6–7 percent of children lived in families in the fifth (top) quintile, and only 12–13 percent were in the fourth quintile. These results indicate that throughout the 40 years from 1939 to 1979, children have been concentrated in families with relatively low incomes per family member.

ways: They do not adequately account for (1) economies of scale in consumption and (2) changing inequality in the income distribution.

Economies of scale in consumption refer to the fact that in order to maintain a specific standard of living when an additional member has been added to a family, the family need not increase its income proportionally. For example, a family of three that adds one member has increased in size by 33 percent, but it can maintain the same standard of living by increasing its income by less than 33 percent. The reason is that the larger family does not need to spend additional money for some consumer items, and it does not need to spend 33 percent more money for other consumer items. The larger family may not need a more costly (or larger) car, television, or radio, for example; and it may not need to spend one-third more for a slightly larger home, the energy costs of maintaining a slightly larger home, or foods that are less costly per unit when purchased in larger packages.

Changing inequality in the income distribution refers to the fact that in one historical period, families near the bottom (or top) part of the income distribution may be further removed from a typical standard of living than families who are near the bottom (or top) part of the income distribution in another historical period. Focusing on the family income distribution, for example, families at the bottom quintile of the income distribution in 1939 had incomes that were only 42 percent as large as the median, but similar families in 1959 had incomes that were 50 percent as large as the median. Focusing on family income per family member as a second example, families at the bottom quintile in 1939 had family incomes per family member that were only 36 percent as large as the median. By 1959, however, similar families had incomes per family member that were 50 percent as large as the median.

Emphasizing that poverty must be defined in comparison to contemporary standards of living, Adam Smith defined economic hardship more than two centuries ago as the experience of being unable to consume commodities that "the custom of the country renders it indecent for creditable people, even of the lowest order, to be without."[8]

More recently, in 1958, John Kenneth Galbraith also argued that "[p]eople are poverty-stricken when their income, even if adequate for survival, falls markedly behind that of the community. Then they cannot have what the larger community regards as the minimum necessary

---

[8]Adam Smith, *Wealth of Nations* (London: Everyman's Library, 1776), p. 691. The basic normative, and hence relative, nature of experience with poverty has been highlighted, in part through this quotation from the *Wealth of Nations*, in recent research focusing on the measurement of poverty in the United States, including "Alternative Measures of Poverty," A Staff Study Prepared for the Joint Economic Committee (of the U.S. Congress), October 18, 1989, p. 10; and Patricia Ruggles, *Drawing the Line* (Washington, DC: Urban Institute, 1990), p. 20.

for decency; and they cannot wholly escape, therefore, the judgment of the larger community that they are indecent. They are degraded for, in a literal sense, they live outside the grades or categories which the community regards as respectable."[9]

Also arguing for relative measures of poverty in preference to absolute measures, Victor Fuchs urged that "[i]t is more reasonable, therefore, to think of poverty in terms of relative incomes. . . . In any given society at any given point in time the 'poor' are those in the bottom tail of the income distribution. While there will always be a bottom tail, how far those in it are from those in the middle is probably of critical importance."[10] Based on this idea, Fuchs proposed that the annual poverty threshold be established at one-half of the median income for that year.

In a comprehensive review of existing U.S. studies, Lee Rainwater concluded in 1974 that "[i]f we put together the evidence from professionals, standard-of-living budgets and public judgments from 1937 through the 1960s concerning living levels, we can sketch out a very rough approximation of qualitative living levels along the following lines."[11] The evidence reviewed by Rainwater consists of conclusions drawn by family-budget experts, conclusions based on extant family-budget studies, and conclusions drawn from public opinion surveys conducted throughout this era.

Rainwater's review indicates that Americans throughout the era have regarded a "low" or "poverty" level income in any given year as an amount that is equal to less than 50 percent of the median family (disposable) income in that year; "enough to get along" translates into an amount equal to at least 50 percent but less then 75 percent of the median; "comfortable or prosperous" is seen as an amount that is at least 75 percent but less than 150 percent of the median; and "rich or super-rich" entails an amount that is at least 150 percent of the median.[12]

[9]John Kenneth Galbraith, *The Affluent Society* (Boston: Houghton Mifflin, 1958), pp. 323–324.

[10]Victor Fuchs, "Towards a Theory of Poverty." In *The Concept of Poverty* (Washington, DC: Chapter of Commerce of the United States, 1965), pp. 71–91.

[11]Lee Rainwater, *What Money Buys: Inequality and the Social Meanings of Income* (New York: Basic Books, 1974), p. 62.

[12]As the culmination of this and subsequent research, an Expert Committee convened by the U.S. Bureau of Labor Statistics, and chaired by Harold W. Watts, developed and recommended an approach that viewed the "prevailing family standard" as the living level experienced by the typical two-parent, two-child family. Report by the Expert Committee on Family Budget Revisions, *New American Family Budget Standards* (Madison, WI: Institute for Research on Poverty, 1980). The Watts Committee also specified three additional expenditure standards. The lowest, "social minimum" standard, set at 50 percent of the prevailing family standard, was developed to mark the boundary below which it is nearly impossible to maintain a living standard that is recognized as a part of the normal social structure. Living levels that fall below this boundary raise issues of defi-

Using this general approach to measuring relative income, this chapter presents a long-term series of historical statistics that classify families (and their members) as living in (1) relative poverty or economic deprivation, (2) near-poor frugality, (3) middle-class comfort or prosperity, and (4) luxury. Specifically, we classify a family's income level as "relatively poor" if it is less than one-half as large as the median family income; as "near-poor" if it is above the relative poverty level but less than three-fourths as large as the median; as "middle-class comfort" if it is above the near-poor level but less than 50 percent more than the median; or as "luxurious" if it is at least 50 percent more than the median.[13]

In addition, however, because the needs and economies of scale experienced by a family depend upon its size and composition, we adjust our thresholds for relatively poor, near-poor, and luxury living by applying the interfamily "equivalence scales" used for the official poverty thresholds since 1979.[14]

The resulting historical estimates of relative poverty are consistent with perhaps the best-known statement about poverty made during the

---

ciency and deprivation. The second, "lower living" standard, set at two-thirds of the prevailing standard, was developed to mark the boundary reflecting public consensus about "how much it takes to get along in this community." The third, "social abundance" standard, set at 50 percent more than the prevailing standard, was developed to reflect the living level at which families can enjoy numerous luxury consumption items available in the U.S. economy. Report by the Expert Committee on Family Budget Revisions, *New American Family Budget Standards* (Madison, WI: Institute for Research on Poverty, 1980), p. 57–60. The most important difference between the recommendations of the Watts Committee in measuring relative poverty and the approach adopted here is that the committee based its recommendations on consumer expenditure data rather than on income data.

[13]Another recent study of poverty and luxury living was presented by James P. Smith, "Children Among the Poor," *Demography* 26, 2 (May 1969): 235–248. Our approach and Smith's are similar in assuming that each $1.00 increase in median income is associated with a $0.50 increase in the relative poverty threshold. But he uses the median income of white families, while we follow Rainwater's assessment of past evidence in using the median for all families as the basis of comparison. Also, in measuring affluence or luxury living, Smith adopted the top 25 percent of white families in 1960 as the threshold point, and he argued that "in my view the standard for affluence should grow at least as rapidly as real income" (p. 247), presumably white real income. Again, we follow Rainwater's assessment of past evidence indicating that the threshold of luxury living is equal to 150 percent of the median for all families, with its implicit increase in threshold equal to $1.50 for every $1.00 increase in the median. These differences in measurement appear to account for the occasional large differences between the estimates presented here and by Smith.

[14]The two-adult, two-child family is taken as the standard for which the median family income is the most appropriate threshold for gauging relative poverty, comfort, and the like. This threshold is then adjusted with the interfamily equivalence scale for families that consist of other sizes and compositions. Between 1940 and 1980, the median dependent number of siblings in the homes of parents varied between 1.8 and 2.1 dependent siblings. Hence, it seems likely that expert and public judgments reviewed by Rainwater were in effect using the two-adult, two-child family as the standard.

Great Depression. In his Second Inaugural Address on January 20, 1937, President Franklin Delano Roosevelt portrayed poverty in the United States, declaring, "I see one-third of a nation ill-housed, ill-clad, and ill-nourished."[15] Our measure of relative poverty indicates that 32 percent of Americans lived in relative poverty in 1939 (Table 7.1).

More recently, when the first official approach to estimating poverty in the United States was developed, the results indicated that 19 percent of Americans lived in poverty in 1963, while our estimate of relative poverty in 1963 (20 percent) is nearly identical.[16] Of course, the more removed one moves from the early 1960s, either backward or forward in time, the greater the difference between the relative and official poverty rates, because the official poverty thresholds do not take into account the enormous changes in the typical standard of living that occurred between 1940 and 1970. Hence, relative poverty rates are much lower than official poverty rates in 1939 and 1949, but substantially higher than official poverty rates since 1969 (Table 7.1).

In addition, in a recent comprehensive review of alternative poverty measures, Patricia Ruggles suggests that in view of other changes in "necessary consumption" since 1970, our relative poverty estimates may *underestimate* actual poverty during the late 1970s and the 1980s.[17] As

[15]John Bartlett *Familiar Quotations*, 14th ed. rev. and enl.. Emily Morison Beck, ed. (Boston: Little, Brown, 1968), p. 971.

[16]The official estimate is from p. 4, Mollie Orshansky, "Who's Who Among the Poor: A Demographic Profile," *Social Security Bulletin* 28, 7 (July 1965): 3–32. The relative poverty rate for 1963 is estimated by assuming that the proportion of change in relative poverty between 1959 and 1969 that had occurred by 1963 was the same as the proportion of change that had occurred in the official poverty rate. Since the decline in relative poverty between 1959 and 1969 was only 3.5 percentage points, this procedure produces no more than a small bias in the relative poverty rate, compared to calculations based on actual income data.

[17]Patricia Ruggles, *Drawing the Line* (Washington, DC: Urban Institute, 1990). Our relative poverty measure corresponds most closely with Ruggles' "Relative threshold—4 person standard," (for example, pp. 43–53, and 55). Small differences between these estimates by Ruggles and our estimates probably result from the fact that we ignore "negative" incomes (by treating them as zero), and we calculate the median family income based on the specific reported dollar value of income for each family in the CPS sample, while the U.S. Census Bureau officially (presumably the medians used by Ruggles) estimates median family income based on broader income categories that produce slightly higher estimates of the median family income, at least during the late 1980s. In Ruggles' view (p. 46), the two most important limitations of a relative poverty measure are as follows. First, relative measures would allow the relative poverty thresholds to fall in real terms whenever median income fell, as during recessions. But as Ruggles notes (p. 46, Footnote 19), Harold W. Watts has proposed a solution to this difficulty, suggesting a "ratchet," which would allow thresholds to rise with median income or expenditure levels but remain constant during times of declining real median income. Second, relative poverty thresholds are less closely linked to the concept of "minimum adequacy" of income than are more direct approaches that set the poverty threshold based on actual consumption patterns. On the other hand, Ruggles' proposed "minimum needs" approach, adjusting for changes in consumption patterns every decade, would also allow for discontinuous

noted above, the approach to measuring relative poverty used in this book is based on research, conducted between the 1930s and the 1960s, that documents professional and public judgments about the minimum income levels needed to live at various levels of comfort.

Consequently, it is possible that the relative measure of poverty used here actually *does* understate the poverty increase since 1970, aside from issues of taxation and noncash benefits discussed below. On the other hand, in view of the relatively small increases in median family income that have occurred since 1970, despite the large increases in the labor force participation of wives and mothers (discussed especially in Chapters 3, 4, 9, and 10), it seems unlikely that a drop has occurred since 1970 in the amount of income that people feel is necessary to get along. All together, then, it seems unlikely that the measure of relative poverty used in this book overstates the increase in poverty that occurred between 1969 and 1988, but it should be kept in mind that this measure may understate somewhat the increase in poverty that has occurred since 1969.

Relative Poverty and Family Income for Children

The relative poverty rate among children dropped sharply after the Great Depression (by 11 percentage points) from 38 to 27 percent between 1939 and 1949 (Figure 7.1 and Table 7.1). The 1950s brought a continuing but smaller decline to 24 percent, and the 1960s brought a slight further decline to 23 percent in 1969. The 4 percentage point decline of the 1950s and the 1960s was reversed by the 4 percentage point increase that occurred between 1969 and 1988. Most of this increase

jumps in poverty thresholds and rates whenever the adjustments actually were implemented. Ruggles also suggests (p. 19) that "[t]he specific set of poverty thresholds constructed using the two approaches may not be significantly different at any given point in time, since "expert" opinions on the minimum (income) needed for subsistence are quite likely to correspond at least roughly to popular ideas based on relative income or consumption levels. Over time, however, an absolute standard that is adjusted only for price changes will decline in relative terms if there is any growth at all in family incomes." In fact, Ruggles' "minimum needs" estimates (pp. 55, 57) indicate that poverty rates based on a "housing consumption standard" or on an "updated multiplier standard" are substantially higher than our relative poverty estimates for the late 1970s and 1980s. Hence, our estimate of poverty increases during these decades may be somewhat too low. (See also "Alternative Measures of Poverty," A Staff Study Prepared for the Joint Economic committee of the U.S. Congress, October 18, 1989.) As noted in the text, however, our relative poverty estimates are quite similar to the official (minimum needs) estimate for the early 1960s, since the official thresholds around 1963 were quite similar to the relative thresholds or standards of the time.

FIGURE 7.1

Children, by Relative Income Levels: 1939–1988

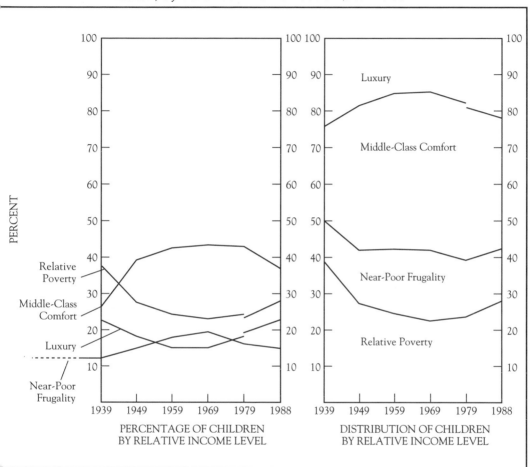

SOURCE: Table 7.1.

occurred during the 1980s, and by 1988, the proportion of children living in economically deprived families had returned to the comparatively high level of 27 percent that had been experienced almost 40 years earlier, in 1949. As a result of this increase in relative poverty among children, the total number of children living in economically deprived families increased from 15.8 million to 17.2 million between 1969 and 1988, despite the 5.7 million decrease during these years in the total number of children in the United States.

TABLE 7.1

Children and Adults, by Relative Income Levels and Official Poverty Rates: 1939–1988

Relative Economic Circumstances, Age, and Family Status	1939	1949	1959	1969	Census 1979	CPS 1979	CPS 1988
Relative Poverty							
Children aged 0–17	37.9	26.9	24.4	22.7	23.8	23.0	27.0
Adults aged 18 and over	29.2	23.4	18.9	17.9	17.0	15.3	16.6
Parents aged 18 and over	27.9	18.0	16.1	14.6	15.9	14.9	18.3
Potential parents aged 18–44	28.1	24.5	17.3	15.1	16.4	11.6	14.2
Post-parental adults aged 45–64	25.5	22.0	16.8	14.0	12.4	12.3	12.7
Post-parental adults aged 65+	42.8	41.7	34.3	37.0	27.1	27.5	22.7
Post-parental adults aged 65+ adjusted for housing cost	39.3	NA	27.6	29.6	19.8	19.2	15.9
Total population	31.7	24.5	20.9	19.6	18.9	17.5	19.3
Near-Poor Frugality							
Children aged 0–17	11.6	15.2	18.1	19.0	15.4	15.7	14.4
Adults aged 18 and over	10.8	10.7	13.0	13.4	12.3	12.5	12.0
Parents aged 18 and over	12.3	12.6	15.3	16.2	13.7	13.8	13.2
Potential parents aged 18–44	9.3	9.5	9.5	10.6	9.8	9.5	9.9
Post-parental adults aged 45–64	9.9	8.3	9.2	8.6	8.5	8.8	8.6
Post-parental adults aged 65+	12.1	12.1	16.4	16.8	19.2	20.4	17.7
Middle-Class Comfort							
Children aged 0–17	27.5	39.3	42.1	42.8	42.4	42.1	36.5
Adults aged 18 and over	25.2	32.3	37.5	38.2	37.5	37.9	33.7
Parents aged 18 and over	30.1	43.0	46.6	47.4	45.5	45.2	38.8
Potential parents aged 18–44	24.5	26.3	32.5	35.5	35.1	36.2	31.0
Post-parental adults aged 45–64	22.3	25.3	29.6	31.8	30.7	30.6	28.7
Post-parental adults aged 65+	18.9	23.8	27.4	26.2	32.6	33.7	34.6

TABLE 7.1 (continued)

Relative Economic Circumstances, Age, and Family Status	1939	1949	1959	1969	Census 1979	CPS 1979	CPS 1988
Luxury							
Children aged 0–17	23.0	18.6	15.3	15.4	18.4	19.3	22.1
Adults aged 18 and over	34.9	33.6	30.6	30.5	33.2	34.2	37.8
Parents aged 18 and over	29.7	26.4	22.1	21.9	24.9	26.1	29.7
Potential parents aged 18–44	38.1	39.6	40.8	38.9	38.7	42.7	44.9
Post-parental adults aged 45–64	42.3	44.4	44.4	45.6	48.5	48.3	50.0
Post-parental adults aged 65+	26.2	22.4	22.0	20.0	21.2	18.4	25.0
Official Poverty							
Children aged 0–17	71.8	47.6	25.8	16.1	16.3	16.2	19.7
Adults aged 18 and over	57.7	37.8	20.1	12.9	10.7	9.5	10.8
Total Population	61.8	40.8	22.2	14.0	12.3	11.4	13.1
Total (in thousands)							
Children aged 0–17	29,647	44,340	64,121	69,434	63,816	63,488	63,747
Adults aged 18 and over	67,889	100,717	111,888	128,408	157,122	159,527	179,783
Parents aged 18 and over	25,503	38,819	50,474	53,566	56,207	57,333	59,543
Potential parents aged 18–44	26,009	27,995	21,253	26,677	43,657	45,093	53,990
Post-parental adults aged 45–64	12,243	22,400	24,966	29,139	33,277	33,125	37,382
Post-parental adults aged 65+	4,134	11,504	15,195	19,026	23,981	23,977	28,868

SOURCES: Estimates derived from 1940–1980 census PUMs, and March CPS for 1980 and 1989.

NOTES: Parents aged 18 and over: persons aged 18 and over with a biological, step, or adopted child aged 0–17 in home. Potential parents, aged 18–44: persons aged 18–44 without a biological, step, or adopted child aged 0–17 in home. Post-parental adults aged 45–64: persons aged 45–64 without a biological, step, or adopted child aged 0–17 in home. Post-parental adults aged 65+: Persons aged 65+ without a biological step or adopted child aged 0–17 in home. See text and especially footnotes for methods of calculating relative poverty, near-poor frugality, middle-class comfort, luxury income levels, and for housing cost adjustment.

247

As relative poverty declined among children between 1939 and 1969, so, too, did the proportion of children who lived in relative luxury. In the Great Depression year of 1939, 23 percent of children lived in relative luxury, but this figure declined to 15 percent in 1959 and 1969. Hence, the proportion of children living in middle-class comfort increased from 28 percent in 1939 to 39 percent in 1949 and 43 percent by 1969. Meanwhile, the proportion of children living in near-poor frugality increased from 12 to 19 percent, mainly between 1939 and 1959.

Overall, then, children experienced a sharp reduction in economic inequality between 1939 and 1959, as the proportion of children living in either relative poverty or relative luxury dropped from 61 to 40 percent. This trend was reversed during the 1970s and the 1980s, however, as the proportion of children living in either relative poverty or relative luxury climbed from 38 percent in 1969 to 49 percent in 1988, eliminating half of the gains made during the 1940s and the 1950s. As inequality increased, the proportion of children living in middle-class comfort declined from 43 percent in 1969 to 37 percent in 1988, and the proportion living above the relative poverty threshold but not achieving middle-class comfort declined from 19 to 14 percent.

As a result of these changes, the proportion of children living in either middle-class comfort or luxury increased from 51 percent in 1939 to 57–58 percent in 1949–1969 and 61 percent in 1979, but by 1988 the proportion had declined to 59 percent. In other words, throughout most of the era since the Great Depression, the proportion of children living in relatively poor or near-poor circumstances has exceeded 40 percent.

Relative Poverty and Income Across the Life Course

How do these changes in relative income and poverty for children compare with changes for adults living in various life course situations? Throughout the era since the Great Depression, the economic circumstances of children have been less favorable than those of adults (Table 7.1). In 1939, children were 9 percentage points more likely than adults to live in relative poverty. After the Great Depression, the age gap in relative poverty narrowed by one-half to only 4–6 percentage points in 1949–1969. But then as relative poverty among children increased, the age gap expanded to 10 percentage points in 1988—virtually the same as it was in 1939.

At the upper end of the income distribution, decade-by-decade changes in the proportion living in luxury were nearly identical for adults and children; children were 12 percentage points less likely than adults to live in luxury in 1939, and this expanded slightly to a nearly constant

15–16 percentage points between 1949–1988. Hence, for adults, as for children, a sharp reduction in income inequality followed the Great Depression, but this reversed after 1969. For adults as a whole, relative poverty increased only slightly after 1979, and the increase in economic inequality is largely accounted for by the large 7 percentage point increase in the proportion who lived in luxury between 1969 and 1988. This overview of trends in relative income and poverty among adults masks important differences in trends among adults in various life course situations, however.

Trends among current parents—that is, parents with dependent children (under age 18) in the home—have been most similar to those for children, since such parents and children share the same households. For both children and current parents, relative poverty rates dropped sharply after the Great Depression, then more slowly; but between 1969 and 1988 relative poverty rates increased by about 4 percentage points, returning to the levels recorded for 1949. At the upper end of the income distribution, the proportions living in luxury declined between 1939 and 1959, then increased between 1969 and 1988 to at least the level experienced during the Great Depression. Hence, for both children and current parents, relative poverty rates and economic inequality decreased substantially between 1939 and 1959, but increased substantially between 1969 and 1988.

Trends in relative income and poverty have been quite different for potential parents and for postparental working-age adults—that is, for adults aged 18–44 and 45–64 who have no dependent children in the home.[18] Although these adults were similar to current parents in their chances of living in relative poverty in 1939, the immediate post-Depression decline in their relative poverty rate was slower than that for children and current parents, but by 1959 they were again on a par with current parents. Between 1969 and 1988, however, children and their parents experienced a substantial increase in relative poverty, while potential parents and postparental working-age adults experienced a slight decline in relative poverty.

At the upper end of the income distribution, in 1939 potential parents and postparental working-age adults were more likely than current parents (by 8–13 percentage points) to live in luxury, and they were more likely than children (by 15–19 percentage points) to live in luxury. For potential parents and postparental working-age adults, the proportion living in luxury did not fall substantially after the Great Depression, as it did for children and their parents; the proportion increased.

[18]Of course, some "potential parents" have parented children who are not in their homes because of divorce or out-of-wedlock childbearing, or because the children have reached adulthood and are living independently.

Between 1969 and 1988, the proportion living in luxury continued to increase. By 1988, then, the gap in luxury living that separated potential parents and postparental working-age adults from current parents had expanded to 15–20 percentage points, and the gap separating them from children had expanded to 23–28 percentage points.

Hence, not only did both children and current parents experience increasing economic inequality between 1969 and 1988 but children and current parents also had, on average, fallen further behind potential parents and postparental working-age adults in their relative economic status, since the gaps in relative poverty and luxury living were greater in 1988 than they were in 1939.

The postparental elderly—that is, adults aged 65 and over with no dependent children in the home—experienced another pattern of change in relative economic status. In 1939, the postparental elderly were more likely than children to be living in relative poverty, but, unlike persons in every other life course situation, the proportion living in relative poverty remained essentially unchanged between 1939 and 1949.

By 1959–1969, the relative poverty rate for the postparental elderly finally had declined, but it remained 17–23 percentage points larger than for other adults and at least 10–14 percentage points larger than for children. Hence, by 1959–1969, the relative poverty rate for the postparental elderly remained much higher than the rate experienced by nonelderly adults in 1939, and nearly as high as the level experienced by children during that year.

During the 1970s, however, as Samuel H. Preston has emphasized, poverty among the elderly dropped sharply,[19] and during the 1980s the relative poverty rate for the postparental elderly continued to decline substantially. Sometime during the 1980s, the relative poverty rate for the postparental elderly fell below that of children. By 1988, the postparental elderly were midway between children and current parents in their chances of living in relative poverty. Hence, the postparental elderly remained substantially more likely to live in relative poverty than did other adults who had no dependent children in the home.

At the upper end of the income distribution, the postparental elderly have, since the Great Depression, generally been more similar to children than to current parents in their chances of living in luxury. In other words, they have been substantially *less likely* to live in luxury than were adults who had no dependent children in the home.

The large post-1969 improvements in the relative economic status of the elderly, which finally put them on a par with children and current

[19]Samuel H. Preston, "Children and the Elderly: Divergent Paths for America's Dependents," *Demography* 21 (1984): 435–457; Samuel H. Preston, "Children and the Elderly in the United States," *Scientific American* 251, 12 (1984): 44–49.

parents, appear to have resulted mainly from the relative increases in the value of Social Security pensions that occurred between the early 1970s and the early 1980s.[20]

These estimates probably tend to overstate relative poverty among the elderly and slightly understate actual luxury living, however, because they effectively assume that housing costs for the elderly are similar to housing costs for nonelderly persons. But many elderly persons own their homes outright and, consequently, do not have to devote a large portion of their income to mortgage or rent payments. Hence, postparental elderly who own their homes outright can maintain a specific standard of living with a smaller income than can corresponding families with children (and other adults), because a substantial portion of the income of most nonelderly persons goes toward paying the mortgage or rent.

If we assume, crudely, that the relative poverty threshold for postparental elderly persons who their own homes outright should be lower by about 25 percent, then we obtain relative poverty rates adjusted for homeownership (Table 7.1).[21] The relative poverty rate for the postpar-

[20]Between 1972 and 1977 newly enrolled Social Security recipients received relatively large benefits, compared with earlier and later years. Between the early 1970s and the early 1980s, the Consumer Price Index used to ensure that Social Security benefits kept up with inflation-measured housing costs by focusing on purchase price and current interest rates. But elderly pensioners are especially likely to own their own homes and hence were not likely to pay the inflated prices of that decade. Since then the Consumer Price Index used to keep benefits on a par with inflation has been a "rental equivalency" approach that focuses on the cost of renting a home rather than on homeownership costs. See David Koitz, "The Indexing of Social Security," Report No. 81–119 EPW, HD 7094 U.S., Congressional Research Service (Washington, DC: Library of Congress, May 15, 1981); David Koitz and Barry Molefsky, "Social Security Benefit Increases Pegged to a Consumer Price Index That Measures Rental Equivalency Rather Than Homeownership Costs," Congressional Research Service (Washington, DC: Library of Congress, November 25, 1981); and David Koitz and Geofferey C. Kollman, "The Automatic Benefit Increase in Social Security," Report No. 83–22 EPW, HD 7094 U.S., Congressional Research Service (Washington, DC: Library of Congress, February 22, 1983).

[21]These estimates are crude since they assume that all postparental elderly living in a household in which the householder is a homeowner do in fact own their homes outright, and since they assume that no more or less than 25 percent of the income of such persons at the poverty threshold is needed for rent or mortgage payments. The basic assumption is that if they did not own their own homes outright, the postparental elderly would have to pay about one-fourth of their income for rent or mortgage—roughly the proportion paid by nonelderly persons. Hence, the basic assumption is that the value of outright homeownership is about the same as the typical cost of mortgage or rent.

This approach is quite different from the "home equity" methodology used with regard to home equity in a research and development effort of the Census Bureau reported in John M. McNeil, U.S. Bureau of the Census, Current Population Reports, Series P-60, No. 164-RD-1, *Measuring the Effects of Benefits and Taxes on Income and Poverty: 1986* (Washington, DC: U.S. Government Printing Office, 1988). The Census Bureau's approach ". . . applies a rate of return to equity to obtain an estimate of income that the household would receive if it chose to shift the amount held as home equity into an interest-earning account," (U.S. Bureau of the Census, p. 3). But as the report notes, this methodology is

ental elderly adjusted in this fashion was 3–4 percentage points smaller in 1939 than the unadjusted rate and 7–8 percentage points smaller in 1959–1988.

Hence, the *trend* in relative poverty is not affected by this adjustment after 1959, while the *difference in levels* suggests that the relative poverty rate for the postparental elderly may have fallen below that of children sometime during the 1970s instead of sometime during the 1980s. As late as 1969, however, even with this housing-cost adjustment, the relative poverty rate for the postparental elderly was 30 percent—a level higher than that experienced by nonelderly adults in 1939.

Overall, then, counting income from the Social Security retirement system (and all other sources of income), and taking homeownership into account, it appears that about 16 percent of the postparental elderly lived in relative poverty by 1988, compared with 13–14 percent for other adults who had no dependent children in the home, 18 percent for current parents, and 27 percent for children. Social Security (and other available sources of income) do not assure a middle-class standard of living for many postparental elderly, however. In 1988, the estimated proportion of postparental elderly whose standard of living was below middle-class comfort was 40 percent; the proportion adjusted for homeownership was about 30–32 percent.

Hence, even counting Social Security, other available income, and homeownership in 1988, the chances that the postparental elderly would live below the standard of middle-class comfort (30–32 percent) was about the same as those for current parents (32 percent), and substantially less than those for children (41 percent), but substantially greater than those for other adults who had no dependent children in the home (21–24 percent). At the upper end of the income distribution, for the postparental elderly the chances of living in luxury were probably fairly similar to those for current parents and substantially greater than those for children, but substantially less than those for other adults who had no dependent children in the home.

---

limited by the ". . . lack of home equity data on the CPS data file (used in the report) and the necessity of choosing an appropriate rate of return" (p. 3). In other words, the value of the home and the interest that would be received on the value of the home are not available for estimation purposes in the Census Bureau report.

Effects of Taxes, Health Insurance, and Other Noncash Benefits

Levels of relative poverty and economic inequality depend not only on the cash income that is available to individuals and families but also upon differences in (1) the amount of tax that various persons and families must pay to federal, state, and local governments, and (2) the value of noncash benefits received from private and public sources. In this section we will discuss how changes in taxes paid, and noncash benefits received, for persons with low and high incomes have influenced the relative poverty rate and economic inequality since the Great Depression.

Taxes for Low-, Medium-, and High-Income Families

Part of a family's income is not directly available to the family for purchasing consumer goods and services, because families must pay various federal, state, and local taxes. The total taxes paid by a family depends mainly upon (1) the size of its income, (2) the federal, state, and local income tax rates, (3) the Social Security tax rate, (4) the sales tax rate and excise taxes on consumer purchases, and (5) the value of property owned and property tax rates.

Because of the large number and variety of taxes, estimates of the total tax burden on families in different parts of the income distribution can be derived only by using complicated modeling procedures. Joseph A. Pechman has developed such procedures to estimate the total tax burden of families with low, medium, and high incomes for selected years from 1966 to 1985. Because of ambiguities in who bears the burden of corporation income tax and property tax, Pechman has concluded that it is not clear whether the total tax burden was slightly greater for low-income or high-income families in 1980.[22]

What is clear, however, is that between 1966 and 1985, the overall tax burden increased for families with low incomes while decreasing for families with high incomes.[23] More specifically, a 1–5 percentage point increase occurred between 1966 and 1985 in the proportion of total family income that families in the bottom fifth of the income distribution were required to pay in taxes, while a 3–5 percentage point decrease

[22]Joseph A. Pechman, *Who Paid the Taxes, 1966–1985?* (Washington, DC: Brookings Institution, 1985), pp. 4–6.
[23]Pechman, p. 68, Table 5-2.

occurred during these years in the proportion of total family income that families in the top tenth of the income distribution paid in taxes.

The overall effect of tax-law changes between 1966 and 1985, then, was to magnify the increases in relative poverty and economic inequality as reflected in our measures based only on before-tax income. In other words, if we could incorporate the effect of changes in tax laws into our measure of relative poverty and luxury living, we would find that: the proportion of children living in relative poverty increased from 23 percent in 1969 to more than 27 percent in 1988; the proportion of current parents living in relative poverty increased from 15 percent to more than 18 percent; and the proportion of other adults living in relative poverty either declined by less than our earlier estimates indicate or increased.

In addition, if we restricted our measure of luxury living to focus only on families that have the highest income levels and included the effect of tax-law changes, we would find that the gap between families in the top tenth of the income distribution and the remaining 90 percent of families had expanded even more than would appear to be the case from looking only at changes in before-tax income. Overall, then, our measure of economic inequality based only on before-tax income underestimates the increase in inequality that actually occurred between 1969 and 1988.

Health Insurance and Other Noncash Benefits

What additional effects have private and public health-insurance benefits, and other noncash benefits, had on relative poverty and economic inequality? In order to answer this question, we must look briefly at the historical evolution of health insurance in the United States.[24]

In 1940 only a handful of persons were covered by any form of health insurance, but this figure jumped to 41 percent in 1948, 57 percent in 1953, and 70 percent in 1956.[25] At the same time, the proportion of hospital and medical expenses paid by employers, through health-insurance plans, was growing rapidly.[26] Hence, it appears that sometime between 1950 and 1960 at least one-half of Americans were receiving health

---

[24]For a fascinating history of the medical care system in the United States, see Paul Starr, *The Social Transformation of American Medicine* (New York: Basic Books, 1982).

[25]Odin W. Anderson and Jacob J. Feldman, *Family Medical Costs and Voluntary Health Insurance: A Nationwide Survey* (New York: McGraw-Hill, 1956), pp. 3, 98; and Joseph W. Garbarino, *Health Plans and Collective Bargaining* (Berkeley: University of California Press, 1960), p. 14.

[26]Starr, p. 313.

benefits paid for partly by their employer or by the employer of their family breadwinner(s).

Not surprisingly, individuals with low family incomes were much less likely to be covered by health insurance than were those with high family incomes. For example, in 1953 the proportion of individuals who were covered by hospital insurance was only about 25 percent for those in relative poverty and about 45 percent for those living in near-poor circumstances, compared with 65 and 70 percent, respectively, for those living in middle-class comfort and high-income luxury (Table 7.2). In short, in 1939 virtually no one, regardless of income, was covered by health insurance. But by 1959, a large majority (about two-thirds) of persons in the middle class and above were covered by health insurance, often as a noncash benefit paid for at least partly by employers, while only a minority of persons below the middle class (about one-third) were covered. Consequently, if it were possible to include the value of this noncash benefit in our estimates of the relative poverty thresholds for 1939–1959, and to include the value of this noncash benefit in the income of various families, we would then draw the following conclusions.

The health-insurance adjusted threshold in 1939 would be the same as the unadjusted threshold, but by 1959 the health-insurance adjusted threshold would be significantly higher than the unadjusted value. Hence, changes in relative poverty between 1939 and 1959 based on the health-insurance adjusted threshold would show that the declines in relative poverty and economic inequality actually were smaller than was indicated by our unadjusted estimates. In other words, our inability to include the value of health insurance in our estimates makes the decline in relative poverty between 1939 and 1959 appear larger than it actually was.

After the 1950s, the proportion of the population that had health-insurance coverage continued to expand from 70 to 87 percent between 1956 and 1977, but coverage then declined somewhat to 84 percent in 1987.[27] With expanded coverage between 1956 and 1977, the health-insurance coverage gap separating persons with low, middle, and high incomes narrowed. Between 1953 and 1980, the proportion covered among those in relative poverty increased by about 45 percentage points, while the increase among those living in middle-class comfort or luxury increased by 25–30 percentage points (Table 7.2).

Still, by 1980, among the nonelderly, the health-insurance gap between the poor and those with middle-class and luxury incomes remained wide at 19–27 percentage points, and about 31 percent of Amer-

[27]See sources in Table 7.2.

TABLE 7.2

Approximate Percentage of Persons Covered and Not Covered by Health Insurance: 1953–1987

Economic Circumstances and Coverage Status	All Ages 1953	Under Age 65	
		1980	1986
Covered			
Relative poverty	25	69	65
Near-poor frugality	45	74	78
Middle-class comfort	60	88	93
Luxury	70	96	96
Not Covered			
Relative poverty	75	31	35
Near-poor frugality	55	26	22
Middle-class comfort	40	12	7
Luxury	30	4	4
Economic Circumstances and Source of Insurance			
Relative poverty			
Medicaid coverage	—	28	22
Private coverage	25	39	40
Near-poor frugality			
Medicaid coverage	—	9	3
Private coverage	45	61	72
	1953	1977	1987
Age 65 and over			
Covered	31	95.7	99.1
Not covered	69	4.3	0.9

SOURCES: Tables A-6 and A-11, Odin W. Anderson and Jacob J. Feldman, *Family Medical Costs and Voluntary Health Insurance: A Nationwide Survey* (New York: McGraw-Hill, 1956), pp. 102, 151; Tables 117 and 118, pp. 171–172, U.S. National Center for Health Statistics, Health, United States, 1988 DHHS Pub. No.: (PHS) 89-1232. Public Health Service (Washington, DC: U.S. Government Printing Office, March 1989); Table 1, National Center for Health Services Research, Public Health Service, "Who Are the Uninsured?" *Data Review* 1:2 (Judith A. Kasper, Daniel C. Walden, Gail R. Wilensky); National Center for Health Services Research and Health Care Technology Assessment, Public Health Service, *Uninsured Americans: A 1987 Profile* (Pamela Farley Short, Alan Monheit, and Karen Beauregard); Series G 1-9, 17a, U.S. Bureau of the Census, Historical Statistics of the United States, *Colonial Times to 1970*, Bicentennial Edition, Part 2 (Washington, DC: U.S. Government Printing Office, 1975); and Tables B and 2, U.S. Bureau of the Census, Current Population Reports, Series P-60, No. 166, *Money Income and Poverty Status in the United States: 1988* (Advanced data from the March 1989 Current Population Survey). Washington, DC: U.S. Government Printing Office, 1989.

icans living in relative poverty were not covered by health insurance, compared with only 4–12 percent of persons with middle and upper incomes. The advent of Medicaid, the federal health-insurance program for the poor, accounts for about two-thirds of the increase that occurred in health-insurance coverage among the relatively poor between 1960 and 1980; by 1980 about 28 percent of the relatively poor depended on Medicaid as their health insurance (Table 7.2). Without Medicaid the increase in health-care insurance coverage for the relatively poor between 1960 and 1980 would have been only one-half as large as the increase for the middle- and upper-income groups (14 vs. 25 percentage points), and the health-insurance gap would have widened further instead of narrowing.

Focusing on private health insurance, since the proportion of the population that had private health-insurance coverage increased only slightly from about 70 to 75 percent between 1956 and 1987, since 64 percent of the population in 1987 was covered by private employment-related health insurance, and since private health-care expenditures as a proportion of the Gross National Product (GNP) increased greatly by more than three-fifths between 1960 and 1986 (from 3.9 to 6.4 percent of the GNP), it seems quite likely that the value of noncash, employer-paid, health-insurance benefits increased as a proportion of the typical family income between 1960 and 1987.[28]

Consequently, if it were possible to include the value of this health insurance as a noncash benefit in our estimates of relative poverty thresholds in 1959–1988, and to include the value of this noncash benefit in the income of various families, we would then draw the following conclusions. The health-insurance adjusted threshold was significantly higher than the unadjusted value, and the difference between the adjusted and unadjusted values increased with each passing decade.

Between 1959 and 1979, based on private health insurance alone, health-insurance adjusted relative poverty and economic inequality either fell by less than is indicated by our unadjusted estimates or they increased. But if we also take into account increasing access to public health insurance among the poor and the elderly (through Medicare), relative poverty and economic inequality declined by more than is indicated in our unadjusted estimates.

Between 1980 and 1986, however, the proportion of the total population that benefited from health-insurance coverage declined by about 3 percentage points, mainly because the proportion of the nonelderly relatively poor population covered by Medicaid declined by about 6 percentage points from 28 to 22 percent (Table 7.2). Meanwhile, the decline

[28]See sources in Table 7.3.

in Medicaid coverage among those living in near-poor frugality was more than counterbalanced by the increase in private coverage, producing an overall increase in coverage of about 4 percentage points for the near-poor—an increase that was roughly as large as the 5 percentage point increase in health-insurance coverage for the middle class.

Taking account of the various changes that took place during the 1980s, if we could adjust for health-insurance coverage, then the increases in relative poverty and economic inequality would be greater during the 1980s than is suggested by our unadjusted measures. This is primarily because the value of health insurance as a noncash benefit for the middle class and above probably increased substantially, while a decline occurred in the proportion of the relatively poor who were covered by health insurance.

Among the elderly aged 65 and over, the history of health-insurance coverage is quite different. By 1953, only 31 percent were covered by health insurance—about half the proportion that was covered among other adults and children (Table 7.2). Hence, health-insurance adjusted measures of relative poverty and economic inequality would show, at least until the creation of Medicare and Medicaid in 1965, that relative poverty was higher and declined more slowly among the elderly than our unadjusted measures indicate, and that the economic inequality experienced by the elderly, compared with younger Americans, increased by more than our unadjusted measures suggest. After 1965, however, during the time of rapidly increasing coverage of the elderly under Medicare and Medicaid, health-insurance adjusted indicators of relative poverty would show a larger decline than our unadjusted measure.

What has been the effect of additional noncash benefits on changes in relative poverty and economic inequality among children, working-age adults, and the elderly since the Great Depression? This question is difficult to answer, because little is known about additional noncash benefits received by middle-class and high-income employees. More is known about noncash benefits provided by the government to poor families, but the evidence indicates that the effect on the overall poverty rate is not large. For example, in 1986 the Census Bureau estimated that if the value of publicly funded noncash food and housing benefits were included in income estimates used to derive the official poverty rate, then the official rate would have been smaller by 2.6 percentage points for children and by 0.7–1.1 percentage points for adults.[29]

However, since many white collar workers with middle and upper incomes also have business expenses, such as lunches and dinners, paid

[29]John M. McNeil, U.S. Bureau of the Census, Current Population Reports, Series P-60, No. 164-RD-1, *Measuring the Effect of Benefits and Taxes on Income and Poverty: 1986* (Washington, DC: U.S. Government Printing Office, 1986), Table H.

at least occasionally by their employers, a full accounting of noncash benefits from public and private sources to persons at all income levels would act to reduce, eliminate, or possibly reverse the effect that publicly funded noncash benefits have on relative poverty and economic inequality. Overall, then, noncash benefits other than health insurance probably have little effect on relative poverty rates, and unless many workers who have relatively high incomes receive noncash benefits that are of considerable value, noncash benefits other than health insurance probably have little effect on economic inequality.

Relative Poverty and Inequality Among Preschoolers and Adolescents

The economic circumstances of successive cohorts of American children, as of their preschool and adolescent years, have been determined in large part by the general economic times in which they lived (Table 7.3). Adolescents born during the 1920s and preschoolers born during the 1930s were about equal (at 37–38 percent) in their chances of living in relative poverty in 1939. Comparing successive cohorts as of the preschool years, the proportion who were economically deprived dropped sharply from 38 percent for the 1930s cohort to a nearly constant 24–25 percent for the cohorts born during the 1940s, 1950s, and 1960s. But the proportion of preschoolers living in relative poverty then jumped by 3 percentage points for the 1970s cohort and by an additional 5 percentage points for the 1980s cohort to 30 percent for preschoolers in 1988, reaching a level that exceeded the relative poverty rate recorded for every other cohort born since the 1940s (by 5 percentage points!). For children born between the 1960s and the 1980s, 45 percent of the gains made by cohorts born between the 1930s and the 1960s was lost.

At the upper end of the income distribution, the proportion of preschoolers living in luxury dropped from 23 percent for the 1930s cohort to 12 percent for the 1950s and 1960s cohort, then increased, returning to the Great Depression level at 20 percent for preschoolers in 1988. Hence, for preschoolers, as for children in general, there was an enormous reduction in economic inequality between 1939 and 1969, followed by a sharp increase in economic inequality for preschoolers between 1969 and 1988. The proportion living in either relative poverty or relative luxury dropped from 61 percent for preschoolers in 1939 to only 35 percent for preschoolers in 1969, then jumped to 50 percent for preschoolers in 1988.

As each cohort born since the 1930s moved from the preschool to

TABLE 7.3
Children Born Between the 1920s and 1980s, by Relative Income Levels at Ages 0–5 and 12–17

Relative Economic Circumstances and Age	1920s	1930s	1940s	1950s	Census 1960s	CPS 1960s	Census 1970s	CPS 1970s	1980s
Relative Poverty									
Age 0–5	—	37.9	24.3	24.8	23.6	—	26.4	25.4	30.1
Age 12–17	37.1	29.8	23.3	21.0	21.3	20.4	—	23.2	—
Near-Poor Frugality									
Age 0–5	—	10.9	14.8	20.2	20.7	—	17.0	16.8	15.4
Age 12–17	12.4	14.9	15.2	16.8	13.5	14.2	—	12.8	—
Middle-Class Comfort									
Age 0–5	—	28.3	42.8	43.4	44.1	—	42.5	42.1	34.8
Age 12–17	25.3	35.4	40.2	41.9	42.2	41.6	—	36.8	—
Luxury									
Age 0–5	—	22.8	18.0	11.7	11.7	—	14.2	15.8	19.7
Age 12–17	23.2	20.0	21.3	20.3	23.1	23.8	—	27.2	—
Official Poverty									
Age 0–5	—	71.8	44.7	26.3	16.5	—	18.2	18.1	22.5
Age 12–17	72.4	49.8	24.4	14.9	14.6	14.3	—	16.4	—
Total Number (in thousands)									
Age 0–5	10,640	9,379	17,780	24,625	20,741	—	19,478	19,399	22,232
Age 12–17	—	12,166	18,058	23,837	23,462	23,297	—	20,135	—

SOURCES: Estimates derived from 1940–1980 census PUMs, and March CPS for 1980 and 1989.

NOTES: 1980 age 0–5 and 1970 age 12–17 from CPS in 1988. See text and especially footnotes for methods of calculating relative poverty, near-poor frugality, middle-class comfort, and luxury income levels.

the adolescent years, the proportions living in economic deprivation fell by 8 percentage points for children born during the 1930s and by 1–4 percentage points for children born between the 1940s and the 1970s. For the 1930s cohort, nearly all of the improvement is accounted for by an increase in the proportion living in middle-class comfort, but for subsequent cohorts all of the increase is accounted for by the rise in luxury living. In fact, for virtually every cohort born between the 1940s and the 1970s, the proportions living in relative poverty, near-poor frugality, and middle-class comfort all declined between the preschool and adolescent years, producing increases in the proportion of those living in luxury.

Still, the overall trends across successive cohorts of adolescents in poverty and economic inequality have been similar to those for children as a whole. The proportion of adolescents living in relative poverty dropped from 37 percent for the 1920s cohort to 30 percent for the 1930s cohort and then to 21 percent for the 1950s and 1960s cohorts, only to increase by nearly 3 percentage points to 23 percent for the 1970s cohort. For adolescents born during the 1970s, then, the chances of living in relative poverty had returned to the level experienced by the 1940s cohort.

At the upper end of the income distribution, the proportion of adolescents living in luxury fluctuated between 20 and 24 percent for the cohorts born between the 1920s and the 1960s, then increased to 27 percent for the 1970s cohort. Overall then, among adolescents, economic inequality declined for those born between the 1920s and the 1950s but increased for subsequent cohorts.

The Racial Gap in Relative Poverty and Luxury

In 1939, 76 percent of black children lived in relative poverty, compared with 33 percent of white children, resulting in a very large racial gap of 43 percentage points (Figure 7.2 and Table 7.4). Since 89 percent of blacks lived in slavery in 1860,[30] it appears that compared with subsequent decades, relatively little improvement had occurred in the relative economic status of blacks between the Civil War and the Great Depression. After the Great Depression black children shared in the general economic boom, but by 1959 the racial gap in relative poverty rates for children was the same as it had been in 1939 (at 44 percentage points), and the proportion of black children living in relative poverty

[30]Reynolds Farley and Walter R. Allen, *The Color Line and the Quality of Life in America* (New York: Russell Sage Foundation, 1987), p. 13.

FIGURE 7.2

White and Black Children, by Relative Income Levels: 1939–1988

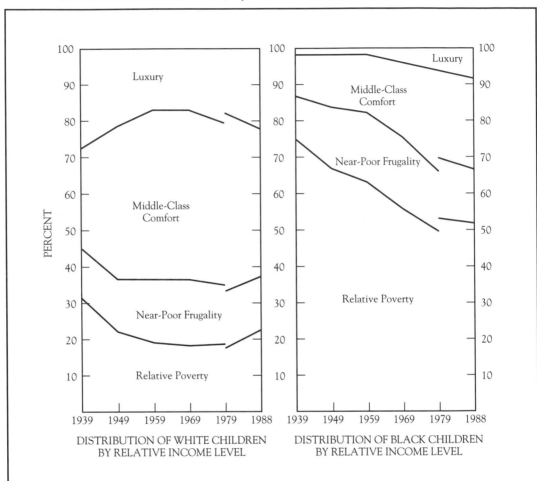

DISTRIBUTION OF WHITE CHILDREN
BY RELATIVE INCOME LEVEL

DISTRIBUTION OF BLACK CHILDREN
BY RELATIVE INCOME LEVEL

SOURCE: Table 7.4

remained very large at 63 percent compared with 19 percent for white children.

Between 1959 and 1979, the relative poverty rate for black children continued to fall. Combined with the slight decline and subsequent turnaround in relative poverty experienced by white children, the racial gap finally narrowed during these decades. But the racial gap in relative poverty rates for children remained quite large (30–35 percentage points)

FIGURE 7.2 (*continued*)

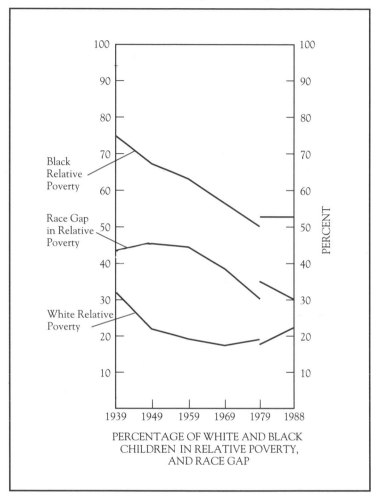

PERCENTAGE OF WHITE AND BLACK
CHILDREN IN RELATIVE POVERTY,
AND RACE GAP

in 1979, and about 50–53 percent of black children still lived in relative poverty (more than two and one-half times the rate for white children).

Despite the improvements experienced by both black and white children after the Great Depression, the 1970s marked the beginning of a new era in childhood poverty. For white children the relative poverty rate increased during the 1970s and the 1980s, and by 1988 it had returned to a level not experienced since the 1940s. For black children, the decline in the relative poverty rate continued during the 1970s. But during the 1980s, the relative poverty rate for black children as a whole appears to have remained stable, and by 1988 it remained at an extraordinary level compared with whites (53 percent—approximately 19 percentage points larger than the relative poverty rate for white children during the Great Depression year of 1939).

Between 1939 and 1959, nearly two-thirds of the decline in relative poverty among black children is accounted for by a corresponding increase in the proportion living in near-poor frugality (8 percentage points), while the remainder (4 percentage points) is accounted for by an increase in middle-class living. Among white children, the increase in the proportion living in frugal circumstances was about 6 percentage points. Hence, for white children, but not for blacks, most of the decline in relative poverty that occurred during the two decades following the Great Depression was accounted for by the rise in middle-class living.

At the upper end of the income distribution, only 2 percent of black children lived in luxury in 1939–1959, compared with 17–26 percent of white children. The proportion of black children living in luxury increased from 4 to 8 percent between 1969 and 1988, resulting in an increase about one-half as large as that for white children (from 17 to 25 percent). Counting middle-class and luxury living together, the proportion of black children who had at least a middle-class level of living increased from only 13 percent in 1939 to 18 percent in 1959 and 31–34 percent in 1979–1988. Meanwhile, the proportion of white children living in middle-class comfort or luxury increased from 55 percent in 1939 to 63–67 percent in 1949–1988.

In other words, the proportion of children living in relative poverty or near-poor frugality declined between 1939 and 1988 from 87 to 67 percent for black children and from 45 to 37 percent for white children. Since the Great Depression, the racial gap in sub-middle-class living has narrowed substantially from 42 to 31 percentage points, but the large gap that remains can be entirely accounted for by the difference in relative poverty rates. The result is that for two-thirds of black children, middle-class living remains only a dream.

The Racial Gap in Relative Poverty for Preschoolers and Adolescents

The broad conclusions regarding trends in the racial gap in relative poverty for children of all ages generally hold true for specific cohorts of children born between the 1920s and the 1980s as of their preschool and adolescent years (Tables 7.4 and 7.5). The reason is that changes in the economic circumstances of successive cohorts of black and white chil-

TABLE 7.4

White and Black Children Aged 0–17, by Relative Income Levels and Official Poverty Rates: 1939–1988

Relative Economic Circumstances, Age, and Family Status	1939	1949	1959	1969	Census 1979	CPS 1979	CPS 1988
Relative Poverty							
White	33.2	21.6	18.9	17.5	19.2	17.9	22.3
Black	75.8	67.0	63.3	55.8	49.6	53.0	52.6
Near-Poor Frugality							
White	11.6	15.0	18.0	18.9	15.2	15.4	14.3
Black	11.2	16.7	19.0	19.6	16.4	16.5	14.6
Middle-Class Comfort							
White	29.6	42.7	45.9	46.3	45.1	45.3	38.7
Black	11.0	14.0	15.4	20.8	27.4	23.8	24.7
Luxury							
White	25.6	20.8	17.2	17.3	20.5	21.5	24.7
Black	2.3	2.3	2.3	3.8	6.5	6.7	8.0
Official Poverty							
White	68.6	42.2	20.2	11.6	12.5	11.9	15.3
Black	97.2	87.7	65.2	44.8	37.6	40.8	43.8
Total Numbers (in thousands)							
White	26,608	39,129	56,157	59,898	54,273	54,142	53,881
Black	3,039	5,211	7,964	9,536	9,543	9,346	9,865

SOURCES: Estimates derived from 1940–1980 census PUMs, and March CPS for 1980 and 1989.

NOTES: 1980 age 0–5 and 1970 age 12–17 from CPS in 1988. See text and especially footnotes for methods of calculating relative poverty, near-poor frugality, middle-class comfort, and luxury income levels.

265

TABLE 7.5

White and Black Children Born Between the 1920s and 1980s, by Relative Income Levels

Relative Economic Circumstances and Age	Birth Cohorts								
	1920s	1930s	1940s	1950s	Census 1960s	CPS 1960s	Census 1970s	CPS 1970s	1980s
Relative Poverty									
White									
Age 0–5	—	33.6	19.0	19.0	18.6	—	21.8	20.3	25.2
Age 12–17	33.1	24.6	18.4	15.7	16.5	15.2	—	18.7	—
Black									
Age 0–5	—	79.2	66.2	63.0	53.4	—	52.5	54.4	57.6
Age 12–17	70.3	66.3	62.7	56.3	48.6	52.4	—	47.3	—
Near-Poor Frugality									
White									
Age 0–5	—	11.0	14.4	20.1	20.6	—	17.1	16.9	15.3
Age 12–17	12.3	14.8	14.9	16.5	13.1	13.6	—	12.6	—
Black									
Age 0–5	—	10.0	17.7	20.7	21.2	—	16.4	16.0	16.0
Age 12–17	13.8	15.5	17.7	18.5	16.0	17.0	—	13.5	—
Middle-Class Comfort									
White									
Age 0–5	—	30.9	46.5	47.7	47.8	—	45.6	45.4	37.4
Age 12–17	30.0	38.2	43.1	45.0	44.5	44.7	—	38.0	—
Black									
Age 0–5	—	8.7	14.1	14.3	21.6	—	25.0	22.7	20.1
Age 12–17	13.2	15.6	16.8	21.0	28.6	23.6	—	30.0	—

TABLE 7.5 (continued)

Relative Economic Circumstances and Age	Birth Cohorts								
	1920s	1930s	1940s	1950s	Census 1960s	CPS 1960s	Census 1970s	CPS 1970s	1980s
Luxury									
White									
Age 0–5	—	25.4	20.1	13.2	13.0	—	15.6	17.3	22.1
Age 12–17	25.7	22.5	23.6	22.7	25.9	26.6	—	30.6	—
Black									
Age 0–5	—	2.1	2.0	1.9	3.8	—	6.0	6.9	6.2
Age 12–17	2.7	2.6	3.0	4.3	6.8	7.0	—	9.2	—
Official Poverty									
White									
Age 0–5	—	66.2	39.2	20.4	12.2	—	14.1	13.6	17.8
Age 12–17	68.3	44.7	19.5	10.5	10.9	10.1	—	12.3	—
Black									
Age 0–5	—	97.9	88.0	65.2	42.2	—	41.1	43.4	48.5
Age 12–17	96.5	85.9	64.2	44.9	36.4	38.9	—	38.1	—
Base Numbers									
Total number (in thousands)									
White									
Age 0–5	—	8,376	15,783	21,390	17,760	—	16,535	16,510	18,850
Age 12–17	9,583	10,659	16,058	20,746	20,008	19,935	—	16,976	—
Black									
Age 0–5	—	1,002	1,997	3,235	2,981	—	2,943	2,889	3,382
Age 12–17	1,057	1,507	2,000	3,091	3,454	3,362	—	3,159	—

SOURCES: Estimates derived from 1940–1980 census PUMs, and March CPS for 1980 and 1989.

NOTES: 1980 age 0–5 and 1970 age 12–17 from CPS in 1989. See text and especially footnotes for methods of calculating relative poverty, near-poor frugality, middle-class comfort, and luxury income levels.

dren have been determined largely by the general economic times in which they lived as well as by factors influencing overall racial differences. But three refinements merit attention.

First, between the preschool and adolescent years, the relative poverty rate has typically declined more for blacks than for whites, but racial differences usually have been within the range of 2–4 percentage points. For example, for the 1930s cohort the declines in relative poverty rates between the preschool and adolescent years for blacks and for whites were 13 and 9 percentage points, respectively. For children born from the 1950s through the 1970s, the corresponding declines in relative poverty by most measures rates were 4–9 and 1–3 percentage points for blacks and whites, respectively.

Hence, between the preschool and adolescent ages, the racial gap in relative poverty narrowed slightly for each cohort born since the Great Depression. For children born between the 1950s and the 1970s, however, the decline in the percent living in near-poor frugality was smaller for black children than for whites, and the racial gap in the chances of living in relative poverty or near-poor frugality was fairly constant across the preschool and adolescent ages for children born since the 1950s. In other words, for children born since the 1950s, the racial gap in sub-middle-class living remained fairly constant between the preschool and adolescent years.

Second, the increase between the preschool years and adolescence in the proportion living in luxury was larger for whites than for blacks for each cohort born since the 1940s. This racial difference was quite large for children born during the 1950s, and it expanded substantially through the 1970s. For example, for the 1950s cohort, between the preschool and adolescent years, the proportion living in luxury increased by 2 percentage points for blacks and by 10 percentage points for whites; but for the 1970s cohort the increases were 2 percentage points for blacks and 13 percentage points for whites. Hence, successive cohorts of white children born since the 1940s have experienced substantial, and increasingly large, increases in luxury living as they reached adolescence; but since the increases for blacks have been slight, the racial gap has increased.

Third, the proportion of preschoolers living in relative poverty or near-poor frugality declined for children born between the 1930s and the 1980s from 89 to 74 percent for blacks and from 45 to 41 percent for whites. Among adolescents, the corresponding declines for children born between the 1920s and the 1970s were from 84 to 61 percent for blacks and from 45 to 31 percent for whites. The racial gaps have narrowed substantially, yet the gaps in sub-middle-class living remain large, at 33 percentage points for preschoolers and 30 percentage points for adolescents.

Focusing on relative poverty, the rates for black preschoolers born during the 1980s and for black adolescents born during the 1970s are nearly twice as large as were the corresponding relative poverty rates for white preschoolers and adolescents born during the 1930s. By 1988, black children continued to experience relative poverty rates that were very large when compared with the experience of white children during the Great Depression.

Relative Poverty Among Hispanic and Non-Hispanic Children

In 1979 Hispanic children (of any race) were much more similar to non-Hispanic black children than to non-Hispanic white children in their chances of living in relative poverty, regardless of whether their family had been in the United States for many generations or for one generation (Tables 7.6 and 7.7). The proportion of children living in relative poverty in 1979 (according to the Current Population Survey, or CPS) was 39 percent for Hispanic children (of any race) and 53 percent for non-Hispanic black children, compared with 16 percent for non-Hispanic white children.

Among Hispanic children (of any race) whose mothers were in the home, according to the census, 45 percent of first-generation children lived in relative poverty in 1979, and 40 percent of old-family Hispanic children lived in relative poverty. By these measures, Hispanics (of all races), many of whose families have been in the United States for three or more generations, have made little more progress than non-Hispanic blacks, most of whom are descended from slaves.

The same is true at the upper end of the income distribution. In 1979, according to the CPS, the proportion of children living in luxury was 9 percent for Hispanics (of any race) and 7 percent for non-Hispanic blacks, compared with 23 percent for non-Hispanic whites, and the differences between old-family and first-generation Hispanic children were slight. Overall, the proportions of children living in relative poverty or near-poor frugality in 1979 according to the CPS were 60 and 69 percent for Hispanics (of any race) and non-Hispanic blacks, respectively, compared with only 30 percent for non-Hispanic whites, and the differences between old-family and first-generation Hispanics (of any race)

TABLE 7.6

Old-Family and First-Generation Hispanic Children and Others,
by Relative Income Levels: 1979 (census-based)

Economic Circumstances	Non-Hispanic			Hispanic Living with Mother	
	White	Black	Total Hispanic	First Generation	Old Family
Age 0–17					
Relative poverty	16.7	49.4	42.5	44.7	40.1
Near-poor frugality	14.8	16.4	18.4	19.9	17.4
Middle-class comfort	46.5	27.6	32.3	29.7	34.6
Luxury	22.0	6.6	6.8	5.7	7.9
Age 0–5					
Relative poverty	19.2	52.3	41.2	43.7	39.9
Near-poor frugality	16.8	16.5	19.2	20.2	17.7
Middle-class comfort	47.2	25.2	33.0	32.2	33.9
Luxury	16.8	6.0	6.6	3.9	8.6
Age 12–17					
Relative poverty	14.0	48.5	43.0	44.5	39.0
Near-poor frugality	12.8	15.9	16.1	18.1	15.7
Middle-class comfort	45.5	28.6	33.6	29.1	37.4
Luxury	27.7	6.9	7.4	8.3	7.9
Official Poverty					
Age 0–17	10.6	37.3	30.4	28.5	30.5
Age 0–5	12.2	40.8	29.7	29.9	30.3
Age 12–17	9.0	36.2	31.0	27.6	29.4
Total Number (in thousands)					
Age 0–17	48,754	9,406	5,656	1,795	3,409
Age 0–5	14,586	2,983	1,999	662	1,201
Age 12–17	18,267	3,401	1,794	508	1,081

SOURCES: Estimates derived from 1980 census PUMs.

NOTE: See text and especially footnotes for methods of calculating relative poverty, near-poor frugality, middle-class comfort, and luxury income levels.

were small compared with the gap separating them from non-Hispanic whites.

During the 1980s, the gap between Hispanics (of any race) and non-Hispanic whites appears to have expanded further, as the economic circumstances of Hispanics (of any race) deteriorated more than was the case for non-Hispanics. For example, the proportion of children living in

TABLE 7.7

Hispanic and Non-Hispanic Children, by Relative Income Levels: 1979–1988
(CPS-based)

	Non-Hispanic White		Non-Hispanic Black		Total Hispanic	
	1979	1988	1979	1988	1979	1988
Age 0–17						
Relative poverty	15.6	18.2	52.9	52.7	38.6	50.0
Near-poor frugality	14.7	14.0	16.5	14.7	21.2	16.6
Middle-class comfort	46.8	40.5	23.8	24.6	31.7	26.5
Luxury	22.9	27.3	6.8	8.0	8.5	6.8
Age 0–5						
Relative poverty	17.5	20.5	54.3	57.3	41.7	55.9
Near-poor frugality	16.4	15.2	16.0	16.2	20.6	15.7
Middle-class comfort	47.4	39.6	22.6	20.3	30.8	23.3
Luxury	18.7	24.7	7.0	6.2	6.9	5.1
Age 12–17						
Relative poverty	13.5	15.3	51.9	47.4	34.2	44.3
Near-poor frugality	12.9	12.0	17.4	13.5	21.3	17.5
Middle-class comfort	45.6	39.5	23.5	29.8	34.4	27.7
Luxury	28.0	33.3	7.2	9.3	10.2	10.5
Official Poverty						
Age 0–17	10.2	12.0	40.7	43.8	27.8	37.9
Age 0–5	11.5	14.0	43.5	48.3	29.6	43.0
Age 12–17	8.8	9.6	38.7	38.2	25.2	32.4
Total Number (in thousands)						
Age 0–17	48,777	47,007	9,228	9,737	5,483	7,003
Age 0–5	14,562	16,341	2,848	3,322	1,988	2,569
Age 12–17	18,229	14,956	3,321	3,129	1,677	2,050

SOURCES: Estimates derived from March CPS for 1980 and 1989.

NOTE: 1980 ages 0–5 and 1970 ages 12–17 from CPS in 1989. See text and especially footnotes for methods of calculating relative poverty, near-poor frugality, middle-class comfort, and luxury income levels.

relative poverty or near-poor frugality appears to have increased for Hispanics (of any race) from 60 to 67 percent between 1979 and 1988, compared with the decline from 69 to 67 percent for non-Hispanic blacks and the increase from 30 to 32 percent for non-Hispanic whites.

Although an increase that occurred between 1979 and 1988 in the proportion of recent immigrants among Hispanics (of any race) may account for part of the jump in sub-middle-class incomes among Hispanic children (of any race), it seems unlikely that immigration accounts for as much as one-half of the jump. Instead, it appears that the economic circumstances of Hispanics (of any race) deteriorated more than did those of non-Hispanic whites during the 1980s.

Conclusions

The absolute income levels of American families increased greatly during the 1940s, 1950s, and 1960s, as real median family income jumped by 35–45 percent per decade. These increases were accompanied by a proliferation of consumer goods and by remarkable increases in the quality of many consumer products. But then income growth nearly ceased, and median family income increased by only 5 percent during the 1970s and 1 percent during the 1980s.

Despite these improvements in absolute income levels, these statistics tell us little about the extent to which children were living in relative deprivation or luxury compared with the standards of the time in which they were growing up, because at a specific time in history, the measure of whether a family is judged to be living in deprivation or luxury is the family's income and whether it is especially low or especially high compared with typical families in the same historical period.

Using median family income as a measure of economic deprivation in various years, the relative poverty rate for children dropped sharply during the 1940s (from 38 to 27 percent), but much more slowly (to 23 percent) in 1969. Subsequently, the relative poverty rate increased for children, largely during the 1980s (to 27 percent in 1988), reaching the same level that was experienced almost 40 years earlier in 1949. These trends are important not only because children in low-income families may, in the short run, experience marked deprivation in nutrition, clothing, housing, or healthcare but also because, in the long run, children from low-income families are less likely to earn high incomes when they reach adulthood than are children from high-income families.

As relative poverty declined among children, so, too, did the proportion living in relative luxury (from 23 percent in 1939 to 15 percent in 1959–1969). Subsequently, however, the proportion living in relative luxury increased to 22 percent in 1988. Overall, then, children experienced a sharp reduction in economic inequality between 1939 and 1969, as the proportion living in either relative poverty or relative luxury dropped from 61 to 38 percent. But economic inequality then increased, and by 1988 the proportion who were living in relative poverty or luxury had climbed to 49 percent, eliminating half of the reduction in inequality that occurred between 1939 and 1959.

Meanwhile, the proportion of children whose families had at least a middle-class income increased from 51 percent in 1939 to 57–61 percent in 1949–1988. Still, although the proportion of children who had a sub-middle-class standard of living fell substantially from 50 percent in 1939 to 42–43 percent between 1949 and 1969, and then to 39 percent in 1979, it increased somewhat during the 1980s to 41 percent in 1988.

Among adults, relative poverty also declined after the Great Depression, but the process was slower than it was for children. Hence, the gap between children and adults living in relative poverty narrowed from 9 percentage points in 1939 to 4–6 percentage points in 1949–1969. The gap expanded, however, and by 1988 children were 10 percentage points more likely to live in relative poverty than were adults.

These estimates of relative economic status are somewhat limited, however, because they ignore historical changes in the tax burden and in access to noncash benefits, such as health insurance, from private and public sources. The overall tax burden as a proportion of family income increased between 1966 and 1985 for low-income families and decreased for high-income families. Health-insurance benefits spread most rapidly to middle- and high-income families between 1939 and 1959, and although the insurance-benefit gap narrowed until about 1980, it expanded substantially during the 1980s.

If we could take these changes in the tax burden and health-insurance benefits into account, the results would show that relative poverty rates and economic inequality actually declined by less than we have indicated for the years between 1939 and 1959; they did not fall as low as we have indicated for 1959–1979, and they actually increased by more than we have indicated during the 1980s.

Finally, the relative economic status of black children appears to have improved comparatively little and comparatively slowly between the Civil War and the Great Depression. At the same time, black children did share in the general economic boom that followed the Great Depression, and the racial gap in relative poverty rates narrowed substantially between 1959 and 1988. Still, by 1988 about 53 percent of black children lived in relative poverty, compared with 22 percent of white children. In addition, as of 1980, both first-generation and old-family Hispanic children (of any race) experienced relative poverty rates that were nearly as high as those for non-Hispanic black children.

To what extent are these historic changes in relative poverty and economic inequality accounted for by changes in fathers' income, mothers' income, and income from relatives other than parents? What has been the role of the rise in mother-only families? To what extent have government welfare programs acted, historically, to either lift children out of relative poverty or ameliorate the income deficit for children who have remained in relative poverty? What underlying causes are responsible for these changes? The answers to these questions will be explored in the following chapters.

8

THE WORKING POOR,
WELFARE DEPENDENCE,
AND MOTHER-ONLY FAMILIES

Introduction and Highlights

IN THE last chapter we saw that the sharp decline in poverty among children after the Great Depression was followed by smaller declines during the 1950s and the 1960s, and then by a turnaround and substantial increase between 1969 and 1988. Despite the large long-term decline, however, we also saw that poverty remained comparatively high for children even at its low point in 1969. In this chapter we will focus on children who lived in poverty between 1939 and 1988, and on the extent to which they lived in working-poor or welfare-dependent families, by addressing the following four questions.

First, to what extent have poor children lived in working-poor families that were partly, mainly, or fully self-supporting but not sufficiently so to lift them out of poverty? Second, to what extent did poor children live in welfare-dependent families that relied partly, mainly, or fully on government welfare programs? Third, to what extent was the rise in mother-only families responsible for changes in poverty and welfare dependence? Fourth, to what extent were increases in the generosity of welfare programs responsible for the rise in the proportion of children living in mother-only families, and hence for changes in poverty and welfare dependence? Briefly, this chapter provides the following answers to these questions (bear in mind that welfare income refers to

275

TABLE 8.1

*Poor Children Aged 0–17 in Self-Supporting and Welfare-Dependent Families:
1939–1988*

Percent by Family Work and Welfare Status	1939	1949	1959	1969	Census 1979	CPS 1979	CPS 1988
			Relatively Poor Children				
Total Number (in thousands)	11,385	NA	14,864	14,938	14,425	14,295	16,852
Fully self-supporting	60–70	NA	69.9	66.5	58.6	49.4	52.5
Mainly self-supporting	12–30	NA	17.3	13.5	14.4	16.3	13.5
Mainly welfare-dependent		NA	6.4	8.6	9.7	16.6	15.7
Fully welfare-dependent	10–18	NA	6.5	11.5	17.3	17.7	18.4
Total		NA	100.0	100.0	100.0	100.0	100.0
			Officially Poor Children				
Total Number (in thousands)	21,348		15,714	10,350	9,629	9,953	12,209
Fully self-supporting	75–80	NA	69.8	61.8	51.0	41.9	44.0
Mainly self-supporting	9–17	NA	18.6	12.5	12.8	14.2	12.6
Mainly welfare-dependent		NA	5.9	9.9	11.5	19.6	18.7
Fully welfare-dependent	8–11	NA	5.7	15.8	24.7	24.3	24.6
Total		NA	100.0	100.0	100.0	100.0	100.0

SOURCES: Estimates derived from 1940–1980 census PUMs and March CPS for 1980 and 1989.

NA Not Available

NOTES: Welfare income and hence welfare dependence is measured as cash income received from the Aid to Families with Dependent Children (AFDC) and Social Security programs. All other cash income is classified as self-support. This approach allows for consistent measurement across all census and CPS years. For additional discussion of welfare programs, see Footnote 1 and Chapters 7 and 11. Fully self-supporting families receive no AFDC or Social Security income. Mainly self-supporting families receive no more than 50 percent of their income from AFDC or Social Security. Mainly welfare-dependent families receive more than 50 percent but less than 100 percent of their income from AFDC or Social Security. Fully welfare-dependent families receive 100 percent of their income from AFDC or Social Security. See Chapter 7 for measurement of relative poverty and official poverty. See Footnote 1 for procedures used to derive estimates for 1939 and 1959, and for limitations to these procedures.

cash income received from major public-assistance programs and Social Security as measured in the Census of the Population).

Throughout the era from 1939–1988, relatively poor children have been much more likely to live in fully self-supporting, working-poor families than in fully welfare-dependent families (Table 8.1). Among relatively poor children, 50–70 percent lived in fully self-supporting families, and 7–18 percent lived in fully welfare-dependent families. As of 1988, 82 percent of relatively poor children lived in working-poor families, 66 percent lived in families that earned at least half of their income through paid labor, and 53 percent lived in fully self-supporting families.

Hence, as of 1988, although 48 percent of relatively poor children lived in welfare-dependent families, only 34 percent depended mainly on welfare for at least one-half of their income, and only 18 percent were fully welfare-dependent.

If the increasing proportion of children living in mother-only families after 1959 had experienced the poverty rates of children remaining in two-parent families, then by 1988 overall poverty rates for children would have been as much as 24–30 percent smaller than they actually were in 1988. However, since many of the fathers who are absent from mother-only families earn comparatively low incomes, even if children in mother-only families had benefited from their fathers' actual incomes, their poverty rates would have been higher than those for children living in two-parent families. Hence, if no increase in mother-only families had occurred after 1959, the number of children in poverty would be more than 70–76 percent as large as it actually was in 1988.

The answer to our fourth question, To what extent were increases in the generosity of welfare programs responsible for the rise in the proportion of children living in mother-only families, and hence for changes in poverty and welfare dependence?, is relevant to the ongoing debate on the impact of federal welfare programs on poor people. Some scholars argue that the increasing value of federal welfare programs has harmed the poor by reducing their incentive to work and by increasing their incentive to bear children out of wedlock, while other scholars argue that these federal welfare programs have helped the poor by reducing financial hardships that resulted from economic dislocations over which they had no control.

Available evidence indicates that increases in the absolute value of welfare programs after 1959 produced an increase of 1–2 percentage points in the proportion of children living in mother-only families, thereby producing an increase of 1–2 percentage points in the overall poverty rate for children by 1988. Hence, even if increases in welfare generosity had produced no increase in mother-only families, the poverty rate for children in 1988 would have been more than 90 percent as large as it actually was. These estimates also suggest that most welfare dependency among poor children in 1988 was *not* the result of the increase in mother-only families produced by increasing welfare generosity after 1959. Let's turn to the detailed results.

Relative Poverty, Work, and Welfare Dependence

We begin our discussion of work and welfare dependence by focusing on children who live in *relative* poverty, because, as we saw in Chapter

7, conclusions pertaining to long-term poverty change are most meaningful when based on the concept of relative poverty. We then briefly compare these conclusions with corresponding conclusions that would be drawn by focusing on children who live in official poverty. Unless otherwise indicated, children are classified in this chapter as being at least partly welfare-dependent if at least one family member in the home received cash income from public assistance programs, most notably, the Aid to Families with Dependent Children program (AFDC) or the Social Security programs. Other welfare-state programs are discussed in greater detail in Chapters 7 and 11.

Because income questions asked in the 1940–1980 censuses and the 1980–1989 Current Population Surveys (CPS) have differed, sometimes greatly, we have developed new procedures to derive maximally comparable estimates of self-support and welfare-dependence for the years 1939, 1959, 1969, 1979, and 1988 (Table 8.1). Estimates for 1979 from the census and the CPS differ noticeably, however, apparently because the CPS asks more detailed income questions that yield a larger, and presumably more accurate, estimate of the number of persons receiving welfare.[1] This census–CPS difference for 1979 suggests that census-based

[1]Since the primary distinction in this chapter is between government cash transfers (that is, welfare-state programs as a source of cash income) and private sources of cash income, estimates of "welfare" income include cash income from the AFDC and Social Security programs, while "earnings" includes wage and salary income, self-employment income, interest, dividend, and net rental income, as well as "all other sources" of income. Since "all other sources" includes not only alimony, child support, and pensions other than Social Security, but also veteran's payments, unemployment insurance benefits, and workmen's compensation cash benefits, income from private sources is overestimated somewhat, while income from government cash-transfer programs is underestimated somewhat. However, this classification system ensures that estimates for 1980 and later are as similar as possible to estimates for earlier years, by collapsing various sources of income to correspond with measurement procedures used in the 1970 census. For further discussion of income sources, see the Census Bureau's technical documentation for the Public Use Microdata Samples (PUMS) for various years.

Census data from the 1940 census cannot be used to directly measure self-support and welfare dependence because no question asked about income from welfare programs. Self-support and welfare dependence have been estimated in this book, however, by using the 1940 census question about labor force participation in "emergency work programs" in conjunction with other data about welfare programs during the late 1930s. Emergency work programs include those associated with the WPA, National Youth Administration, Civilian Conservation Corps, local work relief, and other programs. About 16.6 percent of relatively poor children in 1939 lived in families in which at least one parent in the home was employed in public emergency work, and about 11.1 percent of officially poor children lived in such families. Overall, about 8.25 percent of children lived in families in which at least one parent was employed in public emergency work.

Hence, about 80 percent of children who had a parent who was employed in emergency work lived in relative poverty, and about 96 percent of children with such a parent lived in official poverty. Now overall, households with someone who is employed in emergency work accounted for about 45–55 percent of all households receiving welfare of any kind in March 1940. Hence, we estimate that 30–40 percent of children in relative poverty lived in homes that received welfare at any particular time in 1939 (depending on whether

estimates of welfare dependence in 1959 and 1969 also may be somewhat too low. Still, decade-by-decade changes in census-based estimates
between 1959 and 1979 should be accurate within a few percentage points.

Our results indicate that for relatively poor children in 1939, about

---

it is assumed that all other welfare recipients were in relative poverty vs. 80 percent), and
the proportion for officially poor children is 20–25 percent. See Appendix 9 of *Security,
Work, and Relief Policies*, Report of the Committee on Long-Range Work and Relief Policies to the National Resources Planning Board (Washington, DC: U.S. Government Printing Office, 1942.)

Not all of these children lived in families that were fully welfare-dependent for the
entire year, however, since about 55–65 percent of WPA workers and 60–75 percent of
persons on general relief left the programs within a year. But approximately 40–60 percent
of persons who left one form of welfare simply transferred to another form. Taking both
factors into account, the estimate of the proportion living in fully welfare-dependent families should be smaller by 5–10 percentage points for the relatively poor and by 3–6 percentage points for the officially poor, for revised ranges of 20–35 and 17–22 percent, respectively. See *Security, Work, and Relief Policies*, pp. 108–109; *Social Data on Recipients
of Public Assistance Accepted in 1938–1939*, Social Security Board, Bureau of Research
and Statistics; Bureau of Research & Statistics, Department of Public Assistance, Commonwealth of Pennsylvania, *Pennsylvania Public Assistance Statistics, January 1941*
(Harrisburg, PA: Commonwealth of Pennsylvania, 1941), No. 1, and Tables 2 and 3.

In addition, however, some children in families with parents who depended on welfare for their personal income lived in families with other relatives who earned additional
income from nonwelfare sources. If we assume crudely that this proportion is 50 percent,
then the proportion of children in relative and official poverty who lived in fully welfare-
dependent families was about 10–18 and 8–11 percent, respectively. As a residual, then,
the proportion living in families that depended partly on both self-support and welfare
was 12–30 percent for the relatively poor and 9–17 percent for the officially poor.

A lack of comparable data precludes estimates based on the 1950 census, but the
1960, 1970, and 1980 censuses did ask about income from Social Security and welfare
payments, and with adjustments to 1960 census data, we have derived estimates for 1959
that are roughly comparable to corresponding estimates derived for 1939 and 1969. In the
1960 census, income from AFDC and Social Security was included in the "other income"
category. Hence, the following procedures are used to derive estimates of the working
poor and welfare dependence for 1959 that are as comparable as possible to estimates for
1969 and 1979. First, estimates are derived for 1969 not only as indicated in the text and
in Footnote 1, but also with income sources collapsed as they were for 1959 (that is, with
welfare and other income sources collapsed into a single category that is treated as welfare
income). Second, the difference between these two sets of estimates for 1969 are used to
adjust the estimates derived with the collapsed categories for 1959. The basic assumption
underlying this adjustment procedure is, for each of the four categories of working poor,
that the proportion with "other income" as defined in 1969 was the same in 1959 as it
was ten years later in 1969. If, for example, the proportion with interest income in 1969
was larger than it was in 1959, then the adjustment leads to estimates of the working
poor that are slightly too large in 1959.

Research conducted by George F. Patterson (Table 4, "Quality and Comparability of
Personal Income Data from Surveys and the Decennial Census," presented to the Plenary
Session of the Census Bureau Joint Advisory Committee Meeting, April 25–25, 1985 in
Rosslyn, VA) shows that the estimated number of recipients of Social Security or railroad
retirement and of public assistance was somewhat smaller in the 1980 census than it was
in the 1980 CPS. Since the CPS asked a more detailed set of questions covering 23 individual income sources and amounts, compared with 7 for the census, the CPS processing
estimate of total recipients is presumably more accurate. It should be noted, however,

60–70 percent lived in fully self-supporting families, about 7–18 percent lived in fully welfare-dependent families, and about 12–33 percent lived in working-welfare-dependent families whose income was partly earned and partly derived from welfare programs.

Hence, in 1939 about 30–40 percent of relatively poor children lived in families that were at least partly welfare-dependent. However, 17 percent of all relatively poor children lived in families in which at least one member was employed by the Work Projects Administration (WPA) program and other government-sponsored "emergency work programs" that provided benefits in return for work. Consequently, perhaps as few as 15–30 percent of relatively poor children lived in families that were at least partly dependent on *nonwork* welfare.

What changes occurred following the Great Depression, when jobs became more plentiful and the relative poverty rate for children dropped sharply? The census-based estimates for 1959 indicate that of relatively poor children, about 70 percent lived in fully self-supporting families, and about 7 percent lived in fully welfare-dependent families. Subsequently, between 1959 and 1979, the proportion of children who lived in fully self-supporting families declined from about 70 to 50 percent; the proportion living in working-welfare-dependent families increased from about 24 to 33 percent; and the proportion in fully welfare-dependent families increased from about 7 to 18 percent. Comparatively little change occurred during the 1980s.

Overall, then, for the era from the Great Depression to 1988, relatively poor children have been much more likely to live in fully self-

---

that the census estimate of aggregate income from these public assistance programs is larger than the CPS estimate (Table 1 from Patterson, 1985).

Research conducted by Edward J. Welniak, Jr., of the Census Bureau (Table 1, "Effects of the March Current Population Survey's New Processing System on Estimates of Income and Poverty," presented at the 1990 annual meeting of the American Statistical Association, August 6–9, Anaheim, CA) indicates that changes in the CPS processing between 1978 and 1989 had little effect on estimates of the number of persons who received Social Security, SSI, or public assistance.

For 1939, as discussed in Chapter 7, relative poverty rates are calculated based on children in families that received at least some wage and salary income. The small percentage of children who had no personal or family income reported for subsequent years is ignored, since the living arrangements of these children at the time of the census (or survey) had probably changed since the preceding year. Although most of these children probably had access to cash income during the year preceding the census or survey, the change in living arrangements does not allow this income to be measured. Although some children with reported income also changed living arrangements since the preceding year, recent Census Bureau research indicates that the effect on poverty estimates of "changing versus fixed family composition" was about 0.5 percentage points for the overall poverty rate in 1984–85 (Census Bureau memorandum of May 30, 1989 from Enrique J. Lamas through Gordon W. Green, Jr., to William P. Butz, regarding "Poverty Estimates from SIPP").

supporting families than in fully welfare-dependent families. Still, the proportion of relatively poor children living in fully self-supporting families declined somewhat from 60–70 percent between 1939 and 1969 to 50 percent during the 1980s, while the proportion living in fully welfare-dependent families increased from about 7 percent in 1959 to about 18 percent during the 1980s. Throughout the era since the Great Depression, then, a large minority of relatively poor children have benefited from welfare programs, yet at least one-half of relatively poor children lived in working-poor families that were fully self-supporting.

Official Poverty, Work, and Welfare Dependence

How would these broad conclusions about work and welfare dependence among relatively poor children differ if we focused on children who lived in official poverty (Table 8.1)? First, we have seen that between 1939 and 1988 relatively poor children were much more likely to live in fully self-supporting families than in fully welfare-dependent families. This same conclusion holds true for children whose family incomes were below the official poverty thresholds. But by 1988 the differences would be smaller, because the official thresholds were considerably lower than the relative thresholds, and people whose incomes are extremely low are more likely to depend on government support than are those whose incomes are slightly higher.

Second, we have seen that noteworthy changes occurred in the proportion of relatively poor children living in working-poor and welfare-dependent families. Based on official thresholds the conclusions are broadly similar, but the changes would be somewhat smaller (or in the opposite direction) between 1939 and 1959 and slightly larger between 1969 and 1979. The reason is that the official thresholds count about twice as many children as poor in 1939 (but few of these additional, comparatively high-income children lived in welfare-dependent families), while the official thresholds count about one-fourth fewer children as poor in 1988 (but low-income children below the official threshold are more likely to live in welfare-dependent families).

Third, we have seen that in 1988 most relatively poor children lived in working-poor families, and a majority lived in families that earned at least one-half of their income through paid labor. Again, because the official thresholds are lower in 1988, the estimated proportions of children living in self-supporting families would be smaller. Using the official thresholds, as of 1988, 75 percent instead of 82 percent of poor children would be classified as working-poor (at least partly self-supporting), and 57 percent instead of 66 percent would be classified as living in families that were mainly or fully self-supporting.

Let us turn now to the debate about the causes of rising poverty and welfare dependence since 1959.

Mother-Only Families Among Poor Children

Some scholars argue that poverty has increased since the 1960s because federal welfare programs offered increasingly generous economic rewards that encouraged unemployment, nonemployment, out-of-wedlock childbearing, and welfare dependency, especially among blacks.[2] Other scholars, however, argue that poverty has increased because social and economic dislocations, especially job shortages, acted to reduce incomes and increase family fragmentation—again, especially among blacks.[3]

The debate, then, revolves around two questions. First, to what extent is the rise in mother-only families responsible for the rise in poverty and welfare dependence? Second, to what extent was the rise in mother-only families caused by the increasing generosity of welfare payments versus declining job opportunities? To address these questions for children, we have designated five family situations: two-parent families, mother-only families with unwed (never-married) mothers, mother-only families with ever-married (separated, divorced, or widowed) mothers, father-only families, and no-parent situations.

During the 49 years between 1939 and 1988, two large and counterbalancing changes occurred in the family situations of poor children (Table 8.2). First, the proportion living in mother-only families jumped by 38 percentage points (from 12 to 50 percent) for relatively poor children, and by an even larger 47 percentage points (from 10 to 57 percent) for officially poor children.[4] Second, these increases were counterbalanced

[2]For a prominent statement of this viewpoint, see Charles Murray, *Losing Ground: American Social Policy 1950–1980* (New York: Basic Books, 1984), pp. 125–133, 154–162.

[3]For a prominent statement of this viewpoint, see William Julius Wilson, *The Truly Disadvantaged: The Inner City, the Underclass, and Public Policy* (Chicago: University of Chicago Press, 1987), pp. 62–106.

[4]A small portion of this increase is due to improved measurement procedures implemented during the early 1980s in the Current Population Survey. These procedures made it possible to more fully identify mother-only families. If fully comparable procedures had been employed throughout the era from 1939 to 1987, the proportion of poor children who lived in mother-only families would have increased by about 2 percentage points less for relatively poor children and by about 3 percentage points less for officially poor children. In other words, much of the decline that occurred between 1979 and 1988 in the proportion of poor children who lived in no-parent situations is actually an artifact of improved

by virtually identical declines in the proportions living in two-parent families.

The largest increases in the proportions living in mother-only families occurred during the 1960s, with jumps of 12 and 18 percentage points, respectively, for relatively and officially poor children (Table 8.2). What accounts for the large, five-decade shift? Demographically, two possibilities exist—a family-composition effect, and a poverty-rate effect. The following example illustrates each of these effects.

Let us suppose that at one point in time a population consists of 100 children, with 80 living in two-parent families and 20 in mother-only families. Suppose also that the poverty rates for children in two-parent and mother-only families are 10 and 50 percent, respectively. Then at this time 8 poor children live in two-parent families, 10 poor children live in mother-only families, and the proportion of poor children living in mother-only families is 56 percent (10 of 18 poor children).

Now suppose that the family composition changes so that of 100 children, the proportion living in two-parent families falls to 60 percent, while the proportion in mother-only families increases to 40 percent. If the poverty rates for two-parent and mother-only families remain constant at 10 and 50 percent, respectively, then the new numbers of children living in poverty would be 6 poor children in two-parent families and 20 poor children in mother-only families. Hence, the proportion of poor children living in mother-only families would have increased from 56 percent to 77 percent (20 of 26 poor children). This increase in the proportion of poor children who live in mother-only families is due solely to the change in the family composition of children (that is, the increase in the proportion of all children who live in mother-only families).

On the other hand, suppose the original overall family composition remains unchanged, with 80 percent in two-parent families and 20 percent in mother-only families, but the gap separating the poverty rates for the two groups expands. Suppose, for example, that the poverty rate for children in two-parent families falls to 5 percent but the poverty rate for children in mother-only families increases to 75 percent. In this case the number of poor children living in two-parent families would decline to 4, while the number of children in mother-only families would increase to 15. The overall proportion of poor children who live in mother-only families would then increase from 56 percent to 79 percent (15 of 19 poor children). This increase in the proportion of poor children who

---

identification of mother-only families. These estimates are based on the assumption that the newly identified mother-only families had poverty rates that were identical to the poverty rate for all children in mother-only families. This is a plausible assumption, since the poverty rates for children in mother-only families and no-parent situations are similar.

TABLE 8.2

Poverty Rates and Distribution of Poor Children,
by Parental Presence: 1939–1988

Parental Presence	1939	1949	1959	1969	Census 1979	CPS 1979	CPS 1988
	Parental Presence Among Relatively Poor Children						
Total number (in thousands)	11,439	11,922	15,667	15,791	15,179	14,618	17,189
Percent	100.0	100.0	100.0	100.0	100.0	100.0	100.0
Two parents	77.1	74.5	71.8	59.1	49.3	45.0	42.5
Mother-only	12.4	14.2	20.4	32.0	40.0	45.7	49.7
Ever-married mother	11.0	10.0	19.6	28.5	30.8	36.2	31.2
Never-married mother	0.1	4.2	0.8	3.5	9.2	9.5	18.5
Father-only	2.3	1.7	1.4	2.3	2.4	1.9	3.0
No parent	8.2	9.6	6.4	6.6	8.2	7.5	4.8
	Parental Presence Among Officially Poor Children						
Total number (in thousands)	21,407	21,088	16,517	11,203	10,383	10,275	12,546
Percent	100.0	100.0	100.0	100.0	100.0	100.0	100.0
Two parents	82.1	80.6	72.6	52.8	42.3	37.8	34.9
Mother-only	9.5	10.7	19.8	37.3	46.0	52.4	57.1
Ever-married mother	8.6	7.8	19.0	33.3	34.5	40.6	34.5
Never-married mother	0.9	2.9	0.8	4.0	11.5	11.8	22.7
Father-only	2.1	1.5	1.3	2.3	2.6	1.7	2.9
No parent	6.2	7.2	6.2	7.6	9.1	8.1	5.0
	Relative Poverty Rates						
Two parents	34.6	22.9	19.9	16.1	15.1	13.5	15.7
Mother-only	60.2	57.2	63.4	61.5	57.8	58.5	62.0
Ever-married mother	59.6	53.4	63.1	60.3	54.5	54.8	56.7
Never-married mother	89.2	68.9	72.3	74.1	72.7	78.8	73.8
Father-only	42.0	35.3	30.9	28.8	28.7	25.7	28.7
No parent	58.5	56.1	53.9	48.7	49.4	45.9	52.3
	Official Poverty Rates						
Two parents	69.3	43.9	21.2	10.2	8.9	8.0	9.4
Mother-only	89.5	76.6	64.8	50.9	45.5	47.2	52.1
Ever-married mother	88.5	74.1	64.4	49.9	41.7	43.3	45.7
Never-married mother	100.0	84.1	74.6	61.1	62.2	68.7	66.0
Father-only	73.2	52.5	31.4	20.4	20.8	16.8	20.4
No parent	84.9	74.4	55.5	39.6	37.4	34.9	39.3

SOURCES: Estimates derived from 1940–1980 census PUMs and March CPS for 1980 and 1989.

NOTE: See Chapter 7 for measurement of relative poverty and official poverty. Distributions of poor children in 1939 adjusted by same method used to adjust 1939 poverty rates and discussed in Chapter 17, Footnote 5.

FIGURE 8.1

Childhood Poverty Rate Gaps Separating Two-Parent and Mother-Only Families:
1939–1988

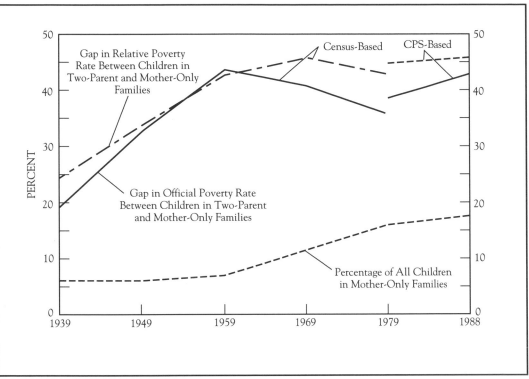

SOURCES: Derived from 1940–1980 PUMS and 1989 CPS, and see Footnote 5.

NOTE: For percent in mother-only families, 1988 results are for 1987 and have been adjusted for CPS procedural improvement and CPS-census differential.

live in mother-only families is due solely to the increase in the gap in the poverty rates between the two groups of children.

Figure 8.1 shows how these two factors—family composition and the poverty-rate gap—actually changed between 1939 and 1988. During the 20 years from 1939 to 1959, the proportion of all children who lived in mother-only families increased by only 1 percentage point, while the gap between the poverty rates of children in mother-only and two-parent families increased greatly (by 18 and 23 percentage points for relatively and officially poor children, respectively). Consequently, most of the increase in the proportion of poor children living in mother-only families that took place during the 1940s and the 1950s can be accounted for by the increasing gap in the poverty rates.

During the next 29 years, the story essentially becomes the opposite. Between 1959 and 1988, the proportion of all children who lived in mother-only families increased by 9 percentage points, compared with the earlier increase of only 1 percentage point. Meanwhile, the gap between the relative poverty rates of children living in mother-only families and those in two-parent families increased between 1959 and 1988 by only about one-sixth as much as it did during the preceding two decades (that is, by only 3 percentage points for relatively poor children), and it decreased by 1 percentage point for officially poor children.[5] Consequently, between 1959 and 1988, most of the rise in the proportion of relatively poor children who lived in mother-only families is accounted for by the rise in the proportion of all children who lived in mother-only families; and all of the rise in the proportion of officially poor children who lived in mother-only families is accounted for by the rise in the proportion of all children who lived in mother-only families. These results suggest why many poverty researchers have focused on the rise in mother-only families.

Mother-only families with unwed mothers have, however, been the particular focus of study. Although less than 1 percent of poor children

[5]During 1982 and 1983, the Census Bureau implemented a change in data collection procedures of the CPS that improved the identification of parent-child relationships, especially mother-child relationships in mother-only families. In addition, published estimates of the proportion of children living in mother-only families pertain to the universe of persons under age 18 only if they live in households and are not reference persons or spouses of reference persons. On the other hand, estimates from the censuses use somewhat different procedures for identifying parent-child relationships and they pertain to all persons under age 18. To take into account these differences in procedures and concepts, in order to develop a consistent time series of estimates of the proportion of children living in mother-only families, we adopted the following adjustment procedures for 1980 and 1988.

Published estimates from the CPS for 1988 of the proportion of children living in mother-only families and mother-only families with never-married mothers (21.42 and 6.81 percent, respectively) were adjusted to preprocedural change levels (19.75 and 5.16 percent, respectively). Then 1980 census estimates were recalculated to correspond to the CPS universe (17.98 and 2.75 percent, respectively). Next the changes from 1980 to 1988 were estimated as the differences between the census-adjusted values for 1980 and the CPS adjusted values for 1988. These differences were then added to the corresponding unadjusted census values (16.15 and 2.97 percent, respectively) to obtain adjusted values for 1988 that were conceptually and procedurally consistent with the census-based series.

These adjusted values for 1988 are somewhat lower (by 3.50 and 1.43 percentage points, respectively) than the official CPS estimates for 1988, but the series in Figure 8.1 should well reflect changes between 1960 and 1988. In fact, all of the reported levels for the percent of children living in mother-only families are probably somewhat too low, especially for 1940 and 1950, because children in secondary subfamilies were not included among those living in mother-only families (in the results presented in this book), and in all the years because census-based procedures have probably tended to miss some children in mother-only families. For further discussion of the procedural change in the CPS, see Arlene F. Saluter, U.S. Bureau of the Census, Current Population Reports, Series P-20, No. 399, *Marital Status and Living Arrangements: March 1984* (Washington, DC: U.S. Government Printing Office, 1985).

lived with unwed mothers as late as 1959, the proportion increased by 3 about percentage points for relatively and officially poor children during the 1960s, by about 6–8 percentage points during the 1970s, and by 10–11 percentage points during the first 9 years of the 1980s (Table 8.2).[6] Rising from less than 1 percent in 1959, as of 1988 children who lived in unwed-mother-only families accounted for 19 percent of relatively poor children and 23 percent of officially poor children.

Although some of this increase is due to the widening gap between the poverty rates of children in unwed-mother-only families and those in ever-married-mother-only families, most of it is due to the rising proportion who lived in unwed-mother-only families. Between 1959 and 1988, the proportion of children in all mother-only families who lived with unwed mothers jumped from 2 percent to 32 percent, and the proportion of poor children in mother-only families who lived with an unwed mother jumped somewhat more from about 4 percent in 1959 to 37–40 percent in 1988.

These results suggest that changes in overall poverty rates among children since the Great Depression, but especially since 1959, may at least partly have been caused by the rise in mother-only families. But these results do not provide direct estimates of the extent to which the change in the overall poverty rate was due to the rise of mother-only families. And it remains the case, as of 1988, that about one-half of poor children (43–50 percent) did not live in such families, and that about four-fifths (77–81 percent) did not live in mother-only families with unwed mothers. We turn now to estimates of the extent to which changes in poverty rates since the Great Depression were due to the rise of mother-only families.

Poverty Trends and the Rise of Mother-Only Families

To measure the extent to which the rise of mother-only families has influenced overall poverty trends for children, we have calculated what hypothetical, overall poverty rates for children would have been if children in mother-only families had experienced the same poverty rates as did children in two-parent families at specific points in time. These hypothetical poverty rates are derived for ten-year intervals from 1939 to 1979 and for the nine-year interval 1979–1988. By comparing the ac-

[6]Since some of the increase that occurred during the 1980s is an artifact of improved identification of mother-only families, the actual increases were probably closer to 3 and 4 percentage points during the 1960s, 6 and 9 percentage points during the 1970s, and 6 and 9 percentage points during the 1980s.

tual and hypothetical poverty rates, we can estimate the effect of mother-only families on the overall poverty rate at specific points in time. Unfortunately, however, our estimates will overestimate, to some degree, the actual effect that the rise of mother-only families had on poverty.

The reason is that even if it were somehow possible to (re)unite each mother-only family with the actual father and his income, the poverty rate for children in the resulting, (re)united but hypothetical, two-parent families would be greater than the poverty rate for children in actual two-parent families. This is because children who enter mother-only families have a higher poverty rate than do children who remain in two-parent families, even before the transition to the mother-only family occurs.[7]

In addition, if, as some researchers argue, much of the rise in mother-only families since 1959 is the result of declining economic opportunities for fathers, then an increasing proportion of poor children in mother-only families would have been poor even if their fathers could somehow have been (re)united with the family, because the additional income earned by the father would not have been enough to raise the family out of poverty. Insofar as this argument is correct, then, our estimates of the effect that the rise of mother-only families had on poverty rates through time will overestimate the actual effect of the rise of mother-only families.

Decade-by-decade comparisons of the actual and hypothetical poverty changes suggest that mother-only families had measurable but small effects on poverty trends (Table 8.3). Changes across each decade in the actual and hypothetical poverty rates were within 0–2 percentage points of each other for the relative poverty rate and within 0–2 percentage points of each other for the official poverty rate.

These differences between changes in actual and hypothetical poverty are, however, cumulative. Consequently, by 1988 the hypothetical relative poverty rate of 20.0 percent was 7.0 percentage points smaller than the actual relative poverty rate of 27.0. Similarly, the hypothetical

[7]For example, Mary Jo Bane (p. 226) reports from the Panel Study of Income Dynamics that of persons who were in poverty after a transition "into a female-headed family from a male-headed household," the proportion who were poor before the transition was 24 percent for whites and 62 percent for blacks. See Mary Jo Bane, "Household Composition and Poverty." In Sheldon H. Danziger and Daniel H. Weinberg, eds., *Fighting Poverty* (Cambridge, MA: Harvard University Press, 1986), pp. 209–231. Similarly, for children Suzanne Bianchi and Edith McArthur report from the Survey of Income and Program Participation that the poverty rate was nearly twice as large for children whose "father leaves" before the transition than for children in two-parent families whose father does not leave (21.3 vs. 12.1 percent). See Suzanne Bianchi and Edith McArthur, U.S. Bureau of the Census, Current Population Reports, Series P-70, No. 23, *Family Disruption and Economic Hardship: The Short-Run Picture for Children* (Washington, DC: U.S. Government Printing Office, 1991), Table B.

TABLE 8.3

Hypothetical Poverty Rates for Children,
if Mother-Only Rates Equaled Two-Parent-Family Rates: 1939–1988

Poverty Rates	1939	1949	1959	1969	Census 1979	CPS 1979	1988
Relative							
Actual	37.9	26.9	24.4	22.7	23.8	23.0	27.0
Hypothetical #1	37.9	26.9	23.9	20.4	19.6	17.9	20.0
Hypothetical #2	—	—	24.4	20.9	20.1	18.4	20.6
Hypothetical #3	35.9	26.4	21.0	17.4	16.8	14.9	17.0
Official							
Actual	71.8	47.6	25.8	16.1	16.3	16.2	19.7
Hypothetical #1	71.8	47.6	25.2	14.1	12.7	11.8	13.3
Hypothetical #2	—	—	25.8	14.5	13.1	12.2	13.8
Hypothetical #3	70.2	45.4	22.3	11.3	10.3	9.1	10.5

Poverty Rate Change	1939–1949	1949–1959	1959–1969	1969–1979	1979–1988
Relative					
Actual	−11.0	−2.5	−1.7	1.1	3.9
Hypothetical #1	−11.0	−3.0	−3.5	−0.8	2.1
Hypothetical #2	—	—	−3.5	−0.8	2.1
Official					
Actual	−24.3	−21.8	−9.6	0.1	3.5
Hypothetical #1	−24.7	−22.3	−11.2	−1.4	1.6
Hypothetical #2	—	—	−11.2	−1.4	1.6

SOURCE: Estimates derived from 1940–1980 census PUMs and March CPS for 1980 and 1989.

NOTES: Hypothetical #1 shows effect of assuming the proportion in mother-only families remained constant after 1939. Hypothetical #2 shows effect of assuming proportion in mother-only families remained constant after 1959. Hypothetical #3 shows effect of assuming all children in mother-only families had poverty rate of children in two-parent families (of the same race). See Chapter 7 for measurement of relative poverty and official poverty.

official poverty rate of 13.3 percent was 6.4 percentage points smaller than the actual official rate of 19.7 percent. However, only a portion of these substantial differences, as of 1988, may have resulted from the post-1959 rise in mother-only families—the rise that has been the focus of controversy.

To estimate the post-1959 effects, we have calculated what hypothetical poverty rates would have been if the proportion of children living in mother-only families had not increased after 1959. The resulting hypothetical, relative, and official poverty rates in 1988 are 6.4 and 5.9 percentage points smaller, respectively, than the corresponding actual rates (Table 8.3). Hence, the rise of mother-only families after 1959 accounts, at most, about nine-tenths of the total effect of mother-only families between 1939 and 1988. Without the post-1959 rise in mother-only families, then, the relative poverty rate might have decreased by as much as 3.8 percentage points instead of increasing by 2.6 percentage points, while the official rate might have decreased by as much as 12.0 instead of 6.1 percentage points.

These results suggest that the rise of mother-only families may have had a substantial influence on poverty trends by increasing poverty among children since 1959, but even if no rise in mother-only families had occurred after 1959, poverty rates would still be at least 70–76 percent as large as they actually were in 1988. Hence, although the relative and official poverty rates for children might be as much as 37 percent and 47 percent smaller (at 17.0 percent and 10.5 percent), respectively, than their actual values if all mother-only families somehow attained the poverty rates of two-parent families, the remaining one-half to two-thirds of childhood poverty in the United States cannot be directly linked to the existence of mother-only families, and no more than 24–30 percent of childhood poverty in this country can be attributed to the post-1959 rise of mother-only families. Still, poverty rates for children might be smaller (by as much as 6 percentage points) if the post-1959 rise of mother-only families had not occurred.

As you will see below, however, this estimate is also too high, since the fathers associated with mother-only families tend to have lower incomes than do other fathers. Taking this into account, the post-1959 rise of mother-only families probably accounts for 2–4 percentage points in current childhood poverty rates.

Although most childhood poverty in the United States is not the result of the post-1959 rise in mother-only families, and although most of the change in childhood poverty since the Great Depression is not the result of the post-1959 rise in mother-only families, the debate about the role of the post-1959 rise in mother-only families, and whether or not this rise was caused by changes in the generosity of welfare programs, remains an important one. The next question addressed in this chapter, then, is, To what extent were changes in the generosity of welfare programs responsible for the post-1959 rise in mother-only families and hence for post-1959 changes in poverty among children?

Absolute Welfare Generosity and the Rise in Mother-Only Families

To study whether changes in the generosity of welfare programs have influenced the prevalence of mother-only families, we present data concerning both trends (Figure 8.2 and Appendix Table 8.1). If, as some scholars argue, low-income persons view welfare benefits as an incentive to separate, divorce, or remain unmarried after the birth of a child, then increases in the generosity of welfare programs should lead to increases in the proportion of children living in mother-only families and decreases in the generosity of welfare programs should lead to decreases in the proportion of children living in mother-only families. The analysis below shows that this effect has been only a small one.

Changes in the generosity of welfare programs are measured using four different indicators in Figure 8.2. The first indicator is the combined AFDC and Food Stamps benefit level for a family of four in which there was no income for each presidential election year from 1960 to 1984 and for each subsequent year between 1985 and 1987.[8] This indicator measures the level of basic income support available from welfare programs to poor families, and these two programs accounted for 82 percent of all welfare expenditures in 1960 and for 63 percent in 1980.[9] Most of this change that occurred during 1960–1980 is due to the increase in Medicaid expenditures, a program that did not exist in 1960 but accounted for 22 percent of welfare expenditures by 1980.

To take some account of Medicaid, the second and third indicators of welfare generosity are the same as the first indicator for the presidential years, except that they include Medicaid benefits valued at 28 percent or 100 percent of market value. Finally, the fourth indicator is the dollar value per mother-only family of total major welfare expenditures.[10]

Although these indicators differ in several important respects, taken together they suggest that there have been three distinct periods of change in the generosity of welfare programs since 1949.[11] The 1950s and the

[8]See Committee on Ways and Means, U.S. House of Representatives, *Background Material and Data on Programs Within the Jurisdiction of the Committee on Ways and Means* (Washington, DC: U.S. Government Printing Office, 1989), Table 35.

[9]See Irwin Garfinkel and Sara S. McLanahan, *Single Mothers and Their Children: A New American Dilemma* (Washington, DC: Urban Institute, 1986), pp. 108–109, Table 7.

[10]Obtained from Garfinkel and McLanahan, Table 7. Results were adjusted to 1988 dollars for Figure 8.3.

[11]Important respects in which the four indicators differ include the following. First, they differ in the number of welfare programs they include. Other things being equal, the larger the number of programs encompassed within an indicator, the better the indicator

FIGURE 8.2

Welfare Generosity and Children in Mother-Only Families: 1939–1987

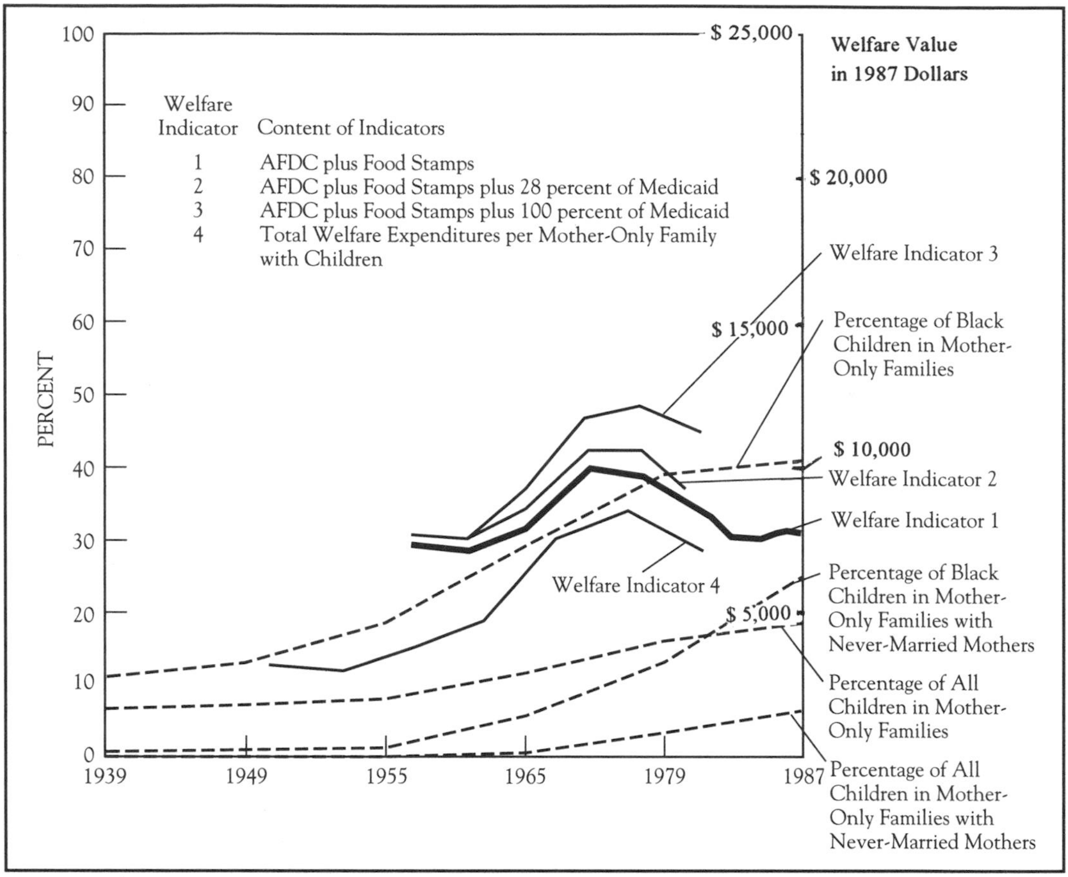

SOURCES: See Footnotes 8–15.

early 1960s brought a small increase in welfare generosity; the late 1960s and the early 1970s brought a rapid increase in welfare generosity; and the late 1970s through 1987 brought a substantial decline in welfare generosity.

---

for present purposes. Indicator number 4 includes the largest number of benefits, although it encompasses more benefits than any specific mother-only family can expect to or will receive.

Second, indicator numbers 1, 2 and 3 differ in the valuation of Medicaid (0 percent, 28 percent, and 100 percent of market value), but the proper valuation of Medicaid benefits is not clear-cut. For two views, see John M. McNeil, U.S. Bureau of the Census,

How closely have changes in mother-only families for children corresponded to these changes in welfare generosity? Figure 8.2 shows that the changes in these trends during the 1950s were fairly similar but that subsequent changes in these trends were quite different.[12] The 1950s brought relatively slow increases in both welfare generosity and the proportion of children living in mother-only families. The 1960s brought much larger increases in both trends. But the 1960s brought the largest increase in welfare generosity, and the 1970s brought a turnaround and a decline in welfare generosity, while the largest increase in the proportion of all children living in mother-only families did not come until the 1970s. For black children this 1970s increase in the proportion living in mother-only families was nearly as large as the 1960s increase (9.1

Current Population Reports, Series P-60, No. 164-RD-1, *Measuring the Effect of Benefits and Taxes on Income and Poverty: 1986* (Washington, DC: U.S. Government Printing Office, 1988), pp. 2–3, 223–224; and Garfinkel and McLanahan, Appendix B. The best approach for valuing Medicaid in the present context probably lies between the two extremes.

Third, indicator number 4 takes into account increases or decreases in the ease of access to AFDC by focusing on total program expenditures that change partly as a function of the proportion of mother-only families that actually receive benefits. This attention to program participation rates is important because various regulatory and court-imposed changes made it easier to receive AFDC between 1961 and 1969, but the tightening of child support regulations, beginning in 1974, might be expected to have reduced AFDC participation rates. In other words, AFDC benefits were effectively made more generous and then less generous by the easing and then the tightening of eligibility requirements. For discussions of ease of access to AFDC, see Murray, *Losing Ground*, pp. 164–165; and Garfinkel and McLanahan, pp. 105–119.

But fourth, indicator number 4 measures program generosity as the average program expenditure across all mother-only families, regardless of whether or not they actually received any welfare benefits. If, as some argue, women become separated, divorced, or bear children out of wedlock in order to receive welfare benefits, then these women may focus mainly on the value of benefits to mother-only families that actually do receive benefits, and the increase in the average value of benefits per mother-only family that actually received benefits would be much less than the increase suggested by indicator 4.

In view of these differences between the four indicators, it is probably best to assume that actual changes in absolute value of generosity levels, as perceived by potential recipients, lie somewhere within the range of estimates. Since increases in generosity, as perceived by prospective recipients, are surely substantially exaggerated by indicator number 4 (with an estimated increase of 128 percent between 1960 and 1975), and since indicators 1 and 2 surely underestimate increases in generosity (with estimated increases of 30 and 38 percent between 1960 and 1976), indicator number 3 may come closest to reflecting increases in absolute generosity levels (59 percent between 1960 and 1976). Fortunately for our purposes, despite differences between the various indicators, the patterns of change in the indicators are broadly similar.

[12]Since census data pertain to living arrangements as of April 1 of the census year, and since survey data pertain to living arrangements as of March 1 of the survey year, the living arrangements as measured for a given year would be little affected by welfare generosity during that year, but living arrangements might be affected by welfare generosity during the preceding year. Since the trends in welfare generosity and living arrangements discussed here pertain to long-term changes of ten years or more, the conclusions drawn here would not be affected by this measurement issue.

versus 10.9 percentage points). Subsequently, the 1980s brought continued decline in welfare generosity but continued (albeit smaller) increases in the proportions of all children, particularly black children,
living in mother-only families.

Perhaps more important, though, are trends in the proportion of
children living in unwed-mother-only families, since much of the debate has centered on these families—especially among blacks. Each successive decade between the 1960s and the 1980s brought a larger increase in the proportion of all children living in unwed mother-only
families. The increases during the 1960s, the 1970s, and the first eight
years of the 1980s were 0.8, 1.9, and about 2.9 percentage points, respectively.

For black children, the corresponding increases in the proportion
living in unwed-mother-only families were 4.0, 8.6, and about 9.6 percentage points.[13] Hence, for all children and for black children, the in-

[13]These results take account of the effect that procedural changes in the CPS (see
Footnote 5) had on estimates for black children. Two methods were used to estimate the
effect of procedural changes. First, the CPS estimates indicate that for 1981–1983 the
number of black children living in two-parent families declined by 198,000 and the total
number of black children declined by 23,000. Of the 175,000 difference, about 81 percent
probably lived in mother-only families, while the remaining 19 percent lived in father-
only families or no-parent situations. Hence, this approach suggests that the actual increase in the number of black children living in mother-only families was 142,000.

The second approach to estimating the effect of procedural changes is as follows.
The decline of 538,000 in the number of children living in no-parent situations that occurred from 1981 to 1983 is subtracted from the increase of 713,000 in the number living
in one-parent families to obtain the estimate that the number of black children living in
one-parent families increased by 175,000. Since 95 percent of black children in one-parent
families live in mother-only families, the newly estimated increase in the number living
in mother-only families is 166,000. Finally, subtracting these two estimates of the actual
increase from the total CPS increase of 715,000 in mother-only families indicates that an
increase of 549,000–573,000 was an artifact of the improved estimation procedures.

We further assumed that all of the artifactual increase occurred among children living in unwed-mother-only families. This reduced the CPS estimate of the proportion of
black children living in unwed-mother-only families from 28.21 to 22.44 percent, and it
reduced the proportion of all black children living mother-only families from 51.13 to
45.36. Finally, differences between the 1980 CPS and census-based estimates were used to
further adjust the CPS results so that they would be comparable with the long-term census-based results.

One might also argue, however, that a portion of the 5.77 percentage point adjustment for the CPS procedural change should be allocated to earlier years. For example, one
might argue that since 90 percent of the 1939–1979 change occurred between 1959 and
1979, 90 percent of the 5.77 percentage point change (5.19 percentage points) should be
allocated to these years. In addition, since 4 percentage points of the 12.6 percentage point
change from 1959–1979 occurred between 1959 and 1969, one might argue that about
one-third of the 5.19 percentage point change probably occurred between 1959 and 1969,
while the additional two-thirds occurred during the next ten years. Based on these assumptions, one would calculate that the percentage point increase in the proportion of
black children living in unwed-mother-only families was 5.7, 12.1, and 9.6 percentage
points during the 1960s, the 1970s, and the first eight years of the 1980s, respectively.
If we "decennialize" the 9.6 percentage points to a ten-year base, the proportion for

creases in the proportions living in unwed-mother-only families that occurred during the 1970s and the 1980s were at least twice as large as corresponding increases that took place during the 1960s (despite the fact that welfare generosity has turned around and declined substantially since the mid-1970s).

Overall, since most of these decade-to-decade comparisons suggest that the trends in welfare generosity and mother-only families are only weakly related, these results indicate that from the perspective of children, changes in welfare generosity have had little effect on the continuing rise in mother-only families. This conclusion is consistent with most of the evidence, as summarized by Irwin Garfinkel and Sara S. McLanahan, from more sophisticated studies of the effects of welfare programs on divorce, out-of-wedlock childbearing, and (re)marriage.[14] According to Garfinkel and McLanahan, the best of these studies estimate that increases in welfare generosity that occurred between 1960 and 1975 accounted for 9–14 percent of the rise in mother-only families.[15]

If we apply this estimate to the total increase of about 6.1 percentage points that occurred in the proportion of children who lived in mother-only families during these 15 years, the result is that increases in welfare generosity are responsible for an increase of only 0.55–0.85 percentage points in the overall proportion of children living in mother-only families during 1960–1979.[16] If, despite the fall in welfare generosity since the 1970s, we assume as a maximum estimate that 9–14 percent of the entire rise through 1988 is accounted for by the earlier increase in welfare generosity, then the welfare-generosity effect produced 1.3–1.9 percentage points of the 13.3 percentage point increase in the overall proportion of children living in mother-only families between 1960 and 1988.

In addition, if as a maximum estimate we assume that of all of these children, 1.3–1.9 percent of those living in mother-only families, were poverty-stricken but would not have been in this condition without the welfare-generosity effect, then the overall relative and official poverty rates for children were 1–2 percentage points larger in 1988 than

---

the 1980s would be 12.0 percent. Hence, the increases for the 1970s and the 1980s would be approximately equal, and about twice as large as the increase for the 1960s. The corresponding estimates of 0.8, 1.9, and 2.9 percentage points for all children (with "decennialization" of the 1980s' estimate) would be 1.2, 2.6, and 3.6 percentage points for the 1960s, 1970s, and 1980s, respectively.

[14]Garfinkel and McLanahan, pp. 55–63.

[15]Garfinkel and McLanahan, p. 63.

[16]Taking into account improved measurement of mother-only families associated with procedural changes in the CPS, the adjusted estimate for 1960–1979 would be 0.62–0.95 percentage points.

they would have been without the welfare-generosity effect.[17] Hence, without the welfare-generosity effect, by 1988 the relative and official poverty rates for children would have been at least 25 and 18 percent, respectively, instead of the actual values of 27 and 20 percent.

The Relative Value of Welfare Benefits

Why did apparent increases in the generosity of welfare programs produce so little increase in mother-only families? Part of the answer may be that published indicators of welfare generosity measure the absolute value of welfare program benefits, not their relative value, thereby ignoring the enormous long-term increase that occurred in the average living level of families in the United States between the Great Depression and 1973.[18] Figure 8.3 shows how different changes in the generosity of welfare programs appear when measured in relative rather than absolute terms.

AFDC and Food Stamps are the two major programs that provide day-to-day economic support of many mother-only families. Figure 8.3 presents the combined value of the benefits from these programs for 1960–1987 as a proportion of both the official and the relative poverty thresholds.[19] The results indicate that in 1960 the value of these welfare

[17]The effect on the overall poverty rates are calculated as follows. If 9–14 percent of the increase in mother-only families for children between 1960 and 1988 was due to the welfare-generosity effect, and none of these children would have been in relative poverty without the welfare-generosity effect, but all were in relative poverty because of the welfare-generosity effect, then the welfare-generosity effect on poverty amounts to 15–23 percent of the increase in mother-only families, since the relative poverty rate was about 60 percent for children in mother-only families throughout the era ($100/60 \times 9$–14). Since about 6.4 percent of all children lived in poverty in 1988 because of the post-1959 rise in mother-only families, as calculated in an earlier section, the product of 15–23 and 6.4 percent indicates that the welfare-generosity effect on relative poverty was about 1.0–1.5 percentage points in 1988. Since the official poverty rate for children in mother-only families was about 50 percent, corresponding calculations indicate that the welfare-generosity effect on poverty amounts to 18–28 percent of the increase in mother-only families, which, multiplied by the 5.9 percentage point effect of the post-1959 rise in mother-only families on the official poverty rate, produces the results that the welfare-generosity effect on official poverty for children was 1.1–1.7 percentage points by 1988.

[18]Median family income reached a peak in 1973 and did not reach this peak level again until 1987, Edward J. Welniak, U.S. Bureau of the Census, Current Population Reports, Series P-60, No. 162, *Money Income of Households, Families, and Persons in the United States: 1987*, U.S. Government Printing Office, Washington, D.C. 1989, Table 11.

[19]As we discussed in Chapter 7, a general rise in the availability of health insurance benefits has occurred since the 1940s. Since only a small portion of the cost of these benefits was paid directly by the employees, much of the actual value cost of the benefits should be viewed as income, but such noncash, benefit-related income is not counted as income in official Census Bureau income measures. If such benefits were included, the

FIGURE 8.3

Value of Welfare Programs
as Percentage of Relative and Official Poverty Thresholds: 1939–1987

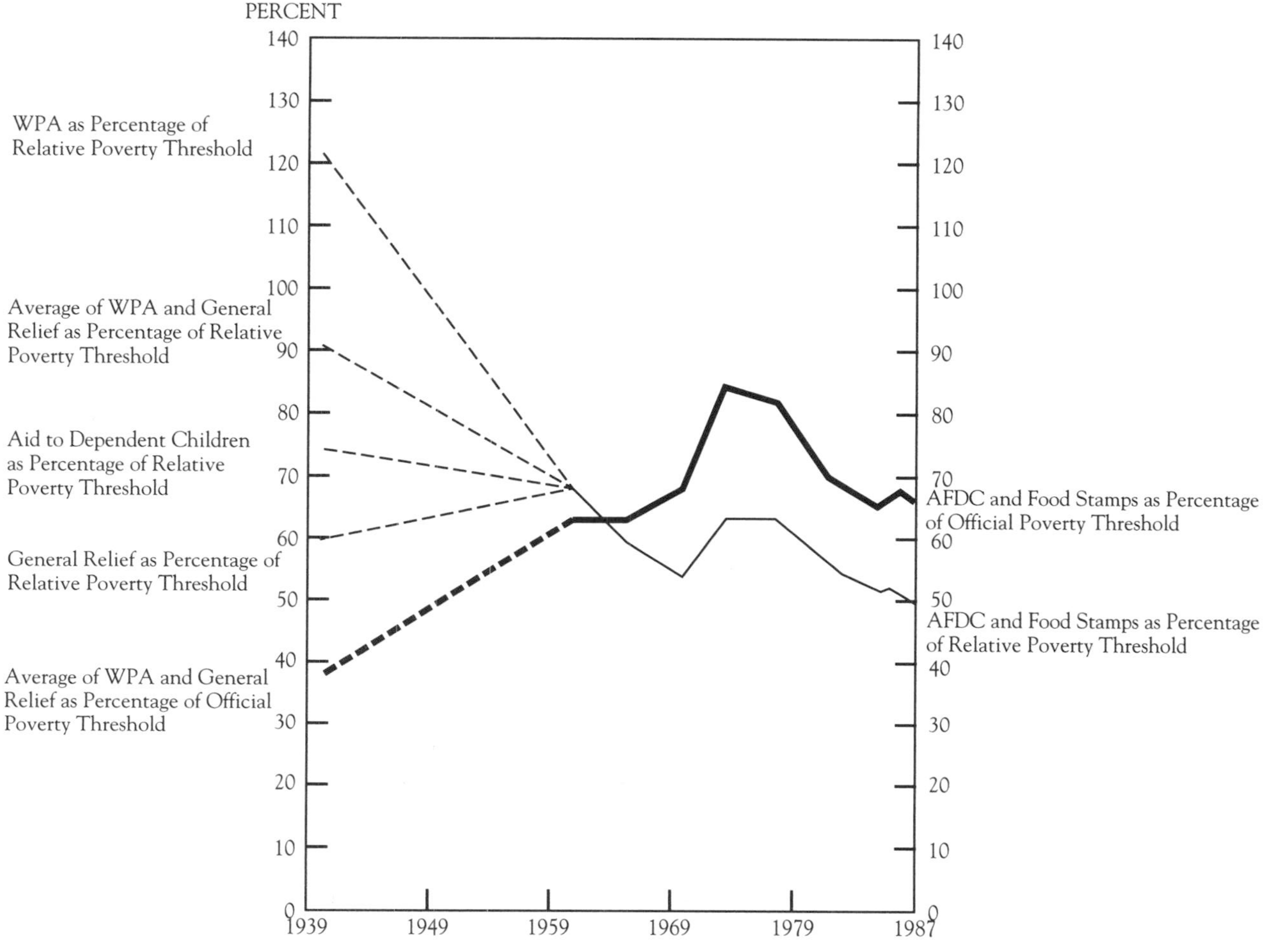

PERCENT

140
130
120
110
100
90
80
70
60
50
40
30
20
10
0

WPA as Percentage of
Relative Poverty Threshold

Average of WPA and General
Relief as Percentage of Relative
Poverty Threshold

Aid to Dependent Children
as Percentage of Relative
Poverty Threshold

General Relief as Percentage of
Relative Poverty Threshold

Average of WPA and General
Relief as Percentage of Official
Poverty Threshold

140
130
120
110
100
90
80
70
60
50
40
30
20
10
0

AFDC and Food Stamps as Percentage
of Official Poverty Threshold

AFDC and Food Stamps as Percentage
of Relative Poverty Threshold

1939   1949   1959   1969   1979   1987

SOURCES: Derived from 1940–1980 PUMS, 1987 CPS, and see Footnotes 1 and 11.

benefits was equal to 64 percent of the official poverty threshold and 68 percent of the relative poverty threshold. Between 1960 and 1972, the value of these benefits as a proportion of the official poverty threshold increased sharply, but as a proportion of the relative poverty threshold their value declined sharply between 1960 and 1968, and the subsequent sharp increase did not fully offset the earlier decline.

The reason for the remarkable differences between these trends is that the American family experienced a large 40 percent increase in median income between 1960 and 1972. Hence, during these 12 years, the value of AFDC and Food Stamps increased by 20.7 percentage points as a proportion of the official poverty threshold, but it declined by 3.7 percentage points as a proportion of the relative poverty threshold. Viewed from the perspective of change in the relative value of these welfare benefits, then, it is not surprising that welfare-benefit changes produced only a small increase in mother-only families. (The sharp increase in the relative value of these benefits that did occur between 1968 and 1972 was not large enough to offset the decline in the relative value of these benefits that occurred during the preceding eight years.)

During the subsequent 15 years from 1972 to 1987, sharp declines occurred in both the absolute and the relative value of AFDC and Food Stamps. By 1987, the absolute value of these benefits had fallen to nearly the level of 1960, while their value as a proportion of the relative poverty threshold had fallen (by a large 18.4 percentage points) to only 50 percent of the relative poverty threshold.

Even at their peak value in the 1970s, AFDC and Food Stamps together provided an income equal to only about 84 percent of the official poverty threshold and 64 percent of the relative poverty threshold, and by 1987 their combined value had fallen to only 67 and 50 percent of the official and relative thresholds, respectively. Hence, since at least 1959, a family that depended only on these welfare programs for support would, despite changes in generosity, have lived substantially below the poverty threshold.

Figure 8.3 also presents crude estimates (for 1940) of the relative value of three different welfare programs that span virtually the entire range of benefit levels of various welfare programs of the time.[20] The

---

relative poverty threshold would need to be adjusted upward (see Chapter 7). In lieu of actual measures of the value such income for the typical (median) family, or for all families across the income distribution, it is probably best to view health insurance (whether an employee benefit or a publicly provided benefit) as separate from day-to-day sources of income that allow families to buy basic necessities, such as food, clothing, shelter, transportation, and the like.

[20]Estimates are in part from Report of the Committee on Long-Range Work and Relief Policies to the National Resources Planning Board, *Security, Work, and Relief Policies*

results indicate that the General Relief program, the Aid to Dependent Children (ADC) program, and the Work Projects Administration (WPA) program provided incomes that were equal, respectively, to about 60, 75, and 122 percent of the relative poverty threshold recorded for 1940.

The relative value of ADC benefits in 1940, then, was probably somewhat more than the relative value of benefits in its successor program, AFDC, 20 years later in 1960. WPA employment benefits had a value that was about 1.6 and 2.0 times as large as the ADC and General Relief benefits. These comparative benefit values are consistent with the ideas that WPA employment income "was intended to provide a minimum standard of living and to make other relief (welfare) unnecessary," and that it "was not to exceed the earnings paid to corresponding occupational groups in private employment."[21] Hence, the value of WPA benefits in 1940 was somewhat above the contemporary relative poverty threshold but well below the median family income of the time.

Finally, since the WPA and General Relief programs were probably the two most important welfare programs from the viewpoint of children in 1940, since approximately equal numbers of persons received benefits from these programs, and since the average benefit level of these two programs was nearly the same as the average benefit level of the two next-largest welfare programs of the time, we estimate that the average benefit level for all welfare programs in 1940 was roughly equal to the average of WPA and General Relief.[22] This average is 91 percent of the relative poverty threshold of the time, but only 39 percent of the official poverty threshold.

In fact, considering the entire series of estimates, the absolute measure suggests that the peak value of welfare benefits probably oc-

---

(Washington, DC: U.S. Government Printing Office, 1942). The monthly values of benefits from these programs are presented on page 161. Since Footnote 76 on page 114 of this report states that "the average general-relief case was about three persons as compared to an average of nearly four (3.76) persons in families of certified WPA workers," the poverty thresholds corresponding to these family sizes (3.00 and 3.75) are used in computing the estimates presented in Figure 8.4. Since Appendix 9 of this report indicates that the total number of children who receive ADC was 831,000 in June 1940, and that they lived in a total of 346,000 families, assuming that each family included one adult (usually the mother), we calculate that the average family size was about 3.4 persons. Since some of these families probably had more than one adult member, we assumed that the average family size was 3.5 persons for purposes of calculating the appropriate poverty thresholds.

[21]Arthur Edward Burns and Peyton Kerr, "Survey of Work-Relief Wage Policies," *American Economic Review* 31 (March 1941): 713, 720.

[22]See National Resources Planning Board, *Security, Work, and Relief Policies* (Washington, DC: U.S. Government Printing Office, 1942), p. 161, Appendix 9. The other two largest programs in 1939 were the Old-Age Assistance program and Unemployment Insurance under the Social Security Act. Since old-age assistance is received by one person, the value of benefits as a proportion of the relative poverty threshold involves the use of a poverty threshold that is much smaller than the threshold for a family of four.

curred during the mid-1970s, and that the value of welfare benefits had fallen substantially by 1987, but to the comparatively high level of about 1970. The relative measure, quite to the contrary, indicates that the relative value of welfare benefits may have fallen to a historic low during the late 1960s. But this was followed by an additional decline, after a sharp but brief increase during the early 1970s, to another historically low level in 1987 that was only slightly more than one-half the average level of welfare benefits documented for 1940.

Taken together, these results suggest that the absolute value of welfare benefits grew greatly after 1940 but that this increase did not keep pace with the general rise in the American standard of living—except during 1968–1972—and that by 1987 the relative benefit levels of AFDC and Food Stamps were lower than they had been at any time since the Great Depression.

If changes in the generosity of welfare programs did not produce most of the rise in mother-only families or most of the associated changes in poverty after 1959, then what did? Is the explanation focusing on declining job opportunities for fathers correct? In Chapters 9 and 10 we address these and other, related questions. But before turning to these issues, we will focus briefly on shifts in welfare dependency among poor children living in various family situations, and on differences among black, Hispanic, and white children in their family structure and welfare dependency.

Welfare Dependence and Family Situation Since 1959

Earlier in this chapter we saw that self-support declined and welfare dependence increased between 1959 and 1988, but mainly during the 1960s and 1970s. Have similar changes occurred among poor children in different family situations? The answer both for relatively poor and officially poor children is yes—for the proportions in mother-only and two-parent families that are mainly and fully welfare-dependent.

Table 8.4 shows that despite large differences in levels of welfare dependence, poor children in mother-only families and two-parent families experienced the same basic pattern of change—increases during the 1960s and 1970s that were noticeably larger than they would be during the 1980s. The similarity of these patterns of change suggests the possibility that regardless of family situation, changes in welfare dependence among poor children were associated, at least in part, with changes in the availability of welfare benefits.

But since, as we saw in the preceding section, the value of welfare

TABLE 8.4

Poor Children in Self-Supporting and Welfare-Dependent Families, by Parental Presence: 1959–1988

Parental Presence	Percent Fully Welfare-Dependent					Percent Mainly or Fully Welfare-Dependent					Percent as least Partially Welfare-Dependent				
	1959	1969	Census 1979	CPS 1979	1988	1959	1969	Census 1979	CPS 1979	1988	1959	1969	Census 1979	CPS 1979	1988
						Relatively Poor Children									
Total	6.5	11.5	17.3	17.7	18.4	12.9	20.1	27.1	34.3	30.1	30.2	33.6	41.4	50.6	47.5
Two Parents	2.5	3.1	4.5	5.5	6.4	5.5	7.2	9.2	12.9	12.1	21.2	18.3	22.4	26.5	22.9
Mother-Only	25.2	27.5	32.9	29.2	29.2	41.7	43.9	47.8	54.2	52.9	59.0	60.7	62.7	71.3	67.8
Father-Only	10.2	14.8	17.2	11.4	11.8	32.4	23.0	25.3	24.9	19.9	45.6	38.1	38.1	46.8	38.7
No Parent	6.1	14.5	21.4	23.9	17.5	18.8	29.5	37.7	45.8	44.6	45.0	48.8	57.4	72.5	65.9
						Officially Poor Children									
Total	5.7	15.8	24.7	24.3	24.6	11.6	25.7	36.2	43.9	43.4	30.2	38.2	49.0	58.1	56.0
Two Parents	2.2	4.9	7.0	8.4	10.8	4.8	10.1	12.9	18.0	18.7	22.0	21.3	26.0	31.5	29.4
Mother-Only	25.0	32.5	40.8	35.4	34.3	41.4	48.2	56.5	61.6	60.2	59.0	61.9	68.6	75.1	73.7
Father-Only	7.9	16.3	23.7	14.7	17.1	31.1	26.6	30.7	33.5	26.3	43.8	43.8	44.4	54.7	43.1
No Parent	4.4	17.4	23.4	30.2	21.5	16.9	35.1	46.7	54.1	44.9	59.0	50.1	61.7	75.2	64.7

SOURCES: Estimates derived from 1960–1980 census PUMs and March CPS for 1980 and 1989.

NOTES: Welfare income and hence welfare dependence is measured as cash income received from the Aid to Families with Dependent Children (AFDC) and Social Security programs. All other cash income is classified as self-support. This approach allows for consistent measurement across all census and CPS years. For additional discussion of welfare programs, and for procedures (and limitations to procedures) used to derive estimates for 1959, see Footnote 1 and Chapters 7 and 11. Fully self-supporting families receive no AFDC or Social Security income. At least partially welfare-dependent families receive at least some income from AFDC or Social Security. Mainly or fully welfare-dependent families receive more than 50 percent of their income from AFDC or Social Security. Fully welfare-dependent families receive 100 percent of their income but less than 100 percent of their income from AFDC or Social Security. See Chapter 7 for measurement of relative poverty and official poverty.

benefits had only a small effect on family structure or poverty rates during the 1960s and 1970s, insofar as changes in access to welfare benefits were associated with changes in welfare dependency, this relationship was mainly a function of the simple fact that welfare eligibility requirements were eased during the 1960s. Benefits that are easier to obtain are more likely to constitute a larger portion of a poor family's income than those that are more difficult to obtain.

Still, overall welfare-dependence levels among poor children were greater in 1979 than they would have been if there had been no increase in mother-only families after 1959.[23] For example, if the increasing proportion of poor children living in mother-only families between 1959 and 1979 had welfare-dependency rates that were equal to those of poor children in two-parent families, then we may estimate that the proportion of poor children living in mainly or fully welfare-dependent families would have increased by 7 instead of 14 percentage points for relatively poor children, and by 13 instead of 25 percentage points for officially poor children.

These results suggest that the rise of mother-only families during the 1960s and the 1970s accounted for substantial increases in overall welfare dependence among poor children. These increases were equal to about one-fourth of the total (main and full) welfare dependence among relatively poor children in 1979 and one-third of the total (main and full) welfare dependence among officially poor children. Consequently, without the rise in the proportion of children living in poor, mother-only families that occurred between 1959 and 1979, the number of welfare-dependent poor children in 1979 might have been approximately 75 percent as large as the actual number for relatively poor children, and about 67 percent as large as the actual number for officially poor children.

Finally, we can make a crude estimate of the effect that the increase in welfare generosity had on welfare dependence through its influence on the rise in mother-only families and poverty. In an earlier section we calculated that if welfare programs had not increased in generosity after the mid-1960s, poverty would have been lower by 1–2 percentage points both for the relative and the official poverty rates. If all of these poor children were welfare-dependent, then by producing a small increase in mother-only families during the 1960s and the 1970s, increasing welfare generosity also produced an increase in welfare dependence among poor

[23]The size of this effect can be estimated crudely by calculating hypothetical welfare-dependency rates. In other words, by calculating what the overall welfare-dependency rates would have been in 1979 if the proportion of poor children living in mother-only families in 1979 had remained the same as the proportion in 1959, and if all of the poor children involved in the actual increase in mother-only families had welfare-dependency rates that were equal to those of children living in two-parent families in 1979.

children that was equal to no more than one-fifth of all welfare-dependent children who lived in relative or official poverty in 1988 (1–2 percent out of 11–13 percent of all children at least partly dependent on welfare).[24]

The Racial Gap in Welfare Dependence and Work

Although black children in 1939 were roughly twice as likely to live in relative poverty as were white children (76 vs. 33 percent), they were equally likely (at 8 percent) to live in a family whose parent was employed in an emergency work program such as the WPA. Hence, among relatively poor children living with at least one parent, black children were about one-third less likely to live with a parent who was employed in emergency work (11 vs. 18 percent) than were white children.

Furthermore, since the proportion of WPA participants who were black was as high as it was in any other Great Depression welfare program, and substantially higher than it was in non-means-tested programs, the overall proportion of poor black children who lived in families that received any welfare benefits was probably only one-third to one-half as large as the proportion for poor white children who lived in such families.[25]

By 1959, among relatively poor children, blacks were 97 percentage points more likely than whites (35 vs. 28 percent) to live in a welfare-dependent family; and this gap more than quadrupled to 23–29 percentage points in 1979, then fell somewhat to 25 percentage points in 1988 (Table 8.5). In 1988, then, the proportion of relatively poor children living in welfare-dependent families was 65 percent for blacks and 40 percent for whites. In 1988, for officially poor children these proportions were 6–8 percentage points greater than they were for relatively poor children.

[24]If we recalculated these results based on the highest estimate of the effect of increasing welfare generosity on mother-only families, as cited by Garfinkel and McLanahan (see page 62, Footnote 23), the resulting estimate would be about three times as large. In other words, the recalculated estimate would indicate that by producing a substantial increase in mother-only families, increasing welfare generosity during the 1960s and the 1970s produced an increase in welfare dependence that was equal to about one-half of welfare-dependent children living in relative or official poverty in 1988.

[25]For crude estimates of the overall representation of blacks and whites in Great Depression welfare programs, see National Resources Planning Board, *Security, Work, and Relief Policies* (Washington, DC: U.S. Government Printing Office, 1942), pp. 116–118. The recipiency levels presented in this welfare policy volume are calculated as a proportion of total black and white populations, not as a proportion of the poor black and white populations.

TABLE 8.5

White and Black Poor Children in Self-Supporting and Welfare-Dependent Families: 1939–1988

	1959		1969		Census 1979		CPS 1979		CPS 1988	
	White	Black	White	Black	White	Black	White	Black	White	Black
	Relatively Poor Children									
Percent by Family Work and Welfare Status										
Total Number (in thousands)	9,980	4,884	9,890	5,048	9,899	4,526	9,395	4,900	11,756	5,096
Fully self-supporting	72.3	65.0	73.1	53.5	65.9	42.6	59.3	30.5	60.0	35.0
Mainly self-supporting	16.4	19.0	11.0	18.2	12.8	17.8	13.4	21.7	12.9	14.8
Mainly welfare-dependent	5.3	8.5	7.3	11.1	8.4	12.5	14.1	21.4	12.9	22.0
Fully welfare-dependent	6.1	7.4	8.6	17.2	12.9	27.1	13.2	26.4	14.1	28.1
Total	100.0	100.0	100.0	100.0	100.0	100.0	100.0	100.0	100.0	100.0
	Officially Poor Children									
Total Number (in thousands)	10,683	5,031	6,352	3,998	6,252	3,377	6,191	3,762	7,983	4,226
Fully self-supporting	72.6	65.1	68.6	51.0	59.6	35.2	52.3	24.8	51.9	29.1
Mainly self-supporting	17.9	19.6	9.8	16.7	11.0	16.1	12.0	17.9	12.3	13.3
Mainly welfare-dependent	4.9	8.0	8.8	11.7	10.2	13.9	16.8	24.1	15.8	24.2
Fully welfare-dependent	4.7	7.4	12.8	20.6	19.2	34.8	18.9	33.2	20.0	33.4
Total	100.0	100.0	100.0	100.0	100.0	100.0	100.0	100.0	100.0	100.0

SOURCES: Estimates derived from 1960–1980 census PUMs and March CPS for 1980 and 1989.

NOTES: Welfare income and hence welfare dependence is measured as cash income received from the Aid to Families with Dependent Children (AFDC) and Social Security programs. All other cash income is classified as self-support. This approach allows for consistent measurement across all census and CPS years. For additional discussion of welfare programs, and for procedures (and limitations to procedures) used to derive estimates for 1959, see Footnote 1 and Chapters 7 and 11. Fully self-supporting families receive no AFDC or Social Security income. Mainly self-supporting families receive no more than 50 percent of their income from AFDC or Social Security. Mainly welfare-dependent families receive more than 50 percent but less than 100 percent of their income from AFDC or Social Security. Fully welfare-dependent families receive 100 percent of their income from AFDC or Social Security. See Chapter 7 for measurement of relative poverty and official poverty.

Hence, a substantial majority of poor black children and a large minority of poor white children depended at least partly on welfare benefits by 1988. But among relatively poor children, only 28 percent of blacks and 14 percent of whites depended fully on welfare, and of officially poor children only 33 percent of blacks and 20 percent of whites were fully welfare-dependent. Hence, the racial gap in complete welfare dependence among poor children was only 13–14 percentage points by 1988; and the proportion living in working-poor families was about two-thirds (or more) for poor black children and about four-fifths (or more) for poor white children.

Overall, then, welfare dependence increased among both poor black and poor white children after 1959, and changed little during the 1980s. Meanwhile, the racial gap widened between 1959 and 1979, then contracted slightly. But it remained the case that a large majority of both poor black and poor white children continued to live in working-poor families throughout the era.

In a National Academy of Sciences report, Martha S. Hill uses Panel Study of Income Dynamics data to focus more broadly on children as a whole, but with greater detail on year-to-year changes that occurred during the 1970s.[26] Hill reports that the proportion of *all* children living in families that received welfare benefits sometime during the 1970s was a large 26 percent for whites and an extraordinary 74 percent for blacks, but that the proportion living in families that were mainly or fully welfare-dependent during at least six of the ten years was only 2 percent for whites and 21 percent for blacks. The large differences between the proportions who ever received welfare and those who depended heavily on welfare for many years highlight the fact that for most children who experience welfare dependence, the experience is short-term and supplementary in a working-poor family.

Hence, although 18–19 percent of white children and 50–56 percent of black children lived in relative poverty during the 1970s (Chapter 7), nearly all white children (98 percent) and most black children (79 percent) lived in families that were mainly or fully self-supporting for five

[26]Martha S. Hill, "Trends in the Economic Situation of U.S. Families and Children: 1970–1980." In Richard R. Nelson and Felicity Skidmore, eds., *American Families and the Economy: The High Costs of Living* (Washington, DC: National Academy, 1983), pp. 9–58. The estimates presented here are from Hill's Tables 12–13. The years of Hill's study are 1970–1979, inclusive. Welfare programs included in Hill's estimates are AFDC, SSI, General Assistance payments, Old-Age Assistance, Aid to the Disabled, and Food Stamps, as received by either the householder or the householder's spouse during specific years (ftn. 14, p. 19). Hill's measures of welfare dependency are based on the value of welfare income as a portion of total annual income of the householder and spouse. A family is mainly or fully welfare dependent (simply welfare dependent in Hill's terminology) if welfare accounts for at least one-half of the total income of the householder and spouse (ftn. 15, p. 19).

TABLE 8.6

Poverty Rates and Distribution of Poor White and Black Children, by Parental Presence: 1939–1988

Parental Presence	1939		1949		1959		1969		Census 1979		CPS 1979		CPS 1988	
	White	Black	White	Black	White	Black	White	Black	White	Black	White	Black	White	Black
Parental Presence Among Relatively Poor Children														
Two Parents	80.4	64.9	79.2	63.2	76.4	62.1	66.4	44.8	58.8	28.3	56.0	23.4	53.6	16.6
Mother-Only	11.5	15.9	12.9	17.4	18.1	25.4	26.7	42.4	32.4	57.0	37.1	62.5	40.2	71.7
Ever-married mother	10.2	14.6	9.7	10.6	17.8	23.4	25.4	34.6	28.9	35.1	33.0	42.4	31.2	31.4
Never-married mother	1.3	1.2	3.1	6.8	0.3	1.9	1.3	7.8	3.5	21.8	4.0	20.1	9.0	40.3
Father Only	2.3	2.5	1.4	2.6	1.2	1.8	1.9	3.1	2.3	2.8	2.2	1.2	3.2	2.6
No Parent	5.8	16.7	6.5	16.9	4.3	10.7	5.0	9.7	6.6	11.9	4.7	12.9	3.0	9.1
Total	100.0	100.0	100.0	100.0	100.0	100.0	100.0	100.0	100.0	100.0	100.0	100.0	100.0	100.0
Parental Presence Among Officially Poor Children														
Two Parents	85.0	66.2	84.5	66.6	77.2	62.6	59.9	41.4	52.7	22.7	48.9	19.0	46.2	13.6
Mother Only	8.7	14.5	9.5	15.3	17.4	25.0	32.4	45.2	37.5	62.1	43.7	67.1	47.4	75.7
Ever-married mother	7.9	13.3	7.4	9.3	17.1	23.1	31.0	37.0	33.0	37.4	38.2	44.6	35.8	32.1
Never-married mother	0.8	1.2	2.0	6.0	0.3	2.0	1.4	8.3	4.5	24.8	5.5	22.5	11.6	43.7
Father-Only	2.0	3.1	1.2	2.6	1.2	1.8	1.8	3.1	2.2	3.3	2.1	1.1	3.3	2.3
No Parent	4.4	16.3	4.8	15.5	4.2	10.7	5.9	10.3	7.6	11.9	5.3	12.8	3.2	8.4
Total	100.0	100.0	100.0	100.0	100.0	100.0	100.0	100.0	100.0	100.0	100.0	100.0	100.0	100.0

TABLE 8.6 (continued)

Parental Presence	1939 White	1939 Black	1949 White	1949 Black	1959 White	1959 Black	1969 White	1969 Black	Census 1979 White	Census 1979 Black	CPS 1979 White	CPS 1979 Black	CPS 1988 White	CPS 1988 Black
Relative Poverty Rate														
Two Parents	31.0	73.4	18.9	62.8	15.9	57.8	13.3	42.9	13.7	29.6	12.1	29.3	15.0	23.0
Mother-Only	54.2	83.6	49.2	80.7	55.1	82.1	52.8	77.3	50.5	70.9	49.2	75.2	55.4	73.4
Ever-married mother	53.0	83.5	46.2	82.0	55.2	81.9	52.5	76.7	49.1	68.0	47.2	72.6	52.6	69.0
Never-married mother	92.2	85.7	61.9	78.8	47.4	84.5	60.8	79.8	64.9	76.0	73.4	81.2	67.8	77.3
Father-Only	38.6	63.6	26.4	64.3	23.8	52.0	20.1	59.1	23.3	48.9	24.1	33.7	26.2	39.6
No Parent	47.5	80.2	45.0	73.0	44.1	66.5	38.7	66.0	42.8	60.9	35.3	58.3	40.5	66.9
Total	33.2	75.8	21.6	67.0	18.9	63.3	17.5	55.8	19.2	49.6	17.9	53.0	22.3	52.6
Official Poverty Rate														
Two Parents	66.8	96.1	39.6	86.5	17.1	60.0	7.9	31.9	8.0	18.0	7.1	18.3	8.9	15.6
Mother-Only	87.3	98.6	71.0	93.1	56.5	83.3	42.5	66.2	38.0	58.5	38.8	62.1	44.8	64.5
Ever-married mother	86.0	97.3	69.1	94.1	56.6	83.0	42.4	65.8	36.5	54.8	36.6	58.7	41.4	58.6
Never-married mother	100.0	100.0	79.0	91.5	49.1	87.1	45.1	67.9	54.5	65.3	65.8	70.1	59.7	69.7
Father-Only	69.0	96.6	43.7	85.2	24.6	52.0	12.8	47.0	14.9	42.7	15.4	23.5	18.4	29.4
No Parent	76.8	100.0	65.3	88.2	45.8	67.9	30.2	55.9	32.4	46.1	26.7	44.6	29.6	51.6
Total	68.6	97.2	42.2	87.7	20.2	65.2	11.6	44.8	12.5	37.6	11.9	40.8	15.3	43.8

SOURCES: Estimates derived from 1940–1980 census PUMs and March CPS for 1980 and 1989.

NOTE: See Chapter 7 for measurement of relative poverty and official poverty.

or more years during the decade. In addition, in specific years between 1959 and 1988, even among relatively poor children, a large majority of both whites and blacks (86–94 and 72–93 percent, respectively) lived in families that were at least partly self-supporting during the year.

The Racial Gap in Poverty and Mother-Only Families

Earlier in this chapter we saw that the proportion of poor children who lived in mother-only families increased during each decade between 1939 and 1988, but especially during the 1960s, and that the increase between 1939 and 1959 was due mainly to the expanding poverty-rate gap between children in mother-only and two-parent families, while the subsequent increase was due to the overall rise in the proportion of children living in mother-only families. Were these patterns of change similar for blacks and whites, and how and why have the racial gaps changed?

The basic pattern of change is the same for both blacks and whites: The proportion of poor children living in mother-only families increased for both black and white children during each post-Depression decade, and the largest increases occurred during the 1960s. But the increases were much greater for blacks, producing an expanding racial gap, and the demographic factors that produced these increases appear to be quite different (Table 8.6). Between 1939 and 1988, the proportion of relatively poor children living in mother-only families increased by 57 percentage points for blacks to reach 72 percent in 1988, and by a much smaller, but substantial, 29 percentage points for whites to reach 40 percent in 1988.

The increase for whites during 1939–1959 was produced mainly by the expanding relative poverty-rate gap between children in mother-only and two-parent families, while the subsequent increase was produced mainly by the overall rise in the proportion living in mother-only families (Figure 8.4). For blacks, however, during each decade increases occurred both in the gap between relative poverty rates for two-parent and mother-only families and in the total proportion living in mother-only families. Hence, for blacks during each decade, each of these two factors was responsible for part of the increase in the proportion of relatively poor children who lived in mother-only families.

How much of the racial gap in overall relative poverty rates resulted from the expanding racial gap in the proportion of relatively poor children living in mother-only families? As we saw in the last chapter, the racial gap in overall relative poverty rates was 43–45 percentage points

FIGURE 8.4

*Childhood Poverty Rate Gaps Separating Two-Parent and Mother-Only Families,
for Whites and Blacks: 1939–1988*

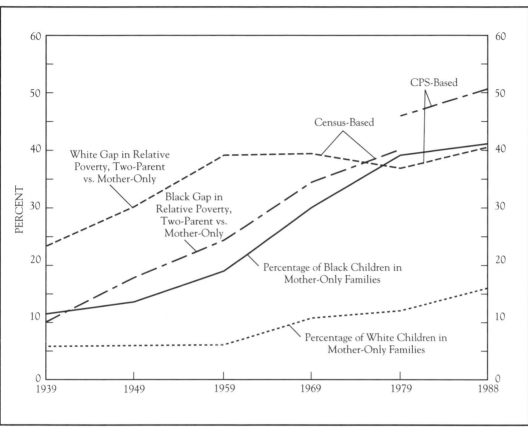

SOURCES: Derived from 1940–1980 PUMS and 1988 CPS, and see Footnote 5.

NOTES: For percent in mother-only families, 1988 results are for 1987 and have been adjusted for CPS procedural improvement and CPS-census differential.

in 1939, 1949, and 1959. If the relative poverty rates of black and white children in mother-only families had been the same as the rates for children of the same race in two-parent families during each of these years, then the resulting hypothetical, overall racial gaps would have been no more than 2 percentage points smaller. However, in 1969, 1979, and 1988, the smaller gaps of 38, 30–35, and 30 percentage points would have been smaller still by 7, 12–15, and 19 percentage points, respectively.

Hence, by 1988 the actual relative poverty rates of 53 and 22 percent for black and white children, respectively, would have been 27 and 16 percent if children in mother-only families had the same relative poverty rates as children of the same race in two-parent families. These estimates suggest that by 1988, about 36 percent of the racial gap in overall relative poverty rates (11 of 30 percentage points) would have existed even if children in mother-only families had the same poverty rate as did children of the same race in two-parent families. Corresponding estimates for the 29 percentage point racial gap in the official poverty rate suggest that about 32 percent of this gap would have existed even if children in mother-only families had the same poverty rate as did children in two-parent families.

But these estimates exaggerate the importance of mother-only families as a cause of poverty (and as a cause of the changing racial gap in poverty), because children in mother-only families would have had higher poverty rates than did children in two-parent families even if they had all been (re)united with their fathers. The reason is that divorce and out-of-wedlock childbearing are more likely to occur among women who have fewer socioeconomic resources than among those who have greater socioeconomic resources.[27]

For example, Arthur J. Norton and Jeanne E. Moorman found an inverse relationship between educational attainment and divorce: For women aged 35–39 in 1985, the proportion who were divorced after their first marriage was 39 percent for women who had received less than 12 years of education compared with only 24 percent for women who had 16 years of education.[28] Norton and Moorman also found an inverse relationship between educational attainment and the percentage of women who remarried. Results derived by Martin O'Connell from the 1988 CPS show that educational attainment and out-of-wedlock childbearing are also inversely related: Never-married women account for 29 percent of births among women who received less than 12 years of education, compared with only 9 percent of births among women who received more than 12 years of education.

Since women who have relatively low educational attainments tend to marry men who have relatively low educational attainments and relatively low incomes, the fact that women with lower educational attainments are more likely to divorce and to bear children out of wedlock

---

[27]As summarized by Greg J. Duncan and Willard Rodgers, most earlier studies have found that differences in family structure account for less than 50 percent of the racial gap in economic status. See "Single-Parent Families: Are Their Economic Problems Transitory or Persistent?" *Family Planning Perspectives* 19, 4 (July/August 1987): 171–178.

[28]Arthur J. Norton and Jeanne E. Moorman, "Current Trends in Marriage and Divorce Among American Women," *Journal of Marriage and the Family* 49 (February 1987): 3–14.

strongly suggests that the children in mother-only families would have had higher poverty rates than those in intact two-parent families even if they could somehow have been (re)united with their fathers. Unfortunately, there are no precise estimates concerning what the poverty levels of black and white children in mother-only families would be if they were (re)united with their fathers. But results derived by Mary Jo Bane for the 1970s and by me for the 1980s can be used to construct an estimate of the poverty rates of such hypothetical (re)united families.[29]

Bane estimates that for the 1970s, among persons who were poor after experiencing a transition from a "male-headed" to a "female-headed" family household, the proportion who were also poor before the transition was 23.5 percent for whites and 61.8 percent for blacks. If we assume that these proportions apply to children who entered mother-only families, then the results indicate that about 75 percent of the racial gap for children in overall poverty rates (both relative and official) would have existed even if all children in mother-only families were (re)united with their fathers in hypothetical two-parent families. Using data from the Survey of Income and Program Participation (SIPP), I have estimated for the mid-1980s that of all children entering poor newly formed mother-only families formed through a marital separation, the proportion already poor in the prior married-couple family was 27 percent for whites and 37 percent for blacks. If we assume that these proportions applied to children who entered mother-only families, then the results indicate that about 50 percent of the racial gap for children in overall poverty rates (both relative and official) would have existed even if all children in mother-only families were (re)united with their fathers in hypothetical two-parent families.

The estimates devised by Bane and myself do not, however, include births; that is, they do not include children who are born out of wedlock. But in 1987, the National Center for Health Statistics estimates that out-of-wedlock births accounted for 62 percent of births among black women and 17 percent among white women.[30] If the incomes of fathers who do not marry their birthing partners are lower than the incomes of fathers who experience a divorce or separation from their wives, as seems likely, then the estimate of 50–75 percent is an underestimate of the

---

[29]See Table 9.5 from "Household Composition and Poverty." In Sheldon H. Danziger and Daniel H. Weinberg, eds., *Fighting Poverty: What Works and What Doesn't* (Cambridge, MA: Harvard University Press, 1986), pp. 209–231. Donald J. Hernandez, U.S. Bureau of the Census, Current Population Reports, Series P-23–179 *When Households Continue, Discontinue, and Form*, U.S. Government Printing Office, Washington, DC, 1992.

[30]National Center for Health Statistics, *Advance Report of Final Natality Statistics, 1987; Monthly Vital Statistics Report*, vol. 38, No. 3, Supplement (Hyattsville, MD: Public Health Service, 1989), Table 18.

proportion of the racial gap in poverty rates for children that would have existed if all children in mother-only families had been (re)united with their fathers.

Taken together, these sets of estimates suggest the following, necessarily crude, conclusions. Of the racial gap for children in overall poverty rates, the proportion not due to racial differences in mother-only families is surely much more than 33–43 percent; it is probably about 50–75 percent and it may be more than 75 percent. Hence, the proportion of the racial gap in poverty rates for children that is due to racial differences in the proportion living in mother-only families is surely less than 57–67 percent, is probably between 25–50 percent and may be less than 25 percent. Consequently, it appears that the (re)unification of fathers with their wives and children in mother-only families, or the transfer of income from fathers to their wives and children in mother-only families, might eliminate as much as one-fourth to one-half of the racial gap in overall poverty rates; but the remaining one-half to three-fourths of the gap would remain. In other words, it appears that at least one-half and perhaps three-fourths or more of the racial gap in poverty among children is due to the racial gap in income levels, not to the racial gap in the proportion who live in mother-only families.

These estimates suggest that if fathers who do not live with their wives and children were (re)united with them, the relative poverty rate probably would have been about 30–37 percent for black children instead of 53 percent, and about 16 percent for white children instead of 22 percent. Similarly, the official poverty rate probably would have been 28–33 percent for black children instead of 44 percent, and about 10 percent for white children instead of 15 percent. Hence, for both blacks and whites the poverty rates would have been about two-thirds as large as their respective actual poverty rates.

As estimates of the effect that transfers of a portion of fathers' income might have on children's poverty rates (through child support or alimony payments), these estimated hypothetical poverty rates are, however, too low, because they assume the economies of scale (in housing, for example) that would be achieved if the fathers lived with their wives and children, and they assume that the fathers' entire incomes are available to these hypothetical two-parent families. Both assumptions are clearly false in the case of child support or alimony payments.[31]

[31]Martha S. Hill has derived estimates, based only on marital breakups (that is, not counting out-of-wedlock births, pp. 13–14). See "The Role of Economic Resources and Dual-Family Status in Child Support Payments" (presented at April 1988 annual meeting of the Population Association of America, revised May 1988). Hill calculates that about 35 percent of the total ex-couple years of official poverty would not have existed for bro-

Consequently, despite the important impact of the rise of mother-only families on poverty and racial gaps in poverty, these results indicate that most of the poverty experienced by both black and white children, and most of the racial gap in overall poverty rates between black and white children, would not be eliminated either by a national mandatory child-support program or by the (re)unification of fathers with their wives or with their nonmarital birthing partners for children currently living in mother-only families.

Racial Gaps in Welfare and Work by Family Situation

Among poor children living in each of the specific type of family situations that have already been designated, racial differences in welfare dependence and work have been comparatively small, and decade-to-decade changes in welfare dependence and work have been quite similar (Table 8.7 and Figure 8.5).

Beginning with relatively poor children living in two-parent families, the proportion living in mainly or fully welfare-dependent families increased somewhat from 5–6 percent in 1959 for both blacks and whites to 14–16 percent for blacks and 8–12 percent for whites in 1979; no change occurred during the 1980s. Corresponding estimates for officially poor children were about the same as those for relatively poor children in 1959 and 3–6 percentage points larger in 1979 and 1988; while the racial gaps for officially and relatively poor children were nearly identical in each year of these years (Table 8.7 and Figure 8.5).

Poor black and poor white children living in mother-only families have been much more likely to depend on welfare for more than one-half of their economic support than have poor children in two-parent families. In 1959, the proportion of (relatively and officially) poor children living in mother-only families who lived in mainly or fully welfare-dependent families was 44 percent for blacks and 39 percent for whites. By 1988, the corresponding proportions were 16–22 percentage points larger for blacks and 8–17 percentage points larger for whites (Table 8.7 and Figure 8.5). However, the racial gap that occurred between 1959 and

---

ken-up couples if it were possible to transfer fathers' incomes to the mothers and children in such a way that the two households experienced the same ratio of income-to-needs (ignoring welfare income). Hence, transferring income from fathers to mothers of ex-married couples would eliminate about one-third of the official poverty. Since the estimate for the near-poor (at 1.25 times the poverty threshold) was also 35 percent, the same proportion would be found using the relative poverty threshold.

TABLE 8.7
White and Black Poor Children, by Parental Presence in Self-Supporting and Welfare-Dependent Families: 1939–1988

Parental Presence Relatively Poor Children	1959 White	1959 Black	1969 White	1969 Black	Census 1979 White	Census 1979 Black	CPS 1979 White	CPS 1979 Black	CPS 1988 White	CPS 1988 Black
Percent Fully Welfare Dependent										
Total	6.1	7.4	8.7	17.2	12.9	27.1	13.2	26.4	14.1	28.1
Two Parents	2.6	2.2	2.7	4.5	3.8	7.6	5.1	7.3	6.0	9.2
Mother-Only	25.5	24.4	23.8	32.0	29.3	37.2	25.7	33.1	25.6	33.8
Father-Only	10.8	9.3	11.2	19.2	16.6	18.3	9.8	16.8	9.4	18.6
No Parent	10.6	3.2	14.5	14.4	15.6	27.8	14.8	29.7	13.0	20.6
Percent Mainly or Fully Welfare Dependent										
Total	11.4	16.0	15.9	28.7	21.3	39.6	27.3	47.8	27.1	50.2
Two Parents	5.9	4.5	6.3	9.6	8.2	13.8	12.4	15.5	11.7	15.5
Mother-Only	39.4	44.0	40.5	48.0	44.2	52.1	49.4	59.6	47.8	59.5
Father-Only	36.1	27.7	20.7	25.8	24.9	26.1	24.4	26.5	18.5	23.5
No Parent	18.2	19.9	23.5	35.1	30.1	45.9	36.9	51.5	39.5	48.1
Percent at Least Partly Welfare Dependent										
Total	27.7	35.0	26.9	46.5	34.1	57.5	40.7	69.5	40.0	65.0
Two Parents	21.2	21.7	15.8	25.7	20.6	30.6	24.1	37.8	22.5	25.6
Mother-Only	56.4	62.0	55.2	67.2	57.4	69.2	64.5	78.9	63.1	73.8
Father-Only	46.0	45.1	33.5	43.7	35.8	42.6	43.7	56.8	36.6	44.6
No Parent	37.9	51.3	37.4	59.6	46.0	69.9	55.9	83.1	53.3	74.6

TABLE 8.7 (continued)

Parental Presence Officially Poor Children	1959 White	1959 Black	1969 White	1969 Black	Census 1979 White	Census 1979 Black	CPS 1979 White	CPS 1979 Black	CPS 1988 White	CPS 1988 Black
Percent Fully Welfare Dependent										
Total	4.7	7.4	12.8	20.6	19.2	34.8	18.9	33.2	20.0	33.4
Two Parents	2.0	2.7	4.5	5.7	5.9	11.5	7.7	11.6	10.4	12.9
Mother-Only	25.0	24.3	29.0	36.4	38.0	43.9	33.1	38.8	30.9	38.3
Father-Only	6.9	8.4	10.3	22.2	26.6	19.4	12.3	21.4	13.9	25.3
No Parent	7.2	2.7	19.0	16.0	20.3	36.9	19.9	36.4	16.7	24.5
Percent Mainly or Fully Welfare Dependent										
Total	9.5	15.4	21.6	32.3	29.4	48.7	35.7	57.3	35.9	57.6
Two Parents	5.0	4.2	9.7	10.9	11.4	19.3	17.4	20.4	18.2	21.3
Mother-Only	38.9	43.6	44.8	51.9	53.8	59.4	56.2	67.4	55.5	65.7
Father-Only	34.5	26.8	22.4	30.8	34.3	25.5	32.7	35.7	24.6	30.5
No Parent	14.6	19.1	29.2	40.1	38.3	55.4	43.3	60.6	36.6	50.2
Percent at Least Partly Welfare Dependent										
Total	27.4	35.0	31.4	49.1	40.4	64.8	47.7	75.2	48.1	70.9
Two Parents	21.7	22.8	18.6	27.5	23.0	38.8	29.2	41.7	29.1	31.2
Mother-Only	56.5	61.5	56.3	68.0	63.8	73.9	67.7	82.9	69.8	78.3
Father-Only	41.4	45.7	33.6	53.9	44.8	43.9	52.1	61.9	41.8	46.3
No Parent	36.0	51.4	40.1	58.6	50.9	72.9	58.0	85.7	47.4	75.5

SOURCES: Estimates derived from 1960–1980 census PUMs and March CPS for 1980 and 1989.

NOTES: Welfare income and hence welfare dependence is measured as cash income received from the Aid to Families with Dependent Children (AFDC) and Social Security programs. All other cash income is classified as self-support. This approach allows for consistent measurement across all census and CPS years. For additional discussion of welfare programs, and for procedures (and limitations to procedures) used to derive estimates for 1959, see Footnote 1 and Chapters 7 and 11. Fully self-supporting families receive no AFDC or Social Security income. At least partially welfare-dependent families receive at least some income from AFDC or Social Security. Mainly or fully welfare-dependent families receive more than 50 percent of their income from AFDC or Social Security. Fully welfare-dependent families receive 100 percent of their income but less than 100 percent of their income from AFDC or Social Security. See Chapter 7 for measurement of relative poverty and official poverty.

FIGURE 8.5

Percentage of White and Black Poor Children Who Are Welfare Dependent: 1988

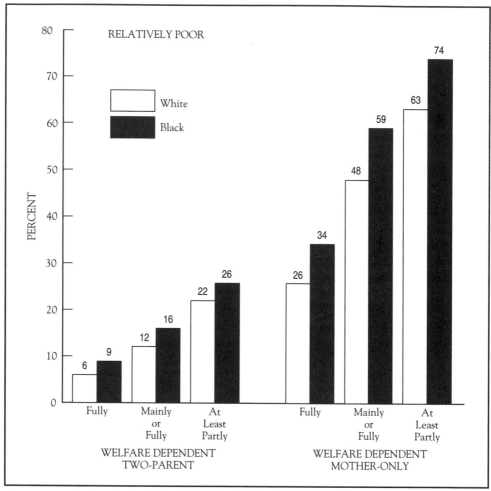

SOURCE: 1989 CPS.

1988 varied within a fairly narrow 5–12 percentage point range (Table 8.7 and Figure 8.5).

The proportions of children who were at least partly dependent on welfare have, of course, been larger than the proportions who were mainly and fully dependent on welfare, ranging between 16–42 percent for black children and white children in two–parent families who were (relatively or officially) poor and between 55–83 percent for poor children in mother-only families. Yet the racial gap, in any specific year, for children living

FIGURE 8.5 (*continued*)

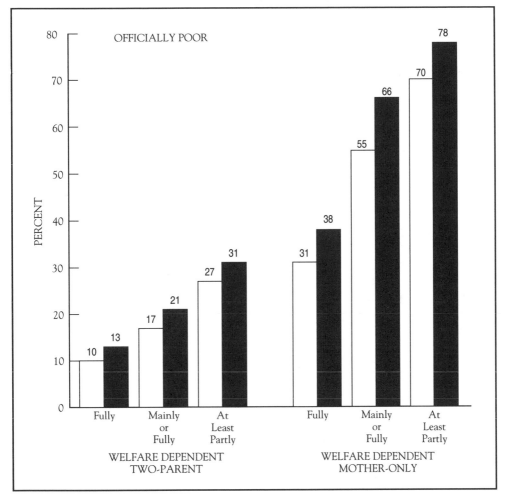

in two-parent families and for those living in mother-only families never surpassed 16 percentage points.

Since the racial gap in welfare dependence (within family situations) has been comparatively small, while the gap in welfare dependence across family situations has been comparatively large (regardless of race), it appears that the increase in the racial gap in overall welfare dependence among poor children that was discussed earlier in this chapter can be accounted for mainly by the much larger increase among blacks than among whites in the proportion of poor children who live in mother-only families. But earlier in this chapter we also saw that perhaps 75 percent or more (but surely more than 50 percent) of the racial gap in the proportion of poor children who were living in mother-only families was the result of racial differences in income.

Hence, these results suggest that much of the increase in the overall racial gap in welfare dependence among poor children also may be due to racial differences in income. To ascertain directly whether this conclusion is correct, it would be necessary to know what the nonwelfare-family incomes of poor black and poor white children in mother-only families would be if they were (re)united with their fathers, since the availability of many fathers' incomes might reduce welfare dependence even while leaving the family below the poverty threshold. Such estimates are not available in the published literature.

Hispanic and Non-Hispanic Work and Welfare Dependence

In 1979 the proportion of poor Hispanic children (of any race) who were welfare-dependent was between the proportions for poor non-Hispanic white children and poor non-Hispanic black children (Table 8.8). Among both relatively poor children and officially poor children, Hispanics (of any race) are somewhat closer to non-Hispanic whites than to non-Hispanic blacks in their chances of living in a fully self-supporting family. But if they do not live in a fully self-supporting family, poor Hispanic children (of any race) are more likely than either poor non-Hispanic white or poor non-Hispanic black children to live in a fully welfare-dependent family.

For example, among relatively poor children in 1979, 59 percent of Hispanics (of any race) and 68 percent of non-Hispanic whites lived in fully self-supporting families, compared with only 43 percent of non-Hispanic blacks. But among relatively poor children who are at least partly welfare-dependent, the proportions who are fully welfare-dependent range from a low of about 32 percent for non-Hispanic whites to 47 percent for non-Hispanic blacks and a high of 54 percent for Hispanics (of any race). However, since the proportion of poor children living in welfare-dependent families is substantially smaller for Hispanics (of any race) than for non-Hispanic blacks, the proportion of poor children living in fully welfare-dependent families is somewhat smaller for Hispanics (of any race) than for non-Hispanic blacks (Table 8.9).

Are first-generation Hispanic children (of any race) especially likely to be welfare-dependent? From the perspective of children, the answer is no as of 1979. In fact, poor first-generation Hispanic children (of any race) whose mothers were *not* born U.S. citizens *are more likely* than poor non-Hispanic white children (by 7–12 percentage points) to live in a fully self-supporting family.[32] However, poor old-family Hispanic children (of any race) *are much less likely* than poor non-Hispanic white children (by 18–21 percentage points) to live in a fully self-supporting family and much more likely (by 18–20 percentage points) to live in a fully welfare-dependent family. As a result, poor old-family Hispanic children (of any race) are generally similar to poor non-Hispanic blacks in their chances of living in a welfare-dependent or self-supporting family.

In addition, although Hispanic children (of any race) have an overall poverty rate that is nearly as high as that for non-Hispanic black children, poor Hispanic children (of any race) and poor non-Hispanic white children are quite similar in their chances of living in a two-parent or mother-only family. The reason is twofold. Hispanic children (of any race) are more similar to non-Hispanic white children than to non-Hispanic black children in their overall chances of living in a mother-only family, and the poverty rate for Hispanic children (of any race) in two-parent families is substantially *higher* than the poverty rates for either non-Hispanic white or non-Hispanic black children in two-parent families.

Again, poor Hispanic children (of any race) differ greatly depending upon whether they are from a first-generation family. Among relatively and officially poor first-generation Hispanic children (of any race), about 80 percent live in two-parent families, compared with only about 50 percent of poor old-family Hispanic children (of any race). Some of this difference, but not all of it, can be accounted for by the fact that, overall, first-generation Hispanic children (of any race) are less likely than old-family Hispanic children (of any race) to live in a mother-only family (13 vs. 27 percent).

The obvious next question, then, is, Why is the proportion of children living in mother-only families higher for old-family than for first-generation Hispanics of any race? The answer to this question is beyond the scope of the present study, but it is plausible that explanations for blacks presented in the next chapter may also be relevant to old-family Hispanics (of any race).

What are the major ethnic similarities and differences in welfare dependence by family situation? For poor children living in two-parent

---

[32]Among relatively and officially poor Hispanic children (of any race), the proportion who do not live with their mothers is 9 percent. The results presented in text comparisons among Hispanic children (of any race) whose mothers were and were not born as U.S. citizens, non-Hispanic white children, and non-Hispanic black children are derived, for all groups, based only on children who live with their mothers.

TABLE 8.8

Old-Family and First-Generation Hispanic Children,
by Poverty and Welfare Dependence: 1979 (census-based)

	Non-Hispanic			Hispanic Living with Mother	
	White	Black	Total Hispanic	First Generation	Old Family
Children in Relative Poverty					
Fully self-supporting	67.6	42.5	59.2	75.8	50.2
Mainly self-supporting	13.0	17.9	12.3	10.0	14.0
Mainly welfare-dependent	9.0	12.7	6.4	3.3	7.8
Fully welfare-dependent	10.4	27.0	22.1	11.0	28.0
Total	100.0	100.0	100.0	100.0	100.0
Children in Official Poverty					
Fully self-supporting	61.9	35.1	51.5	72.3	42.1
Mainly self-supporting	11.3	16.1	10.4	6.8	12.9
Mainly welfare-dependent	10.9	14.0	7.9	3.8	9.1
Fully welfare-dependent	15.8	34.7	30.3	17.2	35.8
Total	100.0	100.0	100.0	100.0	100.0
Relative Poverty Rate					
Total	16.7	49.5	42.5	44.7	40.1
Two parents present	11.7	29.3	33.7	41.4	28.9
Mother-only present	46.7	70.9	70.3	66.8	71.1
Father-only present	22.0	49.3	36.7	NA	NA
No parent present	39.8	60.5	55.5	NA	NA
Official Poverty Rate					
Total	10.6	37.3	30.4	28.5	30.5
Two parents present	6.7	17.6	21.5	22.2	19.2
Mother-only present	33.9	58.6	59.5	50.7	61.7
Father-only present	14.4	43.0	18.9	NA	NA
No parent present	30.3	45.5	41.7	NA	NA
Parental Presence Among Relatively Poor Children					
Two parents present	59.0	28.3	57.1	80.9	53.0
Mother-only present	32.3	57.1	33.1	19.1	47.0
Father-only present	2.5	2.9	1.4	NA	NA
No parent present	6.2	11.7	8.4	NA	NA
Total	100.0	100.0	100.0	100.0	100.0

TABLE 8.8 *(continued)*

| | Non-Hispanic | | | Hispanic Living with Mother | |
	White	Black	Total Hispanic	First Generation	Old Family
Children in Relative Poverty					
Fully Welfare-Dependent					
Total	10.4	27.0	22.1	11.0	28.0
Two parents present	3.1	7.5	6.3	5.4	7.0
Mother-only present	23.3	37.2	50.3	37.0	53.3
Father-only present *	16.3	18.3	18.2	NA	NA
No parent present	12.2	27.2	27.1	NA	NA
Mainly or Fully Welfare-Dependent					
Total	19.4	39.6	28.5	14.3	35.9
Two parents present	8.1	13.8	8.7	7.5	9.9
Mother-only present	38.7	52.2	63.2	45.9	67.2
Father-only present *	26.0	26.1	18.2	NA	NA
No parent present	28.2	45.5	37.7	NA	NA
At Least Partly Welfare-Dependent					
Total	32.4	57.5	40.8	24.3	49.9
Two parents present	20.0	30.4	23.1	17.7	27.9
Mother-only present	53.0	69.4	72.3	54.8	88.8
Father-only present *	36.2	42.6	33.3	NA	NA
No parent present	46.3	70.1	47.1	NA	NA

* Sample size of denominator is 33.

SOURCES: Estimates delivered from 1980 census PUMS.

NOTES: Welfare income and hence welfare dependence is measured as cash income received from the Aid to Families with Dependent Children (AFDC) and Social Security programs. All other cash income is classified as self-support. This approach allows for consistent measurement across all census and CPS years. For additional discussion of welfare programs, see Footnote 1 and Chapters 7 and 11. Fully self-supporting families receive no AFDC or Social Security income. Mainly self-supporting families receive no more than 50 percent of their income from AFDC or Social Security. Mainly welfare-dependent families receive more than 50 percent but less than 100 percent of their income from AFDC or Social Security. Fully welfare-dependent families receive 100 percent of their income from AFDC or Social Security. See Chapter 7 for measurement of relative poverty and official poverty.

TABLE 8.9

Hispanic and Non-Hispanic Children,
by Poverty, Self-Support, and Welfare Dependence: 1979–1988 (CPS-based)

	Non-Hispanic White		Non-Hispanic Black		Hispanic	
	1979	1988	1979	1988	1979	1988
	CPS 1979 and 1988					
Children in Relative Poverty						
Fully self-supporting	60.1	60.4	30.2	35.2	56.4	58.5
Mainly self-supporting	13.9	13.1	22.0	14.9	11.4	12.5
Mainly welfare-dependent	14.9	13.3	21.6	21.8	10.9	12.4
Fully welfare-dependent	11.1	13.3	26.2	28.1	21.4	16.6
Total	100.0	100.0	100.0	100.0	100.0	100.0
Children in Official Poverty						
Fully self-supporting	53.6	50.4	24.5	29.4	48.1	54.1
Mainly self-supporting	12.5	13.1	18.1	13.5	9.9	10.5
Mainly welfare-dependent	17.7	17.1	24.4	23.9	13.6	13.9
Fully welfare-dependent	16.3	19.5	33.0	33.3	28.4	21.5
Total	100.0	100.0	100.0	100.0	100.0	100.0
Relative Poverty Rate						
Total	15.6	18.2	52.9	52.7	38.6	50.0
Two parents present	10.4	12.1	29.0	23.0	29.8	39.0
Mother-only present	45.4	49.4	75.1	73.6	71.9	76.9
Father-only present	22.9	24.6	33.5	39.4	36.6	37.6
No parent present	34.4	35.8	58.1	66.8	42.3	58.0
Official Poverty Rate						
Total	10.2	12.0	40.7	43.8	27.8	37.9
Two parents present	6.0	6.8	18.0	15.7	18.6	25.7
Mother-only present	34.8	38.3	62.1	64.7	62.4	68.1
Father-only present	14.6	17.4	23.1	29.2	25.1	25.6
No parent present	26.0	27.0	44.3	51.4	32.7	39.7
Parental Presence Among Relatively Poor Children						
Two parents present	55.4	54.0	23.0	16.6	58.0	52.1
Mother-only present	37.2	39.4	62.9	71.6	36.3	42.7
Father-only present	2.4	3.7	1.2	2.6	1.5	2.0
No parent present	4.9	2.9	12.9	9.2	4.2	3.2
Total	100.0	100.0	100.0	100.0	100.0	100.0
Parental Presence Among Officially Poor Children						
Two parents present	48.4	46.3	18.6	13.6	50.3	45.3
Mother-only present	43.6	46.5	67.6	75.6	43.8	50.0
Father-only present	2.3	3.9	1.1	2.3	1.4	1.8
No parent present	5.7	3.3	12.8	8.5	4.5	2.9
Total	100.0	100.0	100.0	100.0	100.0	100.0

TABLE 8.9 (*continued*)

	CPS 1979 and 1988					
	Non-Hispanic White		Non-Hispanic Black		Hispanic	
	1979	1988	1979	1988	1979	1988
Children in Relative Poverty						
Percent Fully Welfare Dependent						
Total	11.1	13.3	26.2	28.1	21.4	16.6
Two parents present	5.3	7.7	6.7	9.3	5.1	1.7
Mother-only present	19.9	21.2	33.0	33.8	47.7	36.0
Father-only present	8.0	11.5	17.3	17.4	19.1	2.7
No parent present	13.5	13.0	28.9	20.5	27.2	13.5
Total	100.0	100.0	100.0	100.0	100.0	100.0
Percent Mainly or Fully Welfare Dependent						
Total	26.2	26.6	47.8	49.9	32.3	29.0
Two parents present	12.8	13.8	14.9	15.4	11.5	6.3
Mother-only present	45.1	44.4	59.6	59.2	65.6	56.6
Father-only present	24.6	20.1	27.2	22.4	22.0	14.1
No parent present	36.5	35.2	50.8	48.1	44.3	49.5
Total	100.0	100.0	100.0	100.0	100.0	100.0
Percent At Least Partly Welfare Dependent						
Total	39.9	39.7	69.8	64.8	43.6	41.5
Two parents present	24.9	24.8	37.9	25.7	21.6	16.8
Mother-only present	60.9	60.3	79.1	73.6	77.8	70.5
Father-only present	45.3	35.4	58.4	43.8	32.4	43.1
No parent present	54.4	47.0	82.9	74.6	66.1	67.8
Total	100.0	100.0	100.0	100.0	100.0	100.0

SOURCES: Estimates derived from March CPS for 1980 and 1989.

NOTES: Welfare income and hence welfare dependence is measured as cash income received from the Aid to Families with Dependent Children (AFDC) and Social Security programs. All other cash income is classified as self-support. This approach allows for consistent measurement across all census and CPS years. For additional discussion of welfare programs, see Footnote 1 and Chapters 7 and 11. Fully self-supporting families receive no AFDC or Social Security income. Mainly self-supporting families receive no more than 50 percent of their income from AFDC or Social Security. Mainly welfare-dependent families receive more than 50 percent but less than 100 percent of their income from AFDC or Social Security. Fully welfare-dependent families receive 100 percent of their income from AFDC or Social Security. See Chapter 7 for measurement of relative poverty and official poverty.

families, the proportion who live in welfare dependent families among Hispanics (of any race) generally lies between the proportions for non-Hispanic whites and non-Hispanic blacks. For poor children living in mother-only families, however, the picture is quite different. Poor Hispanics (of any race) are substantially more likely to be mainly or fully welfare dependent than are both non-Hispanic whites and non-Hispanic blacks. Among poor Hispanic children (of any race) in old-family, mother-only families, the chances of living in a welfare-dependent family are usually the same or higher than for poor non-Hispanic black children in mother-only families.

Hence, for poor Hispanic children (of any race), those from first-generation families are substantially less likely to be welfare-dependent than are those from old families, because they are less likely to live in mother-only families and because within family situations the proportions living in welfare-dependent families are much smaller.

In the preceding chapter we saw that the economic disadvantages faced by old-family Hispanics (of any race) in their efforts to enter the economic mainstream of the United States are nearly as formidable as those faced by black children. In this chapter we saw that old-family Hispanics (of any race) also are similar to non-Hispanic black children in the comparatively high proportions of them who are at least partly or mainly welfare-dependent.

Conclusions

Throughout the era since the Great Depression (bearing in mind that welfare is defined here as cash income from public assistance programs, mainly AFDC and Social Security as measured in the Census of the Population), among relatively poor children, 30–50 percent in any given year lived in families that were at least partly dependent on welfare benefits; yet 82–94 percent lived in families that were at least partly self-supporting. In other words, only 7–18 percent of relatively poor children lived in fully welfare-dependent families, while 50–70 percent lived in fully self-supporting families.

Among relatively poor children in any given year since 1959, 27–41 percent of whites and 40–76 percent of blacks were at least partly welfare dependent; but 86–94 percent of whites and 72–93 percent of blacks lived in working-poor families. Hence, although welfare provides at least some support for many relatively poor children of both races, very large majorities live in families that are at least partly self-supporting; and in 1988, only 14 percent of white children and 28 percent of black children in relative poverty lived in families that depended fully on welfare benefits for their economic survival.

More broadly, because many children personally experience poverty (Chapter 9), 26 percent of all white children and 74 percent of all black children lived in families that received welfare benefits sometime during the 1970s. But only 2 percent of white children and 21 percent of black children depended on welfare benefits for at least one-half of their income during at least six of ten years during the 1970s. Hence, although a substantial minority of white children and a large majority of black children experience some welfare dependence, for 92 percent of these white children and 72 percent of these black children during the 1970s, the experience was a comparatively short one in which welfare benefits were a supplementary source of income in a working-poor family.

Still, relative poverty and welfare dependence did increase among children between the 1960s and the 1980s, and the rise of mother-only families, especially for blacks, is often cited as a major contributing factor. If all of the increasing proportion of children living in mother-only families after 1959 experienced the poverty rate of those living in two-parent families, then by 1988 the overall (relative and actual) poverty rate for children would have been 6 percentage points smaller. In fact, however, even if children living in mother-only families were (re)united with their fathers, they would have higher poverty rates than children living in two-parent families, because children entering mother-only families have higher poverty rates than do children who remain in two-parent families even before the transition to the mother-only family, and because fathers of children born out of wedlock probably have substantially lower incomes than do married fathers.

Hence, without the post-1959 rise in mother-only families, the overall (relative and official) poverty rates of children in 1988 might have been 2–4 percentage points lower, and more than 80 percent of poor children still would have been poor. Furthermore, despite the much larger increase in mother-only families that occurred among black children than among white children, if the post-1959 increase in mother-only families had not occurred, it appears likely that the racial gap in relative poverty rates would have been at least 50–75 percent as large as it actually was. It also appears that if a mandatory child-support program transferring part of fathers' incomes to mother-only families were implemented, the racial gap in relative poverty rates would still be more than 50–75 percent as large as it actually was.

Insofar as the increasing absolute value of welfare benefits after 1960 acted as an incentive to separate, divorce, or remain unmarried after the birth of a child, this welfare-generosity effect on childhood poverty rates could be no larger than the effect that the post-1959 rise in mother-only families had on poverty rates. However, additional evidence suggests that without this increase in welfare benefits, the overall relative and official poverty rates for children would have been smaller by only 1–2 percentage points in 1988 (that is, at least 90 percent of poor children would have been poor anyway).

This apparently small welfare-generosity effect may be explained, at least in part, by the fact that the increase in the relative value of welfare benefits was comparatively small and temporary. For example, since median family income increased by 40 percent between 1960 and 1972, the combined value of AFDC and Food Stamp benefits increased by about 21 percentage points as a proportion of the official poverty threshold, but it declined by 4 percentage points as a proportion of the relative poverty threshold. Since the increase in these welfare benefits did not keep up with the general rise in the standard of living in the United States during these 12 years, it is not surprising that insofar as overall increases in welfare benefits acted as an incentive to form mother-only families, the effect was only a small rise in mother-only families and childhood poverty.

In the next two chapters we will turn to other potential explanations of trends and variations in childhood poverty since the Great Depression.

TABLE A-8.1

Welfare Generosity and Children in Mother-Only Families: 1939–1987

	Percent in Mother-Only Families					
Children Aged 0–17	1939	1949	1959	1969	1979	1987*
Mother-Only	6.7	6.4	7.7	11.8	16.2	18.5
Never married	0.1	0.1	0.3	1.1	3.0	5.9
Black Mother-Only	11.6	13.8	19.2	30.1	39.2	40.8
Never Married	0.7	0.7	1.4	5.4	14.0	23.6

	Measure of Welfare Generosity (1987 dollars)				
1987 Dollars	AFDC plus Food Stamps	AFDC plus Food Stamps plus 100 Percent Medicaid	AFDC plus Food Stamps plus 25 Percent Medicaid		Total Welfare Expenditures per Mother-Only Family with Children
1960	7,346	7,658		1950	3,177
1964	7,224	7,532	7,352	1955	2,929
1968	7,798	9,336	8,468	1960	3,699
1972	9,728	11,710	10,582	1965	4,691
1976	9,493	12,159	10,582	1970	7,562
1980	8,188	11,317	9,316	1975	8,442
1983	7,602			1980	7,304
1985	7,699				
1986	7,790				
1987	7,669				
1988	7,699				

SOURCES: See Footnotes 8–16.

NOTE: * 1987 CPS adjusted to be comparable to census-based measure.

327

9

FAMILY INCOME SOURCES, FAMILY SIZE, AND CHILDHOOD POVERTY

Introduction and Highlights

IN CHAPTER 7 we saw that the large decline in childhood poverty that occurred after the Great Depression was followed by smaller declines between 1949 and 1969, then by an increase in childhood poverty between 1969 and 1988. We also saw that the childhood poverty rate remained comparatively high throughout the era. Then in Chapter 8 we saw that most poor children in 1988 would have been poor even if the remarkable post-1959 rise in mother-only families had not occurred. In this chapter we will further explore the reasons for these historic levels and trends in childhood poverty by focusing on the extent to which poverty rates in various years can be accounted for by changes in both family size and the sources of family income.

As in the preceding two chapters, we will focus on *relative* poverty rates, since conclusions pertaining to long-term changes in the rate of poverty are most meaningful when based on this concept (Chapter 7), but we will also briefly discuss how broad conclusions would differ if they were based on analyses of the official poverty rate. To be specific, we will place special focus on the following questions. First, to what extent can changes in childhood relative poverty be accounted for by income received from government welfare programs? Second, to what extent can changes in childhood relative poverty be accounted for by changes in income that is provided by fathers, mothers, and family members other than parents in the homes of children? Third, since larger families need more income than do smaller families in order to lift themselves out of poverty, to what extent can changes in childhood relative poverty be accounted for by changes in dependent sibsize (sibling size) or number of dependent siblings in the home?

In brief, our answers to these questions tell the following story. First, welfare income accounts for a nearly constant reduction of 1–2 percentage points in the relative poverty rate for children during specific years between 1939 and 1988 (Table 9.1). Corresponding estimates for white children are essentially the same, and the corresponding range for black children is 1–4 percentage points for specific years (see Table 9.3). Because the size of the reduction in childhood relative poverty accounted for by welfare income changed little across various years since the Great Depression, most of the large changes in childhood relative poverty that occurred during this era cannot be accounted for by changes in welfare income.

Second, income from family members other than parents accounted for a reduction of 8–9 percentage points in childhood relative poverty in 1939, but this effect fell to a nearly constant 4–5 percentage points for specific years between 1959 and 1988 (Table 9.1). Again, corresponding estimates for white children are essentially the same; but for black children, income from family members other than parents accounted for a nearly constant reduction of 7–9 percentage points in childhood relative poverty throughout the era since the Great Depression (see Table 9.3). These results indicate that changes in income from family members other than parents can neither account for the large post-Depression declines in childhood relative poverty nor for the more recent increases.

Third, changes in available fathers' incomes can account for much of the post-Depression decline and subsequent increase in childhood relative poverty. Based only on available fathers' incomes, childhood relative poverty would have declined by 14.8 percentage points between 1939 and 1969, then increased by 10.3 percentage points between 1969 and 1988, compared with the actual overall decline of 15.2 percentage points and the subsequent overall increase of 5.1 percentage points (Table 9.1).

Meanwhile, changes in mothers' incomes tended to reduce childhood relative poverty by 4.4 percentage points between 1939 and 1969, and by an additional 6.5 percentage points between 1969 and 1988 (Table 9.1). Hence, increasing mothers' incomes acted to speed the earlier relative poverty decline and then slow the subsequent increase, first by effectively counterbalancing the decline in income available from fam-

TABLE 9.1

Changes for Children in Relative Poverty, Parents' Income, and Government Welfare: 1939–1988

All Children Annual Relative Poverty Rates and Effects	Census 1939	Census 1949	Census 1959	Census 1969	Census 1979	CPS 1979	CPS 1988
Relative Poverty Rate							
Based on Father's Income Only	50.9	38.4	35.8	36.1	40.9	40.9	46.4
Effect of Mother's Income	-2.7	—	-5.0	-7.1	-10.4	-10.7	-13.9
Effect of Other Relative's Income	-8.6	—	-4.7	-4.9	-5.2	-5.0	-4.0
Effect of Government Welfare	-1.9		-1.7	-1.4	-1.6	-2.1	-1.5
Actual Relative Poverty Rate	37.9	27.0	24.4	22.7	23.8	23.0	27.0

All Children Relative Poverty Rate Change and Effects Across Decades	Census 1939–1959	Census 1959–1969	Census 1969–1979	CPS 1979–1988
Change in Relative Poverty Rates				
Based on Father's Income Only	-15.1	0.3	4.8	5.5
Effect of Mother's Income	-2.3	-2.2	-3.2	-3.2
Effect of Other Relative's Income	3.9	-0.2	-0.3	1.0
Effect of Government Welfare	0.2	0.3	-0.2	0.6
Actual Relative Poverty Rate	-13.5	-1.7	1.1	-4.0

Children in Two-Parent Families Annual Relative Poverty Rates and Effects	Census 1939	Census 1949	Census 1959	Census 1969	Census 1979	CPS 1979	CPS 1988
Relative Poverty Rate							
Based on Father's Income Only	43.6	30.2	27.8	24.6	25.5	24.3	29.1
Effect of Mother's Income	-1.9	—	-3.8	-5.3	-7.4	-7.3	-11.0
Effect of Other Relative's Income	-5.6	—	-2.6	-2.4	-2.1	-2.3	-1.4
Effect of Government Welfare	-1.8		-1.5	-0.8	-0.9	-1.1	-1.1
Actual Relative Poverty Rate	34.6	22.9	19.9	16.1	15.1	13.5	15.7

TABLE 9.1 (*continued*)

Children in Two-Parent Families Relative Poverty Rate Change and Effects Across Decades	Census 1939–1959	Census 1959–1969	Census 1969–1979	CPS 1979–1988
Change in Relative Poverty Rates				
Based on Father's Income Only	-15.8	-3.2	0.9	4.8
Effect of Mother's Income	-1.9	-1.5	-2.1	-3.7
Effect of Other Relative's Income	3.0	0.2	0.3	0.9
Effect of Government Welfare	0.4	0.7	-0.1	0.0
Actual Relative Poverty Rate	-16.8	-3.8	-1.0	2.2

Children in Mother-Only Families Annual Relative Poverty Rates and Effects	Census 1939	Census 1949	Census 1959	Census 1969	Census 1979	CPS 1979	CPS 1988
Relative Poverty Rate							
Based on Mother's Income Only	82.3	—	81.1	77.1	71.9	71.7	72.9
Effect of Other Relative's Income	-20.5	—	-13.0	-10.7	-10.0	-7.8	-8.0
Effect of Government Welfare	-1.6	—	-4.7	-4.9	-4.1	-5.4	-2.8
Actual Relative Poverty Rate	60.2	57.2	63.4	61.5	57.9	58.7	62.0

Children in Mother-Only Families Relative Poverty Rate Change and Effects Across Decades	Census 1939–1959	Census 1959–1969	Census 1969–1979	CPS 1979–1988
Change in Relative Poverty Rates				
Based on Mother's Income Only	-5.2	-4.0	-5.2	1.1
Effect of Other Relative's Income	9.8	2.3	0.7	-0.2
Effect of Government Welfare	-3.0	-0.2	0.8	2.6
Actual Relative Poverty Rate	7.0	-1.9	-3.6	3.3

SOURCES: Estimates derived from 1940–1980 Census PUMs and March CPS for 1980 and 1989.

NOTE: Government welfare income is income obtained by family from Aid to Families with Dependent Children (AFDC) or Social Security programs. All other income is assigned to recipient within family. See Chapters 7, 8, and 11 for additional discussion of welfare income, measurement of relative poverty, etc. Estimates for 1939 are approximate. See Footnote 9 and Chapter 8, Footnote 1.

ily members other than parents between 1939 and 1969 and then by counterbalancing about two-thirds of the decline in available fathers' incomes between 1969 and 1988.

Once again, the corresponding estimates for the effect of changes in fathers' and mothers' incomes for white children are similar to changes for children as a whole (see Table 9.3). Among black children, however, changes in fathers' incomes generally account for a smaller change in the relative poverty rate than is the case among white children; changes in mothers' incomes generally account for a larger relative poverty rate change than is the case among white children; and after 1969 changes in mothers' incomes among black children accounted for a substantially larger change in relative poverty than did changes in fathers' incomes.

Finally, a separate set of estimates indicates that except for the 1970s, when declining dependent sibsize could account for a reduction of 4 percentage points in the relative poverty rate, decade-by-decade changes in dependent sibsize since the Great Depression can account for changes of only 1–2 percentage points in the rates of childhood relative poverty. Comparing black and white children, the larger dependent sibsizes among black children can account for only about 2–4 percentage points of both the 40 percentage point racial gap in relative poverty rates that occurred in 1939 and the 30 percentage point racial gap that occurred in 1988 (although the size of this effect increased and then decreased during the intervening decades).

Of course, it is unlikely that changes in dependent sibsize are completely independent of changes in income from various sources, especially mothers' incomes. In Chapter 10 we will discuss in detail apparent relationships that link changes in family size, family income, and other important social and economic trends. But let's turn to a more thorough look at reductions in the rates of childhood relative poverty that can be accounted for by various sources of income and dependent sibsize since the Great Depression.

Accounting for Relative Poverty Rates

To account for changes in the rates of childhood relative poverty in terms of changes in income from fathers, mothers, other family members, and welfare benefits, we have calculated a series of hypothetical relative poverty rates for specific years based on income from only one or more of these sources. Because fathers have been the primary source of income for children since at least the Great Depression, we first calculated a hypothetical relative poverty rate based only on the nonwelfare income of fathers in the home.[1] Then, because most children live with two parents, and because mothers have increasingly contributed to their family's economic support since the Great Depression, we calculated a hypothetical relative poverty rate based on the combined non-welfare incomes of fathers and mothers in the home.[2]

The first estimate indicates what the relative poverty rate for children would have been in a specific year if the income of only the fathers in the home had been available to them. The difference between the first and the second estimate indicates the extent to which mothers' incomes acted to reduce the childhood relative poverty rate below what it would have been if children had depended only on the income of fathers in the home for their support.

Next, we calculated a hypothetical relative poverty rate based on the combined nonwelfare income of fathers, mothers, and all other family members in the homes of children. The difference between this estimate and the hypothetical rate based on fathers' and mothers' incomes indicates the extent to which income from family members other than parents in the home acted to reduce the relative poverty rate below what it would have been if children had depended only on the income of parents in the home for their support.

Since the only difference between the actual relative poverty rate and the hypothetical rate based on the nonwelfare income of all family members in the home is the amount of welfare income received by children's families, the difference between the actual relative poverty rate and this hypothetical relative poverty rate indicates the extent to which income from welfare acted to reduce the relative poverty rate below what it would have been if children had depended only on income from parents and other family members in their home for economic support.

Finally, we calculated *changes* across various years in the hypothetical poverty rate based only on the income of fathers and in the reduction of relative poverty rates that can be accounted for by income from mothers, other family members, and welfare programs. The results es-

---

[1]For example, as we saw in Chapter 4, about 85 percent of children in 1940 lived with fathers who were in the labor force, compared with only 10 percent who lived with mothers who were in the labor force. Even as late as 1980, 75 percent of children lived with fathers who were in the labor force, compared with only 49 percent who lived with mothers who were in the labor force. The actual relative poverty thresholds are used to derive the hypothetical relative poverty rates. Hence, the only differences between calculations for actual and hypothetical rates is the amount of income counted. As in Chapter 8, welfare income includes cash income received mainly from Aid to Families with Dependent Children and Social Security. Hence, nonwelfare income includes all cash income received from sources other than these programs. Only the income of fathers in the homes of children is included in this calculation.

[2]In this calculation, mothers' incomes include any alimony, child support, or other income received by the mothers from fathers not living in the home.

timate the extent to which changes in childhood relative poverty can be accounted for by changes in the amount of income that was actually available from these various family members in the home and from welfare programs.

It should be noted at the outset, however, that the estimates described here, concerning the extent to which changes in relative poverty rates can be accounted for by changes in income from fathers, mothers, other family members, and welfare benefits, give no direct indication of how these changes may have influenced one another, or of how other social and economic changes may have influenced the amount of income received from these sources. Instead, they provide a simple accounting, given the actual social, economic, and familial changes that occurred, of the extent to which income from fathers, mothers, other family members, and welfare benefits have become more or less important in reducing childhood relative poverty between two points in time.

For example, across a particular ten-year period, declines in available fathers' incomes might have led to an increase in mothers' employment and income level. Alternatively, changes in available mothers' incomes might (also) have led to changes in fathers' employment and income level. Similarly, changes in the value of welfare benefits may have altered the need to live with and receive support from family members other than parents.[3] The importance of any such causal relationships cannot be ascertained directly from our results. However, we do (in this chapter as well as in Chapter 10) present results and analyses that suggest potentially important causal relationships linking family income and poverty trends for children to other important social and economic changes since the Great Depression.

Welfare Income and Relative Poverty

To what extent can changes in the rates of childhood relative poverty be accounted for by changes in income received from welfare programs? Given the actual evolution of social and economic circumstances and of welfare programs, the effect of government welfare programs on the relative poverty rate for children during specific years has remained small and stable. Without welfare income, the relative

[3]Research cited by Irwin Garfinkel and Sara S. McLanahan indicates, for example, that changes in the value of welfare benefits have influenced such living arrangements of mother-only families. Irwin Garfinkel and Sara S. McLanahan, *Single Mothers and Their Children* (Washington, DC: Urban Institute, 1986), p. 58.

poverty rate for children would have been only 1–2 percentage points above its actual value during specific years (Table 9.1).

Although welfare programs lift few children completely out of poverty, results from Chapter 8 should be remembered: Welfare programs do provide economic support for many children who remain in poverty. Since the effect of welfare programs on childhood relative poverty remained virtually constant throughout the era between 1939 and 1988, the substantial changes in poverty rates that have occurred since the Great Depression cannot be accounted for by changes in income derived from government welfare programs.

Family Members Other Than Parents and Relative Poverty

Turning to income from family members other than parents in the homes of children during the Great Depression year of 1939, income from these family members acted to reduce the relative poverty rate for children by 8–9 percentage points below what it would have been if children had depended only on their parents for economic support.[4] Without the income from these family members, the relative poverty rate for children in 1939 would have been about 47 percent instead of 38 percent (Table 9.1). After the Great Depression, the effect of income from nonparental family members fell by about one-half to 4–5 percentage points during specific years throughout the postwar era between 1959 and 1988.[5]

Clearly, family members other than parents played an important role in reducing relative poverty among children during the Great Depression. But since the salutary effect of these family members was only one-half as large 20 years later, the sharp post-Depression *drop* in childhood relative poverty cannot be accounted for by an increase in the availability of income from such family members. Furthermore, since these family members had a virtually constant 4–5 percentage point effect after the Great Depression, neither the post-Depression decline in

---

[4]The income of relatives other than parents includes income provided by all family members other than the parents, including any income that is provided by children.

[5]Some children may have lived in poverty because it was necessary for family members other than parents who had very low incomes to move in with the child's family in order to survive during the Great Depression or during later years. In such cases, the income of these other relatives may have been so low that the entire family was dragged below the poverty threshold. Hence, for a specific year the estimate of the reduction in childhood poverty due to the presence of other family members in the home may be viewed as a maximum estimate of the size of this effect at that point in time. But for a countervailing factor, see Footnote 6.

childhood relative poverty nor the subsequent increase can be accounted for by changes in income from these family members.

Parents' Income and Relative Poverty

To what extent can changes in the rates of relative poverty for children be accounted for by changes in income provided by fathers and mothers? Based only on the income of fathers in the home in 1939 and 1949, the relative poverty rate for children would have dropped by 12.5 percentage points during the 1940s. Hence, the entire 10.9 percentage point drop in the actual relative poverty rate for children can be accounted for by changes in fathers' incomes. During the 1950s, the income changes of fathers in the homes of children would, by themselves, have led to a 2.6 percentage point drop in relative poverty. Since the actual relative poverty rate for children also declined by 2.6 percentage points, increasing fathers' incomes can account for all of the decline in relative poverty.

To study the changes in relative poverty that occurred for children during the 1940s and the 1950s in greater detail, we must look at changes across the entire 20-year period from 1939 to 1959, because estimates of income from mothers, other relatives, and welfare cannot be distinguished fully in the 1950 census. Taking the 1940s and the 1950s together, all of the decline in childhood relative poverty can be accounted for by changes in fathers' incomes.[6]

Meanwhile, because of mothers' incomes in 1939, the relative poverty rate for children was 2.7 percentage points below what it would have been if children had depended only on their fathers' income. Since this represents about one-third of the 8.6 percent of children whose mothers were in the labor force in 1939, about one-third of children who had working mothers relied on this income to lift them out of poverty. By 1959, because of mothers' incomes, the relative poverty rate for children was 5 percentage points below what it would have been if they had depended only on their fathers' incomes. Since 14.9 percent of children

[6]According to our estimates, the actual relative poverty rate for children dropped by 13.5 percentage points, while the rate based only on fathers' incomes dropped by 15.1 percentage points. Since as many as 2 percent of children in 1939 and 1949 were in "unrelated" subfamilies with one or both parents who lived in the home of a nonrelative, and since our estimates classify these children simply as living with nonrelatives, much of the difference between the estimates of 13.5 and 15.1 percentage points is probably an artifact of the crudeness of our measurement procedures. In addition, a more complete accounting for the proportion of children lifted out of poverty by relatives other than parents might be 2 percentage points higher than in Table 9.1, if children living in unrelated subfamilies were counted. But for a countervailing factor, see Footnote 5.

lived with employed mothers in 1959, about one-third of the substantially larger proportion of children whose mothers were employed that year also depended on their mothers' incomes to lift them out of relative poverty.

Between 1939 and 1959, increasing mothers' incomes can account for a reduction of 2.3 percentage points in the relative poverty rate for children, but this effect acted to counterbalance more than one-half of the increase of 3.9 percentage points in childhood relative poverty that might have occurred because of declining income from family members other than parents. Taken together, then, increases in fathers' and mothers' incomes between 1939 and 1959 appear to have reduced by about one-half the proportion of children who depended on family members other than parents to lift them out of poverty; and increases in fathers' and mothers' incomes also account for the entire 13.5 percentage point reduction that occurred in relative poverty rates for children. Separately, the effect of increasing fathers' incomes was six or seven times larger than the effect of mothers' incomes.

Subsequently, the 1960s has been the only decade during which changes in fathers' incomes account for less change in the rate of childhood relative poverty than did changes in mothers' incomes. During the 1970s and the 1980s, declines in available fathers' incomes would, by themselves, have produced an increase of 10.3 percentage points in the rates of relative poverty for children, but about three-fifths of this effect was offset by increases in mothers' incomes. Overall, during the 1970s and the 1980s, the relative poverty rates for children increased by about 5 percentage points, mainly because the decline in available fathers' incomes was only partly offset by increases in mothers' incomes. This represents an increase in the relative poverty rate of nearly one-fifth from the low of 22.7 percent in 1969. Still, by 1988 about 14 percent of children depended on their mothers' incomes to lift them out of relative poverty.

Family Situation and Relative Poverty

The preceding estimates of the extent to which changes in relative poverty for children can be accounted for by changes in fathers' and mothers' incomes result from two combined effects of (1) changes in the incomes of fathers and mothers living in the homes of children, and (2) changes in family composition, most notably, the loss of access to fathers' incomes associated with the shift toward mother-only families. As we discussed in Chapter 8, the shift toward mother-only families accounts for an increase of about 2–4 percentage points in the rates of relative childhood poverty after 1959. This represents no more than two-fifths of the 10.6 percentage point effect of fathers' incomes on childhood relative poverty between 1959 and 1988, and no more than one-half of the 8.6 percentage point effect of mothers' incomes. Hence, it is not surprising that for children in two-parent families, most estimates of the extent to which relative poverty can be accounted for by fathers', mothers', and other sources of income are fairly similar to estimates for children taken as a whole.

The main difference is that for children living in two-parent families, the increase in relative poverty began a decade later during the 1980s instead of during the 1970s mainly because the corresponding role of fathers' incomes in fostering relative poverty increase was much smaller during the 1970s for children in two-parent families than for children as a whole (Figure 9.1 and Table 9.1). Between 1979 and 1988, the relative poverty rate for children in two-parent families increased by 2.2 percentage points, because the decline in fathers' relative incomes was larger than the increase in mothers' relative incomes. Although this 2.2 percentage point increase in relative poverty for children living in two-parent families between 1979 and 1988 is only about one-half as large as the 5.0 percentage point increase for all children that occurred between 1969 and 1988, both represent increases of nearly one-fifth over the historical low values reached before the turnaround in long-term relative poverty trends.

Focusing on mothers, between 1939 and 1988, changes in mothers' incomes account for a slightly smaller reduction in relative poverty rates for children living in two-parent families than for children as a whole (9.2 vs. 10.8 percentage points). Between 1959 and 1988, the corresponding estimates of the mothers' income effect are 7.3 percentage points for children living in two-parent families and 8.6 percentage points for all children. Between 1969 and 1988, for children living in two-parent families, changes in fathers' incomes would by themselves have led to an increase of 5.7 percentage points in the rates of relative poverty, but this was counterbalanced by changes in mothers' incomes that tended to produce a drop of 5.8 percentage points in these rates.

After 1959 the income from relatives other than parents accounted for a fairly constant reduction in relative poverty of from 1.4 to 2.6 percentage points for children living in two-parent families and from 4.0 to 5.2 percentage points (somewhat higher) for children as a whole. Between 1939 and 1988, government welfare also accounted for a fairly constant reduction in relative poverty of from 0.8 to 1.5 percentage points for children living in two-parent families and from 1.4 to 2.1 percentage points for children as a whole.

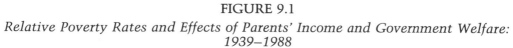

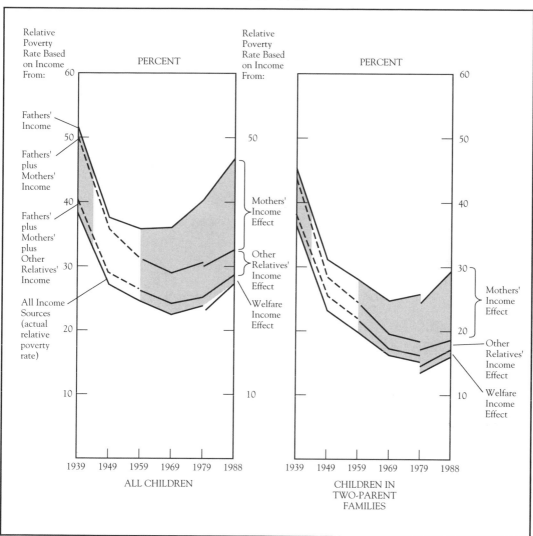

FIGURE 9.1

Relative Poverty Rates and Effects of Parents' Income and Government Welfare:
1939–1988

SOURCE: Table 9.1.

NOTE: Separate estimates of income from mothers and government welfare not available for 1949.

For children living in two-parent families, then, as for children as a whole, the large decline and subsequent increase in relative poverty rates since the Great Depression can be accounted for mainly by changes in fathers' incomes, since the direction of changes in fathers' incomes was usually the same as the direction of changes in the relative poverty rate for children. Meanwhile, changes in mothers' incomes acted to speed the earlier decline and slow the subsequent increase in childhood relative poverty.

Among children living in mother-only families, the relative poverty rate has remained quite high and comparatively stable, varying between 57 and 63 percent (Table 9.1). In 1939, welfare benefits accounted for a reduction of perhaps 1.6 percentage points in the relative poverty rate for children in mother-only families. During specific years between 1959 and 1979, welfare benefits accounted for a somewhat larger and fairly constant reduction of from 4.1 to 4.9 percentage points in the relative poverty rates of children living in mother-only families, but by 1988 the effect of these benefits had declined somewhat to 2.8 percentage points.

Between 1939 and 1959, the relative poverty rate for children living in mother-only families increased by about 3 percentage points—a change accounted for mainly by the 7.5 percentage point effect of income from nonparental family members that was only partly counterbalanced by the effect of income from mothers and welfare benefits. Between 1959 and 1979, all of the decline in relative poverty for children living in mother-only families can be accounted for by the effect of mothers' incomes, which more than compensated for further declines in income that was available from nonparental family members. But between 1979 and 1988, the increase in the rate of relative poverty among children living in mother-only families can be accounted for by the declining effects of income that was available from both mothers and welfare programs.

Family Income Sources and Official Poverty

Most of the broad conclusions presented here about the extent to which changes in relative poverty among children can be accounted for by changes in various sources of income also apply to poverty as measured officially (Appendix Table 9.1).

For example, at least since 1959 welfare income has accounted for a small and nearly stable reduction of about 2–3 percentage points in the official childhood poverty rate, compared with 1–2 percentage points for the relative poverty rate; and the size of both welfare-program effects declined slightly during the 1980s by 0.6–0.8 percentage points. Similarly, nonparental family members in the home accounted for nearly identical reductions in the official and relative poverty rates for children during the years between 1959 and 1988. However, because the official poverty thresholds were much higher than the relative thresholds during the Great Depression, these family members accounted for a notably smaller reduction in the official rate than they did in the relative poverty rate in 1939 (5.4 vs. 8.6 percentage points).

Also, for the official as well as usually for the relative childhood poverty rate, hypothetical changes across decades based on only fathers' incomes were in the same direction as actual overall poverty changes, and mothers' incomes acted to speed the earlier declines and slow the more recent increases in childhood poverty. Hence, based only on the income of fathers in the home, the official childhood poverty rate in 1988 might have been 39 percent instead of 20 percent, and mothers' incomes would have accounted for a reduction of 13 percentage points in this rate, compared with a reduction of 14 percentage points in the rate of relative childhood poverty.

Finally, again for the official as well as the relative childhood poverty rate, for children living in two-parent families, most of the estimates of the extent to which poverty can be accounted for by fathers', mothers', and other sources of income are fairly similar to estimates for children taken as a whole. The main differences result from the fact that since the mid-1960s, the official poverty thresholds have fallen increasingly further behind the relative poverty thresholds.

This difference in thresholds, for example, allows fathers' incomes to play a comparatively more prominent role in official poverty reduction in families in which the fathers are in the home. Hence, by 1988 mothers' incomes accounted for a reduction of 7.3 percentage points in the official poverty rate of children living in two-parent families; this is notably smaller than the reduction of 12.9 percentage points cited among children as a whole. For the relative poverty rate, the corresponding estimates were 11.0 and 13.9 percentage points, respectively.

For children living in mother-only families during specific years since 1969, this difference in thresholds also allows welfare benefits to play larger roles in the reduction of the official poverty rate than in the reduction of the relative poverty rate. In addition, welfare benefits accounted for a decline of 4 percentage points in the official poverty rate of children living in mother-only families between 1959 and 1969 and an increase of 6 percentage points in the rate for children living in mother-only families between 1969 and 1988; but these effects were 3–4 percentage points larger than the corresponding effects of welfare benefits on the relative poverty rate.

Sibsize and Relative Poverty

Since larger families need more income than do smaller families in order to remain above the relative poverty line, changes in sibsize could have a substantial effect on the relative poverty trends of the children during childhood. The extent to which trends in relative poverty can be accounted for by changes in sibsize has differed greatly across decades since 1939 (see Table 9.2 for sibsize distributions and relative poverty rates by sibsize).[7]

The small decline in sibsizes during the 1940s can account for a decline in the relative poverty rate of about 1 percentage point, but this effect is only about one-tenth as large as the overall decline of 12 percentage points. During the 1950s, the increase in sibsizes tended to produce an increase of 1–2 percentage points in the relative poverty rate, but this was more than counterbalanced by other factors, as the relative poverty rate dropped by 2.5 percentage points. The small sibsize change during the 1960s can account for a decline of no more than 0.3 percentage point in the relative poverty rate.

Compared with earlier changes, sibsizes dropped sharply during the 1970s. The proportion of children living in small families in which there were 1–2 children jumped by 16 percentage points, mainly due to the 11 percentage point drop in the proportion living in large families in which there were five or more siblings. Given other social, economic, and family changes that actually occurred, this large shift in sibsizes tended to produce a decline of 4 percentage points in the relative poverty rate for children. Hence, without the sharp drop in sibsizes that occurred during the 1970s, the relative poverty rate for children might

---

[7]These estimated ranges of the effect of changes in sibsize on the poverty rate are derived as follows. First, we calculated what the poverty rate would have been if the sibsize distribution had remained unchanged during the decade, but the poverty rates by sibsize (1–2, 3–4, and 5+) had changed as they actually did. The difference between this hypothetical poverty rate and the actual poverty rate at the end of the decade estimates the size of the effect of change in the sibsize distribution. Second, we calculated what the poverty rate would have been if the poverty rates by sibsize had remained unchanged during the decade, but the sibsize distribution had changed as it actually did. The difference between the hypothetical rate and the actual rate at the beginning of the next decade provides another estimate of the size of the effect of change in the sibsize distribution. It is possible that a more refined analysis, simultaneously considering the interrelationships among changes in sibsize, income (especially mothers' incomes), and family composition (especially the rise of mother-only families), would produce somewhat different results. During the 1940s and the 1950s, however, any differences would be small since the proportion of children living in mother-only families was nearly constant. During the 1960s, 1970s, and 1980s, any differences also would be small since the decade-to-decade changes in relative poverty rates by sibsize and in the sibsize distributions are fairly similar for children living in two-parent and mother-only families.

have increased substantially (perhaps by 5 percentage points) instead of increasing by 1 percentage point.

These changes that occurred during the 1970s cannot be accounted for mainly by the rise in mother-only families, as can be seen by focusing on children in two-parent families (Table 9.2). For children in two-parent families, as for all children, the proportion who lived in small families jumped by 16 percentage points during the 1970s—mainly because of the 11 percentage point drop in the proportion who lived in large families. This drop in sibsizes tended to produce a decline of 4 percentage points in the relative poverty of children living in two-parent families—the same as the 4 percentage point effect for children as a whole. Hence, without the drop in sibsizes, the relative poverty rate for children living in two-parent families might have increased by 3 percentage points during the 1970s instead of declining by 1 percentage point.

During the 1980s (1979–1988), the continuing but smaller decline in sibsizes tended to produce declines of 1–2 percentage points, respectively, in the relative poverty rates of all children and children in two-parent families. Hence, without the 1980s' sibsize decline, the relative poverty-rate increases of 4 and 2 percentage points, respectively, for children as a whole and for children in two-parent families might instead have been 5 and 3–4 percentage points, respectively.

Results in Table 9.2 and Appendix Table 9.2 also show—for children as a whole and for children in two-parent families with specific sibsizes—that both the relative and the official poverty rates dropped substantially between 1939 and 1969, then increased substantially between 1969 and 1988. Results presented thus far for the 1970s and the 1980s suggest that the relative poverty rate increased by 4–5 percentage points for children as a whole, but without the post-baby-boom drop in sibsize an additional increase of 5–6 percentage points might have occurred. Corresponding results for the official poverty rate suggest that the rate increased by 4 percentage points between 1969 and 1988, but without the post-baby-boom drop in sibsizes the official poverty rate would have increased by an additional 4 percentage points.[8]

Of course, changes in sibsize, especially sharply declining sibsizes during the 1970s, may have both contributed to and been fostered by

[8]For the official poverty rate derived using CPI-UX1, an experimental series of the Consumer Price Index, the actual increase was 2 percentage points between 1969 and 1988, but without the post-baby-boom drop in sibsize, the rate would have increased by an additional 4 percentage points. The CPI-UX1 is discussed in Edward J. Welniack, Jr., and Mark S. Littman, U.S. Bureau of the Census, Current Population Reports, Series P-60, No. 166, *Money Income and Poverty Status in the United States: 1988 (Advance Data from the March Current Population Survey)* (Washington, DC: U.S. Government Printing Office, 1989).

TABLE 9.2

Relative Poverty and Dependent Sibsizes for Children: 1939–1988

	Census 1939	Census 1949	Census 1959	Census 1969	Census 1979	CPS 1979	CPS 1988
All Children 0–17							
Total Number (in thousands)	29,647	44,340	64,121	69,434	63,816	63,488	63,747
Number of Dependent Siblings							
Dependent Sibsize Distributions							
Percent	100.0	100.0	100.0	100.0	100.0	100.0	100.0
1–2	49.6	53.0	42.8	43.0	59.1	60.6	65.2
3–4	31.6	31.4	38.6	39.4	34.5	32.5	30.0
5+	18.9	15.6	18.5	17.7	6.4	6.9	4.8
Relative Poverty Rates by Sibsize							
Number of Dependent Siblings							
1–2	25.5	18.5	15.6	15.2	18.2	17.2	21.0
3–4	42.3	26.1	21.0	21.1	28.0	27.9	34.8
5+	66.6	57.1	52.1	44.6	52.5	52.4	58.5
Total	38.6	27.0	24.4	22.7	23.8	23.1	27.0
All Children 0–17 in Two-Parent Families							
Total Number (in thousands)	26,083	38,766	56,542	57,826	49,498	48,637	40,587
Number of Dependent Siblings							
Dependent Sibsize Distributions							
Percent	100.0	100.0	100.0	100.0	100.0	100.0	100.0
1–2	46.2	50.4	40.6	40.8	56.7	58.7	63.4
3–4	33.4	33.3	40.3	41.3	36.8	34.3	31.8
5+	20.4	16.4	19.1	17.9	6.6	7.1	4.8

TABLE 9.2 (continued)

	Census 1939	Census 1949	Census 1959	Census 1969	Census 1979	CPS 1979	CPS 1988
Relative Poverty Rates by Sibsize							
Number of Dependent Siblings							
1–2	20.9	12.3	9.7	7.8	9.4	7.9	10.3
3–4	41.0	23.5	16.8	15.2	19.1	17.5	22.1
5+	65.9	54.7	48.2	37.3	42.3	42.5	44.4
Total	36.7	22.9	19.9	16.1	15.1	13.6	15.7
Dependent Sibsize Distributions							
All Children 0–17 in Mother-Only Families							
Total Number (in thousands)	1,679	2,958	5,046	8,213	10,505	11,406	13,772
Number of Dependent Siblings							
Percent	100.0	100.0	100.0	100.0	100.0	100.0	100.0
1–2	62.3	55.0	45.3	42.2	59.5	59.3	65.8
3–4	26.3	28.9	35.3	36.5	32.8	32.4	28.5
5+	11.4	16.1	19.4	21.3	7.7	8.4	5.6
Relative Poverty Rates by Sibsize							
Number of Dependent Siblings							
1–2	45.8	44.6	44.4	44.8	45.1	45.8	50.1
3–4	66.9	63.5	71.7	66.3	72.8	74.6	82.3
5+	90.1	89.1	92.9	86.5	92.5	88.4	98.7
Total	56.4	57.2	63.4	61.5	57.8	58.7	62.0

SOURCE: Estimates derived from 1940–1980 census PUMs and March CPS for 1980 and 1989.

NOTES: See Chapters 7, 8, and 11 for additional discussion of measurement of relative poverty, etc. Dependent siblings are all siblings aged 0–17 (including the child) who live in the child's home. Estimates for 1939 are not adjusted.

other changes—such as the rise in mothers' labor-force participation and income. Hence, while the simple results presented here indicate that changes in sibsize had little effect on childhood poverty rates (except during the 1970s, when childhood poverty was reduced by these changes), we should remember that this conclusion takes as given the other social, economic, and family changes that occurred during the same time. In the next chapter we will take a more thorough look at the historic links between income changes and other important trends in society, the economy, and the family.

The Racial Gap in Welfare Income and Relative Poverty

Although blacks had less access to welfare programs than did whites during the years of the Great Depression,[9] our crude estimates indicate that welfare programs in 1939 accounted for approximately equal reductions in the relative poverty rates for black and white children at 1 and 2 percentage points, respectively (Table 9.3). After the Great Depression, when many blacks moved to urban areas and gained greater access to the welfare system, welfare during specific years between 1959 and 1988 accounted for a reduction in the relative poverty rate that amounted to a nearly constant 3–4 percentage points for black children and 1–2 percentage points for white children.

Hence, the reduction in relative poverty accounted for by welfare income has been roughly twice as large for black children as for white children during specific years since 1959. This is consistent with the fact that the relative poverty rate for black children during specific years has been roughly two to three times as large as that for white children. Equally important is the fact that the actual size of the difference in the relative poverty reduction accounted for by welfare among black and white children has remained nearly stable and quite small (at 1–2 percentage points) in any given year.

Racial differences for children living in two-parent families follow the same pattern as racial differences for children as a whole. After the Great Depression, the reduction in relative poverty that is accounted for

[9]For crude estimates of the overall representation of blacks and whites in Great Depression welfare programs, see National Resources Planning Board, *Security, Work, and Relief Policies* (Washington, DC: U.S. Government Printing Office, 1942), pp. 116–118. The recipiency levels presented in that volume are calculated as a proportion of total black and white populations. The 1939 welfare program effect estimates in the tables in Chapter 9 are crudely based on these estimates and PUMs results concerning emergency work.

TABLE 9.3

Changes for White and Black Children in Relative Poverty, Parents' Income, and Government Welfare: 1939–1988

All Children Annual Relative Poverty Rates and Effects	Census 1939	Census 1949	Census 1959	Census 1969	Census 1979	CPS 1979	CPS 1988
White							
Relative poverty rates							
based on father's income only	46.3	32.9	29.4	29.8	34.8	34.5	40.5
Effect of mother's income	-2.6	—	-4.8	-6.8	-9.7	-10.3	-13.3
Effect of other relative's income	-8.7	—	-4.1	-4.4	-4.5	-4.6	-3.5
Effect of government welfare	-2.0	—	-1.6	-1.2	-1.4	-1.8	-1.4
Actual relative poverty rate	33.2	21.6	18.9	17.5	19.2	17.9	22.3
Black							
Relative poverty rates							
based on father's income only	88.2	79.5	80.4	76.0	75.6	77.5	78.7
Effect of mother's income	-3.1	—	-5.8	-9.4	-14.0	-13.0	-17.1
Effect of other relative's income	-8.1	—	-8.6	-8.2	-9.0	-7.7	-6.7
Effect of government welfare	-1.0	—	-2.7	-2.6	-2.9	-3.8	-2.3
Actual relative poverty rate	75.8	67.0	63.3	55.8	49.6	53.0	52.6

All Children Relative Poverty Rate Change and Effects Across Decades	Census 1939–1959	Census 1959–1969	Census 1969–1979	CPS 1979–1988
White				
Change in relative poverty rates				
based on fathers income only	-18.1	-0.4	5.0	6.0
Effect of mother's income	-2.2	-2.0	-2.9	-3.0
Effect of other relative's income	4.3	-0.3	-0.1	1.0
Effect of government welfare	-0.4	0.4	-0.2	0.4
Actual relative poverty rate	-14.3	-1.4	1.7	4.4
Black				
Change in relative poverty rates				
based on father's income only	-7.8	-4.4	-0.4	1.3
Effect of mother's income	-2.2	-3.6	-4.6	-4.1
Effect of other relative's income	-0.5	0.4	-0.8	1.0
Effect of government welfare	-1.7	0.1	-0.3	1.0
Actual relative poverty rate	-12.5	-7.5	-6.2	-0.4

347

TABLE 9.3 (continued)

Two-Parent Families Annual Relative Poverty Rates and Effects	Census 1939	Census 1949	Census 1959	Census 1969	Census 1979	CPS 1979	CPS 1988
White							
Relative poverty rates							
based on father's income only	39.9	26.2	23.1	20.8	22.9	22.1	27.4
Effect of mothers' income	−1.8	—	−3.5	−4.7	−6.5	−6.7	−10.0
Effect of other relative's income	−5.6	—	−2.3	−2.1	−1.9	−2.2	−1.4
Effect of government welfare	−2.0	—	−1.4	−0.7	−0.8	−1.0	−0.9
Actual relative poverty rate	31.0	18.9	15.9	13.3	13.7	12.1	15.0
Black							
Relative poverty rates							
based on father's income only	82.8	70.4	71.9	60.1	51.2	49.2	48.8
Effect of mother's income	−3.3	—	−7.0	−10.6	−16.0	−13.8	−22.1
Effect of other relative's income	−4.7	—	−5.0	−4.8	−4.2	−3.8	−1.0
Effect of government welfare	−1.7	—	−2.1	−1.8	−1.4	−2.3	−2.7
Actual relative poverty rate	73.4	62.8	57.8	42.9	29.6	29.3	23.0

Two-Parent Families Relative Poverty Rate Change and Effects Across Decades	Census 1939–1959	Census 1959–1969	Census 1969–1979	CPS 1979–1988
White				
Change in relative poverty rates				
based on father's income only	−16.8	−2.3	2.1	5.3
Effect of mother's income	−1.7	−1.2	−1.8	−3.3
Effect of other relative's income	3.3	0.2	0.2	0.8
Effect of government welfare	−1.0	0.7	−0.1	0.1
Actual relative poverty rate	−15.1	−2.6	0.4	2.9
Black				
Change in relative poverty rates				
based on father's income only	−11.0	−11.8	−8.9	−0.4
Effect of mother's income	−3.7	−3.6	−5.4	−8.3
Effect of other relative's income	−0.3	0.2	0.6	2.8
Effect of government welfare	−0.4	0.3	0.4	−0.4
Actual relative poverty rate	−15.6	−14.9	−13.3	−6.3

TABLE 9.3 (continued)

Mother-Only Families Annual Relative Poverty Rates and Effects	Census 1939	Census 1949	Census 1959	Census 1969	Census 1979	CPS 1979	CPS 1988
White							
Relative poverty rates							
based on mother's income only	79.2	—	74.8	70.2	65.1	64.9	67.0
Effect of other relative's income	-30.1	—	-14.7	-11.9	-10.7	-9.4	-8.4
Effect of government welfare	-1.0	—	-5.0	-5.5	-4.0	-6.3	-3.2
Actual relative poverty rate	54.2	49.2	55.1	52.8	50.5	49.2	55.4
Black							
Relative poverty rates							
based on mother's income only	93.3	—	94.5	89.5	83.9	83.8	83.0
Effect of other relative's income	-10.6	—	-9.1	-8.3	-8.8	-4.9	-7.4
Effect of government welfare	-1.0	—	-3.3	-3.9	-4.3	-3.7	-2.1
Actual relative poverty rate	83.6	80.7	82.1	77.3	70.9	75.2	73.4

Mother-Only Families Relative Poverty Rate Change and Effects Across Decades	Census 1939–1959	Census 1959–1969	Census 1969–1979	CPS 1979–1988
White				
Relative poverty rates				
based on mother's income only	-4.4	-4.6	-5.1	2.1
Effect of other relative's income	15.4	2.8	1.2	1.0
Effect of government welfare	-4.0	-0.5	1.5	3.1
Actual relative poverty rate	0.9	-2.3	-2.3	6.2
Black				
Relative poverty rates				
based on mother's income only	1.2	-5.0	-5.6	-0.8
Effect of other relative's income	1.5	0.8	-0.5	-2.5
Effect of government welfare	-2.2	-0.6	-0.4	1.6
Actual relative poverty rate	-1.5	-4.8	-6.4	-1.8

SOURCES: Estimates derived from 1940–1980 census PUMs and March CPS for 1980 and 1989.

NOTES: Government welfare income is income obtained by family from Aid to Families with Dependent Children (AFDC) or Social Security programs. All other income is assigned to recipient within family. See Chapters 7, 8, and 11 for additional discussion of welfare income, measurement of relative poverty, etc. Estimates for 1939 are approximate. See Footnote 9 and Chapter 8, Footnote 1.

by welfare during specific years was about 1 percentage point greater for blacks than it was for whites (Table 9.3). But for children living in mother-only families, the pattern is reversed (Table 9.3). Despite the higher relative poverty rate among black children, the reduction of 2–4 percentage points in relative poverty that is accounted for by welfare among blacks was generally smaller than the 3–6 percentage point effect recorded for whites.[10] Since reductions in the rates of relative poverty accounted for by the difference in the welfare benefits received by blacks and whites and by family situation have been virtually constant since the Great Depression, changes in welfare programs cannot account for the changes in relative poverty rates that have occurred for black or white children.

The Racial Gap in Income from Relatives Other Than Parents

Income from family members other than parents in the homes of children accounted for reductions of about 8–9 percentage points in the relative poverty rate during the Great Depression year of 1939 for both black and white children (Table 9.3). After the Great Depression, income from family members other than parents accounted for reductions in childhood relative poverty that were two to three times larger than those that were accounted for by welfare programs (that is, reductions of 8–9 percentage points for black children and 4–5 percentage points for white children between 1959 and 1979). This racial difference is again consistent with the fact that the relative poverty rates for black children were two to three times as great as those for white children.

Differences between black and white children living in two-parent families were about one-half as large, since the income of family members other than parents account for reductions of 4–5 and 2 percentage points, respectively, in the relative poverty rates of black and white children during specific years between 1959 and 1979 (Table 9.3). Among children living in mother-only families the effects were much larger,

[10]The poverty reduction accounted for by welfare among children living in mother-only families may be larger for whites than for blacks, at least partly because in any given year whites are more likely than blacks to leave poverty, and hence to have enough non-welfare income in specific years so that the additional income from welfare lifts the child's family above the poverty threshold. For example, of children born during the mid-1960s who lived in official poverty during at least 1 year, the proportion living in official poverty for less than 5 years was 79 percent for whites but only 41 percent for blacks (calculated from Table 1). Greg J. Duncan and Willard L. Rodgers, "Longitudinal Aspects of Childhood Poverty," *Journal of Marriage and the Family* 50 (November 1988): 1007–1021.

and the pattern was reversed. For black children, income from family members other than parents accounted for reductions in relative poverty that were 2–6 percentage points less than those for white children (at 5–9 vs. 9–15 percentage points, respectively). Since income from family members other than parents has accounted for larger effects in relative poverty rates for children living in mother-only families than for children living in two-parent families, the higher concentration of black children in mother-only families, in turn, accounts for much of the overall racial gap in the effect of income provided by nonparental family members.

Despite the importance of income provided by family members other than parents during the Great Depression, changes in the size of this effect that have occurred since then have usually been either small or in the opposite direction of actual changes in relative poverty. Hence, changes in income provided by nonparental family members in the homes of black children and white children do *not* account for major changes in their relative poverty rates since the Great Depression.

The Racial Gap in Parents' Income and Relative Poverty

For white children as a whole, as for all children taken together, given social and economic changes as they actually occurred, the large decline and subsequent increase that have occurred in relative poverty rates since the Great Depression can be accounted for mainly by changes in fathers' income, since the direction of changes in fathers' incomes was usually the same as the direction of changes in relative poverty for children (Tables 9.1 and 9.3). Meanwhile, changes in the income of white mothers acted to speed the post-Depression decline in childhood relative poverty through an effect that is about one-fourth as large as that for white fathers, then to slow the subsequent increase in childhood relative poverty through an effect that is about one-half as large as that for fathers.

In contrast, for black children as a whole, given social and economic changes as they actually occurred, changes in fathers' incomes accounted for an important portion of the decline that occurred in relative poverty between 1939 and 1969, but changes in mothers' incomes accounted for about one-half as much decline in relative poverty as did changes in fathers' incomes during these years. After 1969, changes in mothers' incomes account for much more change in childhood relative poverty than do changes in fathers' incomes. Between 1969 and 1988, changes in fathers' incomes tended to produce a slight increase of 0.9 percentage points in the relative poverty rate for black children, but their relative poverty rate actually declined by 6.6 percentage points, because changes in mothers' incomes acted to produce effects totalling 8.7 percentage points in the opposite direction.

However, as we discussed earlier in this chapter, results of this type estimate two combined effects of (1) changes in the incomes of fathers and mothers living in the homes of children, and (2) changes in family composition, most notably, any loss of access to fathers' incomes resulting from the shift toward mother-only families. To further address these issues, in Chapter 10 we will discuss in detail the nature and possible causes of historic trends in fathers' incomes, mothers' incomes, and family composition among both white and black children. But first we turn here to an overview of changes in relative poverty by race for children in two-parent and mother-only families.

An Overview of Relative Poverty Change by Race

Between 1939 and 1969, the drops in relative poverty rates for black children and white children were fairly similar at 16–20 percentage points. About sixth-tenths of the decline for black children can be accounted for by increasing fathers' incomes, about three-tenths can be accounted for by increasing mothers' incomes, and about one-ninth can by accounted for by increasing welfare income. For white children, increasing fathers' incomes can account for all of the decline in relative poverty that occurred between 1939 and 1969. At the same time, the effect of increasing mothers' incomes were about one-fourth the size of the relative poverty decline, and it about counterbalanced the opposite tendency for decreasing income from nonparental family members to produce a relative poverty increase of 4.3 percentage points.

Between 1969 and 1988, the relative poverty rate declined by a much smaller 3–6 percentage points for black children, while increasing by a substantial 5–6 percentage points for white children. Among black children, the decline in fathers' incomes tended to produce a small increase in relative poverty, as did the decline in welfare income. But these effects were more than counterbalanced by increasing mothers' incomes, which account for all of the decline in relative poverty among black children. Among whites, declining fathers' incomes would by themselves have produced an increase of 11.0 percentage points in relative poverty, but increasing mothers' incomes reduced the actual relative poverty increase by about one-half (that is, by a still substantial 5.9 percentage points).

Overall, then, changes in fathers' relative incomes dominated trends in childhood relative poverty both for black children between 1939 and 1969 and for white children throughout the post-Depression era, but increasing mothers' incomes have become a necessity for many children—especially black children. By 1988, 17 percent of all black children and 13 percent of all white children depended on their mothers' income to lift them out of relative poverty, and an additional 27 percent of black children and 13 percent of white children lived in relative poverty despite their mothers' work. All told, then, mothers' work was as an economic necessity for the 44 percent of black children and 26 percent of white children who either lived in relative poverty despite their mothers' work or were lifted at least somewhat above the relative poverty threshold by this work.

Two-Parent Families and Relative Poverty by Race

For both black and white children, when little change occurred in the proportion who lived in two-parent families between 1939 and 1959, the declines in relative poverty and the salutary effects of fathers' incomes for children in two-parent families were not greatly different than they were for all black children and all white children (Table 9.3).

After 1959, even among the shrinking proportion of children who lived in two-parent families, but especially among black children living in two-parent families, mothers' incomes became increasingly necessary to lift children out of relative poverty. During the 1960s, 1970s, and 1980s, the proportion of black children living in two-parent families who depended on their mothers' income to lift them out of relative poverty grew by 3.6, 5.4, and 8.3 percentage points, respectively. Hence, by 1988, among the one-third of black children who lived with two parents, without their mothers' income the relative poverty rate would have been 22 percentage points higher (at 45 percent instead of 23 percent), and the proportion living with two parents who either depended on their mothers' work to lift them out of relative poverty or lived in relative poverty despite this income was 35 percent.

Although the proportion of white children living in two-parent families by 1988 was more than twice as large as the proportion of black children living in such families (78 vs. 37 percent), white children were only about one-half as likely to depend on their mothers' income to lift them out of relative poverty as were black children. Still, even for white children living in two-parent families in 1988, without their mothers' income the relative poverty rate would have been 10 percentage points higher (at about 25 percent instead of 15 percent), and the proportion who either depended on their mothers' income to lift them out of relative poverty or lived in relative poverty despite this income had increased to 18 percent by 1988.

Mother-Only Families and Relative Poverty by Race

The relative poverty rate for children living in mother-only families declined for blacks from 81–84 percent in 1939–1959 to 71–75 percent in 1979–1988, and it fluctuated between 49 and 55 percent for whites (Table 9.3). Based on mothers' income only, the relative poverty rates for black and for white children living in mother-only families would have declined by 12 and 8 percentage points, respectively, between 1959 and 1988, but mainly between 1959 and 1979.

Hence, by 1979–1988 the proportion of children living in mother-only families in which their mothers' incomes were high enough to keep them above the relative poverty threshold was about 16–17 percent for blacks and 33–35 percent for whites. Also during specific years between 1969 and 1988, relative poverty rates for black and white children living in mother-only families were reduced by an additional 5–12 percentage points as a result of the income of other family members in the home and by an additional 2–6 percentage points as a result of welfare benefits.

Meanwhile, the proportion of black children living in mother-only families increased from 12 to 19 percent between 1939 and 1959 and remained stable for whites at 6 percent. But the proportions living in mother-only families more than doubled between 1959 and 1988 both for black and white children, reaching 50 percent for blacks and 16 percent for whites as of 1988. Overall, then, declines since 1959 in relative poverty rates for children living in mother-only families have been small among black children and negligible among white children, yet the proportions of black and white children living in mother-only families have more than doubled.

The high probability that children living in mother-only families— especially black children—will live in relative poverty, and the fact that relative poverty rates for children living in mother-only families have improved little since 1959, suggest that the forces that lead increasing proportions of women to form mother-only families must be quite powerful. Why else would such large increases in mother-only families have occurred? As we will see in Chapter 10, in which we discuss apparent causes of the rise in mother-only families, they do indeed represent powerful forces that are inherent in some of the most important social and economic transformations of the past half century.

Entering and Exiting Poverty by Race

Results presented thus far have focused mainly on the extent to which income from fathers, mothers, other family members, as well as welfare benefits, acted to reduce relative poverty rates for children during specific years, and on the extent to which the size of these effects changed across various years. But because these results are based on cross-sectional data for specific years, they provide no information about the proportion of children who have ever lived in poverty before reaching adulthood, the number of years that they spend in poverty, or the circumstances associated with entering and exiting specific spells of poverty. Using data from the Panel Study of Income Dynamics (PSID), Greg J. Duncan and Willard L. Rodgers have developed such estimates for the period between the late 1960s and the mid-1980s.[11]

Using the official poverty concept, Duncan and Rodgers found about 34 percent had lived in poverty before reaching 16 for children born during the mid-1960s, and 52 percent had lived within 150 percent of the official poverty threshold.[12] Since the relative poverty threshold was about 125 percent of the official poverty threshold during the 1970s, it seems likely that 40–45 percent of children born during the mid-1960s lived in relative poverty for at least one year before reaching age 16, and that the proportion who lived in relative poverty before reaching age 18 was slightly higher. Hence, among children born during the mid-1960s, the proportion who had ever lived in relative poverty before age 18 was approximately twice as great as the 23–24 percent of children aged 0–17 who lived in relative poverty in 1969 and 1979 (that is, about twice as great as the proportion who lived in relative poverty in any single year).

Duncan and Rodgers estimate that for white children born during the mid-1960s, 25 percent lived below the official poverty threshold for at least one year before reaching age 16, and 44 percent lived below 150 percent of the official poverty threshold for at least one year. For black

[11]Greg J. Duncan and Willard L. Rodgers, "Longitudinal Aspects of Childhood Poverty," *Journal of Marriage and the Family* 50 (November 1988): 1007–1021; and Greg J. Duncan and Willard L. Rodgers, "Single-Parent Families: Are Their Economic Problems Transitory or Persistent?" *Family Planning Perspectives* 19, 4 (July/August 1987): 171–178.

[12]Duncan and Rodgers, "Longitudinal Aspects," Table 1.

children born during the mid-1960s, an extraordinary 79 percent lived in official poverty for at least one year before reaching age 16, and 87 percent lived below 150 percent of the poverty threshold for at least one year. Duncan and Rodgers also estimate that for children born during the mid-1960s, the proportion living in official poverty for five or more years before age 16 was only 5 percent for whites compared with 47 percent for blacks.

In terms of relative poverty rates, these results imply that for children born during the mid-1960s, the proportion who lived in relative poverty for at least one year before reaching age 18 was approximately 30–40 percent for whites and 80–85 percent for blacks, compared with relative poverty rates of 18–19 percent for whites and 50–56 percent for blacks among children aged 0–17 in 1969 and 1979.

Turning to the relationship between family composition and official poverty, Duncan and Rodgers go on to calculate the proportion of years spent by children in official poverty according to their family circumstances.[13] Between the late 1960s and the early 1980s, 53 percent of the years during which children lived in official poverty were spent in two-parent families, 28 percent were spent in one-parent families that children experienced from birth, and 19 percent were spent in one-parent families that children experienced following the parents' separation or divorce.

For whites, an even larger 65 percent of years during which children lived in official poverty were spent in two-parent families, while 19 percent were spent in one-parent families from birth and 16 percent were spent in one-parent families following separation or divorce. For blacks, only 37 percent of the years during which children lived in official poverty were spent in two-parent families, while 40 percent were spent in one-parent families from birth and 23 percent were spent in one-parent families following separation or divorce. Hence, a large majority of official poverty years among white children, and a substantial minority of official poverty years among black children, occurred while they lived in two-parent families.

Duncan and Rodgers also present results concerning the extent to which changes in family employment, parental disability, and family composition were associated with entering and existing official poverty for children between the late 1960s and the early 1980s. To be specific, they calculate the proportions of children who one to two years before entering official poverty experienced (1) the loss of a parent from the home through separation, divorce, or death, (2) the reduction in employment of a father, mother, or other family member in the home because

[13]Duncan and Rodgers, "Single-Parent Families," Table 6.

of unemployment or fewer hours worked, or (3) the disability of a parent.[14] Excluded are transitions into poverty through birth into an officially poor one-parent or two-parent family. Similarly, they calculate the proportions of children who one or two years before exiting official poverty experienced (1) the entry of a parent into the home through parental reconciliation or (re)marriage, (2) the increased employment of a father, mother, or other family member in the home through obtaining a job or increased hours of work, or (3) the end of a spell of parental disability.

For both white and black children these results indicate that only 8–9 percent of transitions into or out of official poverty were associated with the loss or gain of a parent in the home. Much more important were changes both in fathers' and in mothers' employment or disability status. Changes in fathers' employment or disability status for white and black children were associated with 39–40 and 15–25 percent, respectively, of the transitions into or out of official poverty, while changes in mothers' employment or disability status were associated with 16–22 and 27–33 percent, respectively, of transitions in the rates of official poverty.

Comparing changes in fathers' and mothers' employment and disability status between the late 1960s and the early 1980s, then, changes for fathers were more important for white children, but changes for mothers were more important for black children. Furthermore, among white children changes in mothers' employment status for children living in two-parent and mother-only families were associated with approximately equal proportions of total poverty transitions (8–13 vs. 7–8 percent, respectively). But among black children, changes in mothers' employment status for those living in two-parent families were less often associated with poverty transitions than were changes in mothers' employment status for children living in mother-only families (7–12 vs. 17–19 percent, respectively).

Finally, changes in the employment of family members other than

[14]Duncan and Rodgers, "Longitudinal Aspects," Table 5. In these PSID estimates, relatives in the home are identified as being the "head" or "wife" in a family, but since these persons are apparently usually the parents of the children, we simply refer to them in our summary as parents. For other distinctions and more precise definitions of the concepts and calculations used by Duncan and Rodgers, see their original article. In our forthcoming study of household transitions during the mid-1980s using SIPP data, the results are similar. Of all transitions into poverty during one-year periods among family households with own children present, the proportions accounted for by newly formed mother-only family households created through marital separations of married-couple households were 8.5 percent, overall, and 8.6 and 6.0 percent, respectively, for whites and blacks. Donald J. Hernandez, U.S. Bureau of the Census, Current Population Reports, Series P 23–179, *When Households Continue, Discontinue, and Form* (Washington, DC: U.S. Government Printing Office, 1992).

parents in the homes of children were associated with about 18–29 percent of transitions in childhood poverty for both whites and blacks—a level roughly comparable to changes in mothers' employment and disability status.

Although the conclusions of Duncan and Rodgers address questions that differ from the ones we address using cross-sectional data, their results and our results are complementary in that they portray a broadly consistent picture of racial differences in childhood poverty. First, black children experience much higher poverty rates than do white children, and their experience with poverty tends to last much longer than it does among white children. Second, poverty for black children is much more likely to occur within the context of mother-only families. Third, poverty changes and transitions among white children are more likely to be associated with changes in fathers' incomes than with those in mothers' incomes, but the reverse has been true for black children since at least the late 1960s. Fourth, poverty changes and transitions are substantially more likely to be associated with changes in the income of family members (fathers, mothers, or others) in the homes of children than with changes in family composition involving the loss (or gain) of a parent from the home.

Dependent Sibsizes and Relative Poverty by Race

Another potential source of the racial gap in the rates of childhood relative poverty is the racial gap in dependent sibsizes. To what extent can the racial gap in relative poverty rates for children be accounted for by the larger dependent sibsizes that exist among black children than among white children, and to what extent can changes in the racial gap in relative poverty rates be accounted for by changes in the dependent sibsize gap? The answers to these questions are (1) that most of the racial gap in annual relative poverty rates cannot be accounted for by the racial gap in dependent sibsizes, and (2) that about one-half of the expanding relative poverty gap that occurred during the 1940s can be accounted for by the expanding dependent sibsize gap, but that subsequent reductions in the dependent sibsize gap had, by 1988, offset this deleterious effect.

Hence, although the racial gap in relative poverty rates was about one-fourth smaller in 1988 than it was in 1939 (down from 40 to 30 percentage points), the racial gap in dependent sibsizes accounted for a nearly identical 2–4 percentage points in the racial gap that occurred in relative poverty rates in 1939 and 1988. Let's explore these results in more detail. (See Table 9.4 for the basic data on dependent sibsizes and relative poverty rates by race.)

In 1939, the racial gap in relative poverty rates for children was 39.8 percentage points, but if blacks and whites had had the same dependent sibsize distribution, the gap in relative poverty rates would have been smaller (by only 2–4 percentage points).[15] Hence, at least nine-tenths of the overall racial gap in relative poverty rates for children in 1939 can be accounted for by racial differences in relative poverty rates for families that have the same number of dependent siblings. It therefore appears that racial differences in income for families of the same size, not differences in the family-size distributions of blacks and whites, accounted for most of the racial gap in relative poverty for children in 1939.

During the 1940s, when the relative poverty rate for children as a whole dropped sharply (by 12 percentage points), the declines for black and white children were 7 and 13 percentage points, respectively. Of this 6 percentage point widening of the racial gap in relative poverty rates, about one-half (2–3 percentage points) can be accounted for by increasing dependent sibsizes among black children and decreasing dependent sibsizes among white children. During the 1950s, changing dependent sibsizes can account for no more than a change of 0–2 percentage points in the racial gap in the relative poverty rates of children.

For black children, the 1960s brought a large decline of 7.5 percentage points in relative poverty, compared with a decline of only 1.4 percentage points for whites. Of this 6.1 percentage point narrowing of the racial gap in relative poverty, declining dependent sibsizes among black children and nearly stable dependent sibsizes among white children can account for 2 percentage points of the 6 percentage point change.

During the 1970s, dependent sibsizes dropped substantially for both black and white children. For example, the proportions who had small dependent sibsizes of 1–2 increased by 17 percentage points for blacks and 14 percentage points for whites. Without these large drops in dependent sibsizes the relative poverty rate for black children would have remained constant instead of dropping by 6 percentage points; and the relative poverty rate for white children would have increased by about

---

[15]All of the annual effects of racial gaps in dependent sibsize are estimated here in two different ways: (1) by applying the black dependent sibsize distribution to the white poverty rates and (2) by applying the white dependent sibsize distribution to the black poverty rates. Since these results sometimes differ somewhat, they may provide a range of estimates that bound the probable actual effect of dependent sibsize change, independent of changes in poverty rates within sibsizes. The three dependent sibsize categories employed in these analyses are 1–2, 3–4, and 5 or more. The dependent sibsize is the total number of siblings aged 0–17 living in the child's home. A dependent sibsize of 1 means that the only-child has no siblings in the home.

TABLE 9.4

Relative Poverty and Dependent Sibsizes for White and Black Children: 1939–1988

All Children 0–17	Census 1939	Census 1949	Census 1959	Census 1969	Census 1979	CPS 1979	CPS 1988
		Dependent Sibsize Distributions					
White							
Number of dependent siblings							
1–2	50.3	54.5	44.2	44.0	60.2	61.6	66.2
3–4	32.0	32.2	39.9	40.6	34.5	32.4	29.7
5+	17.8	13.3	15.8	15.4	5.3	6.1	4.1
Black							
Number of dependent siblings							
1–2	43.6	42.1	33.0	36.0	52.7	54.9	60.0
3–4	27.9	25.2	29.6	31.9	34.5	33.1	31.5
5+	28.5	32.7	37.4	32.1	12.8	12.0	8.5
		Relative Poverty Rates by Sibsize					
White							
Number of dependent siblings							
1–2	21.8	14.6	12.3	11.8	14.7	13.2	17.3
3–4	38.7	22.1	17.2	17.0	23.3	22.3	29.3
5+	63.1	48.8	41.7	34.8	43.8	42.1	51.9
Total	34.5	21.5	18.9	17.5	19.2	17.9	22.3
Black							
Number of dependent siblings							
1–2	63.6	56.8	46.7	41.5	40.9	43.0	43.6
3–4	78.7	61.1	57.1	53.5	54.3	59.6	63.5
5+	86.2	82.3	82.9	74.3	73.0	82.5	75.9
Total	74.3	67.0	63.3	55.8	49.6	53.2	52.6

TABLE 9.4 (*continued*)

All Children 0–17 in Two-Parent Families	Census 1939	Census 1949	Census 1959	Census 1969	Census 1979	CPS 1979	CPS 1988
Dependent Sibsize Distributions							
White							
Number of dependent siblings							
1–2	47.6	52.5	42.4	42.1	57.9	59.5	64.1
3–4	33.4	33.6	41.2	42.1	36.4	33.9	31.6
5+	18.9	13.9	16.4	15.8	5.7	6.6	4.3
Black							
Number of dependent siblings							
1–2	30.7	29.5	23.9	28.8	44.8	48.9	55.5
3–4	33.0	29.9	32.1	34.2	40.3	39.0	34.3
5+	36.3	40.7	44.0	37.0	14.9	12.1	10.2
Relative Poverty Rates by Sibsize							
White							
Number of dependent siblings							
1–2	19.1	10.7	8.5	7.0	8.8	7.3	10.0
3–4	37.7	20.1	14.3	13.3	17.4	15.6	21.5
5+	62.6	47.4	39.1	30.1	38.4	38.0	42.0
Total	33.5	18.9	15.9	13.3	13.7	12.1	15.0
Black							
Number of dependent siblings							
1–2	51.9	40.0	30.2	18.9	16.7	15.4	13.6
3–4	78.6	61.7	47.8	38.0	33.7	34.9	28.4
5+	85.1	80.0	80.2	66.1	57.1	70.2	55.7
Total	72.7	62.7	57.8	42.9	29.6	29.6	23.0

TABLE 9.4 (continued)

All Children 0–17 in Mother-Only Families	Census 1939	Census 1949	Census 1959	Census 1969	Census 1979	CPS 1979	CPS 1988
Dependent Sibsize Distributions							
White							
Number of dependent siblings							
1–2	65.3	60.0	52.3	47.8	64.5	65.9	70.9
3–4	25.9	29.0	34.8	37.0	31.1	29.8	25.0
5+	8.8	11.0	12.9	15.2	4.3	4.3	4.1
Black							
Number of dependent siblings							
1–2	51.4	40.2	29.8	32.0	50.6	47.6	57.1
3–4	27.8	28.7	36.3	35.5	35.8	36.8	34.6
5+	20.7	31.1	33.9	32.5	13.7	15.6	8.3
Relative Poverty Rates by Sibsize							
White							
Number of dependent siblings							
1–2	39.4	38.6	40.2	39.3	39.6	39.1	45.4
3–4	61.9	58.3	65.1	59.0	67.3	67.0	76.4
5+	83.6	83.2	88.0	80.4	91.0	81.8	100.0
Total	49.1	49.2	55.0	52.8	50.4	49.3	55.4
Black							
Number of dependent siblings							
1–2	75.4	70.7	60.8	59.7	57.5	62.2	60.1
3–4	83.5	78.9	85.7	79.9	81.1	85.4	89.6
5+	100.0	95.2	97.0	91.7	93.3	91.6	97.6
Total	82.7	80.7	82.1	77.3	70.9	75.3	73.4

SOURCE: Estimates derived from 1940–1980 census PUMs and March CPS for 1980 and 1989.

NOTES: See Chapters 7, 8, and 11 for additional discussion of measurement of relative poverty, etc. Dependent siblings are all siblings aged 0–17 (including the child) who live in the child's home. Estimates for 1939 are not adjusted.

5 percentage points instead of 2 percentage points. Overall, during the 1970s the racial gap in relative poverty narrowed by 8 percentage points, and the greater dependent-sibsize decline among blacks can be said to account for about one-fourth (2 percentage points) of this change.

During the 1980s, continuing dependent-sibsize declines were smaller than they were during the 1970s, accounting for relative poverty declines of about 0.1–1.5 percentage points for black children and 0.8 percentage point for white children. Hence, the slight racial convergence in dependent sibsizes during the 1980s tended to produce a racial convergence in the relative poverty rate that amounted to no more than 1 percentage point. By 1988, racial differences in dependent sibsizes accounted for only 2 percentage points of the large 30 percentage point gap in relative poverty rates for black and white children.

The extent to which trends in the racial gap in dependent sibsizes can account for trends in the racial gap in relative poverty rates for children living in two-parent families and mother-only families are generally similar to the trends for children as a whole, but they indicate that dependent sibsize effects were somewhat larger for children living in two-parent families throughout the era and for mother-only families beginning in about 1959. Still, even in 1949–1959, when the racial gap in dependent sibsizes was largest, the dependent sibsize gap accounted for less than three-tenths of the racial gap in relative poverty rates for children living in two-parent families and for less than two-fifths of the relative poverty gap for children living in mother-only families.

After 1959 the racial gap in dependent sibsizes became much smaller. By 1988, for children living in two-parent families the racial gap in dependent sibsizes accounted for 2–3 percentage points of the 8 percentage point racial gap in relative poverty rates; for children living in mother-only families the dependent sibsize gap accounted for 4–5 percentage points of the 18 percentage point gap in the rate of relative poverty. These dependent sibsize effects by family situation are no more than about 3 percentage points larger than the effect for children as a whole, which accounted for about 2 out of 30 percentage points of the racial gap in the relative poverty rate in 1988.

Overall, then, changes in dependent sibsize between 1939 and 1988 can account for a fairly small portion of the racial gap in relative poverty rates for children. Most of the large reduction in the racial gap in relative poverty since the Great Depression is due not to changes in dependent sibsize but to changes in family income. Equally important is the fact that most of the large remaining racial gap in relative poverty rates for children is due not to differences in dependent sibsize but to differences in family income.

Hispanic Family Income and Relative Poverty in 1979

Hispanic children (of any race) are generally similar to black non-Hispanic children in their relative poverty rates and in the extent to which fathers' incomes and sibsize accounted for poverty reductions in 1979.

Although relative poverty rates for Hispanic children (of any race) and non-Hispanic black children in 1979 were much larger than those for non-Hispanic white children (by 26 and 33 percentage points, respectively), government welfare programs account for small and similar reductions of 1–3 percentage points in the relative poverty rates for all three groups (Table 9.5).

Income from family members other than parents in the homes of children can account for a larger reduction of 8–9 percentage points in relative poverty rates for Hispanic children (of any race) and non-Hispanic black children, and for a reduction of 4 percentage points for non-Hispanic white children. Since relative poverty-rate reductions accounted for by family members other than parents are somewhat larger for Hispanic children (of any race) and non-Hispanic black children than for non-Hispanic white children, the overall gaps in the relative poverty rates separating the two minorities from the non-Hispanic white majority would have been somewhat greater were it not for the income received from these other family members.

Mothers' incomes can account for a still larger reduction in relative poverty rates. If mothers' incomes had not been available in 1979, relative poverty rates for Hispanic children (of any race), for non-Hispanic black children, and for non-Hispanic white children would have been larger by 11, 14, and 10 percentage points, respectively.

Since income from welfare benefits, nonparental family members, and mothers together account for reductions in relative poverty rates that do not differ greatly across ethnic and racial groups, differences in fathers' incomes can be said to account for most of the large ethnic and racial gaps in relative poverty rates. If they depended only on the income of fathers in the home, the relative poverty rates for Hispanic children (of any race) and non-Hispanic black children would have exceeded the relative poverty rate of non-Hispanic white children in 1979 by 31 and 44 percentage points, respectively, instead of by 25 and 33 percentage points. Hence, most of the ethnic and racial gaps in relative poverty are accounted for by differences in fathers' incomes.

The patterns across ethnic and racial groups are broadly similar for children in two-parent families and those in mother-only families. Among children living with two parents across Hispanic origin and racial groups, welfare income accounts for a small reduction in the relative poverty rate of about 1 percentage point; the income from nonparental family members accounts for a somewhat larger reduction of 2–4 percentage points; and mothers' incomes account for a still larger reduction of 6–16 percentage points. But if only fathers' incomes were available, the gaps in relative poverty rates between Hispanic children (of any race) and non-Hispanic black children, on one hand, and non-Hispanic whites, on the other, would have been 29 and 31 percentage points, respectively, instead of 22 and 18 percentage points.

Compared with children living in two-parent families, for those in mother-only families, welfare income accounts for somewhat larger reductions in relative poverty rates of about 4 percentage points, and income from other nonparental family members accounts for a larger reduction of 9–11 percentage points. But for children living in mother-only families, differences in mothers' incomes account for most of the ethnic and racial differences in relative poverty rates.

Differences between first-generation Hispanic children (of any race) and old-family Hispanic children (of any race) were also small for virtually all of the results presented thus far in this section. For example, in 1979 the relative poverty rates for first-generation and old-family Hispanic children were 45 and 40 percent, respectively. The most noteworthy difference between first-generation and old-family Hispanic children (of any race) was that for those living in two-parent families, the relative poverty rates in 1979 were 41 and 29 percent, respectively. But even in this case, the relative poverty rate of 29 percent for old-family Hispanic children (of any race) was the same as the relative poverty rate of 29 percent for non-Hispanic black children.

Hispanic Income and Relative Poverty Between 1979 and 1988

A major difference between Hispanic children (of any race) and non-Hispanic children in family income and relative poverty is that relative poverty appears to have increased quite sharply among Hispanic children (of any race) during the 1980s (Table 9.5).

The relative poverty rate for Hispanic children (of any race) jumped by a large 11 percentage points between 1979 and 1988, compared with no change for non-Hispanic black children and an important but much smaller increase of 3 percentage points for non-Hispanic white children.

TABLE 9.5

Relative Poverty, Parents' Income, Government Welfare, Dependent Sibsizes, by Hispanic Origin: 1979–1988

| 1980 Census Data | Non-Hispanic | | Total Hispanic | Hispanic Living with Mother | |
Annual Relative Poverty Rates and Effects	White	Black		Old Family	First Generation
All Children					
Relative poverty rates					
based on father's income only	31.7	75.4	63.1	63.8	59.0
Effect of mother's income	–9.6	–14.1	–10.8	–11.3	–12.0
Effect of other relative's income	–4.2	–8.9	–7.5	–6.5	–4.6
Effect of government welfare	–1.3	–2.9	–2.2	–1.4	–2.3
Actual relative poverty rate	16.7	49.5	42.5	44.7	40.1
Two-Parent Families					
Relative poverty rates					
based on father's income only	20.3	51.0	49.7	58.6	44.2
Effect of mother's income	–6.1	–16.1	–10.3	–10.6	–10.1
Effect of other relative's income	–1.7	–4.2	–4.4	–5.4	–3.7
Effect of government welfare	–0.8	–1.3	–1.4	–1.1	–1.6
Actual relative poverty rate	11.7	29.3	33.7	41.4	28.9
Mother-Only Families					
Relative poverty rates					
based on mother's income only	61.7	83.9	82.9	83.8	82.6
Effect of other relative's income	–11.1	–8.7	–8.6	–13.5	–7.3
Effect of government welfare	–3.9	–4.4	–4.1	–3.5	–4.2
Actual relative poverty rate	46.7	70.9	70.3	66.8	71.1

TABLE 9.5 (continued)

| 1980 and 1989 CPS Data Annual Relative Poverty Rates and Effects | Non-Hispanic | | | | Hispanic | |
| | White | | Black | | | |
	1979 CPS	1988 CPS	1979 CPS	1988 CPS	1979 CPS	1988 CPS
All Children						
Relative poverty rates						
based on father's income only	31.8	36.0	77.5	78.7	60.0	71.7
Effect of mother's income	−10.2	−13.4	−13.1	−17.0	−11.3	−13.1
Effect of other relative's income	−4.3	−3.0	−7.8	−6.7	−7.2	−7.1
Effect of government welfare	−1.7	−1.4	−3.8	−2.3	−2.9	−1.3
Actual relative poverty rate	15.6	18.2	52.9	52.7	38.6	50.0
Two-Parent Families						
Relative poverty rates						
based on father's income only	19.5	23.5	48.9	48.8	47.7	59.6
Effect of mother's income	−6.3	−9.6	−13.9	−22.1	−11.0	−14.0
Effect of other relative's income	−1.9	−1.0	−3.8	−1.0	−5.1	−5.4
Effect of government welfare	−1.0	−0.9	−2.3	−2.7	−1.8	−1.3
Actual relative poverty rate	10.4	12.1	29.0	23.0	29.8	39.0
Mother-Only Families						
Relative poverty rates						
based on mother's income only	61.6	61.5	83.7	83.2	84.4	86.2
Effect of other relative's income	−9.9	−8.5	−5.0	−7.4	−6.2	−7.8
Effect of government welfare	−6.3	−3.6	−3.7	−2.2	−6.3	−1.5
Actual relative poverty rate	45.4	49.4	75.1	73.6	71.9	76.9

TABLE 9.5 (continued)

1979–1988 Change	All Children			Two-Parent Families			Mother-Only Families		
	White	Black	Hispanic	White	Black	Hispanic	White	Black	Hispanic
Change in relative poverty rates based on father's income only	4.2	1.2	11.7	4.0	-0.1	11.9	-0.1	-0.5	1.8
Effect of mother's income	-3.2	-3.9	-1.9	-3.3	-8.2	-3.0	1.4	-2.4	-1.6
Effect of other relative's income	1.3	1.1	0.1	0.9	2.8	-0.3	2.7	1.5	4.8
Effect of government welfare	0.3	1.5	1.6	0.1	-0.4	0.5	4.0	-1.5	5.0
Actual relative poverty rate	2.6	-0.2	11.4	1.7	-6.0	9.2			

	Non-Hispanic				Hispanic	
	White		Black			
	1979 CPS	1988 CPS	1979 CPS	1988 CPS	1979 CPS	1988 CPS

Dependent Sibsize Distributions

All Children — Number of dependent siblings						
1–2	63.0	68.2	55.0	59.9	48.4	52.5
3–4	31.7	28.5	33.0	31.6	38.6	37.9
5+	5.3	3.3	12.0	8.5	13.1	9.6

Relative Poverty Rates by Sibsize

Number of dependent siblings						
1–2	11.8	14.7	43.0	43.8	30.2	40.2
3–4	19.8	24.0	59.5	63.3	41.9	56.3
5+	36.9	40.2	82.7	75.8	61.3	79.3
Total	15.7	18.2	53.2	52.7	38.8	50.0

Dependent Sibsize Distribution

Two-Parent Families — Number of dependent siblings						
1–2	60.9	65.9	49.1	55.1	45.3	49.6
3–4	33.3	30.5	38.8	34.6	40.1	40.5
5+	5.8	3.6	12.1	10.3	14.6	10.0

TABLE 9.5 (continued)

Relative Poverty Rates by Sibsize

Number of dependent siblings

1–2	6.4	8.4	15.3	13.4	19.2	27.9
3–4	13.9	17.7	34.2	28.5	31.8	45.0
5+	33.0	32.4	70.6	55.6	57.8	70.2
Total	10.5	12.1	29.3	23.0	29.9	39.0

Dependent Sibsize Distributions

1–2	68.7	75.5	47.5	57.1	49.3	54.3
3–4	28.0	21.9	36.9	34.6	40.9	36.3
5+	3.4	2.6	15.6	8.4	9.8	9.4

Mother-Only Families

Number of dependent siblings

Relative Poverty Rates by Sibsize

1–2	36.3	41.3	62.1	60.4	63.1	65.3
3–4	64.0	71.1	85.4	89.5	79.8	88.3
5+	79.4	100.0	91.5	97.6	87.3	100.0
Total	45.5	49.4	75.3	73.6	72.3	76.9

SOURCE: Estimates derived from 1980 census PUMs and March CPS for 1980 and 1989.

NOTES: Government welfare income is income obtained by family from Aid to Families with Dependent Children (AFDC) or Social Security programs. All other income is assigned to recipient within family. See Chapters 7, 8, and 11 for additional discussion of welfare income, measurement of relative poverty, etc. Dependent siblings are all siblings aged 0–17 (including the child) who live in the child's home.

Since the corresponding increases would have been 12, 1, and 4 percentage points for the three ethnic and racial groups if only changes in fathers' incomes had occurred, ethnic and racial differences in fathers' incomes were the most important factor in the rapidly widening relative-poverty gap between Hispanic children (of any race) and non-Hispanic children.

If the relative poverty rate was dramatically higher among Hispanic children (of any race) in families that immigrated during the 1980s than it was among Hispanic children (of any race) in families that were already in the United States in 1980, then we might suspect that rapid immigration during the 1980s brought many newcomers with very high relative poverty rates and that this acted to increase sharply the overall relative poverty rate for Hispanic children (of any race). But as we have seen, at least as of 1979 the relative poverty rate of first-generation Hispanic children (of any race) was only 4–5 percentage points larger than it was for old-family Hispanic children (of any race). Hence, even if the gap in the relative poverty rates between 1980s' immigrants and the resident 1980 population were several times as large, no plausible increase in immigration during the 1980s could account for as much as one-half of the sharp 11 percentage point jump that occurred in the relative poverty rate among Hispanic children (of any race) as a whole during the decade.

Dependent Sibsizes and Relative Poverty for Hispanics

The comparatively high relative poverty rates among Hispanic children (of any race) are not accounted for by large dependent sibsizes. If the dependent sibsizes of Hispanic children (of any race) and non-Hispanic white children had been equal in 1979 and 1988, the gaps in relative poverty rates would have been reduced slightly from 23 to 20–21 percentage points in 1979 and from 32 to 28–29 percentage points in 1988. Since the dependent sibsize distribution of Hispanic children (of any race) is similar to that of non-Hispanic black children, the comparatively small reduction in the relative poverty gap separating Hispanic children (of any race) from non-Hispanic white children is about the same as the reduction in the racial gap in relative poverty that would be achieved if the dependent sibsize distributions of non-Hispanic black and non-Hispanic white children were equal.

Hence, it is comparatively high relative poverty rates within families of the same size, rather than comparatively large dependent sibsizes, that account for the comparatively high relative poverty rates that exist among Hispanic children (of any race).

Conclusion

The large historic decline in childhood relative poverty after the Great Depression and the more recent increase were mirrored most closely by the changes in relative poverty that would have occurred if children had depended only on the income of fathers in their homes. The actual relative poverty rate for children and the hypothetical rate based only on fathers' incomes both declined by 14–15 percentage points between 1939 and 1969. Subsequently, between 1969 and 1988, the actual relative poverty rate increased by about one-half as much as did the hypothetical rate based only on fathers' incomes (5.1 vs. 10.3 percentage points).

The additional and increasingly large reductions in childhood relative poverty that can be accounted for by mothers' incomes acted to speed the earlier decline and slow the subsequent increase in childhood relative poverty. In 1939, mothers' incomes acted to reduce the childhood relative poverty rate by about 3 percentage points below what it would have been if children had depended only on their fathers' incomes, representing one-third of the 9 percent of children whose mothers were in the labor force. By 1988, 14 percent of children depended on their mothers' incomes to lift them out of relative poverty, and an additional 15 percent remained in relative poverty despite their mothers' incomes. Hence, close to one-half of children whose mothers were in the labor force in 1988 (29 of 59 percent) depended on their mothers' employment for basic necessities, and the proportion was only slightly lower as measured by the official poverty rate (23 of 59 percent).

Meanwhile, the additional reduction in the rates of childhood relative poverty that can be accounted for by family members other than parents in the home declined from about 8–9 percentage points during the Great Depression year of 1939 to about 4–5 percentage points for the years between 1959 and 1988. This suggests that rising parental income after the Great Depression may have allowed children and their parents to become more independent of other family members for economic support. Beyond the role of income from these sources, a fourth and final income source, welfare programs, accounted for an additional small and nearly stable reduction in childhood relative poverty of only 1–2 percentage points for the years between 1939 and 1988.

The results for white children are similar to those for all children, but the experiences of black children have been quite different in some important respects. Black children have higher poverty rates, they tend to remain in poverty for longer periods, and they spend more than half of their poverty years living in mother-only families. Compared with white children, changes in relative poverty for black children across various decades were usually less likely to be accounted for by changes in fathers' incomes and more likely to be accounted for by changes in mothers' incomes. But despite racial differences, changes and transitions in the poverty rates for black children, as for white children, are more likely to be associated with changes in the incomes of family members (fathers, mothers, and others) in the homes of children than with changes in welfare income or in family composition involving the loss (or gain) of a parent from the home.

More limited results since 1979 for both old-family and first-generation Hispanic children (of any race) indicate that they were generally more similar to non-Hispanic blacks than to non-Hispanic whites in their relative poverty rates and in the extent to which fathers' incomes were not high enough to lift them out of poverty. The most important difference between Hispanic children (of any race) and all non-Hispanic children is the extraordinary 11 percentage point increase in relative poverty for these Hispanics during the 1980s—an increase that can be accounted for mainly by the decline in the ability of their fathers' incomes to lift them out of poverty.

A separate analysis of family size indicates that dependent sibsizes can account for a change of only a 1–2 percentage points in the rate of childhood relative poverty during each decade between 1939 and 1988 except one. During the 1970s, the large decline in dependent sibsize can account for a reduction of 4 percentage points in the rate of relative childhood poverty. Although the racial gap in dependent sibsizes first increased then decreased between 1939 and 1988, at both the beginning and the end of the era, when the racial gaps in relative poverty rates were 40 and 30 percentage points, respectively, the racial gaps in dependent sibsizes accounted for a small and nearly identical 2–4 percentage points in the racial gaps in relative poverty. In 1979 and 1988 the dependent sibsizes of Hispanic children (of any race) were similar to those of non-Hispanic black children, with similar consequences for relative poverty.

Of course, as has been noted throughout the chapter, these results concerning the extent to which changes in relative poverty can be accounted for by changes in income from fathers, mothers, other family members, welfare, and dependent sibsize provide no indication of how these changes may have influenced one another, or of how other social and economic trends may have influenced these changes. Instead, the results provide a simple accounting of the extent to which these factors became more or less important in reducing the rates of childhood relative poverty between various points in time, given the social, economic, and familial changes that actually occurred. In the next chapter we will turn our attention to the subject of how these changes and other social and economic trends discussed in earlier chapters appear to have influenced one another since the Great Depression.

TABLE A-9.1

Changes for Children in Official Poverty, Parents' Income, and Government Welfare: 1939–1988

All Children Annual Official Poverty Rates and Effects	Census 1939	Census 1949	Census 1959	Census 1969	Census 1979	CPS 1979	CPS 1988
Poverty rates							
Based on Father's Income Only	80.6	57.4	37.3	29.2	33.8	34.2	38.8
Effect of Mother's Income	-1.6	—	-5.1	-6.4	-10.2	-10.1	-12.9
Effect of Other Relative's Income	-5.4	—	-4.7	-4.7	-5.1	-4.9	-4.0
Effect of Government Welfare	-1.0	—	-1.7	-1.9	-2.2	-3.0	-2.3
Actual Official Poverty Rate	71.8	47.6	25.8	16.1	16.3	16.2	19.7

All Children Official Poverty Rate Change and Effects Across Decades	Census 1939–1959	Census 1959–1969	Census 1969–1979	CPS 1979–1988
Change in Official Poverty Rates				
Based on Father's Income Only	-43.3	-8.1	4.6	4.6
Effect of Mother's Income	-3.5	-1.3	-3.8	-2.8
Effect of Other Relative's Income	0.7	0.0	-0.4	0.9
Effect of Government Welfare	-0.7	-0.2	-0.3	0.7
Actual Official Poverty Rate	-46.0	-9.7	0.2	3.5

Children in Two-Parent Families Annual Official Poverty Rates and Effects	Census 1939	Census 1949	Census 1959	Census 1969	Census 1979	CPS 1979	CPS 1988
Poverty Rates							
Based on Father's Income Only	77.2	51.8	29.6	16.4	16.5	15.7	19.0
Effect of Mother's Income	-1.6	—	-3.9	-3.6	-5.0	-4.7	-7.3
Effect of Other Relative's Income	-4.4	—	-2.6	-1.8	-1.4	-1.7	-1.1
Effect of Government Welfare	-1.0	—	-1.9	-0.8	-1.2	-1.4	-1.2
Actual Official Poverty Rate	69.3	43.9	21.2	10.2	8.9	8.0	9.4

TABLE A-9.1 (*continued*)

Children in Two-Parent Families Official Poverty Rate Change and Effects Across Decades

	Census 1939–1959	Census 1959–1969	Census 1969–1979	CPS 1979–1988
Change in Official Poverty Rates				
Based on Father's Income Only	−47.6	−13.2	0.1	3.3
Effect of Mother's Income	−2.3	0.3	−1.5	−2.6
Effect of Other Relative's Income	1.8	0.8	0.4	0.6
Effect of Government Welfare	−0.9	1.1	−0.4	0.2
Actual Official Poverty Rate	−48.1	−11.0	−1.3	1.4

Children in Mother-Only Families Annual Official Poverty Rates and Effects

	Census 1939	Census 1949	Census 1959	Census 1969	Census 1979	CPS 1979	CPS 1988
Poverty rates							
Based on Mother's Income Only	96.1	81.7	81.6	71.1	61.7	63.7	64.9
Effect of Other Relative's Income	−5.5	—	−12.4	−11.7	−10.0	−7.8	−8.1
Effect of Government Welfare	−1.0	—	−4.4	−8.5	−6.2	−8.8	−4.7
Actual Official Poverty Rate	89.5	76.6	64.8	50.9	45.5	47.2	52.1

Children in Mother-Only Families Official Poverty Rate Change and Effects Across Decades

	Census 1939–1959	Census 1959–1969	Census 1969–1979	CPS 1979–1988
Change in Official Poverty Rates				
Based on Mother's Income Only	−14.5	−10.5	−9.4	1.2
Effect of Other Relative's Income	−6.9	0.7	1.7	−0.3
Effect of Government Welfare	−3.4	−4.1	2.3	4.1
Actual Official Poverty Rate	−24.7	−13.9	−5.4	4.9

SOURCES: Estimates derived from 1940–1980 census PUMs and March CPS for 1980 and 1989.

NOTES: Government welfare income is income obtained by family from Aid to Families with Dependent Children (AFDC) or Social Security programs. All other income is assigned to recipient within family. See Chapters 7, 8, and 11 for additional discussion of welfare income, measurement of official poverty, etc. Estimates for 1939 are approximate. See Footnote 8, Chapter 8, Footnote 1.

TABLE A-9.2

Official Poverty by Dependent Sibsizes for Children: 1939–1988

Official Poverty Rates by Sibsize

Age	Census 1939	Census 1949	Census 1959	Census 1969	Census 1979	CPS 1979	CPS 1988
All Children 0–17							
Number of dependent siblings							
1–2	58.1	33.6	16.6	10.9	12.4	11.7	14.9
3–4	80.9	52.9	22.4	13.8	18.7	19.6	25.4
5+	94.7	84.4	54.0	34.0	38.8	39.0	48.6
Total	72.2	47.6	25.8	16.1	16.3	16.2	19.7
All Children 0–17 in Two-Parent Families							
Number of dependent siblings							
1–2	53.8	26.4	10.5	5.0	5.4	4.4	5.7
3–4	80.3	50.7	18.3	8.4	11.0	10.2	13.4
5+	94.5	83.6	50.3	26.5	27.2	27.1	32.7
Total	70.9	43.9	21.2	10.2	8.9	8.0	9.4
All Children 0–17 in Mother-Only Families							
Number of dependent siblings							
1–2	80.3	66.2	45.8	33.2	33.6	34.1	40.5
3–4	95.1	84.2	73.4	55.8	57.8	62.1	70.3
5+	97.8	98.3	93.5	77.6	84.1	82.6	94.6
Total	86.2	76.6	64.8	50.9	45.5	47.2	52.1

SOURCE: Estimates derived from 1940–1980 census PUMs and March CPS for 1980 and 1989.

NOTE: See Chapters 7, 8, and 11 for additional discussion of measurement of official poverty, etc. Dependent siblings are all siblings aged 0–17 (including the child) who live in the child's home. Estimates for 1939 are not adjusted.

TABLE A-9.3

Changes for White and Black Children in Official Poverty, Parents' Income, Government Welfare: 1939–1988

All Children Annual Official Poverty Rates and Effects	Census 1939	Census 1949	Census 1959	Census 1969	Census 1979	CPS 1979	CPS 1988
White							
Official poverty rates							
based on father's income only	78.1	52.6	31.0	22.9	27.7	27.8	32.7
Effect of mother's income	-1.8	—	-4.9	-5.8	-9.3	-9.4	-12.0
Effect of other relative's income	-5.9	—	-4.1	-4.0	-4.1	-4.1	-3.4
Effect of government welfare	-1.0	—	-1.8	-1.5	-1.8	-2.3	-2.0
Actual official poverty rate	68.6	42.2	20.2	11.6	12.5	11.9	15.3
Black							
Official poverty rates							
based on father's income only	99.8	93.7	81.7	68.4	68.1	71.2	72.3
Effect of mother's income	-0.5	—	-6.0	-10.0	-15.6	-14.1	-17.8
Effect of other relative's income	-1.0	—	-8.2	-9.1	-10.3	-9.3	-7.2
Effect of government welfare	-0.5	—	-2.3	-4.5	-4.6	-7.1	-3.5
Actual official poverty rate	97.2	87.7	65.2	44.8	37.6	40.8	43.8

All Children Official Poverty Rate Change and Effects Across Decades	Census 1939–1959	Census 1959–1969	Census 1969–1979	CPS 1979–1988
White				
Change in official poverty rates				
based on father's income only	-47.1	-8.1	4.8	4.9
Effect of mother's income	-3.1	-0.9	-3.5	-2.6
Effect of other relative's income	1.8	0.1	-0.1	0.7
Effect of government welfare	-0.8	0.3	-0.3	0.3
Actual official poverty rate	-48.4	-8.6	0.9	3.3
Black				
Change in official poverty rates				
based on father's income only	-18.1	-13.3	-0.3	1.1
Effect of mother's income	-5.5	-4.0	-5.6	-3.7
Effect of other relative's income	-7.2	-0.9	-1.2	2.1
Effect of government welfare	1.8	-2.2	-0.1	3.6
Actual official poverty rate	-32.0	-20.4	-7.2	3.4

TABLE A-9.3 (continued)

Children in Two-Parent Families Annual Official Poverty Rates and Effects	Census 1939	Census 1949	Census 1959	Census 1969	Census 1979	CPS 1979	CPS 1988
White							
Official poverty rates							
based on father's income only	75.1	47.9	24.9	13.1	14.6	14.0	17.8
Effect of mother's income	-1.7	—	-3.6	-3.0	-4.3	-4.2	-6.6
Effect of other relative's income	-4.7	—	-2.4	-1.5	-1.3	-1.5	-1.2
Effect of government welfare	-1.0	—	-1.8	-0.7	-1.1	-1.2	-1.2
Actual official poverty rate	66.8	39.6	17.1	7.9	8.0	7.1	8.9
Black							
Official poverty rates							
based on father's income only	99.2	91.0	73.9	47.5	35.8	34.8	32.8
Effect of mother's income	-0.7	—	-7.1	-9.1	-12.7	-9.3	-15.0
Effect of other relative's income	-1.3	—	-5.0	-4.3	-3.1	-4.0	-0.7
Effect of government welfare	-0.5	—	-2.7	-2.3	-2.0	-3.3	-1.5
Actual official poverty rate	96.1	86.5	60.0	31.9	18.0	18.3	15.6

Children in Two-Parent Families Official Poverty Rate Change and Effects Across Decades	Census 1939–1959	Census 1959–1969	Census 1969–1979	CPS 1979–1988
White				
Change in official poverty rates				
based on father's income only	-50.2	-11.8	1.5	3.8
Effect of mother's income	-1.9	0.6	-1.3	-2.4
Effect of other relative's income	2.3	0.9	0.2	0.3
Effect of government welfare	-0.8	1.1	-0.4	0.0
Actual official poverty rate	-49.7	-9.2	0.1	1.8
Black				
Change in official poverty rates				
based on father's income only	-25.3	-26.4	-11.7	-2.0
Effect of mother's income	-6.4	-2.0	-3.6	-5.7
Effect of other relative's income	-3.7	0.7	1.2	3.3
Effect of government welfare	-2.2	0.4	0.3	1.8
Actual official poverty rate	-36.1	-28.1	-13.9	-2.7

TABLE A-9.3 (continued)

Children in Mother-Only Families / Annual Official Poverty Rates and Effects	Census 1939	Census 1949	Census 1959	Census 1969	Census 1979	CPS 1979	CPS 1988
White							
Official poverty rates							
based on mother's income only	95.0	77.2	75.7	63.6	53.6	56.3	58.1
Effect of other relative's income	−5.0	—	−14.5	−12.5	−9.6	−8.8	−8.1
Effect of government welfare	−0.5	—	−4.7	−8.7	−5.9	−8.7	−5.2
Actual official poverty rate	87.3	71.0	56.5	42.5	38.0	38.8	44.8
Black							
Official poverty rates							
based on mother's income only	100.0	94.9	94.3	84.6	76.0	76.9	76.4
Effect of other relative's income	−1.3	—	−7.8	−10.2	−10.7	−6.0	−8.0
Effect of government welfare	−0.1	—	−3.2	−8.3	−6.7	−8.8	−3.9
Actual official poverty rate	98.6	93.1	83.3	66.2	58.5	62.1	64.5

Children in Mother-Only Families / Official Poverty Rate Change and Effects Across Decades	Census 1939–1959	Census 1959–1969	Census 1969–1979	CPS 1979–1988
White				
Official poverty rates				
based on mother's income only	−19.3	−12.1	−10.0	1.8
Effect of other relative's income	−9.5	2.0	2.8	0.7
Effect of government welfare	−4.2	−4.0	−0.3	3.5
Actual official poverty rate	−30.8	−14.0	−4.5	6.0
Black				
Official poverty rates				
based on mother's income only	−5.7	−9.7	−8.6	−0.5
Effect of other relative's income	−6.5	−2.4	−0.5	−2.0
Effect of government welfare	−3.1	−5.1	1.6	4.9
Actual official poverty rate	−15.3	−17.1	−7.7	2.4

SOURCE: Estimates derived from 1940–1980 census PUMs and March CPS for 1980 and 1989.

NOTES: Government welfare income is income obtained by family from Aid to Families with Dependent Children (AFDC) or Social Security programs. All other income is assigned to recipient within family. See Chapters 7, 8, and 11 for additional discussion of welfare income, measurement of official poverty, etc. Estimates for 1939 are approximate. See footnote 9 and Chapter 8, Footnote 1.

TABLE A-9.4

Official Poverty by Dependent Sibsizes for White and Black Children: 1939–1988

	Official Poverty Rates by Sibsize						
Age	Census 1939	Census 1949	Census 1959	Census 1969	Census 1979	CPS 1979	CPS 1988
All Children 0–17							
White							
Number of dependent siblings							
1–2	54.6	29.0	13.2	8.2	9.6	8.7	11.5
3–4	79.2	49.0	18.7	10.5	14.9	14.9	20.0
5+	93.8	80.1	45.6	24.2	29.9	29.6	41.9
Total	69.4	42.2	20.2	11.6	12.5	11.9	15.3
Black							
Number of dependent siblings							
1–2	94.0	78.5	48.5	31.6	30.3	31.7	35.4
3–4	97.8	89.7	58.4	40.8	40.8	46.4	53.7
5+	99.6	97.9	85.2	63.6	59.6	66.6	66.4
Total	96.7	87.7	65.2	44.8	37.6	40.8	43.8
All Children 0–17 in Two-Parent Families							
White							
Number of dependent siblings							
1–2	51.6	24.1	9.2	4.4	5.1	4.1	5.4
3–4	78.7	47.2	15.8	7.0	9.9	8.9	12.9
5+	93.6	79.5	40.9	19.7	24.4	24.9	30.8
Total	68.6	39.6	17.1	7.9	8.0	7.1	8.9
Black							
Number of dependent siblings							
1–2	90.8	68.0	32.1	12.3	8.9	9.1	9.0
3–4	97.3	89.8	49.1	24.4	20.8	23.0	18.3
5+	99.5	97.6	83.1	54.0	37.7	40.4	42.1
Total	96.1	86.5	60.0	31.9	18.0	18.3	15.6

TABLE A-9.4 (continued)

Official Poverty Rates by Sibsize

Age	Census 1939	Census 1949	Census 1959	Census 1969	Census 1979	CPS 1979	CPS 1988
All Children 0–17 in Mother-Only Families							
White							
Number of dependent siblings							
1–2	76.7	60.7	41.4	29.1	28.1	28.6	35.5
3–4	93.6	82.4	66.9	49.1	52.9	55.9	62.3
5+	96.4	96.7	89.4	68.4	78.6	75.2	98.7
Total	82.8	71.0	56.5	42.5	38.0	38.8	44.8
Black							
Number of dependent siblings							
1–2	97.0	90.2	63.1	44.0	46.1	47.4	51.2
3–4	100.0	89.6	87.1	68.6	65.3	71.0	80.2
5+	100.0	100.0	97.0	85.4	87.1	86.2	91.2
Total	98.5	93.1	83.3	66.2	58.5	62.1	64.5

SOURCE: Estimates derived from 1940–1980 census PUMs and March CPS for 1980 and 1989.

NOTE: See Chapters 7, 8, and 11 for additional discussion of measurement of official poverty, etc. Dependent siblings are all siblings aged 0–17 (including the child) who live in the child's home. Estimates for 1939 are not adjusted.

TABLE A-9.5

Official Poverty, Parents' Income, Government Welfare, and Dependent Sibsizes, by Hispanic Origin: 1979–1988

Annual Official Poverty Rates and Effects 1980 Census	Non-Hispanic		Total Hispanic	Hispanic Living with Mother	
	White	Black		Old Family	First Generation
All Children					
Official poverty rates					
based on father's income only	25.1	67.8	51.7	48.3	49.4
Effect of mother's income	−9.1	−15.6	−10.8	−10.7	−13.8
Effect of other relative's income	−3.8	−10.3	−7.4	−4.1	−4.6
Effect of government welfare	−1.7	−4.6	−3.1	−3.1	−2.6
Actual official poverty rate	10.6	37.3	30.4	30.5	28.5
Two-Parent Families					
Official poverty rates					
based on father's income only	12.7	35.5	34.4	29.6	42.0
Effect of mother's income	−3.9	−12.8	−7.9	−5.7	−11.4
Effect of other relative's income	−1.1	−3.0	−3.2	−3.1	−3.4
Effect of government welfare	−1.0	−2.1	−1.7	−1.6	−1.9
Actual official poverty rate	6.7	17.6	21.5	19.2	25.2
Mother-Only Families					
Official poverty rates					
based on mother's income only	49.5	76.2	74.5	75.6	70.3
Effect of other relative's income	−9.9	−10.8	−8.0	−6.9	−12.7
Effect of government welfare	−5.7	−6.8	−7.0	−7.0	−7.0
Actual official poverty rate	33.9	58.6	59.5	61.7	50.7

TABLE A-9.5 (*continued*)

Annual Official Poverty Rates and Effects 1980 and 1989 CPS	Non-Hispanic				Hispanic	
	White		Black			
	1979 CPS	1988 CPS	1979 CPS	1988 CPS	1979 CPS	1988 CPS
All Children						
Official poverty rates based on father's income only	25.6	28.7	71.3	72.3	47.9	60.2
Effect of mother's income	−9.3	−11.9	−14.2	−17.7	−10.4	−12.5
Effect of other relative's income	−3.9	−2.9	−9.3	−7.2	−6.3	−6.5
Effect of government welfare	−2.2	−1.9	−7.1	−3.5	−3.4	−3.3
Actual official poverty rate	10.2	12.0	40.7	43.8	27.8	37.9
Two-Parent Families						
Official poverty rates based on father's income only	12.3	14.8	34.6	32.9	31.9	42.6
Effect of mother's income	−3.9	−6.1	−9.4	−15.1	−8.6	−10.8
Effect of other relative's income	−1.3	−0.8	−4.0	−0.6	−3.7	−4.0
Effect of government welfare	−1.1	−1.1	−3.3	−1.5	−1.9	−2.2
Actual official poverty rate	6.0	6.8	18.0	15.7	18.6	25.7
Mother-Only Families						
Official poverty rates based on mother's income only	53.0	51.7	76.9	76.6	76.1	80.8
Effect of other relative's income	−9.3	−8.1	−6.0	−8.0	−5.7	−8.4
Effect of government welfare	−8.9	−5.4	−8.8	−4.0	−8.0	−4.3
Actual official poverty rate	34.8	38.3	62.1	64.7	62.4	68.1

1979–1988 Change	All Children			Two-Parent Families			Mother-Only Families		
	White	Black	Hispanic	White	Black	Hispanic	White	Black	Hispanic
Change in official poverty rates based on father's income only	3.0	1.0	12.4	0.3	−7.5	7.6	−1.3	−0.3	4.7
Effect of mother's income	−2.7	−3.6	−2.1	0.5	3.4	−0.3			
Effect of other relative's income	1.0	2.1	−0.2	0.0	1.8	−0.3	1.2	−1.9	−2.7
Effect of government welfare	0.4	3.6	0.1	0.9	−2.3	7.0	3.4	4.8	3.7
Actual official poverty rate	1.7	3.1	10.0	0.0	0.0	0.0	3.4	2.6	5.7

TABLE A-9.5 (continued)

Official Poverty Rates by Sibsize	Non-Hispanic				Hispanic	
	White		Black			
	1979 CPS	1988 CPS	1979 CPS	1988 CPS	1979 CPS	1988 CPS
All Children						
Number of dependent siblings						
1–2	7.6	9.7	31.8	35.6	20.9	27.9
3–4	13.1	15.3	46.3	53.4	28.5	44.2
5+	23.7	31.2	66.6	66.3	51.3	66.9
Total	10.2	12.0	40.7	43.8	27.8	37.9
Two-Parent Families						
Number of dependent siblings						
1–2	3.6	4.5	9.1	9.0	10.4	15.5
3–4	7.9	10.0	22.4	18.4	18.0	30.9
5+	19.6	22.6	40.3	42.1	45.9	54.5
Total	5.9	6.8	18.0	15.7	18.6	25.7
Mother-Only Families						
Number of dependent siblings						
1–2	25.7	31.7	47.4	51.5	53.1	53.9
3–4	53.2	54.0	70.8	80.0	67.8	81.2
5+	69.7	97.4	86.1	91.1	87.3	100.0
Total	34.8	38.3	62.1	64.7	62.4	68.1

SOURCE: Estimates derived from 1980 Census PUMs and March CPS for 1980 and 1989.

NOTES: Government welfare income is income obtained by family from Aid to Families with Dependent Children (AFDC) or Social Security programs. All other income is assigned to recipient within family. See Chapters 7, 8, and 11 for additional discussion of welfare income, measurement of official poverty, etc. Dependent siblings are all siblings aged 0–17 (including the child) who live in the child's home.

10

FATHERS' INCOMES,
MOTHERS' INCOMES,
AND MOTHER-ONLY FAMILIES

Introduction

EARLIER chapters discussed profound changes in the lives of children that were associated with major trends in (1) family size and composition, (2) parents' education, work, and income, and (3) child care arrangements and childhood poverty. We also sometimes identified the important relationships that link these trends. In this chapter we will focus broadly on the ways in which these and other trends are related by exploring the reasons for changes in fathers' incomes, reasons for the rise of mothers' labor-force participation, and reasons for the rise in mother-only families. Our goal is to make sense of these trends from the perspective of children and their parents. In a single chapter, it is not possible to provide a complete and richly detailed explanation of the many historic changes discussed here. Our more limited purpose is to portray with a broad brush some of the fundamental causes of these changes.

Fathers' Incomes and Childhood Poverty

Since the poverty rate among children reflects the extent to which they are living in material deprivation, it is important to understand why changes have occurred in childhood poverty since the Great Depression. We have seen that the sharp drop in childhood poverty that occurred after the Great Depression was followed by a slower decline and then by a turnaround and an increase, and that changes in childhood poverty generally mirrored changes in fathers' incomes (Chapters 7 and 9). Part of the explanation for changes in childhood poverty, then, lies in the explanation of changes in fathers' incomes.

Much of the 11 percentage point drop that occurred in the relative poverty rate for children between 1939 and 1949 can be attributed to the 9 percentage point drop in the proportion of children whose fathers were unemployed (Chapter 4). Subsequently, the postwar economic boom brought, from the perspective of children, large increases in the absolute incomes of fathers and families, as well as greater equality in the distribution in fathers' incomes and hence a continuing decline in relative poverty (Chapters 7 and 9). The postwar economic boom and the associated rise in relative incomes also appear to have contributed to the postwar baby boom between 1946 and 1964 (Chapter 2).

But between 1969 and 1979, the rise in the proportion of children whose fathers' incomes were below the relative poverty threshold contributed to the rise in the relative poverty rate for children, and between 1979 and 1988 both the relative and the official poverty rates for children increased with relative and absolute declines in fathers' incomes for children in the bottom half of the income distribution. These post-1969 increases in the proportion of children whose fathers had comparatively low incomes resulted, no doubt, from many factors, but one of the most prominent demographic factors was that the baby boomers were entering adulthood.

When rapid increases occur in the number of persons who are available to work in the economy, competition for available jobs tends to increase, and employers can more easily hire workers who are willing to work for comparatively low pay. As a result, wages and salaries tend to increase more slowly or to decline, compared with times of slower growth in the pool of persons who are available to work. When children born during the high-fertility, postwar baby boom reached working age, they represented a large pool of potential workers. Between 1946 and 1964, the average annual number of births was 45 percent larger than it had been during the preceding 37 years (3.99 million vs. 2.75 million). Baby boomers began to enter the labor force during the early 1960s.

Using 1960 as the starting point, the total labor force increased by 18.3 percent as of 1970 and by an additional 36.0 percent as of 1980. But if the baby-boom cohorts had been similar to earlier cohorts in size, the total labor force would have increased by only 10.9 percent as of 1970 and by an additional 2.6 percent as of 1980. Hence, increased births during the baby boom accounted for about two-fifths of the large labor-force increase during the 1960s and for more than nine-tenths of the even larger increase during the 1970s.[1]

Overall, then, the total labor-force increase after 1960 was 18.3 percent by 1970 and 54.3 percent by 1980. In comparison, using 1940 as the starting point, the total labor force increased by only 10.4 percent as of 1950 and by only 28.4 percent as of 1960. Since the rate by which the total labor force expanded between 1960 and 1980 was nearly double the expansion rate that occurred between 1940 and 1960, and since the influx of the baby-boom cohorts accounts for this doubling, it seems likely that intensified competition for jobs, especially beginning-level jobs for new labor-market entrants, contributed to the sharp post-1959 slowdown and subsequent stagnation in family income growth, and to the stagnation and subsequent deterioration in fathers' relative incomes for children in the bottom half of the income distribution.

Using a detailed study of men's incomes between 1947 and 1977, but especially between 1959 and 1969, Valerie Kincade Oppenheimer has concluded that relative cohort size does appear to have been an important factor influencing changes in the relative incomes of young men.[2] However, she also cites two other factors that contributed to the decline in the relative incomes of young men and that made it unlikely that the smaller baby-bust cohorts subsequently would experience increases in relative income when they entered the labor force after 1980.[3] First, the historic increase in educational attainments (Chapter 6) involves a later age of entry into comparatively permanent occupational commitments and a shift toward occupations in which entry-level earnings are relatively low compared with earnings for older men. Second, various institutional and legal changes provided greater job and income security to older workers through measures that favored seniority and reduced age discrimination.

It should be noted, however, that not all of the baby-boom rise in the labor force was due to a sheer increase in cohort size; part of it was due to the fact that female baby boomers had much higher labor-force participation rates than did earlier generations of young women. Be-

---

[1]The number of labor force participants aged 16–23 in 1970 (baby boomers born between 1946 and 1953) is subtracted from the number of labor force participants aged 16–23 in 1960 to estimate the labor force increase between 1960 and 1970 that is due to the baby boom. Similarly, the number of labor force participants aged 16–34 in 1980 (baby boomers born between 1945 and 1964) is subtracted from the number aged 16–34 in 1960 to get an estimate of the labor force increase between 1960 and 1980 that is due to the baby boom. Age 34 is used as the upper age limit in the latter estimate because of the availability of published data.

[2]Valerie Kincade Oppenheimer, *Work and the Family* (New York: Academic, 1982), pp. 121–122.

[3]Oppenheimer, pp. 99–103.

tween 1960 and 1980, the proportion of women aged 16–34 who worked in the labor force jumped from 40.3 percent to 61.1 percent. If the labor-force participation rate for women aged 16–34 had remained constant between 1960 and 1980, the total labor force would have increased by about 43 percent instead of the actual 54 percent. Later in this chapter we will discuss reasons for the post-Depression increase in labor-force participation rates among women, particularly mothers.

Increasing immigration to the United States represents another potential source of workers. As a result of immigration, the labor force increased by about 1.9 million between 1940 and 1960 and by about 3.2 million between 1960 and 1980.[4] Compared with the period from 1940 to 1960, then, the next two decades of immigration brought 1.3 million additional workers. Since the total labor force grew by about 36.8 million between 1960 and 1980, an *increased number of immigrants after 1960* accounted for about 3–4 percentage points of the overall 54 percentage point increase in the labor force between 1960 and 1980. Hence, increasing immigration after 1960 may also have contributed to increasing job competition, but increased immigration was small compared with the increased size of birth cohorts associated with the baby boom.[5]

Parents' Work and Mother-Only Families

The rise of mother-only families represents a second historic change in the lives of children (Chapters 3, 5, 8, and 9). By 1989, about one-fifth

[4]These crude estimates are derived from estimates of net civilian immigration obtained from Table 6, Frederick W. Hollmann, U.S. Bureau of the Census, Current Population Reports, Series P-25, No. 1045, *United States Population Estimates by Age, Sex, Race and Hispanic Origin: 1980 to 1989* (Washington, DC: U.S. Government Printing Office, 1990). Estimates for the 1940s, 1950s, 1960s, and 1970s are obtained from the years 1940–1949, 1949–1959, 1959–1969, and 1969–1979. The total for 1940–1949 is adjusted to a 10-year interval through multiplication by 10/9. Years ending in 9 are used as the end of each decade, because during such years immigrants are potentially available for work during the following year. Labor-force participation rates for immigrants are assumed to be 40 percent, a figure that is close to the corresponding estimate for the United States as a whole throughout the era. Insofar as immigrants are slightly more concentrated in the main working ages than are nonimmigrants, these estimates may slightly underestimate the labor force participation of immigrants.

[5]All of these estimates are somewhat crude. Insofar as immigrants are concentrated in the young working ages, a small portion of actual "immigrant effect" is incorrectly assigned here to the "baby-boom effect." The size of such an error, however, is unlikely to be more than a few percentage points of the growth in the labor force between 1960 and 1980. Total post-1960 immigration accounted for about 9 percent of the labor force increase that occurred between 1960 and 1980, compared with 13 percent between 1940 and 1960. Census data for 1990, at least for Hispanics, suggest that these estimates of immigrants for the 1980s are somewhat too low.

of children lived in mother-only families; of these, 63 percent lived with divorced or separated mothers, 31 percent lived with never-married mothers, and only 6 percent lived with widowed mothers.[6] Hence, to explain most of the post-Depression rise in mother-only families, we must explain the historic, long-term increase in divorce rates that had begun by 1860.

Kingsley Davis has argued that changes in the conditions of life associated with the Industrial Revolution were ultimately responsible for the long-term rise in divorce. Specifically, Davis argues that the rise in divorce can be traced to the rise in the breadwinner-homemaker family, which involved the shift to production outside the home (Chapter 4): "With this shift, husband and wife . . . were no longer bound together in a close face-to-face division of labor in a common enterprise (farming).[7] On farms, husbands and wives were deeply mutually-dependent on each other, because each contributed large amounts of labor to their common enterprise. But this mutual dependence weakened greatly off the farm, because a husband could, if he desired, depend on his own work alone for his income. Freed from rural and small-town social controls censuring divorce, this weakening of economic interdependence fostered the historic rise in divorce.

As we will see in the following section, rising divorce, in turn, contributed to the increase in working wives because, for wives, work during marriage represents a hedge against the possible loss of their husbands' incomes through divorce. At the same time, the growing need for wives and families to increase their relative economic standing through wives' paid employment further separates family members, because ". . . it puts both husband and wife in the labor market—not together, as in the household (farm) economy, but separately."[8] Thus wives, like husbands, increasingly had independent incomes from their own jobs, contributing further to increased divorce. Consequently, the dramatic jump in divorce between the mid-1960s and late 1970s may be both a cause and a consequence of the equally dramatic jump during these years of dual-earner families (Chapter 4).

From the perspective of children, economic insecurity and need also appear to have contributed to the rise in separations and divorces that have occurred since at least the mid-1960s. Economic recessions since the mid-1960s have involved both increases in unemployment and drops

---

[6]Arlene F. Saluter, U.S. Bureau of the Census, Current Population Reports, Series P-20, No. 445, *Marital Status and Living Arrangements; March 1989* (Washington, DC: U.S. Government Printing Office, 1990), Tables 5 and 6.

[7]Kingsley Davis, "Wives and Work: The Sex Role Revolution and Its Consequences," *Population and Development Review* 10, 3 (1984): 410.

[8]Davis, p. 414.

in median family income for married-couple families—that is, income drops for families that are near the middle of the income distribution.[9] But research by Glen H. Elder, Jr., and his colleagues, for example, has found that the consequences of economic recessions for specific families, such as instability in husbands' work, a drop in family income, and a low ratio of family income-to-needs can in turn lead to increased hostility between husbands and wives, decreased marital quality, and increased risk of divorce.[10] It is not surprising, then, to find that during economic recessions since the mid-1960s, comparatively large jumps have occurred in the average annual increase in the proportion of "own children" living in mother-only families.[11]

In the nonrecession years of 1968 and 1969, the proportion of children living in mother-only families increased by .34 percentage points per year, but the 1970 recession brought a doubling of this increase to .66 percentage points during 1970 and 1971. The increase that occurred during the subsequent nonrecession years of 1972 and 1973 remained at .65 percentage points per year, then the recession of 1974 and 1975 brought another jump in the increase to .92 percentage points per year. During the subsequent nonrecession years of 1976 through 1979, the increase in mother-only families fell by two-thirds (to only .35 percentage points per year, a level equal to that for the nonrecession years of 1968 and 1969), but the recessions of 1980 and 1982 brought a doubling of the increase (to .61 percentage points per year). Finally, during the most recent nonrecession years of 1983 through 1988, the increase in mother-only families dropped again by two-thirds (to only .19 percentage points per year).

These results suggest that recession-induced economic insecurity

[9]For trends in median income for married-couple families, see Arlene F. Saluter, U.S. Bureau of the Census, Current Population Reports, Series P-23, No. 163, *Changes in American Family Life* (Washington, DC: U.S. Government Printing Office, 1989), Figure 20, and for changes during recessionary periods, see Carman DeNavas and Edward J. Welniak, Jr., U.S. Bureau of the Census, Current Population Reports, Series P-60, No. 174 *Money Income of Households, Families, and Persons in the United States: 1990* (Washington, DC: U.S. Government Printing Office, 1991), Figure 5.

[10]Rand D. Conger, et. al, "Linking Economic Hardship to Marital Quality and Instability," *Journal of Marriage and the Family* 52 (August 1990): 643–656; Glen H. Elder, Jr., E. Michael Foster, and Rand D. Conger, "Families Under Economic Pressure" (presented at the 1990 annual meeting of the American Sociological Association); and Jeffrey K. Liker and Glen H. Elder, Jr., "Economic Hardship and Marital Relations in the 1930s," *American Sociological Review* 48 (1983): 343–359.

[11]Estimates of the increases in mother-only families for "own" children are derived from Table 4: "Household Relationship and Presence of Parents, for Persons Under 18 Years, by Age, Sex, Race, and Spanish Origin," from various years of Arlene F. Saluter, U.S. Bureau of the Census, Current Population Reports, Series P-20, *Marital Status and Living Arrangements* (Washington, DC: U.S. Government Printing Office). These particular data were used because they provide the longest available annual time series concerning the detailed family living arrangements of children.

may have contributed substantially to the large rise in mother-only families between the mid-1960s and the early 1980s. We may calculate a rough estimate of the size of the recession effect for children by assuming that without each recession the average annual increase in mother-only families would have been the same during recession years as during the immediately preceding nonrecessionary period.

Based on this assumption, recessions appear to account for 30 percent of the total increase in mother-only families for children between 1968 and 1988—that is, 3.2 percentage points of the total 10.7 percentage point increase. Similar calculations for children in mother-only families with never-married mothers indicate that about 14 percent of the increase between 1970 and 1988 was recession-induced—that is, 0.8 percentage points of the total 6.0 percentage point increase. Hence, these results suggest that without recession-induced increases, the proportion of children living in mother-only families with separated, divorced, or widowed mothers might have increased by only 2.1 percentage points (less than one-half of the actual increase of 4.5 percentage points that occurred between 1970 and 1988).

Mothers' Work and Incomes

The rise in mothers who work outside the home for pay represents a third historic change in the lives of children—one that has important implications both for the day-to-day care of children and for family income and poverty levels (Chapters 4, 5, and 9). Other historic changes in the family and economy appear to have fostered the rise in mothers' labor-force participation.

Between the early years of the Industrial Revolution and about 1940, two important ways in which couples sought to maintain or improve their relative economic standing were by having husbands work in comparatively well-paid jobs in the growing urban-industrial economy and by limiting their family size so that available family income could be spread less thinly among ever-smaller families (see Chapters 2 and 4). For example, during the half century between the 1880s and the 1930s, the proportion of Americans who lived on farms dropped by nearly one-half (from 44 to 25 percent), and the average number of children born to ever-married women also dropped by one-half (from 4.9 to 2.4 children).[12]

[12]The proportions of children who lived on farms pertain to 1880 and 1930. U.S. Bureau of the Census, *Historical Statistics of the United States, Colonial Times to 1970, Bicentennial Edition, Part 1* (Washington, DC: U.S. Government Printing Office, 1975),

In addition, as higher educational attainments became more widespread, they also became increasingly necessary in order to obtain a comparatively high-paying job. Hence, advanced education became an increasingly important third avenue to maintaining or improving one's relative economic status. As we saw in Chapter 5, with the shift from farming to industrial jobs, with child labor and compulsory education laws, and with rising affluence, the proportion of days in the year that children aged 7–14 spent in school more than doubled between 1870 and 1930 (from 15 to 38 percent). For increasing proportions of young persons, full-time work was further postponed by high school and college attendance. For example, between 1870 and 1940, new high school graduates as a proportion of persons aged 17 increased from 2 to 49 percent, and college students as a proportion of the population aged 18–24 increased from 1 to 9 percent.[13]

By 1940, then, for many couples two of the major avenues to maintaining or improving their relative economic status had run their course— only 23 percent of Americans lived on farms, and 70 percent of parents had only one or two dependent children in the home. In addition, since most men and women reach their highest educational attainments during early adulthood, by age 25, about 40 years of potential labor force participation remain once adults have completed their schooling. Hence, for most parents after 1940, the main avenue available for maintaining or sharply improving the family's relative economic status after age 25 was for the wife to enter paid employment outside the home.

Equally important, perhaps, movement off the farm and increasing school enrollment of children implied a sharp constriction in the role of mothers as providers of personal and economic support—that is, both as child care providers for their children and as family farm laborers (see Chapter 5). Under these conditions, as Kingsley Davis argues, "[a] woman who is at home full-time and yet has only one to three children who are at school most of the day has less than a full-time vocation."[14] Moreover, by 1940 young women were often as highly educated as young men, since they accounted for 53 percent of all high school graduates and 41 percent of all bachelor's or first professional degrees from institutions of higher education in that year.[15] Between 1880 and 1940, then,

---

(Series K 2); U.S. Bureau of the Census, *Statistical Abstract of the United States: 1989* (109th ed.) (Washington, DC: U.S. Government Printing Office, 1989), Tables 2 and 1077; and Kingsley Davis, "Wives and Work: The Sex Role Revolution and Its Consequences," *Population and Development Review* 10, 3 (1984): 408.

[13]U.S. Bureau of the Census, *Historical Statistics*, Series H 599 and H 707.

[14]Davis, p. 408.

[15]U.S. Bureau of the Census, *Historical Statistics*, Series H 598–601 and H 752–754.

mothers represented an increasingly available and well-educated pool of potential employees.

Hence, by 1940, for many couples and mothers over age 25, mothers' work for pay outside the home had become both the main potential avenue—and an increasingly attractive one at that—to maintaining or improving their family's relative economic status. With the continuing historic rise in divorce, increasing proportions of married women and mothers would also be faced at some time with the loss of most, if not all, of their husbands' income. For this reason, too, paid employment outside the home became increasingly attractive for mothers as a hedge against such an economic disaster, and paid work was becoming a necessity for many of the increasing proportion of women who actually did experience divorce.[16]

Turning to changes in the economy itself, Valerie Kincade Oppenheimer has shown that the historic backbone of the female (nonfarm) labor force—namely young and unmarried women—was either stationary or in the process of declining in size during the two decades between 1940 and 1960, but the economic demand for female workers was increasing during these decades.[17] Consequently, increasing demand for female workers, at least between 1940 and the mid-1960s, came at a time when no increase was occurring in the number of young and unmarried women who were available to fill the demand, but when a substantial and rising proportion of wives and mothers were both potentially available and increasingly attracted to employment outside the home.

Oppenheimer's study of postwar changes in work and the family also portrays how social and economic pressures on families to maintain or improve their relative economic status fostered the rise in mothers' labor-force participation, and how this rise then led to increased social and economic pressure to obtain additional income through mothers' work.[18]

Suggesting that families judge the adequacy of their social and economic status at least partly by comparing themselves with other families in which the husbands have a similar occupational status, Oppenheimer finds that in 1960 and 1970 wives were more likely to be employed (1) if their husbands had relatively low incomes compared with others

---

[16]Davis, pp. 409–413.

[17]Valerie Kincade Oppenheimer, *The Female Labor Force in the United States*, Population Monograph Series, No. 5, Institute of International Studies (Berkeley: University of California Press, 1970), pp. 188–189; and Valerie Kincade Oppenheimer, *Work and the Family* (New York: Academic, 1982), pp. 291, 304–308.

[18]Oppenheimer, pp. 255–352, but especially pp. 314–352.

in the same occupational group and (2) if they (the wives) were able to make a comparatively large contribution to the family's income.[19] In fact, Oppenheimer finds ". . . that whether or not wives worked extensively during the year, and despite low earnings, they (working wives) had a considerable impact on family income—enough in many cases to eliminate the income difference between a working wife's family and the family of a man with a much higher-paying occupational group whose wife did not work at all."[20]

From these results, Oppenheimer has concluded that the relative economic disadvantage associated with having a husband whose income is comparatively low for his occupational status encourages wives to enter the labor force as a means of raising their family's income. But insofar as we live in a competitively consumer-oriented society, where a family's social status depends partly on the number and quality of consumer goods and services they can afford to buy, the entry of such wives into the labor force tends to increase their family's income to such a degree that it has two effects.

First, families in which the husband's income is comparatively low can, by virtue of the wife's work, often jump economically ahead of families in which the husbands have the same occupational status and a comparatively high income, placing the latter families at a social and economic disadvantage. Second, families in which the husband's income is comparatively low can also, by virtue of the wife's work, often jump economically to a level that is equal to that of families in which the husbands have a higher occupational status but no working wife, thereby reducing or eliminating the social and economic-status advantage of the latter group. In response, the latter two groups of families, Oppenheimer argues, are motivated to have their wives enter the labor force in order to reestablish their relative social and economic advantage.[21]

In addition, Oppenheimer effectively shows and argues that the same process operates among other relatively disadvantaged groups of families—for example, among young families after 1960 who experienced high expenses involved in furnishing a "normal" family home but had husbands who earned comparatively low incomes. Increased labor force participation by wives in such a relatively disadvantaged group of families tends, in turn, to encourage increased labor force participation by wives among older groups who can thereby maintain or reestablish their relative social and economic advantage compared with younger families.[22]

[19]Oppenheimer, especially pp. 314–315.
[20]Oppenheimer, pp. 320–321.
[21]Oppenheimer, pp. 321–322.
[22]Oppenheimer, pp. 322–340.

Of course, the desire to maintain or improve their family's relative social and economic status is not the only reason that wives and mothers enter the labor force. Additional reasons to work include the personal nonfinancial rewards of the job itself, the opportunity to be productively involved with other adults, and the satisfactions associated with having a career in a high-prestige occupation. At the same time, sheer economic necessity also appears to be an increasingly common reason for mothers' employment—even in two-parent families, since substantial increases have occurred since 1940 both in the proportion of children who would be living in poverty if their mothers did not work and in the proportion who remain in poverty even though their mothers do work (Chapter 9).

Such economic necessity results, at least partly, from the continuing high proportion of children (24–32 percent between 1950 and 1980) who live with fathers who do not work full-time, year-round (Chapter 4). Between 1939 and 1988, the proportion of all children who would have lived in relative poverty if they had depended only on their fathers' incomes but were lifted out of relative poverty by their mothers' incomes increased from only 3 percent to 14 percent, and the corresponding increase for children in two-parent families was almost as large (from 2 to 11 percent). Nearly twice as large are the proportions of children who were either lifted out of relative poverty by their mothers' incomes or lived in relative poverty even though their mothers worked. The proportion of children who experienced one of these two situations jumped from 7 to 29 percent for children as a whole between 1939 and 1988, and from 5 to 20 percent for children living in two-parent families.

Ironically, some of this increasing need for mothers' work to provide for basic necessities resulted from the general rise in wives' labor-force participation rates, which tended to raise median family income and hence the relative poverty threshold. For example, given social and economic changes as they actually occurred, if no wives had worked in 1988, the median family income and relative poverty threshold would have been about 25 percent lower in 1988—implying a relative poverty threshold roughly equal to the official poverty threshold. Even if the more stringent official poverty threshold is used, however, 23 percent of all children in 1988 depended on their mothers' incomes to either lift them out of official poverty or supplement their below-official-poverty income; the corresponding proportion for children living in two-parent families was 12 percent.

Nevertheless, as we saw in Chapter 7, judgments about economic needs at a specific time in history depend upon one's economic position relative to the general standard of living of the times, and the relative poverty threshold reflects the amount of income that is generally believed to be the *minimum* necessary to get by at various points in time. Hence, by 1988 the official poverty standards appear to underestimate the extent to which children lived in families in which mothers worked out of economic necessity; the higher estimates based on the relative poverty threshold are more appropriate.

Still, by either measure a large proportion of children (12 –20 percent of children in two-parent families and 23–29 percent of all children) depended upon their mothers' work in 1988 to either lift them out of poverty or supplement a below-poverty income. By 1988, then, mothers' work had become an economic necessity for about one in four American children. These results suggest that one important driving force that fostered increasing work among children's mothers after 1940 was the increasing need and opportunity for many to augment the below-poverty incomes that their husbands were able to provide; wives' incomes might either lift these families out of poverty or at least somewhat improve a bleak, poverty-stricken situation.

In sum, as children's parents after 1940 sought to meet the basic economic needs of their families and, when possible, to maintain or improve their relative social and economic standing compared with other families, they continued to pursue the three major avenues to achieving economic advancement that had been followed since the early years of the Industrial Revolution. They also increasingly relied on a fourth avenue—increasing mother's employment outside the home. Hence, the proportion of children who lived on farms declined from 26 to only 2 percent between 1940 and 1988; the proportion who lived in small families with only one to two dependent children declined temporarily by only 10–12 percentage points during the postwar economic boom but jumped from 41 to 65 percent between 1970 and 1989; and between 1940 and 1988 the proportion whose mothers had completed fewer than four years of high school plummeted from 83 to 19 percent, while the proportion whose mothers had completed at least one year of college jumped from 6 to 38 percent (Chapters 2, 4, and 6).

Meanwhile, the proportion of children whose mothers were employed jumped from 9 to 59 percent between 1940 and 1989; for children living in two-parent families, there was an equal jump (from 7 to 62 percent). In fact, by the mid-1970s, one-half of all families with wives aged 20–44 had a working wife, and America had reached the point where the typical standard of living could be achieved by many families only if the wife worked for pay outside the home. During the 1980s, employment of wives aged 20–44 continued to rise, reaching 70 percent in 1988—a level only 10 percentage points below the rate for never-married women of the same age.

By 1990, then, it has become quite clear that the breadwinner-homemaker family that emerged with the Industrial Revolution—a family in which the father provided economic support and the mother provided personal care to family members—will soon be only a memory or simply past history for most persons. As we move toward the twenty-first century, the mothers of many children are again directly contributing in major ways to the economic support of the family, as they did on family farms before, and to a declining degree during, the Industrial Revolution. Profound differences distinguish the new and old work, however. In preindustrial times parents worked together, often with their children by their side, to support the family. Now, however, parents usually work at two separate locations, and their children often spend much of the day at a third location where they receive care or formal education.

Black Mother-Only Families: 1940–1960

In 1940, 11.5 percent of black children lived in mother-only families, compared with 6.0 percent of white children—a difference that is accounted for mainly by differences in the proportions who had either separated or divorced mothers (4.4 vs. 2.8 percent) or widowed mothers (6.5 vs. 3.2 percent). Between 1940 and 1960, the proportion of children who lived in mother-only families increased by 7.6 percentage points for black children, compared with only 0.2 percentage points for white children. Most of the increase for blacks can be accounted for by the rise in the proportion who had separated or divorced mothers (9.1 percentage points). Meanwhile, the proportion of black children living in mother-only families with never-married mothers increased by only 0.8 percentage points, and the proportion with widowed mothers declined by 2.3 percentage points.

Why did such a comparatively high proportion of black children live in mother-only families with separated or divorced mothers in 1940, and why was there such a comparatively large increase in these families between 1940 and 1960? To answer these questions, we'll begin by identifying relevant socioeconomic trends in which blacks have either trailed or led whites.

First, as of 1940, blacks substantially trailed whites in moving off the farm and in reducing fertility and family size. For example, black children were 16–17 percentage points more likely than white children to live on farms (43 vs. 27 percent) and to have five or more dependent siblings in the home (37 vs. 20 percent). Still, by 1940 a majority of black children lived off farms and a majority lived in families that had only a small or medium number of children.

At the same time, despite the comparatively high proportion of them who lived on farms in 1940, black children, overall, were 5 percentage points more likely than whites to live in dual-earner families (11 vs. 6 percent); and among children living with two parents, blacks were 10 percentage points more likely than whites to live in dual-earner families (17 vs. 7 percent).[23] Much larger than any of these differences, though, was the racial gap in relative poverty rates. In 1940 black children, overall, and black children living in two-parent families were 42–43 percentage points more likely than corresponding whites to live in relative poverty (73–76 vs. 31–33 percent), despite the fact that they were 5–10 percentage points more likely than whites to live in dual-earner families.

These extraordinarily high relative poverty rates for blacks suggest that they were experiencing extremely high levels of economic insecurity and need compared with whites. Since the important but comparatively small increases in economic insecurity associated with recessions after 1970 appear to account for a 2–3 percentage point rise in mother-only families among children as a whole due to separation and divorce between 1970 and 1988, it seems likely that the extraordinarily large racial gap (of 42–43 percentage points) in the relative poverty rate in 1940—along with the 5–10 percentage point racial gap in dual-earner family living—can account for the 1–2 percentage point racial gap in the proportion of children who lived in mother-only families with a separated or divorced mother in 1940.

The vast racial gap in relative poverty rates that existed in 1940 was also, no doubt, a major force behind the startling drop in the number of blacks who lived on farms during the next two decades. Between 1940 and 1960, the proportion of children who lived on farms dropped by 33 percentage points for blacks compared with 16 percentage points for whites. Hence, mass migration by blacks off farms to take advantage of jobs in the industrial war and postwar economies led, by 1960, to virtual equality with whites in the proportions of children who lived on farms (about 10–11 percent). It seems plausible that the remarkably speedy exodus of blacks from farm life involved high levels of family stress and insecurity, however.

In addition, as blacks sought to maintain or improve their relative

[23]It is possible that the racial gap was slightly larger (or smaller), since these estimates exclude children in unrelated or "secondary" subfamilies (that is, families with one or two parents living in a household maintained by a nonrelative), and since the black children were probably slightly more likely than the white children to live in such unrelated subfamilies in 1940.

economic status between 1940 and 1960, black children living in two-parent families continued to lead white children in two-parent families (by 10, 7, and 14 percentage points, respectively, in 1940, 1950, and 1960) in their chances of having both parents in the labor force. Despite mass migration off farms and rising dual-earner families, however, economic insecurity and need remained extraordinarily common among blacks, as the racial gap in relative poverty remained essentially unchanged (at 42–45 percentage points) for children in 1939, 1949 and 1959 and the relative poverty rate had remained very high by 1959 (at 58–63 percent for black children overall and for those living in two-parent families).

Since economic stress, insecurity, and need appear to contribute substantially to family conflict, marital separation, and divorce, it seems likely that within the context of the already high proportion of black children living in mother-only families with separated or divorced mothers in 1940, the precipitous exodus of blacks from farms after 1940, the comparatively high and rising levels of dual-earner families among black children after 1940, and the continuing extraordinary racial gap in relative poverty after 1940 may be responsible for much of the increase in mother-only families among blacks with separated or divorced mothers that occurred between 1940 and 1960.

Black Mother-Only Families: 1960–1988

Subsequently, between 1960 and 1988, when mother-only families were increasing sharply for both white and black children, about 70 percent of the increase for white children was accounted for by the rise in separation and divorce, but about 80 percent of the much larger increase for black children was accounted for by the rise in never-married mothers (Chapter 3).

Hence, much of the increase in mother-only families that occurred among white children after 1960 is probably due to the historic causes discussed earlier in this chapter—namely, the continuing shift toward nonfarm breadwinner-homemaker families and the more recent rise in mothers' labor-force participation, reflecting parents' continuing efforts to maintain or improve their relative economic standing, as well as economic insecurity and need, which was at least partly associated with economic recessions. For black children, we must look further, however, to explain why the post-1960 increase in mother-only families was much larger than it was for whites and why most of this increase was associated with never-married mothers rather than with parents' separation and divorce. After discussing the rise of mother-only families among black children in more detail, we will address these two issues in turn.

By 1960, 19.1 percent of black children lived in mother-only families; of these, 13.5 percent had separated or divorced mothers, 4.2 percent had widowed mothers, and only 1.4 percent had never-married mothers. Between 1960 and 1970, the proportion of black children who lived in mother-only families with separated or divorced mothers increased from 13.5 to 20.0 percent, while the proportion with never-married mothers increased somewhat less from 1.4 to 5.4 percent. Subsequently, however, the proportion of black children living with separated or divorced mothers remained comparatively stable (at 21.7 and 19.8 percent in 1980 and 1988, respectively), but the proportion living with never-married mothers jumped to 14.0 percent in 1980 and 27.4 percent in 1988 (Chapter 3).

Overall, then, each decade between 1960 and 1988 brought a 10–11 percentage point increase in the proportion of black children living in mother-only families with separated, divorced, or never-married mothers, compared with a 2–4 percentage point increase in the proportion of white children living in such families. By 1988, 50 percent of black children and 16 percent of white children lived in mother-only families. The continuing overall rise in mother-only families among blacks after 1960 may be explained by the same general, historic factors that appear to explain the rise in mother-only families among whites (that is, the continuing movement off the farm, the continuing increase in dual-earner families, and the pressures of economic insecurity and need).

But why was the increase in mother-only families so much greater for black children after 1960, and why, especially after 1970, did the source of this increase shift from separation and divorce to out-of-wedlock childbearing? The answers to these questions may be mainly that blacks have been much more likely to experience severe economic pressure and dual-earner family living than have whites.

For example, despite a 14 percentage point decline in relative poverty among black children between 1959 and 1979, and a similar racial convergence, in any specific year at least 50 percent of black children lived in relative poverty, compared with only 17–22 percent of white children (Chapter 7). Equally important is the fact that an extraordinary 80–85 percent of black children born during the mid-1960s spent at least one year in relative poverty before reaching age 18 compared with only 30–40 percent of white children (Chapter 1). In addition, of the total years spent in official poverty by children between the late 1960s and early 1980s, the proportions that were *not* experienced in families resulting from out-of-wedlock childbearing were 60 percent for blacks and 81 percent for whites (Chapter 9).

Finally, excluding transitions into official poverty at the time of birth, only 8–9 percent of the transitions into or out of poverty for both black and white children were associated with the loss (or gain) of parent(s) from (into) the household; but more than 70 percent were associated with a change in the employment status, hours worked, or disability status of a parent or other relative in the home (Chapter 9). These results indicate that compared with white children, after 1960 black children continued to experience extraordinarily high rates of economic insecurity and need that were often associated with changes in the employment of parents or other relatives.

The comparatively great economic pressures experienced by blacks may explain why, among children in two-parent families, the proportion living in dual-earner families has also remained comparatively high. Despite these racial differences in parents' employment, by 1988 black children living in two-parent families continued to experience a relative poverty rate that was 1.5 times as large as the corresponding rate for white children (23 vs. 15 percent).

The extraordinary economic pressures experienced by black families, combined with the continuing racial gap in dual-earner family status among children in two-parent families, is so large as to provide a plausible explanation for why the increase in mother-only families was much greater for black than for white children after 1960. But the question remains: Why did the source of increase in mother-only families among blacks shift from separation and divorce to out-of-wedlock childbearing, especially after 1970? The results that we present toward answering this question also provide more detailed support for the idea that the much larger increase in mother-only families among blacks resulted from the comparatively severe economic pressures they experienced after 1960.

Part of the explanation for the large increase in never-married mothers among black children after 1960 may be that as the proportion of black children in mother-only families with separated or divorced mothers approached 20 percent, increasing proportions of black women decided that there was little point in marrying the fathers of their children if it appeared that the marriage might end in separation or divorce within a few years anyway. Why should they experience the emotional rollercoaster of a marriage and early divorce, especially if the father would contribute little to the family's income either during the marriage or following the separation and divorce, these women may have reasoned. In fact, I have recently found for the mid-1980s that poor black married-couple households with children were twice as likely to dissolve within two years as nonpoor ones (21 verses 11 percent).[24]

[24]Donald J. Hernandez, U.S. Bureau of the Census, Current Population Reports, Series P 23–179, *When Households Continue, Discontinue, and Form* (Washington, DC: U.S. Government Printing Office, 1992), Table I.

Another part of the explanation appears to rest with changes in the incomes of black men, and hence changes in their potential economic contribution to their families. After about 1970, relative improvements in the median income of black men ceased. Among men who had any income, the median income for blacks as a proportion of the median for whites increased from 41 percent to 58 percent between 1939 and 1969; but 19 years later, in 1988, the proportion was 60 percent—virtually identical to the proportion in 1969.[25] More important, though, as William Julius Wilson has highlighted, employment opportunities for black men during the main family-forming ages dropped sharply after the mid-1950s (Figure 10.1 and Table 10.1).

In 1955, black and white men aged 16–24 were about equally likely to be employed, while among men aged 25–34, blacks were about 8 percentage points less likely than whites to be employed. By 1965 a disadvantage in the proportion of blacks who were employed had emerged, and this expanded for men aged 16–17 and 18–19 to 9 and 5 percentage points, respectively. By 1975, among men aged 16–19 the racial disadvantage in the proportion who were employed had expanded to 24 percentage points; among men aged 20–24 a 15 percentage point disadvantage had emerged for black men; and the earlier 8 percentage point disadvantage for black men aged 25–34 had increased slightly to 10 percentage points. Since 1975, these economic disadvantages among black men have fluctuated within fairly narrow ranges, and by 1989 they remained quite high for men aged 16–19, 20–24, and 25–34 (at about 20–24, 16, and 11–13 percentage points, respectively).

These changes represent corresponding increases between 1955 and 1975 in the racial gap in the proportion of young men who earned *any* income that might be used to support a family. By 1975–1989, the proportion of young black men who were *not* employed, and hence could *not* contribute to the support of a family, was 79–88 percent for ages 16–17, 60–71 percent for ages 18–19, 34–46 percent for ages 20–24, and 18–29 percent for ages 25–34.

Wilson notes, in addition, that (1) high black-male mortality rates imply that many black male children do not reach the young adult ages; (2) high incarceration rates among blacks imply that additional young black men are not available for marriage or family support because they are in prison; and (3) the undercount of young black men in the Census of the Population and in the Current Population Survey probably tends

[25]Reynolds Farley and Walter R. Allen, *The Color Line and the Quality of Life in America* (New York: Russell Sage Foundation, 1987), p. 298; and Edward J. Welniak, Jr., U.S. Bureau of the Census, Current Population Reports, Series P-60, No. 166, *Money Income and Poverty Status in the United States: 1988 (Advance Data from the March 1989 Current Population Survey)* (Washington, DC: U.S. Government Printing Office, 1989).

FIGURE 10.1

Percentage Points by Which White Male Employment Exceeds Black Male Employment: 1955–1988

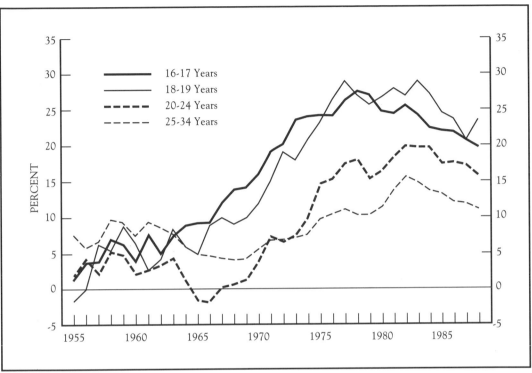

SOURCE: Table 10.1.

to occur especially among men who do not have a stable attachment to labor force or family.[26]

Hence, focusing only on joblessness, it appears that young black men aged 16–24 experienced the emergence and rapid expansion of a racial disadvantage in employment after 1955, but especially between 1965 and 1975, and by 1975–1989 the gap amounted to at least 15–25 percentage points for young black men. Faced with this large and rapid reduction in the availability of black men during the main family-building ages who might provide significant support to a family, many young black women appear to have decided to forgo a temporary and unre-

[26]William Julius Wilson, *The Truly Disadvantaged: The Inner City, the Underclass, and Public Policy* (Chicago: University of Chicago Press, 1987), p. 204. In the employment-population ratios presented in the text for years beginning with 1972, the population is the noninstitutional population (that is, the population excluding persons in prisons, nursing homes, and similar places of confinement).

TABLE 10.1
Civilian Employment-Population Ratios for White and Black Men Aged 16–34: 1955–1988

		White Men			
Year	Total 16–19 Years	16–17 Years	18–19 Years	20–24 Years	25-34 Years
1955	52.0	42.2	64.2	80.4	95.2
1956	54.1	45.5	64.8	82.3	94.7
1957	52.4	43.7	63.6	80.5	94.5
1958	47.6	39.8	58.0	76.6	91.8
1959	48.1	38.6	61.2	80.8	93.8
1960	48.1	39.3	59.7	80.5	93.6
1961	45.9	37.0	56.2	78.8	92.9
1962	46.4	36.4	58.0	79.6	93.8
1963	44.7	34.8	58.2	79.1	93.6
1964	45.0	36.5	57.7	79.3	94.6
1965	47.1	38.0	58.3	80.2	94.9
1966	50.0	41.2	59.6	81.0	95.5
1967	50.2	41.8	60.1	80.5	95.6
1968	50.3	41.8	60.3	78.6	95.5
1969	51.1	42.7	61.1	78.7	95.4
1970	49.6	41.3	59.3	76.8	93.7
1971	49.2	40.8	58.6	75.4	92.5
1972	51.5	42.0	62.3	77.1	92.8
1973	54.3	44.7	65.1	80.2	93.3
1974	54.4	44.7	65.2	79.8	92.9
1975	50.6	41.6	60.3	74.3	89.7
1976	51.5	41.6	62.2	76.9	90.5
1977	54.4	44.3	65.2	78.7	91.2
1978	56.3	46.0	67.2	80.6	92.3
1979	55.7	46.4	65.4	81.1	92.5
1980	53.4	43.7	63.3	77.5	90.2
1981	51.3	41.2	61.4	77.0	90.0
1982	47.0	37.4	56.4	73.9	87.1
1983	47.4	36.3	58.0	74.3	86.7
1984	49.1	37.8	60.1	78.0	89.5
1985	49.9	39.2	60.8	78.0	90.2
1986	49.6	39.7	60.2	79.2	89.9
1987	49.9	40.1	60.4	79.6	90.6
1988	51.7	41.4	62.2	80.1	90.9

SOURCES: Table 16, U.S. Department of Labor, Bureau of Labor Statistics, *Handbook of Labor Statistics, Bulletin 2340* (August 1989); and calculated from Tables A-4, A-13, A-16, *Employment and Training Report of the President*, 1982, U.S. Government Printing Office, Washington, DC.

TABLE 10.1 *(continued)*

Black Men

	Total 16–19 Years	16–17 Years	18–19 Years	20–24 Years	25–34 Years
1955	52.4	41.1	66.0	78.6	87.6
1956	52.4	41.8	65.0	78.1	88.9
1957	48.0	39.8	57.6	78.2	88.0
1958	41.9	32.9	52.6	71.4	82.1
1959	41.5	32.4	52.5	75.9	84.5
1960	43.6	35.3	53.3	78.4	86.1
1961	40.8	29.3	53.7	76.1	83.6
1962	41.7	31.4	53.8	76.3	85.2
1963	37.4	27.2	50.0	74.8	85.9
1964	37.9	27.6	51.8	78.1	88.7
1965	39.6	28.8	53.4	81.6	90.0
1966	40.5	31.9	50.7	82.8	90.8
1967	39.0	29.6	50.1	80.3	91.3
1968	38.6	27.8	51.2	77.9	91.4
1969	39.0	28.5	51.0	77.3	91.2
1970	35.4	25.1	47.3	72.9	87.9
1971	31.8	21.6	43.5	68.2	85.9
1972	31.6	21.8	43.1	70.4	85.9
1973	32.8	20.9	47.0	72.6	86.1
1974	31.4	20.5	44.3	69.9	85.1
1975	26.3	17.3	36.8	59.4	79.9
1976	25.8	17.2	35.5	61.3	80.0
1977	26.4	17.9	36.0	61.0	80.0
1978	28.5	18.3	40.0	62.2	81.9
1979	28.7	19.2	39.4	65.5	82.0
1980	27.0	18.8	36.3	60.9	78.7
1981	24.6	16.5	33.3	58.3	76.1
1982	20.3	11.7	29.2	53.9	71.3
1983	20.4	11.8	29.0	54.5	71.7
1984	23.9	15.1	32.6	58.0	75.6
1985	26.3	16.9	36.0	60.4	76.6
1986	26.5	17.5	36.2	61.3	77.6
1987	28.5	19.3	39.1	62.1	78.5
1988	29.4	21.4	38.2	63.9	79.5

NOTES: The employment-population ratio represents the percentage of the total designated population who are employed. Data for blacks 1955–1971 pertain to all nonwhites (black and other).

warding marriage—in fact, a marriage in which a jobless or poorly paid husband might act as a financial drain. Furthermore, the size of this reduction is at least two-thirds as large as the 23 percentage point increase that occurred between 1960 and 1988 in the racial gap in the proportion of children living in mother-only families with never-married mothers. Hence, the increasing racial gap in joblessness among young males between 1960 and 1988 may well be the major cause of the increasing racial gap in the proportion of children living in mother-only families with never-married mothers.

Of course, in response to this drop in the availability of potential husbands who are able to provide financial support to a family, many black women who bore children out of wedlock could instead have decided to not bear any children, or to postpone childbearing until they had completed additional education that might allow them to earn a higher income. Why didn't they follow this path? The answer may be as follows. Most adults spend most of their time and reap most of their personal satisfactions in one or both of two distinct realms of life—family life or work/career life. Since only two main possibilities exist for most people, if one is effectively closed or appears to be closed as an option, the other realm of life is likely to become, perforce, the major focus of attention and activity.

When the relative incomes of young men declined after 1960 with the entry of male baby boomers into the labor force, blacks were harder hit than whites, in part because blacks were more likely to be in the bottom half of the income distribution. Despite the impressive economic gains made by some blacks during the postwar economic boom and the civil rights era, a large proportion were, as we have seen, left behind. The relative poverty rate for blacks remained remarkably high, and the sharp drop in the relative economic opportunities for many young black men after 1955, but especially after 1965, meant that from the mid-1970s through the late 1980s at least 15–25 percent were unable to find well-paid, full-time employment, let alone long-term opportunities for career advancement.

Living side by side with these young black men, many young black women may have given up hope of achieving substantial economic improvement in their life situation through the educational and career advancement of either their potential husbands or themselves. Under these conditions many young black women may have found little reason to delay childbearing and family life as a parent, since this was the only remaining realm of life they felt was available for obtaining personal satisfaction.[27]

[27]This interpretation is developed and relevant research is discussed by William Julius Wilson, pp. 74–75.

During the same time, however, blacks did sharply limit their fertility—presumably to maintain the highest possible ratio of income per family member—within the constraints set by realistic or perceived economic opportunities and the desire to become a parent by bearing children. Thus, between 1960 and 1989, the racial gap in the proportion of children who lived in families in which there were 1–4 dependent siblings in the home fell from 26 to 4 percentage points, and the racial gap in the proportion living in families in which there were 1–2 dependent siblings fell from 18 to 6 percentage points. By 1989, the proportions living in families in which there were 1–4 dependent siblings for black children and white children were 92 and 96 percent, respectively, while the proportions living in families with 1–2 dependent siblings were 60 and 66 percent, respectively.

It appears, then, that the same general factors that produced the rise in mother-only families among whites may also be responsible for the rise in mother-only families among blacks—namely, the continuing desire to maintain or improve one's relative standing, movement off the farm, the rise in dual-earner families, and economic insecurity and need. But for blacks the 1940–1960 move off the farm was a mass exodus that far outstripped the speed of the move for whites, and the historically large racial gap in relative poverty rates both continued and contributed to the continuing comparatively high proportion of blacks who lived in dual-earner families. These racial differences in turn led to increases in mother-only families formed through separation and divorce that were larger than increases experienced by whites.

Finally, and more recently, these factors, along with the especially large and rapid deterioration in the relative economic standing of young black men in the bottom half of the income distribution, and the associated jump in economic insecurity after the mid-1950s, appear large enough to account not only for the especially rapid rise in mother-only families among blacks but also for the shift from divorce and separation toward out-of-wedlock childbearing as the primary mode of forming mother-only families.

Joblessness Among Blacks After 1960

Why did the post-1960 decline in employment opportunities and relative income for persons in the bottom half of the income distribution hit blacks especially hard, with its apparent implications for black mother-only families? In seeking an explanation for this comparatively large and long-lasting increase in joblessness among young black males, William Julius Wilson discusses four key factors.

First, and most generally, he emphasizes that blacks are concentrated in America's inner cities.[28] Second, he presents research findings by Frank Levy indicating that blacks were especially susceptible to job loss during the recent period of weakness in the national economy, because they have been concentrated at low educational levels and in low-wage jobs as newly hired workers in manufacturing industries.[29]

Third, he presents research findings by John D. Kasarda indicating that many urban centers have lost lower-skill jobs in recent years, and the growth in entry-level and other jobs requiring comparatively low educational levels has occurred mainly in suburbs and other areas that are removed from inner cities.[30] Hence, the effective movement of jobs that might have been filled by low-education blacks to suburbs far from their inner city neighborhoods led to a substantial increase in joblessness among young black men.

Fourth, Wilson suggests that historically, during hard economic times middle- and working-class black families would provide ". . . mainstream role models that help keep alive the perception that education is meaningful, that steady employment is a viable alternative to welfare, and that family stability is the norm, not the exception."[31] But he argues further that there was an exodus of middle- and working-class black families from inner-city neighborhoods during the 1970s and that the resulting increase in the concentration and social isolation of poor blacks in inner cities had deleterious consequences for their perceptions about work and family.[32]

Insofar as these factors may account for the extraordinary post-1960 rise in joblessness among young black men, the stage was set by the sharp increase that occurred in residential segregation in U.S. cities between 1910 and 1930, and by subsequent continuing high levels of residential segregation.[33] Especially noteworthy is the lack of change in residential segregation between 1940 and 1960, which occurred despite the

[28]The subtitle of Wilson's book highlights this emphasis.

[29]Wilson, pp. 44–45.

[30]Wilson, pp. 41–42. Black children living in nonmetro areas also experience especially high poverty rates. See also Carolyn C. Rogers, U.S. Department of Agriculture, Economic Research Services, Rural Development Report, No. 83, *The Economic Well-Being of Nonmetro Children* (Washington, DC: U.S. Government Printing Office, 1991). It may be that employment opportunities in nonmetro areas have also declined with the suburbanization of economic activity.

[31]Wilson, p. 56.

[32]Wilson, pp. 46–62.

[33]Citations and data concerning these trends are presented in Reynolds Farley and Walter R. Allen, *The Color Line and the Quality of Life in America* (New York: Russell Sage Foundation, 1987), pp. 139–145.

potential opportunity for desegregation inherent in the large changes in residence associated with the rapid suburbanization of the United States and the massive migration of blacks off farms during these decades.[34]

Why has residential segregation remained at high levels since the 1940s? Reynolds Farley and Walter R. Allen discuss studies indicating that racial animosity appears to have combined with discriminatory housing practices to maintain high levels of residential segregation during the postwar era.[35] Discussing the roots of suburbanization in the United States, Kenneth T. Jackson identifies federal housing and highway policies that also may have contributed to continuing post-1940 residential segregation,[36] and hence to the post-1960 rise in joblessness among black males.

Comparing the postwar policies of the Federal Housing Authority and the federal public housing programs with those of European countries, such as England and France, Jackson concludes that ". . . the basic direction of federal policies toward housing has been the concentration of the poor in the central city and the dispersal of the affluent to the suburbs. American housing policy . . . helped establish the basis for social inequities (and) contributed to the general disbenefit of the cities and to the general prosperity of the suburbs."[37] Jackson also suggests that federal highway policy, especially the interstate highway system, which subsidized automobile transportation to the neglect of mass transportation, fostered deconcentration not only of housing but of jobs.[38] Thus, these federal policies may have contributed to making it increasingly necessary for an individual to own an automobile in order to reach jobs that have increasingly become scattered beyond central cities.

Taking a long-run view, then, as blacks left farms on a massive scale between 1940 and 1960, in the hope of maintaining or improving their relative economic standing in America's major industrial cities, they were confronted with discriminatory practices and attitudes that tended to limit them to living in deteriorating inner cities. At the same time, many whites migrated to newly built suburbs, which ultimately led to a shift

---

[34]The virtually constant level of residential segregation between 1940 and 1960 (for 109 cities) is reported by Annemette Sorensen, Karl E. Taeuber, and Leslie J. Hollingsworth, Jr., *Social Focus* 2, 2 (1975): 131. Although they report a small decline in racial segregation between 1960 and 1970, for the 25 central cities with the largest black populations, the 1960s brought virtual stability in residential segregation, and a noteworthy but small decline did not occur until the decade of the 1970s, according to results presented by Reynolds Farley and Walter R. Allen, *The Color Line and the Quality of Life in America*, p. 141.

[35]Farley and Allen, pp. 150–155.

[36]Kenneth T. Jackson, *Crabgrass Frontier: The Suburbanization of the United States* (Oxford: Oxford University Press, 1985), pp. 170–250.

[37]Jackson, p. 230.

[38]Jackson, p. 191.

of many economic activities to suburbs that became essentially inaccessible except by automobile.[39]

Since by 1960 blacks still tended to be concentrated in the bottom half of the income distribution, they were especially hard hit by subsequent declines in relative income, and increasing joblessness among blacks may have been accentuated by the suburbanization of jobs for persons who had comparatively low educational levels and the continued concentration of low-education blacks in inner cities. These changes may in turn have contributed to both the rise in mother-only families with never-married mothers and a continuing high rate of relative poverty among black children.

Hispanic Parents' Work and Mother-Only Families

Since we have not analyzed long-run historical data for Hispanics (of any race) concerning changes in fathers' and mothers' incomes, sibsize, family structure, and the like, we cannot discuss the nature and causes of these changes among Hispanics in any detail. However, we have discussed data for 1979 and 1988, and these results suggest the possibility that Hispanics (of any race) have been confronted with social and economic circumstances that are generally similar to those faced by blacks, and hence that similar factors may have influenced the familial and economic situation of Hispanic children (of any race).

We have seen that the relative poverty rate for Hispanic children (of any race) is about the same as that for black children, even among old-family Hispanic children (of any race), many of whose grandparents and great-grandparents were born U.S. citizens (Chapters 7 and 9). Hence, Hispanic families (of any race) who have lived in the United States for 50–100 years appear to have achieved no more economic success than have non-Hispanic black families.

At the same time, since the sibsize distribution for old-family Hispanic children (of any race) is quite similar to the sibsize distribution for non-Hispanic white and non-Hispanic black children, the high relative poverty rate for old-family Hispanic children (of any race) cannot be accounted for by high fertility and family size. In addition, it seems likely that the striking similarity of sibsize distributions across the three ethnic-race groups results from the same factors—namely, actions by cou-

---

[39]For a fascinating case study of Chicago that suggests how local discriminatory practices and politics fostered the creation of inner-city slums, in part by influencing federal policy, see Arnold R. Hirsch, *Making the Second Ghetto: Race and Housing in Chicago, 1940–1960* (London: Cambridge University Press, 1983).

ples to limit their fertility as a means of maintaining or improving their relative economic standing (Chapter 2).

Turning to patterns of residence, in 1930, when the U.S. Bureau of the Census classified Mexicans as a race, and when Mexicans constituted the vast majority of Hispanics in the United States, the proportion living in urban areas was 50.9 percent for Mexicans, compared with 57.7 and 43.7 percent for whites and blacks, respectively.[40] These Mexicans of 1930 were the grandparents of many of the old-family Hispanic children (of any race) in 1980. But by 1980, old-family Hispanic children (of any race) were substantially more likely than non-Hispanic white or non-Hispanic black children to live in a metropolitan area.

These results suggest that many Hispanics (of any race), like many non-Hispanic blacks and non-Hispanic whites, moved to urban areas after the Great Depression in search of greater economic opportunities. Equally important, we saw earlier that the migration of blacks off farms was much more rapid than it was for whites, and that this difference may have contributed to family stress and disruption and hence to the rapid rise of mother-only families among blacks. Since the proportion of Mexicans living in urban areas in 1930 was roughly midway between the proportions for blacks and whites, these Hispanic families probably experienced a rate of migration to cities that is also midway between that for blacks and whites. As a result, they may have experienced greater family disruption than did whites but less family disruption than did blacks.

In a further partial parallel to the black experience, as Hispanics moved to metropolitan areas, Frank Bean and Marta Tienda report that they experienced moderate levels of residential segregation by 1970. This means that 32–65 percent of Hispanics (of any race) would have had to move into neighborhoods that consisted predominantly of non-Hispanic whites in order to eliminate residential segregation. But "[d]uring the 1970s the four largest Hispanic communities seemed to be converging toward a common high level of residential segregation, with Los Angeles, New York, and Chicago beginning to approach the very high levels typical of blacks in American cities."[41]

In addition to moving to cities and limiting their family size as approaches to maintaining or improving their relative economic status, two other approaches adopted by many Americans were to obtain ever-higher levels of education and to have wives enter the paid labor force. Old-family Hispanics (of any race) appear to have followed the same

---

[40]U.S. Bureau of the Census, *Fifteenth Census of the United States: 1930, Population, Volume II* (Washington, DC: U.S. Government Printing Office, 1933), p. 27.

[41]Frank D. Bean and Marta Tienda, *The Hispanic Population of the United States* (New York: Russell Sage Foundation, 1987), p. 171.

course. But by 1980, the educational attainments of parents of old-family Hispanic children (of any race) were somewhat below those of parents of non-Hispanic black children (Chapter 6), and the proportion of old-family Hispanic children (of any race) living in two-parent families with a working mother was similar to that for non-Hispanic white children but lower than that for non-Hispanic black children.

For black children, we saw that the rapid rise in mother-only families after 1960, compared with white children, may have been largely the result of parents' desire to maintain or improve their own relative economic standing as well as that of their children (through continuing migration off farms, continuing increases in mothers' employment in two-parent families, and especially through sharp reductions in fertility), combined with deteriorating relative economic opportunities and increasing joblessness among blacks in the bottom half of the income distribution. During the past 50 years it appears that old-family Hispanics (of any race) may have pursued the same path in their search for economic opportunities, but they faced many of the same difficulties experienced by blacks—though perhaps less severely.

The broad similarities in the evolving situations faced by Hispanics (of any race) and blacks, but the slower pace of some changes and the apparently less extreme residential segregation (at least until recently) among Hispanics (of any race), may explain why the proportion of old-family Hispanic children (of any race) in 1980 who lived in mother-only families was about twice as large as for non-Hispanic whites but substantially below the proportion for non-Hispanic blacks.

In fact, no doubt reflecting the attitudes of the time, in 1930 the U.S. Bureau of the Census classified Mexicans as a distinct race and reported that they were the second-largest minority race (after blacks). In addition, Mexicans ceased to be classified as a race in the 1940 census, at least partly in response to the "unfavorable reactions" of the Mexican government and the U.S. Department of State.[42]

If Hispanics were widely viewed as a distinct racial group, like blacks, at the time of the Great Depression, and if many of the social and economic changes and constraints faced by Hispanics have been similar to those faced by blacks, then it seems plausible that at least part of the explanation for continuing high relative poverty rates among blacks also apply to the continuing high relative poverty rates among old-family Hispanics (of any race). Of course, membership in a racial minority cannot by itself explain high relative poverty rates, since some racial minorities have experienced considerable economic success.[43]

[42]Leo Grebler, Joan W. Moore, and Ralph C. Guzman, *The Mexican-American People* (New York: Free Press, 1970), p. 601.

[43]Asian-Americans, for example, experience comparatively low poverty rates and

Conclusion

This chapter portrays with a broad brush some fundamental causes of changes in fathers' incomes, the rise of mother-only families, and the rise of mothers' labor-force participation since the Great Depression.

With the economic boom following the Great Depression and World War II, children experienced a large drop in fathers' unemployment, a large increase in fathers' absolute income levels, greater equality in the distribution of fathers' incomes, and large declines in relative poverty. But the relative poverty rate for children increased after 1969, and the official childhood poverty rate increased after 1979. Rising childhood poverty mirrored the increases in the proportion of children whose fathers had comparatively low incomes and in the proportion who lived in mother-only families.

A prominent demographic factor that contributed to the rise in the proportion of children whose fathers had comparatively low incomes was the fact that baby boomers were reaching adulthood. The entry of the very large baby-boom cohorts into the labor force after 1960 tended to intensify competition for available jobs and hence to depress wages and relative incomes for young men. This in turn contributed to the sharp post-1959 slowdown and subsequent stagnation in the growth of family income, the stagnation and subsequent deterioration in fathers' relative incomes for children in the bottom half of the income distribution, and hence to rising relative and official poverty among children.

Increased immigration after 1960 also tended to intensify competition for available jobs, but increased immigration had a much smaller effect on the labor force than did the baby boomers. Additional factors that tended to depress the relative incomes of young men were (1) the historic increase in educational attainments, because it involved a later age of entry into permanent work commitments and a shift toward occupations that offered comparatively low entry-level earnings; and (2) institutional and legal changes that provided greater job and income security and reduced age discrimination for older workers, because these increased the comparative disadvantage of younger workers.

Much of the historic rise in mother-only families appears to have grown out of transformations in the family economy that occurred as

comparatively high family incomes, though partly because they have comparatively large number of workers per family. See Claudette Bennett, U.S. Bureau of the Census, Current Population Reports, Series P-20, No. 459, *The Asian and Pacific Islander Population in the United States: March 1991 and 1990* (U.S. Government Printing Office, Washington, DC: 1992).

individuals sought to maintain or improve their relative economic standing in the face of changing economic circumstances. With the Industrial Revolution, couples sought to maintain or improve their relative economic position, in part by having fathers work at comparatively well-paid jobs in the nonfarm economy. But this work greatly weakened the mutual economic interdependence of husbands and wives, because the husband could, if he desired, depend on his own work alone for his income. More recently, mothers' work outside the home has also increased sharply, as families sought to maintain or improve their relative economic standing. This trend has provided mothers, too, with independent incomes from their own jobs.

This increasing work by parents away from the family home, and the associated weakening of the economic independence of husbands and wives, combined with the decline of rural and small-town social controls censuring divorce, have fostered the large historic rise in separation and divorce that accounts for about two-thirds of the rise in mother-only families among children.

Economic insecurity and need also apparently contributed substantially to the rise in separation and divorce, at least after 1970. Instability in husbands' work, drops in family income, and a low ratio of family income-to-needs have been found to lead to increased hostility between husbands and wives, to decreased marital quality, and to increased risk of divorce. Hence, it is not surprising that each economic recession since the early 1970s brought a substantially larger increase in mother-only families for children than did the preceding nonrecessionary period.

The increase in mothers' work for pay outside the home also appears to have resulted largely from the continuing desire of individuals to maintain or improve their relative economic standing, and from economic insecurity and need in the face of changing socioeconomic circumstances. From the onset of the Industrial Revolution through 1940, the major avenues available to couples seeking to maintain or improve their relative economic standing were by having husbands work in comparatively well-paid nonfarm jobs, by limiting their family size to a comparatively small number of children, and by seeking increased educational attainments that would provide greater access to well-paid jobs.

By 1940, the first two avenues had run their course for most couples, and since most persons achieve their ultimate educational attainments by age 25, additional schooling beyond age 25 is often difficult or impractical. Instead, a fourth major avenue to improving family income emerged between 1940 and 1960—namely, paid work by wives and mothers, because the traditional source of female nonfarm labor (unmarried women) was either stationary or in the process of declining in size, while the demand for female workers was increasing.

Meanwhile, mothers were also becoming increasingly available and increasingly well qualified for work outside the home. Although the breadwinner-homemaker family had emerged as the dominant family form during the Industrial Revolution, by 1940 the substantial time spent by children in school combined with declining family size had greatly constricted the homemaker role of mothers, making them potentially available for paid work outside the home. As of 1940, in fact, childhood school attendance had effectively released mothers from personal child-care responsibilities for a time period equivalent to about two-thirds of a full-time adult work year, except for the few years before children entered elementary school. In addition, the educational attainments of women and mothers had increased along with those of men, and by 1940 young women were more likely than young men to graduate from high school and about two-thirds as likely to graduate from college.

Finally, paid work outside the home for mothers was also becoming increasingly attractive in our competitive, consumer-oriented society. For example, families in which the husband's income was comparatively low could, by virtue of the wife's work, jump economically ahead of families in which the husbands have the same occupational status but lack a working wife. Similarly, families of young men with low relative incomes after 1960 could, by virtue of wives' work, jump economically ahead of other young families in which there was no working wife, or ahead of older families that had no working wife. But this in turn placed families with comparatively well-paid husbands at a disadvantage, which made wives' work more attractive for them. In addition, with rising divorce rates, work became increasingly attractive to mothers as a hedge against the increasingly possible economic disaster of losing most or all of their husbands' income through divorce.

Economic insecurity and need have also made mothers' work increasingly attractive. Both among the increasing proportion of children living in mother-only families and among an increasing proportion of children now living in two-parent families, mothers' incomes have become essential either to lift the family out of poverty or to provide basic support at a subpoverty level.

In short, by 1940 mothers' work had become the only major avenue available to most couples over age 25 who wanted to either maintain or improve their relative economic status. In fact, after 1940 not only did the economic demand for married women to work increase, but the potential availability, attractiveness, and sheer family need for mothers to work also increased.

Although black children are sometimes viewed as having experiences that are markedly different from those of white children, results presented here suggest that factors responsible for declines in fathers' relative incomes after 1960, and for long-term increases in mothers' employment and mother-only families among children in general, have played the same role for black children. The main difference is that blacks began the postwar era with extraordinarily high levels of economic insecurity and need, and because of that, as well as a high level of residential segregation, changes in the economy have affected them more severely than whites. This in turn has led to a much larger increase in mother-only families among blacks than among whites. Much more limited results for old-family Hispanic children (of any race) are consistent, at least, with the view that they have faced changes and constraints similar to, but in some ways less severe than, those experienced by black children.

11

RESOURCES FOR CHILDREN
PAST, PRESENT, AND FUTURE

Introduction

REVOLUTIONARY changes in the life course, the economy, and society have transformed childhood, and the resources available to children, during the past 150 years. A revolutionary decline in the number of siblings in the families of children occurred during the past 100 years. Historically, a substantial minority of children did not spend their entire childhood in a two-parent family, but this will expand to a majority for children born during the past decade. The role of grandparents in the home, as surrogate parents filling the gap left by absent parents, has been important but limited during at least the past half century.

The family economy was revolutionized twice during the past 150 years, first as fathers and then mothers left the home to spend much of the day away at jobs as family breadwinners. With these changes, with instability in fathers' work, and with increasing divorce and out-of-wedlock childbearing, never during the past half century were a majority of children born into "Ozzie and Harriet" families in which the father worked full-time year-round, the mother was a full-time homemaker, and all of the children were born after the parents' only marriage.

Corresponding revolutions in child care occurred first as children over age 5 and then as younger children began to spend increasing amounts of time in formal educational or other settings in the care of someone other than their parents. Since today's children are tomorrow's parents, the spread of universal compulsory education led to revolutionary increases in the educational attainments of parents during the past half century, to the benefit of successive cohorts of children. But as opportunities to complete at least a high school education became substantially more equal for children during the past century, opportunities to go beyond high school and complete at least one year of college became less equal.

The absolute income levels of families increased greatly after the Great Depression and World War II through the 1960s but have changed comparatively little since then. Meanwhile, childhood poverty and economic inequality declined after World War II through the 1960s, then increased mainly during the 1980s. Most poor children throughout the era lived in working-poor families, and only a minority of poor children were fully welfare-dependent.

These historic changes in the resources available to children, and the causes and consequences of these changes, are discussed in some detail in this book. In this last chapter we will summarize major conclusions, highlighting the circumstances of black and Hispanic children (of any race), and we draw upon selected international data to show broadly how the contemporary life course of children in the United States compares with that of children in other industrialized countries. Finally, we suggest the possible implications these historic changes have for children in the future.

Family Composition

Because siblings are the family members who are usually closest in age, needs, and activities, they may be among a child's most important companions and most important competitors for family resources. The typical child born in 1890 lived, as an adolescent, in a family in which there were about 6.6 siblings, but the typical child born in 1994 is expected to live in a family that is only one-third as large—with 1.9 children.

About one-half of this decline in family size had occurred by 1945, and the typical child born during that year lived in a family that had 2.9 siblings. Subsequently, during the postwar baby boom that occurred between 1945 and 1957, the annual number of births jumped by 55 percent (from 2.7 to 4.3 million births per year) and the Total Fertility Rate jumped by 52 percent (from 2.4 to 3.7 births per woman), but the family size of the typical adolescent increased by only 17 percent (from 2.9 to 3.4 siblings).

Changes in the distribution of adolescents by family size tell a similar story. The proportion living in families in which there are 5 or more siblings is expected to decline from 77 percent for children born in 1890 to only 6 percent for children born in 1994. Again, about one-half of the decline had occurred for children born in 1945, 32 percent of whom as adolescents lived in families in which there were 5 or more children, and again the increase during the baby boom was comparatively small at about 6 percentage points. At the opposite extreme, the proportion of adolescents living in families in which there are only 1-2 children is expected to increase from only 7 percent for children born in 1890 to 57 percent for children born in 1994. Among children born in 1945, about 30 percent lived in such small families, and this fell by 10 percentage points to 20 percent during the baby boom.

Historically, black children have tended to live in families in which there were substantially larger numbers of siblings than did white children, but trends in the family sizes of both black and white children were generally similar between the Civil War and 1925. Then for about 20 years, however, the racial gap expanded, apparently because the comparatively large decline in tuberculosis and venereal disease led to increased family sizes among blacks. Since about 1945, the number of siblings in the families of both black and white children have been converging.

Among children born in 1994, family-size differences between blacks and whites, as well as between Hispanic children (of any race) and non-Hispanic children, are expected to essentially vanish. Of the racial convergence in family size that is expected to occur for children born between 1945 and 1994, more than two-thirds had occurred among children born in 1973 who are now about 18 years old and approaching college age.

What are the consequences of this decline for children? First, children with larger numbers of siblings have greater opportunities to experience caring, loving sibling companionship. Hence, the family-size revolution drastically reduced the number of siblings who were available as potential companions during childhood and through adulthood. On the other hand, childhood family size appears to have little effect on psychological well-being later during adulthood. But because children growing up in large families—especially families with 5 or more siblings—tend to complete fewer years of schooling than do children from smaller families, they are less likely to enter high-status occupations with high incomes when they reach adulthood. Hence, the family-size revolution led to greatly improved opportunities for educational, occupational, and economic advancement among successive cohorts of children.

Overall, then, since we were roughly midway through the family-size revolution by the end of the Great Depression, about half of the effects expected to occur had done so for cohorts born by then. Since the postwar baby boom had only a small and short-lived effect on family size, it is best viewed as a brief lull in the revolution rather than as a sharp reversal. Since about two-thirds of the expected change had occurred for children born by 1965, who are now about twenty-five years old, about two-thirds of the consequences have already been felt.

Finally, if, as expected, the proportion of children whose families consist of 5 or more siblings becomes approximately stable for children born after 1983, then the remaining one-third of the potential improvement in educational opportunities associated with the family-size revolution will have occurred by the year 2010—only 17 years from now—when the 1983 cohort passes through the main ages of college enrollment. The universality of the family-size revolution among industrialized countries is reflected in the very low current fertility levels in these countries. For example, the overall Total Fertility Rate in North America and Europe for 1990–2010 is projected to be an average of 1.8–1.9 children per woman.[1]

Most children depend mainly on the parents in their homes for financial support and day-to-day care. Hence, it would be surprising if important differences in current welfare and future life chances were not found when children who do spend their entire childhood in a two-parent family are compared with those who do not.

In the short run, for many children the separation or divorce of their parents brings a sharp drop in family income and substantial psychological trauma. When the lone parent in a one-parent family marries to form a stepfamily, however, the children often experience a sharp jump in family income. Still, children in stepfamilies are more likely to have a low family income than are children in intact two-parent families. In addition, since one parent is absent from the home in one-parent families, children in these families may receive substantially less day-to-day care and attention from parents than do children in two-parent families.

Children in one-parent families are more likely, on average, to be exposed to parental stress than are children in two-parent families, more likely to exhibit behavioral problems, more likely to receive or need professional psychological help, more likely to perform poorly in school, and more likely to have health problems. In addition, on average, step-

[1]Frank Hobbs and Laura Lippman, U.S. Bureau of the Census, *Children's Well-Being: An International Comparison,* International Population Reports, Series P-95, No. 80 (Washington, DC: U.S. Government Printing Office, 1990), Table 4.

children are virtually indistinguishable from children in one-parent families in their chances of having behavioral, psychological, academic, and health problems.

Over the long run, children who do not spend most of their childhood in an intact two-parent family tend, as they reach adulthood, to complete fewer years of schooling, enter lower-status occupations, and earn lower incomes than do adults who did spend most of their childhood in an intact two-parent family. Some children from one-parent families may finish fewer years of school because fathers who can afford to provide financial support in college do not in fact do so when the child reaches college age. Many of the disadvantages associated with living in a one-parent family may result from the low family incomes of many children who live in such families.

In view of the potential disadvantages of not living with two parents, how typical has it become for children not to spend their entire childhood in a two-parent family? Historically, about 90 percent of newborn children under age 1 have lived with both biological parents. Still, between the late 1800s and 1950, a large and nearly stable minority of about 33 percent spent part of their childhood before age 18 with fewer than two parents in the home. Little change occurred during the first half of the twentieth century, despite the rise in parental separation and divorce, because this rise was counterbalanced by declining parental mortality.

Since about 1950 the link between marriage and the bearing and rearing of children has loosened. Because of the rise in out-of-wedlock childbearing that occurred between 1950 and 1980, the proportion of newborn children under age 1 who did not live with two parents doubled, climbing from 9 to 19 percent. Combined with the rise in separation and divorce, the proportion of children who will ever live with fewer than two parents is expected to increase from about 33 percent for the era between the late 1800s and 1950 to about 55–60 percent of children born in 1980.

Since at least the Civil War, white and black children have been quite different in their chances of spending part of their childhood living with fewer than two parents. For example, in 1940 the proportion of newborn children under age 1 who did not live with two parents was about 25 percent for blacks, compared with 7 percent for whites. Historically, it appears that for children born between the late 1800s and 1940, a majority of blacks (55–60 percent) spent part of their childhood in families in which there were fewer than two parents. For whites born between the late 1800s and 1940, a minority (but a large minority of approximately 29–33 percent) spent part of their childhood in families in which there were fewer than two parents.

Since 1940, the racial gap in out-of-wedlock childbearing more than doubled, and in 1980 about 55 percent of newborn black children under age 1 did not live with two parents, compared with 13 percent for whites. However, separation and divorce have increased less for blacks than for whites since 1940. Hence, the proportion of children ever living with fewer than two parents between ages 0 and 17 will increase fairly equally (by about 16–23 percentage points) for both blacks and whites born between 1940 and 1980.

For children born between 1940 and 1980, the proportion who have ever lived with fewer than two parents is expected to increase from about 60 to about 80 percent for black children and from about 30 to about 46 percent for white children. The experience of living with fewer than two parents by age 17, then, was historically common for both black and white children, but the postwar era brought large increases.

Hispanic children (of any race) in 1980 were much more similar to non-Hispanic whites than to non-Hispanic blacks in their chances of living in two-parent or one-parent families. Among both newborns and children aged 17 in 1980, most of the difference between Hispanic children (of any race) and non-Hispanic whites is accounted for by old-family Hispanic children (of any race), since the parental living arrangements of first-generation Hispanic children (of any race) and non-Hispanic whites were relatively similar.

In at least some other developed countries, the proportion of children who live in one-parent families has also increased during recent decades. Despite increases, however, the proportions living in one-parent families in Sweden and the United Kingdom, for example, were still no more than two-thirds as large as those in the United States, reflecting in large part corresponding differences in divorce rates.[2]

To what extent have grandparents in the home acted to fill the gap left by absent parents among children in the United States since 1940? The answer is that grandparents have played an important role in easing the difficulties associated with living in a one-parent family, especially for black children. But in any single year between 1940 and 1960, among both black and white children living in one-parent families, only 20–27 percent had a grandparent in the home. Hence, a large majority of 73–80 percent of the children who lived in one-parent families did not have a grandparent in the home to fill the gap left by the absent parent.

With the rise in one-parent families after 1960, the proportion of children who had a grandparent in the home declined. In 1970 and 1980, only 10–15 percent of children living in one-parent families had a grandparent in the home, with little difference between black children and

[2]Hobbs and Lippman, Tables 8 and 10.

white children. All together, the proportion who at some point during childhood lived in a one-parent family with a grandparent in the home, or in a grandparent-only family, remained roughly constant at 5–10 percent for white children and somewhere between 20 and 35 percent for black children.

Family Work and Education

As children were experiencing a revolutionary decline in family size and a large increase in one-parent family living, they also were experiencing two distinct transformations in parents' work and living arrangements. On the family farm, economic production, parenting, and child care were combined, as parents and children worked together to support themselves. This changed with the Industrial Revolution, however. Fathers became breadwinners who took jobs located away from home in order to support the family, and mothers became homemakers who remained at home to personally care for the children as well as to clean, cook, and perform other domestic functions for the family. Following the Great Depression, parents' work and the family economy were again transformed. Today most children live either in dual-earner families in which both parents work at jobs away from home or in one-parent families.

More specifically, between about 1840 and 1920 the proportion of children who lived in two-parent farm families fell from at least two-thirds to about one-third, while the proportion who lived in breadwinner-homemaker families climbed from 15–20 percent to 50 percent. Although a majority of children lived in breadwinner-homemaker families between about 1920 and 1970, this figure never reached 60 percent.

In fact, even during the heyday of the breadwinner-homemaker family, a second transformation in parents' work was under way. Between 1920 and 1970, as the proportion of children living in two-parent farm families continued to fall, the proportion who had breadwinner mothers working at jobs that were located away from home increased, and after 1960 the proportion living in one-parent families with their mothers also increased. The rise in the proportion of children living in dual-earner or one-parent families was extremely rapid, since the increase from 15–20 percent to 50 percent required only 30 years—about one-third as long as the time required for the same rise in the breadwinner-homemaker family to take place.

By 1980, nearly 60 percent of children lived in dual-earner or one-parent families, by 1989 about 70 percent lived in such families, and by the year 2000, only 7 years from now, the proportion of children living in such families may exceed 80 percent. Equally striking is the fact that even between 1920 and 1970, only a minority of children aged 0–17 lived in families that conformed to the mid-twentieth century ideal portrayed, for example, on the "Ozzie and Harriet" television program (that is, a nonfarm breadwinner-homemaker family in which the father works full-time year-round, the mother is a full-time homemaker, and all of the children were born after the parents' only marriage).

In fact, only a minority of newborn children under age 1 lived in such families in any year between 1940 and 1980. During these years a large majority of newborns (75–86 percent) did live with employed fathers, but only 42–49 percent lived with two parents in families in which the father worked full-time year-round and all of the children were born after the parents' only marriage. Still smaller proportions of newborns lived with two parents in families in which the father worked full-time year-round, all of the children were born after the parents' only marriage, and the mother was a full-time homemaker. Between 1940 and 1960, 41–43 percent of newborns lived in such families, and with rising mothers' labor-force participation this fell to only 27 percent in 1980. By age 17, children were even less likely, historically, to live in such families, as the proportion declined from 31 to 15 percent between 1940 and 1980.

These estimates imply that for children born between 1940 and 1960, an average of 65–70 percent of their childhood years were spent in a family situation that did not conform to the mid-twentieth century ideal. Looking ahead, it appears that children born in 1980 may spend an average of 80 percent of their childhood in families that do not conform to this ideal. In addition, children who lived on farms were likely, historically, to experience a parental death or other parental loss, or the economic insecurity associated with drought, crop disease, collapse of commodity prices, and similar catastrophes. Consequently, it is clear that neither historically nor during the industrial era have a majority of children experienced the family stability, the economic stability, and the homemaking mother that was idealized in mid-twentieth century America.

For white children, the chances of living in an idealized "Ozzie and Harriet," breadwinner-homemaker family were only slightly larger than for children as a whole. Among newborn black children at least since 1940, however, no more than 25 percent lived in such idealized families, and this figure fell to only 8 percent for black newborns in 1980. By the end of childhood, among blacks born in 1922, only 15 percent still lived in such families by age 17, and among blacks born in 1962, only 3 percent still lived in such families by age 17. Looking across the entire childhood experience of black children, the average proportion of childhood years not spent in idealized "Ozzie and Harriet" families increased from about 70–80 percent for the 1920s cohort to at least 95 percent for the 1980s cohort.

In 1980 Hispanic children (of any race) were roughly midway between black and white children in their chances of living in an idealized "Ozzie and Harriet" family. Only 10 percent of Hispanic 17-year-olds (of any race) lived in such families in 1980, only 21 percent of Hispanic newborns (of any race) lived in such families in 1980, and among these newborns more than 85 percent of the childhood years will be spent in families that do not conform to the mid-twentieth century ideal.

With these two historic transformations in parents' work and living arrangements, children simultaneously experienced two revolutionary increases in nonparental care, first among those over age 5 and then among younger children.

As farming became overshadowed by an industrial economy in which fathers worked for pay at jobs located away from home, compulsory school attendance and child labor laws were enacted to ensure that children were protected from unsafe and unfair working conditions, that they were excluded from jobs that were needed for adults, and that they received at least a minimal level of education. Also, as time passed increasing affluence allowed families to support themselves without child labor, and higher educational attainments became increasingly necessary in order to obtain jobs that offered higher pay and higher social prestige.

Hence, in 1870 only 50 percent of children aged 5–19 were enrolled in school, and their attendance averaged only 21 percent of the total days in the year. But 70 years later, in 1940, 95 percent of children aged 7–13 were enrolled in school, 79 percent of children aged 14–17 were enrolled in school, and the average attendance amounted to 42 percent of the days in the year. Even as mothers were increasingly viewed as full-time child care providers and homemakers, the need for them to act as full-time child care providers was diminishing, both because of the revolutionary decline in family size and because of the quadrupling in the amount of nonparental child care provided by teachers in school.

Since a full adult workday amounted to about 8 hours per day, 5 days per week (plus commuting time) after 1940, a full adult work year amounted to about 65 percent of the days in a year. But by 1940, school days of 5–6 hours (plus commuting time) amounted to about two-thirds of a full workday for about two-thirds of a full work year. As of 1940, then, childhood school attendance had effectively released mothers from personal child care responsibilities for a time period equivalent to about two-thirds of a full-time adult work year, except for the few years before children entered elementary school.

By reducing the time required for a mother's most important home-maker responsibility—the personal care of her children—this first child-care revolution contributed to the large increase in mothers' labor-force participation after 1940, not only for school-age children but for pre-schoolers as well. Increasing mothers' labor-force participation and the rise in one-parent families then ushered in the second child-care revo-lution for preschool children aged 0–5. Between 1940 and 1989, the pro-portion of children who had no specific parent at home full-time tripled for school-age children (from roughly 22 to 66 percent) and quadrupled for preschoolers (from about 13 percent to about 52 percent).

Today these proportions are probably fairly typical for children in industrial countries, since by 1980 labor-force participation rates for women who were in main parenting ages in the United States were av-erage when compared with other industrial countries. For example, the labor-force participation rates for women aged 30–39 were 70–90 per-cent in Sweden, Denmark, and Norway, 60–70 percent in the United States, France, and Canada, and 45–60 percent in the United Kingdom, West Germany, Italy, Belgium, Switzerland, Australia, and Japan.[3]

The increase in the proportion of preschoolers who had no specific parent at home full-time effectively reduced the amount of parental time that was potentially available to care for preschoolers and effectively increased the need for nonparental care. Yet the proportion of pre-schoolers who had a relative other than a parent in the home who might act as a surrogate parent also declined. For preschoolers living in dual-earner families, the proportion with a potential surrogate parent in the home declined from 19–20 percent in 1940 to only 4–5 percent in 1980. Meanwhile, the proportion of preschoolers living in one-parent families in which there was a potential surrogate parent in the home declined from 51–57 to 20–25 percent.

Time-use studies of nonemployed mothers indicate that the actual time devoted to child care as a primary activity probably increased by about 50–100 percent between 1926–1935 and 1943 and may have in-creased a bit more during the 20 years that followed. But between the 1960s and the early 1980s, the average amount of time that all mothers of preschoolers devoted to child care as a primary activity declined be-cause an increasing number of mothers were employed outside the home and because employed mothers of preschoolers devote about one-half as

[3]Data from the U.S. Bureau of the Census for the following years: 1985 (Norway), 1984 (France), 1983 (Sweden), 1982 (U.S.), 1981 (Canada, Denmark, United Kingdom, Italy, Australia), 1980 (Japan, West Germany, Switzerland), 1977 (Belgium).

much time to child care as a primary activity as do nonemployed mothers (1.2 vs. 2.2 hours per day during the mid-1970s).

By 1989, then, about 48 percent of preschoolers had a specific nonemployed parent at home on a full-time basis (usually the mother), another 12 percent had dual-earner parents who personally provided for their preschoolers' care (often by working different hours or days), and the remaining 40 percent were cared for by someone other than their parents for a large portion of time. Since the proportion of preschoolers who have a specific parent at home full-time declined from about 80 to about 48 percent during the 29 years between 1960 and 1989, we appear to be halfway through the preschool child-care revolution, and we are probably within 30–40 years of its culmination and will then see a very large proportion of preschool children spending increasingly more time in the care of someone other than their parents.

Overall, black children in 1940 were 24 percentage points less likely to have a specific parent at home full-time than were white children, but this racial gap had narrowed to 12 percentage points by 1980. Essentially all of this convergence occurred among older children, since the racial gap among adolescents declined from 27 to 6 percentage points, while the racial gap among preschoolers remained nearly constant at 18–23 percentage points. In 1980, about one-half of the racial gap among preschoolers was accounted for by differences in parental employment, and about one-half was accounted for by differences in the proportion of preschoolers who have no parent in the home.

Also in 1980, Hispanic children (of any race) were generally quite similar to non-Hispanic white children in their parental working and living arrangements, except that Hispanics (of any race) were somewhat more likely to live in one-parent families in which the parent was not employed and somewhat less likely to live in dual-earner families in which at least one parent worked part-time.

The importance of mothers' employment in contributing to family income is discussed below, but what other consequences do mothers' employment and nonparental care have for preschoolers? Past research suggests, broadly, that mothers' employment and nonparental care are neither necessarily nor pervasively harmful to preschoolers. This research also suggests that nonparental care is not a form of maternal deprivation, since children can and do form attachments to multiple caregivers if the number of caregivers is limited, the child-caregiver relationships are long-lasting, and the caregivers are responsive to the individual child.

Available evidence also suggests that the quality of care that children receive is important, and that some children, especially those from low-income families, are in double jeopardy from psychological and economic stress at home as well as exposure to low-quality nonparental child care. Additional potentially beneficial and detrimental effects of mothers' employment and nonparental care for preschoolers have been identified, but most of the results must be viewed as preliminary and tentative. Overall, research on the consequences of nonparental care for preschoolers is itself in its infancy, and much remains to be done.

The first revolution in child care—that is, the advent of nearly universal elementary and high school enrollment between ages 6 and 17—as well as large increases in high school and college graduation, led in due course to a revolutionary increase in parents' education. For example, among children born during the 1920s, the proportions whose fathers completed only 0–8 years of schooling or 4 or more years of high school were 73 and 15 percent, respectively; but these proportions were nearly reversed (at 5 and 85 percent, respectively) among children born only 60 years later during the 1980s. For the same children, those with fathers who had completed 4 or more or 1 or more years of college climbed from 4 and 7 percent, respectively, to 28 and 47 percent. Increases were generally similar for mothers' education, except for a somewhat smaller rise in the proportion with mothers who were college-educated.

Black children, as well as white children, experienced revolutionary increases in parents' education, but blacks continued to lag behind whites, as the black disadvantage effectively shifted higher on the educational ladder but constricted substantially in size. For example, among the 1920s cohort, the maximum racial disadvantages of 38–43 percentage points were in the proportions whose fathers or mothers had completed at least 7–8 years of schooling. But among the 1980s cohort, the maximum racial gaps were only two-fifths as large at 15–16 percentage points, and were in the proportions whose fathers or mothers had completed 13–15 years of schooling.

Measured in terms of the number of decades by which blacks lagged behind whites, the 2–3 decades by which black children born during the 1940s and the 1950s lagged behind whites in having parents who received at least 8 years of education had essentially vanished for the 1970s cohort. But despite a temporary racial convergence among children born during the 1960s and the 1970s, black children born during the 1980s, like black children born during the 1940s and the 1950s, lagged about 2–3 decades behind whites in the proportion whose fathers and mothers had completed at least 4 years of college.

Old-family Hispanic children (of any race) born during the 1960s and the 1970s were fairly similar to non-Hispanic black children in their parents' educational attainments. But first-generation Hispanic children (of any race) were much less likely (by 32–42 percentage points) to have parents who had completed at least 8 years of schooling, presumably because many of their parents had immigrated from countries in which the general educational levels were much lower than those in the United States.

This revolution in parents' education, and continuing differentials by race and Hispanic origin, are important for children both in the short run and throughout their adult years. In the short run, parents with higher educational attainments are more likely to have higher incomes than those with lower educational attainments. In the long run, children whose parents have comparatively high educational attainments also tend, when they reach adulthood, to complete more years of education and thus obtain jobs that offer higher social prestige and income.

Consequently, successive cohorts of children benefited from increasing parents' education both because it contributed to the large increases in family income for children that occurred between World War II and approximately 1970, as described below, and because it contributed to increasing educational levels among children and therefore to higher prestige and income for successive cohorts of children when they reached adulthood. At the same time, the continuing disadvantage of black and Hispanic children (of any race) in their parents' educational attainments tends to limit their current family incomes and their future chances of achieving occupational and economic success during adulthood.

Historically, children's educational attainments, and hence their chances of achieving economic success as adults, were influenced not only by parents' educational attainments, number of siblings, and one-parent family living but also by parents' occupational prestige, living in a farm family, and being black. Since the advantages of some children are the disadvantages of others, differences in these features of family origins led to substantial inequality in the educational opportunities experienced by various children.

For children born between the beginning and the middle of the twentieth century, educational opportunities became substantially more equal, but the overall increase in the equality of educational opportunities was restricted to the opportunity to achieve only as much as a high school education. Beyond the high school level, educational opportunities became less equal, as fathers' education, number of siblings, not living in a two-parent family, and farm origins became more influential in determining whether a child continued beyond high school to finish at least one year of college.

Insofar as these features of family origins have continued to influence children's educational attainments, changes across successive cohorts in their distribution with regard to these family origins taken as a whole place more recent cohorts at an advantage compared with earlier cohorts. The revolutionary increase in parents' education and fathers' occupational prestige, the revolutionary decline in family size, and the near extinction of the family farm all contributed to higher educational attainments among later cohorts of children, although the rise in one-parent families was a partially countervailing influence.

Distinguishing children by race, as we have seen, the racial gap in parents' education has narrowed substantially, although a large gap remains; the racial gap in the proportion of children who live with a large number of siblings has narrowed substantially; and the racial gap in the proportion who live in farm families has essentially vanished. These changes tended to reduce racial inequality in educational opportunities, although this was probably partly counterbalanced by an increasing racial gap in one-parent family living after 1940. Beyond these features of family origins, however, black children born in 1920 faced an additional, large disadvantage in their educational opportunities, but this disadvantage declined sharply in size and essentially vanished for black children born after about 1940. This further contributed to the reduction in racial inequality in educational opportunities.

Taking these features of family origins as a whole, old-family Hispanic children (of any race) born by the 1970s were about as likely as non-Hispanic blacks to be disadvantaged in their family origins, and first-generation Hispanic children (of any race) were somewhat more disadvantaged.

Family Income, Poverty, and Welfare Dependence

Family income, another major feature of family origins, also has important consequences for children's current well-being and future life chances. On a day-to-day basis, whether children live in material deprivation, comfort, or luxury depends mainly on their family's income level. Of particular interest are children in low-income families because they may experience marked deprivation in such areas as nutrition, clothing, housing, or healthcare.

During the 1940s, 1950s, and 1960s, the absolute income levels of American families increased greatly, as real median family income jumped by 35–45 percent per decade, bringing corresponding decreases in absolute want. Associated with this rapid expansion in the ability to purchase consumer products was an unprecedented proliferation in the number and kinds of products that became available, as well as remarkable increases in the quality of these products. By the 1970s the typical American lived in a world of abundance that Americans 30 years earlier could hardly have imagined. Since the beginning of the 1970s, however, real family income has increased comparatively little, despite the ongoing revolution in labor force participation by wives and mothers, and during the 1970s and the 1980s median family income increased by only 5 and 1 percent, respectively.

Despite large improvements in absolute income levels between 1939 and 1969, however, these statistics tell us little about the extent to which children lived in relative deprivation or luxury compared with the standards of the time in which they grew up, because at a specific point in history, the measure of whether a family is judged to be living in deprivation or luxury is that family's income and whether it is especially low or especially high compared with typical families in the same historical period.

Measuring economic deprivation in comparison with median family income in various years, the "relative poverty rate" for children dropped sharply during the 1940s (from 38 to 27 percent) but then much more slowly (to 23 percent in 1969). Subsequently, the relative poverty rate for children increased—mostly during the 1980s—to 27 percent in 1988, reaching the same level experienced almost 40 years earlier in 1949.

As relative poverty declined among children, so, too, did the proportion who lived in relative luxury (from 23 percent in 1939, to 19 percent in 1949, to 15 percent in 1959 and 1969). Subsequently, however, the proportion who lived in relative luxury increased to 22 percent by 1988. Overall, then, economic inequality among children declined substantially between 1939 and 1969, as the proportion living in either relative poverty or luxury dropped from 61 to 38 percent. But economic inequality subsequently increased, and by 1988 the proportion of children who lived in relative poverty or luxury had climbed to 49 percent, eliminating one-half of the reduction in inequality that had occurred between 1939 and 1969.

Meanwhile, the proportion of children who had at least a middle-class family income increased from 51 percent in 1939 to 57–61 percent between 1949 and 1988. Still, although the proportion of children who had a sub-middle-class standard of living fell substantially from 50 percent in 1939 to 42–43 percent in 1949 through 1969, and then to 39 percent in 1979, it increased during the 1980s to 41 percent in 1988.

Among adults, relative poverty also declined after the Great Depression—but more slowly than for children. Hence, the gap between children and adults in relative poverty rates narrowed from about 9 percentage points in 1939 to 4–6 percentage points in 1949–1969. This gap then expanded, however, and by 1988 children were 10 percentage points more likely than adults to live in relative poverty—virtually the same gap that existed during the Great Depression year of 1939.

These estimates of relative economic status are somewhat incomplete, however, because they ignore historical changes in the tax burden and in access to noncash benefits—such as health insurance from private and public sources. If we could explicitly take these changes into account, the results would show that relative poverty rates and economic inequality actually declined by less than we have indicated between 1939 and 1959; they did not fall as low as we have indicated between 1959 and 1979, and they actually increased more than we have indicated during the 1980s.

Among black children, the relative poverty rate probably changed comparatively little between the Civil War and the Great Depression, and by 1939 about 76 percent of black children lived in relative poverty, compared with 33 percent of white children, for a racial gap of 43 percentage points. But black children also shared in the general economic boom that followed the Great Depression and World War II, and the racial gap in relative poverty rates narrowed for children between 1959 and 1988. Still, by 1988 black and white children had relative poverty rates of 53 percent and 22 percent, respectively, for a racial gap of 31 percentage points (seven-tenths as large as in 1939).

Since the relative poverty rates for first-generation and old-family Hispanic children (of any race) in 1980 were 45 and 40 percent, respectively, compared with 49 and 17 percent for non-Hispanic black and non-Hispanic white children, respectively, both first-generation and old-family Hispanic children (of any race) had relative poverty rates that were nearly as high as those for non-Hispanic blacks.

With movements into and out of relative poverty, the proportion of children who ever live in relative poverty is much higher than the proportion who live in relative poverty at any single point in time. For example, among children born during the mid-1960s, about 40–45 percent lived in relative poverty at least one year before reaching adulthood. By race, the proportion of the mid-1960s cohort experiencing at least one year of relative poverty was about 30–40 percent for whites and about 80–85 percent for blacks.

Internationally comparable estimates of relative poverty for children are not available, but comparable estimates differing only slightly from the official U.S. approach to measuring poverty have been calculated for five developed countries and the United States for circa 1980.[4] These poverty rates for Australian and American children were about the same (at 17 percent), but much lower in the United Kingdom, Canada, West Germany, and Sweden (at 11, 10, 8, and 5 percent, respectively). Hence, compared with the latter four countries this poverty rate

[4]Hobbs and Lippman, Table 12.

for children in the United States was at least three-fifths to more than three times higher.

Although portions of these international differences are accounted for by differences in the proportions of children who lived in one-parent families, even among children in one-parent families the poverty rate for American children is at least one-third and as much as six times higher than those of other countries. For children living in one-parent families, these estimated poverty rates were 51 percent for the United States, compared with 37 percent for the United Kingdom, 35 percent for Canada, 32 percent for West Germany, and 9 percent for Sweden.

Focusing only on relatively poor children in the United States, and counting as "welfare" any cash income received from public assistance or Social Security, 30–50 percent of relatively poor children during specific years since the Great Depression have depended at least partly upon welfare benefits for their economic survival. Yet only 7–18 percent lived in families that were fully dependent upon these programs. In other words, as many as 82–93 percent of relatively poor children lived in working-poor families that were at least partly self-supporting, while 50–70 percent lived in families that were fully self-supporting.

Among relatively poor children during specific years since 1959, 27–41 percent of whites and 40–76 percent of blacks were at least partly welfare-dependent, but 86–94 percent of whites and 72–93 percent of blacks lived in working-poor families. Hence, although welfare provides at least some support for many relatively poor children of both races, very large majorities live in families that are at least partly self-supporting, and in 1988, only 14 percent of white children and 28 percent of black children in relative poverty lived in families that depended fully on welfare benefits for their economic survival.

More broadly, because many children personally experience poverty sometime before adulthood, 26 percent of all white children and 74 percent of all black children lived in families that received welfare benefits (including food stamps) sometime during the 1970s. But only 2 percent of all white children and 21 percent of all black children depended on welfare benefits for at least one-half of their income during at least 6 of 10 years during the 1970s. Hence, although a substantial minority of white children and a large majority of black children experience some welfare dependence, for 92 percent of these white children and 72 percent of these black children who did experience some welfare dependence during the 1970s, the experience was a comparatively short one in which welfare was a supplementary source of income in a working-poor family.

In fact, compared with families that have poor children in other developed countries, families with poor children in the United States are much less likely to receive government support, the average amount of support received is much smaller, and it is much more likely (except for Australia) to flow from "means-tested" welfare programs than to come from more broadly based social insurance programs that are similar to Social Security.[5]

With a poverty definition that differs slightly from the official United States definition, 99–100 percent of poor families with children in Australia, Canada, West Germany, Sweden, and the United Kingdom receive economic support from their governments, compared with only 73 percent in the United States. The average amount of government support provided for poor families with children in the United States was about $2,400 in 1980, compared with a range of $2,800–$6,400 in the other five developed countries (that is, 18–170 percent more than in the United States).

Finally, the proportion of government support provided for poor families with children coming from means-tested welfare programs was 71 percent in the United States and 87 percent in Australia, compared with only 11–48 percent in Canada, the United Kingdom, Sweden, and West Germany. In the latter four countries, then, government support to poor families with children is provided to citizens mainly as a matter of course, while in the United States and Australia it is provided only insofar as these families undergo a "means test" to demonstrate to the government that they are, indeed, poverty-stricken.

Although government support to poor families with children is less generous in the United States than in these other developed countries, as relative poverty among American children was increasing between the 1960s and the 1980s, children who lived in poverty also became somewhat more likely to receive welfare benefits. The rise in mother-only families, especially among blacks, is often cited as a major factor contributing to the increases in both poverty and welfare recipiency.

We have calculated that if all of the increasing proportion of children in mother-only families after 1959 had the poverty rate of children in two-parent families, then by 1988 the overall relative and official poverty rates for children would have been 6 percentage points smaller. In fact, however, even if children in mother-only families were (re)united with their fathers, they would have higher poverty rates than children who remained in two-parent families. The reasons for this are that children entering mother-only families have higher poverty rates than do those who remain in two-parent families even before the transition to the mother-only family, and that fathers of children born out of wedlock probably have substantially lower incomes than do married fathers.

[5]Hobbs and Lippman, p. 12 and Table 12.

Hence, without the post-1959 rise in mother-only families, the overall relative and official poverty rates of children in 1988 might have been 2–4 percentage points lower, and more than 80 percent of poor children would still have been poor. Furthermore, despite the much larger increase in mother-only families among black than among white children, if the post-1959 increase in mother-only families had not occurred, it appears that the racial gap in relative poverty rates would have been at least 50–75 percent as large as it actually was. It also appears that if a mandatory child-support program transferring part of fathers' incomes to mother-only families were implemented, the racial gap in relative poverty rates would still be more than 50–75 percent as large as it actually was.

Insofar as the increasing absolute value of welfare benefits after 1960 acted as an incentive for women to become separated, divorced, or bear children out of wedlock, this "welfare-generosity" effect on childhood poverty rates could be no larger than the effect that the post-1959 rise in mother-only families had on poverty rates. However, available evidence suggests that without this increase in welfare benefits, the overall relative and official poverty rates for children would have been smaller by only 1–2 percentage points in 1988—that is, at least 90 percent of poor children would have been poor anyway. This apparently small welfare-generosity effect may be explained, at least partly, by the fact that the increase in the relative value of welfare benefits was comparatively small and temporary.

If historic levels and changes in childhood relative poverty rates cannot be attributed primarily to the rise of mother-only families and changes in welfare generosity, to what can we attribute them? Most immediately, what determines whether a child lives in poverty is the income that is available from fathers, mothers, other relatives, and welfare programs.

Looking across decades, the large historic decline in childhood relative poverty after the Great Depression and World War II, and the more recent increase, were mirrored most closely by changes in relative poverty that would have occurred if children had depended only on the income of fathers in their homes. Both the actual relative poverty rate for children and a hypothetical rate based only on fathers' incomes declined by 14–15 percentage points between 1939 and 1969. Subsequently, between 1969 and 1988 the actual relative poverty rate increased by about one-half as much as the hypothetical rate based only on fathers' incomes (that is, 5.1 vs. 10.3 percentage points).

The additional and increasingly large reductions in the rates of childhood relative poverty that can be accounted for by mothers' incomes acted to speed the earlier decline and slow the subsequent increase in childhood relative poverty. In 1939, mothers' incomes acted to reduce the childhood relative poverty rate by about 3 percentage points below what it would have been if children had depended only on their fathers' income, representing about one-third of the 9 percent of children whose mothers were in the labor force. By 1988, 14 percent of children depended on mothers' incomes to lift them out of relative poverty, and an additional 15 percent remained in relative poverty despite mothers' incomes. Hence, close to one-half of children who had mothers in the labor force in 1988 (29 of 59 percent) depended on their mothers' employment for basic necessities, and the proportion was only slightly lower as measured by the official poverty rate (23 of 59 percent).

Meanwhile, the additional reduction in childhood relative poverty that can be accounted for by family members other than parents in the home declined from about 8–9 percentage points during the Great Depression year of 1939 to about 4–5 percentage points for the years between 1959 and 1988. This suggests that rising parental incomes after the Great Depression may have allowed children and their parents to become more independent of other family members for economic support. Beyond the role of income from these sources, a fourth and final source of income, welfare programs (public assistance and Social Security), accounted for an additional small and nearly stable reduction in childhood relative poverty of only 1–2 percentage points for the years between 1939 and 1988.

The results for white children are similar to those for children as a whole, but the experiences of black children differ in important respects. Black children have higher poverty rates, they tend to remain in poverty for longer periods, and they spend more than half of their poverty years living in mother-only families. Compared with white children, changes in relative poverty for black children across various decades were usually less likely to be accounted for by changes in fathers' incomes and more likely to be accounted for by changes in mothers' incomes. But despite racial differences, poverty changes and transitions for black children, as for white children, are more likely to be associated with changes in the incomes of family members (fathers, mothers, and others) in the homes of children than with changes in welfare income or in family composition involving the loss (or gain) of a parent from the home.

More limited results since 1979 for both old-family and first-generation Hispanic children (of any race) indicate that they were generally more similar to non-Hispanic blacks than to non-Hispanic whites in the relative poverty rates and in the extent to which fathers' incomes were not high enough to lift them out of poverty. The most important difference between Hispanic children (of any race) and all non-Hispanic children is the extraordinary 11 percentage point increase in relative poverty for these Hispanics during the 1980s—an increase that can be accounted for mainly by the declining extent to which fathers' incomes lifted them out of poverty.

Since larger families require more income than do smaller families in order to maintain a specific standard of living, changes in family size might also account of poverty trends since the Great Depression. A separate analysis of family size indicates that dependent sibsizes can account for a change of only 1–2 percentage points in childhood relative poverty during each decade between 1939 and 1988 except one. During the 1970s, the large decline in dependent sibsizes can account for a reduction of 4–5 percentage points in the rates of relative childhood poverty.

Although the racial gap in dependent sibsizes increased and then decreased between 1939 and 1988, at both the beginning and the end of the era, when the racial gaps in relative poverty were about 40 and 30 percentage points, respectively, the racial gaps in dependent sibsizes accounted for a small and nearly identical 2–4 percentage points in the racial gaps in relative poverty. During the 1970s, the dependent sibsizes of Hispanic children (of any race) were similar to those of non-Hispanic black children, with similar consequences for relative poverty.

This approach to accounting for changes in relative poverty in terms of changes in income from fathers, mothers, other family members, welfare, and dependent sibsize is limited, however, because it provides no direct indication of how these changes may have influenced one another or of how other trends in the family, the economy, and society may have influenced these changes. Instead, the results provide a simple accounting of the extent to which these factors became more or less important in reducing childhood relative poverty between various points in time, given the social, economic, and familial changes that actually occurred.

Why Children's Family Life Changed

A complete and richly detailed explanation of historic changes in family income, family work, family composition, and other features of children's life course is not possible within the confines of this book. But to make some sense of these trends from the perspective of children and their parents, we do discuss important ways in which these and other trends are related by exploring some of the fundamental causes of historic change in fathers' incomes, the rise of mothers' labor-force participation, and the rise of mother-only families.

With the economic boom following the Great Depression and World War II, children experienced a large drop in fathers' unemployment, a large increase in fathers' absolute income levels, greater equality in the distribution of fathers' incomes, and a large decline in relative poverty. But the relative poverty rate for children increased after 1969, and the official childhood poverty rate increased after 1979. Rising childhood poverty mirrored the increases both in the proportion of children whose fathers had comparatively low incomes and in the proportion of those who lived in mother-only families.

A prominent demographic factor that contributed to the rise in the proportion of children whose fathers had comparatively low incomes was the fact that the baby boomers were reaching adulthood. The entry of the comparatively large baby-boom cohorts into the labor force after 1960 tended to intensify competition for available jobs and therefore depress the wages and relative incomes of young men. This in turn contributed to the sharp post-1959 slowdown and subsequent stagnation in the growth of family income, to the stagnation and subsequent deterioration in fathers' incomes for children in the bottom half of the income distribution, and hence to rising relative and official poverty rates among children.

Increased immigration after 1960 also tended to intensify competition for available jobs, but increased immigration had a much smaller effect on the labor force than did the baby boomers. Additional factors that tended to depress the relative incomes of young men were (1) the historic increase in educational attainments, because it involved a later age of entry into permanent work commitments and a shift toward occupations that were characterized by comparatively low entry-level earnings; and (2) institutional and legal changes that provided greater job and income security and reduced age discrimination for older workers, because these increased the comparative disadvantage of younger workers.

Much of the historic rise in mother-only families appears to have grown out of transformations in the family economy that occurred as individuals sought to maintain or improve their relative economic standing in the face of changing economic circumstances. With the Industrial Revolution, couples sought to maintain or improve their relative economic position in several ways. Parents had smaller families with fewer children so that available resources might be spread less thinly among family members, thereby providing greater opportunities for current consumption and greater resources needed by children to advance their own relative economic status during adulthood. Parents also moved off the farm so that fathers could work at comparatively well-paid jobs in the nonfarm economy. But this work greatly weakened the mutual economic interdependence of husbands and wives, because the husband could, if he desired, depend on his own work alone for his income. More recently, mothers' work outside the home has also increased sharply, as families sought to maintain or improve their relative economic standing. But this trend provided mothers, too, with independent incomes from their own jobs, incomes with which they might support themselves. Hence, the weakening of the economic interdependence of husbands and wives, combined with the decline of rural small-town controls that once censured divorce, fostered the large historic rise in separation and divorce that accounts for about two-thirds of the rise in mother-only families among children.

Economic insecurity and need also apparently contributed substantially to the rise in separation and divorce, at least after 1970. Instability in husbands' work, drops in family income, and a low ratio of family income-to-needs have been found to lead to increased hostility between husbands and wives, to decreased marital quality, and to increased risk of divorce. Hence, it is not surprising that each economic recession since the early 1970s brought a substantially larger increase in mother-only families for children than did the preceding nonrecessionary period.

Increased mothers' work for pay outside the home also appears to have resulted largely from the continuing desire of individuals to maintain or improve their relative economic standing, and from economic insecurity and need, in the face of changing socioeconomic circumstances. From the onset of the Industrial Revolution through 1940, major avenues available to couples who sought to maintain or improve their relative economic standing were to have husbands work in comparatively well-paid nonfarm jobs, to limit family size to a comparatively small number of children, and to increase educational attainments that would provide greater access to well-paid jobs.

By 1940, the first two avenues had run their course for most couples, and since most persons achieve their ultimate educational attainments by age 25, additional schooling beyond age 25 is often difficult or impractical. Instead, a fourth major avenue to improving family income emerged between 1940 and 1960—namely paid work by wives and mothers—because the traditional sources of female nonfarm labor (unmarried women) were either stationary or in the process of declining in size, while the demand for female workers was increasing.

Meanwhile, mothers also were becoming increasingly available and increasingly well qualified for work outside the home. Although the breadwinner-homemaker family had emerged as the dominant family form with the Industrial Revolution, by 1940 the substantial time spent by children in school and declining family size had greatly constricted the homemaker role of mothers, making them potentially available for paid work outside the home. As of 1940, in fact, childhood school attendance had effectively released mothers from personal child-care responsibilities for a time period equivalent to about two-thirds of a full-time adult work year, except for the few years before children entered elementary school. In addition, the educational attainments of women and mothers had increased along with those of men, and by 1940 young women were more likely than young men to graduate from high school and about two-thirds as likely to graduate from college.

Finally, paid work outside the home for mothers was also becoming increasingly attractive in our competitive, consumer-oriented society. For example, families in which the husband's income was comparatively low could, by virtue of the wife's work, jump economically ahead of families in which the husbands had the same occupational status but lacked a working wife. Similarly, families of young men with low relative incomes after 1960 could, by virtue of wives' work, jump economically ahead of both other young families and older families that had no working wife. But this in turn placed families with comparatively well-paid husbands at a disadvantage, which made their wives' work more attractive. In addition, with the rising divorce rate, work became increasingly attractive to mothers as a hedge against the possible economic disaster of losing most or all of their husbands' income through divorce.

Economic insecurity and need have also made mothers' work increasingly attractive. Both among the increasing proportion of children living in mother-only families and among an increasing proportion of children who live in two-parent families, mothers' incomes have become essential as a means of either lifting the family out of poverty or providing basic support at a subpoverty level.

In short, by 1940 mothers' work had become the only major avenue that was available to most couples over age 25 who sought to maintain or improve their relative economic status; and after 1940 not only did the economic demand for married women to work increase, but so did the potential availability, attractiveness, and sheer family need for mothers to work.

Although black children are sometimes viewed as having very different experiences from those of white children, results presented in earlier chapters suggest that factors responsible for the declines in fathers' relative incomes after 1960, and for long-term increases in mothers' employment and mother-only families among children in general, have played the same role for black children. The main difference is that blacks began the post–World War II era with extraordinarily high levels of economic insecurity and need, and because of that, as well as a high level of residential segregation, changes in the economy have affected them more severely than whites. This in turn has led to a much larger increase in mother-only families among black children. Much more limited results for old-family Hispanic children (of any race) are consistent, at least, with the view that they have faced changes and constraints similar to, but in some ways less severe than, black children.

Looking Toward the Future

A detailed description of future change in the childhood life course is not possible, of course, because it would require a detailed knowledge of future changes in the family, the economy, the society, and public policy. We can, however, outline plausible directions of change in the immediate future, and possible implications, viewing current trends in historical perspective.

During the past century, the average number of siblings in the families of children is expected to decline by a total of 4.7 siblings per family (from 6.6 to 1.9). But the largest possible future decline is much smaller (from 1.9 to 1.0 child per family), since an only-child lives in a one-child family. Less extreme, for example, is the fact that if the average family size of women declined by 50 percent (from 2.1 to 1.0 children per woman), with one-third of women each having 0, 1, and 2 children, then the average family size of children would decline by only 10–20 percent (from 1.9 to 1.67 children per family), since one-third of children would be only-children and two-thirds would be in two-child families.

Hence, any future decline in children's family size would be small by historical standards. At the extreme, a continuing decline might effectively eliminate potential sibling companionship for a comparatively large proportion of children. But the beneficial effect that less sibling competition for parental resources would have on children's educational attainments would probably be comparatively small by historical standards, since the negative effects that living in small families with different numbers of siblings would have on educational attainments are relatively small compared with the large negative effects of living in families in which there are 5 or more siblings.

Insofar as the increasing costs and decreasing benefits that children now represent for their parents were responsible for the historic fertility decline, a continuing desire by adults to maintain or improve their relative economic status compared with others may lead to further reductions in family size in the future. On the other hand, parent-child relationships have historically been—and at least to this point in history remain—one of the two major realms of activity from which most adults could reap substantial personal satisfaction. Such familial satisfactions—the benefits of having children—may place a lower limit on family size of 1–2 children per family for many adults.

During the 1960s and the 1970s, the proportion of children who experienced mother-only families increased greatly with rising separation and divorce, especially among whites. But since the late 1970s, divorce rates have changed comparatively little. If divorce continues on this plateau, children born during the 1980s will be the first to experience these historically high divorce rates throughout childhood, and they may experience the highest proportion ever living in mother-only families.

The comparatively small changes in divorce rates during the past 10–15 years suggest that forces that foster marital disruption reached a point of equilibrium as the transition from farming to nonfarm work reached its end. Future increases or decreases are possible, of course. But a continuing rise in mothers' labor-force participation, which might potentially provide the basis for economic independence among a growing proportion of mothers, may be counterbalanced as two-parent families approach nearly universal dependence on two adult earners in order to maintain the typical standard of living now prevalent in the United States.

Rising out-of-wedlock childbearing also contributed to the increase in mother-only families after 1960, especially among black children. Out-of-wedlock births as a proportion all births have increased almost without interruption since the early 1950s, reaching 64 percent for blacks and 18 percent for whites by 1990. Insofar as these increases result from apparently limited economic opportunities, particularly the lack of steady employment—especially for black men—future changes may depend mainly upon the extent to which such economic opportunities improve or deteriorate further during the coming years. Despite major progress in narrowing the racial gaps in educational attainments and income, racial gaps remain large, and a disproportionately large proportion of blacks continue to lag far behind typical whites.

The second revolution in parents' work, the rapid rise in mothers' labor-force participation, was more than half complete by 1989. Historically, declining family size and increasing school attendance of children over age 5 increased the potential availability of mothers for work outside the home. Today school attendance through age 17 is nearly universal, and insofar as women continue to bear any children, additional potential declines in family size are limited. Still, mothers' educational attainments continue to rise, making them increasingly employable. In addition, economic insecurity among families in which the fathers' incomes are relatively low makes mothers' work virtually essential, while the ever-smaller proportion of two-parent families in which only the father works is becoming increasingly disadvantaged in its relative family income compared with the rising proportion of dual-earner families.

Hence, powerful historical forces provide continuing incentives for increasing mothers' employment, as does the rising proportion of children who live in mother-only families. By the turn of the century, perhaps 80 percent of children or more will live in dual-earner or one-parent families, and even among newborn children under age 1, fewer than 20 percent may live in the idealized "Ozzie and Harriet" type of family in which the father works full-time year-round, the mother is a full-time homemaker, and all of the children were born after the parents' only marriage.

The second child-care revolution, the expansion of nonparental care for children under age 6, is occurring in tandem with the rise in dual-earner families. By 1987, although about 12 percent of children lived in dual-earner families in which the parents worked different hours or days and were therefore able to personally care for their children, about 40 percent of preschoolers spent considerable time in the care of someone other than their parents while the parents worked. Insofar as mothers' labor-force participation continues to rise, and unless a major change in time commitments required by many jobs regardless of parental status occurs, nonparental child care will also continue to rise to include at least a majority of preschoolers, and perhaps a substantial majority, by the turn of the century. The cost and quality of expanded preschool child care and the consequences for children remain uncertain.

When the first child-care revolution led to nearly universal school enrollment for children aged 6–17 by the 1950s or the 1960s, high school and college enrollment and graduation rates continued to climb upward until the mid-1970s, at older ages. It goes without saying that each generation of children becomes the next generation of parents, and we have been in the midst of an ongoing revolutionary increase in parents' educational attainments. Ever higher educational attainments for children have been seen by parents as a major pathway to ensuring their children's relative economic success during adulthood. Hence, it would appear that the revolutionary increase in children's, and thereby parents', educational attainments might be expected to continue as long as parents continue to desire greater success for their children and to have the ability to send them to ever-higher levels of schooling.

Education through high school is available throughout the United States at public expense as a society-wide commitment to basic education. The public also supports college education through an infrastructure of junior college and university systems, but the direct cost of college or university attendance may be substantial for students and their families, and relatively low-income families may find the potential loss of income associated with college attendance particularly burdensome. Consistent with nearly free high school but much higher costs in educating children beyond high school, opportunities to complete at least 4 years of high school among children with differing family origins became much more equal for children born between the beginning and middle of the twentieth century, but opportunities to go on to college have become somewhat more unequal during the same era.

Because of public and parental support, the proportion of persons aged 25–29 who have completed at least 4 years of high school reached 85 percent by the mid-1970s, although little change has occurred since then.[6] Lagging about 10 years behind whites, blacks aged 25–29 did not reach 83 percent of completing this level of schooling until 1986. The proportion of persons aged 25–29 who completed at least 4 years of college also reached a plateau during the mid-1970s (at about 22–23 percent).[7] Among blacks aged 25–29, the proportion who completed at least 4 years of college has also changed little since the mid-1970s, but at the much lower level of 11–13 percent. Since persons aged 25–29 between 1975 and 1989 were born between 1946 and 1964, educational attainments have changed little for successive cohorts of children born during the baby-boom era of increasing fertility.

In addition, post-1975 estimates of educational attainments for persons aged 25–29 are similar in size to the proportion of children aged 0–5 in 1985 whose parents had completed corresponding levels of education. Hence, unless high school and college enrollment and graduation rates increase, the proportions of children whose parents completed at least 4 years of high school or college will probably change little in the future. School enrollment did increase for persons aged 18–21 during the 1980s, however, suggesting that as these young adults become parents, parental education for children born during the 1990s may drift upward slightly.[8] Overall, then, revolutionary increases in children's ed-

[6]Robert Kominski, U.S. Bureau of the Census, Current Population Reports, Series P-20, No. 451, *Educational Attainment in the United States: March 1989 and March 1988* (Washington, DC: U.S. Government Printing Office, 1991), Table 18.

[7]The temporary jump of as much as 5 percentage points that occurred for men, but not women, can apparently be explained by the passing of the "Vietnam cohort" through ages 25–29. See Rosalind R. Bruno, U.S. Bureau of the Census, Current Population Reports, Series P-20, No. 415, *Educational Attainment in the United States: March 1982 to 1985* (Washington, DC: U.S. Government Printing Office, 1987), pp. 1–2. Table 18. Robert Kominski, U.S. Bureau of the Census, Current Population Reports, Series P-20, No. 451, *Educational Attainment in the United States: March 1988 and March 1989* (Washington, DC: U.S. Government Printing Office, 1991), Table 12.

[8]Rosalind R. Bruno, U.S. Bureau of the Census, Current Population Reports, Series P-20, No. 443, *School Enrollment—Social and Economic Characteristics of Students: October 1988 and 1987* (Washington, DC: U.S. Government Printing Office, 1990), Table A-3.

ucation appear to have ended with children of the baby boom and, consequently, revolutionary increases in parents' education may have ended as of the early 1980s cohort of children.

Historical precedence suggests that future changes in childhood poverty and in the amount of inequality in the distribution of family income for children will depend mainly on future changes in fathers' incomes and mothers' incomes. But changes in parents' income will in turn depend upon a variety of social and economic factors, including changes in the economy itself with regard to the kinds of jobs that are created and the amount of inequality in the incomes that are associated with different kinds of jobs. Since economic and social trends during the past two decades, but especially during the 1980s, led to increased poverty and economic inequality among children, a continuation of current economic and social trends may lead to continued, comparatively high levels of childhood poverty and economic inequality, if not to increases, in future years.

Of course, public polices may also influence the amount and distribution of family income available to children, both by affecting the economy and by providing income and services directly to children's families. Among the many historical and contemporary public policies that affect children, their family income, and the economy, only a few of the more prominent can be mentioned here.

Free public education for all children through elementary school and, subsequently, through high school led to revolutionary increases in knowledge and the skills of both children and workers. These advances contributed greatly to the historic economic expansion associated with the Industrial Revolution during the past century and hence to the resulting multiplication of family income levels.

Public support for education beyond high school has also been substantial but more restricted, and the proportion of young adults who completed at least 4 years of college appears to have stalled at 22–23 percent since the mid-1970s. Moreover, continuing inequality in opportunities to go beyond high school among children with differing family origins especially hinders black and Hispanic children (of any race) in their efforts to close the economic gap with non-Hispanic whites. Public support for education (and child care) at the opposite end of the age spectrum, for children under age 5, has been still more limited.

In view of the important historic role that public support for elementary and high school education played in fostering income growth, further extensions of public support to both higher and lower levels of schooling might have a similarly salutary effect. In addition, it appears that a substantial minority of mothers with young children would seek

employment or work more hours if child care were available at a reasonable cost.[9] Since the constraining effect of available child care on mothers' employment seems most prevalent among mothers who are young,
black, single, and have low education and little income, additional public support for child care for young children might help raise the amount
of income that is available to many children who are especially disadvantaged.

With regard to the economy itself, minimum-wage laws influence
the extent of income inequality by setting a lower limit to the amount
of income earned by many low-income workers and tax laws influence
income inequality by placing a lesser or greater tax burden on persons
and families who have comparatively high or comparatively low incomes. More broadly, public expenditures can influence the income distribution by leading to the creation of a specific array of jobs involving
a particular distribution of income to employed persons. For example,
the interstate highway program, the space program, and specific health
and defense programs each led to particular combinations of low-, me-
dium-, and high-paying jobs. Of course, while public policies may have
a great influence on the economy and society, they do not directly control economic growth or the precise shape of the income distribution.

Public policies can, however, ameliorate at least some of the negative consequences for children and families that flow from economic
and social change. For example, programs that directly provide cash or
noncash benefits, such as Aid to Families with Dependent Children and
Food Stamps, and their predecessors, have helped a substantial minority
of children and families through difficult economic times from the Great
Depression to the present. As we have seen, however, the effect of these
programs on the poverty rates of children and families in the United
States is small compared with the social welfare and insurance programs in other major developed countries. Similarly, public service-ori-
ented programs, such as Medicaid and Medicare, have made essential
health services available to many poor children and families during recent decades, but coverage is far from universal.[10]

[9]Harriet B. Presser and Wendy Baldwin, "Child Care as a Constraint on Employment: Prevalence, Correlates, and Bearing on the Work and Fertility Nexus," *American
Journal of Sociology* 85, 5 (March 1980): 1202–1213.

[10]For example, see Figure 43, Terry Lugaila, U.S. Bureau of the Census, Current Population Reports, Series P 23–181, *Households, Families, and Children: A Thirty-Year Perspective*, (Washington, DC: U.S. Government Printing Office, 1992).

Conclusion

America's children experienced several interrelated revolutions in their life course, as the family, economy, and society were transformed during the past 150 years. Family size plummeted. One-parent family living jumped. Family farms nearly became extinct, as first fathers and then mothers left the home for much of the day in order to serve as family breadwinners. Formal schooling, nonparental care for children, and parents' educational attainments have increased greatly, although educational opportunities to go beyond high school have become less equal since the turn of the century.

Absolute family incomes multiplied, but the past two decades brought little change in average income and increasing economic inequality among children, despite increasing mothers' labor-force participation. Relative and official poverty rates for children climbed during the past decade. Welfare dependence increased during recent decades, but most poor children historically and today live in working-poor families.

Currently, it appears that many of these revolutionary changes will be most extreme among children born within a decade of this writing. By historical standards, family size can decline comparatively little below the level expected for children born in the mid-1990s. Divorce, the major contributor to one-parent family living, has changed little since the late 1970s. By the year 2000, a large majority of children will live in dual-earner or one-parent families, a majority of preschoolers will receive substantial nonparental care while parents work, and only a small minority, even among newborns, will live in idealized "Ozzie and Harriet" families. Future changes in parents' education, in real income, poverty, and income inequality, and in welfare recipiency appear less certain, partly because they may be more responsive to specific public policies than are family size, divorce, and whether fathers and mothers work outside the home.

Regardless of future public policies, however, it seems likely that the fundamental transformations that have occurred during the past 150 years in the family, the economy, and the society will not be undone. Today, as throughout America's history, most children live with their parents and rely on them to provide for their economic support and day-to-day care. Yet a majority of children—both historically and today—have experienced either the loss of a parent from the home or economic insecurity, or both. Nevertheless, as a result of 150 years of revolutionary change in parents' work, in the family economy, and in the broader economy and society, America's children have entered a new age.

Bibliography

Adam, Smith *Wealth of Nations.* London: Everyman's Library, 1776.

Alwin, Duane F. "Trends in Parental Socialization Values: Detroit, 1958–1984." *American Journal of Sociology* 90, 2 (September 1984):359–382.

Alwin, Duane F., and Arland Thornton "Family Origins and the Schooling Process: Early Versus Late Influence of Parental Characteristics." *American Sociological Review* 49 (1984): 784–802.

Anderson, Odin W., and Jacob J. Feldman *Family Medical Costs and Voluntary Health Insurance: A Nationwide Survey.* New York: McGraw-Hill, 1956.

Bane, Mary Jo "Household Composition and Poverty." In Sheldon H. Danziger and Daniel H. Weinberg, eds., *Fighting Poverty.* Cambridge, MA: Harvard University Press, 1986, pp. 209–231.

Bartlett, John *Familiar Quotations.* 14th ed. rev. and enl., Emily Morison Beck, ed. Boston: Little, Brown, 1968.

Bean, Frank D., and Marta Tienda *The Hispanic Population of the United States.* New York: Russell Sage Foundation, 1987.

Belsky, Jay "Developmental Risks Associated with Infant Day Care: Attachment Insecurity, Noncompliance, and Aggression?" In S. Chehrazi, ed., *Balancing Working and Parenting: Psychological and Developmental Implications of Day Care.* New York: American Psychiatric, 1990, pp. 37–68.

Bernert (Sheldon), Elenor H. *America's Children,* prepared for the Social Science Research Council in cooperation with the U.S. Department of Commerce, Bureau of the Census, New York: Wiley, 1958.

Blake, Judith "Family Size and the Quality of Children." *Demography* 18, (1981):321–342.

——— "Number of Siblings and Educational Mobility." *American Sociological Review* 50 (1985):84–94.

———"Differential Parental Investment: Its Effects on Child Quality and Status Attainment." In Jane B. Lancaster, et al., *Parenting Across the Life Span: Biosocial Dimensions,* New York: Aldine de gruyter, 1987, pp. 351–375.

——— *Family Size and Achievement.* Berkeley: University of California Press, 1989.

——— "Fertility Control and the Problem of Voluntarism." In Scientists and World Affairs Proceedings of the Twenty-Second Pugwash Conference on Science and World Affairs, September 7–12, 1973, London, pp. 279–283.

——— "Demographic Science and the Redirection of Population Policy." In Mindel C. Sheps and Jeanne Clare Ridley, eds., *Public Health and Population Change,* Pittsburgh: University of Pittsburgh Press, 1965.

———, **and Prithwis Das Gupta** "Reproductive Motivation Versus Contraceptive Technology: Is Recent American Experience an Exception?" *Population and Development Review* 1:229–249.

Blau, Peter M. and Otis Dudley Duncan *The American Occupational Structure.* New York: Wiley, 1969.

Broderick, Carlfred B. "To Arrive Where We Started: The Field of Family Studies in the 1930s." *Journal of Marriage and the Family* 50 3 (August 1988):569– 584.

Bureau of Research & Statistics, Department of Public Assistance Commonwealth of Pennsylvania. *Pennsylvania Public Assistance Statistics, January 1941.* Harrisburg, PA: Commonwealth of Pennsylvania, 1941.

Burns, Arthur Edward and Peyton Kerr "Survey of Work-Relief Wage Policies." *American Economic Review* 31 (March 1941): 713– 720.

Bumpass, Larry L. "Children and Marital Disruption: A Replication and Update." *Demography* 21 (1984):71–83.

—— "Bigger Isn't Necessarily Better: A Comment on Hofferth's "Updating Children's Life Course." *Journal of Marriage and the Family* 48 (1985):797– 798.

Carter, Hugh, and Paul C. Glick *Marriage and Divorce: A Social and Economic Study.* Cambridge, MA: Harvard Press, 1970.

Cherlin, Andrew, J. "The Weakening Link Between Marriage and the Care of Children." *Family Planning Perspectives* 10 (December 1988):302–306.

Clarke-Stewart, K. Allison "Infant Day Care: Maligned or Malignant?" *American Psychologist* 44 (1989):266–273.

Conger, R. D., et al "Linking Economic Hardship to Marital Quality and Instability." *Journal of Marriage and the Family* 52 (1990):643–656.

Davis, Kingsley "The Theory of Response and Change in Modern Demographic History." *Population Index* 29 (1963):345–366.

—— "The American Family in Relation to Demographic Change." In U.S. Commission on Population Growth and the American Future, pp. 237–265. Charles F. Westoff and Robert Parke, Jr., eds., *Demographic and Social Aspects of Population Growth*, vol. 1 of Commission Research Reports. Washington, DC: U.S. Government Printing Office, 1972.

—— "Wives and Work: The Sex Role Revolution and Its Consequences." *Population and Development Review* 10:397–417.

Desai, Sonalde, P. Lindsay Chase-Lansdale, and Robert T. Michael "Mother or Market? Effects of Maternal Employment on Intellectual Ability of 4-Year-Old Children." *Demography* 26 (1989):545–561.

Duncan, Greg J. *Years of Poverty, Years of Plenty.* Michigan: Survey Research Center, Institute for Social Research, University of Michigan, Ann Arbor, 1980.

——, **and Willard Rodgers** "Lone-Parent Families and Their Economic Problems: Transitory or Persistent?" In *Lone-Parent Families*, Organization for Economic Co-operation and Development, Social Policy Studies No. 8, Organization for Economic Co-operation and Development.

——, **and Willard L. Rodgers** "Longitudinal Aspects of Childhood Poverty." *Journal of Marriage and the Family* 50 (November 1988):1007–1021.

——, **and Willard Rodgers** "Single-Parent Families: Are Their Economy Problems Transitory or Persistent?" *Family Planning Perspectives* 19, 4 (July/August 1987):171–178.

Durand, John D. *The Labor Force in the United States 1890–1960.* New York: Social Science Research Council, 1948.

Easterlin, Richard A. *Birth and Fortune: The Impact of Numbers on Personal Welfare.* New York: Basic Books, 1980.

Elder, Glen H., Jr. *Children of the Great Depression: Social Change in Life Experience.* Chicago: University of Chicago Press, 1974.

—— "Perspectives on the Life Course." In Glen H. Elder, Jr., ed., *Life Course Dynamics:* Ithaca, NY: Cornell University Press, 1985, pp. 23–49.

——, **Rand D. Conger, E. Michael Foster, and Monika Ardelt** "Families Under Economic Pressure." *Journal of Family Issues* (in Press).

—— "Household, Kinship, and the Life Course: Perspective on Black Families and Children." In M. Spencer, G. Brookins, and W. Allen, eds., *Beginnings: The Social and Affective Development of Black Children,* New York: Erlbaum, 1985, pp. 39–43.

——, **Avshalom Caspi, and Geraldine Downey** "Problem Behavior and Family Relationships." In Age Sorenson, Franz Weinert, and Lonnie Sherrod, eds., *Human Development: Multi-Disciplinary, Perspectives,* Hillsdale, NJ: Erlbaum, (in Press), pp. 293–340.

——, **Avshalom Caspi, and Tri van Nguyen** "Resourceful and Vulnerable Children: Family Influences in Stressful Times." In R. K. Silbereisen and K. Eyferth, eds., *Development as Action in Context: Integrative Perspectives on Youth Development,* New York: Springer, 1986, pp. 167–187.

—— "Scarcity and Prosperity in Postwar Child Bearing: Explorations from a Life Course Perspective." *Journal of Family History:* 5 410–433.

——, **and Tamara K. Hareven** "Rising Above Life's Disadvantage: From Great Depression to World War." In Glen H. Elder, Jr., John Modell, and Ross Parke, eds., selections from *Children in Time and Place,* Cambridge: Cambridge University Press, 1992.

Employment and Training Report of the President. Washington, D.C: U.S. Government Printing Office, 1982.

Espenshade, Thomas J. *Investing in Children: New Estimates of Parental Expenditures.* Washington, DC: Urban Institute, 1984.

Expert Committee on Family Budget Revisions *New American Family Budget Standards,* Madison, WI: Institute for Research on Poverty, 1980.

Farley, Reynolds and Walter R. Allen *The Color Line and the Quality of Life in America.* New York: Russell Sage Foundation, 1987.

Featherman, David L. "Life-Span Perspectives in Social Science Research." In Paul B. Bates and Orville G. Brim, Jr., eds., *Life-Span Development,* vol. 5. New York: Academic Press, 1983, pp. 1–51.

——, **and Robert M. Hauser** *Opportunity and Change.* New York: Academic Press, 1978.

Fuchs, Victor "Towards a Theory of Poverty." In *The Concept of Poverty.* Washington, DC: Chapter of Commerce of the United States, 1965, pp. 71–91.

Furstenberg, Jr., Frank F., Christine Winquist Nord, James L. Peterson, Nicholas Zill "The Life Course of Children of Divorce: Marital Disruption and Parental Contact." *American Sociological Review* 48, 5 (1983):656–668.

Galbraith, John Kenneth *The Affluent Society.* Boston: Houghton Mifflin, 1958.

Garbarino, Joseph W. *Health Plans and Collective Bargaining.* Berkeley: University of California Press, 1960.

Garfinkel, Irwin, and Sara S. McLanahan *Single Mothers and Their Children.* Washington, DC: Urban Institute, 1986.

Gershuny, Jonathan, and John P. Robinson "Historical Changes in the Household Division of Labor." *Demography* 25, 4 (November 1988):537–552.

Glick, Paul C. "The Family Cycle." *American Sociological Review* 12 (1947):164–174.

———— "The Life Cycle of the Family." *Marriage and Family Living* 17 (1955):3–9.

————, and Robert Parke, Jr. "New Approaches in Studying the Life Cycle of the Family." *Journal of Marriage and the Family* 39 (1977): pp. 5–13.

———— *Marriage and Divorce: A Social and Economic Study.* New York: Wiley, 1957.

Grebler, Leo, Joan W. Moore, and Ralph G. Guzman *The Mexican-American People.* New York: Free Press, 1970.

Greehalgh, Susan "Toward a Political Economy of Fertility: Anthropological Contributions." *Population and Development Review* 16, 1 (March 1990):85–106.

Greenberger, Ellen, and Laurence Steinberg *When Teenagers Work: The Psychological and Social Costs of Adolescent Employment.* New York: Basic Books, 1986.

Hareven, Tamara K. and Maris A. Vinovskis, eds. *Family and Population in Nineteenth-Century America.* Princeton, NJ: Princeton University Press, 1978.

Haskins, Ron "Beyond Metaphor: The Efficacy of Early Childhood Education." *American Psychologist* 44 (1989):274–282.

Hayes, Cheryl D., and Sheila B. Kamerman, eds. *Children of Working Parents: Experiences and Outcomes.* A report of the Panel on Work, Family and Community of the Committee on Child Development and Public Policy. Washington, D.C: National Academy, 1983.

Hayes, Cheryl D., John L. Palmer, and Martha J. Zaslow, eds. *Who Cares for America's Children?* A report of the Panel of Child Care Policy, Committee on Child Development Research and Public Policy. Washington, DC: National Academy, 1990.

Hernandez, Donald J. "Childhood in Sociodemographic Perspective." In Turner, Ralph H., and James F. Short, Jr., eds., *Annual Review of Sociology,* vol. 12, Palo Alto, CA: Annual Reviews, 1986, 159–180.

———— "A Comment on Barbara Entwisle's Measuring Components of Family Planning Program Effort." *Demography* 26, 1 (1989): 77–80.

———— *Success or Failure Family Planning Programs in the Third World.* Westport, CT: Greenwood, 1984.

———— "Organizing for Effective Family Planning Programs." A review of a National Research Council report in *Population and Development Review* 14, 1 (1988):198–201.

———— "Population Policy." In Adam Kuper and Jessica Kuper, eds., *The Social Science Encyclopedia,* London: Routledge, 1958, p. 628.

Hetherington, E. Mavis, M. Cox, and R. Cox "The Aftermath of Divorce." In J. H. Stevens, Jr., and M. Matthews, eds. *Mother-Child, Father-Child Relationship,* National Association for the Education of Young Children, Washington, DC, 1978.

———— "Long-term Effects of Divorce and Remarriage on the Adjustment of Children." *Journal of the American Academy of Child Psychiatry* 24:518–530.

Hill, Martha S. "The Role of Economic Resources and Dual-Family Status in Child Support Payments." Presented at April 1988 annual meeting of the Population Association of America, May 1988.

———— "Trends in the Economic Situation of U.S. Families and Children: 1970–1980." *American Families and the Economy: the High Costs of Living.* Washington, DC: National Academy, 1983.

Hill, Martha S., and Greg J. Duncan "Parental Family Income and the Socioeconomic Attainment of Children." *Social Science Research* 16, 1 (March 1987):39–73.

Hirsch, Arnold R. *Making the Second Ghetto: Race and Housing in Chicago, 1940–1960.* London: Cambridge University Press, 1983.

Hoffman, Lois Wladis "Effects of Maternal Employment in the Two-Parent Family." *American Psychologist* 44 (1989):283–299.

Hoffman, Saul D. and Greg J. Duncan "What Are the Economic Consequences of Divorce?" *Demography* 25 (November 1988): 302–306.

Jackson, Kenneth T. *Crabgrass Frontier: The Suburbanization of the United States.* New York: Oxford University Press, 1985.

Juster, Thomas J., and Frank P. Stafford "Introduction and Overview." In F. Thomas Juster and Frank P. Stafford, eds., *Time, Goods, and Well-Being,* Ann Arbor: Survey Research Center, Institute for Social Research, University of Michigan, 1985, pp. 1–18.

Juster, Thomas F. "A Note on Recent Changes in Time Use." In F. Thomas Juster and Frank Stafford, eds., *Studies in the Measurement of Time Allocation,* Ann Arbor: Institute for Social Research, University of Michigan, pp. 397–422.

Kohn, Melvin L. *Class and Conformity.* Homewood, IL: Dorsey, 1969.

———**, and Carmi Schooler** *Work and Personality.* Norwood, NJ: Ablex, 1983.

Levy, Frank *Dollars and Dreams: The Changing American Income Distribution.* New York: Russell Sage Foundation, 1987.

Longfellow, Cynthia "Divorce in Context: Its Impact on Children." In George Levinger and Oliver C. Moles, eds., *Divorce and Separation,* New York: Basic Books, 1979, pp. 287–306.

Miller, Herman P. *Income of the American People.* New York: Wiley, 1955.

Modell, John *Into One's Own: From Youth to Adulthood in the United States 1920–1972.* Berkeley: University of California Press, 1989.

Moorman, Jeanne E., and Donald J. Hernandez "Married-Couple Families with Step, Adopted, and Biological Children." *Demography* 26 (1989):267–277.

Mortimer, Jeylan T., Michael D. Finch, Michael Shanahan, and Seongryeol Ryu "Work Experience, Mental Health and Behavioral Adjustment in Adolescence." 1990 Bientenial Meeting of the Society for Research in Adolescence, Atlanta, and 1990 Meeting of the World Congress of Sociology, Madrid.

Mortimer, Michael D. Finch, Seongryeol Ryu, and Michael Shanahan "Evidence from a Prospective Longitudinal Study of Work Experience and Adolescent Development" (forthcoming).

Murray, Charles *Losing Ground: American Social Policy 1950–1980.* New York: Basic Books, 1984.

National Center for Health Service Research, Judith A. Kasper, Daniel C. Walden, Gail R. Wilensky "Who Are the Uninsured?" Public Health Service. *Data Review* 1:2.

National Center for Health Services Research and Health Care Technology Assessment, Pamela Farley Short, Alan Monheit, and Karen Beauregard *Uninsured Americans: A 1987 Profile.* Public Health Service Series G 1–9, 1a.

National Center for Health Statistics *Vital Statistics of the United States,* 1988, Vol. I, Natality, DHHS Pub. No. (PHS) 90–110. Public Health Service, Washington, DC: U.S. Government Printing Office, 1990.

——— *Advance Report of Final Natality Statistics, 1987; Monthly Vital Statis-*

tics Report, vol. 38, no. 3, Supplement. Hyattsville, MD: Public Health Service, 1989.

—— Health, United States, 1988 DHHS Pub. no. PHS 89–1232. Public Health Service. Washington, DC: U.S. Government Printing Office, March 1989.

—— Heuser, Robert L. *Fertility Tables for Birth Cohorts by Color, United States, 1917–73*. Washington, DC: U.S. Government Printing Office, 1990.

—— *Monthly Vital Statistics Report 39, 4. Advance Report of Final Natality Statistics 1988*. Suppl. Hyattsville, Maryland: Public Health Service, August 15, 1990.

—— *Vital Statistics of the United States, 1973. Volume II, Section 5. Life Tables* Rockville, MD: 1975.

—— *Vital Statistics of the United States, 1985, Vol. III, Marriage and Divorce*, DHHS no. 9 PHS 89–1103. Public Health Service. Washington, DC: U.S. Government Printing Office, 1989.

—— *Vital Statistics of the United States, 1986, Vol. I, Natality*, DHHS no. PHS 88–1123. Public Health Service. Washington, DC: U.S. Government Printing Office, 1988.

National Research Planning Board *Security, Work, and Relief Policies*. Report of the Committee on Long-Range Work and Relief Policies. Washington, DC: U.S. Government Printing Office, 1942.

Oppenheimer, Valerie Kincade *The Female Labor Force in the United States.* Population Monograph Series, no. 5, Institute of International Studies, Berkeley: University of California Press, 1970.

—— *Work and the Family*. New York: Academic Press, 1982.

Orshansky, Mollie "Who's Who Among the Poor: A Demographic Profile." *Social Security Bulletin* 28, 7 (July 1965): 3–32.

Passel, Jeffrey S., and Barry Edmonston "Immigration and Race: Recent Trends in Immigration to the United States." Paper presented at conference on "Immigration and Ethnicity; The Integration of America's Newest Immigrants." Washington, DC: The Urban Institute, June 1991.

Pechman, Joseph A. *Who Paid the Taxes, 1966–1985?* Washington, D.C: Brookings Institute, 1985.

Phillips, Deborah A., and Carollee Howes "Indicators of Quality in Child Care: Review of Research." In Deborah A. Phillips, ed., *Quality in Child Care: What Does Research Tell Us?* Washington, DC: National Association for the Education of Young Children, 1987, pp. 1–20.

Pleck, Joseph H. *Working Wives/Working Husbands.* Beverly Hills: Sage Publications, 1985.

Presser, Harriet, B. "Can We Make Time for Children? The Economy, Work Schedules, and Child Care." *Demography* 26 (1989):523–543.

—— "Place of Child Care and Medicated Respiratory Illness Among Young American Children." *Journal of Marriage and the Family* 50 (1988):995–1005.

——, **and Wendy Baldwin** "Child Care as a Constraint on Employment: Prevalence, Correlates, and Bearing on the Work and Fertility Nexus." *American Journal of Sociology* 85, 5 (March 1980):1202–1213.

Preston, Samuel H. "Children and the Elderly: Divergent Paths for America's Dependents." *Demography* 21 (1984): 435–457.

—— "Children and the Elderly in the United States." *Scientific American* 251, 12 (1984):44–49.

Rainwater, Lee *What Money Buys: Inequality and the Social Meanings of Income.* New York: Basic Books, 1974.

Robinson, Joseph P. *How Americans Use Time.* New York: Praeger, 1977.

Rones, Philip L. "Moving to the Sun: Regional Job Growth, 1968 to 1978." *Monthly Labor Review* 103, 3 (March 1980):3–11.

Ross, Christine, Sheldon Danziger, and Eugene Smolensky "The Level and Trend of Poverty in the United States, 1939–1979." *Demography* 24, 4 (November 1987): 587–600.

Ruggles, Patricia *Drawing the Line.* Washington, DC: Urban Institute, 1990.

Ryder, Norman B. "The Cohort as a Concept in the Study of Social Change." *American Sociological Review* 30 6 (1965):843–861.

———— "Components of Temporal Variations in American Fertility." In R. W. Hiorns, ed., *Demographic Patterns in Developed Societies,* London: Taylor & Francis, 1980.

Sewell, William H., Robert M. Hauser, and Wendy C. Wolf "Sex, Schooling, and Occupational Status." *American Journal of Sociology* 83, 3 (1980):551–583.

Sewell, William H., and Robert M. Hauser *Education, Occupation and Earnings.* New York: Academic Press, 1975, pp. 71–75.

Smith, James, P. "Children Among the Poor." *Demography* 26, 2 (May 1969): 235–248.

Smith, Shirley J. "The Growing Diversity of Work Schedules." *Monthly Labor Review* 109, 11 (November 1986:7–13).

Smolensky, Eugene, Sheldon Danziger, and Peter Gottschalk "The Declining Significance of Age in the United States: Trends in the Well-Being of Children and the Elderly Since 1939." In John L. Palmer, Timothy Smeeding, and Barbara Boyle Torrey, ed., *The Vulnerable.* Washington, DC: Urban Institute, 1988.

Sørensen, Annemette, Karl E. Taeuber, and Leslie J. Hollingsworth, Jr. "Indexes of Racial Residential Segregation for 109 Cities in the United States, 1940–1970." *Sociological Focus* 2, 2 (1975):131.

Spanier, Graham B., and Paul C. Glick "The Life Cycle of American Families: An Expanded Analysis." *Journal of Marriage and the Family* 45 2 (May 1983):267–275.

Spitze, Glenna D. "Women's Employment and Family Relations: A Review." *Journal of Marriage and the Family* 50, 1988: pp. 595–618.

Starr, Paul *The Social Transformation of American Medicine.* New York: Basic Books, 1982.

Taeuber, Richard C., and Richard C. Rockwell "National Social Data Series: A Compendium of Brief Descriptions." *Review of Public Data Use* 10, 1–2 (May 1982):23–111.

Timmer, Susan Goff, Jacquelynne Eccles, and Kerth O'Brien "How Families Use Time." *ISR Newsletter.* Ann Arbor: Institute for Social Research, University of Michigan, Winter 1985–86, pp. 3–4.

U.S. Bureau of the Census, Bohme, Frederick G. *200 Years of Census Taking: Population and Housing Questions 1790–1990.* Washington, DC: U.S. Government Printing Office, 1989.

————, *1980 Census of Population, Volume 1, Characteristics of the Population. Chapter D. Detailed Characteristics of Population. Part 1. United States Summary. PC80–1D1–A. Section A: United States.* Washington, DC: U.S. Government Printing Office, March 1984.

————, Bachu, Amara *Fertility of American Women: June 1988. Current Population Reports,* series P-20, no. 436. U.S. Government Printing Office, Washington, DC: 1989.

————, Bennett, Claudette *The Asian and Pacific Islander Population in the*

United States: March 1991 and 1990. Washington, DC: U.S. Government Printing Office, 1992.

——, Bianchi, Suzanne, and Edith McArthur "Family Disruption and Economic Hardship: The Short-Run Picture for Children." *Current Population Reports,* series P-70, no. 23. Washington, D.C: U.S. Government Printing Office, 1991.

——, Bruno, Rosalind R. "After-School Care of School-Age Children: December 1984." *Current Population Reports,* series P-23, no. 149. Washington, DC: U.S. Government Printing Office, 1987.

——, Bruno, Rosalind R. "Educational Attainment in the United States: March 1982 to 1985." *Current Population Reports,* series P-20, no. 415. Washington, D.C: U.S. Government Printing Office, 1987.

——, Bruno, Rosalind R. "School Enrollment—Social and Economic Characteristics of Students: October 1988 and 1987," *Current Population Reports,* series P-20, no. 443. Washington, DC: U.S. Government Printing Office, 1990, p. 168.

——, *Census of the Population: 1970. Vol 1, Characteristics of the Population. Part 1, United States Summary—Section 2.* Washington, DC: U.S. Government Printing Office, 1973.

——, DeNavas, Carmen and Edward J. Welniak, Jr. "Money Income of Households, Families, and Persons in the United States:1990." *Current Population Reports,* series P-60, no. 174. Washington, DC: U.S. Government Printing Office, 1991.

——, *Fifteenth Census of the United States: 1930, Population, Volume II.* Washington, DC: U.S. Government Printing Office, 1933.

——, Garcia, Jesus, M. and Patricia A. Montgomery "The Hispanic Population in the United States: March 1990." *Current Population Reports,* series P-20, no. 499. Washington, DC: U.S. Government Printing Office, 1991.

——, Hanlon, Ruth A. Sanders. "Child Support and Alimony: 1985 (Supplement Report)." *Current Population Reports,* Series P-23, no. 154. Washington, DC: U.S. Government Printing Office.

——, Hernandez, Donald J. "When Households Continue, Discontinue, and Form: Studies in Household Formation." *Current Population Reports,* series P-23, no. 179. Washington, DC: U.S. Government Printing Office, 1992.

——, *Historical Statistics of the United States, Colonial Times to 1970,* Bicentennial Edition, Part 1, Washington, DC: U.S. Government Printing Office, 1975.

——, *Historical Statistics of the United States, Colonial Times to 1970,* Bicentennial Edition, Part 2, Washington, DC: U.S. Government Printing Office, 1975.

——, Hobbs, Frank and Laura Lippman *Children's Well-Being: An International Comparison. International Population Reports,* series P-95, no. 80. Washington, D.C: U.S. Government Printing Office, 1990.

——, Hollman, Frederick W. "United States Population Estimates by Age, Sex, Race and Hispanics Origin: 1980 to 1989." *Current Population Reports,* series P-25, no. 1045. Washington, DC: U.S. Government Printing Office, 1990.

——, Kominski, Robert "Educational Attainment in the United States: March 1989 and March 1988." *Current Population Reports,* series P-20, no. 451. Washington, DC: U.S. Government Printing Office, 1991, Table 18.

——, Kominski, Robert "What's It Worth? Educational Background and Economic Status, Spring 1987." *Current Population Reports,* series P-70, no. 21. Washington, DC: U.S. Government Printing Office, 1990.

———, Lamas, Enrique J. "Poverty Estimates from SIPP." Census Bureau memorandum of May 30, 1989 to William P. Butz.

———, Lugaila, Terry "Households, Families, and Children: A 30-Year Perspective." *Current Population Reports*, series P-23, no. 181. Washington, DC: U.S. Government Printing Office, 1992.

———, "Measuring the Effects of Benefits and Taxes on Income and Poverty: 1986." *Current Population Reports*, series P-60, no. 164-7RD-1. Washington, DC: U.S. Government Printing Office, 1988.

———, Miller, Louisa M. and Jeanne E. Moorman "Married-Couple Children with Step, Adopted, and Biological Children." *Current Population Reports*, series P-23, no. 162. Washington, DC: U.S. Government Printing Office, 1989.

———, and Mark S. Littman "Money Income and Poverty Status in the United States: 1987." *Current Population Reports*, series P-60, no. 156. Washington, DC: U.S. Government Printing Office, 1986.

———, "Money Income and Poverty Status in the United States: 1988" (Advanced data from the March 1989 Current Population Survey). *Current Population Reports*, series P-60, no. 166. Washington, DC: U.S. Government Printing Office, 1989.

———, *Negro Population 1790–1915*. Washington, DC: U.S. Government Printing Office, 1918.

———, *Negroes in the United States*. Bulletin 8. Washington, DC: U.S. Government Printing Office, 1940.

———, Norton, Arthur J., and Jeanne E. Moorman "Current Trends in Marriage and Divorce Among American Women." *Journal of Marriage and the Family* 49 (February 1987):3–14.

———, Norton, Arthur J., and Louisa F. Miller "The Family Life Cycle: 1985." *Work and Family Patterns of American Women. Current Population Reports*, series P-23, no. 165. Washington, DC: U.S. Government Printing Office, 1992.

———, O'Connell, Martin "Late Expectations: Childbearing Patterns of American Women for the 1990's." *Studies in American Fertility, Current Population Reports*, series P-23, no. 176. Washington, DC: U.S. Government Printing Office, 1991.

———, O'Connell, Martin, and Amara Bachu "Who's Minding the Kids? Child Care Arrangements: Winter 1984–1985." *Current Population Reports*, series P-70, no. 9. Washington, DC: U.S. Government Printing Office, 1987.

———, O'Connell, Martin, and Amara Bachu *"Who's Minding the Kids? Child Care Arrangements: 1986–87.* Washington, D.C: U.S. Government Printing Office, 1990.

———, Patterson, George, F. "Quality and Comparability of Personal Income Data from Surveys and the Decennial Census." Presented to the Plenary Session of the Census Bureau Joint Advisory Committee Meeting; Rossyln, VA: April 25–26, 1985.

———, *Population, Differential Fertility 1940 and 1910, Fertility for States and Large Cities*. Washington, DC: U.S. Government Printing Office, 1943.

———, *Population, Volume I, 1910*. Thirteenth Census of the United States taken in the year 1910. Washington, DC: U.S. Government Printing Office, 1913.

———, Press Release, CB91–100. Washington, DC: U.S. Government Printing Office, Monday, March 11, 1991.

———, Rawlings, Steve W. "Household and Family Characteristics," March 1985. *Current Population Reports*, series P-20, nos. 153 and 411.

———, *Report on the Population of the United States at the Eleventh Census: 1890, Part II.* Washington, DC: U.S. Government Printing Office, 1897.

———, Saluter, Arlene F. Changes in American Family Life. *Current Population Reports*, series P-23, no. 163. Washington, DC: U.S. Government Printing Office, 1989.

———, Saluter, Arlene F. "Marital Status and Living Arrangements: March 1990." *Current Population Reports*, series P-20, no. 450. Washington, DC: U.S. Government Printing Office, 1990.

———, Saluter, Arlene F. "Marital Status and Living Arrangements: March 1984." *Current Population Reports*, series P-20, no. 399. Washington, DC: U.S. Government Printing Office, 1985.

———, Siegel, Paul M., and Rosalind R. Bruno "School Enrollment—Social and Economic Characteristics of Students: October 1982." *Current Population Reports*, series P-20, no. 408. Washington, D.C: U.S. Government Printing Office, 1986.

———, Spencer, Gregory *Projections of the Population of the United States, by Age, Sex, and Race: 1988 to 2080.* Washington, DC: U.S. Government Printing Office, 1989.

———, *Statistical Abstract of the United States: 1989* (109th ed.) Washington, DC: U.S. Government Printing Office, 1989.

———, *U.S. Census of Population: 1960. Vol. I, Characteristics of the Population. Part 1. United States Summary.* Washington, D.C: U.S. Government Printing Office, 1986.

———, Welniak, Edward Jr. "Effects of the March Current Population Survey's New Processing System on Estimates of Income and Poverty." Presented at the 1990 annual meeting of the American Statistical Association. Anaheim, CA: August 6–9.

———, "Money Income of Households, Families, and Persons in the United States: 1984." *Current Population Reports*, series P-60, no. 156. Washington, DC: U.S. Government Printing Office, 1986.

———, "Money Income of Households, Families, and Persons in the United States: 1987." *Current Population Reports*, series P-60, no. 162. Washington, DC: U.S. Government Printing Office, 1987.

U.S. Bureau of Labor Statistics *Handbook of Labor Statistics*, Bulletin 2340. Washington, DC: U.S. Government Printing Office, August 1989.

———, Handbook of Labor Statistics, Bulletin 2217. Washington, DC: U.S. Government Printing Office.

U.S. Congress "Alternative Measures of Poverty." A Staff Study Prepared for the Joint Economic Committee, October 18, 1989.

U.S. Congressional Research Service "The Indexing of Social Security." Report no. 81–110 EPW, HD 7094. Washington, DC: Library of Congress, May 15, 1981.

——— "Social Security Benefit Increases Pegged to a Consumer Price Index that Measures Rental Equivalency Rather than Home-ownership Costs." Washington, DC: Library of Congress, November 25, 1981.

———"The Automatic Benefit Increase in Social Security." Report no. 83-22 EPW, HD 7094. Washington, DC: Library of Congress, February 22, 1983.

U.S. Department of Agriculture, Economic Research Services, Rural Development, no. 83. *The Economic Well-Being of Nonmetro Children.* Washington, DC: U.S. Government Printing Office, 1991.

U.S. House of Representatives, Committee on Ways and Means *Background*

Material and Data on Programs Within the Jurisdiction of the Committee on Ways and Means. Washington, DC: U.S. Government Printing Office, 1989.

Vanek, Joann "Time Spent in Housework." In Alice H. Amsden, ed., *The Economics of Women and Work.* New York: St. Martin's, pp. 83–90. Reprinted from *Scientific American* 231 (November 1974):116–120.

Wallerstein, Judith, S. and Joan Berlin Kelly *Second Chances.* New York: Ticknor & Fields, 1989.

—— *Surviving the Breakup.* New York: Basic Books, 1980.

Wallerstein, Judith S., Shauna B. Corbin, and Julia M. Lewis "Children of Divorce: A 10-Year Study." In E. Mavis Hetherington and Josephine D. Arasteh, eds. *Impact of Divorce, Single Parenting and Stepparenting on Children,* Hillsdale, NJ: Lawrence Erlbaum, 1988.

Watts, Harold W. and Donald J. Hernandez eds. *Child and Family Indicators: A Report with Recommendations.* NY: Social Science Research Council, 1982.

Watts, Harold W. and Fredricka Pickford Santos, *The Allocation of Human and Material Resources to Childbearing in the United States: A Theoretical Framework and Analysis of Major Data Sources,* prepared for the Foundation for Child Development New York: Center for Social Sciences, Columbia University, 1978.

Weiss, Robert S. "The Impact of Marital Dissolution on Income and Consumption in Single-Parent Households." *Journal of Marriage and the Family* 46 (1984):115–127.

Wilson, William Julius *The Truly Disadvantaged: The Inner City, the Underclass, and Public Policy.* Chicago: University of Chicago Press, 1987.

Name Index

Boldface numbers refer to figures and tables.

A

Allen, Walter R., 49, 49n, 50, 50n, 100n, 121n, 261n, 402n, 408n, 409, 409n
Alwin, Duane F., 30n, 192n
Amsden, Alice H., 165n
Anderson, Odin W., 254n, **256**
Arasteh, Josephine D., 60n, 61n, 62n
Ardelt, Monika, 100n, 121n

B

Bachman, Jerald, 134
Bachu, Amara, **24**, **29**, 39n, 112n, 149n, 169n, 170n, 185n
Baldwin, Wendy, 446n
Baltes, Paul B., 5n
Bane, Mary Jo, 288n, 311
Bartlett, John, 243n
Bean, Frank D., 8n, 411, 411n
Beauregard, Karen, **256**
Beck, Emily Morison, 243n
Belsky, Jay, 173, 173n
Bennett, Claudette, 413n
Bernert, Eleanor H., 2, 2n, 129, 129n, 132n,
Bianchi, Suzanne, 288n
Blake, Judith, 19, 19n, 36, 36n, 39, 39n, 194, 194n, 195n, 198, 198n, 199n, 206, 206n, 209
Blau, Peter M., 19, 19n, 62, 62n, 192n
Bohme, Frederick G., 2n
Brim, Orville G., Jr., 5n
Broderick, Carlfred B., 4n
Brookins, G., 100n, 121n
Bruno, Rosalind R., 132n, 149n, 167, 167n, 198, 198n, 212, 213n, 444n
Bumpass, Larry, 71, 71n, 87n
Bureau of the Census. *See* U.S. Bureau of the Census

Bureau of Research and Statistics, 279n
Burns, Arthur Edward, 299n
Butz, William P., 280n

C

Carter, Hugh, 4n
Caspi, Avshalom, 100n, 121n
Center for Demography and Ecology, 2n
Chase-Lansdale, P. Lindsay, 172, 172n
Chehrazi, S., 173n
Cherlin, Andrew J., 96, 96n
Civilian Conservation Corps, 278n
Clarke-Stewart, K. Alison, 173, 173n
Committee on Long Range Work and Relief Policies, 279n, 298n
Committee on Ways and Means, 291n
Conger, Rand D., 100n, 121n, 390n
Corbin, Shauna B., 60n
Cox, M., 60n
Cox, R., 60n

D

Danziger, Sheldon H., 238n, 288n, 311n
Davis, Kingsley, 36, 36n, 37n, 69n, 101n, 138, 389, 389n, 392, 392n, 393n
DeNavas, Carmen, 390n
Desai, Sonalde, 172, 172n
Downey, Geraldine, 100n, 121n
Duncan, Greg J., 58, 58n, 59n, 234n, 310n, 350n, 355–356, 355n, 356n, 357n, 358
Duncan, Otis Dudley, 19, 19n, 62, 62n, 192n
Durand, John D., 129n

461

Subject Index

Boldface numbers refer to figures and tables.

A

adolescents, 6, 6*n*, 17, 175, 427; causes in change of family size for, 50; family size of, 17, 27, 30–36, 31*n*, 55, 419; family size of Hispanic, 51, **52**; labor force participation of, 101, 129, 132; living in luxury, **260**, 261; mortality of, 47, **48**; racial gap in relative poverty for, 265, **266–267**, 268–269; racial gap in sibsizes of, 40, **42, 43, 45**, 45–46; relative poverty and inequality among, 259, **260**, 261; school enrollment of, 136; sibsizes of, **29, 32–33, 34**, 51, **54**; work transformation of, 128–129, 132–134, 135–136

adults: economic circumstances of, 248; relative poverty among, 236, 254, 273, 431; strategies for improvement in relative social and economic standing of, 17–18; trends in relative income and poverty for, 249–252

age, 6–7, 6*n*, 8*n*, 248

Aid to Dependent Children (ADC) program, 299, 299*n*

Aid to the Disabled, 305*n*

Aid to Families with Dependent Children (AFDC), 291, **292**, 296, 299, 305*n*, 324, 446; benefits, 293*n*, 300; income from, **276**, 278, 278*n*, 279*n*, **301, 304, 315, 321, 323, 331**, 333*n*, **350, 369, 379, 384**; as percentage of relative poverty threshold, **297**; value of, **297**, 298, 326, **327**

American dream, 189

America's Children (E.H. Bernert), 2

Australia, 426, 432, 434

automobile, 409–410

B

baby boom, 20, 38–39; changes in family size during, 27, 418–419; and education, 445; effect of, 386–388, 388*n*; and family size, 16, 17, 26, 45, 55, 199, 420; number of children ever born during, 25

baby boomers: and blacks, 406; entering the labor force, 386, 387, 413, 438; female, 387

baby bust, 38, 39; cohorts, 387; and family size, 16, 17, 27, 46; number of children ever born during, 25

behavioral problems, 57, 420–421; of children in one-parent families, 61, 62, 63, 93; of infants, 173; potential, due to day care, 174; of stepchildren, 61

births, 20, 39, 310, 418; expected, **21**, 23, **24**; out-of-wedlock, 67, **70**, 77, 311

black children, 7, **368**, 412, 415–416; chances of living in idealized families for, 100, 424–425; changes in family life for, 440; changes in family size for, 47, 49–50; changes in parents' incomes for, 332, **347–349**, 351–352, **377–379**; changes in official poverty for, **377–379**; changes in relative poverty for, 351, 371, 436; changes in relative poverty rates for, 352–354, 359, **360–363**, 432; disadvantages experienced by, 215, **216**, 217–218, 223–224, 428–430, 445; distribution of poor, **306–307**; educational disadvantage of, 190, 201, 215, 218–219; educational opportunities for, 428, 430; ever living with fewer than two parents, 84–88, **85, 86**, 96, 421–422; family sizes of, 47, 55, 419; income from relatives other than parents for, 350–351; increase in

born, number of, 20, **21, 24**, 25; by fathers' amount of work, **110, 112**; by fathers' labor force status, **106**; future life chances of, 16, 56; historic change in lives of, 388–397; home-care, 174; in idealized families, 105, **113**; importance of parents' educational level for, 190; from large families, trends, 17; life course of, 4–7, 9; living in poverty, 355–358; by mothers' amount of work, **112**; by mothers' education, family size, and farm origin, **200**; by mothers' labor force status, **111**; national study on, 2; needs of, 1; not living in two-parent families, 57, 84; with parent at home full-time, 175; by parents' work status, **108–109**; projections for, 71; by relative income levels, **245, 246–247, 262**; three major family forms of, **103, 104**; ways of spending time for, 10. *See also* adolescents; black children; Hispanic children; newborns; preschoolers; white children

children ever living with fewer than two parents, 66, 69, **70**; expected proportion of, 71, 96, 97, 218, 421, 422; racial differences among, 84, **85, 86**, 88

children living in no parent situations, 282, 294n; distribution of poor, **284, 301**; among Hispanics and non-Hispanics, **92, 94–96, 184–185, 320–323**; in the home, **65, 67, 68**, 69; in the home, increase of, 71–72, 186; parental presence and employment status among, **151, 152, 155, 161, 184–185**; poverty rates and distribution of poor children in, **306–307**; procedures for estimating proportion of, 137, 139, 140, 142; proportion of, in home, 102, **103, 104**, 426; racial differences among, **78–83, 176–178, 182–183, 314–315**

child support, 3, 59, 313

cohorts, 5–7

college: attendance, 443; chances of completing one year of, 207, 222, 396; effect of family origin on access to, 207–208; enrollment, 147n, 213, 443, 444; four years of, completed, 198, 212, 443, 444, 445; likelihood of graduating from, 212, 415, 440

college education, 11, 418, 428, 443; annual earnings of men with, 191; of black

mothers and fathers, 213; effects of race on levels of parents', **210**, 210, 213, 214, 224; of fathers, **196, 197**, 197, **210**, 210, **211**; for Hispanic children, 219; of mothers, **196, 197**, 197, **200, 210, 211**

comfort, children living in, 11, 234, 236, 430. *See also* middle-class comfort

companionship, 16, 35, 47, 52, 55

competition among siblings, 35–36, 441; for family resources, 52, 418–419; for parental attention, 18, 27; racial gap in, 47

Consumer Price Index, 251n, 343n

contact time, 60–61, 163–166

couples, ways of improving economic standing for, 391, 392, 393, 414, 438–439

Current Population Survey (CPS), 2, 15, 31n, 64n, 66n, 76n, 102n, 220, 237n, **247**, 252n, **260, 265, 266–267**, 269, **276**, 280n, 282n, **284**, 286n, **289, 301, 304, 306–307, 314–315, 323, 330–331, 344–345, 347–349, 360–362, 367, 374–381, 383–384**; income questions asked by, 278, 279n; Marital and Fertility Histories of, 59; median family income according to, 58; effect of procedural changes in, 294n, 294n; undercount of young black men by, 402

custodial child care, 164

D

daughters, 192–193

day care, 169; effects of, 171, 173–174

death: of parents, 66, 67, 69, 69n, 85–87, 424; of parents, experienced by children, 100, 121, 125, 128, 135, 356; of siblings, 47. *See also* mortality

deprivation: adolescents living in economic, 261; children living in material, 11, 234, 430; children living in relative, 12, 236, 239, 272, 431; economic, 242, 245, 272, 431

disadvantage: among black and white children, 214–219; black, in parents' education, 214, 223–224; economic, 63, 394, 402; educational, 190, 201–202, 204, 214, 218–219; educational, among Hispanic children, 219–222, **221**; experi-

97, 398–399; of 17–year-olds, **68, 81, 83**;
transformations in, 423–425, 427; of
white children, **78, 80**
low-income families, 11, 234, 253, 255.
See also near-poor frugality
luxury, 251, 254; adolescents living in,
260, 261; children living in, 11, 12, 234,
239, **245, 247**, 430, 431; children living
in relative, 235, 236, 248, 272; definition
of relative, 235*n*, 242; health-insurance
coverage for individuals living in, 255,
256, 257; Hispanic children living in,
269, **270, 271**; likelihood of living in,
248–250, 252; preschoolers living in,
259, **260**; racial gap for living in, 261,
262, 264, **265, 267**, 268

M

marital disruption, 63, 71, 442
marital dissolutions, 87. *See also* divorce;
separation
married women, 137–138, 139
Medicaid, 257, 258, **292**, 446; coverage,
256, 257, 258; expenditures, 291; valuation of, 292*n*, 293*n*, **327**
Medicare, 257, 258, 446
men: annual earnings of, 191; black, 402–
403, **405**; civilian employment-population ratios for white and black, **404–405**;
and contact time with children, 60; educational attainments of, 193, 205–208;
family work time for, 166; incomes of,
387, 402; primary-activity child care for
all, 166; racial disadvantage among, 402;
racial gap in employment of, **403**. *See
also* fathers; husbands; young men
Mexicans, 411, 412
middle-class comfort: adolescents living
in, **260**, 261; children living in, **245, 246**,
248; definition of, 235*n*, 242; elderly living below, 252; health-insurance coverage for individuals living in, 255, **256**,
257, 258; Hispanic children living in,
270, 271; preschoolers living in, **260**; racial gap in, **262**, 264, **265, 266**. *See also*
sub-middle-class living
middle-income families, 234, 253, 273, 408
migrants, 220, 222, 411
minimum-wage laws, 446
mortality: childhood, 36, 46–47; parental,

85–87, 88, 96, 421; of siblings, 35–36,
35*n*, **48**
mother-avoiding behavior, 173–174
mother-only families, 275, **285**, 385; black,
14–15, **79, 82**, 397–401, 407; changes in,
390; children living in, **65**, 66, **70**, 71,
327, 415; comparison of ethnic and racial groups in, 364–365; dependent sibsizes of, **362**, 363, **376, 381, 384**; disadvantages of, 62, 63; effects of poverty
thresholds for children living in, 341;
with ever-married mothers, 282, **284**,
287, **306–307**; with a grandparent in the
home, 57, **73, 74**, 88, **89**, 91, **96**; Hispanic and non-Hispanic children in, **92**,
93, **94–96**, 319, **320–323**, 324, **366–369**;
and Hispanic parents' work, 410–412;
incomes of, 59; with never-married
mothers, 282, **284**, 286–287, **292, 306–
307**, 327, 397; newborns living in, **67**,
74, 80, 82; official poverty rates for children in, **375, 379, 381, 382–283**; parents'
work and, 388–391; among poor children, 282–283, **284**, 285–287, 302, 308;
poverty rates of children in, 434; poverty
rates and distribution of poor children
in, **306–307**; proportion of children in,
72, 277, 286, 291, 293, 325; racial gap in,
308, **309**, 309–313, **314–315**, 316–318,
350–351, 406; relative poverty and dependent sibsizes for children in, **345**;
and relative poverty by race, 354; relative poverty rates and effects for children in, **331**, 340, **349**, 350; 17–year-olds
living in, **68, 81, 83**; shift toward, 337,
352; trends in proportion of children living in unwed-, 294–295, 294*n*; welfare
dependence in, 300, **301**, 302, **316–317**,
316–318; among whites, **78, 80, 81**
mother-only families, rise in, 76*n*-77*n*,
439, 443; absolute welfare generosity
and, 291, **292**, 293–295, 296, 296*n*;
among blacks, 213, 354, 372, 440–441;
effects of, 64, 76, 282, 325, 326, 435; reasons for, 14, 77, 283, 385, 391, 410, 442;
poverty trends and, 275, 287–288, **289**,
289–290; racial differences leading to,
407; reasons for historic, 275, 388–389,
397–401, 413–414, 438; role of, 290, 416
mothers, 25, 351; amount of work of, **112**;
as breadwinners, 135, 417; changing role

and, 365, 370; disadvantages due to family origin of, 220, **221**, 225; educational attainments of, 190; effects of parents' incomes and government welfare for, **366–368, 382–383**; family sizes of, 51, 55, 419; grandparents in homes of, **74**, 91, 93, **96**; parental living arrangements of, 91, **92**, 93; parental presence and employment status for, **184–185**; parental time and child care for, 182, 185; by parents' work status, **130–131**; by parents' years of education, 219, **230–233**; relative poverty among, 269, 270–273, **270–271**, 364–365, 372; work and welfare dependence among, 318–319, **320–323**, 324

nonparental child care, 143–144, 418, 443; effects of, 145, 187–188, 341, 427, 428; need for, 158, 163, 167, 181, 187, 426; potential effects of, 170–175; racial gap in, 179–181; revolutions in, 185, 186, 188; for school-age children, 146–149; sources of, 168

nonparental family members. *See* nonrelatives

noncash benefits, 253–255, 257–259, 273

nonrelatives, 335, 336n, 340, 351, 352; care of school-age children by, 149; child care by, 145, 170, 187; Hispanic, 185, 364, 365

nursery school: enrollment in, **156, 161, 162**, 167–168; Hispanic and non-Hispanic preschoolers enrolled in, 182; racial differences in enrollment, **182–183**

O

occupational achievements, 17, 63, 192–193, 419

occupational status, 190, 394; of fathers, 193, 205

occupations, 19, 49; high-status, 419; lower-status, 62, 93, 421

officially poor children, **276**, 279n, 281–283; of Hispanic origin, 318, 319, **320, 322**; living in mother-only families, 286–287; parental presence among, **284, 301, 306**; racial differences among, **304**, 313, **315, 317**; welfare dependence of, 305

official poverty, 281, 340–341, 413;

changes for children in, **374–375**; changes for white and black children in, **377–379**; children in, 278, 356–357; and dependent sibsizes for children, **376, 380–381**; by Hispanic origin, **382–384**; racial differences in proportion living in, 350n; standards, 396; thresholds, 238, 243, 341, 355, 395; transition in or out of, 357, 400

official poverty rate, 238, 310, 328, 341; for children, 238, **260**, 340; for children, increase in overall, 277

official poverty rates, 243, **284**, 326, **374–384**, 435; among children, **246–247, 267, 289**, 289–290; changes in children's, 295–296; drop in, 343; increase in, 386, 438; racial gap in children's, **265**

Old-Age Assistance program, 299n, 305n

one-parent families, 10, 98; advantages and disadvantages of, 58–64, 93, 202; black children in, **79, 82–83**; children in, **65**, 66, 69, **70**; forecast for children in, 57, 71, 443; with a grandparent in the home, 10, 57, 74; Hispanic and non-Hispanic children in, **92, 94–96**, 181, **184–185**, 225; international comparisons of, 422, 433; newborns in, **67, 80, 82, 94**; poor children in, 356; preschoolers in, 150, 153, 162, 168, 426; presence of surrogate parents in, **156**, 157, **159–162, 180**, 181, **182–183**; problems of children in, 57, 420–421; proportion of children in, 58, 72, 98–99, 135, 137–140, 142; proportion of children in, by parental presence and employment status, **151, 152, 154–155, 158, 176–178**; proportion of children in, by three major family forms, **103, 104**; racial differences in, 175, **176–178**, 179, **180**, 181, 224, 422–423; rise in, 90, 102, 104, 105, 151; rise in proportion of children living in, 201, 202, 423; 17-year-olds in, **68, 81, 83, 95**; white children in, **78, 80–81**, 356. *See also* mother-only families; specific groups and issues

out-of-wedlock childbearing, 86n-87n, 421; among blacks, 400, 401, 406, 407, 442; due to welfare benefits, 277, 435; and education, 310; effects of, 69, 71, 96, 223, 417, 442; racial gap in, 97, 311, 422. *See also* births